The Collected Works of
Marie-Louise von Franz

MLvF

Volume 2

General Editors

Steven Buser

Leonard Cruz

Marie-Louise von Franz
1915-1998

Volume 2

Archetypal Symbols in Fairytales

The Hero's Journey

Marie-Louise von Franz

Translated by Roy Freeman and Tony Woolfson
in collaboration with Emmanuel Kennedy

CHIRON PUBLICATIONS • ASHEVILLE, NORTH CAROLINA

Logo of the Foundation of Jungian Psychology, Küsnacht Switzerland:
Fons mercurialis from Rosarium Philosophorum 1550 (Fountain of Life).

Original title: *Symbolik des Märchens – Versuch einer Deutung*
Copyright © 1952, 1960 Bern, revised edition 2015
Verlag Stiftung für Jung'sche Psychologie, Küsnacht ZH

www.ChironPublications.com

Interior and cover design by Danijela Mijailovic
Cover Image by Martina Ott
Printed primarily in the United States of America.
Translated by Roy Freeman and Tony Woolfson
Copyediting by Margaretha le Roux

ISBN 978-1-63051-950-6 paperback
ISBN 978-1-63051-951-3 hardcover

"Everything is simpler than you think
and at the same time more complex than you imagine."

"Alles ist einfacher, als man denken kann, zugleich verschränkter,
als zu begreifen ist."

Johann Wolfgang von Goethe, *Maxims and Reflections*

❖❖❖ Table of Contents ❖❖❖

Introduction

1 In Volume 1 we showed that there are two spheres in fairytales, the profane and the magical, and that these reflect the human world of consciousness and the unconscious. We believe that the main processes described in fairytales comprise statements about the unconscious. Furthermore, we focused on four figures that are of general importance and appear again and again in fairytales with only minor variations. First, the figure of the half-light and half-dark father, a spirit hidden in nature. Then there is the Great Mother, matter and nature in her life-fostering and death-bringing aspects. Next was the shadowy companion of the hero, partly a miscreant, partly an animal, and partly a divine prince. Finally, we presented the anima, the soul image of a man with all her dazzling and iridescent, sometimes high and sometimes low, manifestations.

2 All these figures are, however, woven together. They merge one into the other, and often are very difficult to separate. The behavior and characteristics of these figures depend on human consciousness, an ego, that refers them to a center of consciousness.[1] The fairytale always presumes the presence of human consciousness because only then is it useful to represent what happens to the individual who behaves in one way or the other, and what logic is inherent in his or her experience in the magical. It then reveals that humans are not merely playthings of those unconscious powers, but that an intention underlies the plot, a striving for the realization of an individual destiny, a meaningful development that, through suffering and dramatic conflicts, pushes through to the final goal. This thread, which runs through the fairytale, is usually laid bare by the interpretation of the *peripeteia*. In the following we will focus on uncovering this meaningful thread.

3 The constellated archetype that steers and determines the inner course of events is most commonly represented in fairytales as the "Great Journey"[2] the

---

[1] See Jung, "Unless the conscious mind intervened, the unconscious would go on sending out wave after wave without result, like the treasure that is said to take nine years, nine months, and nine nights to come to the surface and, if not found on the last night, sinks back to start all over again from the beginning." C.G. Jung, CW 12, *Psychology and Alchemy* ¶111.

[2] In this context, the meaning of the verb *fara* is interesting. [In German, the word for journey is *Fahrt*.] See Ninck:

> No less significant is that the verb *fara* has in Nordic lands many strikingly different meanings. One "journeys," or "goes" to sleep, one journeys to Hel (death) . . . Just *fara* corresponds to [German] "procedural act, behaviour" . . . but *fara skapa* means "damage suffered," in the

adventurous quest to find the "precious treasure that is hardest to reach." This is a symbol of the Self,[3] and this journey – interpreted psychologically – is the process of inner development (individuation) in a temporal sequence of events. Whether the hero wanders aimlessly or follows a clearly defined goal, this objective is often only ambiguously circumscribed. This goal (the Self) is always a symbol whose meaning can only be deduced in relation to the recurring adventures and the whole dynamic process. Jung writes of this:

4   The heroes are usually wanderers, and wandering is a symbol of longing, of the restless urge which never finds its object, of nostalgia for the lost mother. The sun comparison can easily be taken in this sense: the heroes are like the wandering sun, from which it is concluded that the myth of the hero is a solar myth. It seems to us, rather, that he is first and foremost a self-representation of the longing of the unconscious, of its unquenched and unquenchable desire for the light of consciousness. But consciousness, continually in danger of being led astray by its own light and of becoming a rootless will-o'-the-wisp, longs for the healing power of nature, for the deep wells of being and for unconscious communion with life in all its countless forms.[4][5]

5   The quest is a journey over unknown ways, it is "... the perilous adventure of the night sea journey . . . whose end and aim is the restoration of life, resurrection, and the triumph over death . . . "[6] It is the same basic idea as the journey to Hades to renew the inner being, which is rooted in many ancient mystery cults. It is a return to the archetypal images out of which all religious and artistic experience arises. This descent constitutes a significant risk because the human feels a deep fear of drowning in himself. "If it were only resistance that he felt, that would not be so bad. In actual fact, however, the psychic substratum, that dark realm of the unknown, exercises a fascinating attraction that threatens to become the more overpowering the further one

---

dative it means "kill, exterminate" . . . Impersonally or in passive construction, "it concerns me, it concerns us, it happens," or even "to die, to perish." Associated to the same word root is *fern*, "to travel, the way, the road, travel company, carry. . . (M. Ninck, *Wodan*, Jena 1935 p. 111.)

[3] See C.G. Jung, CW 9i, *The Archetypes and the Collective Unconscious* ¶248, also C.G. Jung, CW 6, *Psychological Types* ¶423f, ¶434.

[4] C.G. Jung, CW 5, *Symbols of Transformation* ¶299. [This quote follows that in CW 5, which differs slightly from the older version quoted by von Franz and von Beit.]

[5] See also Carus:

The spirit of mankind that has come to consciousness, the self-knowing soul . . . aims . . . towards, when viewing and comprehending the world, arising from the eternal trans-formations of itself . . . from the sea of restless sinking and restless self-renewing reality to save itself and reach an eternal, an unchangeable, with one word, a primordial spiritual goal that has become objective, as the highest cause of all reality and its own proper existence, and all this we call the "the soul's search for God." This search, this longing, this yearning is an undercurrent flowing through the whole history of mankind's coming to consciousness. . . (C.G. Carus, *Psyche*, Leipzig 1931 p. 399).

See also, *ibid*, p. 401.

[6] C.G. Jung, CW 12, *Psychology and Alchemy* ¶436.

penetrates into it."⁷ The human is in danger of losing himself completely to the images of the unconscious, in whose flood he becomes alienated from the world.⁸

6   A well-known example of the hero's journey as a metaphor for a temporary entry into the unconscious is the Jonah motif: being swallowed up by the whale and being reborn out of the maternal monster.⁹ In the fairytales already discussed, the night sea journey, or being swallowed up by the whale dragon, is represented in "Tseremsaaks," "Makonaura and Anuanaitu," "Giviok (Kiviok)," "The Visit to Heaven," "The Witchdoctor Makanaholo" and "The Strange Boy."¹⁰ Not only in these, but also in many fairytales that we have not mentioned, this motif signals a journey to the magical kingdom, differing only in the symbols chosen to represent the unconscious. An example of a final engulfment without return was given in "The Disowned Princess."

---

⁷ C.G. Jung, CW 12, *Psychology and Alchemy* ¶439.
⁸ See C.G. Jung, CW 7, *Two Essays in Analytical Psychology* ¶233.
⁹ For more on this see C.G. Jung, CW 5, *Symbols of Transformation* ¶538–546, ¶237, ¶246, ¶285–290. Cf. further C.G. Jung, CW 8, *The Structure and Dynamics of the Psyche* ¶68; O. Rank, *Myth of the Birth*, Baltimore 2004 p. 65, 80; de Gubernatis, *Zoological*, London 1872 p. 103f; L. Frobenius, *Zeitalter*, Berlin 1904 *passim*. See also the fairytale, "Sun and Moon" [Maidu People (California), original in Roland Dixon, "Maidu Myths" in: *Bulletin of the American Museum of Natural History*, 17 (2) [1902] pp. 76–78, German in Walter Krickeberg (ed.), *Indianermärchen aus Nordamerika*, (MdW), ed. by Fr. van der Leyen and P. Zaunert, Eugen Diederichs, Jena 1924 No. 39) in which the sun god (female in the original)] is swallowed by a mother frog. The sun swelled up in the stomach of the frog woman and became so large that it soon protruded from the frog's mouth. The sun continued to swell and burst the frog.
¹⁰ See also, "Why the Boa Constrictor Does Not Eat People" from "Adventures of Manabusch," "Mäshenomak, the Great Fish," "Mänäbush and Buzzard Päskose"; also, "The Origin of the Stars," from "The Raven Legends," "Yetl the Raven and the Whale," "Tsetlwalakame," "Coyote Remains Coyote" and "Djulek Batür," which will be discussed later in detail.

◆

Chapter 1

The Three Feathers

7   The big question that has so far remained unanswered is: if the fairytale with all its characters is interpreted as the inner drama of a human being, who actually is this "hero," who experiences and suffers all the action in this drama? Light is shed on this question in those fairytales that describe the initial situation of the hero before he sets off on his journey. In these scenes we see his place within the human wholeness. A good example of this, giving insight into our question, is the Grimm's fairytale "The Three Feathers" to which we now turn:

8   Once upon a time there was a king who had three sons, two of them were clever, but the third one did not talk very much. He was simpleminded and the name they gave him was "the Simpleton." When the king became old and weak and contemplated his end, he did not know which of his sons should inherit the kingdom after him. And one day he said to them, "Go forth, and the one of you who brings me the finest carpet, he shall be king after my death."

9   So that there would be no dispute among them, he led them to the front of his castle, blew three feathers into the air and said, "As they fly, so shall you go forth."

10   One feather flew to the east, the other to the west, and the third feather flew straight ahead. It did not go far but fell quickly to the ground. One brother followed the first feather to the right, the other to the left, and they laughed at the Simpleton who had to stand there where the third feather had fallen.

11   The Simpleton sat down and was sad. Suddenly he noticed that there was a trapdoor just next to his feather. He lifted it up, found a stairway, and climbed down inside. Then he came to another door and knocked, whereupon he heard someone calling out from within:

12

> Maiden green and small,
> Hopping toad,[1]
> Hopping toad's puppy,
> Hop hither and thither,
> Quickly see who is outside.

13

The door opened, and he saw a big, fat toad sitting there, surrounded by a large number of little toads. The fat toad asked what he wanted. The Simpleton answered, "I would like the most beautiful and finest carpet." Then the fat toad called to a young toad, saying:

14

> Maiden green and small,
> Hopping toad,
> Hopping toad's puppy,
> Hop hither and thither,
> Bring me the big box.

15

A young toad brought the box, and the fat toad opened it, then gave the Simpleton a carpet from inside that was so beautiful and so fine, the like of which could never have been woven in the world above. He thanked the toad and climbed back up.

16

Now the other two sons thought that their brother was so stupid he would certainly not find anything to bring home. "Why should we spend a lot of effort looking for a special carpet?" they said, so they took some pieces of coarse cloth from the first shepherd woman they came to and took these back to the king.

17

At the same time, they returned home, the Simpleton also arrived, bringing with him his beautiful carpet. When the king saw it, he was astonished, and said, "It is only right that the kingdom should go to my youngest son."

18

The two other sons gave their father no peace, however, saying that it would be impossible for the Simpleton to become king, he lacked understanding in all things. They asked their father the king to declare another contest. The father acquiesced and said, "He who brings me the most beautiful ring shall inherit the kingdom." Again, he led the three brothers outside and blew three feathers into the air that they were to follow.

---

[1] [The translator of this line in H. Silberer, *Problems of Mysticism*, New York 1917 p. 220, has "shrunken old crone." the German *Hutzelbein* means literally "hopping leg."]

19 Again, the Simpleton followed his feather to the fat toad who gave him a beautiful ring. The elder brothers made no effort and drove nails out of old wagon rings and brought these to the king. When the Simpleton presented his golden, bejeweled ring, the king said once again, "The kingdom belongs to him."

20 The two eldest sons did not cease from tormenting the King until finally he declared a third contest, saying that he who would bring home the most beautiful woman should have the kingdom. Once again he blew three feathers into the air and they flew in the same directions as before. Without hesitating, the Simpleton went back down to the fat toad and said, "I am supposed to take home the most beautiful woman."

21 "Yipes!" answered the toad. "The most beautiful woman! She is not here at the moment, but you shall nevertheless have her." The fat toad gave him a hollowed-out carrot, to which were harnessed six little mice. The Simpleton said very sadly, "What am I to do with this?"

22 The toad answered, "Just put one of my little toads inside it." Then he grabbed one of them from the group and set it inside the yellow coach. The little toad was scarcely inside when it turned into a beautiful young lady, the carrot into a coach, and the six mice into horses. He kissed her, raced away with the horses, and brought her to the king.

23 His brothers came along afterward. They had given no effort to find a beautiful woman, but simply brought along the first good peasant women they had come upon. After looking at them, the king said, "After my death the kingdom belongs to my youngest son."

24 The two eldest sons deafened the king's ears all over again, yelling, "We cannot allow the Simpleton to become king!" They demanded that the choice should go to the brother whose woman could jump through a hoop that was hanging in the middle of the hall. They thought the peasant women would manage that much better than the delicate lady.

25 The old king gave in to this as well. Then the two peasant women jumped through the hoop, but they were so plump they fell and broke their legs. Then the beautiful lady that the Simpleton had brought home sprang through the hoop as lightly as a deer. After this all the protests stopped. The Simpleton received the crown, and he ruled wisely for a long time.[2]

---

[2] Slightly modified from J. and W. Grimm, *Complete Grimm's*, London 1975 pp. 319–322, original German in *KHM*, final edition (1857), no. 63. The Grimm Brothers modified this from the version they gave in the first edition (1812).

26 Here the hero belongs initially to a group of four people.[3] He himself is the fourth, the one despised and regarded as the most backward (since he does not "understand all things"). This initial tetrad (a father or a mother with three sons or with three daughters) is a very common fairytale motif.[4] The quaternary in itself indicates a wholeness, complete within itself, to which nothing can be added. As we discussed above in relation to the Self, the quaternary indicates the secret center in the unconscious. This is almost always represented as a mandala and frequently appears as a circle divided into four parts. If we look at this fairytale situation in terms of this pattern (a quartered circle), the hero, like the anima, is an image of one particular psychic function, one part of a higher psychic wholeness.

27 One can ask, how appropriate is such a perspective? Jung[5] found that when an unconscious image appears, it does not necessarily concern the overtly represented object, but rather, at least as much if not primarily, symbolizes subjective parts of the psyche. In the case of a literary work, this would be parts of the soul of the poet or writer. For fairytales, this kind of psychological interpretation is not immediately evident because their characters, such as the hero, are relatively autonomous, independent, and rounded-out; they are not clearly recognizable as parts of a system. On the other hand, they do not exhibit the changeability and shifting quality of dream figures. The exposition in many fairytales where the hero initially belongs to a group of four lends support to our interpretation that these figures represent parts of the psyche. If we were to waive the idea that the group of figures is part of a whole being, then the story disintegrates into a multiplicity of characters and actions that could make some degree of sense, but from which no real unifying meaning can be recognized.[6]

---

[3] [This fairytale is interpreted in detail in M.-L. von Franz, *Interpretation of Fairytales*, New York 1970 p. IVff.]

[4] See for example, "The Gnome" (king and three daughters), "Cinderella" (mother and three daughters), "The Golden Bird," "The Water of Life," "The Frog Princess," "The Virgin Tsar," "The Three Sons of the Padishah," "Prince Hassan Pasha," "Djulek Batür" (all a king, tzar or padishah with three sons), "The Poor Miller's Boy and the Cat" (miller and three apprentices), "The Singing, Soaring Lark" (man and three daughters), "The Treasures of the Devil," "Tritill, Litill, and the Birds," "Móirín" (widow and three daughters), and "The White Dog from the Mountains" (king and three daughters). In North America, the number four is especially dominant. Cf. L. Lévy-Bruhl, *How Natives Think*, New York 1966 p. 209. The same is true for the Aztecs. In Aztec cosmology, "World Time Age," the supreme couple (two gods forming one unit) first created four sons, whereby the fourth was Huitzilopochtli, at birth only bones and no flesh and who remained six hundred years in that state. Noteworthy here is that it is stated: "During all this time nothing happened on the part of the gods. . . " W. Krickeberg, *Azteken und Inka*, Jena 1928 p. 4.

[5] See C.G. Jung, CW 6, *Psychological Types* ¶817.

[6] See Novalis:

> A truly synthetic person is a person who is several persons at once – a genius. Every person is the seed of an infinite genius. Though divided into various persons it is nevertheless also capable of being a single person. True analysis of a person as such produces several persons – a person can only break up, divide, and dissolve into several persons. . . (Novalis, *Fragmente*, Dresden 1929 No. 1123.)

See also E. Jung, "Beitrag zum Problem des Animus," Zürich 1934 p. 296ff.

28   The division into four is an archetype that is found all over the world and appears to be of central importance. Jung writes:

29   The *quaternarium* or quaternary has a long history. It appears not only in Christian iconology and mystical speculation but plays perhaps a still greater role in Gnostic philosophy and from then on down through the Middle Ages until well into the eighteenth century.[7]

30   Reviewing these sources, Jung discerns a basic scheme: the representation of the given psychic condition by four basic psychological functions:[8]

31   Like the four seasons and the four quarters of heaven, the four elements are a quaternary system of orientation which always expresses a wholeness. . . The orienting system of consciousness has four aspects, which correspond to four empirical functions: thinking, feeling, sensation (sense-perception), and intuition. This quaternary is an archetypal arrangement.[9]

32   The quaternity is an archetype of almost universal occurrence. It forms the logical basis for any whole judgement. If one wishes to pass such a judgement, it must have this fourfold aspect. For instance, if you want to describe the horizon as a whole, you name the four quarters of heaven. . . There are four elements, four prime qualities, four colors, four castes, four ways of spiritual development in Buddhism, etc. So, too, there are four aspects of psychological orientation, beyond which nothing fundamental remains to be said. . . The ideal of completeness is the circle or sphere, but its natural minimal division is a quaternary.[10]

---

[7] C.G. Jung, CW 11, *Psychology and Religion* ¶62, ¶97f; also G. R. S. Mead, *Fragments*, London 1931 p. 374; H. Leisegang, *Die Gnosis*, Leipzig 1924 p. 68, 186.
[8] C.G. Jung, CW 13, *Alchemical Studies* ¶207. See further:
    It is as if we were confronted with a pre-existent ground plan, a kind of Pythagorean *tetraktys*. I have very frequently observed the number four in this connection. It probably explains the universal incidence and magical significance of the cross or of the circle divided into four. (C.G. Jung, CW 12, *Psychology and Alchemy* ¶189.)
    Further:
    Surveying those facts as a whole, we come, at least in my opinion, to the inescapable conclusion that there is some psychic element present which expresses itself through the quaternary. . . No daring speculation or extravagant fancy is needed for this. If I have called the center the "Self," I did so after mature consideration and a careful appraisal of the empirical and historical data. (*Ibid* ¶327.)
    See also C.G. Jung, CW 12, *Psychology and Alchemy* ¶109 and C.G. Jung, CW 6, *Psychological Types passim*, C.G. Jung, CW 11, *Psychology and Religion passim* also Plato's X-shaped layout of the soul in *Timaeus*.
[9] C.G. Jung, CW 13, *Alchemical Studies* ¶207.
[10] C.G. Jung, CW 11, *Psychology and Religion* ¶246.

33   Of the four functions there is one that is the most used and, therefore, the one that is most developed and differentiated. With this dominant function the individual adapts to the objective world, and it determines the psychological typology of the person. Whereas the two auxiliary functions are not in opposition to the main function, but can even complement it, the fourth function is a diametrical opposite to the main function. For example, feeling is the fourth function when thinking is dominant. The fourth function can become a problem for the individual because it lives at the border to the unconscious or can even persist in the unconscious, and negate all conscious values acquired by the dominant function.[11]

34   Two short Caucasian anecdotes about Alexander the Great illustrate the problems of the fourth function graphically. According to the first:

35   When Alexander of Macedonia had just come into the world, he ran around his room. When he came to the fourth corner, an angel knocked him down and let him understand that he would only conquer three continents.[12]

36   The other anecdote told that Alexander had conquered three regions of the world:

37   The fourth part was inhabited by the "poor and righteous" and remained unconquered. It was separated from the rest of the world by an ocean with the same name as the people. Alexander wanted then to conquer this last part. He gathered a large army and set off to that ocean. He erected a bridge and was about to order his army to march

---

[11] Jung writes:
[The term "inferior function"] is used to denote the function that lags behind in the process of differentiation. Experience shows that it is practically impossible, owing to adverse circumstances in general, for anyone to develop all his psychological functions simultaneously. The demands of society compel a man to apply himself first and foremost to the differentiation of the function with which he is best equipped by nature, or which will secure him the greatest social success. Very frequently, indeed as a general rule, a man identifies more or less completely with the most favored and hence the most developed function. . . As a consequence of this one-sided development, one or more functions are necessarily retarded. These functions may properly be called *inferior* in a psychological but not in a psychopathological sense, since they are in no way morbid but merely backward as compared with the favored function. (C.G. Jung, CW 6, *Psychological Types* ¶763.
See also *ibid* ¶589, ¶670-71. See A. Wolff, "Grundlagen," *Festschrift*, Berlin 1935 p. 62ff. On the one-sidedness of people in their main function see also Schiller: Eternally bound to only a single small fragment of the whole, the individual forms himself only as a fragment, eternally only the monotonous noise of the wheels that he turns in his ears; he never develops the harmony of his whole being, instead of unfolding humanity in his nature, he is merely an imprint of his business, his science. (Translated from Schiller 6th letter, *Über die ästhetische Erziehung*, Stuttgart, 1879).
[12] A. Dirr, *Kaukasische Märchen*, Jena 1922 p. 259.

across when an angel of God appeared to him and said, "Alexander, by God's command, you may not wage war in that land. If your ambition does not permit you to retract from this endeavor, then let your army cross over first. Then look to see if even one man keeps his head on his shoulders, and then you can go yourself over the bridge." Alexander did what was said, he let his army cross over the bridge and saw that every soldier lost his head. Spurred by his ambition, he went across himself – and lost his own head. The Poor and Righteous people gathered and stoned him and his whole army.[13]

38 The fourth corner of the room and the fourth part of the world are especially emphasized in these stories. There, an otherworldly power resides, which poses a threat to the individual. The three accessible corners or parts of the world symbolize conscious orientation points, while the fourth manifests forces of the Beyond. On the other hand, there is the belief that the Trinity is holy and three is the number of wholeness, which according to Aristotle signifies the beginning, middle, and the end. In this respect, the Trinity is associated with the deity.[14] The human psyche, however, which encompasses both this reality and the reality of the Beyond, the conscious mind and the unconscious, is characterized by the archetype of the four. A four-part structure is a symbol of earthly wholeness.[15]

39 Of the four figures in "The Three Feathers" (which reflect the natural movement in the human soul),[16] the three sons are less differentiated among themselves from their father, the king, as the two elder brothers and their father are from the youngest brother, the one who is familiar with the magical world. In the above legends about Alexander, the two elder brothers and the king correspond to the accessible parts of the world and represent functions of consciousness; the youngest son, the fourth function, is characterized by his relationship to the unconscious world, and therefore symbolizes a function that draws its power from that realm.[17]

40 The interpretation of the four persons at the outset of a fairytale as the four functions of consciousness is supported by the fact that usually one of

[13] Ibid

[14] See H. Usener, Dreiheit, Bonn 1903 p. 1f, and passim on the graphic and rhythmic application of the trinitarian concept.

[15] According to Carus, at the stage of development he called "emerging awareness of the self," there appears "the great threefold higher psychic life as cognition, feeling, and volition clearly differentiated one from the other." (C.G. Carus, Psyche, Leipzig 1931 p. 153.) After that stage, one can interpret the three kings' sons in fairytales as the above three functions. But as soon as the old king becomes involved as the previously dominant conscious attitude there is again a quaternity of figures.

[16] On the incompleteness of the three in the human soul, see, C.G. Jung, CW 9i, The Archetypes and the Collective Unconscious ¶419–453.

[17] See R. Meyer, Weisheit Schweizer, Schaffhausen 1944 p. 165ff for the anthroposophical view of the threefold soul forces and ibid p. 48 on fourness of the elements as structural factors in the construction of the human being.

them is described as being "old" (the old king, the old father, the old mother) and the fourth as inferior (the youngest as stupid, backward, or clumsy). The essence of the hero is recognized by carefully considering how he (or she) behaves and reacts: his or her awkwardness and foolishness is the expression of the general lack of differentiation of the fourth function, which is in an archaic undeveloped state.[18] This is often depicted as foolishness or poverty, whereby in the latter case, poorness refers to the weak allocation of energy in this function and the poor ability to stand up for itself against the other, more developed functions.[19] In the fairytale "The Gnome" it is said of the youngest, significantly, "he was not quite of this world." This fairytale focuses on the fate and the deeds of this fourth, "poor" figure, and he quickly gains the central importance in the tale. Thus, it is likely that a time of psychic events has been chosen in which old is replaced by new; familiar values give way to previously unrecognized ones. This usually occurs in the middle of life: that is when, in general, people tend psychologically to consider adjusting their relationship from the hitherto most differentiated function in favor of the less well-developed function(s). Whereas the goal of the first half of life seems to be establishing oneself in the world, procreation, expanding and enhancing conscious awareness, a reversal begins in midlife. The focus turns towards death, which entails an exploration of the inner realities. Only then does the confrontation of the ego with the figures of the shadow, and the anima and animus gain importance.[20]

41   Hence the great initiation rites of the ancient mysteries occurred at this stage (see also the "night in mid-Autumn" at the outset of the tale "The Lady of the Moon" when the emperor embarks on his journey to the moon). At first there comes a downward movement, a "regression," and an adaptation to the psychic inner world. Jung refers to this in the context of the myth of the whale-dragon in Frobenius' *Das Zeitalter Des Sonnengottes* [*The Age of the Sun God*] and writes:

42   The hero is the symbolic exponent of the movement of the libido. Entry into the dragon is the regressive direction, and the journey to the East (the "night sea journey") with its attendant events symbolizes the effort to adapt to the conditions of the psychic inner world. The complete swallowing up and disappearance of the hero in the belly of the dragon represents the complete withdrawal of interest from the outer world. The overcoming of the monster from within is the achievement of adaptation to the conditions of the inner world, and

---

[18] See C.G. Jung, CW 6, *Psychological Types* ¶671.
[19] See the frequent abandonment or upbringing of the hero with poor people or shepherds in myths, O. Rank, *Myth of the Birth*, Baltimore 2004 p. 47f.
[20] For more on this problem see, C.G. Jung, CW 8, *The Archetypes and the Collective Unconscious* ¶749f and 796ff, C.G. Jung, CW 5, *Symbols of Transformation* ¶680.

the emergence ("slipping out") of the hero from the monster's belly with the help of a bird, which happens at the moment of sunrise, symbolizes the recommencement of progression. It is characteristic that the monster begins the night sea journey to *the East*, i.e., towards sunrise, while the hero is engulfed in its belly. This seems to me to indicate that regression is not necessarily a *retrograde* step in the sense of a *backwards* development or *degeneration*, but rather represents a necessary phase of development.[21]

43   This regression is shown in the tale, "The Three Feathers" by the descent of the Simpleton to the toad. This happens to fulfill the king's wish for the "most beautiful carpet," whose knotting of colored threads can be understood as a "colorful life" with all its entanglements and embroilments. The king's longing expresses that he has succumbed to a lifeless rigidity, he has distanced himself too far from the roots of life, and when we replace this figure with the first and main function of the psychic personality, or the prevailing attitude, it shows that this power no longer suffices. The symbol of the superior function carried by the old king is typically the only part of his own ego that a person is aware of,[22] and that is often developed to the point of one-sidedness. "This means, on the one hand, the possibility of human freedom, but on the other it is a source of endless transgressions against one's instincts."[23]

44   Around the middle of life, at the height of earthly vigor and "secular" self-confidence, the unconscious forces a turn to the magical, for there are the images and insights that give meaning to the second half of life. The approach to the unconscious leads away from the usual one-sidedness of the developed and familiar conscious mind and shifts the psychic emphasis to that soul part that always stood closer to the magical realm and that is essential for the new orientation. In fairytales this soul part appears as the image of the son, while the father symbolizes the representatives of the traditional spirit or worldview (*Weltanschauung*).[24] If this father-figure, as is often seen in fairytales, appears

---

[21] C.G. Jung, CW 8, *The Archetypes and the Collective Unconscious* ¶68 [emphasis by von Franz and von Beit]. See also C.G. Jung, CW 5, *Symbols of Transformation passim*, esp. ¶251 and ¶306ff, and, "To take an example, the daily course of the sun and the regular alternation of day and night must have imprinted themselves on the psyche in the form of an image from primordial times. We cannot demonstrate the existence of their image, but we find instead more or less fantastic analogies of the physical process. Every morning a divine hero is born from the sea and mounts the chariot of the sun. In the West a Great Mother awaits him, and he is devoured by her in the evening. In the belly of a dragon he reverses the depths of the midnight sea. After a frightful combat with the serpent of night he is born again in the morning." (C.G. Jung, CW 8, *The Archetypes and the Collective Unconscious* ¶326.) See also H. Zimmer, *Maya*, Stuttgart and Berlin 1936 p. 302.
[22] See C.G. Jung, CW 12, *Psychology and Alchemy* ¶137; see also C.G. Carus, *Psyche*, Leipzig 1931 p. 160.
[23] C.G. Jung, CW 9i, *The Archetypes and the Collective Unconscious* ¶276.
[24] See here especially H. Silberer, *Problems of Mysticism*, New York 1917 p. 299; C.G. Jung, CW 7, *Two Essays in Analytical Psychology* ¶389, C.G. Jung, CW 12, *Psychology and Alchemy* ¶59, ¶92, C.G. Jung, CW 9i, *The Archetypes and the Collective Unconscious* ¶69.

as a king, this represents the importance of collective values and dominant authority, which can certainly be attributed to the ego. In the imagination of people from early cultures, as, for example, the ancient Egyptians, the king is the only individual and as such the representative of the whole people, which itself is only an undifferentiated mass. He is the divine Sun, the symbol of conscious awareness.[25]

45   At the outset of many fairytales, this father-king finds himself in an emergency situation. He is sick and often blind, or his secret values have been stolen without trace of the thief. This represents symbolically the failure of the hitherto prevailing conscious attitude. (According to Silberer the father in dreams often refers to the "symbol of an outgrown attitude."[26] The feeling of the intensity of life leaves without being noticed, one finds oneself unable to see how to get along (blindness). Such a situation existed in the Irish fairytale, "The Knight With the Sinister Laugh," in which the king who handed out the tasks represented the prevailing conscious attitude, and needed the exploits of Cathal to complete the building of his new palace. This means, to gain a rounding-out of his personality, and a husband for his daughter. He needed a son-in-law to take over his inheritance. This was only possible through the redemption of the dark knight, the shadow.

46   A tale from the collection, *German Fairy Tales Since Grimm,* "The Diligent and the Lazy Fishermen" tells particularly clearly that the plight causing the hero to embark on his journey is a meaningful situation and at the same time

---

[25] See the exposition by van der Leeuw:
In the primitive world the king is the power bearer, the savior; and for quite a long time he remained so. . . Since kingly potency is no personal capacity, all conceivable salvation is expected of it. The king's power ought to overflow; and the next most closely related consequence of this is that he bestows gifts. . . But royal power likewise manifests itself in matters which we moderns consider quite beyond human attainment. As a genuine savior the king also *heals*. . . The classic land of the royal power, however, was ancient Egypt where the king was addressed as follows: "Thou are indeed he who canst veil the horizon, the sun rises at thy pleasure; we drink the water of the river when thou wilest it, and breathe the air of heaven when thou permittest.". . . The king, then, is also a god: indeed, he is one of the first and oldest gods. Power has been embodied in a living figure. For the King is no rigid god, he is rather a living, active, changeable power, a god who walks among men. But undoubtedly a god. . . Far from being an "important," or even an unimportant, "personality," the king rises and sets as often as the orb with which he is frequently so intimately connected. . . The Egyptians likewise treated the ascension as a parallel to the commencement of all things. Thus, the gospel of the new monarch is of cosmic significance. . . the old deposed ruler is presupposed, so that the king's first proud year succeeds the last sad year of his predecessor. (G. van der Leeuw, *Religion in Essence*, Vol. 1 pp. 115–122.)
Cf. also A. Erman, *Religion der Ägypter*, Berlin and Leipzig 1934 p. 56, M. Ninck, *Wodan*, Jena 1935 p. 195ff; E. Mogk, *Germanische*, Berlin and Leipzig 1927 p. 121f. See also L. Lévy- Bruhl, *The "Soul" of the Primitive*, New York 1928 p. 228f. See the role of the old king in alchemy in C.G. Jung, CW 12, *Psychology and Alchemy* ¶491.
[26] See H. Silberer, *Problems of Mysticism*, New York 1917 p. 250, "Marcinowski found in his analysis that the father in dream life often was a 'symbol of an outlived, obsolete attitude." (J. Marcinowski, "Gezeichnete Träume," *Zentralblatt* 1912), See also the anthroposophical view of R. Meyer, *Weisheit Schweizer*, Schaffhausen 1944 pp. 53–54, who writes that the authority of the old king is founded on tradition.

it is seemingly "intended" by the unconscious to enable the conscious mind to gain access to new values.

47   Once there was a very diligent but poor fisherman who in the space of one year caught no fish and to make matters worse, lost his wife and his only son. But he submitted to his fate and held through with trust in God and patience. One evening – it was the eve of St. Andrew, his patron saint – as he was out walking near the sea, he could not help from crying out loud. It became darker and darker, but in his sadness he did not notice. When he finally came to himself, it was pitch black, he wanted to go home but saw in the distance a small flame dancing on the waves and coming towards the shore. He watched as it came swiftly to shore, busied itself around a little hut, and then returned again to the sea. At a certain place, it lit up more brightly, and then flitted again to the shore.

48   Now the fisherman had heard legends of a light at sea that pointed to sunken treasure, but he was so timid that he turned his back and started to go to his home. Suddenly he heard someone calling his name. The poor fisherman turned and saw behind the ruins of the old hut a pale old man wearing clothes foreign to this place. The strange figure looked at him with such pleading eyes that the brave fisherman felt sorry for him and asked, "Did you call my name, master? Tell me what you wish from me?"

49   The old man answered, "Andrew, you have cried so hard over your misfortunes that I would like to make you a rich man. But to grant this, you must do as I say." Now the poor fisherman became afraid, for he believed the man to be the Devil incarnate. He touched his crucifix and answered. "No, I do not need your help, I would rather remain poor than take from you."

50   Then the old man laughed and said, "You think that I am the Devil and you are mixed up. You can have complete trust in me and it will certainly turn out in your favor. If you will, then take this ring here and come back three days from now. Go right at midnight just a short way out into the sea. You will find three upside-down pots. You must lift up the middle one. This will redeem a poor unfortunate drowned soul. Then you must return to the shore, and do not pay attention to anything you see or hear, I will reward you richly, you will become a happy human in this world." With these words the old one disappeared and at that moment an old rusty ring fell at the foot of the fisherman. But the fisherman could not muster the courage to carry out the task and spoke to himself, "Why should I bother myself

with the souls of the drowned? Why are they so crazy as to be kept in a pot turned upside-down?"

51 The fisherman turned and went indifferently back to his house and thought no further about the strange happenings. But this was not correct, as was soon apparent. In the very next days he lost the rest of the money he had saved over the years. Then he became sick and landed in the hospital for nine months. When he came out, he was as poor as Job and there was nothing else to do but to go begging.

52 [Then he met again the flame and the old man. He found the ring and decided to dare the adventure. He came to the land of the dead and the drowned, and as a result of the advice of the old man he escaped the dangers there and returned home with treasures. Nearby was a lazy fisherman who had heard the story and tried to imitate the adventure but failed miserably.][27]

53 This story shows more clearly than many other examples just how the initial distress seems to some extent to be intentionally brought about by the unconscious, because it wants to force the individual to change some conscious attitude.

54 "All true wisdom is only to be learned far from the dwellings of men out in the great solitude, and is only attained through suffering. Privation and suffering are the only things that can open the mind of man to those things that are hidden from others."[28]

55 Thus spoke one Inuit shaman about the tortures of their initiations. Individuals who do not want to get into a hopeless conflict situation with the all-powerful unconscious should ask themselves, "what is meant by this emergency and what is required of me?" And give themselves the answer that, as in this tale, the new life values are contained in the unconscious (the sea) and have to be won by a new conscious attitude that is opposite to a previous one. A different form is chosen in "The Three Feathers." There the king seeks the most beautiful carpet because as the embodiment of an outdated and infertile conscious standpoint, he must turn to the resource of archetypal images. The carpet is a fabric and thus a product of the Great Mother, nature's weaver. The colorfulness of the sought-after carpet indicates the diversity and fulness of life. The king desires the invigorating variety of natural connections of fate, from which he has apparently distanced himself. In fairytales, a flying carpet sometimes appears that carries one at one's will through the air. The

---

[27] Translated, original in P. Zaunert, *Deutsche Märchen seit Grimm*, Jena 1922 p. 63ff.
[28] Igjugarjuk, an Inuit shaman, quoted in Rasmussen p. 81.

fabric – and the images woven into the carpet – symbolize fantasies and call attention to how imagination can shape reality.

56   The king blows three feathers in three directions and orders his sons to follow them.[29] This action is similar to folk customs of interrogating an oracle.[30] Fate is left to chance or, better, to the spirit that "bloweth where it listeth,"[31] that is, it is entrusted to the soul. The breath is something psychic or mental (compare [ανεμος] *anemos–anima*, *spiritus–pneuma*, and so forth), or spiritual, which here emerges from traditional consciousness. This is not capable of accomplishing the task by itself, but in that the will turns to the magical, thus creating space for objective psychic events, which is equivalent to taking a risk,[32] in that the individual must desperately resist the dictates of reason, as we understand it, and give up the supremacy of egohood, regarded by reason as sacrosanct. What this means in practice is complete capitulation to the objective powers of the psyche, with all that this entails; a kind of figurative death. . .[33]

57   The feathers as parts standing for the whole are the same as birds (in other versions arrows appear)[34] and contain a mystical power. Like hair, they signify something spiritual, which is now allowed to take on a guiding function. Whereas the feathers of the elder brothers fly east and west, the feather of the youngest falls right in front of him and leads into his own inner depths, to the mother.[35] That he should go this way is founded in his own being as the

---

[29] H. Silberer, *Problems of Mysticism*, New York 1917 p. 226, explains (paraphrasing Hitchcock) in anagogic allegory, the trinity of the three sons as symbolizing the body, soul, and spirit. The two older sons are "wise in the worldly sense," meaning reason and emotion, and the third is conscience.

[30] See J. Bolte and L. Mackensen, *Handwörterbuch* Berlin 1930, under *Die drei Federn* [The Three Feathers].

[31] John 3: 8.

[32] See here Jung:

The resistance of the conscious mind to the unconscious and the depreciation of the latter were historical necessities in the development of the human psyche, for otherwise the conscious mind would never have been able to differentiate itself at all. But modern man's consciousness has strayed rather too far from the fact of the unconscious. We have even forgotten that the psyche is by no means of our design, but is for the most part autonomous and unconscious. Consequently, the approach of the unconscious induces a fear in civilized people, not least on account of the menacing analogy with insanity. The intellect has no objection to 'analyzing' the unconscious as a passive object; on the contrary such an activity would coincide with our rational expectations. But to let the unconscious go its own way and to experience it as a reality is something that exceeds the courage and capacity of the average European. He prefers simply not to understand this problem. For the spiritually weak-kneed this is the better course, since the thing is not without its dangers. (C.G. Jung, CW 12, *Psychology and Alchemy* ¶60.)

[33] C.G. Jung, CW 11, *Psychology and Religion* ¶846.

[34] See J. Bolte and L. Mackensen, *op. cit.*, under *Federn* [feathers] and *Die drei Federn*. See also J. Bolte and G. Polívka, *Anmerkungen*, Vol. 1, Leipzig 1913 p. 37f on blowing feathers in ancient customs and folk sayings about giving direction or giving a new direction to something.

[35] According to J. Bolte and G. Polívka, *Anmerkungen*, Vol. 2, Leipzig 1915 p. 30, the feathers of the Simpleton in the Hessian version fly "onto a rock not far from the palace." The Simpleton sits on the stone, which moves by itself and exposes the trap door. See Bächtold-Stäubli under *durchkriechen*, *durchlaufen*, *durchziehen* [creep through, crawl through, run through] an opening as a healing ceremony and symbolic rebirth in superstitious beliefs. See also C.G. Jung, CW 5, *Symbols of Transformation* ¶549

Simpleton, because as such he naturally gropes for what is closest, most natural, and this very simplicity of his reactions, his utter lack of pre-suppositions, leads him to the goal. Meister Eckhart says of this attitude:

58   How much more should we remove ourselves from all things, gather our powers together, in order to see and to know the sole, immeasurable, uncreated truth? For this you should gather all your senses, your faculties, the whole of your intellect and memory, drawing it all into the ground in which this treasure lies buried. If this is to happen, then we know that you must strip yourself of all other works and must enter a state of unknowing, if you are to succeed in finding this.[36]

59   Thanks to his inner willingness, the Simpleton gains access to the inside of the earth. The earth is the receptive, the mother, and also means physicality and reality. That it is the youngest son who finds the way there is, of course, natural because within the whole personality he represents the earthy part of the human soul.[37] The hole in the earth is the entry into the unconscious, the passage to rebirth (see the hole from which the people came to earth in "The Legend of Okonoróté" or the birth hole in the sky in "Kaboi").[38] The ladder or stairs symbolize the path of a change or transformation that takes place in stages.[39]

60   When the Simpleton knocks, a strange verse comes from the inside, full of contradictions. It contains in germinal form a multiplicity of ideas, a not-yet-clearly-drawn primordial image, that is, a typical manifestation of the

---

fn. 95 where Jung equates the image of a youth crawling through a hollow oak tree to "entering into the mother, becoming immersed in oneself." This entry into one's own inner world, is often symbolized by crawling or going through something. See Jung:

> [T]he libido sinks "into its own depths" (a favorite image of Nietzsche's) and discovers in the darkness a substitute for the upper world it has abandoned – the world of memories . . . It is the world of the child, the paradisal state of early infancy, from which we are driven out by the relentless law of time. In this subterranean kingdom slumber sweet feelings of home and the hopes of all that is to be . . . For if the libido gets stuck in the wonderland of this inner world, then for the upper world man is nothing but a shadow, he is already moribund or at least seriously ill. But if the libido manages to tear itself loose and force its way up again, something like a miracle happens: the journey to the underworld was a plunge into this fountain of youth, and the libido, apparently dead, wakes to renewed fruitfulness." (*Ibid* ¶448-449.)

[36] Meister Eckhart (trans. Davies), *Selected Writings*, London 1994 p. 219, Original German in Pfeiffer's edition p. 13 *Predigten* No. 2 on *Matthew*, 2: 2. See also the *Chandogya Upanishad*, "But just as one who does not know the spot, does not find the gold-treasure concealed under it, although he again and again goes over that spot, so also all these creatures do not find the world of Brahman, although they enter into it every day (in deep sleep); because they have been forced away by untruth." (*Chandogya Upanishad* Chapter VIII, Part 3, Verse 2. Deussen, *Sixty Upanishads* pp. 193–94.)

[37] See C.G. Jung, CW 12, *Psychology and Alchemy* ¶192–193 on the connection between the fourth function and the unconscious.

[38] See also "Help in Need," and "The Coming of the Hopi from the Underworld," and the note in W. Krickeberg, *Nordamerika*, Jena 1924 p. 410 and T.-W. Danzel, "The Psychology of Ancient Mexican Symbolism," *Spiritual Disciplines*, Princeton 1960 p. 112.

[39] ["Stairs mean gaining consciousness step by step." (C.G. Jung, *Children's Dreams*, Princeton 2008 p. 75).]

unconscious. The contents flow over into one another and avail themselves of a more comprehensive language than that of consciousness, which in order to make itself clearly understood is forced to exclude other viewpoints.[40]

61   The first verse of the poem in "The Three Feathers" begins "Maiden green and small." As evident from the following images, this seems to refer to a toad. On the other hand, the salutation "Maiden (damsel)" is an allusion to the princess, the anima figure. The green color is that of vegetation and a symbol of life.[41] ("The green of life's golden tree.") Green is associated in the Christian doctrine with the Holy Spirit, who is a "Quickener."[42]

62   In Tibetan mythology green is the color of the "all-effecting wisdom."[43] In Egypt, "to do green things" meant something like to do beneficial things, and for the Aztecs, the "green gemstone [that is, jade]" was the animating principle.[44] Green is the color of growth,[45] and in the Muslim world, the servant of Allah is Chider (Khidr), the Green, son of the water depth, who in his lively and arcane but wise ways ministers his master's works on Earth.[46] For the individual, this is about the strength and life-productive base on which to stand in life, and eventually to find oneself. Thus, the hero in "The Three Feathers" obtains the renewal of life on Earth from an insignificant little green creature. Through the encounter with the toad:

---

[40] See Jung, "Differentiation is the *sine qua non* of consciousness. Everything unconscious is undifferentiated, and everything that happens unconsciously proceeds on the basis of non-differentiation. . . " C.G. Jung, CW 7, *Two Essays in Analytical Psychology* ¶329.

[41] On the meaning of the color green, see Dossetor p. 16,
> The very first manifestation of life is green slime on the mud. Green is the color of the grass that feeds cattle, the corn that feeds man, the leaves of the tree . . . It [green] symbolizes the green earth from which our own life comes, and to which we must return to renew our strength. "Hunting the Green Lyon" is one of the alchemical symbols for the way of psychological development . . .(R. Dossetor, *Gawain*, London 1942)

[42] See C.G. Jung, CW 11, *Psychologie und Religion* ¶118, C.G. Jung, CW 12, *Psychology and Alchemy* ¶317–320. See also Silesius, "God is Green" (The Godhead Brings Forth Growth), "The Godhead is my sap; what in me greens and flowers / It is the Holy Ghost who all the growth empowers." A. Silesius, *The Cherubinic Wanderer*, New Jersey 1986 p. 43, No. 90.

[43] See C.G. Jung, CW 11, *Psychology and Religion* ¶850.

[44] See also the Chinese tale "Sky O'Dawn" in which an old wise man says, "The pupils of my eyes have gradually acquired a green glow, which enables me to see all hidden things." For Egypt see A. Erman, *Religion der Ägypter*, Berlin and Leipzig 1934 p. 39. On the Aztecs, W. Krickeberg, *Azteken und Inka*, Jena 1928 p. 323, 330 notes to "Two gods become the Sun and Moon" and "Quetzalcuatl's Youth."

[45] See C.G. Jung, CW 12, *Psychology and Alchemy* p. 207. See also the Chinese fairytale, "Dschang Liang" in which the hero receives the command:
> Green the garments you should wear,
> If to heaven's gate you'd fare; There the Golden Mother greet,
> Bow before the Wood Lord's feet!

When Dschang Liang heard this, he bowed before the youths, and said to his friends: "Those are angel children of the King Father of the East. The Golden Mother is the Queen of the West. The Lord of Wood is the King Father of the East. They are the two primal powers, the parents of all that is male and female, the root and fountain of heaven and earth, to whom all that has life is indebted for its creation and nourishment. The song of the angel children shows us the manner in which the hidden knowledge may be acquired." Green is the color of the Lord of the Wood. See also "And green the golden tree of life." Lines 2038-2039 from J. W. von Goethe *Faust*, Stuttgart 1949 Part 1.

[46] See C.G. Jung, CW 5, *Symbols of Transformation* ¶282ff, C.G. Jung, CW 9i, *The Archetypes and the Collective Unconscious* ¶240-258.

63   [A] new and powerful life springs up just where there had seemed to be no life and no power and no possibility of further development. It comes streaming out of the unconscious, from that unknown part of the psyche which is therefore disregarded by all rationalists. From this discredited and rejected region comes the new afflux of energy, the renewal of life. But what is this discredited and rejected source of vitality? It consists of all those psychic contents that were repressed because of their incompatibility with conscious values – everything hateful, immoral, wrong, unsuitable, useless, etc. which means everything that at one time or another appeared so to the individual concerned.[47]

64   The toad or "maiden"[48] is also described as *Hutzelbein* [hop-leg]. Toads and old people are "wrinkled." Such is the mysterious creature small like a seed and shriveled like an ancient being. It is at this moment engaged in a transformation like a new seed that falls to the ground and breaks down to sprout new life. Moreover, the "maiden/spinster" is still addressed as "hopping toad's puppy." This probably means that "hop-leg" is the name of the old toad, and "maiden" is her servant who opens the door and fetches things for the old toad. The term "puppy" is already a clue that this mysterious maiden is a warm-blooded animal at a significantly higher level than frogs. This hints at the anima's development, which also extends through the plant kingdom (turnip). The dog is a common manifestation of the chthonic primordial mother or her companion, like Hecate and the wild hunt. He is in almost all religions the guardian of the land of the dead and guide of the dead souls[49] and, in contrast to wild animals, represents domesticated instinct.

65   As the door opens, the youngest son of the king sees the big fat toad surrounded by a circle of small toads. As already mentioned, the old toad is an image of the Great Mother. That she is also an image of the principle of evil, as the causative agent of disease, as well as its antidote.[50] It

---

[47] C.G. Jung, CW 6, *Psychological Types* p. 449.
[48] [Can also be translated as "spinster."]
[49] See M. Ninck, *Wodan*, Jena 1935 p. 65 fn. 4, C.G. Jung, CW 5, *Symbols of Transformation* ¶354, ¶577; G. Roeder, *Urkunden*, Jena 1923 p. XXI; also, "The Three Realms of the Dead," "Tales of the Toad" and notes in W. Krickeberg, *Azteken und Inka*, Jena 1928 pp. 326–327. See also, "Sedna's World, Version 4" and notes in W. Krickeberg, *Nordamerika*, Jena 1924 pp. 367–368.
[50] See H. Silberer, *Problems of Mysticism*, New York 1917 p. 219 [who analyses this tale in detail], W. Laiblin, "Urbild," *Märchenforschung und Tiefenpsychologie*, Darmstadt 1936 p. 94, 96, 147, O. Tobler, *Epiphanie*, Kiel 1911 pp. 25–28, O. Rank, *Myth of the Birth*, Baltimore 2004 p. 81 fn. 52. On the partly frightening, partly auspicious meaning of the toad in superstition see Bächtold-Stäubli under *Kröte* [toad], J. Bolte and L. Mackensen, *Handwörterbuch* Berlin 1930, under *Frosch, Kröte* [frog, toad]. There it is stated that, "Tlalteucli, the ancient Mexican earth goddess takes the form of a toad." See *ibid* under *Froschkönig* [Frog King], "The toad encompasses a wide range in folklore and folk medicine and is a soul animal. On All Souls' Day in Tirol, it is forbidden to kill toads because perhaps some poor soul lives in their skin. . . " See also C.G. Jung, CW 5, *Symbols of Transformation* ¶367 fn. 77 and, E. Mogk, *Germanische*, Berlin and Leipzig 1927 pp. 33–34. See in addition notes to the Peruvian tale "Uallallo and Pariacaca" and the notes

corresponds here to the treasure-hoarding dragon, found in many myths and fairytales.[51]

66 In a fairytale from the Tirol region of Austria "The Strange Marriage" it is the old toad herself who later transforms into the bride of the simpleton-hero.[52]

67 She is also the anima as mother-lover.[53]

68 A Norwegian fairytale "The Youth Who Wanted to Win the Daughter of the Mother in the Corner" describes a parallel process to our tale:[54]

69 There was once a useless, lazy boy who danced around and did nothing the whole day long. He continually outgrew all his clothes and ate more and more each day. Finally, his mother could not keep up with the mending and cooking and she said he must now really go to work or they shall starve. The boy said he was not going to work; he would marry the daughter of the mother in the corner. This turned out to be a rat who lived in the swamp and carried a bunch of keys hanging from her tail.[55] She bestowed on him great riches, gave him linen and woolen threads, which he had to trail behind him, constantly repeating the words, "Short before, long behind," whereby the fabric lengthened and grew.[56] In the end, perhaps in response to his somewhat flippant greeting at the beginning, she required that he marry her. On the way to the wedding, the rat traveled in a frying pan through the swamp and the young man had to walk beside. But gradually the road became more passable, and the rat transformed into a beautiful princess and the rat's hole changed into a beautiful castle.

70 The rat is, like the toad, an animal of the earth, the darkness, and a symbol of the mother goddess. The rat may also have a witchlike character, here she appears as a generous and giving mother.

---

in W. Krickeberg, *Azteken und Inka*, Jena 1928 p. 385, and notes in T. Koch-Grünberg, *Südamerika*, Jena 1921 p. 324 to the tale from an Amazon tribe, "The Kurupira and the Woman."
[51] On the dragon who guards the pearl in China see E. Rousselle, "Drache," *Eranos*, Zürich 1935 p. 22 and in general C.G. Jung, CW 5, *Symbols of Transformation* ¶569f, ¶578. See also "Ngeraod's Bundle," where the vitally important symbol was also in the possession of the Great Mother.
[52] In Zingerle pp. 306–310.
[53] See the fairytale from the Donau region, "Hansel Croak-Croak" and the literary parallels in A. Wesselski, *Versuch*, Reichenberg i. B. 1931 p. 162.
[54] [Here summarized.]
[55] She opens up the secrets of the unconscious!
[56] In this way, she revealed to him that "short in front," that is, what appears unimportant to the conscious mind, will be compensated "behind" by the unconscious through values that evolve or develop naturally. The rat thus forces the hero to recognize the long past that is behind him, the "fabric" of ideas in the unconscious.

71   Similarly, in "The Three Feathers" the toad expresses her bestowing motherly nature, which in turn is symbolized and emphasized by the large box containing all that one could wish for[57] including the magical carpet that the Simpleton takes to his father.

72   Despite the undeniable success of the Simpleton in the eyes of the king, it takes four tests to finally come to what is his right; the two elder brothers do not accept the successes of their younger brother. They embody the resistance of the conscious mind that is reluctant to acknowledge the value of the unconscious skills and opportunities personified by the youngest brother.[58] Thus, for his second task, the Simpleton brings back a beautiful ring. This assignment represents a development over the previous task.[59] Whereas the carpet generally symbolizes the "fullness of life," the ring is something formed, complete in itself, and integrally whole. Its circular shape makes it a mandala, and, therefore, a symbol of the Self. This was already foreshadowed in the circular arrangement of the small toads around the big one. Silberer[60] suggests that the toad's ring symbolizes nature's cycles, ". . . for nature always returns upon herself in a cycle." This accords also with the Gnostic-Alchemical idea of the dragon that bites its own tail.[61]

73   The ring is a symbol of bonds and relationships, especially the relationship between body and soul.[62] Like the carpet, the ring stands for the connection

---

[57] See the interpretation of the box as womb by Silberer:
>   The toad's box (= mother) is also the womb. From it indeed the female symbols, in this connection, sister, are produced for the simpleton. The box is, however, also the domestic cupboard – food closet, parcel, bandbox, chamber, bowl, etc. – from which the good mother hands out tasty gifts, toys, etc. (H. Silberer, *Problems of Mysticism*, New York 1917 p. 225.)

[58] Also R. Meyer, *Weisheit Schweizer*, Schaffhausen 1944 pp. 95–96, interprets the secular-minded brothers as no longer appropriate cognitive powers; on pp. 165–174ff he calls them – seen anthroposophically – sensory and rational soul parts; the youngest, however, the conscious soul. See Bächtold-Stäubli under *Jüngster* [youngest] on the role of the youngest son in popular belief and in legal instruments, "the right of the youngest."

[59] See J. Bolte and G. Polívka, *Anmerkungen,* Vol. 2, Leipzig 1915 p. 34ff. In parallel fairytales there are different task series. Noteworthy variants are: shirt-bread-dance, or canvas-dog-bride, and especially mirror-image of the bride-bride.

[60] In H. Silberer, *Problems of Mysticism*, New York 1917 p. 228.

[61] See H. Leisegang, "Schlange," *Eranos*, Zürich 1940 pp. 187–188, and H. Leisegang, *Die Gnosis*, Leipzig 1924 p. 140f.

[62] See Guentert:
>   For us the wedding ring is foremost a symbol of the marital bond, and when an engagement is dissolved, the first act is the return of the symbolic golden fetters, as given in a verse by Josef von Eichendorff, *Das zerbrochene Ringlein* [The broken little ring]: She promised me faithfulness,
>   and gave me a ring;
>   she has broken the trust:
>   and my little ring broke in two.
>   The ring is a symbol of power and domination, and bestows mystical power, see Balder's ring *Draupnir* and the Sigurd (Siegfried) legend of Andvari's Ring, which he gave to Brynhildyr (Brünnehilde) The great ring of kingship [ribboned diadem (cydaris)], as shown with the Ahura Mazda on reliefs and even the God usually interpreted as "Opinn" on the golden Horn next to a rod in his left hand. . . is certainly also intended here. . . We already know that one liked to designate family members as "allies". . . Those without such a "relationship" have no rights. (H. Güntert, *Weltkönig*, Halle a. S. 1923 pp. 71–72.)

to the feminine principle. In the fairytale, "The Story of the Blind King Who Lived in the Western Lands," a ring is given to the hero by a winged woman so that he will later be recognized. The ring is a symbol of the Self. "This 'the round' thing is the great treasure that lies hidden in the cave of the unconscious, and. . . represents the higher unity of conscious and the unconscious."[63] This totality can only be represented by a symbol because only a symbol can express the unconscious and at the same time correspond to the presentiment of consciousness. It indicates the possibility of a new manifestation of life.[64]

74   Only the fourth, that function of the ego standing closest to the unconscious, can bring forth this symbol. The two elder brothers are unable to discern the value and retrieve only things from the secular and collective world.[65]

75   The symbol of the anima is of such important and yet difficult to recognize values that here even the Simpleton, who otherwise had direct access to the gifts of the Earth Mother, is put to a test of confidence, in that the princess appears in the most unassuming form. He must accept her as a toad in a carrot-carriage drawn by mice. As Silberer recognized, the carrot, as a root [tuber], represents the vegetative life, the body.[66] They are the root force of all beings. Just as the carrot grows under the ground, so, too, the mice are underground creatures, shy nocturnal animals, which reproduce very quickly. They symbolize unconscious instinctual emotions, erotic desires, which are grouped around that root strength.[67] While the toad as the Great Mother dominates the center of the circle, the anima lives on the periphery. Psychologically the anima is a derivative, a rejuvenated form of the mother

---

See also M. Ninck, *Wodan*, Jena 1935 p. 60, 311 on Odin's miracle ring Draupnir, also called *Träufler*, from which new rings continue to fall like golden drops. See also the miraculous Ring of Gyges [mentioned by Plato in *The Republic*], that makes one invisible, and, according to J.

J. Bachofen, *Mutterrecht*, Stuttgart 1861 p. 52, is an image of chthonic power. [See also the One Ring from J. R. R. Tolkien's *The Hobbit* and *The Lord of the Rings*.] See also the miraculous ring in C. Guest, *Mabinogion*, London/New York (1906) 1937 p. 159. Such wishing rings are also found in fairytales, for example, in "The Creation of the World," "Don Juan and the Magician- Witch," "Hans One and a Half," "The Story of the Old Witch," and "Diarmuid Donn and the Magic Flute."

[63] C.G. Jung, CW 9i, *The Archetypes and the Collective Unconscious* p. 248.

[64] Jung: "The symbol is the primitive exponent of the unconscious but at the same time an idea that corresponds to the highest intuitions of the conscious mind." See C.G. Jung, CW 13, *Alchemical Studies* ¶44f. See also C.G. Jung, CW 6, *Psychological Types* ¶789f.

[65] See here Jung:

It may well be . . . that beneath the neglected functions there lie hidden far higher individual values which, though of small importance for collective life, are of the greatest value for individual life, and are therefore vital values that can endow the life of the individual with an intensity and beauty he will vainly seek in his collective function. (*Ibid* ¶113.)

[66] See H. Silberer, *Problems of Mysticism*, New York 1917 p. 228.

[67] On the mouse as a totem animal and a complement to lighter and higher deities, see:

A. Lang, *Custom and Myth*, London 1885 pp. 103–120. Starting with the Iliad, I, 39, on the relation between the mouse and Apollo (in the temple of Apollo Smintheus where mice were kept) Lang relates mice also to Rudra and other figures, and brings a wealth of amplificatory material.

image. The anima's obligatory command to accept her in a lower or even repulsive shape has many parallels. In one of these:

76   The Simpleton went under a stone on which his feather had landed, and then into the ground. There, a maiden directed him onwards to a vault where he should find the most beautiful woman in the world. The Simpleton went there and came to a chamber where everything glittered and shimmered with gold and precious stones. But instead of a beautiful woman, a disgusting frog sat in the middle of the room. The frog called out to him, "Embrace me and lose yourself!" He was repulsed and the frog called out a second and third time, "Embrace me and lose yourself!" Then the Simpleton picked up the frog and carried her up to a pond and jumped in with her. Hardly had they touched the water, then he found himself holding in his arms the most beautiful maiden in the world. They climbed out of the water and he went with her to his home and presented the woman to his father. She was indeed a thousand times more beautiful than the women whom the other princes had brought home.[68]

77   The anima's close relationship to the Great Mother, that partly good and partly evil representative of the unconscious, is the reason that their first appearance elicits repugnance. As far as the unconscious is represented as female, it can be personified by the anima.[69]

78   The Simpleton represents that part of the soul that is related to the conscious personality, but reaching into the unconscious; a connection to the anima represents, therefore, the continuation of the fourth function into the unconscious. Once the youth has overcome his last suspicions and, laying aside his critical judgement, complies with the commands of the toad, all the spiritual forces blossom into unimaginable beauty and the toad [the Great Mother aspect of the anima], becomes a lovely princess.

79   But even after gaining the anima, the resistance of the elder brothers does not stop; they stipulate that the women jump through a hoop. The mandala symbol appears once again in this hoop as a leitmotif. The new psychic powers

---

[68] See J. Bolte and G. Polívka, *Anmerkungen,* Vol. 2, Leipzig 1915 p. 31. See also, "The Princesses as a Monkey." There the anima is initially an ape.

[69] See C.G. Jung, CW 12, *Psychology and Alchemy* ¶145. Perhaps the following quote from Jung might help to understand this better:

    In the [masculine] psychology of the functions there are two conscious and therefore masculine functions, the differentiated function and its auxiliary, which are represented in dreams by, say, father and son, whereas the unconscious functions appear as mother and daughter. Since the conflict between two auxiliary functions is not nearly as great as that between the differentiated and the inferior function, it is possible for the third function – that is, the unconscious auxiliary one – to be raised to consciousness and thus made masculine. It will, however, bring with it traces of its contamination with the darkness of the unconscious. (*Ibid* ¶192.)

only have value when they can pass freely through this ring and fit in with the psychic wholeness, full of life vigor and movement. Remarkably, this soul figure coming from the Earth Mother succeeds without difficulty in jumping through, while the seemingly down-to-earth, reality-oriented peasant women of the brothers break their legs. Both make the connection to the earth, to daily reality on this side. It turns out that, despite their apparently secular realism, the two functions standing closest to the conscious mind just do not have the power to make the connection to life. Around the middle of life, a new force leads to the way to actual reality, which, on the one hand, is a piece of nature, but on the other hand, appears in the shape of a spiritual wholeness in mandala form that leads beyond merely chaotic nature.

80   The two elder brothers take on in a characteristic way the role of the shadow. This is also shown, for example, in a Gypsy (Roma) tale "Threeson,"[70] in which the two elder brothers take over the role of the slanderer (that is, Ferdinand the Unfaithful). This results in a complementary illumination of the figure of the shadow: he is actually dangerous, being connected, on the one hand, to the conscious mind, and simultaneously, on the other hand, to the unconscious. Thus, the shadow possesses neither the innocence of pure unconscious nature nor the unambiguous clarity of pure consciousness.

81   Because the youngest brother has found real new life values, he is the rightful heir to the throne, and as expressly stated, rules long and wisely. This ending is a typical conclusion to many fairytales.[71] Therein is expressed psychologically that the person who was previously seen as carrying the dominant attitude and the differentiated mental function, has been cast aside to make way for the "hero," the hitherto despised fourth function. Thus the total personality, symbolized as the "kingdom," develops with new leadership and a younger force, which can complement the paternal tradition through its contact with the netherworld.[72] Novalis speaks of an "absolute, wonderful synthesis" that is "often the axis of a fairytale or the goal itself."[73]

82   By interpreting the characters represented in fairytales as inner psychic events and goals, the figure of the hero can now be even more clearly outlined. He embodies the emerging personality, who develops from inconspicuous beginnings to the power that sees the person through to real values in life.

---

[70] A parallel to "Ferdinand the Faithful and Ferdinand the Unfaithful." For more parallels see J. Bolte and G. Polívka, *Anmerkungen,* Vol. 3, Leipzig 1918 p. 18ff.

[71] See J. Bolte and L. Mackensen, *Handwörterbuch* Berlin 1930, under *Erbschaft* [inheritance]. See also Parsifal as heir of Amfortas.

[72] See C.G. Jung, CW 7, *Two Essays in Analytical Psychology* ¶347 on the development of the unconscious into the leading power, while the conscious mind lets itself be indiscernibly led. In another place Jung writes:

> But if the unconscious can be recognized as a co-determining factor along with consciousness and if we can live in such a way that conscious and unconscious demands are taken into account as far as possible, then the centre of gravity of the total personality shifts its position. (C.G. Jung, CW 13, *Alchemical Studies* ¶67.)

[73] Novalis, *Fragmente,* Dresden 1929

According to how the fairytale dramatically personifies the individual psychic functions, the part of the psyche that is most closely bound to the unconscious is portrayed as the youngest or "dumbest" of the three brothers, or, as the fourth figure of a given group of four quaternity that includes the father. This soul part mediates all the living wealth of the unconscious to which the conscious functions do not have access. As mediator of the highest magical values, the fourth gains a great significance. As far as the fairytale portrays a psychic process whose carrier is a hero initially represented as a simpleton, one can view this as the personification of a striving for self-realization, as the embodiment of the inner superior personality,[74] that is, the Self, which "includes the experience of the ego and therefore transcends it."[75] This superhuman, or supernatural, side of the Self as experienced as something more than the ego, is often expressed in fairytales through the divine or animal attribute of the hero, and the more ego side as his humanity.[76]

83   Many fairytales focus solely on the fate of the hero, he just emerges somehow out of the unconscious. Suddenly he stands there as in "The Two Travelers" or "Ferdinand the Faithful and Ferdinand the Unfaithful." He passes the usual tests and battles with enemies who arise from the opposing nature of the unconscious itself, or who, in their secular nature (for instance, the king in "Ferdinand the Faithful and Ferdinand the Unfaithful"), clearly reveal that they embody the prevailing conscious powers that defend themselves against the emerging Self. The conscious mind takes a hostile position towards the Self because through the confrontation, it experiences a relative devaluation. Sometimes at the end of the tale the king, as personification of the conscious mind, is deposed or killed and then replaced by the hero. The present tale, "The Three Feathers," shows more clearly the position and evolution of the previously ruling conscious attitude, shown by the three feathers. Initially he appears as the carrier of the dominant conscious attitude as a father-king within the tetrad, and at the end of the story he abdicates and the hero is declared to be the proper heir to his throne. The different depictions of the origin of the hero correspond to a paradoxical psychological truth: the Self is, on the one hand, that which has always been there "in me," although perhaps unrecognized or even despised. At the same time, it is a completely foreign, unknown power emerging from far away. (In myths this combination appears in the figure of the royal child, who is abandoned and then years later returns as someone totally unknown.)[77] The hero personifies the. . .

---

[74] On this, see C.G. Jung, CW 7, *Two Essays in Analytical Psychology* ¶121 on the transcendent function, C.G. Jung, CW 5, *Symbols of Transformation* ¶536 on the impersonal and universal nature of the hero, and C.G. Jung, CW 5, *Symbols of Transformation* ¶592f on the symbol of the hero.

[75] C.G. Jung, CW 11, *Psychology and Religion* ¶885.

[76] On this see this C.G. Jung, CW 9i, *The Archetypes and the Collective Unconscious* ¶281. For the non-human and superhuman aspects of the hero and the other characters in fairytales, see Lüthi p. 11ff, 14f, 58.

[77] See O. Rank, *Myth of the Birth*, Baltimore 2004 *passim*.

84   . . . vital forces quite outside the limited range of our conscious mind; of ways and possibilities of which our one-sided conscious mind knows nothing; a wholeness, which embraces the very depths of Nature. It [the child hero] represents the strongest, the most ineluctable urge of nature, namely the urge to realize oneself. It is, as it were, an incarnation of *the inability to do otherwise*, equipped with all the powers of nature and instinct, whereas the conscious mind is always getting caught up in its supposed ability to do otherwise. The urge and compulsion towards self-realization is a law of nature and thus of invincible power, even though its effect, at the start, is insignificant and improbable.[78]

85   From the beginning this self-realization was already marked out in the group of four (the father and his three sons), because the quaternary is in itself a psychic image of the Self.[79] Thus the four quarters are the Self, and the fourth quarter alone is also the Self.

86   The mandala appears in our story a second time, and that is in the ring of tiny toads under the earth with the big toad in the middle. (A transition mandala shows up in a parallel tale in which a marble slab with a ring is the starting point for the descent into the earth.)[80] While the first mandala consisted of four males, the second is purely feminine. The first is an organizing distribution without a central point, the second, in contrast, has the large toad in the middle, who in one parallel version herself turns into the princess.[81] That this mandala lies in the earth expresses that it has the character of reality, which is highlighted by the female element. The fourth function, which is almost always in the male psyche connected to the female principle, is psychologically the mediator between the conscious functions and the earth and feminine principle. Thus, it is the Simpleton who finds the way to that earthy hidden mandala, whose center is represented by an animal mother deity. There is so far no relationship to the upper world, which is probably due to the absence of interest, participation, or involvement by the conscious mind (that is, the old king). Winning the anima is seen here to be an enrichment of the personality through the incorporation of the female element. Thus, in this tale, as in others we have studied, awareness of the anima and inclusion of the feminine element into the conscious personality is considered to be the essential condition for the renewal of the personality.

---

[78] C.G. Jung, CW 9i, *The Archetypes and the Collective Unconscious* ¶289.
[79] See C.G. Jung, CW 12, *Psychology and Alchemy* ¶327.
[80] See J. Bolte and G. Polívka, *Anmerkungen*, Vol. 2, Leipzig 1915 p. 30.
[81] *Ibid* p. 31.

◆

Chapter 2

The Poor Miller's Boy and the Cat

87 Another fairytale that takes a similarly simple course, focusing again on the anima problem, is the Grimm Brothers' tale, "The Poor Miller's Boy and the Cat":

88 In a certain mill lived an old miller who had neither wife nor child but three apprentices who served under him. As they had been with him for many years, he one day said to them: "I am old and want to sit in the chimney-corner. Go out, and whosoever of you brings me the best horse home, to him will I give the mill, and in return for it he shall take care of me till my death. The third of the boys was, however, the dunce, who was looked on as foolish by the others and they called him Stupid Hans. They begrudged the mill to him; after all, he was not even interested and most likely did not even want it. Then all three went out together, and when they came to the village, the two said to Stupid Hans, "You may just as well stay here, as long as you live, you will never get a horse." Hans went with them, however, and when it was night they came to a cave in which they lay down to sleep. The two sharp ones waited until Hans had fallen asleep, then they got up and went away, leaving him where he was. And they thought they had done a very clever thing, but it was certain to turn out ill for them.

89 When the sun arose and Hans woke up, he was lying in a deep cavern. He clambered out of the cave, went into the forest, and thought, "Here I am quite alone and deserted, how shall I obtain a horse now?" Whilst he was thus walking full of thoughts, he met a small tabby-cat that said, "Hans, where are you going?" "Alas, thou canst not help me." "I well know your desire," said the cat. "You wish to have a beautiful horse. Come with me, and be my faithful servant for seven years long, and then I will give you one more beautiful than any you have ever seen in your whole life."

90 So she took him with her into her enchanted castle, where there were nothing but cats that were her servants. They leapt nimbly upstairs and downstairs, and were merry and happy. In the evening when they

sat down to dinner, three of them had to make music. One played the bassoon, the other the fiddle, and the third put the trumpet to his lips, and blew out his cheeks as much as he possibly could. When they had dined, the table was carried away, and the cat said, "Now, Hans, come and dance with me." "No," said he, "I won't dance with a pussy cat. I have never done that yet." "Then take him to bed," said she to the cats. So, one of them lighted him to his bedroom, one pulled his shoes off, one his stockings, and at last one of them blew out the candle. The next morning, they returned and helped him out of bed, one put his stockings on for him, one tied his garters, one brought his shoes, one washed him, and one dried his face with her tail. He had to serve the cat, however, and chop some wood every day, and to do that, he had an axe of silver, and the wedge and saw were of silver and the mallet of copper. So, he chopped the wood into small pieces, stayed there in the house and had good meat and drink, but never saw anyone but the tabby-cat and her servants. Once she said to him, "Go and mow my meadow, and dry the grass," and gave him a scythe of silver, and a whetstone of gold, but bade him deliver them up again carefully. Hans went thither, and did what he was bidden, and when he had finished the work, he carried the scythe, whetstone, and hay to the house, and asked if it was not yet time for her to give him his reward. "No," said the cat, "you must first do something more for me of the same kind. There is timber of silver, a carpenter's axe, square, and everything that is needful, all of silver, with these build me a small house." Then Hans built the small house. The seven years went by as if they were six months. The cat asked him if he would like to see her horses, then she opened the door of the small house, and there stood twelve horses; such horses, so bright and shining, that his heart rejoiced at the sight of them. And now she gave him to eat and drink, and said, "Go home, I will not give thee thy horse away with thee; but in three days' time I will follow thee and bring it." So, Hans set out, and she showed him the way to the mill. She had never once given him a new coat, however, and he had been obliged to keep on his dirty old smock-frock, which he had brought with him, and which during the seven years had become too small for him. [In the meantime, the other miller boys had brought home a blind horse and a lame one. They laughed at Hans and did not believe that his horse would follow in three days. The old miller sent him away from the table because of his torn clothes and he had to sleep in the goose house.]

91 In the morning when he awoke, the three days had passed, and a coach came with six horses and they shone so brightly that it was delightful to see them! A servant brought a seventh as well, which was

for the poor miller's boy. And a magnificent princess alighted from the coach and went into the mill, and this princess was the little tabby-cat whom poor Hans had served for seven years. She asked the miller where the miller's boy and dunce was. Then the miller said, "We cannot have him here in the mill, for he is so ragged; he is lying in the goose-house." Then the king's daughter said that they were to bring him immediately. So, they brought him out, and he had to hold his little smock-frock together to cover himself. The servants unpacked splendid garments, and washed him and dressed him, and when that was done, no king could have looked more handsome.

92 Then the maiden desired to see the horses which the other apprentices had brought home with them, and one of them was blind and the other lame. Then she ordered the servant to bring the seventh horse, and when the miller saw it, he said that such a horse as that had never yet entered his yard. "And that is for the third miller's boy," said she. "Then he must have the mill," said the miller, but the king's daughter said that the horse was there, and that he was to keep his mill as well, and took her faithful Hans and set him in the coach, and drove away with him. They first drove to the little house which he had built with the silver tools, and behold it was a great castle, and everything inside it was of silver and gold; and then she married him, and he was rich, so rich that he had enough for all the rest of his life. After this, let no one ever say that anyone who is silly can never become a person of importance.[1]

93 Once again, the story begins with an initial division into a tetrad of people whose nature is not further characterized other than being associated with the symbol of the mill. In the large waterwheel there is another mandala motif. Flowing water is a symbol of how time weaves together the happenings of life, which is why one speaks of the "flow of time." The ever-turning wheel signifies, particularly in Eastern symbolism, the wheel of eternal rebirth, the fateful course of life. In the negative sense, it can express the eternal restless wandering, or being thrown about in life, or being caught in the wheels of hell.[2] Since the mill represents the well-known motif of the eternal return, folklore knows examples of the rejuvenating wheel. According to Bächtold-Stäubli under *Mühle* [mill], in gratitude for the nourishing food prepared by

---

[1] Slightly shortened and modified from J. and W. Grimm, *Complete Grimm's*, London 1975 pp. 482–485. The version is the original English translation by Margaret Taylor (1884).
[2] See *Ixion* in the Greek underworld and the fairytale "How a Scholar Chastised the Princes of Hell." For more on the wheel symbol see the Irish tale, "Fionn and Lorcán," where to conquer a fortress the hero must first overcome a poisonous wheel that turns in a huge circle around the palace. He succeeds in bringing the wheel temporally to a halt and in this moment jumps into the interior of the fortress.

the mill, there has arisen the idea of a miracle mill. (More likely it is the transformation of the grain in the milling process that forms the basis for this idea.)

94   Grinding and the mill have a mystical, erotic meaning; to mill, to grind (Latin, *mollere, mola*; Greek, μυ´λλειν *(mýllein)*). This is why in many legends the mill is a place for love adventures and of many heroes it is said that they were born out of wedlock.[3]

95   The location of mills, usually standing alone and apart from other houses, and the often alleged dishonesty or stinginess of the miller complement the superstition, just as the mystery of the flow of water and the mill wheel that seemingly turns of itself. As the place of origin of the fairytale hero, the mill points to a background with a predisposition to magical happenings.

96   The aging miller, who wants to retire from his mill, is like the old king of the previously discussed fairytale, and symbolizes the prevailing conscious attitude. On the one hand, he yearns for renewal of life (in the image of the horse), and, on the other hand, he expresses the wish to give up the reins of the mill, to relinquish being the captain and sufferer of his own fate, and to find peace outside the seat of action by allowing someone else to take over the steering wheel. This again hints at a midlife crisis, in which the person begins to lose interest in the happenings of the outer world and turns to questions concerning what lies behind the ways of fate. Initially there is an uncertainty about which soul part will actually take over the lead and by which means the new vitality should be found.

97   The horse, which first symbolizes this new life energy, "as a beast of burden. . . is closely related to the mother archetype."[4] As an animal used for riding, a horse is located beneath the human and symbolizes the world of instinct, animal-physical body life, and movement in general.

98   The wish of the old miller is directed in general to the renewal of the life force behind which, as already hinted, stands the anima problem. This is similar to the old king's desire for a rug in, "The Three Feathers," which led down to the toad mother. In the present tale, the miller's request for a horse steers the boy into the realm of the cat, which also represents the female principle. In this regard it is interesting that the princess in, "The Three Feathers," is, in some parallels, a cat.[5]

---

[3] Bächtold-Stäubli under *Mühle*.
[4] See C.G. Jung, CW 16, *Practice of Psychotherapy* ¶347. See also C.G. Jung, CW 5, *Symbols of Transformation* ¶657ff. The horse is also connected with the Demeter cult. See K. Kerényi, *Kore*, Princeton, 1969 p. 41f. On the maternal role of the horse see also E. Rousselle, *Dragon and Mare*, Princeton 1970 p. 113ff. Frau Holle sometimes wears the head of a mare, see J. Bolte and G. Polívka, *Anmerkungen*, Vol. 1, Leipzig 1913 p. 224.
[5] See J. Bolte and G. Polívka, *Anmerkungen,* Vol. 2, Leipzig 1915 p. 32ff.

99   The cat is an animal of the Great Mother, the animal of Freya and Frau Holle, and thus in fairytales often the companion animal of witches.[6] But the cat is also a maternal, helpful animal. The cat can even appear in fairytales as the embodiment of a dead mother.[7] One of many indications that the cat symbolizes feminine instinctual life is a folk belief found in Tirol according to which girls who want to marry should caress a cat.[8]

100   The kitten that "stupid" Hans (who again stands for the fourth and despised function within the conscious personality) finally meets after sleeping in the cave and traveling through a forest –that is, deep in the unconscious – corresponds to an anima figure like the toad princess in "The Three Feathers." And just as there the king had asked for a colorful carpet, so here it is the cat itself that is colorful. This animal thus bears the characteristic of living diversity, the variety and richness of life. The anima appears at first as an animal, but is later transformed into human form not by a violent intervention, such as the theft of her animal garment (usually only a temporary success), rather she requires the hero to trust her and submit himself into her service. She is thereby permanently released from her animal shape.

101   Hans's ministry lasts for seven years. Seven is the number of stepwise transformation. The realm of the anima appears in its double aspect (all unconscious symbols have a double aspect): on the one hand, its inhabitants are animals, and, on the other hand, it is endowed with precious gold and silver plates. This points to the actual royal descent of the cat anima. So too must the hero, on the one hand, perform menial labor without wages and, on the other, he is regaled by the other cats.

---

[6] See M. Führer, *Nordgermanische*, München 1938 p. 90. See the tales "Djulek Batür," "Sura and the Witches" and "The Witch and Prince Golden Hair."

[7] See, for example, "Móirín." See Bächtold-Stäubli under *Katze* [cat]:

> According to general [folk] belief something sinister and demonic dwells in this animal, which is treated, therefore, always with a certain awe. To even a greater degree than other domestic animals the cat can foretell when something will happen in the future... In popular belief a cat, especially a black cat, brings evil or bad luck. For instance, if a black cat crosses your path in the morning or runs between your legs (Bächtold-Stäubli under *Katze*). One should not chase a black cat away, otherwise disaster will result. But also due to the cat's shyness, they can also be good luck charms: blessings reign where cats like to linger in a house. If on the way to the dance a girl is followed by a spotted cat, she will soon find a boyfriend... A white cat, or one with white paws, is a herald of good fortune, also a cat of four colors... If one sees a foreign or strange cat, one should be very careful, because they may really be demons, nightmares, incubi, witches, or even the devil himself... Even poor souls go around in the form of cats... Numerous legends tell of demons, wizards, and witches in the shape of a tomcat or a cat.

[8] See the legend retold in *The Lost Child* that expresses the identity of the cat and anima in a childlike but tragic way:

> A little boy on the way to school once saw a *beautiful kitten*, that was very friendly. He played with it and slipped with it under the balcony of the house nearby... Nine days later people found the boy still sitting there. He did not want to go home, but begged that he might stay there where he got to eat much better things than ever before. All brought to him by a *little white damsel* in gold and silver bowls... Not long after, the little boy died. (O. Tobler, *Epiphanie*, Kiel 1911 p. 71.)

102   Let us look at the possible meaning in the order of the tasks that Hans has to perform. The first is cutting up wood, the primordial matter, and the second is to mow and dry the grass, and the third is to build a house. His tools are precious metals. The hero is forced to have a real confrontation with the substance of reality until he can master it creatively. This passage of the hero through a time in which he must humbly serve the mother, matter, and the material, is an archetypal motif and corresponds roughly to the service of Hercules under Omphale. The great danger is getting stuck in epicurean life. But Hans proves to be a true hero, and after seven years service, he leaves the paradisal kingdom of cats without gain or a moment's hesitation. Thus, the test of trust is raised to the highest level. With only a promise he is released, and brings nothing but the knowledge of the world of the anima back home after seven years. For him this is a big reward, for the secular youths it is meager. And although the other apprentices had brought useless and unfit animals, they pour out all the more mockery over him and reject any fellowship whatsoever. But, "in the morning when he awoke, three days had passed." Because he had stayed in the timeless realm of the anima, time has become relative for him. In the eighth year and on the fourth day (eight and four are numbers of perfection compared to three and seven) the anima-princess appears in all her splendor and brings exaltation to the poor shadow-hero.

103   The beautiful garments that the princess gives Hans prove to the outer world that he has undergone an internal change: the redemption of the anima and of the (previously) unknown spiritual strength embodied in the youngest out of the worthless appearance imposed by the secular-oriented conscious mind. A royal couple, a symbol of the Self, emerges in the unconscious by the action of the fourth function, that is, through its work in the material world.[9]

104   One result of this whole process, which runs mostly unconsciously, is that the conscious mind, embodied by the old miller, acquires the desired horse, a renewal of the life force. On the other hand, the new couple does not take over his poor mill, but rather they move into a realm corresponding to its value, the redeemed royal palace of the cat-anima. The conscious attitude remains in its old ways until it dies, but there has been a shift in intrinsic value: to the creation of a supra-individual inner center.

105   The little silver house that Hans had built [in the kingdom of the cats] in which he already saw the beautiful horses at his farewell, has since expanded into a great castle. It is a mandala whose building materials, gold and silver, also suggests a union of male and female, of the opposites. Not only the kingdom is transformed and become wide and beautiful, but also the

---

[9] In a Low German parallel version "The People Like Cats" the redemption is more strongly emphasized than the work of the hero, and is much more dramatic.

inhabitants are freed from the bondage of the animal form. The couple remains in the realm of the anima, however, in which the hero is caught and into which he retreats.[10] In "The Three Feathers" there is a direct replacement of the old king by the new couple and, significantly, this shift of values to a new inner center is sanctioned by the prevailing conscious attitude. In "The Poor Miller's Boy and the Cat" only a new influx of vitality and happiness is experienced, whereby the actual process appears just for only a moment in the narrow field of consciousness, namely, when the princess picks Hans up in a splendid fashion, but then the pair vanishes back into the unconscious.

---

[10] [German: *entrücken.*]

Chapter 3
Tritill, Litill, and the Birds

106   The sphere of the royal family becomes a symbol of the transfigured, redeemed, and enhanced value of inner life, while the world of the miller signifies the intellectual framework of the common man. At a more basic cultural level the king is often a symbol of divine power, what happens in its dazzling realm carries the stamp of the archetypal, what is in general good and right. "The fact that the figures are royal expresses, like real royalty, their archetypal character; they are collective figures common to large numbers of people."[1] If the archetypal course of the story is realized in the space of everyday life, then often the gravity of such intrapsychic events is expressed by an elevation to a royal state or otherwise a rise in rank.[2] [In fairytales, therefore, the hero who has proven his supernatural abilities becomes the king.] This is clearly shown in the Icelandic tale, "Tritill, Litill, and the Birds":

107   There once reigned a king and a queen, and in the same country there also lived a poor old man and his wife. The king had an only daughter, called Enid, who was greatly beloved by both her father and mother. They spared no expense, and she had the best masters and governesses, and a number of servants to wait upon her; but desite the fact that she was so carefully watched, she suddenly disappeared. Inquiries were made of everyone, but nothing was heard of the princess. No one had seen her; she had vanished in the most mysterious manner. The king, in despair, sent out messengers in all directions, and spent a great part of his treasure searching for her; but all in vain. Then, at last, he vowed that he would give the princess in marriage to whoever should be fortunate enough to find her, and also give him the half of his kingdom. But though many of the knights and nobles about the court, eager to secure so great a prize, went off in search of her, they one and all returned empty-handed.

---

[1] C.G. Jung, CW 16, *Practice of Psychotherapy* ¶421. See also ¶469 on "trans-subjective union of archetypal figures."

[2] *Ibid* ¶473 about the ordinary man being the natural man, but the king or the hero is the "supernatural" man.

108   Now the poor old man who lived outside the palace grounds had three sons. Their names were Osmond, Tostig, and Harald. The two eldest boys were greatly beloved by their parents; but Harald, the youngest, was disliked by his father and mother, and both his elder brothers ill-treated him and made him do all the work, while they went out shooting and fishing.

109   When the boys were grown up, Osmond came to his parents, and said he would like to start off and see the world, and try to win fame and riches for himself. His father and mother were quite willing that he should do so, and provided him with a new pair of boots and a large bag of food. So, he started off on his journey. After he had gone a long way, he arrived at a little hillock. Here he sat down to rest and unpacked his bag of provisions.

110   Just as he was beginning to eat, a tiny man, dressed in grey, came up to him, begging for a morsel of food. Osmond ordered him away. After he had rested, Osmond went on again a long, long way, till he came to another hillock. Here he again sat down to rest and began to eat. But he had hardly commenced than a still smaller and shabbier man, dressed in green, came up to him and asked him for a morsel of food. Osmond sent him away with a volley of abuse.

111   He then went on again a long way, till he reached a large open glade in the wood. Here he sat down for another morsel. But no sooner had he opened his bag and taken out the food, than a whole flock of birds flew down beside him. He chased them away, and continued on until he came to a big cave. Looking in, and seeing no one, only a herd of cattle, he thought he would go in and wait till the dawn arrived.

112   Just as the sun was setting, an enormously big giantess walked in. Osmond took courage, went up to her, and asked whether he might stay the night there.

113   She agreed, on condition that in the morning he would do the work she would require of him. This he promised he would do. The next morning the giantess told him to clean out the cave, and put down fresh bedding for the cattle, and that the work must be finished before the evening or she would take his life. With these words she went away.

114   No sooner did Osmond begin to turn up the straw than the pitchfork stuck fast in the bedding. In vain he pushed and pulled and tried to drag it out and when in the evening the giantess returned and found that the cave had not been cleaned, she took hold of Osmond and hung him up on a nail in the cave.

115   Meanwhile Tostig, the second son, also set out to seek his fortune but he was no more fortunate than Osmond and followed the same course as his brother.

116   Now there was only the youngest son, Harald, left. But though he was the only one at home, his parents did not love him any better, so he also decided to go away. His parents agreed; but instead of nice strong boots, they gave him an old pair of his brother's and his sack contained nothing but dry crusts. Despite this Harald started off with a light heart, and as it chanced, he took the same road his brothers, and presently came to the first hillock. No sooner did he sit down when the little old man in grey stood beside him.

117   Harald pitied the old man and shared his meal. When they had done, the old man said, "My name is Tritill. If ever you are in need of help, call me, and I will come to you." Harald then continued his journey until he came to the second hillock. Again he sat down, opened his bag, and took out another crust. Hardly had he done so when the little old man dressed in green appeared and asked for a morsel of food. Harald also shared a crust with him. When they had finished eating, the little green man said "Call me, if ever you think I can do you a service. My name is Litill." Harald then continued his journey until he came to the large open glade in the wood.

118   There he sat down and took out another crust. No sooner had he done so than a great flock of birds came down. They circled round him, and Harald's heart was filled with pity, and he broke up the remaining crusts and threw the crumbs among them. When they had eaten up every crumb, the biggest bird alighted on Harald's shoulder and whistled, "If ever you think we can do you a service, call us. We shall hear you wherever we are." Harald then continued his journey, until he, too, came to the big cave. Looking in, he saw it was full of cattle, and hanging from a beam in one corner he saw the bodies of his two brothers.

119   Startled at the sight, Harald's first impulse was to go away; but he thought he must first bury his brothers. He took down the bodies, and seeing a spade near the entrance, he dug a grave and buried them in the sand outside the cave. Just as he had finished, the giantess arrived. Harald, who was tired, asked her if he might stay the night there. She allowed him on the same condition she had set his brothers.

120   The next morning, Harald set upon the task but finding it impossible he called: "Oh, dear Tritill, come and help me!"

121 The little grey man appeared and called out: "Prick pitchfork and shovel spade!" and in no time the work was done.

122 When the giantess came home in the evening and saw that the work was done, she said to Harald, "Oh, man, you human! You have not done this by yourself! But I will let it pass!" and she retired into the inner cave. The next morning the giantess had fresh work for Harald. He was to carry her bedding outside the cave, take out all the feathers, spread them out in the sun to air, and then put them back again.

123 This time Harald called all of his helpers: "Dear Tritill, dear Litill, and all my dear birds oh, come and help me if you can!" And almost before the words had passed his lips, Tritill, Litill, and the whole flight of birds, came bringing the feathers with them; and while Tritill and Litill helped Harald to fill the bed and the pillows, and sew them up again, the birds flew round picking up all the stray feathers, so that none were missing. But out of each pillow they took one feather, and, tying them together, told Harald that when the giantess missed them and threatened to kill him, he was to tickle her nose with the feathers.

124 When the giantess came home in the evening, she went up to her bed, and threw herself down on it so heavily that the whole cave shook. Then she began carefully feeling all over the bed, and when she came to the pillows she cried out, "Aha, man! I have caught you! There is a feather missing in each pillow! Now I shall hang you like your brothers!"

125 But as she took hold of him, Harold pulled the two feathers out of his pocket and tickled her nose with them. In an instant the giantess fell back on her bed looking terribly white and frightened; but Harald gave her back her feathers. "Ah, man, human!" said the giantess, "I know you did not do this alone; but I will let it pass this time!"

126 The third night Harald also passed in the cave, and in the morning the giantess ordered him to kill one of her oxen, scrape and clean the skin to make a leather bag; cut up the animal in joints ready for cooking, clean the entrails, and make spoons out of its horns. Harald also had to pick the right one from her herd of fifty oxen. If he should do the work correctly, she would release him and, as a reward, allow him to choose three things from her treasures.

127 This time Harald called on Tritill and Litill. Hardly had the words passed his lips, than he saw them approaching, leading an ox between them. They at once set to work and killed him, and while Harald cleaned the entrails and cut up the joints, Tritill scraped the skin and prepared it for making the bag, and Litill began fashioning the spoons

out of the horns. The work sped along quickly and merrily, and all was ready ere the sun sank to rest. Harald now asked his friends' advice on what he should choose.

128 Then they told him he should first ask for that which was over her bed, then for the chest which stood beside her bed, and lastly for that which was behind the wall of her bed.

129 When the giantess came home in the evening and found that Harald had finished all the tasks she had set him, she exclaimed. "Ah, man, human! You never did all this alone, but you have conquered, so I must let it pass." The next morning, the giantess called Harald into the inner cave and told him he might choose the reward she had promised him.

130 When Harald spoke his choice, she cried out, "Ah, man, human! You have not chosen these things by yourself, but I cannot refuse you." So saying, she mounted some steps above her bed cut into the rock, and, opening a secret door, she led forth a beautiful maiden. This was none other than the fair Princess Enid, who had disappeared so mysteriously. "Take her back to her father, and he will reward you as you deserve," said the giantess.

131 She then opened the lid of the chest beside her bed. This was filled with gold, pearls, and precious stones; and then moving aside the bed, she touched a secret spring, and the wall sliding back, they saw the blue sea, and anchored close to the cave lay a ship completely fitted out, its sails all set, and its pennant flying, and possessing the power of sailing wherever its owner wished, without aid of either captain or crew.

132 The couple quickly departed, and reached the country of the princess' father. The delight of the king and queen on recovering their long-lost daughter can be more easily imagined than described. They never tired hearing of Harald's wonderful adventures, and the king ordered a great feast, which ended with the wedding of Enid and Harald.

133 The king then made Harald his prime minister; and so well and so wisely did he rule the country, that on the king's death he was chosen to succeed him.[3]

---

[3] This is the modified Icelandic version referred to by von Franz and von Beit as found in A. Hall, *Icelandic*, London 1897 pp. 210–223. The editors of the Hall collection state that they have removed all "objectionable" material to make the tales in their collection more suitable for young children. The oldest (original?) version appears to come from Hungary.

134   The description of the situation at the outset is very striking. On the one hand, a trinity of figures lives at the royal palace and at the end this is increased by the addition of the cottagers' son raised to a prince, making a tetrad (a quaternity). Comparing this situation to the one in "The Three Feathers," the king again represents the hitherto dominant conscious attitude, the cottagers' son, the despised fourth function, who is the bearer of the development process and becomes a symbol of the Self. This shadow-prince figure is at the same time the third and last son of a cottager, similar to Hans in "The Poor Miller's Boy and the Cat." On the other hand, here there is the cottager with his wife and the three sons. Thus, in the initial situation the hero (the third son) is more precisely the fifth person.

135   Five is considered the number of materiality and the natural man.[4] In China five is the number of the earth: the centre and the four corners, and according to the tale "How the Five Ancients Became Men," the five elders are the elemental spirits or the basic forces that bring about creation (they are the rulers of earth, fire, water, wood, and the mistress of the metals). To them are assigned the four directions and the center.[5]

136   The cottager quintet at the beginning of "Tritill, Litill, and the Birds" includes a female figure indicating the possibility of a natural ordering. Thus, at the outset two issues are indicated: first, the completion of the royal foursome as a symbol of psychic wholeness, and, second, a transformation process emanating from the natural human. That the king's son and the cottager people actually comprise a unity, is indirectly suggested by the fact that in other fairytales the one and the same king is simultaneously the owner of the stolen treasure and also the father of three sons who are given the task to find it. The milieu of the cottager expresses the plainness of the hero from the standpoint of the secular world. As soon as the process begins to focus on the essential quaternity, the other brothers perish and the parents are no longer mentioned. First comes the report that the king's daughter has disappeared, as we learn later, stolen by an evil giantess. Thus arises the hero's task to retrieve the lost treasure. This process reflects the initial motif of many fairytales. Sometimes, like in "The Three Feathers" or "The Poor Miller's Boy and the Cat," the precious object is from the outset to be sought in the magical kingdom. That the anima, or another symbol of the Self, must, after the middle of life, be found in the unconscious is immediately evident. On the other hand, the initial motif describing the loss of something that was initially present in the secular ego-sphere, is a new psychological fact. The archetype of the Self also carries the first half of life. The life-sustaining energy streams out of the

---

[4] See Volume 1, p. 187.
[5] See R. Bernoulli, *Symbolik geom. Figuren*, Zürich 1935 p. 383. See also the similar idea with the Aztecs, W. Krickeberg, *Azteken und Inka*, Jena 1928 p. 324, and also the five in the religion of India and Manichaeism, R. Reitzenstein, *Iranische*, Bonn a. Rh. 1921 p. 154 and esp.160ff.

unconscious and is the actual source and sustaining power of the conscious mind. People only realize the value of this root power when they lose control over their secular life. The fairytale expresses this by indicating that the anima, or some other precious treasure that symbolizes the Self, was already present at the court, that is, in the sphere of consciousness, before she disappeared.

137   The reference to the psychic life situations of both halves of life solves the apparent contradiction. It could be that the anima figure appearing in many of the fairytales of the first volume were daughters of a dark demon, whereas in the present tale, she appears as the daughter of a secular king. Such a father of the anima acts as a mirror reflection of the demonic father and as a center of the unconscious in consciousness. Thus the anima can be the daughter of two worlds. The magical background of the anima in the present tale is not presented as a demonic father, but rather in the image of the giantess, who suddenly and apparently without reason appropriates the anima. But she has a secret right to her, since the giantess is a manifestation of the Great Mother, with whom the anima stands in close relationship. Psychologically, the process described at the beginning means that all the images of life-creating soul force that the conscious mind carries, are lost in the dark sphere of matter. They lose their efficacy (that is, they are held prisoner), such that the natural flow between the unconscious and consciousness is dammed up and the call for the redeeming hero and mediator becomes manifest.

138   Then the story begins, as if, for the second time and describes the origin of the hero. This forms a parallel to "The Poor Miller's Boy and the Cat" and can be interpreted accordingly. The hero symbolizes the scorned fourth function that stands in opposition to the conscious attitude as the main function with the two auxiliary functions. The two elder sons of the cottager do not – because of their close relationship to the prevailing attitude – undertake a quest to find the princess, but rather to gain riches and honor, that is, worldly goals. They support the pursuit of ego-consciousness, which prefers to adapt to the external world. But they do get to the hill in the magical realm and are immediately approached by a being whom they treat with incomprehension and feelingless hubris. The brothers entertain no notion that this unassuming, begging dwarf could be a magical helper offering his unprecedented abilities if only one were to make a real relationship with him. The brothers succumb to "material reality," therefore, the duties of "matter."

139   The third son, the scorned one, is humble enough not to "want" something, but is satisfied just to get by. Strictly speaking, he is content to serve life as it is.

140   As a result, he greets every phenomenon with a trusting and open mind. His poverty in the secular world is his wealth in the magical. And, thus, he gains his helpful assistants. First, he meets two dwarves, one right after the other, who ask him for a bite of his bread. We have already met this motif of

asking for a morsel of bread in "The Two Travelers" in which the frivolous tailor sold his bread to the evil shoemaker for the price of his eyesight. Here, as in that tale, the giving of bread is a sharing of one's own reality and, at the same time, an entering into a community (cf. the *agape*, a shared meal as a worship service, or ritual feast as a sign of the community). In contrast to the two elder brothers, who have distanced themselves from the dark forces of the unconscious in order to align with the differentiating conscious mind, the youngest strikes up a relationship with the dwarves. Within the total personality, dwarves represent unconscious creative forces in a deep layer of the soul. Herein lies the meaning of the fourth function, behind which stand the deep-rooted hidden life powers that reach into the physiological, bodily realm. Dwarves are known for their omniscience concerning hidden things, and are often magical helpers. They are the guardians of secret treasures, the "Lords of the Forest" and almost identical to the chthonic father god (like the little man in "The Story of Longa-Poa"). In the Mediterranean cultural sphere they were held in high esteem as Dactyls or Cabiri. The latter term means "powerful." They acted as companions of the Great Mother.[6] In "Tritill, Litill, and the Birds," therefore, they know the secret of the evil giantess. As small but powerful creatures, dwarves are related to child deities[7] and at the same time with the figure of the wise old man.[8] When the hero goes into the community of dwarves, he is subordinating himself to the inconspicuous yet powerful, which has approached him in his own unconscious.

141   The occurrence of dwarves as a duality with similar, but not quite identical names, indicates a slight contrast within this dwarf-helper figure. The motif of two equal or slightly differentiated companions of a hero or a divinity is archetypal and appears frequently.[9] Just as the hero is at first flanked by his

---

[6] See the comprehensive review in C.G. Jung, CW 5, *Symbols of Transformation* ¶180–184. See also C.G. Jung, CW 12, *Psychology and Alchemy* ¶203f; J. Przyluski, "Mutter-Göttin," Zürich 1939 pp. 48–49. See also the numerous dwarf legends in F. F. A. Kuhn, *Mythologische Studien,* Gütersloh 1886 Vol. 2, pp. 21–79.

[7] See Jung:

> This archetype of the 'child god' is extremely widespread and intimately bound up with other mythological aspects of the child motif. . . in folklore the child motif appears in the guise of the *dwarf* or the *elf* as personifications of the hidden forces of nature. (C.G. Jung, CW 9i, *The Archetypes and the Collective Unconscious* ¶268)

[8] In the Grimm's tale, "The Gnome," a "little earth man" appears. In some parallels he is an old bearded man. See J. Bolte and G. Polívka, *Anmerkungen,* Vol. 2, Leipzig 1915 p. 299. See also the vision in the Gnostic *The Gospel of Eve* (*Epiph.,* xxvi. 3), describing one of these visions on the Mount. "I stood on a lofty mountain and saw a mighty Man, and another, a dwarf, and heard as it were a voice of thunder, I drew nigh for to hear; and it spake unto me and said: 'I am thou and thou art I; and wheresoever thou art I am there, and I am sown (or scattered) in all; from whencesoever thou willest, thou gatherest Me, and gathering Me thou gatherest Thyself.' [Mead writes on this:] "The 'dwarf' presumably corresponds to the 'man of the size of a thumb in the ether of the heart' of the *Upanishads*; as yet he is smaller than the small, but as the spiritual nature develops he will become greater than the great, and grow into the stature of the Heavenly Man – the Supreme Self." (G. R. S. Mead, *Fragments,* London 1931 p. 439.) Here, too, the dwarf is combined with the almighty great deity.

[9] The Great Mothergoddess of Anatolia (Asia Minor), for example, often has two Cabiri or other male acolytes at her side. See J. Przyluski, *Ursprünge,* Zürich 1939 p. 28ff,33, J. Przyluski, *Mutter-Göttin,*

two elder secular brothers, so is he again in the unconscious surrounded by their mirror images, the two magic helpers from the underworld. This trinity in the Magical (the hero with two companions) or the group of four (when the birds as a unit are included) corresponds to the archetypal need of the soul for wholeness. (Not in all, but in many fairytales we find such a correspondence of figures from the two spheres, for instance, in "Ferdinand the Faithful and Ferdinand the Unfaithful.") At the climax of the story, the group dissolves and takes on another form after the return to the secular world.

142   Here, the double appearance of the magical helper signifies that he could be effective in different ways.[10] In the multitude of birds that associate with the dwarves, the figure of the magical helper dissolves into collective psychic stirrings; here the essential being of humans lies deep in nature composed as it is out of a chaos of many different elements, such as ancestral traits. The occurrence of a multiplicity indicates that the unity of the person has not yet evolved, but is still in an unconscious identity with surrounding figures such that the personality experiences itself as seen only in the group.[11] The hero of the fairytale, psychologically the core personality, joins with the externally as yet inconspicuous soul parts, the animals, which as instinctual drives embody the unconscious wisdom of nature. It should be noted that here we are dealing with the image of birds, which are a symbol of spiritual content: wishes, ideas, and helpful hunches [intuitions]. Insofar as nature itself has both a spiritual and a material aspect, symbolized by the image of the primordial couple, the chthonic Father and Great Mother, respectively, one could say that here the hero gains the masculine-spiritual side of the unconscious as a helper against the feminine-material. Here the hero does not himself overcome the mother goddess but, to add a phrase of Pseudo-Democritus, to help the dwarves and birds, "nature rejoices in nature, nature conquers nature, nature rules over nature."[12]

Zürich 1939 p. 42. In fairytales, frequently two guardian animals occur, such as in, "How a Scholar Chastised the Princes of Hell," where an ox and a horse flank the sovereign of the cave; or in "The Strange Boy," where the gate is guarded by two bears. Odin also is accompanied by two ravens (M. Ninck, *Wodan*, Jena 1935 p. 175, and the Egyptian Sun God [not Ra] had two Wazti-snakes on either side of his skull (G. Roeder, *Urkunden*, Jena 1923 p. 232).

[10] See A. Wolff, *Grundlagen*, Berlin 1935 p. 138:

> New, that is, still unconscious material often appears in dreams and fantasies in pairs, such as twins, or doubled figures. A content of the objective psyche is evaluated by conscious awareness as having many meanings, being paradoxical and possibly ambiguous. Phenomena of the objective psyche when left to themselves consistently exhibit an *enantiodromic* character. [Italics by Wolff.] See also *ibid* p. 105.

[11] See C.G. Jung, CW 9i, *The Archetypes and the Collective Unconscious* ¶279f.

[12] Berthelot, *Alchemistes Grecs*, Paris 1888 p. II,3. The image of this intuition of the natural philosophy of late antiquity was the *ouroboros*, the snake biting its own tail, where the head represented the psychic or mental aspect and the tail represented the material aspect. For the Pseudo-Democritus quote see C.G. Jung, CW 16, *Practice of Psychotherapy* ¶469,¶454 and for images of the ouroboros, see C.G. Jung, CW 12, *Psychology and Alchemy* p. Fig. 46, Fig. 47.

143   The tests that the giantess imposes on the hero are typical heroic tasks.[13] The first is to clean out the cave of the giantess, which recalls the task that Eurystheus imposes on Heracles to clean the Augean Stables. The mythical hero is, according to his nature, essentially a culture-bringer and thereby often forced to eliminate antiquated, spoiled things, the dust and dirt of the past, and to take on the fight against inert, dead matter.

144   The second task, to air the bedding and the feather pillows of the ogress, follows along the lines of the previous test. The bed is a base, a foundation, a material support and here the epitome of the material nature of the Great Mother. Just as in the middle of life everything outdated and dead must first be removed, so must also the material substance in the soul be exposed to the light of discerning consciousness. Then the wind whirls up the feathers, another multiplicity, an appearance of psychic dissolution, that the hero can only manage by setting the living multiplicity of birds against the inanimate multiplicity of the feathers in the wind. (This struggle happens, as so often, according to the law of similars: *similia similibus curantur*, like cures like).[14]

145   The hero's friendship with the birds proves to be a conscious relationship with disintegrating tendencies, an awareness that prevents the loss of what holds the personality together, the "glue," of the personality. In itself, the feather – as stated above – is a symbol of a psychic fact, and it follows that the image of the heavy, dead, and evil matter (the giantess) is based on a multiplicity of unconscious psychic impulses. When the hero penetrates into this area and brings his part into the light, a whirlwind arises, that is, the psychic side of matter appears as a natural phenomenon. This is of such super-personal power that a fragmentation and dissolution of the personality threatens, the danger of being carried away and enraptured by the experience of the unconscious. Against this the hero can only rally his instinctual, helpful intuitions, which enable him to reunite his personality. He thus invokes the advice of his magical helper, and keeps back one feather from each pillow. In doing this he demonstrates at the same time that he has the ability to discriminate. He retains the power of choice and, therefore, despite the whirlwind of emotional impulses, remains conscious. He thus proves his superiority over the giantess, which flows to him from the secretly hidden forces of nature. In that he tickles the giantess's nose, he performs to a certain extent a generative action, which in a metaphorical form, in the sense of realization, figuratively indicates a mental penetration. The nose serves to give an intuitive orientation (cf. the English word "flair") and, with the help of the dwarves and their natural wisdom, the hero steals this ability from the giantess. Actually, it is the dwarves who defeat the giantess. They are another

---

[13] See the similar tests in an Icelandic parallel tale "The Helpful Animals."
[14] [Attributed to Paracelsus, the 16th Century Swiss doctor and philosopher.]

aspect of her, and the fact that the giantess is defeated by herself finds expression in that she is conquered by her own feathers.

146   The last task that the hero must perform is the slaughter and butchering of an ox, which he has to pick from a herd of fifty-odd oxen. This is to be accomplished in an unusually short time and represents a sacrifice, the sacrifice of instincts in the service of the Mother Goddess. Only through such a sacrifice can the hero overcome inert, heavy, matter and gain the spiritual forces that lie in its spell, that is, to free the anima. To fulfill the task within the very tight time schedule and make the right choice of ox proves his conscious superiority over his own instinctual nature.[15] The fact that the hero must carve a human tool (a spoon) from the horns, which are a symbol of primitive power, points that the sacrifice of the instincts is connected to their domestication, a transformation. A state of creative fertility often follows this steering of the instinct in the service of culture.[16]

147   In that the hero confronts and engages in an *auseinandersetzung* with the nature and driving forces of matter, he becomes the master of these forces and they are transformed into gifts that are valuable for humans: a ship – a human construction – so that one can sail over the waters (the unconscious) and not sink; the treasures; and, especially, the princess. The liberation of the beautiful maiden, the anima, by defeating the demonic mother is a widespread archetypal motif, for instance, in tales where the hero must fight a dragon to win the fair maiden. The anima who had been imprisoned inside a box (again, a maternal symbol) and could, therefore, neither appear nor in any way act – being bound up in the power of the dark, impenetrable unconscious – is now redeemed. The treasures and the ship are synonyms for the princess, symbols of the highest value and independent, superior mastery over the unconscious. When the hero with the anima boards the ship that can easily reach any desired destination, he joins himself with her, just as Connla (in, "Connla and the Fairy Maiden") did with the mermaid in the crystal ship.[17] But unlike in that tale, however, here the hero is not abducted by the anima figure into the unconscious, but is, on the contrary, the one who returns her to the king's court where she once was. He had gained his superiority from taking on and winning the fierce battle with the giantess. He had overcome the death side of the unconscious, which was, in the tale of Connla, working behind the figure of the anima.

148   Upon their return to court, the young couple become heir to the old royal couple and the cottager's son, like Hans in "The Poor Miller's Boy and the Cat"

---

[15] See C.G. Jung, CW 5, *Symbols of Transformation* ¶397f, ¶671, on the sacrifice of the "animal nature" (the bull) by Mithras and the interpretation as overcoming of the Great Mother.
[16] *Ibid* ¶354.
[17] See also "Prince Hlini" where the couple return on a moving bed, in "The Helpful Animals" on a flying jacket, and in "The Son of the Old Woman" on a flying bed.

and the simpleton in "The Three Feathers" he becomes prime minister. The old cottager and the secular brethren of the hero have disappeared and the worldly pursuits of the ego have become insignificant. At the same time, the number of persons at the royal court have been supplemented into a quaternity in which the male and female forces are balanced. The old king is no longer the sole representative of consciousness, he is rather to be seen in universal terms as a power of light that was at the root of what generated the emergence of the ego-feeling, an archetype of consciousness. Since this is a decidedly masculine figure, he stands in opposition to the evil dark feminine power, to which he had lost his soul power, his anima. In this moment of changeover from the masculine-light to the feminine-dark principle, a mediator enters, the redeemer hero, just there where he was least expected.[18] This hero, as a part of the ego, was at first unaware of his real mission, but unintentionally is drawn into the dark forest. The dwarves and birds, with their promises of aid, guide him and then make it possible for him to complete his task. Thus, they worked in the same direction as the hero. This is of fundamental importance: hero and magical helpers are largely one and the same. They both belong to the unknown side of the ego, whereby the magical helpers are more unconscious, more animal, and belong more to the transpersonal side of the core personality. (See also the white horse in "Ferdinand the Faithful and Ferdinand the Unfaithful.") He is actually the true Self, which realizes its intentions in life. The hero of the Icelandic tale would be best described, therefore, as the personification of the fourth function, which in its simplicity could best serve the higher intentions of the Self. The dwarves, on the other hand, possessed the insight that guides destiny and embody the spirit of autonomous nature.[19]

149   The hero, who in the conscious world is only one part of the personality – the despised part – is, through his attachment to the Self in the unconscious, a symbol of the whole personality. The process of esteeming more highly a previously scorned part of one's nature – in the sense of becoming more whole – is exemplified in a particularly elemental and graphic way in the Sulawesi fairytale "The Half":

150   The Half sat on the seashore next to the border of the king's land. There he drew in the sand a horse with seven heads. The king's servants came out and watched as The Half drew the horse with seven heads. They returned and told the king. Thereupon the king said, "Go and get him!" They went there, got him, and brought him to the king. Then the king asked, "Do you understand the art of drawing a horse

---

[18] See C.G. Jung, CW 6, *Psychological Types* ¶439.
[19] See C.G. Jung, CW 8, *The Structure and Dynamics of the Psyche* ¶642 on the psychological phenomenon of the guiding spirit.

with seven heads?" The Half replied, "No, I was only playing." The king said to him, "Go and find me a horse with seven heads!"

151   So The Half went off. After a while he came to a house and was invited to sit down there. After he had chewed his betel nut, he asked, "Have you not seen a horse with seven heads?" The people there said, "That of which you speak, we hear of for the first time." Then they lit a fire, which blazed as high as a house, and they threw him into the flames. Then they took him back out and beat him with hammers, and they made a whole person out of the half a body that he had been so far. Then they said to him: "Get up and go into that house, there you will find the horse with seven heads."

152   The Half – he kept his name even though he was now a whole, complete person – went there and when he came to that house, he went behind and whispered softly. An old woman came out and said, "Little one! Little one! Do not whisper like that! Don't you see all the bones here? The Tiger and the Garuda Bird have eaten almost all of us up!" They went into the house. The Old One cooked for him, handed out the food, and they both ate together. The Half said, "Grandmother! Do we not eat the rice that is left in the pot, too?" "No," she replied, "that we leave inside the pot." While they were eating, a girl came out of a closet. He looked at her and found her so beautiful that he desired her and wanted to have her as his wife. He asked the old woman, "Grandmother! Is the horse with seven heads here?" She said, "Little one, little one! Well, now that you first mention that, we hear about it for the first time! Now we know that there is such a horse!" She was joking of course, because just behind the house, there was tethered the horse. The Half asked again, "Granny! If I make a noise will the Tiger and the Garuda Bird come?" She said, "If we beat the gong, they will come." So he went and struck the gong, and see there, the air became dark. A Garuda came flying by. First came the female and said, "Ha! Ha! Comrade! Are you there?" "Yes, I am here." Then she dove down and tried to grab him, but he reached out after her and cut off one of her heads. "Ho! Ho! Comrade! one of my heads you cut off, but I still have eight heads and they all have poison fangs." She again came back down to get him, but he struck again, and another head fell off. And so it went until he had cut off all the heads and the Garuda died. Soon after the male Garuda appeared and said, "You have killed my wife, now I will have the end of you!" He had seven heads. He dove at The Half and tried to seize him, but the boy swung and one head came down. This went on until he had cut off all the seven heads, and the male Garuda was dead. Thereafter

came a snake and attacked The Half, but he found a bamboo stick and thrust it up her throat, so that she also had to die.

153 Then he ascended into a carriage with his new wife. He untethered the horse with seven heads, which had been tied up behind the house, and invited him to come with them. Again a snake came after them. They threw rice up all around. The rice became huge heaps as big as a city. The snake came upon them and ate and ate until it ate itself to death. Now the couple could leave, and they came to the city of the king, where they tethered the horse and carriage near a beautiful garden.

154 Soon thereafter, the servants of the king went fishing and saw that The Half had returned. They hastened to the king and reported what they had seen. The king summoned the pair before him. Seven times did his minions have to go to fetch them; every time he refused to go along. Then the king himself went and said, "I want to buy that horse with seven heads." But The Half did not agree to the deal. Finally, the king said, "If you give me the horse with seven heads, then your wife will be queen and my children will serve her, and you will be king, and I will be your servant." To this offer The Half agreed, and he became king and his wife queen.[20]

155 Here it is emphasized that the hero not only has a socially insignificant position (like the son of the cottager in, "Tritill, Litill, and the Birds"), but he is even referred to as "The Half." This name connects him to a figure in another Sulawesi legend of the origin of human gender: "The first people were twins. When the woman was pregnant for the second time, a flood destroyed their field. She cursed the rain and soon after gave birth to a half-child that was called *Badangima-sononga*, the half body."[21] In a Japanese tribal saga "Brother and Sister" a brother and his sister tie their hair and so hang themselves on the branch of a tree and escape the great flood as the only people to survive. Then they marry. Their children have only one eye, half a nose and their lips are split in the middle. The next generation is also incomplete, and it is only with the third generation that the children are whole. As in many legends,[22] demons are described as "half-people," the half measure is a characteristic of an unconscious figure. This suggests that the human being is either still partly bound to the unconscious and is, therefore, not a "whole" person, or conversely, that he or she is split off from the unconscious part.[23]

---

[20] Translated from the German of P. Hambruch, *Malaiische*, Jena 1922 pp. 104–107.
[21] Cited from a note in *Ibid* p. 320. Original source for this is same as for "The Half," M. van Baarda, *Loda*, 's-Gravenhage 1904 p. 442.
[22] Cf. L. Laistner, *Das Rätsel*, Berlin 1889 p. II, 91.
[23] Cf. the same meaning but differently formulated concept of the stepwise progress of becoming conscious in "Kaboi."

156   In the Sulawesi legend, the "half body" is – like in the Japanese tale – the child of the primordial twin couple of the tribe. There too, the birth is preceded by a flood and thus indicates an overpowering by the unconscious, which apparently tries to prevent the birth or entry of the heroes into the world. This overpowering is the cause of being "half" and the revenge by the unconscious. In "The Half" revenge is clearly the result of the mother's cursing the rain. This turning of the mother against the oppressive tide of the unconscious, against nature, symbolizes the emergence of a clearly defined ego-consciousness that has grown organically out of the primordial wholeness and stands in contrast to it. (In the Japanese legend, the primordial pair escape the flood by hanging "above" the waves on the World Tree, that is, isolated from the events in the unconscious. The children that are born into the world are, however, at first, "half.") The child in the Sulawesi tale is marked by the unconscious as a "half" human, that is, from now there is the duality of consciousness and the unconscious. The half which, in spite of the flood, is born into the world of human ego-awareness, no longer belongs to the world of the unconscious, against which his mother took a position.

157   Compared to the symbolic figure of the primordial original human or the Self who encompasses the two spheres in a sense, more "whole," and in a higher sense, knowing, The Half is more unconscious. He is thus as much a "half" as the magical creatures that rational consciousness lacks. According to Plato (in *Timaeus*), the original human was once "whole" and was later divided into two parts. This archetypal idea is also reflected in the Sulawesi and Japanese narratives. There, the primordial pair of twins corresponds to the original "whole" human being. The actual "splitting" is only transferred to the following generation. This parallel positioning leads to the conclusion that the "hero" corresponds at the beginning to one half of the original man and the goal of his adventure is the making-whole-again. Insofar as the half of the man, "The Half" is human, therefore, he must seek wholeness to overcome his one-sided orientation, and gain higher consciousness. Thus, he becomes a hero as the symbol of the conscious whole human.[24]

158   At the beginning of the present tale, The Half is sitting on the beach, a border area. This symbolizes a psychic location at the edge of the unconscious. His counterpart, his other half, is initially the sea, an infinity of vague, unknown, psychic stirrings. Goethe says of this condition: "Whoever seriously

---

[24] In a tale from the Iban Dayak people of Borneo, "Simpang Impang," the hero is also born after a flood as half-man, whose father was a vine plant that the mother used to make the first fire. He is later made whole by the wind demon (spirit!). The half-person is also found in other myths. Thus, for example, in *The Mabinogion*, King Arthur is challenged to battle by the "Hanner Dyn," the half man, and although Arthur initially scorned his opponent he overcame him only with the greatest effort (see in C. Guest, *Mabinogion*, London/New York (1906) 1937 p. 322 see this same reference, page 105, where another half man, Kynvelyn Keudawd Pwyll, appears). And a tale from India tells of a hero named Half-A-Son, a cripple, who has to overcome his six hostile brothers. (Cf. J. Bolte and G. Polívka, *Anmerkungen*, Vol. 2, Leipzig 1915 p. 480.)

descends deep down into himself will always realize that he is only half a being; let him find a girl or a world, no matter which, and he will become a whole."[25] The Half lets vague, indefinite images arise, which he tries to bring into a consciously tangible form. He plays, as he himself explicitly emphasizes.

159   The horse that The Half draws has seven heads and is thus a mythical creature, a symbol.[26] The king of the land covets this miracle horse, like the king in "The Three Feathers" who wants to have a rug, and the miller in, "The Poor Miller's Boy and the Cat" who desires a particularly good horse. It is the initial image that leads to a long psychological transformation process describing his journey into the realm of the Great Mother to becoming whole. The seven-headed horse is here an image of an unconscious goal, as Jung writes:

160   [T]he psychic process, being goal-directed, apparently sets up of its own accord, without any external stimulus. . . The goal which beckons to this psychic need, the image which promises to heal, to *make whole*, is at first strange beyond all measure to the conscious mind, so that it can find entry only with the very greatest difficulty.[27]

161   The initial difficulty is here expressed not as a resistance of the prevailing conscious attitude (the king greedily grabs at the possibility to get the horse), but rather in the fact that The Half himself first refuses his task, which amounts to practically the same thing. Yet the hero is induced by an order of the king to embark on his quest, and due to the fact that the conscious mind has decided to pursue the symbol of his soul, the parallel process in the unconscious succeeds: the higher personality, personified by the hero, becomes whole. Basically, the conscious mind succumbs to a fascination, for it streams out from that. . .

162   . . . psychic stratum, that dark realm of the unknown, [which] exerts fascinating attraction that threatens to become the more over-powering the further he penetrates into it. The psychological danger that arises here is a *disintegration* of personality into its functional components, i.e., the separate functions of consciousness, the complexes, hereditary units, etc.[28]

163   The Half comes to a house where "people" throw him into the fire and then, suddenly, like with a piece of hot metal, they beat him with hammers until he

---

[25] J. W. Goethe, *Maxims and Reflections*, New York, 1893 (nr. 935).
[26] It is not possible for us to interpret the meaning of the *seven* heads without regard to the number symbolism of the Sulawesi, which, because of their syncretic culture, would require a specific study.
[27] C.G. Jung, CW 12, *Psychology and Alchemy* ¶328, [Italics by von Franz].)
[28] C.G. Jung, CW 12, *Psychology and Alchemy* ¶439. [The first part of this quote was cited earlier on page 5. Italics by von Franz and von Beit .]

is a whole person. As long as he is half, they do not disclose any information about the horse he seeks, but afterwards they show him the way to where the horse is tethered. With the transformation into a whole human in the fire, The Half is redeemed from his incompleteness; from the shadowy ego there arises the hero who has been called. The making whole of The Half represents a rebirth,[29] the eternally recurring archetypal process of torture, death, and transformation of the primordial human being.[30] The sufferer cannot be identified as the empirical ego, but rather

164   . . . with a 'divine nature' quite distinct from it, and hence, psychologically speaking, with a conscious-transcending content issuing from the realm of the unconscious.[31]

165   The Ukrainian fairytale, "Och" tells how the hero – initially a lazy, oafish farmer's son – is thrice burned by Och, the Forest King, and then revived and made into a fine, "usable" and nimble fellow who later accomplishes various heroical tasks. In the legend from the Bakairi people of Brazil, "Keri and Kame," the hero twins, Keri and Kame, come first to the world in jaguar, not human, form. Kame fell into a fire and Keri blew on him and made him into a human being. Soon after, Keri caught fire and Kame blew him to life and into human form. Thus, the natural man must go through a painful transformation process to become his true self or so that a higher consciousness can emerge. The image of the fire, through which the conversion takes place, indicates emotional arousal, the outbreak of passions,[32] in a conflict situation.[33]

---

[29] Cf. also, "The Old Man Made Young Again," and the parallels in J. Bolte and G. Polívka, *Anmerkungen,* Vol. 3, Leipzig 1918 p. 193ff.

[30] On this theme see C.G. Jung, CW 13, *Alchemical Studies* ¶139.

[31] See C.G. Jung, CW 11, *"Psychology and Religion"* ¶154. Likewise, in alchemy, the transformative substance was represented as a human hero who is dismembered and painfully recombined by cooking. See C.G. Jung, CW 13, *Op. cit.* ¶86,III,vbis. The Indian primordial human being, *Purusha* is fragmented and then reassembled in the form of the visible world. See J. Przyluski, *Erlösung,* Zürich 1938 p. 104. The transformation of The Half in the fire also recalls an Indian tale of a "misshapen demon," with a headless torso, long arms and powerful chest, who was cursed by a saint to have this shape. He blocked the god Rama from continuing on his path. He begged Rama to transform him which Rama did by burning him in a pit. After he was consumed in the fire, he took on his divine form and went redeemed up to heaven. See H. Zimmer, *Maya,* Stuttgart and Berlin 1936 pp. 271–272.

[32] See the ancient Germanic view of the fire, of which M. Ninck, *Wodan,* Jena 1935 pp. 58– 59 fn. 4 writes: "the skald poets [of 9th-11th century Scandinavia and Iceland], often called fire: wolf or dog . . . Old Icelandic *ólmr* (angry, furious) an epithet of dogs and oxen, is related to Old Icelandic *ylja* (warm up), Old English *welm,* boil up, cook, flame up, become angry, Old High German *walm,* heat, embers, German *wel* boil, hot flush, see also German *Welle* [wave]. The basic meaning is then: to seethe, flush, fly into a rage.

[33] See Jung:

The stirring up of a conflict is a Luciferian virtue in the true sense of the word. Conflict engenders fire, the fire of affects and emotions, and like every other fire it has two aspects, that of combustion and that of creating light. On the one hand, emotion is the alchemical fire whose warmth brings everything into existence and shoe heat burns all superfluities to ashes (*omnes surperfluitates comburit*). But on the other hand, emotion is the moment when steel meets flint and a spark is stuck forth, for emotion is the

166   When The Half is made whole in the fire, still another simile plays a role, he is annealed and hammered like a piece of metal, which remarkably is reminiscent of the alchemical speculations on the conversion of base metals into gold, an image that is widespread. Angelus Silesius wrote:

167   I myself am the metal, the spirit is fire and the hearth,
          Messiah the tincture, which glorifies the body and the soul.[34]

168   A similar motif to the whole-making of The Half in the forge can be found in a fairytale from the Caucasus region, "Batrás Birth" in which the hero lets himself be tempered (literally"steeled") to become victorious in war. Batrás spoke:

169   "So, as I am, I am made of flesh and bone, I cannot go to war with the people. I will let myself be steeled," He put sixty *Tuman*[35] in his pocket and went to Kurdálägon[36] and said "God grant us mercy! Steel me, that I may become as hard as steel." "I could indeed do this. But you would be burnt!" objected Kurdálägon. "Whatever becomes of me, I must let myself be steeled." Then Kurdálägon brought stones, built a furnace, and laid Batrás in it. He lit the fire and blew on it from one sundown to the next. "Now I want to see what has become of Batrás," Kurdálägon said. He opened the fire a crack and lo, there sat Batrás in the fire and looked around. "No good," he said, "if you want to steel me, then do it properly; if not, then do not joke with me, give me a Fändý[37] to play!" Kurdálägon thus began again anew to build an oven and light the fire. He blew on the fire for a whole week. He opened the oven and looked in, Batrás said, "Be merciful and throw me into the sea!" This did Kurdálägon do. The sea dried up from the heat, there was not water in it for one whole week. When Batrás rose out of the sea, the waters came back. (Thereafter the hero was invincible.)"[38]

---

chief source of consciousness. There is no change from darkness to light or from inertia to movement without emotion. (C.G. Jung, CW 9i, *The Archetypes and the Collective Unconscious* ¶179.)

[34] A. Silesius, *The Cherubinic Wanderer*, New Jersey 1986 p. 15, No. 103 (according to title of No. 102), "The spiritual gold-making." See also p. 63 No. 163: *God works like the fire*:
The fire melts and makes you one: you sink into the Origin,
This is how your mind (spirit) is melted into one with God.

[35] Original Persian coins – A. Dirr, *Kaukasische Märchen*, Jena 1922 p. 175.

[36] According to a footnote in A. Dirr, *Kaukasische Märchen*, Jena 1922 p. 175, the mythical smith of the Osseten, who dwells in heaven or in the land of the dead.

[37] A two-stringed, guitar-like instrument – A. Dirr, *Kaukasische Märchen*, Jena 1922 p. 175

[38] A. Dirr, *Kaukasische Märchen*, Jena 1922 pp. 173–175. [Legends and myths revolving around the smith forging the hero feature prominently in the Nart sagas which tell of the relationship between the great mother Satanay and the great smith, Aynar or Lhepesh.]

170   The Half comes rather involuntarily under the power of the magical smith, reminiscent of the Idaean Dactyls (fingers, a Tom Thumb), who had learned from the great mother of the gods the blacksmith's art, and who live as mysterious creative deities in the earth.[39] The narrative as we have it states only vaguely that The Half came to "people," who hammered him together. The transformation process takes place deep in the unconscious. The hero is beaten by the "people." In many rites, beating has the meaning of making fertile.[40]

171   An Inuit fairytale "Kagsagsuk" strikingly portrays the transformation of the hero by beating:

172   There was once a poor orphan boy who lived among a lot of uncharitable men. His name was Kagsagsuk, and his foster-mother was a miserable old woman. These poor people had a wretched little shed adjoining the house-passage[41] and they were not allowed to enter the main room. Kagsagsuk did not even venture to enter the shed, but lay in the passage, seeking to warm himself among the dogs. In the morning, when the men were rousing their sledge-dogs with their whips, they often hit the poor boy as well as the dogs. He then would cry out, "Na-ah! Na-ah!" mocking himself in imitating the dogs. When the men were feasting upon various frozen dishes, such as the hide of the walrus and frozen meat, the little Kagsagsuk used to peep over the threshold, and sometimes the men lifted him up above it, but only by putting their fingers into his nostrils; these enlarged accordingly, but otherwise he did not grow at all. They would give the poor wretch frozen meat, without allowing him a knife to cut it with, saying his teeth might do instead; and sometimes they pulled out a couple of teeth, complaining of his eating too much. His poor foster-mother procured him boots and a small beard-spear, in order to enable him to go outside the house and play with the other children,

---

[39] [The Dactyls of Mount Ida in Phrygia invented the art of working metals into usable shapes with fire] See C.G. Jung, CW 5, *Symbols of Transformation* ¶183. See also "The Chaifi" a tale with a demiurgic primordial smith Chaifi:

> Chaifi forged souls in his furnace so that he had slaves who were able to serve him. He stoked the fire that burst the forge. Red-hot stones and fiery streams poured down on the earth, and then one soul flew out of Sasalaguan. It fell down on the country Guahan Funia and turned to stone. But the sun warmed the stone, the rain softened it, and the sea gave it human form. Then the man saw that it was beautiful on earth. He formed other men of the dust and other water and forged them the fire of the sun souls, as he had learned from the Chaifi, and called them sons of earth.

[40] See W. Mannhardt, *Wald- und Feldkulte*, Vol. 1, Berlin 1875 pp. 292–303; C. Picard, *Grosse Mutter*, Zürich 1939 p. 113. Stroking with a "rod of life," such as a freshly cut twig, bestows fertility, G. van der Leeuw, *Religion in Essence*, Vol. 1 p. 195 and Leeuw p. 347. See also beatings and stroking administered by medieval masters and in the rituals of knighthood.

[41] [Or doorway, a long and very narrow, sometimes half- subterranean, tunnel, leading by an upward step to the main, or rather the only, room of the winter hut, and adapted to keeping out the cold air. Its ends we have called the outer and the inner entrance. – footnote included in the original, H. Rink, *Eskimo*, Edinburgh & London 1875]

but they would turn him over and roll him in the snow, filling his clothes with it, and treating him most cruelly in various ways. The girls sometimes covered him all over with filth. Thus the little boy was always tormented and mocked, and did not grow except about the nostrils.

173   At length he ventured out among the mountains by himself, choosing solitary places, and meditating how to get strength. His foster-mother had taught him how to manage this. Once, standing between two high mountains, he called out: "Lord of strength, come forth! Lord of strength, come to me!" A large animal now appeared in the shape of an *amarok* [a fabulous animal, originally a wolf], and Kagsagsuk got very terrified, and was on the point of taking to his heels. But the beast soon overtook him, and, twisting its tail round his body, threw him down. Totally unable to rise, he heard the while a rustling sound, and saw a number of seal-bones, like small toys, falling from his own body. The amarok now said: "It is because of these bones that thy growth has been stopped." Again it wound its tail round the boy, and again they fell down, but the little bones were fewer this time; and when the beast threw him down the third time, the last bones fell off. The fourth time he did not quite fall, and at the fifth he did not fall at all, but jumped along the ground. The amarok now said: "If it be thy wish to become strong and vigorous, thou mayst come every day to me."

174   On his way home, Kagsagsuk felt very much lighter, and could even run home, meanwhile kicking and striking the stones on his way. Approaching the house, the girls who nursed the babies met him, and shouted, "Kagsagsuk is coming – let us pelt him with mud," and the boys beat him and tormented him as before. But he made no opposition, and following his old habits, he went to sleep among the dogs. Afterwards, he met the amarok every day, and always underwent the same process. The boy felt stronger every day, and on his way home he kicked the very rocks and, rolling himself on the ground, made the stones fly about him. At last the beast was not able to overthrow him, and then it spoke: "Now, that will do. Human beings will not be able to conquer thee anymore. Still, thou hast better stick to thy old habits. When winter sets in, and the sea is frozen, then is thy time to show thyself. Three great bears will then appear, and they shall be killed by thy hand." That day Kagsagsuk ran all the way back, kicking the stones right and left, as was his wont. But at home he went on as usual, and the people tormented him more than ever.

175 One day, in the autumn, the kayakers[42] returned home with a large piece of driftwood, which they only made fast to some large stones on the beach, finding it too heavy to be carried up to the house at once. At nightfall, Kagsagsuk said to his mother, "Let me have thy boots, mother, that I too may go down and have a look at the large piece of timber." When all had gone to rest, he slipped out of the house, and having reached the beach, and loosened the moorings, he flung the piece of timber on his shoulders and carried it up behind the house, where he buried it deep in the ground. In the morning, when the first of the men came out, he cried, "The driftwood is gone!" and when he was joined by the rest, and they saw the strings cut, they wondered how it could possibly have drifted away, there being neither wind nor tide. But an old woman, who happened to go behind the house, cried, "Just look! Here is the spar!" Whereat they all rushed to the spot, making a fearful noise, shouting, "Who can have done this? There surely must be a man of extraordinary strength among us!" And the young men all gave themselves great airs, that each might be believed to be the great unknown strong man – the impostors!

176 In the beginning of the winter, the housemates of Kagsaguk ill-treated him even worse than before; but he stuck to his old habits and did not let them suspect anything. At last the sea was quite frozen over, and seal-hunting out of the question. But when the days began to lengthen, the men one day came running in to report that three bears were seen climbing an iceberg. Nobody, however, ventured to go out and attack them. Now was Kagsagsuk's time to be up and doing. "Mother," he said, "let me have thy boots, that I too may go out and have a look at the bears!" She did not like it much, but, however, she threw her boots to him, at the same time mocking him, saying, "Then fetch me a skin for my couch, and another for my coverlet, in return." He took the boots, fastened his ragged clothes around him, and then was off for the bears. Those who were standing outside cried, "Well, if that is not Kagsagsuk! What can he be about? Kick him away!" and the girls went on, "He must surely be out of his wits!" But Kagsagsuk came running right through the crowd, as if they had been a shoal of small fish; his heels seemed almost to be touching his neck, while the snow, foaming about, sparkled in rainbow colors. He ascended the iceberg by taking hold with his hands, and instantly the largest bear lifted his paw, but Kagsagsuk turned round to make himself *hard*, that is, invulnerable by charm. Seizing hold of the animal by the forepaws, flung it against

---

[42] [Men in their kayaks, or skin canoes, made for the purpose of seal hunting, with room only for a single person. – footnote, *ibid.*]

the iceberg, so that the haunches were severed from the body, and then threw it down on the ice to the bystanders, crying, "This was my first catch; now, flense away[43] and divide [the meat] up amongst yourselves!"

177   The others now thought, "The next bear will be sure to kill him." The former process, however, was repeated, and the beast thrown down on the ice. But the third bear he merely caught hold of by the forepaws, and, swinging it above his head, he hurled it at the bystanders, crying, "This fellow behaved shamefully towards me!" and then, smiting another, "That one treated me still worse!" until they all fled before him, making for the house in great consternation. On entering it himself he went straight to his foster-mother with the two bearskins, crying, "There is one for thy couch, and another for thy coverlet!" After which he ordered the flesh of the bears to be dressed and cooked. Kagsagsuk was now requested to enter the main room. In answer to which request he, as was his wont, only peeped above the threshold, saying, "I really can't get across, unless someone will lift me up by the nostrils." But nobody else venturing to do so now, his old foster-mother came and lifted him up as he desired. All the men had now become very civil to him. One would say, "Step forward" another, "Come and sit down, friend." No, not there where the ledge[44] has no cover," cried another, "Here is a nice seat for you!" But rejecting their offers, he sat down, as usual, on the side-ledge. Some of them went on, "We have got boots for Kagsagsuk" and others, "Here are breeches for him!" and the girls rivaled each other in offering to make clothes for him.

178   [Kagsasusk refused all courting offers and killed all those men who had mocked him. He spared the poor people who had helped him and became a great hero of the tribe.][45]

179 As noted by Krickeberg,[46] the encounter with the *amarok* describes the initiation of a shaman (*angakok*). The wolf demon is a future totem animal that does not devour (German: *verschlingen*) but violently entwines (German: *umschlingen*) the boy and squeezes him. This corresponds to the trial by fire and the beating of The Half (in one variant Kagsagsuk is beaten by his brothers

---

[43] [I.e., "Take off the skin and blubber." – footnote, *ibid.*]

[44] [The main ledge or bench; a low and broad bench for sitting and sleeping places, occupying the whole length of the wall opposite to the windows, the narrower side-ledge and window ledge bordering the other walls. It is generally known in Greenland as the *brix*. – footnote, *ibid.*]

[45] This version from H. Rink, *Eskimo*, Edinburgh & London pp. 93–99. See also R. Trebitsch and M. Haberlandt, *Bei den Eskimos*, Berlin 1910 pp. 92–98 where there are several other stories from the Inuit of West Greenland featuring the hero Kagsagsug [as his name is spelled there].

[46] Editor of the German collection of North American tales, W. Krickeberg, *Nordamerika*, Jena 1924 p. 369.

with a whip, from which whipping he gets his strength). Whereas with The Half his initial state of poverty was portrayed as an incompleteness, with Kagsagsuk it is attributed to a remarkable origin: the hero is full of bones and these evidently have prevented him from growing. These bones are organic elements that are not connected to the rest of his body. Psychologically they mean inherited psychic components, inherited possibilities that are difficult or impossible to combine into a single coherent personality. As a consequence of this, primitive people often believe that human beings take on different ancestral souls.

180   An inner core personality, represented here by the hero, must first be built up from these different elements. Some of these elements (soul parts) inherited from the ancestors can cause serious developmental disorders and inhibitions when they do not let themselves be assimilated – or eliminated. Kagsagsuk's growth remains regressed, therefore, until the "Lord of Strength," the totem ancestor himself, wraps himself around the boy and "concentrates" him whereby the unneeded soul parts fall off. (In another version of the same tale, "Qaudjaqdjuq," it is the man in the moon, a divine being, who makes the boy stronger and stronger by whipping cycles.) Just as The Half, on his way to the seven-headed horse, an animal god, is made whole, so too is Kagsagsuk unified, completed, and granted potency through the reconnection to the divine totem animal. In the subsequent battle with the polar bears, he performs a second ritual action that also expresses wholeness: he turns three times[47] around himself.[48] So he turns to the magical, establishes the connection, and creates a magic circle: a mandala in which he is protected from the power of the bears. This rounding out of his personality makes him invulnerable.

181   The Half also, after his rebirth as a whole person, was able to conquer the seven-headed horse. Following the advice of the people who hammered him, he comes to the house of an old woman in whom we can recognize the figure of the Great Mother. She appears in her full double aspect: on the one hand, she is well disposed towards him, offers good advice, and he finds – as so often – the anima with her, whom he later wins. On the other hand, she is surrounded by tigers and demonic Garuda birds that threaten him, and, moreover, conceal the existence of the magical horse.

182   To gain possession of the horse, he must contend with the many-headed Garuda bird representing the "inconceivable," ephemeral, and obstructive nature of the unconscious that must be overcome before the desired treasure can be assimilated by the conscious mind. There hostile resistance in the unconscious is first embodied as a bird demon, that is, in a more psychic

---

[47] [The original has "turned around to make himself hard." The authors assume that Kagsaksuk repeated the turning before the fight with each of the other two bears.]

[48] See the magical effect of turning in Bächtold-Stäubli under *drehen* [turning, rotating].

aspect, then it reveals itself for the second time as a snake, a symbol of the earthly world of instinct. The hero survives the usual battle with the dragon as a fight against the hostile Great Mother, against the dark lethargic power of the unconscious. On the way back, he must a second time overcome a snake that is tracking him and turns its greed for rice against itself. This shows again that the secret of the hero's overcoming the unconscious is that he lets his evil side destroy itself, a common motif in many fairytales.

183   The conclusion of the story is like the end of the previously discussed tale: as in "The Poor Miller's Boy and the Cat" the father figure gets his desired horse that gives him a new lease on life, while the hero together with the anima remain in an intermediate zone, with a beautiful garden that surrounds them. There in passive quiet, he can await the reactions of the ego consciousness symbolized in the king. But later he steps forth and demands the complete subjugation of the former ruler and, as in "The Three Feathers" and "Tritill, Litill, and the Birds" becomes heir of the empire, that is, the central dominant principle of the personality. This does not mean that we should entirely abandon the precious acquisition of our forefathers, namely, the intellectual differentiation of consciousness. It is rather a question of the *man* taking the place of the *intellect. . .*[49]

184   The Half who has now become whole is just "the man" – the realized conscious personality.

---

[49] C.G. Jung, CW 12, *Psychology and Alchemy* ¶84, italics in the original.

◆

Chapter 4

The Devil with the
Three Golden Hairs

185   So far, the father or king, who portrays the intellect, has only contempt or little understanding for the hero and forces him into the position of an unknown or unacknowledged core of the personality. In the following tale, "The Devil with the Three Golden Hairs," the king vehemently opposes the hero because he suspects his future significance and cannot, or will not, accept it. This resistance creates an exaggerated conflict situation, not as in the previous tales between the hero and the forces of the unconscious, but here directly between the hero and prevailing secular conscious attitude. Thus, the hero is pushed into a kind of solidarity stance with the powers of Hell.

186   There was once a poor woman who gave birth to a little son; and as he came into the world with a caul,[1] it was predicted that in his fourteenth year he would have the King's daughter for his wife. It happened that soon afterwards the King came into the village, but no one knew that he was the King. He asked the people what news there was, and they answered, "A child has just been born with a caul; whatever anyone so born undertakes will turn out well. It is prophesied, too, that in his fourteenth year he will have the King's daughter for his wife."

187   The King, who had a bad heart, and was angry about the prophecy, went to the parents and feigning charity, said, "You poor people, let me have your child, I will take care of it." At first they refused, but when the stranger offered them a large amount of gold for their child, they thought, "It is a good luck child, and everything must turn out well for it." At last they consented and gave the child to the King. The King put the child in a box and rode away with it until he came to a deep stretch of water; then he threw the box into it and thought, "Now I have freed my daughter from her unwanted suitor!"

---

[1] [A caul (Latin: *Caput galeatum*, literally, "helmeted head") is a piece of membrane that can cover a newborn's head and face immediately after birth.]

188 The box did not sink, however, but floated like a boat, and not a drop of water made its way into it. And it floated to within two miles of the King's chief city, where there was a mill, and it came to a standstill at the mill dam. A miller's boy, who by good luck was standing there, noticed it and pulled it out with a hook, thinking that he had found a great treasure, but when he opened it, there lay a pretty boy inside, quite fresh and lively. He took him to the miller and his wife, and as they had no children they were very glad, and said, "God has given him to us." They took great care of the foundling, and he grew up in all goodness.

189 It happened that once in a storm, the King went into the mill, and he asked the mill-folk if the tall youth was their son. "No" answered they, "he's a foundling. Fourteen years ago he floated down to the mill dam in a box, and the mill-boy pulled him out of the water."

190 Then the King knew that it was none other than the lucky child that he had thrown into the water, and he said, "My good people, could not the youth take a letter to the Queen. I will give him two gold pieces as a reward?" "As the King commands," they answered, and they told the boy to hold himself in readiness. Then the King wrote a letter to the Queen, wherein he said, "As soon as the boy arrives with this letter, let him be killed and buried, and all must be done before I come home."

191 The boy set out with this letter, but he lost his way, and in the evening came to a large forest. In the darkness he saw a small light; he went towards it and reached a cottage. When he went in, an old woman was sitting by the fire quite alone. She started when she saw the boy, and said, "Whence do you come, and whither are you going?" "I come from the mill," he answered, "and wish to go to the Queen, to whom I am taking a letter, but as I have lost my way in the forest I should like to stay here over night." "You poor boy," said the woman, "you have come into a den of thieves, and when they come home they will kill you." "Let them come," said the boy, "I am not afraid, but I am so tired that I cannot go any farther," and he stretched himself upon a bench and fell asleep.

192 Soon afterwards the robbers came, and asked what strange boy was lying there. "Ah," said the old woman, "it is an innocent child who lost himself in the forest, and out of pity I have let him come in. He has to take a letter to the Queen." The robbers opened the letter and read it, and in it was written that the boy as soon as he arrived should be put to death. Then the robbers tore up the letter and wrote another, saying, that as soon as the boy arrived, he should be married at once to the

King's daughter. Then they let him lie quietly on the bench until the next morning, and when he awoke they gave him the letter, and showed him the right way.

193 The Queen, when she had received the letter and read it, did as was written in it, and had a splendid wedding-feast prepared, and the King's daughter was married to the lucky child, and as the youth was handsome and agreeable she lived with him in joy and contentment.

194 After some time the King returned to his palace and saw that the prophecy was fulfilled, and that the lucky child had married his daughter. The King was in a passion and said, "You shall not have everything quite so much your own way; whosoever marries my daughter must fetch me from Hell three golden hairs from the head of the devil. Bring me what I want, and you shall keep my daughter." In this way the King hoped to be rid of him forever. Thereupon he took leave of them and began his journey.

195 The road led him to a large town, where the watchman by the gates asked him what his trade was, and what he knew. "I know everything," answered the lucky child. "Then you can do us a favor," said the watchman, "if you will tell us why our market-fountain that once flowed with wine, has become dry, and no longer gives even water?" "That you shall know," answered he, "only wait until I come back."

196 Then he went farther and came to another town, and there also the gatekeeper asked him what his trade was, and what he knew. "I know everything," answered he. "Then you can do us a favor and tell us why a tree in our town that once bore golden apples now does not even put forth leaves?" "You shall know that," answered he, "only wait until I come back."

197 Then he went on and came to a wide river over which he had to cross. The ferryman asked him what his trade was, and what he knew. "I know everything," answered he. "Then you can do me a favor," said the ferryman, "and tell me why I must always be rowing backwards and forwards, and am never set free?" "You shall know that," answered he, "only wait until I come back."

198 When he had crossed the water he found the entrance to Hell. It was black and sooty within; the Devil was not at home, but his grandmother was sitting in an armchair. "What do you want?" said she to him. "I should like to have three golden hairs from the devil's head," answered he, "else I cannot keep my wife." "That is a good deal to ask for," said she. "If the devil comes home and finds you, it will cost you your life; but as I pity you, I will see if I can help you."

She changed him into an ant and said, "Creep into the folds of my dress, you will be safe there." "Yes," answered he, "so far, so good. But there are three things besides that I want to know: why a fountain which once flowed with wine has become dry, and no longer gives even water; why a tree which once bore golden apples does not even put forth leaves; and why a ferryman must always be going backwards and forwards, and is never set free?"

199 "Those are difficult questions," answered she, "but only be silent and quiet and pay attention to what the devil says when I pull out the three golden hairs."

200 As the evening came on, the devil returned home. No sooner had he entered than he noticed that the air was not pure. "I smell man's flesh," said he, "all is not right here." Then he pried into every corner, and searched, but could not find anything. His grandmother scolded him. "It has just been swept," said she, "and everything put in order, and now you are upsetting it again; you have always got man's flesh in your nose. Sit down and eat your supper."

201 When he had eaten and drunk he was tired, and laid his head in his grandmother's lap, and before long he was fast asleep, snoring and breathing heavily. Then the old woman took hold of a golden hair, pulled it out, and laid it down near her. "Oh!" cried the devil, "what are you doing?" "I have had a bad dream," answered the grandmother, "so I seized hold of your hair." "What did you dream then?" said the devil. "I dreamed that a fountain in a marketplace from which wine once flowed was dried up, and not even water would flow out of it; what is the cause of it?" "Oh, ho! If they did but know it," answered the devil. "There is a toad sitting under a stone in the well. If they killed it, the wine would flow again."

202 He went to sleep again and snored until the windows shook. Then she pulled the second hair out. "Ha! what are you doing?" cried the devil angrily. "Do not take it ill," said she, "I did it in a dream." "What have you dreamt this time?" asked he. "I dreamt that in a certain kingdom there stood an apple tree which once bore golden apples, but now would not even bear leaves. What, think you, was the reason?" "Oh! If they did but know," answered the devil. "A mouse is gnawing at the root; if they killed it, they would have golden apples again, but if it gnaws much longer the tree will wither altogether. But leave me alone with your dreams. If you disturb me in my sleep again you will get a box on the ear."

203   The grandmother waited until he fell asleep again. Then she took hold of the third golden hair and pulled it out. The devil jumped up, roared out, and would have treated her ill if she had not quieted him once more and said, "Who can help bad dreams?" "What was the dream, then?" asked he. "I dreamt of a ferryman who complained that he must always ferry from one side to the other, and was never released. What is the cause of it?" "Ah! The fool," answered the devil. "When anyone comes and wants to go across, he must put the oar in his hand, and the other man will have to ferry and he will be free." As the grandmother had plucked out the three golden hairs, and the three questions were answered, she let the old serpent alone, and he slept until daybreak.

204   When the devil had gone out again the old woman took the ant out of the folds of her dress, and gave the lucky child his human shape again and gave him the three golden. The answers he had heard for himself. He thanked the old woman and was on his way.

205   When he came to the ferryman he was expected to give the promised answer. "Ferry me across first," said the good-luck child, "and then I will tell you how you can be set free," and when he reached the opposite shore he gave him the devil's advice: "The next time anyone comes who wants to be ferried over, just put the oar in their hand."

206   He went on and came to the town in which the unfruitful tree grew. There the young man told the watchman what he had heard from the devil: "Kill the mouse that is gnawing at its root and it will again bear golden apples." Then the watchman thanked him, and gave him as a reward two asses laden with gold.

207   At last he came to the town whose well was dry. He told the watchman what the devil had said: "A toad is in the well beneath a stone. You must find it and kill it, and the well will then again give wine in plenty." The watchman thanked him, and also gave him two asses laden with gold.

208   At last the good luck child got home to his wife, who was heartily glad to see him again. To the King he took the devil's three golden hairs, and when the King saw the four asses laden with gold he was quite content, and said, "Now all the conditions are fulfilled, and you can keep my daughter. But tell me, dear son- in-law, where did all that gold come from?" "I was rowed across a river," answered he, "and when I got to the other side; gold was lying on the shore instead of sand." The King set out in all haste, and when he came to the river he beckoned to the ferryman to put him across. The ferryman came and

bade him get in, and when they got to the other shore he put the oar in his hand and sprang out. But from this time forth the King had to ferry as a punishment for his sins. Perhaps he is ferrying still? If he is, it is because no one has taken the oar from him.

209 A parallel tale[2] closes with the words: "Therefore anyone who is not afraid of the devil can pluck his hair out and gain the whole world."

210 The hero's poverty comes to light when he is set out in the water and then found and adopted by the miller and his wife. He was born, however, with a feature that stamps him as a "called" person. This is a sign to the king of his superior significance: he was born with a caul. This is a piece of amniotic membrane that surrounds the child at birth and, if not removed, hinders its breathing. According to old Germanic ideas the caul is a special sign of good luck. Ninck writes:

211 *Hamr* means skin, shadow, shape, guardian spirit, the feminine form *hamingja* means guardian spirit, good luck. The corresponding Old High German word *hamo* designates skin, shell, clothes and is found in the modern German word *Hemd* [shirt]

212 . . . Middle Low German *ham* and *hamel*, English *heam* means "afterbirth." In Wallonian (language of French-speaking Belgium) *hamelette* means caul, skin of the uterus in which lucky children are born. [Once removed] this membrane was carefully preserved or buried, because it served as a guardian spirit of the child (cf. *fylgja* [afterbirth], originally "guardian spirit.") The development of this expression is very insightful. It is part of the common concept associated with the image . . . shadow . . . or the figure of the person that can detach itself from the body, such as in a dream, or in a deep sleep. In a paroxysm of rage it can even completely free itself from the person and perform independent acts. *Hamr* is the soul in its transformative aspect; *hamr*, *hamingja* are at the same time expressions for guardian spirits and good luck, because they denote something outside the ego that is experienced as the fulfillment of a deep desire, the liberation of the soul.[3]

213 The hero is thus special, he has a kind of twin, a guardian spirit born with him and he can change his shape and become an animal [or insect]. He is called to achieve a great destiny and has the characteristics of one who has to carry

[2] See J. Bolte and G. Polívka, *Anmerkungen*, Vol. 1, Leipzig 1913 pp. 278–282.
[3] M. Ninck, *Wodan*, Jena 1935 p. 43, 294. See further Bächtold-Stäubli under *Glückshaube* [caul].

out a specific assignment.[4] Such a calling can be a curse or a vocation. It is the same as being addressed by a deity.[5] It determines the hero's journey that in this fairytale leads him to Hell and in a parallel tale, to God![6]

214   This hero, who is appointed by the otherworldly powers, must survive against the king. The king, whom we again consider representing the prevailing conscious attitude, sets all his efforts against the "lowly born" as his son-in-law and, therefore, as his future heir. That the king himself has no son symbolizes the sterility of this ruling principle, which can gain new life only through an initially unknown psychic power; the anima plays here the role of a mediator. The king thinks he alone has all the power, and this is the reason why he becomes so deeply troubled when a being emerges who should replace him. The fear of being displaced by a successor is not unwarranted, as at a primitive stage of culture the old king was in some places actually killed in favor of a young new king.[7] Symbolically this means that consciousness needs to "die and become."[8]

---

[4] On this Jung writes:

    [W]hat is commonly called *vocation* [is] an irrational factor that destines a man to emancipate himself from the herd and from its well-worn paths. True personality is always a vocation and puts its trust in it as in God, despite its being, as the ordinary man would say, only a personal feeling. But vocation acts like a law of God from which there is no escape. The fact that many a man who goes his own way ends in ruin means nothing to one who has a vocation. He *must* obey his own law, as if it were a daemon whispering to him of new and wonderful paths. Anyone with a vocation hears the voice of the *inner man*; he is *called*. That is why legends say that he possesses a private daemon who counsel him and whose mandates he must obey. . . The original meaning of *to have a vocation is to be addressed by a voice.* (C.G. Jung, CW 17, *The Development of Personality* ¶300, italics by Jung.)

[5] See also Schopenhauer:

    [W]e can quite generally imagine as possible that, just as everyone is the secret theatrical director of his dreams, so too by analogy that fate that controls the actual course of our lives, ultimately comes in some way from the *will*. This is our own and yet here, where it appears as fate, it operates from a region that lies far beyond our representing individual consciousness; whereas this furnishes the motives that guide our empirically knowable individual will. Hence such will has often to contend most violently with that will of ours that manifests itself as fate, with our guiding genius, with our 'spirit which dwells outside us and has its seat in the stars above,' which surveys the individual consciousness and thus, in relentless opposition thereto, arranges and fixes as external restraint that which it could not leave the consciousness to find out and yet does not wish to see a miscarriage. Schopenhauer pp. 218–219 slightly edited.

Cf. on the calling to initiants in the Mysteries, see R. Reitzenstein, *Hellenistic*, Pittsburgh 1978 p. 170, 252-56. See also the *Mundaka Upanishad*, III,2,3:

    This Atman cannot be attained through teaching,
    nor through reason, nor by studying the scriptures
    (Vedas)
    He whom Atman chooses – he alone understands.
    To him does Atman reveal his own [i.e., the seeker's] true nature.

(P. Deussen, *Sechzig Upanishad's*, Leipzig 1921 p. 557, [translated comparing other English translations. The last line is in accordance with Deussen's reading.])

[6] See J. Bolte and G. Polívka, *Anmerkungen*, Vol. 1, Leipzig 1913 p. 285.

[7] See the evidence in G. van der Leeuw, *Religion in Essence*, Vol. 1 p. 106ff, especially about the Egyptian Set festival.

[8] [The phrase *Stirb und Werde* [die and become] used by in the *West-Eastern Divan*, "Und so lang du das nicht hast / Dieses: Stirb und werde! / Bist du nur ein trüber Gast / Auf der dunklen Erde." ("And so long as you have not attained that, this 'die and become!', you will be only a gloomy guest on this dark earth.") This in turn plays on the passage from John 12: 24-25: "Truly, truly, I say to you, unless a

215   In addition to his early dangers (the caul at his birth, coming from the magical) in the course of his development the hero is driven three times by the hostile king into situations where he is nearly devoured again by the magical. It is the familiar motif of the threatened child hero, and, as Jung explains:

216   It is a striking paradox in all child myths that the "child" is on the one hand delivered helpless into the power of terrible enemies and in constant danger of extinction, while on the other hand he possesses powers far exceeding those of ordinary humanity. This is closely related to the psychological fact that although the child may be "insignificant," unknown, a "mere child," he is also divine. From the conscious standpoint we seem to be dealing with an insignificant content that has no releasing, let alone redeeming character. . . It is therefore easily overlooked and falls back into the unconscious. At least, this is what we should have to fear if things turned out according to our conscious expectations. Myth, however, emphasizes that it is not so, but that the "child" is endowed with superior powers and, despite all dangers, will unexpectedly pull through. The "child" is born out of the womb of the unconscious, begotten out of the depths of human nature, or rather out of living Nature herself. It is a personification of vital forces quite outside the limited range of our conscious mind; of ways and possibilities of which our conscious mind knows nothing; a wholeness which embraces the very depths of Nature. It represents the strongest and most ineluctable urge in every being, namely the urge to realize itself. It is, as it were, an incarnation of the *inability to do otherwise*, equipped with all the powers of nature and instinct, whereas the conscious mind is always getting caught up in its supposed ability to do otherwise. The urge and compulsion to self-realization is a law of nature and thus of invincible power, even though its effect, at the start, is insignificant and improbable. . . The size and invincibility of the "child" are bound up in Hindu speculation with the nature of the Atman, which corresponds to the "smaller than small, yet bigger than big" motif.[9]

217   The initial threat to the savior as a child is portrayed in countless myths in the form of abandonment. Rank comprehensively treated this motif in his book, *The Myth of the Birth of the Hero*. He describes the pattern of this particular hero's fate:

---

grain of wheat falls into the earth and dies, it remains alone; but if it dies, it bears much fruit. Whoever loves his life loses it, and whoever hates his life in this world will keep it for eternal life."]

[9] C.G. Jung, CW 9i, *The Archetypes and the Collective Unconscious* ¶289.

218   The hero is the child of most distinguished parents; usually the son of a king. His origin is preceded by difficulties, such as continence, or prolonged barrenness, or secret intercourse of the parents, due to external prohibition or obstacles. During or before the pregnancy there is a prophecy in the form of a dream or an oracle, waning about the birth, which usually threatens the father. As so often with this motif, the newborn is destined to be killed or abandoned at the instigation of the father or his proxy; as a rule he is consigned to a box surrendered to water. He is then saved by animals, or by lowly people (shepherds) and is suckled by a female animal or by a humble woman. After he has grown up, he finds distinguished parents in a highly varied fashion; he takes his revenge on his father, in some cases, or is acknowledged, in others, and finally achieves rank and honor.[10]

219   The basic types of this fate are the Sargon legend, the story of Krishna, the story of the birth of Moses, and in India the birth of the hero Karna in the *Mahabharata*. The same motif is found in the heroic tales, among many, of Perseus, Oedipus, and Romulus[11] and also in many fairytales. The hero is usually set out, abandoned, or exposed in a basket, a chest, or a box, which Bachofen saw as a symbol of the nourishing womb.[12] The box, drawer, basket, and barrel are symbols of the womb, so that it was natural to imagine that the child was swimming in the amniotic fluid. Here also we find a connection to concepts of the sun's course. As a god traversing the sea, the sun dives every evening into the maternal sea and is born again out of the sea in the morning. Aligning these concepts in parallel, all those "outcasts" become immortal divine hero and sun symbols who for the "night sea journey" (Frobenius) are placed in a box, basket, or ark. The sun god enclosed in the maternal womb is often threatened by all kinds of dangers. Ninck identifies the little boat in which the newborn hero of our tale drifts as the Germanic death ship.[13]

---

[10] O. Rank, *Myth of the Birth*, Baltimore 2004 p. 61.

[11] See *ibid* pp. 12–58.

[12] See J. J. Bachofen, *Gräbersymbolik*, Basel 1859 pp. 127–128. See also H. Silberer, *Problems of Mysticism*, New York 1917 p. 143, O. Rank, *Myth of the Birth*, Baltimore 2004 p. 55f, about the *Lohengrin saga* on the little box in which the child is exposed as "fruit basket in the womb," and in the German O. Rank, *Myth of the Birth*, Baltimore 2004 p. 97f) the Sceaf legend (from the Song of Beowulf). On the identity of the hero rescued from the flood with beings from the netherworld see H. Usener, *Sintfluthsagen*, Bonn 1899 *passim*. See also C.G. Jung, CW 5, *Symbols of Transformation* ¶306ff.

[13] See also his remarks on page 218: "For if Old Norse *lúðr* is the name of the frost giant Bergelmir's boat, meaning also "flour-bin," coffin, chest, ark, and also "bed for the newborn child," this probably comes from the Old High German *ludara* [cradle], finally the *Lur* of worship and war called, like arca never means "ship," but rather cell, coffin, box, water trough, and mystical box (Latin *arcanus*, mystical, mysterious). Thus the box is obviously to be understood as a symbol of a boll [seed vessel] floating on the waters which contains the seeds, like the flour bin contains the flour, and like the ark that carries the progenitors and the seeds (sperm) of the new organisms." M. Ninck, *Wodan*, Jena 1935 p. 210, 218. Cf. here also O. Rank, *Myth of the Birth*, Baltimore 2004 p. 60 on the English-Lombardian heroes Sceaf son of the *Schaffing* [barrel or ship].

Actually, the hero is threatened by water, that is, the danger of sinking into the unconscious, or being devoured by the tide as the mother dragon. But a generous destiny drives him into the safety of the mill, which symbolizes how the course of fate works to create (in the sense of a grinding wheel) reality.[14]

220   The miller and his wife become the adoptive parents of the child, hinting at the widespread motif of dual ancestry. In some native tribes and in India and Central Europe there is the custom of the quasi adoption, according to which children are set out for credit or sold to people of lower social standing and the child even takes on the names of its foster-parents. The expensive repurchase represents a rebirth.[15] This shows that humans are children of two worlds, one is the universal human sphere, and the other a godlike transpersonal realm. As in "Tritill, Litill, and the Birds" the hero in "The Devil with the Three Golden Hairs" actually belongs to the royal court, but is at first the son of some poor parents. Here the hero's destiny to be the son of the king is revealed from the outset by the caul and the associated prophecy. In a Russian parallel, "Marco the Rich and Vasily the Luckless," a child abandoned in the snowy woods displays his magical character in that a warm wind melted the snow and when he was found, he was surrounded by green grass and flowers in bloom. In this version, instead of the caul, an angel of God comes flying down and declares that the boy's fate will be to inherit the wealth of Marco the Rich. Later it is the same figure, but as an old man, who reverses the words in a letter that demands the bearer be killed so that the letter is an order to marry the bearer to the daughter of Marco.

221   The king in the Grimm's tale finds the lucky child at the miller's and sends him with a "Letter of Uriah" to the queen.[16] On the way the boy falls prey to robbers in the forest, where an old woman helps him. These robbers in the forest with the good-natured woman are in many ways a precursor to the actual principle of evil: the devil and his grandmother. Due to the female principle being kindly disposed towards him, the hero quickly gains access to the anima at the court of the king. But the achievement of an easy "magical marriage" (discussed in Volume 1 of this work, from page 392, and onwards) is never permanent, unless an *auseinandersetzung* with the god of the magical kingdom, usually the father of the anima, has taken place. This time it is not the usual dangerous escapade, however, but that the hero must consciously make a decision to embark on a dark and dangerous journey to win the devil's three golden hairs. How far gaining the anima depends on an *auseinandersetzung* with the lord of the chthonic world, here the devil, is shown

---

[14] [The authors use here the singular expression *wirklichkeitsverarbeitenden Schicksalablaufes*, literally: reality-manufacturing course of fate.]

[15] See here O. Rank, *Myth of the Birth*, Baltimore 2004. [See also the moving Inuit tale of a mother giving away her sick child in the 1870s in Hall, *Icelandic Fairy Tales*, London 1897 p. 248.]

[16] On the origin of this motif see J. Bolte and L. Mackensen, *Handwörterbuch* Berlin 1930, under *Brief* [letter].

in a Danish fairytale "The Tree of Health" in which the anima (a very choosy princess) gives herself to the hero only after he brings her the "three oldest blazes in hell."[17] Maria Führer noted that the present tale "The Devil with the Three Golden Hairs" can be attributed to an old Germanic legend of Thor's journey to the dead and the underworld god Utgard-Loki:

222   Thorkill (corresponding to Thor) was sent to the underworld Ugarthilokus (= Utgard-Loki, Utgard-Loke) by king Gorm. Thorkill had to journey over a wide lake, since the underworld is separated from the upper world by a large water or a strongly flowing river. Underway Thorkill meets gruesome giants who offer to help him find the right path only when he twice tells them three indubitable truths. Finally, Thorkill came to the land of eternal darkness, where he beheld Utgard-Loke bound to a rock with heavy fetters, from whom he snatched a foul-smelling hair of beard.[18]

223   Like the three-headed Satan in Dante's *Inferno*, the devil in the fairytale has three golden hairs. This chthonic triad mirrors the Heavenly Trinity. At the same time the gold color points back to its original light nature, and thus to the fallen "Lucifer."[19]

224   The hero has to pluck out three golden hairs, or, in the Grimm's parallel tale "The Griffin" to bring back three tailfeathers. Hair in its meaning of spiritual power arising from the head is also a symbol of generating force, especially red or golden hair that points to the hero's sun power. In Indian mythology, Rama and Krishna emerge from a light and dark hair of Vishnu.[20] The red-gold color of the hair points to demonic and connection [relation] to fire. The devil's golden hair marks him both as Lord of the Earthfire and

---

[17] [A young suitor remembered the raven, the devil's apostle, whom he had once helped. He called the raven and told him his troubles. The raven promised to do what he could, and soon returned with the three blazes. The lad took them, ran as fast as he could to the castle, and threw them into the princess's lap. They at once flamed up and she was well-nigh choked by the fire and smoke.]

[18] M. Führer, *Nordgermanische*, München 1938 p. 73. [In Norse mythology, Utgarda-Loke was the ruler of the castle Útgarðr in Jötunheimr. He was one of the Jötnar (a mythological race of giants, later trolls) and his name means literally, "Loki of the Outyards" to distinguish him from Loki, the companion of Thor.]

[19] Note also that the Aztec God of the Land of the Dead was called "falling down head over heels" in "The Origin of People and Plants."

[20] See R. Thurnwald, "Primitive Initiationsriten," *Eranos*, Zürich 1940 p. 379f, where the change in a hairstyle during initiation rites represents a transformation of the personality. See also L. Lévy-Bruhl, *The "Soul" of the Primitive*, New York 1928 p. 110ff, 120f, 149ff , G. van der Leeuw, *Religion in Essence*, Vol. 1 p. 291 , E. Abegg, "Krishnas Geburt," *Mitteilungen*, Zürich 1937/1938 p. 35, H. Zimmer, *Maya*, Stuttgart and Berlin 1936 p. 321. See further that hair in Germanic superstition may indicate descendants, in M. Ninck, *Wodan*, Jena 1935 p. 194. See also the tale from the Native North American Kootenay tribe, "How Wildcat's Sons Became the Sun and the Moon," [only in German] in which the two animal heroes are born from four hairs laid in the vagina of a girl. See also the Italian parallel to the above narrated Grimm's tale, in which the three hairs of the devil are intended to impregnate the queen and give her children. In J. Bolte and G. Polívka, *Anmerkungen*, Vol. 1, Leipzig 1913 p. 289.

possessor of the highest value, as symbolized by the gold. The symbol for gold and the sun is from ancient times identical;[21] gold occurs often in myth and usually comes from the region of darkness, the North, from the bowels of the Earth, from dirt. It can also be found in the hats of dragons, from which it must be snatched away.[22] Psychologically, this means that the new light (gold symbolizes fire and light[23]), that is, new knowledge and consciousness, arises from the chthonic depths, the region of the darkest foundations of the soul. In the parallel version, "The Griffin," it is not the hairs of the devil, but the feathers of the griffin bird, which is, like the phoenix, a symbol of the sun. In another parallel[24] it is the phoenix itself from which three feathers must be fetched. Also, in a Russian fairytale, "The Farmer and the Golden Sun," the sun is partially a demon who eats humans. An old woman protects the hero from being eaten. At the same time, the sun is called: "the just, red sun" and Saint George is his companion. The devil in hell is also a similar deity, a midnight sun. In the French fairytale, "Thirty-From-Paris," which seems to be a fusion of "Ferdinand the Faithful and Ferdinand the Unfaithful" with the present tale, is, significantly, the Lord "Monseigneur le Soleil" [Lord the Sun] who lives at the end of the world, solves all riddles, and almost burns the hero to death. Like the miracle bird in the Grimm's, "The Griffin," this figure is also a symbol of the spirit, and even in some ways, a symbol of the Self. Thus the strange conclusion that the hero as the "human" Self snatches the most precious from the devil as the "demonic" Self.[25] The treasure, in whatever form it is represented, is, in turn, a symbol of the central value. Raising this treasure into conscious awareness brings a new orientation and the recovery of the possibility of living life more fully and intensively.[26] Such a new symbol unites all opposites in its living beauty: light and dark, good and evil, past and future, these form a harmonious unity. For this reason, a new life movement can commence since the jewel, or the treasure, is "divine" nature.[27]

---

[21] See D. Bernoulli, *Spiritual*, Princeton 1960 p. 333, H. Silberer, *Problems of Mysticism*, New York 1917 p. 149, 209.

[22] See C.G. Jung, CW 12, *Psychology and Alchemy* ¶445; M. Ninck, *Wodan*, Jena 1935 p. 245.

[23] See R. Wilhelm, *Secret of the Golden Flower*, London 1962 p. 9, 23.

[24] See J. Bolte and G. Polívka, *Anmerkungen*, Vol. 1, Leipzig 1913 p. 276ff and also see also "Na'n Kiwitsbarg."

[25] See the *Bhagavad Gita* VI, 4-6:

> One (should) raise himself by the self; one (should) not
> bring down the self; The self is one's own friend, the self is
> also one's own enemy.
> The self becomes one's own friend, when the self is defeated by the self;
> But if one struggles with the outer world, then the self becomes the enemy
> himself. (Translated from the German consulting the English translation by
> Kisari Mohan Ganguli.)

[26] See C.G. Jung, CW 6, *Psychological Types* ¶300f.

[27] On the "unifying symbol" see *ibid* ¶211,¶319f,¶366f,¶434,¶441ff; further C.G. Jung, CW 9i, *The Archetypes and the Collective Unconscious* ¶293, and C.G. Jung, CW 13, *Alchemical Studies* ¶44f.

225   The hero soon obtains the anima with the help of the dark forces of nature, including the well-meant, albeit fraudulent exchange of letters by the robbers. However, the real treasure, which brings him into final possession of the king's daughter and the inheritance of the kingdom, he must wrestle loose from hell, with the help of the devil's grandmother. Because the dark powers are well-inclined to the hero, he is able to fulfill the tasks and this retrograde motion, which pulls him deeper and deeper into the unconscious, is reversed, thus enabling him to return to the royal court. The tale describes in simple terms a descent into "inferno," the characteristic midlife experience of the individual. At this time the conscious attitude to life changes most dramatically in the sense that values that consciousness had hitherto considered important lose their importance relative to previously disregarded unconscious values. Thus, the image of a countermovement appears.[28] In a broader sense, this tells us how light and knowledge were hidden in the unconscious and are lifted by humans into consciousness. The meaning here is similar to the theft of fire by Prometheus.

226   With the help of the devil's grandmother[29] the lucky fellow tricks the devil into answering his questions. By revealing the ultimate causes of obstruction and destruction the hero returns the pervasively stagnating and covertly sick life back into a healthy development. Possessing the devil's hair lends the hero a certain power over his [the devil's] doings.[30] The knowledge gained is actually identical to the stolen hair, in so far as the mental power of the devil and at the same time, gold, means insight, perception, and knowledge. With every plucked hair the hero receives an answer from the devil to one of his questions. Just how much hair is related to questions and answers is shown by Bolte-Polívka.[31] Of particular interest is a Hungarian version mentioned there in which the Griffin lets a student pull out one of his feathers that grants all-knowledge. Bolte-Polívka also mention a Roma (Gypsy) legend, in which three hairs from the beard of the devil turn stones into gold. See also the motif of hair as the wisdom of the world in the aforementioned Serbian tale, "The Wonderful Hair," in which the hair of a spring goddess, as radiant as the sun, contains the secrets of creation, which God wants to reveal to the world.

---

[28] See the description of such reverse or counter-movement (*enantiodromia*) in Dante's *Divine Comedy*, where Dante [who describes himself as thirty-five years old, "halfway along life's path"], with his guide Virgil, travel to the center of the Earth and then over the legs and feet of Satan who is chained there. They pass through this zone after which [due to the consequent change in the direction of gravity] Dante at first thinks he is upside down and returning to Hell. But they continue and finally emerge in the other hemisphere.

[29] [The word in the German edition is *Ellermutter* [southern German dialect for grandmother]. Of interest here is that this word gained popular usage through just this particular Grimm's fairytale.]

[30] See L. Lévy-Bruhl, *The "Soul" of the Primitive*, New York 1928 p. 115, 247, 252. Lévy-Bruhl For many primitive cultures, possession of hair or the skull of an enemy gives power over the latter. It converts the enemy into a protector, helper, or slave. See also the fairytale, "The Three Hunters," in which the Russian archwitch, Baba Yaga, asks for hairs of one of the hunters. She blows on them and the man turns into stone.

[31] J. Bolte and G. Polívka, *Anmerkungen*, Vol. 1, Leipzig 1913 p. 282ff, esp. 286, 289.

227 But again (as in, "Tritill, Litill, and the Birds") it is not the hero himself who actually performs the deeds, rather, he lets the benevolent side of dark nature, the grandmother of the devil, work for him. The same motif is found in Grimm's "The Griffin"[32] and also the Gilgamesh epic in which the wife of Utnapishtim takes pity on Gilgamesh and gives him the herb of immortality.[33] In a Low German variant "Na'n Kiwitsbarg" the figure of the grandmother, in this case the wife of the phoenix bird, is identical with the sought after princess, that is, the anima. In this tale, the image of the mother appears merged with that of the anima, a feature of many fairytales.

228 The hazards of the unconscious threaten the hero four times: at birth by the caul, at his abandonment, in the den of thieves, and on his descent into hell. The road to hell is again divided into four stages: the city with the desiccated well, the town with the withered tree, the river of the dead with the ferryman, and finally Hell itself. The rhythm of the four stations points to four as the number of orientation in this [conscious] world, a symbol of wholeness on earth, to which the God-man, or the hero himself must bow.

229 With the fourth station, the visit to hell, the process reaches a kind of completeness, a definitive transformation. The withered life begins to bloom anew, the secret damage to the roots – certainly the work of the devil himself – is overcome through knowledgeable insight. The compilation by Bolte-Polívka describes the kind of difficulties that confront the hero:

230 Soon the wanderer will find out why an apple tree no longer bears fruit, soon why a fountain has dried up, where the lost keys to the treasury are to be found, and how the king's sick daughter is to be healed, why two mountains are constantly smashing, why strife always ensues during the monastery midday meal . . .[34]

---

[32] See also "The Devil and his Grandmother" where:
Three soldiers deserted the king's army because he paid them so little. They hid in a cornfield because they thought the army was going to move on. But all the soldiers remained in the same camp. After three days of eating nothing, the three soldiers were starved and desperate. A fiery dragon flew by overhead, spotted them and landed. It asked them what they are doing there. They explained and the dragon offered to save them if they would serve him for seven years. They agreed. It turned out that the dragon was the devil himself. He gave them all the money they wanted and said that after seven years living a luxurious life, they would become his property. He proposed first to ask them a riddle, and if they were able to answer it correctly, then he would set them free from his power forever. The youngest of the three found the way to the devil's grandmother, who hid him so that he could overhear the dragon-devil when she asked him about the riddle at his supper. The soldier heard the answers, told his comrades, and thus outwitted the devil and were freed from his power. (Summarized from J. and W. Grimm, Complete Grimm's, London 1975 pp. 563–566.)

[33] See also fairytales discussed above, "The Story of Haburi," "Makunaima and Pia" and "The Daughter of the King Vultures" in each of which the Great Mother helps the hero to overcome the Great Father deity. See also "Tsetlwalakame."

[34] J. Bolte and G. Polívka, Anmerkungen, Vol. 1, Leipzig 1913 p. 293. See also the Low German fairytale, "De dre Gesell'n un de Düwel" (The Three Companions and the Peg), in which it is also a question of overhearing the devil's secret and redeeming knowledge. See also, Vogel Strauss [The Ostrich] J. Jegerlehner, Herdfeuer, Bern 1929 p. 125. There (p. 129) the question is asked: why was the baker's

231   This very often has to do with an ossified tension of opposites that the hero can release. Possessing the precious hair of the devil, he is both mediator and savior. The hero knew this in advance: on the way to the gatekeepers he said: "I know everything."

232   The redemption of life is here construed, as in Manichean Gnosticism, to be insight into the relations between matter and evil. Liberation arises through knowledge.[35] The hero makes a mystery journey to learn the workings of the other side.[36] Because he now knows the mystery of evil, its power is broken, it is demystified and life is freed from its spell. The realization of the hero acts creatively – the word "gnosis" (= knowledge) has the same root as the Latin *gignere* (= generate)[37] (hence the significance of hair as knowledge and, at the same time, a phallic symbol). Consequently, the source of life begins to flow again and the golden tree blooms anew.

233   The third question that the hero has to answer concerns another problem, namely, the strange figure and story of the ferryman. He is like Charon, who establishes the connection to the realm of the dead. This ferryman can be released from the endless and agonizing going back and forth if he can find a substitute for his job. The name Charon is unexplained.[38] In modern Greek folklore, this ferryman lives on as a death demon, even as the devil himself. "*Charuns*" is pictured on an Etruscan wall painting as the devil but not a ferryman.[39] The resulting possibility of deriving the essential identity of the devil and the ferryman can be shown by the following forms of mythologems: as mentioned above for the ancient Egyptians, the crocodile enemy of Osiris is called "turning face" or "changing face" (*Wendegesicht*), and is thus a manifestation of the dark deity.[40] At the same time, according to Erman, the ferryman of the underworld has the name, "he who looks backwards" or, "turning face" (because he turns his head when he rows as he stands in his boat).[41] Perhaps here the similar name points to a similar meaning. Moreover, in Germanic mythology, Odin is both ferryman and guide to the dead.[42]

---

daughter turned into a toad? The answer, however, is, "The old one (i.e., the parents) should put their pride aside and bury the toad one day in dung. Then she will again get a ponytail and skirt!" The unconscious indicates that the hubris has been compensated in the form of a toad and that therefore an inner transformation can lead to healing.

[35] See Puech pp. 250ff, 268-71, 283-84, and 313.

[36] See G. R. S. Mead, *Fragments*, London 1931 p. 46f [page numbers approximate.]. Odin's journey to Mimir also served the purpose of obtaining secret knowledge.

[37] See H. Leisegang, *Die Gnosis*, Leipzig 1924 p. 32.

[38] [The name Charon is most often explained as a proper noun from χαρων (charon), a poetic form of χαρωπο΄ς (charopós), "of keen gaze," referring either to fierce, flashing, or feverish eyes, or to eyes of a bluish-gray color. The word may be a euphemism for death. Liddell & Scott, *Greek-English*, Oxford 1843 pp. 1980–1981, entries on χαροπο΄ς and χαρων, Brill, *Greek-English*, Leiden and Boston 2003 pp. 202–203.

[39] See J. Bolte and L. Mackensen, *Handwörterbuch* Berlin 1930, under *Fährmann* (ferryman).

[40] See G. Roeder, *Urkunden*, Jena 1923 p. 87. See also the material in Bächtold-Stäubli under*Fährmann* [ferryman].

[41] A. Erman, *Religion der Ägypter*, Berlin and Leipzig 1934 p. 217.

[42] See M. Ninck, *Wodan*, Jena 1935 pp. 13, 88,133. See also Bächtold-Stäubli under *Wolf* where it is

234   In the figure of the ferryman a part, or an emanation, of the underworld god himself stands opposite the hero, namely, the aspect of suffering. The toad in the well and the mouse gnawing at the root of the tree of life represent the purely destructive effects of the demons that, above all, affect the inhabitants of the towns and cities. Contained in the image of the ferryman is an unknown evil agent and the agonizing consequent is concentrated in one figure in desperate need of salvation, who aimlessly toils in vain back and forth in a pendulum-like motion at the border between consciousness and the unconscious. Unlike the devil, the ferryman reaches the shore of the secular world. He is a figure of the border area, psychologically belonging half to the ego, half to the unconscious.[43]

235   The ferryman thus corresponds to the figure of the shadow. This identification is supported in that this figure is in myths often replaced by a fish, which in turn may be considered to be a figure of Hermes as psychopomp.[44] According to a Russian parallel to the Grimm's fairytale,[45] a merchant takes the place of the king. There the journey of the merchant's son takes him to his grandfather, himself the ferryman, who escorts the hero across a fiery river. The merchant is the son of the old ferryman and he takes over as the ferryman at the border to the magical realm. Thus, the dark deity, appearing here in the father and the son, through this tale gains two new aspects: first there is an intimate connection between them and the figure personifying secular consciousness, a topic which will be discussed more thoroughly later. And second, this divine figure is not only powerful both in

---

mentioned that Charon had wolf ears, and keeping in mind that the wolf is frequently represented as a devilish demon and lord of the spirit world.

[43] His work is reminiscent of the pointless efforts of Sisyphus or the Danaides. The back-and-forth movement expresses an unresolved problem of the opposites comparable to the clashing cliffs.

[44] Psychopomp (Greek) is "a guide of the souls." For more on fairytale personifications of this figure see the reference in J. Bolte and L. Mackensen, *Handwörterbuch* Berlin 1930, under *Fährmann*, note no. 14 to H. Usener, *Kleine Schriften*, Vol. 4 Leipzig and Berlin 1913 Vol. 4, p. 386f. H. Usener, *Sintfluthsagen*, Bonn 1899 p. 80ff, 115ff considers the chest, fish, and ship to be parallel motifs. In this sense, the hero's crossing the river to the underworld is a repetition of his "abandonment" to the unconscious at a conscious level. See also the discussion on the ferryman who connects the two sides of the river in R. Meyer, *Weisheit Schweizer*, Schaffhausen 1944 pp. 61–67. In Goethe's "The Tale of Snake and the Lily" (J. W. von Goethe, *Das Märchen*, Boston 1904 (1904)), which is included in Goethe's *Unterhaltung deutscher Ausgewanderter* [Entertainment for German Emigrants], the hero must cross a river where there is a ferryman and clashing cliffs. There, the hero does not know how to cross and ask the snake for help. The snake informs him that a giant lives nearby and one way to cross the river is to walk on the shadow of the giant when it is cast on the waters. This interpretation of the ferryman coincides with his being part of the underworld ruler himself. In that he connects a realm controlled by the unconscious (i.e., a river) with a more conscious-oriented land, he functions as a bridge. He overcomes the dangers, which, according to the mythical tradition, are caused by a snake inhabiting the river. Whereas the ferryman is related to the demon and thus – psychologically as a shadow – full of life energy, he is unconscious and, therefore, unreliable as a bridge. As an escort on the way to the underworld god and shadowy figure, he is associated with the "grim ferryman" mentioned in stanzas 1547 and 1559 of *The Lay of the Nibelungs*. There Siegfried's murderer, Hagen, makes a deal with the ferryman to plot the demise of the Burgundians as they cross the river Danube to their fateful meeting with King Etzel [Attila the Hun]. As predicted by an elfin mermaid none of the Burgundians survive the crossing. See J. Bolte and L. Mackensen, *Handwörterbuch* Berlin 1930, under *Fährmann*.

[45] See J. Bolte and G. Polívka, *Anmerkungen*, Vol. 1, Leipzig 1913 p. 285.

the positive and negative sense, not only to be feared as a demon, but at the same time he suffers and needs to be redeemed by a human act, which the hero accomplishes.[46] The ferryman's replacement by the king is the result of both the king's not knowing the situation and his greed for the gold inflamed by the hero's winning of the treasures. He is completely possessed by the desire for the treasures and this obsession banishes him to the border area of the magical sphere.[47] The Swedish fairytale "The Rooster, the Hand-Mill, and the Swarm of Hornets" also brings up the subject of supersession at the border of Hell. There, a farmer goes to Hell to sell his pig.

236   When he came to the devil's place, there stood a man out by the woodpile chopping wood. The peasant went to him and asked whether he could tell him if they wanted to buy a pig in the devil's place. "I'll go in and ask," said the man, "if you will chop wood in my stead while I am gone." "Yes, I will do that gladly," said the peasant, took the axe, stood at the woodpile, and began to make wood. And he worked and worked until evening came; but the man did not return to tell him whether they would or would not buy a pig in the devil's place. At length another man came that way, and the peasant asked him whether he would make wood in his stead, for it was impossible to lay down the axe unless another took it up and went on working.[48]

237   Essential in all these cases is the obsession that arises out of, and is energized by, the underworld and whose victims are those whose behavior towards the unconscious is either too weak, too arrogant, or too indifferent. This desperate suffering springs from the underworld deity itself, because it is its own victim, as illustrated in the Grimm's tale by the figure of the ferryman. The unredeemed state, or the illness of the chthonic ruler, corresponds to the one-sided rigidity of the "old" consciousness that is cut off from its living foundations. The motif of the replacement or substitution is the fairytale's expression for the transformation of the personality, which goes hand-in-hand

---

[46] See also the Icelandic tale, "The Enchanted Giant," in which the giant demon is really an enchanted prince, who is redeemed at the end by the hero's feats.

[47] See the legends retold in L. Laistner, *Das Rätsel*, Berlin 1889 Vol. I, pp. 166f, 189–90, 198f, with the motif of replacement. There it is the aggressive attitude of consciousness towards the unconscious circumstances, i.e., obsession, which causes the replacing of one figure by another. See also in retrospect the Chinese fairytale, "The Ghost of the One Who Hung Herself," in which the ghosts seek replacements among those who appear to be powerless and at their mercy, even when consciousness intervenes to set things in order. A figure similar to the ferryman is the demonic servant in "Lasse, My Servant" (see Volume 1 of the work, p. 332) who laments that he had to race around for a thousand years, and only now is freed by the fact that the Duke relieves him from his hard services by undertaking some of the work himself and abandoning his anyway illegitimate claim to enrichment by the forces of the unconscious. (In contrast to the arrogance of the King in "The Devil with the Three Golden Hairs," who perseveres in his old position and constantly opposes the intentions of the unconscious to engender a higher personality).

[48] K. Stroebe, *The Swedish Fairy Book*, New York 1921 p. 202.

with the transformation of the shadow, that is, the forces in the background of the personality.[49]

238   Once the symbolic carriers of the self and the anima take control, the demonic shadow figure of the ferryman dissolves and as a consequence the former traditional consciousness assumes, logically, the role of the shadow. The negative attitude in which the old king remains stuck, his resistance to the notion that approaches him and could bridge the gap between this world and the hereafter, and his deprecating judgement towards this chance to recreate his personality arising from the foundations of the psyche, are the reason why he cannot partake of the redemption that is realized in his unconscious. He thus finds himself doomed to the painful and unredeemed ferrying back-and-forth between consciousness and the unconscious, a suffering that was previously carried by the unconscious part of his personality. He is dethroned and must create the connection of the secular, profane world to the magical realm. In taking this job on, he performs something quite correct, since serving to mediate between the conscious mind and the unconscious is a task befitting the empirical ego.[50] But due to his resistance this role takes on a ghostly, painful, and, in its spastic convulsiveness, a senseless aspect. The Self asserts itself, as it were, unconcerned if the ego recognizes it or not.[51]

---

[49] Jung discusses the simultaneous mirroring of processes in the fate of the ego with processes in the unconscious in his review of Spitteler's *Prometheus and Epimetheus*, in C.G. Jung, CW 6, *Psychological Types* ¶275-460 esp. ¶295f.

[50] Cf. also R. Meyer, *Weisheit Schweizer*, Schaffhausen 1944 p. 67, who emphasizes that the prevailing ruling power must now serve and become a "bridge."

[51] See Jung on the unconcern of the unconscious with the suffering of the conscious mind. But when we look deeper, we find that this unconcern of the unconscious has a meaning, indeed a purpose and a goal. There are psychic goals that lie beyond the conscious goals; in fact, they may even be inimical to them. But we find that the unconscious has an inimical or ruthless bearing towards the conscious only when the latter adopts a false or pretentious attitude. (C.G. Jung, CW 7, *Two Essays in Analytical Psychology* ¶346.)

◆

Chapter 5

The King of the Golden Mountain

239 Another Grimm fairytale in which a young hero was also delivered to the devil by an uncomprehending and greedy father, yet in this case manages to complete his journey, is "The King of the Golden Mountain."

240 A certain merchant had two children, a son and a daughter; both very young, and could not yet walk. Two richly-laden ships of his sailed forth to sea with all his property on board. Just as he was expecting to win much money by this action, news came that they had gone to the bottom, and now instead of being a rich man he was a poor one, and had nothing left but one field outside the town. In order to drive his misfortune a little out of his thoughts, he went out to a field, and as he was walking forwards and backwards in it, a little black mannikin stood suddenly by his side and asked why he was so sad, and what he was taking so much to heart. Then said the merchant, "If thou couldst help me I would willingly tell thee." "Who knows?" replied the black dwarf. "Perhaps, I can help thee." Then the merchant told him that all he possessed had gone to the bottom of the sea, and that he had nothing left but this field. "Do not trouble thyself," said the dwarf. "If thou wilt promise to give me the first thing that rubs itself against thy leg when thou art at home again, and to bring it here to this place in twelve years' time, thou shalt have as much money as thou wilt." The merchant thought, "What can that be but my dog?" and did not remember his little boy, so he agreed and gave the man a written and sealed promise, and went home.

241 When he reached home, his little boy was so delighted that he tottered up to him and seized him fast by the legs. The father was shocked, for he remembered his promise, and now knew what he had pledged himself to do. As he still found no money in his chest, however, he thought the dwarf had only been jesting. A month afterwards he went up to the garret, intending to gather together some old tin to sell, and saw a great heap of money lying there. Then he was happy again, made

purchases, became a greater merchant than before, and felt that his world was well-governed.

242 In the meantime the boy grew tall, and at the same time clever. But the nearer the twelfth year approached, the more anxious grew the merchant. One day his son asked what ailed him, but his father would not say. The boy, however, persisted so long, that at last he told him that, without being aware of what he was doing, he had promised him to a black dwarf, and had received much money for doing so. He said likewise that he had set his hand and seal to this, and since twelve years had now passed, he would have to give him up. Then said the son, "Oh, father, do not be uneasy, all will go well. The little man has no power over me." The son had himself blessed by the priest, and when the time came, father and son went together to the field, and the son made a circle and placed himself inside it with his father. Then came the black dwarf and said to the old man, "Hast thou brought with thee that which thou hast promised me?" They spoke for a long time, and at last they agreed that the son, as he did not belong to the arch-enemy, nor yet to his father, should seat himself in a small boat floating on water that was flowing away from them, and that the father should push it off with his own foot, and then the son should remain at the mercy of the waters. So, the boy took leave of his father, placed himself in a little boat, and the father had to push it off with his own foot. The boat soon capsized so that the keel was uppermost, and the father believed his son was lost, and went home and mourned for him.

243 The boat, however, did not sink, but floated quietly away, and the boy sat safely inside as it floated for a long time until at last it touched down at an unknown shore. There the boy went ashore, saw a beautiful castle before him, and set out to reach it. But when he entered, he found that it was bewitched. He went through every room, but all were empty until he reached the last, where a snake lay coiled up. The snake, however, was an enchanted maiden, who rejoiced at seeing the boy, and said, "Hast thou come, oh, my deliverer? I have already waited twelve years for thee; this kingdom is bewitched, and thou must set it free." "How can I do that?" he inquired. "Tonight twelve black men, covered with chains, will come. They will ask what thou art doing here; keep silent; give them no answer, and let them do what they will with thee; they will torment thee, beat thee, stab thee; let everything pass, only do not speak; at twelve o'clock, they must go away again. On the second night twelve others will come; on the third, four-and-twenty, who will cut off thy head, but at twelve o'clock their power will be over, and then if thou hast endured all, and

hast not spoken the slightest word, I shall be released. I will come to thee, and will have, in a bottle, some of the water of life. I will rub thee with that, and then thou wilt come to life again, and be as healthy as before." Then said he, "I will gladly set thee free." And everything happened just as she had said. The black men could not force a single word from him, and on the third night the snake became a beautiful princess, who came with the water of life and brought him back to life again. She threw herself into his arms and kissed him, and there was joy and gladness in the whole castle. After this their marriage was celebrated, and he was King of the Golden Mountain.

244   [They lived happily together and the queen gave him a beautiful boy. When eight years had passed, the king remembered his father, and he wished to visit him. The queen wanted to prevent it because she suspected misfortune, but she finally agreed. She gave him a ring which would take him to any place he wanted, but he had to first promise not to use it to wish her, his wife, away from her kingdom to his father. He promised and then wished himself back home. In a moment he found himself outside his home town, but the guard would not let him in because he was wearing strange and yet rich and splendid clothes. So he exchanged them with those of a shepherd and went to his father, who did not recognize his son because he thought him long dead. When the son showed his parents a hidden birthmark, they finally believed him. He told them of his kingdom and his wife and son. The father demurred that a king would not go about dressed in rags. Then the son became angry and turned the ring, wishing his wife and son to come to him. The queen came but silently wept over the broken promise. He told her he had been careless and had no evil intent, and although she accepted, she pondered revenge. He led her to his father's field and showed her the spot where the boat was turned adrift the river. Then he fell asleep with his head in her lap. She took the ring from his finger, and holding her child wished them back to her kingdom, leaving only a slipper behind. When he woke up, finding himself alone, he said to himself he could not return to his father's house because they would believe him to be a sorcerer. He decided to go wherever the path takes him to find his wife and child and the kingdom. He came to a mountain, in front of which three giants were fighting each other over an inheritance. They called him to make a decision, because "little people have sharp wits." The inheritance consisted of a sword that obeyed the command "All heads off but mine," a cloak that made the bearer invisible, and a pair of boots that would take one to wherever one so desired. He asked the giants if he could try out the three things. At first they would not be fooled, but

then he promised not to use them against the giants and so they agreed. He tried them all and with the boots on wished to be taken to the kingdom of the golden mountain. He was immediately transported there, where he discovered that his wife was celebrating her wedding with another man. He put on the coat that makes one invisible and ate everything off her plate and drank her glass empty. Dismayed and ashamed, she arose and went to her chamber and wept, but he followed her there. She said, "Has the devil power over me, or did my deliverer never come?" Then he struck her in the face, and said, "Did thy deliverer never come? It is he who has thee in his power, thou traitor. Have I deserved this from thee?" Then he made himself visible, went into the hall, and cried, "The wedding is at an end, the true king has returned." The kings, princes, and councilors who were assembled there, ridiculed and mocked him, but he did not trouble to answer them, and said, "Will you go away, or not?" On this they tried to seize him, but he drew his sword and said, "All heads off but mine," and all the heads rolled on the ground, and he alone was master, and once more King of the Golden Mountain.][1]

245   The merchant, who is again the worldly father of the hero, represents the empirical ego. He has lost his fortune to the sea, that is, to the unconscious. His plight follows from his greed for money, and is thus like the situation of the aging king in "The Three Feathers" with his desire for a carpet and like that of the old miller in "The Poor Miller's Boy and the Cat" who needed a horse. The merchant has lost his life energy, in the form of money, that made possible his previous existence.[2] The fact that the energy flows to the unconscious amounts to an increase of its intensity, and brings up its deepest content: the little black man who appears on the scene. This small black dwarf is, as the parallels show,[3] and confirmed by the development of the story in "The King of the Golden Mountain," the devil himself. He appears in the field "outside the town," that is, in a region known to the conscious mind but not controlled by it, in a border area. In a parallel tale he appears in the form of a large millstone, rolling down the mountain,[4] remarkably reminiscent of the

---

[1] [Shortened, original collected and edited by the Brothers Grimm, translated from German to English by Margaret Taylor (1884), published in J. and W. Grimm, *Complete Grimm's*, London 1975 pp. 425–430.] See also the Low German Parallel "Op 'n Goll 'n marker Sloss" (On the Gollenmarker Castle), and from P. Zaunert, *Deutsche Märchen seit Grimm*, Jena 1922, "The Iron Boot," also two tales from the German-speaking Danube region "Saint Anthony and Charles the Murderer" and "The Black-Brown Michel." The latter two tales exploit only the initial motif of being handed over to the devil as their central plot.

[2] See J. Bolte and G. Polívka, *Anmerkungen*, Vol. 2, Leipzig 1915 p. 318ff for instances in which the father figure is a fisherman. This points to his meaning as the embodiment of the conscious mind that wrests unconscious contents from the sea.

[3] See *ibid* p. 318ff.

[4] See *ibid* p. 320.

rolling skull demons in the Native American tales related before. In this sense, he represents the negative, self-destructive side of the Self. He is the dark shadow side of the small son of the merchant who represents the light, that is, the conscious side of the Self. Both sides of the Self thus appear suddenly and immediately in the moment of need. But the merchant does not recognize the inner possibilities of the situation. Frantic to replace what has been lost, he stubbornly continues to orient himself towards the outer world where he had previously been effective. Abandoning former goals, which is the main problem of midlife, and that alone can open up new sources of life, is not an option for him. As a result, he falls prey to the negative side of the unconscious. He becomes "possessed by the devil," who demands the merchant's small son as a sacrifice. As always, the actual game of opposites is not played out between the conscious mind and the unconscious, but within the unconscious psyche. Consciousness has no choice but to join one or the other, or – "free from contradictions" – neither side. The devil knows that the future hero is his real opponent and he tries to bind the boy to himself, that is, to ensure that the future personality remains forever in the unconscious and ineffective.

246   The merchant carelessly agrees to the little man's proposal. It is not that he does not love his son, but that he thinks it will be his dog that will rub against his leg when he later arrives home. He thinks of the lowly, little-valued, the animal-like, the shadow, that anyway stands far from the conscious mind. Indeed, it is the undeveloped part of the Self, lingering in the unconscious in the form of a child that is still close to the animal in its expressions of life who reaches out to him as a greeting. It is as if this movement actually indicates a desire to realize the correct togetherness. The merchant senses, but too late, the inner values that he has sacrificed.

247   His encounter with the negative side of the unconscious brings about an initial enrichment, but this is "above the ground," that is, entirely in his conscious mind, not in the root forces of life. Once again something worn-out and worthless, like old scrap, has been transformed into gold, a sure value, in the worldly view of the conscious mind. But this renewal cannot be sustained and is paid for with the subsequent disaster, the loss of his son.

248   The boy is not afraid and feels himself up to facing the little black man.[5] He also knows that a magic circle, a mandala, will protect him, thereby preventing

---

[5] The fact that this is owing to the blessing of a priest is probably attributable to a later Christian revision that also made the dark little fellow into the "devil." Every hero is inherently superior to the dark demonic forces of nature.

his being completely at the devil's mercy. He strengthens the position of his father, who here symbolizes a helpless conscious attitude confronted with his demonic contract partner. From the view of the total personality, the Self assumes leadership and the little black one cannot completely exploit his power. Significant is the reason for the decision: the son no longer belongs either to the father nor to the arch-enemy! He stands in the middle between the two; this characterizes the nature of the hero well: he is the Self appearing in *human* form, which in this form is on the one hand connected with the consciousness, and on the other hand participates in the demonic and natural forces of the unconscious. Thus, he even has to float away on the river, for his boat leads him from the anchor of the father to the golden mountain until either light or darkness triumphs over him. The river represents the "flow of life," which is located at the border between the two spheres because, like it, life is a happening that takes place between the, in itself rigid, consciousness and the timeless, and therefore motionless, unconscious. The hero, as he who in the core of his being can consciously experience his fate, is able to entrust his being to the flow of the river, and thus begins the inner realization of his being. This process is similar to the motif of being cast adrift in a basket on a river, an archetypal beginning to many heroic quests in legends and fairytales.

249   It turns out that the boat tips over so that the father, from the worldly view on the bank, falls into the delusion that he had gambled and forever lost his son, his heir, and his own future. Humans caught in purely mundane ways of thinking inevitably assume that things do not happen if they are no longer comprehensible to their way of seeing things.

250   The transition into the magical realm is depicted particularly clearly in this fairytale: the ship capsizes but the youth sits safe. The unconscious is indeed an "upside-down world" as seen from consciousness, but the supra-personal core of the psyche is not bound to such a one-sided orientation. Seen from the point of view of the Self, what is below is above, and vice versa. In addition, the unconscious – according to the remarkable diversity of place names – corresponds to the flowing water, in which the human remains alive: the far shore, the castle, and finally the golden mountain. According to the titles of the many parallel tales, the distant realm carries some very expressive names,[6] such as: "(King of the) Rose Mountain," "(The Kingdom of the) Morning Star," "(The Queen of) Deep Valley," "(The Castle of) the Golden Sun," "Golden-Pearl Castle" the "Cursed City." Castles and towns take the form of mandalas and are therefore symbols of the Self. The fortified castle signifies the unshakable invulnerability of the Self. According to Eastern concepts, the godhead itself dwells there. Chinese philosophy calls it the innermost center, which can be found through meditation. This center has names like "terrace of life," the "ancestral land," the "yellow castle" or the "realm of former

---

[6] See J. Bolte and G. Polívka, *Anmerkungen*, Vol. 2, Leipzig 1915 pp. 320–321.

heaven."[7] In symbolism, the town or castle as a mandala has a female character, it is the container, the vessel, the "Footstool of the Godhead."[8] It also corresponds to the heavenly Jerusalem, which comes down from heaven as an "adorned bride."[9] Thus symbolically the feminine castle or city is in some respects identical with its inhabitants. In the above tale, it is identical with the snake that lay coiled in a ring, which turned out to be an enchanted maiden, the anima. The hero's emerging male consciousness-to-be finds its female-earthy complement. This is because the feminine mandala and especially the snake as a chthonic being, signify the earth, darkness, and bodily reality. In so far as the mandala is itself also a symbol of wholeness and as such, of union. The previously not-yet-firm male conscious part of the Self, which was still an unattached "daimonion" (as apparent from his almost arrogant behavior towards the devil), now becomes the actual inner core by being connected with the soul. The profound mystery of the union of male and female takes place in the mandala palace, deep in the unconscious, as the name "Deep Valley" implies. The hero as the spiritual unites with the nature-bound side of the soul in that castle, which is actually located at the bottom of the waters. It corresponds to the Dragon Palace in the depths of the sea in which I Liu in "The Disowned Princess" obtained immortality from the daughter of the Dragon King.[10] In the Grimm's fairytale "The Raven" the princess, bewitched as a raven, lives in the "golden castle of Stromberg," which stands on a glass mountain.

251   The deep unconsciousness of the castle center at the bottom of the waters corresponds to the figure of the anima as a snake. According to her own words, she has been bewitched for twelve years in this form (the same length of time since the hero has been sold!), and it seems it was the devil who cursed her.[11]

---

[7] See R. Wilhelm, *Secret of the Golden Flower*, London 1962 p. 22, see also *ibid*, Plate 10 and description. In the Western alchemical philosophy of Christian imagination the symbol of the temple or the castle plays a central role. See C.G. Jung, CW 13, *Alchemical Studies* ¶86, III, 1, 3, C.G. Jung, CW 12, *Psychology and Alchemy* ¶138f on the name of the alchemical vessel as "city" or "castle," which protects the precious substance from the outside world. See also H. Silberer, *Problems of Mysticism*, New York 1917 p. 389, on the Jewish tabernacle and the Holy Ark as alchemistic symbols.

[8] See C.G. Jung, CW 11, *Psychology and Religion* ¶123, and C.G. Jung, CW 12, *Psychology and Alchemy* ¶246 footnote 125. "Just as the stupas preserve relics of the Buddha in their innermost sanctuary, so in the interior of the Lamaic quadrangle, and angle in the Chinese earth-square, there is a Holy of Holies with its magical agent, the cosmic source of energy, be it the god Shiva, Buddha, a bodhisattva, or a great teacher And equally in the Western mandalas of medieval Christendom the deity is enthroned at the center, often in the form of the triumphant Redeemer together with the four symbolical figures of the evangelists." (*Ibid* ¶169).

[9] See Revelations 21: 2. See also Silesius' verses on "Maria":
    Mary is named a Throne, the Lord's own Tabernacle,
    An Ark, Keep, Tower, House, a Spring, Tree, Garden, Mirror,
    A Sea, a Star, the Moon, a Hill, the Blush of Morning.
    All these how can she be? She is another world!
(A. Silesius, *The Cherubinic Wanderer*, New Jersey 1986 p. Book IV, no. 42).

[10] See the mystical castle of Corbenic where the Grail was kept.

[11] [It may be of interest to note that the story opens saying that there are two children, a boy and girl. Nothing more is said of the girl.]

She later relates in tears: "Has the devil power over me, or did my deliverer never come?" That it is the same number of years is salient: at the very moment when the soul falls into the dark power, the same happens to her future redeemer, since the whole game of the opposites has its roots in the unconscious itself. The fact that the anima initially appears in animal form can be explained in reference to the motif of the magical marriage. In the fairytale under discussion, the otherwise rare extension indicates that some event that occurred prior to the beginning of the fairytale is the cause for her appearance in animal form. We have met this previously only in "The Mermaid and the Great Dubhdach." There, also, it is a demonic father figure who enchants his daughter and binds her to the magical world until the time of her redemption.

252   The point of this idea can be illuminated by glancing at a Gnostic scripture, *The Book of Baruch* by Justin.[12] This tells of the Edem,[13] the female principle, who is "virgin above and viper below." Elohim, the demiurgic "father of all things," falls in love and marries the "half-virgin Edem." Before their separation, they produce twenty-four angels – twelve paternal, and twelve maternal. The twelve angels of Elohim took from the best earth (upper part) of Edem and created man. Edem provided the soul and Elohim the spirit (*pneuma*). After the creation:

253   Elohim chose to rise to the highest part of heaven to see if their creation lacked any elements.
He took his angels with him and rose, as was his nature, and he abandoned Edem below,
who being earth declined to follow her husband upward.[14]

254   The abandoned Edem initially expects the return of Elohim, and tries to attract him with her adornments. But to no avail, since the highest god, the "good," refused to let Elohim return. Edem then takes revenge on the *pneuma* of Elohim in mankind by causing adultery among the people and as a consequence evil prevails among humans next to good.[15] Edem, or world soul (*anima mundi*), is:

255   . . . "the divine soul imprisoned in the elements," which is to be redeemed. . . Now, all these mythical images represent a drama of the

---

[12] [Note that this is not the Deuterocanonical *The Book of Baruch*.]
[13] ["The spelling Edem is used for Eden, as in the garden of Eden in Genesis, both in the Book of Baruch and in the Septuagint translation of Genesis – hence also in our translation here."]
[14] [See B. Willis and M. Meyer, *The Gnostic Bible* 2003 p. 128.]
[15] See H. Leisegang, *Die Gnosis*, Leipzig 1924 p. 158ff [for the English, see B. Willis and M. Meyer, *The Gnostic Bible* 2003 p. 119ff].

human psyche beyond our consciousness, showing *man as both the one to be redeemed and the redeemer.*"[16]

256   These archetypes are also reflected in the fairytale, and the sought-after salvation can only happen when the human being knowingly and humbly takes on the suffering of the darkness on herself or himself. As long as the anima remains excluded from conscious life and remains in the unconscious, she has a non-human, animal-demonic quality. Indeed, she can even stand in for the devil himself as in the tale "The Tailor and the Treasure" in which she appears as a crocodile, a toad, and finally as a black goat, which clearly indicates her relationship with the devil.[17] As a result of this similar nature, in myths both [that is, anima and devil] often take on the form of a snake or dragon. Along with the interrelated bodily and earthly aspects, these two represent psychic impulses. The snake represents the underworld, the chthonic, the anxiety-causing, the instinctually driven, and the dark mother.[18] Particularly in the Gnosis the snake had the greatest importance and that was an ambivalent one. It sometimes symbolized a redeeming deity and sometimes the principle of evil, sometimes the female as the world soul, and sometimes the male as Chronos, Leviathan, or Satan.[19] As a good demon, the snake stands in relation to the solar system. The winged serpent is a picture of Helios,[20] because it is the creative bringer of new consciousness. Also, in this tale the redeemed snake princess confers rule over the "golden mountain." Gold is inextricably bound up with the notions of "light" and "Sun." The task is to wrest this new gold or light from the dark earth, like the three golden hairs from the head of the devil in "The Devil with the Three Golden Hairs."

---

[16] C.G. Jung, CW 12, *Psychology and Alchemy* ¶413-14 slightly altered to conform with authors' reading.

[17] See Jung:

A man's unconscious is . . . feminine and is personified by the anima. The anima also stands for the "inferior" function and for that reason frequently has a shady character; in fact, she sometimes stands for evil itself. She is the dark and dreaded maternal womb, which is of an essentially ambivalent nature. (*Ibid* ¶192.)

[18] See C.G. Jung, CW 5, *Symbols of Transformation* ¶155 ¶680f. On the snake in general see G. F. Hartlaub, "Schlange," Berlin 1940 (1940).

[19] On the partly light, partly dark character of the snake see H. Leisegang, *Die Gnosis*, Leipzig 1924 p. Chap. 4. In medieval alchemistic philosophy, the snake is the animal of Mercurius, and [as the planet Mercury] also a god of revelation who discloses the secrets of the [alchemical] arts, and he is himself, "the soul of the bodies," "a spirit that has become earth," "a spirit that penetrates into the depths of the material world and transforms it. Like the *nous*, he is symbolized by the serpent." C.G. Jung, CW 11, *Psychology and Religion* ¶356. The medieval Melusine is a similar figure, which was represented as a serpent virgin. See C.G. Jung, CW 13, *Alchemical Studies* ¶179f. According to the Gnostic view it is the task of the redeemer to raise back this soul that has sunk into substance and matter. Often the Redeemer himself has snake-like attributes. "*The hero is himself the snake*, himself the sacrificer and the sacrificed, which is why Christ rightly compares himself with the healing Moses-serpent, and why the savior of the Christian Ophites was a serpent, too. It is both Agathodaimon and Cacodaimon." C.G. Jung, CW 5, *Symbols of Transformation* ¶593, also ¶575f. [Italics by von Franz and von Beit.]

[20] See H. Leisegang, "Schlange," Zürich 1940 p. 186. [Note also the Aztec Quetzalcoatl who was known as a winged serpent and sun god. M. Graulich, *Myths*, Norman 1997 p. 82, 165f.]

257 The virgin-to-be-redeemed in the shape of the snake is a common motif in Germanic legends.[21] Sometimes the maiden secretly carries a snake in her heart, which means danger for the hero.[22] Usually she is redeemed through accepting her animal form by, for example, the hero kissing her.[23] In a Norwegian parallel to our stories, "The Three Princesses of Whiteland," the princess-to-be-redeemed and her two sisters are buried up to their heads in the ground, clearly showing the chthonic aspect of the anima and her bond to the unconscious. The hero must let himself get whipped by a troll – which is the cause of the curse – for three nights. Every night the princesses rise a little further out of the earth. The demon, who at the outset of the tale claimed the hero for himself, is a water spirit. In the Grimm's version [narrated here], the redeemer must let himself be tortured and remain silent for two nights by twelve, and on the third night, by twenty-four black men covered in chains. This signifies that the reason for the inferiority of the soul image, or anima, is not due to the image itself, but to its indistinguishability from the shadow figures, which also cause the hero to suffer. By this suffering consciousness recognizes and experiences the shadow. In fact, the dark side of the Self is connected with the light side and through such suffering joined into a wholeness. Only after this is the real connection with the anima possible.

258 The number twelve almost always points to some given situation in space-time, and, therefore, to the fate that is therein actualized.[24] Horoscopes are divided into twelve sections, the twelve signs of the zodiac.[25] The twelve zodiac signs are also in the Gnostic scripture, *The Book of Baruch*, as the twelve angels of the snake virgin Edem.[26] These signify fate-bringing demons or archons, whose influence act over time. In some Gnostic systems there are more than twelve aeons, in which case the thirteenth plays a special role. The thirteenth unites with the twelve aeons to lure the divine world soul, here Sophia, into matter through a false light.[27] In the *Corpus Hermeticum*, Discourse XIII, called the "Consecration of prophets," there is an exhortation to the initiates

---

[21] See L. Laistner, *Das Rätsel*, Berlin 1889 p. 99ff (and on a magical marriage that ran an unhappy course, see *ibid*, page 119f.).

[22] See J. Bolte and G. Polívka, *Anmerkungen*, Vol. 1, Leipzig 1913 p. 50.

[23] See also the note above parallel to "The Three Feathers" in *ibid* p. 31ff where the anima as frog calls out to the hero, "Embrace me and lose yourself!" and then becomes a beautiful maiden.

[24] The doubling of the number in the third night to twenty-four men might here be viewed as an amplification, a reinforcement, an accentuation, which often occurs in the third test in fairytales.

[25] See R. Bernoulli, "Symbolik geom. Figuren," *Eranos*, Zürich 1935 p. 400, 402f.

[26] See H. Leisegang, *Die Gnosis*, Leipzig 1924 p. 180. See also, *ibid*, p. 22 on the twelve winds of ancient compass (windrose) with their animal heads.

[27] See translation of *Pistis Sophia* G. R. S. Mead, *Fragments*, London 1931 p. 469f and *ibid* p. 325 about the number twelve.

to clean themselves, ". . . and there are twelve evil spirits who follow humans and torture them. . . You can cleanse yourself with the support of the divine *Dynamis* [also translated as 'powers' or 'intelligibles']."[28] The dodecagon is geometrically a triple square. The consulted diagrams show that the figure three seems to represent the potential triad or trinity latent in all manifestation, and that this triad, acting within the tetrad of the squares, produce the infinite ordering into twelves or dodecads.[29]

259   The center, the thirteenth, is the immovable in the developing process[30] and, therefore, often a picture of the godhead, either in its dark or light aspect. In Eastern mandalas the one, the great *dorje* [thunderbolt power] is usually shown surrounded by twelve smaller *dorjes*.[31] The relationship of time to the twelve men in the present fairytale is shown in that the princess is cursed for twelve years and that the effectiveness of the men ceases at twelve o'clock.

260   The hero of the present tale represents the thirteenth, the core of the personality. His task is to endure the nocturnal rounds of torture by twelve black shackled figures, like the initiants of the ancient mysteries who had to pass through the twelve hours of the night in their transformation. In this process they assumed twelve animal forms to obtain their divine immortal form.[32] The hero must accept without complaint the fate of his earthly existence, in order to obtain the connection with the feminine and together with the anima form a psychic wholeness.

261   As with the ferryman in "The Devil with the Three Golden Hairs" where the dangerous dark side of the deity in need of salvation also came to light, so do the twelve demons of the present tale carry chains suggesting that they themselves are not free and are suffering. Chain-rattling figures in the dark night are usually ghosts of the dead; it follows that the hero, therefore, in his night sea journey enters the other side as the land of the dead.

---

[28] W. Bousset, *Hauptprobleme der Gnosis*, Göttingen 1907 p. 364. [English, Copenhaver p. 50f.] On the twelve as lords of the twelve hours of the night in Hell see, R. Reitzenstein, *Iranische*, Bonn a. Rh. 1921 p. 245, and the same reference, *passim* on "the Twelve."

[29] G. R. S. Mead, *Fragments*, London 1931 p. 536. In the present fairytale note that with the tetrad there are triadic groupings of people or events: 1 father + 3 sons = 4, or: 3 brothers + 1 maiden = 4, or: 3 futile efforts or stations + 1 successful one (the goal) = 4, etc.

[30] Cf. R. Bernoulli, "Symbolik geom. Figuren," Zürich 1935 p. 409.

[31] See C.G. Jung, CW 12, *Psychology and Alchemy* Fig. 43 ¶139, fn. 12. A similar phenomenon is Jacob, the perfect human being as the central figure of the twelve tribes of Israel, just as Jesus is the thirteenth in the center of the circle of his twelve disciples. In Germanic mythology, the king is sometimes surrounded by twelve of Odin's *berserkers*. See M. Ninck, *Wodan*, Jena 1935 pp. 102–03, fn. 1. See also in general E. Böklen, "Die 'Unglückszahl' Dreizehn und ihre mythische Bedeutung" in: *Mythologische Bibliothek*, Vol. 5, no. 2, Leipzig 1913 p. 27ff. especially *ibid* p. 27ff for information on the thirteenth as the "youngest."

[32] See R. Reitzenstein, *Hellenistic*, Pittsburgh 1978 p. 40. [See also Hugh Bowden, *Mystery Cults of the Ancient World*, London 2010.]

262　The main condition that the snake requires for her redemption is that the hero *silently* endures the tortures. Therein lies, on the one hand, a test of courage, but on the other hand, also a deeper meaning: silence means here "not responding," that is, not making contact,[33] that is, remaining differentiated. Similarly, on their way to the underground Persephone, initiants (mystes) in the ancient mystery cults had to veil themselves and remain silent. The word μυε῾ειν (myéein, dedicate) comes from μυ῾ειν (myein) and means to close one's eyes and ears.[34] In the *Mithras Liturgy* when new demons or images confront the initiant, he or she must call out the word, "silent!" This is a protective gesture to avoid being overwhelmed by emotions,[35] which is probably similar in meaning to the commandment of silence in the present tale.

263　The hero, as the perfect man, must descend into the dark chaos in which the soul is held captive, and allow its powers to work on him while he remains passive. Thus he preserves his purity and suffers [consciously] the conditions of his earthly and individual contingency. Gnosticism developed in particular the myth of the redemption of the imprisoned soul. For instance, according to Philo of Alexandria the soul itself torments the structure of the perfect human being. As Leisegang explains:

264　She comes from above, from the Spirit. Only through her can spirit and matter be bound together. By entering into the connection to dead matter in the earthly human body, she puts herself into captivity. She suffers, and through this suffering comes into the world, because with her the Spirit suffers, the divine cosmos suffers in its own creation, in the earthly human being.[36]

265　From this parallel it is understandable that in "The King of the Golden Mountain" the redeemer appears on earth at the moment when the soul falls into the captivity of matter. But through the descent of the perfect human into

---

[33] See "The Mountain Spirit and the Cooper" where a Yamachichi [a Japanese supernatural monster with one eye and one leg] once visited a barrel maker at work. He repeated exactly what the cooper was thinking without the man saying a word. Realizing that the Yamachichi could read his thoughts, the cooper just continued calmly to work on his barrels. Without any forethought whatsoever, a bamboo strip he was bending sprang loose and hit the Yamachichi in the face. The monster thought to himself, "If this fellow can do this without even thinking, who knows what else he can do?" and then fled as quickly as he could. Thus, the man proved his superiority to demonic thinking.

[34] See Meister Eckhart, "Therefore, a master says, if someone is to perform an inner work, they must draw in all their powers as if in the corner of their soul, hiding from all images and forms, and then they shall be able to act. Where this word is to be heard, there must be stillness and silence." Meister Eckhart (trans. Davies), *Selected Writings*, London 1994 p. 220. See K. Kerényi, *Kore*, Princeton, 1969 p. 182, (*Epilogmena*). See also the theme of the closing of the eyes at the start of a heavenly journey in Volume 1, above, page **30**.

[35] See A. Dieterich, *Eine Mithrasliturgie*, Leipzig and Berlin 1923 pp. 7, 9, 42–43.

[36] H. Leisegang, *Die Gnosis*, Leipzig 1924 p. 118.

the realm of matter, the transformative redemption emerges.[37] In that the hero, coming out of the sphere of consciousness, carries light into the darkness, and the darkness accepts this suffering, the anima is freed from her oppressive aspect, "and can take up the living and creative function that is properly her own."[38]

266   This is reflected in our tale in that the snake-woman-anima is in possession of the living water, with which every morning she heals the hero again. It is "the living psychic being," of which she lets him partake. This process is a very common theme in fairytales.[39] Usually it is the anima, being intimately connected with her source of life, that saves the hero, for example, in the Grimm's tale, "The Water of Life" in which a prince, the third son, must find the water of life for his sick father. He comes to an enchanted castle and must pass by two lions and get the water before midnight otherwise the gate of the castle will slam shut. In the castle he meets a maiden whom he redeems with a kiss. She then leads him to the water of life. Even more similar to "The Devil with the Three Golden Hairs" is another Grimm's tale, "The King's Son Who Feared Nothing." In this fairytale, the hero lands in an enchanted castle where a black virgin lives. In order to redeem her, he must let himself be brutally tortured and tormented by little devils for three nights without uttering a sound. The virgin cures him every morning with a small bottle containing the water of life. By the third morning she has become white and shows him how to deliver the castle from its curse.[40] She revives the hero not because she is "good" and not because she is "beautiful," but because the anima desires life above all.[41] In "The King of the Golden Mountain" after the mutual

---

[37] On the self-sacrifice of the hero and in general the problem of the sacrifice, see C.G. Jung, CW 11, *Psychology and Religion* ¶296–448, and C.G. Jung, CW 13, *Alchemical Studies* ¶91 ¶139. See also:
> By a certain "synchronicity" of events, man, the bearer of a soul submerged in the world and the flesh, is potentially related to God at the moment when he, as Mary's Son, enters into her, the *virgo terrae* and representative of matter in its highest form; and potentially at least, man is fully redeemed at the moment when the eternal Son of God returns again to the Father after undergoing the sacrificial death. The ideology of this *mysterium* is anticipated in the myths of Osiris, Orpheus, Dionysus, and Hercules, and in the conception of the Messiah among the Hebrew prophets. These anticipations go back to the archaic hero myths where the conquest of death is already an important factor. (C.G. Jung, CW 12, *Psychology and Alchemy* ¶415.)

See also *ibid* ¶184.

[38] *Ibid* ¶242.

[39] See for example, "Dat Könirik von Mornstêrn" (The Kingdom of the Morning Star) and the French fairytale mentioned in G. Huet, *Les contes*, Paris 1923 p. 125ff, where the demons chop up, cook, and devour the hero, bones and all. Then the princess resurrects him by rubbing the nail of his little toe.

[40] See "The Story of the Blind King Who Lived in the Western Lands" and "The Story of the Magpie who had Ringworm" in which it is told that a youth must retrieve the calabash with the water of life first from the Land of the East and then from the Land of the West. From each land he must also bring with him the princess who watches over the water. See further the tales "The Journey into the Underworld to the Whirlpool Cave Fafá" and "The Water of Life of Ka-Ne."

[41] See Jung:
> Because the anima wants life, she wants both good and bad. These categories do not exist in the elfin realm. The anima believes in the καλόν καλαθόν, the "beautiful and the good," a primitive conception that antedates the discovery of the conflict between aesthetics and

redemption is accomplished, the union is consummated. From this a child is born, which means the Self has become one. The hero becomes King of the Golden Mountain, in the realm of the psyche, in the sphere of the unconscious female principle. This kingdom is reminiscent of the common human dream of the Golden Age that is present in every eschatology. It can be construed progressively, as a future longed-for goal, or regressively, as a temptation to return to the outgrown childhood paradise.[42] The symbol of becoming whole appears – projected in time – as what has always been and at the same time as the distant goal of life.[43] When the hero joins the anima, a union of consciousness and the unconscious takes place. This is the same image as the union of the sun and the snake that was of central importance in the Orphic mysteries. By uniting with the life-snake the hero transforms into the new sun, that is, a source of new life and wholeness.[44]

267   This state of unification, the inner harmony of personality, lasts for seven years. Because the connection has taken place in the depths of the unconscious and the father, the merchant, who represents the prevailing conscious attitude, takes absolutely no part in this process, the hero is seized with homesickness in the eighth year and longs to see his father again. With the completion of the eight-year cycle, the rhythm of wholeness would also have been realized, since eight, like four, is a symbol of the Self.[45]

268   Numbers that contain a multiple of four occur throughout this tale: in the twelve-year-old hero, in the twelve men, in the torture that lasts until twelve o'clock in the night, and now in these eight years. But just before reaching the fulfilling eight, an event occurs that causes the hero to take a long detour. His longing to return to the secular world now overwhelms him. This is understandable considering that although the situation seems very pleasant, it is actually unsatisfactory: the sphere of worldly thinking has been left out. The queen suspects calamity and wants to prevent the hero's return because she knows how dangerous rational and purposeful thinking can be to the experience of the objective psyche when it reacts with one-sided

---

morals. It took more than a thousand years of Christian differentiation to make it clear that the good is not always the beautiful and the beautiful is not necessarily good. (C.G. Jung, CW 9i, *The Archetypes and the Collective Unconscious* ¶59.)

[42] See C.G. Jung, CW 6, *Psychological Types* ¶123ff. See also the image of the Golden Age in Bächtold-Stäubli under *Goldenes Zeitalter* [Golden Age].

[43] On this see C.G. Jung, CW 9i, *The Archetypes and the Collective Unconscious* ¶294.

[44] See H. Leisegang, "Schlange," Zürich 1940 *passim*. See also the concept of the Feathered Serpent (Quetzelcoatl) in Mexico.

[45] On the meaning of the number eight, see C.G. Jung, CW 12, *Psychology and Alchemy* ¶239ff. On eight as a symbol of equal measure and the limit in Gnostic concepts, see G. R. S. Mead, *Fragments*, London 1931 p. 379. Chinese philosophy as expressed in the *I Ching* represents the wholeness of the universe as built from eight characters or images. See Wilhelm/Baynes, *I Ching*, Princeton, 1967 pp. 283f, 357ff. See also the fairytale, "The Eight Immortals (1)." Among the Aztecs, the Healer Quetzalcoatl eight days after his death became the "great star" [Venus, the Morning Star] that is, God. M. Graulich, *Myths*, Norman 1997 p. 202f.

formulations.[46] But neither the conscious mind nor the anima, as parts of the Self hidden in the unconscious, are able decisively to assert their essence. Dire consequences arise, therefore, from the encounter with the profane world. If the hero were to remain in the golden kingdom, however, it would result in lifeless stagnation. Thus, the departure of the hero to his father is correct, because through this detour the newly gained knowledge of inner values can be connected to the reality reflected in secular thinking. Certainly, this creates more problems, but it also brings broadened possibilities of life and living.

269   The queen gives her husband a wishing ring to take with him. The finger ring is a symbol of connectedness, bonding, and relationship.[47] It also means the connection between body and soul. Thus, according to old German superstition, the ring of the berserker opens when his soul travels out of his body and closes when it returns. In death, the ring falls off or it is stolen.[48] As something round, like a mandala, it encompasses all the forces of the unconscious and can bring wishes, that is, things imagined, into reality.

270   In our tale the wishing ring is meant to preserve and protect the connection between the anima and the hero, but he may not misuse it to lure the anima into the secular world. He promises her that he will let her remain in *her* world. This obligation corresponds to the imposition of a command of silence, as is almost always the case in "magical marriages." The anima is the figure that mediates at the border to the unconscious and she may not be drawn into a situation where she must interact with the outer world, because she could then be "falsified" and be delivered to the mercy of overestimation or contempt.

271   The hero now passes into the profane world, but he wears "strange clothes" and is not recognized by the sentries. This indicates that the division between the old attitude and the inner essence of the personality has become so great that the personality no longer recognizes its own deeper values as belonging to itself. Since the empirical ego does not recognize the Self, which was honored as king in the unconscious, the Self is again forced into an apparently soulless, inferior, and mean role; the hero dons the vestments of a shepherd. By an outer mark on the hero's skin, the father then does indeed recognize his son, but he cannot and will not believe that he is King of the Golden Mountain. The secular conscious mind is evidently incapable of recognizing the values of the other side of life, since they mean nothing to his conscious, goal-oriented view. This feebleness and inability of the conscious mind faces an equally vaguely formed figure, representing the core of the personality or the

---

[46] See C.G. Jung, CW 6, *Psychological Types* ¶830ff.
[47] See C.G. Jung, CW 7, *Two Essays in Analytical Psychology* ¶178.
[48] See M. Ninck, *Wodan*, Jena 1935 p. 60, 291. See also the fairytale "Diarmuid Donn and the Magic Flute" in which it is told that three drops of liquid flow from the ring of a sorceress that can revive the dead. In "The Specter in Fjelkinge" the ghost of a murdered man is calmed by placing a ring near him.

center of the soul: in his weakness the hero falls prey to the temptation and reveals the values of the unconscious realms. If a human betrays unconscious secrets, this is partly due to a conscious disbelief (because if he really believed then he would not reveal the secrets), and partly due to a weakness at the core of his inner consciousness. Despite her ban, the hero summons the queen and her child to appear. (In a parallel from Slovakia he displays the ring – also against warnings not to do this.)[49] As a result of this betrayal, the anima immediately acquires a negative aspect, which she reveals before the eyes of the unrefined consciousness. As it later turns out, she falls back under the power of the devil, and the whole work of redemption comes to naught. So it comes to a tragic separation, which in magical marriages always follows a betrayal. But this separation is just an episode of the great journey, because the hero follows the anima into her realm to get her back.[50]

272 The Grimm's fairytale "The Drummer" relates the same process in quite a similar fashion. There, the hero obtains the Princess of the Glass Mountain and returns home, also with a wishing ring. Despite the ban of his wife he kisses his parents on their right cheeks (the right side is the side of consciousness) and immediately forgets his princess.

273 Our hero goes with his queen to the border area by the river, the place where the encounter with the devil took place. There, he slips under the spell of the anima and falls asleep (that is, he becomes unconscious). But she disappears with the most valuable things: the child and the ring. The abandoned slipper – according to the idiomatic usage, "standing under the slipper" means to be henpecked – is a derisive indication of his dependence on the betrayed princess. A shoe is also a sign of earthiness and a symbol of the sexual-feminine.[51] This expresses that only the secular world remains understandable to the forsaken hero because, in the eyes of the uncomprehending conscious mind, the soul (the objective psyche, or empirical consciousness) appears in the profane world as an admixture of inferior instinct and whim.[52]

274 On his renewed journey the hero encounters the fighting giants. In the parallels mentioned by Bolte-Polívka[53] he meets instead huge magical creatures: the king of the fish, birds and winds; three witches; three dwarves; three robbers; the moon, sun, and dew; the "Lord of Feathered Beasts and Fish"; the sun, moon, and wind; and the devil. From their names it appears

---

[49] See J. Bolte and G. Polívka, *Anmerkungen*, Vol. 2, Leipzig 1915 p. 325. See also *ibid* page 326 on Brunhilde (Brynhildr) whose relationship to Sigurd (Siegfried) must be kept secret.
[50] Like the hero in "Rakian."
[51] See Dr. Aigremont, *Fuss- and Schuh-Symbolik*, Leipzig 1909b.
[52] In some of the parallels mentioned in J. Bolte and G. Polívka, *Anmerkungen*, Vol. 2, Leipzig 1915 pp. 321, 323, 334, we find lead shoes or iron boots in place of the slipper, emphasizing the cumbersome, clumsy, ponderous and inhibiting, the material, in contrast to the light [i.e. the nature of the anima].
[53] J. Bolte and G. Polívka, *Anmerkungen*, Vol. 2, Leipzig 1915 p. 321ff.

that these giants are nature powers. In an Iranian tale "Saʿd and Saʿīd" it is even said that these three contending figures, who so often occur in fairytales but are not otherwise included in the main plot, are actually sons of the dark opponent. The wanderer must, therefore, repeat his conquest of the twelve black men. This *auseinandersetzung* is, however, less tortuous and more a matter of cunning. The hero has now acquired knowledge of the contradictory nature of the dark ones, that is, the opposites in the unconscious (the competing giants!). Using his experience, he obtains a coat that makes the wearer invisible, a symbol of the ability to transform. This perhaps arises from the same concept as the wishing-coat of Odin, just as the sword is the equivalent of Odin's spear. When he calls out, "Odin has you all," he mows down all his enemies with his sword.[54] On its return journey the conscious mind is gradually devoured by the unconscious and thus again merges with the demonic dark forces of nature from which it emerged. As a third gift, the hero acquires boots with which he can wish himself anywhere. In two of the parallels mentioned by Bolte-Polívka[55] the wind gives the boots or the wanderer exchanges his horse for the magic boots. The wind is an element of Odin.

275   Once at the Golden Mountain, the hero behaves so much like a demon, so similar to Odin himself, that the queen doubts her redemption. In fact, she has now completely fallen for a "false bridegroom,"[56] the dark aspect of the unconscious. Although she is no longer a snake, she is again surrounded by a multitude of shadowy beings and celebrates her wedding with a man who is not further described. This man undoubtedly represents a shadow figure, since the anima is psychologically almost always connected to the shadow, especially if she has not been freed by conscious effort from her captivity in the unconscious. She often appears at the beginning of a fairytale, therefore, with a shadowy husband, as the case in "Tapairu, the Beauty from the Land of the Fairies" (see Volume 1 page 449), or after the tragic separation of a magical marriage, she unites with an animal shadow, as in "Ititaujang."

276   The hero punishes the queen for her infidelity with a slap in her face, but his upbraiding is only partly justified, since he himself was actually the traitor.

277   With the cry, "All heads off but mine!" he then kills the whole court and reestablishes himself as king. The sword represents rational cognition that the shadow figures are "headless," that is, they are marked as senseless, instinct-driven psychic impulses. In some versions of this fairytale his revenge extends also to include the princess herself, who is either permanently or temporarily transformed into an ass.[57] Because of her association with the shadow, she is

---

[54] See M. Führer, *Nordgermanische*, München 1938 p. 32.
[55] J. Bolte and G. Polívka, *Op. cit.* pp. 320, 322.
[56] On the motif of "false bride" and "false groom," see the next volume of this work.
[57] See J. Bolte and G. Polívka, *Anmerkungen*, Vol. 2, Leipzig 1915 pp. 321, 324.

rejected and banned again into animal form. The unresolved and un-satisfactory features of this process result from the incomplete nature of all the characters throughout the whole tale: the empirical consciousness is portrayed by a greedy, unbelieving merchant, and the unknown core of the ego by a weak hero, vacillating between the spheres. Both the hero and the anima remain, therefore, associated with the dark powers, and the fairytale sinks into the magical.

278　　In "The Devil with the Three Golden Hairs" the father-king was punished; the hero, however, obtained the anima and is exalted. There, both the vigor and penetrating power of the new personality was greater, and the resistance of the prevailing conscious attitude was more intense, whereas in "The King of the Golden Mountain" the tension between the antagonists is lower and thus all figures are more vague, less clear-cut, and less differentiated. In addition, the original purpose of the hero's return, to make contact with his father again, remains unfulfilled. The tale actually expresses pessimistically that the unconscious is insurmountable, because as in the aforementioned parallels, the redeemed princess returns again to animal form, and the hero that was called to renew life disappears into the kingdom of the golden mountain, the realm of the midnight sun, that is, the unconscious.

279　　A variant that is rich in images and supports the above interpretation, is found in the collection, *German Fairy Tales Since Grimm*, and is called "The Iron Boot":

280　　Once there was a king who had a fine castle and a wonderful queen. But they were not happy because although they had no want of riches, servants, mansions and horses, they lacked the best and fairest of all; they had no children. This made their lives bitter and quite often their hearts were so heavy that they had to cry. And to make matters worse, one day a great fire broke out, and engulfed the whole palace. The king and queen escaped with their lives but they lost all of their treasures. The only thing they could save was an iron box full of gold. With this gold they constructed a new and even more beautiful castle, but again, their joy was short-lived. A second fire devoured the new castle and nothing was saved, just the iron box – now completely empty. They were suddenly as poor as the poorest man in their own country. No, even poorer, because a poor man can at least work and earn his bread, but he was not the king. With this king, however, all his servants, courtiers, and friends left. The king then took his wife's hand and they both went into the forest, deeply saddened. There they found an abandoned shepherd's hut and made do as poor people do. The king himself went into the forest, cut and brought the firewood home, and the queen made a fire, stirred the soup, and cooked potatoes. That was very unusual work for them, so it was quite bitter at first; but little by little all went better. It actually became even better than when they were still sitting on their thrones and had all that they wanted.

281 One day[58] when the king went into the forest to cut wood as usual, a strange man appeared and asked the king why he, a king, was cutting wood. The king explained all that had happened and the strange man promised to fill the king's empty iron box with gold if he would sign a contract stating that he would give the strange man "everything that he did not know." The king thought this to be trivial and so he right away signed the contract. This turned out to be a careless act. The strange man laughed in an odd way and said, "Now stop your wood cutting and go home!"

282 When the king went back to his hut, his wife sprang out to greet him, "My lucky king! Our iron box is full of gold and our greatest happiness we shall soon have: I am with child! The king was very glad; he began at once to assemble all possible craftsmen, masons and carpenters, and it was not long before they stood in the midst of a most beautiful castle in place of their hut in the woods. And not three weeks more had passed and his greatest wish was fulfilled, the queen gave birth to a beautiful young son. Now there was nothing left to be desired.

283 The king and queen gave the boy the name Ferdinand and he grew up in happiness with his parents. When it came time to see to his education, they sent the endangered child to a priest. There Ferdinand learned not only piety but all the arts and ways of the world. On the boy's fifteenth birthday, according to the contract with the strange man, the priest went with the young prince to the forest, gave him a magic staff and told him what he should do and how he should act. Then Ferdinand went to the place where his father had first met with the strange man. There he waited and listened and observed the forest. Suddenly a ship came sailing through the sky. It was full of singing devils that had come to take Ferdinand up into their vessel. But Ferdinand resisted with his staff and beat the demons so hard that they fled. Then a second ship came sailing through the clouds. This time the crew of devils were even angrier and louder. But the prince again courageously beat them off with his staff and they sailed away, howling in the wind. After a while a golden chariot driven by fiery horses came at him accompanied by a terrible din that confounded his mind. Inside was the Evil One himself, furious and bent on taking what was his. Only with great difficulty did Ferdinand defend himself

---

[58] [From here on the tale is summarized.]

again the Evil One. When the devil brought out the signed contract and pointed at the words and the king's signature, Ferdinand hit him so hard with his staff that the devil dropped the paper and drove off in a terrible mood. The prince returned to his teacher, but then soon left again. He explained that now the time had come for him to seek the Kingdom of Heaven.

284 Prince Ferdinand now set off and soon came to a gray-bearded hermit living on the shore of a large lake. When asked the way to the Kingdom of Heaven, the hermit responded that he himself did not know, but his brother did. He pointed and said his brother lived still farther on through an even larger forest and there at the edge of an even bigger lake. The prince went on and on the further shore met a white-bearded hermit. This one also said he did not know the way but surely the third brother did. Ferdinand went on and on, deeper and deeper, and met the third hermit. This one also admitted that he did not know the way, but in his hut upstairs there lived birds that surely did. Ferdinand entered the hut and climbed to the upper floor. There he met screeching birds that told him to wait for the griffin, which would soon come back from Heaven. When the griffin appeared, Ferdinand asked him if he could take him to the Kingdom of Heaven. The griffin agreed, took Ferdinand up in his claws and flew with him to the Kingdom of Heaven. There, the prince found a magnificent garden, a golden castle, and a pond with a huge, terrifying snake. Ferdinand went directly to the pond and the snake spoke to the fearless Ferdinand: "I have waited a long time for you to come and save me, no one else can redeem me but you alone." She[59] told him that to save her he had to endure three nights in the golden castle without reacting, no matter what happened.

285 On the first night a company of wild people appeared at midnight who tempted Ferdinand to dance with them, but he remained motionless. On the second night, the same company came again, and this time beat him because he did not join them. On the third night they dismembered and ripped him apart because he again refused to join. They danced and trod upon the pieces of his body. When the clock struck one, the ghosts disappeared, the rescued princess entered, and revived the prince. They embraced and rejoiced and celebrated the redemption of the princess. She showed him all around the palace and the gardens but forbade him to look into a small shed that they passed, explaining that it would cause his misfortune. They were then married and lived happily together.

---

[59] [In German, *Schlange* (snake) is feminine.]

286 After some time, the prince was no longer able to resist and peeped into the shed. There in the darkness he made out down below his father's castle and was overcome with homesickness. He tried to keep it from the princess but she forced him to tell her what was wrong. When she heard the reason for his depression she agreed to let him make a visit to his old home. She added that if in distress, he should call her name, but only if he met with real hardship. He returned "down to earth." There, many things had changed, his mother had died and his father had married a young and beautiful woman. The king was overjoyed to see his son after all these years and called for a great feast. At the table the king boasted of the unsurpassed beauty of his wife. The prince could not resist and said that he knew of another woman even more beautiful. The king challenged Ferdinand to prove his claim and the prince thereupon called the name of his wife. She appeared in all her beauty, truly beyond compare. But she wore a pale complexion and carried a sad face. She spoke not but wrote some golden letters on the table with her fine white fingers: "It is impossible for you to rip apart a pair of iron boots, and equally impossible to travel back into the heavenly paradise."

287 Ferdinand only too late realized his grave mistake. He ordered a pair of iron boots to be forged and restlessly tramped around the world for years, through ice and heat, mountain and vale. When the boot soles wore very thin, he again journeyed to the three hermits and waited for the griffin. He implored the bird once again to take him to the Kingdom of Heaven. This the griffin did and underway told the prince that the princess had found a second husband and they were just then getting married.

288 Upon arriving, the prince crept into the castle and placed his shredded iron boots just outside the princess's bedroom door and hid himself nearby. When the princess came to her room she recognized the boots and told the groom to wait in the main hall. She did not see Ferdinand, but rejoiced that he must be alive and somewhere near. She returned to the wedding guests and asked them for advice. She explained that she had an iron box where she kept her pearls and precious stones. One day she lost the key.

289 Having searched all over to no avail she had ordered a new key to be made. But just before she was about to use the new key, she found her old lost key. She asked the gathered guests: "Which key should I take now, the old one or the new one?" All the guests voted unanimously that she should take the old key. When he heard this the new

bridegroom crept away and the princess was again happily united with Ferdinand.

290   In this fairytale, the weakness of the dominant conscious mind is clearly marked relative to the powers of the unconscious that favor another attitude. Not one but two fires are needed to finally bring about the utter impoverishment of the king. By retiring to the woods, the king approaches – out of necessity – a confrontation with the unconscious but then avoids a direct conscious struggle by selling off all his future possibilities – unknown to the ego – in order to gain that which appears to his profane mind to be of value. He builds his new palace over the same place where his cottage stood, pompously underlining the small step that had brought him closer to the unconscious world. At the end of the story he has, in a youthful worldly way, taken a young woman to wife. He evidently thinks he can compare her with the real, operative image in the foundations of his soul. His own uncertainty is reflected in the encounter with his son as the higher Self and in the confrontation between the two female characters. The son is from the beginning placed between the light and the dark aspects of the magical and knows how to resist diabolical nature, even when confronted with the sensual temptation of demonic music.

291   The hermits are both steps on his path and also shadow figures, as is the ferryman in "The Devil with the Three Golden Hairs." They live on this side of the water, but they have the means to communicate with the other world. The "upper floor" (that is, in the head) of the third hermit's cottage, is inhabited by "birds" (symbolizing thoughts and spirit) and the hermit as a sort of "Lord of the Birds." He is described almost as a chthonic deity. Since the house is located deep in the realm of the unconscious, the spiritual possibilities appear in indefinite multiplicity. Here also lives the griffin, a figure we have met before, and which occurs in a number of fairytales, often taking the place of the devil or the chthonic godhead itself. Here he is the last bridge to the center and goal in the magical kingdom. The princess is not only an enchanted snake, but she also lives in the water, in the depths of the unformed. During his three nights of tests the hero withstands the alluring temptations and dissolves – he is dismembered – into the unconscious only soon to come to life again, reassembled by the anima figure who has become a figure of light.

292   Seen from the perspective of the total personality, a conversion has occurred in the unconscious, an uplift, a rising upwards. Ego consciousness in the form of the old king, however, has not yet been included. He evidently believes that orientating oneself completely to the transformed soul image is identical to achieving worldly happiness. This uncomprehending and mistaken identification reflects the weakness of the core personality in that the hero cannot resist the temptation to return to the secular world and betray

his precious inner secret. Thus, a renewed and difficult effort must follow. The way passes through the same stations, so that the hermits here stand formally for the same role taken by the quarrelling giants in "The King of the Golden Mountain." This position within the constellation confirms their interpretation as shadow figures related to the demonic father.[60] As in "The King of the Golden Mountain" the ending symbolizes the restoration of blissful harmony in the whole person, without the ego consciously taking any fruitful part.[61]

293   Noteworthy is that many fairytales, especially those of primitive peoples, describe such a regression of the hero into the realm of the anima as a satisfactory end result of his efforts. This may be the reason that fairytales have been characterized as "dreams of a clan, or a people," that is, as a direct statement of the unconscious, largely ignoring the problem of secular thinking and the striving of the individual.[62] A large part of psychic cultural problems is, however, disregarded in this process and have become historical elements. The real exponent of this problem, the individual person with his and her empirical conscious attitude, is thereby ignored. The fairytale reckons only with the unchanging natural human circumstances, and in this it differs from all consciously shaped religious systems and all mythological-philosophical formulations of psychic problems (such as the Gnostic or alchemical philosophy in Europe, or the Taoist alchemy in China, etc.). For such reasons it is possible that the fairytale ends the career of a hero – as the symbol of the perfect inner human being – after the night sea journey and his exploits in the magical realm of the anima, that is, in the unconscious. The tale extols this retreat[63] to the maternal womb, the return to the ancestral land, as the supreme state of bliss. Especially to those peoples who are exposed to extraordinary hardships of existence in their real life owing to an undeveloped civilization, the fairytale reveals – like a wish-dream – an unconscious wonderland, in which the individual can forget his or her distress.[64]

294   Still, there are many fairytales in which the ego's relationship to the secular framework is respected, insofar as the ego is the psychic element, which, as a hostile rational, leaves the subtle wonderworld of unconscious secrets and threatens it unwittingly or, with the right serving attitude, indirectly

---

[60] See the parallel "The Jew and the Padlock" in which the "Jew" plays the role of the devil. There, also giants are encountered along the second journey, the first is the "The Lord of the Animals," the second and the third want to kill the hero, but are appeased and turn helpful.

[61] This interpretation parallels that of the conclusion of "The Poor Miller's Boy and the Cat" where the old miller indeed acquires his longed-for horse, but only partakes very briefly of the good luck of his youngest son and the cat princess.

[62] [For more discussion of this point, see M.-L. v. Franz, *Interpretation of Fairytales*, New York 1970 p. II, 2.]

[63] [The German word here *Wiedereinkehren* carries the meaning of "going (or returning) into a state of inner contemplation or reflection."]

[64] Precisely due to this "regressive" tendency, some teachers object to the telling of fairytales believing that they will mollycoddle the children, make them dreamy, and unable to cope with the harshness of life.

participates in the blessings of the heroic journey. Thus, the aging king in "The Three Feathers" receives his sought-after carpet, and one can imagine how he partakes of the young couple's happiness. Even the old miller in "The Poor Miller's Boy and the Cat" receives the best horse that he ever could want, even though the young pair, after a short glamorous appearance, retire to "their" (the cat-anima's) realm. This represents just a short flash, a realization of that which was going on in the deepest unconscious. Tragically, on the other hand, is the decision by the king in "The Devil with the Three Golden Hairs" who in his greediness wants to copy what the hero has accomplished. He becomes hopelessly attached to the unconscious, and turns into a ghostly shadow.[65] Thus, the glorified apotheosis of the hero in the magical realm has, like everything else, a double aspect. What is a gain there can, on the other hand, be seen from the conscious side as a loss or even death. It is rare that a fairytale indicates a way in which the obligations of the human towards both this world *and* the other world can be harmoniously combined.

---

[65] See Jung on the profound consequences that can follow being engulfed by an inner vision: "Many fathomless transformations of personality, like sudden conversions and other far-reaching changes of mind . . . can cause such a high degree of inflation that the entire personality is disintegrated." (C.G. Jung, CW 7, *Two Essays in Analytical Psychology* ¶233.)

Chapter 6
Stupid Ivanko

²⁹⁵ One fairytale that describes the heroic career as a complete regression into the unconscious, and gives the impression of being a somewhat farcical journey into the land of milk and honey, is a Russian fairytale, "Stupid Ivanko."

²⁹⁶   There was once a father who had three sons. Two of them were sensible and the third one was a simpleton. The more intelligent sons were his favorite. The third was just called "stupid Ivanko" and spent most of the day sitting on his oven. One day the father went to market with his two smart sons and ordered Ivanko to stay at home. If everything was in order when they returned, he would get a red shirt. As soon as the father and brothers left, Ivanko's sisters-in-law ordered him to go and fetch water. But as everyone knows, "the dumb one always has the luck!" Along with the water, Ivanko scooped up a golden fish. The fish pleaded that it be set free and promised that it would later be of great help to Ivanko. "You only have to say 'By the command of the little fish, by my own request, I wish that such-and-such happens.'" The next day, Ivanko's sisters-in-law sent him out to gather firewood in the forest. Upon "his own wish" and "the little fish's command," the sled drove into the woods without even a horse having been hitched. Ivanko asked and the firewood stacked itself up on the sled without Ivanko doing anything. On his return trip, he had to go through the marketplace. It was very crowded with people all over, but Ivanko did not go right or left, he just drove straight through. The people ran out of the way, astounded at this sled that went by itself without horses. They wanted to grab him, but Ivanko was gone again in a flash. This angered the people all the more, and the next day they set out to find him. Sure enough, there he was in his hut sitting on his oven, laughing. They accused him of having run over and squashed many people at the marketplace with his heavily-laden sled. He cried out, "No! I did not do that!" But they were relentless. Ivanko finally called out, "By the command of little fish, by my own request, bring on the fire hooks and drive these people out of my hut!"

Immediately fishhooks appeared and thrashed the people, driving them out the doors and windows as fast as they could escape.

297   The townspeople put their accusations on paper and sent it to the tsar: there was a crazy man in a hut who knew all the tricks of magic and whom they could not bring to justice. The tsar read the grievance and commanded that they should bring Ivanko to him with the help of a sack full of sweetmeats. When they found Ivanko and offered him the bag of confectionery, he let them in and quickly ate all the sweets in the sack. But when they said, now come with us to the tsar, he answered, "Without my oven, I am going nowhere!" Again the townspeople wrote up what happened and went to the tsar with Ivanko's answer. The tsar considered the situation and declared that Ivanko could come to him with his oven. With the help of the little fish, Ivanko drove on his oven to the tsar. Once at the tsar's palace, Ivanko was adamant that only riding upon his oven would he go up to his room. The tsar was at a loss what to do with this impossible Ivanko and finally let him ride up to his room on his oven. Everything and everybody had to be brought up to him and it was mostly the sweets of the tsar that Ivanko wanted. How much candy and sweet things he ate, could never be counted! The tsar's daughter also went up to see Ivanko, fell in love with him, and wanted to marry him. In spite of the tsar's fury at hearing this, the princess jumped up on the oven with Ivanko. And no one could bring her down. There was nothing that could be done and the tsar had to allow his daughter to marry Ivanko. But as soon as they had become a couple, the oven disappeared.

298   The tsar ordered that a great barrel be made. When it was finished, he himself stuffed his daughter and Ivanko inside, had the barrel shut tight, and threw it into the sea. For three years the pair drifted willy-nilly on the ocean and then they were washed up on a beach. With the help of the little fish, Ivanko made the barrel fall apart, and they climbed up on the shore. There was nobody around, it was beautiful, like in Paradise. Ivanko wished a wonderful palace be built that was even more magnificent than that of the tsar. In this splendid castle he lived with his wife. The animals and the birds brought them food and drink and the bees made sweets for them with their honey.[1]

299   The beginning of this tale is reminiscent of "The Fisherman and His Wife." The simpleton, the youngest son, gains access to the creative resources of the

---

[1] [Translated from the authors' summary referring to the German translation of the original Russian. A. v. Löwis of Menar, *Russische Volksmärchen*, Jena 1921 pp. 43–48.

unconscious. He wins all his good fortune not by performance but by favorable circumstance. But, like the fishermen, he becomes inflated and arrogant. In his inflation he willfully harms his fellow man, who never understood him but neither did they do anything for which they should be guilty. The whole story portrays an undeveloped function becoming overly powerful in its shadow aspect. This aspect could become so strong because the Self stands behind it with its vibrant, fascinating values. Here the hero is completely negative because he turns to the wrong side: to the outer, instead of taking the journey inward. Thus, he shows only the early infantile aspect of the destined personality. This can be seen in that he only wants to sit on his oven and eat sweets. The oven is a mother symbol,[2] and also the sweets point to the maternal bond (see "Hansel and Gretel"). Of similar importance as the oven is the self-propelling sled. This corresponds to the carriage, which is also a symbol of the feminine. It symbolizes the supporting and moving forces that the little golden fish, the Self, gives the shadow hero in a completely unconscious form. The stove also carries the hero and at the same time offers him warmth and heat. But the hero just sits on it, totally passive. He remains bound to the unconscious, the mother.

300   The importance of the wonder-carriage is illustrated by another Russian fairytale, "The Miracle Sleigh."

301   There once were six children of a merchant who, putting their few kopecks together, purchased a miracle sleigh with golden runners. This wonderful sled traveled without horse and whip. They wanted to take the sleigh into the woods to the evil Baba Yaga. But, as if on its own, the sleigh took off against their will and whisked them into the forest. Soon they came upon the hut of the Baba Yaga with its chicken legs and guarded by a grey wolf. Immediately, Baba Yaga also appeared and took five of the crying children into her hut. Only the sixth, little Ilya, whose head did not even stick up above the snow, did she overlook. And this little thing scared the big grey wolf and even frightened away the black cat Vaska who was guarding the children

---

[2] Frau Holle in "Mother Holle," has an oven, which the heroine must tend, and the witch in "Hansel and Gretel," is destroyed in her own oven in which she wanted to stuff the children. See W. Laiblin, "Urbild," *Märchenforschung und Tiefenpsychologie*, Darmstadt 1936 pp. 84, 87, 88:

> The oven, the *womb* in its most real meaning, emerges from other contexts, of which Otto Schmidt in an essay reports humorously, "The womb was considered like an oven, from which little children were drawn. Someone once reported that a few days earlier a Swabian peasant held out his two-day-old boy with the words, 'Fresh from the baking oven!' Another example is when we experience pure joy when we suddenly understood the full meaning of the term, which one gets hit with three times every day on the head when it is said (in Swabian and Swiss-German), 'You are not baked enough!' [meaning in English something like: "Born yesterday, you have not yet understood."].

See also C.G. Jung, CW 5, *Symbols of Transformation* ¶245 and C.G. Jung, CW 9i, *The Archetypes and the Collective Unconscious* ¶156.

in the hut, and then freed his brothers and sisters. Once again on the miracle sled they dashed home, just as they had come. It flew like a whirlwind through the dark forest, across the wide fields, along the river, and over the bridge – all by itself, with neither horses nor whip. Soon houses appeared, and the village came upon them and the sleigh stopped dead in the middle of the big square. All six children stepped out and went into their home, greeted their parents, drank some hot tea, and were soon fast and deep asleep. Outside the moon rose in the sky and looked down in amazement at the empty miracle sleigh. The wind whistled through the streets and blew the sled away. And no one has ever seen it since."[3]

302   The carriage symbolizes the descent into the unconscious on the path of a small child's imagination. The dreamlike nature of the whole experience is clear from the tale. But it is no coincidence that the children go to Baba Yaga. This episode is equivalent to the German fairytale episode of the well-known Grimm's tale "Hansel and Gretel" and represents the infantile stage of dealing with the Terrible Mother.

303   From the contents of this tale we can make deductions about the maternal role of the oven and the sleigh in the story of Ivanko. He also makes a regression into the realm of the mother. The previous process takes place, as it were, exclusively in the region of the soul, relatively unnoticed by the empirical consciousness, in that the undeveloped function simply exploits the words of the Self, and thus associates itself with the power of the Self. Thus, it acquires potency in the secular world, which makes the rational consciousness aware of the phenomenon. The *auseinandersetzung* with the tsar brings a confrontation with the secular consciousness, embodied this time not by the father, but by the ruling collective attitude.[4] The tsar even deigns to allow Ivanko to be served sitting on his stove because he suspects the power that lies behind him. But his daughter becomes fascinated and overcome by the powers of Ivanko. This means that the collective goal-oriented thinking and also the female-unconscious forces both flow to the higher personality that is still veiled in its shadow aspect. As a result, the oven disappears because the anima replaces the mother. The bond with the anima, which is otherwise the aim of the hero's journey, is here realized through natural attraction without any effort on the hero's part. Thus it holds no particular value for the total personality and mirrors the unclarified close relation between the shadow and

---

[3] [Translated from the authors' summary of the German translation of the original Russian, A. Loepfe, *Russische*, Olten 1941 pp. 130–131.]
[4] About this doubling see also "Tritill, Litill, and the Birds."

anima that often occurs at the beginning of fairytales.⁵ A supremacy of the unconscious arises gradually through the completely undifferentiated union of the shadow, the little fish (as the Self), and the anima, resulting in a concentration of powers.⁶ Because the infantile and shadowy features outweigh the positive aspects, this combination is subsequently rejected in toto by the tsar, who represents the attitude of secular consciousness. He puts the couple together in a barrel and throws it into the sea, that is, back into the unconscious. The barrel (like the sleigh, carriage, and the oven) is a maternal-female symbol. The abandonment of the young hero, alone or with his mother, in the barrel is a common motif in legends, about which Rank has written extensively.⁷ It is usually the initial motif of a heroic career, whereas in the present tale it appears towards the end and needs, therefore, to be assessed differently, namely as a regression. Ivanko begins, apparently, a great journey, but then he does not return. Rather he remains stuck on a paradise island. He is cut off from the secular world and encapsulated in the unconscious world, coddled and free in the realm of wishful thinking. From the point of view of this world, the fact that he never returns and does not partake of life, signifies that essentially nothing comes out of his island experience. Due to the overwhelming attraction of psychic imagery,⁸ the core personality is lost to the unconscious. The weakness manifests itself in Ivanko's inactive laziness, on the one hand, and in his position of helpless protest, on the other hand, and finally also in the predominance throughout of the mother symbolism, which emphasizes regression, such as crouching on the stove, eating candy, the island of milk and honey etc. These tendencies are also clearly shown in the German versions of this tale, which slide over into the farcical and bring out the childlike and playful elements of the dream world.

304   Of many parallel tales, here is a Low German variant called "Fuldôwat." The following is a summary.⁹

305   Once there was a mother who had such a lazy son that she called him Fuldôwat ["Ne'er-do-well," lit., "Lazy one do something!"]. Once, when he fetched and poured out a bucket of water, there remained a small

⁵ Remember the couple, Tapairu and her companion, at their initial state in the fountain in "Tapairu, the Beauty from the Land of the Fairies" (See Volume 1 of the work, p. 449).
⁶ This state is underscored, even if only in a distant and assonant way, in the Finnish tale "The Living Kantele" in which the anima first appears as a squirrel that the simpleton does not shoot and because of this turns into a wish-fulfilling beautiful woman.
⁷ See O. Rank, *Myth of the Birth*, Baltimore 2004 (2004). See also C.G. Jung, CW 5, *Symbols of Transformation* ¶311ff, ¶405.
⁸ See C.G. Jung, CW 7, *Two Essays in Analytical Psychology* ¶233f on the psychological inflation caused by such an attraction, which is based on a weakness of the personality relative to the autonomy of unconscious contents.
⁹ [Used here without the humorous linguistic nuances of the Low German original. This fairytale and the next, "The Child with the Golden Apple," appeared as footnotes in Von Franz's original text.]

fish at the bottom. The fish spoke and promised to fulfill his every wish if he were to let it go again. So the boy put it back in the water. The first thing that happened was that the water remained in the basket. Then the boy wished that the butcher's chopping block take him home. As he passed the castle and the princess teased him, he wished that she be with child. Indeed, soon after she gave birth to a boy.

306   After some time, the King wanted to know who the father was. He gave the child a golden apple and to whomever the child handed the apple, he must be the father. He invited all the fine young princes in the land to come and visit the princess. Surely one of them would be given the apple and to him the king would grant his daughter and later his kingdom. The child refused to present the apple to any of the invited guests. Then Fuldôwat asked to be admitted into the room. The child reached the apple out to Fuldôwat and the court was astounded. The king himself was outraged, but had to carry out his promise. He then had a ship built for the honeymoon, but with two chambers separated by a glass wall. One chamber was for his daughter, the other for Fuldôwat. The princess was to get food, but Fuldôwat none. He would surely soon starve to death and the princess would return alone. So the ship set forth. Now when Fuldôwat became hungry, he just called on the little fish and wished himself the finest foods. When the Princess looked through the glass she saw Fuldôwat eating the most delicious foods. She learnt from him that he could ask for anything he wanted and it would be granted. She then asked that he be allowed to come into her chamber. She also asked that he wish for her the most beautiful clothes, and that he would stop blowing his nose with his fingers. Finally she asked that the ship turn around and sail home. When the ship arrived, the astonished King went aboard and when he opened the door to her chamber, he saw both of them in bed. When he asked how Fuldôwat got there, he learned of Fuldôwat's wishing abilities and now had nothing to say against him. Fuldôwat wished a castle for him and the princess and therein they lived happily from then on. "There they had taught everybody the ropes in a week." And when the King died, Fuldôwat himself became King.[10]

307   See also another German fairytale "The Child With the Golden Apple."

308   There was once a widow who had a simpleton, named Michel, for a son. One day when Michel went to fetch water, he found a pike in his

---

[10] Summarized from W. Wisser, *Plattdeutsche*, Jena 1922 p. 192f.

bucket. The fish asked to be free again, and for his freedom he would fulfill every wish that the boy might have. Michel said, "Well, jump back in the water." And that was just what the pike did. Michel went back home. That evening he thought to test if the pike was telling the truth. He wished that the daughter of the king in the golden and silver royal palace would become pregnant with child that very day before nightfall. Exactly this came to be, just as Michel had wished. The child had a golden apple in his hand. The girl's father, the king, became very upset at this and commanded all the wise men in his land to get together and find out who the father was. By all their powers, the wise men could not find the answer. An old gypsy woman, who was sitting in prison awaiting her death, heard of the plight of the wise men and called on the king. If he were to grant her freedom and as much money as she needed to survive, she would see that the matter found a good end. The king granted her wishes. Whether she continued to steal or not, I do not know, but what is sure is that she advised the king to call on all the bachelors of the land to gather around the child in the castle. Surely the child would throw the apple to his real father and then the king would know what he wanted to know! So the king did as advised.

309 But when all the men had gathered around in a circle around the child, the little boy did not budge. Exasperated, the king called on all princes, dukes, lords, and counts to come, and then again all the ministers and all the merchants of the land to come to his castle, and then the farmers and day-laborers and servants. All went by but the child did not stir. Then in stumbled a boy wearing a tar skirt and a three-pointed hat. Michel's mother had forced him out of the house with violence and had led him all the way to the castle. As soon as the child saw Michel, he threw him the golden apple.

310 Now the child had a father and the princess a husband, but the king went completely red with fury and would have nothing more to do with his daughter, nor his grandchild, and least of all with Michel. He had a glass globe made with a screw so that one could open and close the sphere. He commanded the princess, the boy, and Michel to get in, then he screwed the globe shut and set it out on the waters. The globe drifted out to sea. The princess became sad that she had such a father for she and her child now would have to die in misery. Michel took pity on her and wished that they land on an island. In that moment the glass sphere was standing on the beach, it burst open and all three jumped out healthy and happy. Michel wished a wonderful castle to arise with all that a royal palace needed and in a wink of an

eye, there stood a magnificent palace. Michel wished beautiful clothes both for the princess and himself. Now they looked quite stately together and lived on the island with the child. By-and-by the princess got homesick, she told Michel this, and he wished for a bridge of gold and silver to her father's kingdom. They climbed into a splendid carriage and rode over the bridge to the land of the king. As soon as he saw them arrive in such magnificence and that his daughter was well and happy, his anger melted. Now the pair lived in happiness and love together until their end.[11]

311 Here the link to the secular world is even more clearly established than in the Low German variant.[12] A Russian parallel, "Emelya the Simpleton"[13] includes an especially appealing characteristic: Emelya does not want to leave either the stove or the barrel because there it is warm (as in the womb). After a brief contact with the king on the occasion of the Emelya's wedding, the ending brings about Emelya's rejection of her inheritance, so that the king and Emelya each return to their own kingdom.[14]

312 Incidentally, in the final words of "Stupid Ivanko" the narrator hints at the negative result of remaining in the magical with the lines:

313 I was with them, I drank mead and wine, I ate candy, and I spoke with Ivanko. But when he gave me a shove, I flew and hit my nose on the ground and my head on a poor tree, and this is the end of the story.[15]

314 Suddenly, the narrator himself embodies the secular ego attitude, in that he rudely awakens and notices that he is not entitled to partake in a share of the unconscious. This explains psychologically the widespread form of fairytale endings in which the narrator announces his or her sober awakening and disappointment at not sharing in the happy fate of the hero and heroine.

315 On this Bolte-Polívka write:

Storytellers in Sicily often end the tale with: "And they remained happy and satisfied, but we are left empty-handed." Or, "We stand here barefoot like pack mules, like a bunch of roots, or candlesticks, or fires

---

[11] Summarized from P. Zaunert, *Deutsche Märchen seit Grimm*, Köln 1964 pp. 51–53.
[12] See also the second half of the tales, "Martti," and, "Lazybones, or: Good is Rewarded with Good."
[13] [This version gives the most complete telling of "Stupid Ivanko" explaining where the stove came from and other features.]
[14] See, in contrast, the positive effect of the attachment to the mother in "Dumb Peter" where the hero accomplishes all his deeds with a little hammer, a gift from his mother.
[15] See also the ending to "The Prince and his Servant": "There I was also a guest, I drank mead and ale in haste and it flowed over my moustache. But nothing came into my mouth; one offered us meat of the house, but I remained unfed." See similar endings to other Russian tales such as "The Three Brothers," "Och," "The Tsar's Daughter in the Underground Kingdom," "Father's Daughter and Mother's Daughter" and "Koshchey the Deathless."

that have fizzled out. We just lick our teeth because we have nothing to chew on."[16] Sometimes the narrator concludes by saying that from all the delicious gifts there was nothing left for her, or that she had been thrown out of the festivities because she had made a stupid blunder, or even that on the way home she was robbed of everything she had gathered for herself. In Schleswig (Jutland Peninsula, Germany), it is related: "Seven years and a day they celebrated their marriage; I drank a glass or two, and danced my way back home. Then I stumbled on a stone. Bing! I saw stars and went on my way."[17]

316   In Jutland, the narrator reports that at the wedding he (or she) received bread in a bottle, beer in some cloth, a coat of paper, a hat of butter, and shoes of glass, and when he lost all of these gifts, at a gun salute he jumped on a cannonball and flew away. In French from Brittany:

317   J'étais par là aussi, avec mon bec frais (I was there, with my fresh nose),
       Et comme j'avais faim, je mordis tôt (And as I was hungry, I soon took a bite);
       Mais, un grand diable de cuisinier qui était là (but a big devil of a cook who was there),
       Avec ses sabots à pointe de Saint-Malo (with his pointed boots from Saint-Malo),
       Me donna un coup de pied dans le derrière (gave me a kick in the behind),
       Et me lança sur le haut de la montagne de Bré (and sent me sailing on high to the mountains of Bre),
       Et je suis venu de là jusqu'ici (And from there I came here),
       Pour vous raconter cette histoire (To tell you this tale).[18]

318   . . . In some Spanish fairytales it is often said at the end, "To me they gave shoes of lard that melted on the road home." Or even: "And I got nothing." . . . In Romanian, "I too was there, but since I am lame in one foot, I arrived just when the wedding was already over. With great difficulty I found a bowl with only clear broth. I looked in vain for a bite of meat but found not a morsel. I sipped what was left from a sieve. Just imagine how much I had and how I passed the time!" Greek, "He gave me 300 pounds and when I arrived back home, a dog tore it away and ran off." Russian, " If I was there with them, I

---

[16] This and the rest of the indented text is from J. Bolte and G. Polívka, *Anmerkungen*, Vol. 4, Leipzig 1930 pp. 24–30.
[17] [Original rhymes in dialect, translation approximate.]
[18] See also the ending of the tale, "The City of Roses," "I was there and when someone asked me what I was doing they gave me a kick in the ass such that I landed right here." And the ending to a tale from Raon-l'Etape [northwestern France]: "There were endless large parties and banquets. I remember well since I was the one who removed the dishes. When I dropped one of the plates, the head cook – to teach me that I should be more careful – gave me such a kick in the butt that it left a hole, which I could show you now!" (Notes from E. Tegethoff, *Französische Volksmärchen*, Vol. 2, Jena 1923 p. 328.)

drank mead and wine; it flowed down my beard, but my mouth remained dry."
... "There was such a banquet that the smoke rose to the sky and hung in the clouds. When I left the banquet I looked up to the sky and was taken into the clouds. They carried me away and then I suddenly fell down. You asked for a fairytale and now I have told you one." ... Ukrainian, "They gave me a cart of straw and a horse of wax, the car burned and the horse melted."[19]

319   The ending of the Spanish folktale, "A Tale of Evil Peter," describes the essence of the tale as an intuition or a notion, "This story came in through one door, and went out through another. . . " which means the same as: "It just occurred to me and then I forgot it immediately, without ever again thinking about it."

320   All these formulae express a conscious departure from the wealth of unconscious images so as not to fall prey to their life-alienating aspect. Occasionally the narrator hints at how difficult it is to comprehend the tale, which causes a "headache" as soon as one tries to make sense of it with the rational mind: "As long as I do not cook my millet in a thimble, or stir it with a needle, or spoon it out with a fingernail, just as long will those who have listened to this story not get a headache!"[20] Another tale from the Caucasus

321   "The Bald Goose-Herder" ends with:

> Suffering there, joy here,
> Bran there and flour here.
> I dragged a wagon up the mountain,
> It became itself like a mountain,
> Call me from this life
> Into the eternal.
> Elesah, Melasa.
> A glass hung around my neck,
> May the listener marry the storyteller.[21]

---

[19] J. Bolte and G. Polívka, *Anmerkungen,* Vol. 4, Leipzig 1930 pp. 24–30. Similar endings in "The Dragon from the Rosebush": "They gave me a little doll made of butter, but since it was summer, it melted." See also "Fionn and Lorcán": "From all that I myself got only Fenier socks, paper shoes, and suspenders of sour milk. I found the ford, but the others drowned. I arrived home healthy – thank God!" See also "Páidin O'Dalaigh" – "As for this tale, I did not get it complete. It was only shoes of paper and suspenders of sour milk." Also, "King Dragon," "They were very happy and had many children, and the last time I visited them they gave me a tin sandwich in a sieve. "And "Hans Married" ends: " 'Were you even at the wedding too?' 'Yes, indeed I was there, and in full dress. My hat was of snow; then the sun came out, and it was melted. My coat was of cobwebs, and I had to pass by some thorns which tore it off me. My shoes were of glass, and I trod on a stone and they said 'Klink,' and broke in two,' "(J. and W. Grimm, *Complete Grimm's,* London 1975 p. 388). See also the conclusion of "Seághan's Story" – "They came to the ford, and I had to jump over on stepping stones. They were drowned and I got away unscathed." There are also terse, quick endings such as (among many others) that of "Kari Woodencoat": "Spin, span, spun, Now our tale is done!" (C. Stroebe, *Norwegian Fairy Book,* New York 1922 p. 151. See in general the discussion in J. Bolte and G. Polívka, *Anmerkungen,* Vol. 4, Leipzig 1930 pp. 24–32 and also J. Bolte and L. Mackensen, *Handwörterbuch* Berlin 1930, *Formel* [formula]. We also mention Robert Petsch, *Formelhafte Schlüsse im Volksmärchen,* Weidmann 1900, which was unfortunately not available to us.
[20] From "The Rose of Paradise" in A. Dirr, *Kaukasische Märchen,* Jena 1922 p. 35.
[21] A. Dirr, *Kaukasische Märchen,* Jena 1922 p. 65. [This tale begins with, "It was and it was not, there is nothing better than God. Once upon a time there was a farmer. . . "]

322   The first two lines are a general philosophical reference to the inequality of human destiny, which is to be accepted as fact. The next lines show, however, the effort it takes to tell a fairytale and to drag the "heavy" images from the unconscious into the conscious mind. The following lines hint at the desire for the beyond, the unconscious, which is awakened by hearing the tales. To help separate oneself from this pull, the verse ends with a droll and nonsensical conclusion.

323   To evaluate a fairytale from the point of view of ego consciousness is difficult because the tale hardly concerns itself in any way with the realities of conscious life. Higher value lies probably in those fairytales in which the events are described in a dramatic form and the individual aspects of the archetypes are more differentiated. Curiously, and also in terms of the tale's contents, this often occurs where the figure that represents the empirical consciousness [objective psyche], often the father-king, is more involved in the plot. Another question remains, however, and that is the form of the ending in which the attained goal of a further level of inner human development should be expressed. Fairytales that are formally effective from a structural point of view often end in an apparently more "regressive" state, like the simple fulfillment of a magical fantasy such as a state of bliss or eternal happiness. The intensity of the composition and design of the plot coupled with the natural ability of the individual storytellers and their listeners do not always go hand-in-hand with the particular cultural level. Sometimes a tale told relatively pallidly and colorlessly represents psychologically deep developments, while more colorful tales that are rich in imagery express relatively simple psychological facts. And yet one cannot completely separate the formal structure, composition, and storytelling from the psychological content. Graphic, vivid images and words arise from psychologically appropriate tendencies. A motif expressing significant psychological content usually generates a meaningful symbolic manifestation that brings this content to life in ways that exhaustively differentiate it into all its possible shapes and forms.

324   A review of the previously discussed tales of this section from this perspective, shows that the first "The Three Feathers" is not insignificant both formally and in terms of the psychological content and the level of development reached at the end. In contrast, the tale, "The Poor Miller's Boy and the Cat," contains primitive images and ends unconsciously without creating any permanent connection of the realms. On the other hand, "Tritill, Litill, and the Birds" and "The Half" are both richer in content and psychologically more differentiated. Also "The Devil with the Three Golden Hairs," is formally led to a logical conclusion, but psychologically ends in a tragic conflict between consciousness and unconscious without a completely satisfactory solution. The same applies to the tale "The King of the Golden

Mountain" but here the progress of the plot is not formally so consistent in that towards the end a series of relatively unconnected episodes follow one after the other. Psychologically, the tales obviously do not represent ideal models, but rather the objective psychic realities in typical pictures in which the tragic and unresolved can also be expressed.

Chapter 7
The Virgin Tsar

325   Less unconscious and childishly unreal than "Stupid Ivanko" but also unfolding with many primitive and undifferentiated aspects, is the Russian fairytale "The Virgin Tsar."[1] The ending of this tale, however, allows us to make additional psychological conclusions. The battle with the primordial maternal foundation of the unconscious and its dual aspect, and the representation of the anima experience are drawn in succinct, strong, strokes and thus allow us to sense the soul's significance[2] through form:

326   Once there was a tsar who had three sons, the first one was Feodor Tsarevich, the second Dimitri Tsarevich, and the third one Ivan Tsarevich. One day the tsar gave a memorial feast and addressed his assembled generals and counts: "What do you think, gentlemen? I have three sons: which of them is able to pluck my flowers and to follow in my footsteps?" The eldest son, Feodor Tsarevich, stepped before him and asked: "Dearest Father, give me your blessings and permission to pluck your flowers and follow in your footprints!" The tsar was pleased and let him proceed. He ordered that his best horse be fetched from the stable and given to his eldest. His servants went to the stable and brought out the best horse, saddled and bridled it, and the bold lad rode out onto the open fields. He came to a pillar at a crossroads, and on this pillar it was written, "He who takes the road to the right will get plenty of food, but his horse will remain hungry. He who rides to the left will remain hungry but his horse will be satiated, he who takes the middle way, he will suffer death. Feodor Tsarevich thought hard and then took the right path. He came to a mountain of copper, dismounted from his horse and climbed the mountain. Reaching the top, he wandered all around, but could find nothing more than a copper serpent, which was, however, very

---

[1] [This tale, as "The Virgin Czarina," is extensively interpreted in von Franz, *Animus*, New York 2001 pp. 79–121. Note that this tale is not "The Maiden Tsar" the main fairytale interpreted in the book by Robert Bly and Marion Woodman, titled *The Maiden King: The Reunion of Masculine and Feminine*, Henry Holt and Company, New York 1998.]

[2] [German: *Seelisch-Bedeutsame.*]

beautiful. He put it in his pocket and went back to his kingdom. And he came unto his father, joined him in the secret chambers, and showed him the copper serpent. The tsar grew angry and shouted, "What sort of monster did you bring me here? It will certainly destroy our kingdom!"

327
After this the tsar was very angry for a long time. But then he eventually became more cheerful, and one day as he was walking in the garden, decided to again call for a special feast. It was a great banquet and all got drunk. In the midst of merriment the tsar rose and said: "My lords and generals, dukes and counts! Although my children are all grown up, none of them has yet been able to pluck my flowers nor follow in my footsteps." Then Dimitri Tsarevich, the second son, stepped forward. Bowing to his father, he asked him for his blessing and said: "Honorable Father give me your blessing and permission to pluck your flowers and follow in your footsteps." The tsar was pleased and ordered his best horse be given. Dimitri Tsarevitch came to the crossroads and took the left path, saying "my steed will be fed and then maybe he can help me out of trouble." He came to a great edifice with gold plated columns. A maiden ran up to him, greeted him in a most polite fashion. The tables were richly covered with all sorts of delicious food. The hostess urged him to eat his fill and brought drink and all he desired. When he had finished, she brought him to his room to rest in a luxurious bed. But no sooner had he lain down than she turned the bed upside down, and he flew down to the basement!

328
The tsar waited and waited for his son and when he did not return was sad for a long time. Then he organized another great feast, at which he announced. "What do you think, my lords and generals? Three sons, I have brought up, and no matter how eager and diligent in the service of the kingdom, none of them have yet succeeded in plucking my flowers or following in my footsteps!" Then Ivan Tsarevich rose up and came to his father and asked for his blessing. "Oh, Ivan Tsarevich, son of the tsar! Your brothers are stronger and cleverer than you and what have they brought forth? You would do better to lie near the stove and not worry about strange adventures." But Ivan Tsarevich leapt up and continued, "Dear Father, magnificent Lord! If you grant me permission and give me your blessings, then I will ride forth. If you do not give me your blessings and withhold permission, then I will still ride out!" So the tsar ordered to give him the best horse that remained, so he could ride wherever he wanted to go.

329 Instead of the best horse, Ivan Tsarevitch chose an old mare. He mounted the old mare and sat with his face turned towards the tail. All the men of the court laughed at how the tsar's son rode out in such an awkward and unfitting fashion. As soon as Ivan Tsarevich came out into the open fields he pulled the nag at the tail and hung the skin on a nail. "Here you have her, crows and magpies! God has provided you with a meal!" Then he roared like an animal in the forest and whistled like a dragon. Soon a horse came galloping so that the moist mother earth trembled, flames blazed from its mouth, sparks flew from its nostrils, smoke poured out of its ears, and steam rose in pillars! Fire apples fell from its behind! Ivan Tsarevich took this loyal steed by the reins, stroked it, and suddenly it became so quiet that a lad of three years could have sat on it, and indeed, would even have been able to ride it! Then Ivan Tsarevich went into the great deep cellar that his dear grandfather had given him, and ate and drank his fill. He chose the most beautifully plaited bridle and a Circassian saddle, mounted this on his gallant steed, pulled the straps tight, picked up his sharp sword, rose up on his steed, and rode out into the open fields.

330 And he rode until he came to the same pillar at the crossroads where his two brothers had come passed. He chose the middle path that had written "he who rides down the middle road will suffer death." Ivan Tsarevich began to weep. He pulled himself together and thought, "Neither honor nor glory endorse this brave lad, he will ride into the jaws of death." With powerful bounds he sprang across the open field and drove his good steed onwards. Rivers and lakes passed under the hooves, the horse's mane flowed in a grand arc, his tail swept over the earth! The horse and rider soon came to a green meadow and saw a cottage turning around on legs of a chicken with spindle feet. The young man called out: "Stay still, little hut. Turn your back to the forest and your door towards me!" The hut spun around until its door was right in front of him and then it stood still. The daring lad jumped down from his faithful steed and cried, "I do not want to stay forever, but one night only. I go in and will soon come out again!" And the young hero went into the house, touched the cross, as it was written, and bowed, as was the custom. Inside sat a little old grandmother, poking the fire with her nose she stirred the coals in the oven; with her eyes, she watched over the geese in the field; with her hands, she spun silk threads. "Fie, fie, fie! So far the black raven has never brought back any Russian bones here, but now a living Russian himself stands before my very eyes! How is it with you, child? Did you ride here on your own free will, or by compulsion?" The young man jumped at the

old woman and said, "I will smash your ears together, your asshole will become the stove door! I will grind your brains with my hands until sand flies out of your ass! My dear old one, you should know that you do not question a hero, but serve him food and drink!" The old hag set the table, fed and gave drink to the tsar's son. She prepared a place for him to rest and then asked, "Do you ride here on your own free will or by compulsion?" And he replied, "Willingly, but thrice as much unwillingly. We were three brothers, the first rode out and brought home only a copper serpent from the Copper Mountain. My father, the tsar threw this brother in jail. The second rode out and we know nothing about what happened to him. And then I had to take on the service myself, to pluck his flowers and to follow in his footsteps. Tell me, dear Grandmother, did our father ride far in his time?" "Lie down and sleep, my child. The morning is wiser than the night, the day brings rewards." In the morning the old woman woke the brave young man, gave him food and drink, her own good horse, took him out on the road, and said to him: "My elder sister still lives down the way and she knows more about your business than I."

331 He blasted off on his steed and passed rivers and lakes and came to green fields as the day was drawing to a close. Then he saw a little hut standing in the field. It was perched on one bison's leg and a distaff. "Little hut! Stand still! I do not want to stay for long, only until the night is gone. I am coming inside and I shall come out again too!" The little house stood still with its back to the forest and its front door towards the rider. The young hero jumped down from his loyal steed and entered the hut. There sat a woman, even older than her sister! She was spinning silk threads, stirring the coals in the oven with her nose, and watching over the geese in the field with her eyes. She asked the same question as her sister and Ivan Tsarevitch swore back at her in the same way as before. She gave him food and drink and again they had the same conversation. In the morning she gave him food and drink and her own gallant steed. The horse he had ridden she kept for herself, and mounted upon this one, she accompanied him out onto the open field and said to him, "My elder sister still lives down the way and she knows more about your business than I."

332 Once again the bold lad rode on, ever urging his steed forwards. From mountain to mountain, from hill to hill, rivers and lakes passed under hoof until he came to the house of the third sister. Again he had the same conversation her as with her sisters.

333 Early next morning, the old woman woke him up, gave him her own trusty steed, led him to the road and instructed him, "Ride forth, my

child. Around midday you will come to the kingdom under the sun. There rules a virgin as tsar, she is called the beautiful Marya with the long tresses. Her bed is raised on nine pillars. She sleeps on this resting place until noon. But then you must be quick and jump straight over the walls of the city. In the garden there stands a young apple tree and nearby lies the water of both life and death. For this reason did your father once ride here. Fill two glasses, one with the water of life, and one with the water of death, but first test their power: rip apart a young raven. On the right side of the pool is the water of life, on the left hand the water of death."

334   Ivan Tsarevich rode off and came to the kingdom under the sun, he went into the garden, caught a young raven and tore it into two pieces. He sprinkled it with the water of death and the raven's body grew back together. Then he sprinkled it with the water of life and the raven flew away! Now the young hero wanted to enter the chambers of the Virgin Tsar, Marya the Beautiful, with the long tresses, and observe how she slept until noontime. He wandered through the halls and rooms, and saw how all the young chambermaids slept on their beds. And then he came into the chamber of the beautiful Virgin Marya with the long tresses. The maiden was more beautiful than he had ever imagined. When she drew in her breath, the doors closed; when she let her breath out, the doors opened again. "What does my honor matter!" the young hero said in his heart, "I will give my horse to drink by this virgin." He could see her perfect body right through her nightgown, right through to her heart. He was on fire and wished to fulfill his pleasure. The maiden noticed nothing of what he had in mind. And he lay with her and took his pleasure. Then he went softly and quietly out of the chambers and came to a wide courtyard. There stood his horse and it was very tired. He led it to the well and washed it with fresh water from head to foot. He then gathered the apples of youth from the apple tree, filled his knapsack, drew the water of life and death into two glasses, and rode out of the realm as fast as he could.

335   As he mounted his brave steed and they sped away, he spurred it on, striking its strong thighs and they sprang over the wall of the city. But the horse struck a piece of copper with its left hoof as it jumped over the wall. Suddenly the bells and alarms rang out all over the city. The Virgin Tsar awoke and roused all her company. They all mounted horses swift as with wings and they flew out after the hero. "A thief has trespassed in our kingdom and has watered his horse at my well! He has stolen our apples of youth and the water of life and death!" Ivan Tsarevich rode on, all the way to the old woman. She led out his

faithful steed, the tsar's son jumped down from his exhausted horse, mounted the fresh one and rode away.

336   Now up the road came her niece, the Virgin Tsar. The old woman came out of her hut and offered her tea and coffee, and bade her visit awhile. "Oh, Auntie, I have not the time to rest! Did you not see an idiot ride past here?" "Ah, my dear child, he will not escape from you, he only rides on a hobby-horse. Come and stay with me for a little while as my dear guest!" As they were entertaining themselves, the tsar's son spurred his steed onwards and came to the second old woman. She exchanged the tired horse for his loyal steed, and bade him to immediately ride onwards.

337   When the Virgin Tsar arrived, the second witch had a similar story as her sister. She related that the simpleton's horse was already stumbling. The third old woman gave Ivan Tsarevich his own horse back and told the Virgin Tsar that the idiot's horse is only fur and bones. Meanwhile Ivan Tsarevich rode on and came to the pillar at the crossroads upon which the inscription was written. He thought to himself, "Have I not won glory as a brave hero? I have made my way on unknown paths, I have fulfilled the wishes of my dear father. Now I will go and seek my brother, Dmitri Tsarevich!" He took the left path and came upon a green meadow and saw an enormous house and headed for it. He rode through the gate, reigned his horse, and gave him fresh white millet grains. The horse of his brother immediately recognized the newcomer and neighed wildly with all its might. The hero strode to the elegant columns and climbed up the golden staircase. There a marvelously beautiful woman came toward him, greeted him warmly, and invited him to her chambers, took him to a table, gave him food and drink, and treated him with all kinds of delicacies. When she had fed him, she showed him to a fine bed where he could rest. She wanted Ivan Tsarevich to lie on the side nearest the wall, but the lad demanded that she herself instead should lie there. For a long time they argued over who should lie where. Then Ivan Tsarevich grabbed her around the waist and threw her against the wall. The revolving bed tipped over and the woman flew down into the deep cellar! He heard the cries of those who had fallen down and were imprisoned there. "God has given us a new companion!" Ivan Tsarevich yelled back, "Tear her into pieces, for she was your destruction!" The bold boys grabbed her, one tore off a hand, the other a foot, the third her head! Then Ivan Tsarevich let a rope down to them and pulled the adventurous young men back up to their freedom. When he saw his brother Dimitri, he seized him by his white hands, pressed him to his golden chest, kissed

him on his sweet lips, and called him his dear brother Dimitri Tsarevich. He then gave his brother food and drink, and they rode back towards their father's castle.

338 But when they came out to the open country, Ivan Tsarevich was overcome by a deep, irresistible sleepiness. Nine days and nine nights had he ridden without sleeping, without eating, and without drinking. They pitched their tents and took care to rest awhile. Ivan Tsarevich fell into a deep sleep. On the third day, Dimitri Tsarevich took the apples of youth and the water of life together from his brother's knapsack and rode off into the kingdom. When Ivan Tsarevich awoke, there was nothing of his possessions to be seen! He quickly saddled up and rode to the edge of the kingdom. There he removed his Circassian saddle and the plaited reins and said to his horse, "Grey-brown one! Run to the fields to rest! I shall not need you for a while!" Ivan Tsarevich went into the town on foot and wandered around, staying at the inns with the laborers and visiting the taverns like the idlers and lay bouts of the city. Meanwhile, with great honors the tsar welcomed Dimitri Tsarevich and commanded that there should be revelry and dancing. Quickly told is slowly lived; after these events three years passed. Then the Virgin Tsar came in the middle of the night, and at the first hour commenced to bombard the tsar's city with cannons and guns. She demanded the surrender of the guilty one. The tsar did not know what to do: who was the criminal that he should deliver? So he assembled his ministers and said: "My dear advisors and boyars! Let us take counsel if we should answer the Tsarina's wishes and deliver up a criminal."

339 "Merciful Tsar!" answered his assembled ministers, "If you so wish it, then we can advise you: did not Feodor Tsarevich make mischief in distant lands? Has he not perhaps committed some crime in a foreign kingdom?" And they brought Feodor Tsarevich out of prison and sent him out to the ship. The beautiful Marya with the long tresses saw him coming, and ordered the gangway laid and had it covered with a red carpet. Then two wonderfully beautiful little boys ran up and called, "Dear mother, dear mother, is our father coming?" "No, my little children," she said, "That is not your dear father, but your eldest uncle who comes. Seize him and stretch him out on the deck. Cut three scars on his thighs and three scars on his back. He should not meddle in foreign affairs!"

340 And again she bombarded the tsar's city night and day with her canons and muskets. This time they sent Dimitri Tsarevich to the tsarina's ship but everything happened as before. The Virgin Tsar then

opened fire and bombarded the town with her cannons and muskets. Again she demanded the surrender of the real guilty one.

341   And again the tsar assembled his counselors. "What do you think, my lords? Who among us has committed the crime? Advise me!" One of them dared to be brave and answer the tsar. "Your Imperial Highness! It is your third son who is to blame!" He spoke further, "Vanshka,[3] stay-at-home, the stove-sitter, is also a son of the tsar. It may not be seemly to tell you, but he hangs around in taverns and butteries and spreads lies all around." The tsar demanded, "Find him at once and bring him here! Maybe he has committed the crime!"

342   They searched for Vanshka in all the pubs and taverns throughout the city. They found him, the tsar's son, and called him to come to the tsar and commanded him to look into his father's face.

343   His father demanded that Ivan Tsarevitch take the blame he deserved. Vanshka went immediately to the ship, but not by the cleanest way, rather through dirt and rubbish. No one commented. The waiting tsarina again let down the gangway and covered it with a red carpet as before. The two boys came running, and cried out, "Dear mother, dear mother, does not our father come?" Then said the Virgin Tsarina, "Dear children! Take him by his white hands and embrace his golden chest, because your true dear father has come!" And the beautiful Marya with the long tresses took his hands so white and named him her chosen husband.

344   "By the seeds that you have sown, I will enter into holy marriage with you." And they began to celebrate. The tsar invited them to a feast with great honor. Ivan Tsarevich told of all his deeds and what had befallen him. And he asked his father for his blessing, which is unshakeable through all eternity, to marry the Virgin Tsar according to the law of the land. "Because my strength and my wisdom were rest enough, I reached the water of life and death and the apples of youth, and now you, our dear father, shall become younger through them, and may God grant you many years of health! And now I ask you for permission to go with the Virgin Tsar into the kingdom under the sun, because I do not wish to sit on a throne in our realm." And he went away into the kingdom under the sun, and lived there happily and joyfully, and wished himself, his tsarina, and their children long-lasting peace.

345   Now I have told this story, just as I heard it.[4]

---

[3] [Vanshka is a form of endearment for Ivan; also Ivanka; Ivanshka.]
[4] [Translated from *Die Jungfrau Zar*, August von Löwis of Menar (ed.), *Russische Volksmärchen*, (*MdW* Jena 1921 pp. 236–251, referring to the English translation by E.C. Elstob and R. Barber, A. v. Löwis of

346 The tsar wants to send his sons to the realm of the past and the ancestors, a realm which also contains the seeds of a future rejuvenation. Particularly telling is the phrase, "Which of you is able to pluck my flowers [that is, gather my laurels] and follow in my footsteps?" Also the Russian arch-witch, Baba Yaga, reveals that the father did indeed "pass this way," that is, he made the journey.[5] "To know *the footprints* that lead to the path of the gods is. . . a great wisdom and a deep mystery."[6]

347 In general, flowers signify feelings, and for a man, his relationship to the feminine. The Garden of Paradise, the land of the blessed, is full of flowers and therefore they belong to the world beyond. Individually, flowers represent a mandala and are, therefore, symbols of the Self. To "follow in the footsteps of the father" and "to pluck his flowers" mean, therefore, to investigate the unconscious roots of the empirical ego,[7] whereas this irrational, fully blooming other-world (the beyond), that is, the world of the feminine, is – as is clearly apparent from the tsar's formulation – only accessible through feeling and imagination. To travel on this "path to the gods" in a new sense, the sense of final maturation of the total personality, is not the job of the prevailing conscious mind. At first the idea appears strange that the same path leading to worldly awareness, which gradually evolves in adulthood, should be travelled once again – repeating the same footsteps – since this development leads, apparently, away from the unconscious into the world, the realm of collective views. Yet they basically lead to the *auseinandersetzung* with the same powers, the same ecstatic rapture, and to the same goal as Ivan Tsarevich's journey into the unconscious, only in the secular world. By experiencing the archetypes in reality – in their morphogenesis in matter, the material world – consciousness develops into a principle that then remains dominant until, having become too one-sided, it requires a new orientation in midlife, a different – reversed – perspective. Since the conscious mind is focused exclusively on outward goals, "life" lies behind it, the highest point has been reached, the culmination surpassed. The former point of departure before the conscious conquest of the world, the unconscious home, becomes the new goal, and the human being must recognize that just those instinctual drives that supported and hindered him in the battle of life, are powers of the unconscious world. Only that function that is averted from this world, and is

---

Menar, *Russian Folktales*, London 1971 pp. 119–32. The original Russian source is the journal *Živaja Starina*, VII, p. 113-120. Collected in the region of Za-Onež'je, Olonets, Republic of Karelia.

[5] On the magic power of footprints see Bächtold-Stäubli under *Fußspur* [footprint].

[6] H. Güntert, *Weltkönig*, Halle a. S. 1923 p. 298, see also *ibid*, pp. 297–301, on the footprints of Vishnu and the secret way to the Land of the Dead. "So it is said of Varuna . . . Although they knew them, the wise did not reveal the secrets of the footprints." See *ibid* on the gods gaining immortality through "secret footprints."

[7] See Jung "It is easy to understand why it is his father who leads the dreamer to the source of life, since he is the natural source of the latter's life. We could say that the father represents the country or the soil from which life sprang." (C.G. Jung, CW 12, *Psychology and Alchemy* ¶159.)

considered undeveloped from the point of view of the conscious mind, has direct access to the magical world. In this and other fairytales, this function is portrayed by the youngest sibling, for whom the secret of life lies "ahead."

348   In our present tale, the conscious mind initially has lost its relationship to the unconscious world, and thus is unable to believe in the ability of the despised youngest son. The fact that the Tsar supposedly once himself completed the journey implies the conclusion that the conscious world built up in the first half of life, which later stands as the "secular realm," opposed to the unconscious, represents a mirror image of the magical realm.[8] In principle, there is only *one* path, *one* big battle, and *one* goal, that is, *one* archetype of the course of life. The hero is thus the primordial image of the human being aspiring to become complete, who moves through the whole process. He is the image of the youthful person and the inner child who remains forever young and is always open to new encounters. This difficult to comprehend mirror image relationship between the secular and magical realm will be observed frequently in the course of our investigation.[9]

349   Here this theme is only slightly hinted at in the young's taking the same journey as his father. And yet his father was not able to repeat it, because suddenly the goals lay there, just where he did not expect them.[10]

350   At the end of the tale, Ivan Tsarevith tells his father that he (that is, his father) will become younger through the apples of youth and the water of life, so it can be assumed that the old tsar needed these, like the old king needed the carpet in "The Three Feathers" and the miller needed the horse in "The Poor Miller's Boy and the Cat." Through the inner return flow of the unconscious stream of life he had lost connection to it, to the anima, to his soul, and the task he presented to his sons is not only an invitation to a competition, but an inner necessity.

351   As in other fairytales presented here, the three sons successively embark on a journey on which the two elder sons fail to reach the goal. Psychologically, the two other sons represent the auxiliary functions and are differentiated from each other. The three sons together with the tsar make up the complete quaternity of the psychic personality. This is also expressed abstractly in the

---

[8] See C.G. Jung, CW 11, *Psychology and Religion* ¶391 and on the reversal of values C.G. Jung, CW 12, *Psychology and Alchemy* ¶224–225.
[9] See also the commentary on *I Ching*:
    The ultimate meaning of the world – fate, the world as it is, how it has come to be so through creative decision *ming* – can be apprehended by going down to the ultimate sources in the world of outer experience (nature) and of inner experience (mind, psyche). Both paths lead to the same goal. (Wilhelm/Baynes, *I Ching*, Princeton, 1967 pp. 263–264. [This rendering is augmented by words from the German version (in parentheses).]
[10] On this theme see also "Youth Without Age and Life Without Death" where the father was ultimately the cause of the hero's taking on the journey to the anima because he believed that he could manipulate the powers of life to fulfill his own purposes.

image of the inscribed pillar and the crossroads, which represents a mandala and is a symbol of the Self. This is illustrated in the following diagram:

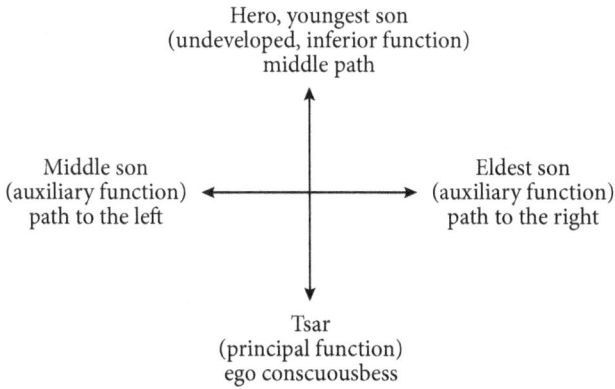

```
                    Hero, youngest son
                (undeveloped, inferior function)
                        middle path
                             ▲
                             |
  Middle son                 |                    Eldest son
(auxiliary function) ◄────────┼────────►      (auxiliary function)
  path to the left            |                   path to the right
                             |
                             ▼
                           Tsar
                   (principal function)
                    ego conscuousbess
```

352   In folk superstition the crossroads is a place where ghosts spook, as it is considered as the hub, the middle point of the world; the place of decisions.[11] The tsar, who represents secular consciousness, stands on that very same vertical line on which the youngest moves insofar as he finds himself on the middle path between the right and left, which lead to two completely opposite worlds. This is because the discursive, conscious mind that dominates the first half of life aims at the goal of uniting the primordial opposites (spirit and instinct, good and bad). This, in turn, confirms the image of the reflection. This mundane consciousness moves in only one direction, diametrically opposed to the fourth function. Whenever an internal shift of weight occurs that reverses the flow of conscious life force, in other words, begins to prepare the hero's journey to take the opposite direction, the opposites first fall into a right and a left path, corresponding to a conflict situation. The diametrically opposite path (here the middle road) is then felt to be the way of death. At the same time, this process can also be understood as a shift in the activity of the functions; if the main function has become sterile, then as a rule one of the auxiliary functions becomes active. This is the journey taken by the eldest son, he chooses the road to the right, which leads to the copper mountain.

353   The right is the side of the conscious mind; the first auxiliary function is still relatively close to ego consciousness. The path followed by the eldest son leads his conscious mind to only moderately new values in that he brings a copper snake back from the mountain, in ancient times a symbol of the *nous* or *logos*. The second son, symbolizing the second auxiliary function, goes

---

[11] See C.G. Jung, CW 5, *Symbols of Transformation* ¶401ff ¶577, L. Lévy-Bruhl, *The "Soul" of the Primitive*, New York 1928 p. 259; Bächtold-Stäubli under *Kreuzweg* [crossroad].

down deeper into the unconscious. He apparently follows his feeling and, led by instinctual drives, falls into the whore's cellar.[12] This second auxiliary function is in complete contrast to the first, but does not lead to increased awareness, and thus does not contribute to bringing new life. Ivan Tsarevich penetrates, however, deep into the unconscious realm and provides a wealth of intuitively perceived inner images and possibilities, which are the sought after, living complements of the personality.

354 The opposing positions between the auxiliary functions are here more strongly developed than in other tales. The contrast between being conscious and being in an unconscious state plays a role here, which is otherwise mainly operative between the prevailing dominant conscious attitude and the hero. In this fairytale this often extreme tension between the opposites is relatively low, the tsar is haughty and uncomprehending, but not hostile. When secular consciousness assumes a relatively generous attitude in this way, the main and unavoidable tension of opposites is constellated in the unconscious. The latter in turn assumes the aspect of a natural being that fights itself and at the same time seeks reconciliation within itself. Immediately upon entry into the magical realm, therefore, all the tsar's sons are presented at the crossroads with the decision between right and left, and whoever wants to avoid this, is threatened with death.

355 The cross is a symbol of being torn apart by the conflict of opposites.[13] Accordingly, at the crossroads the knight in his wholeness as animal and human, is not offered any possibility of survival. One or the other must be sacrificed, and – at least apparently – the third way threatens both with death. To the right, the horse will perish, because traditionally the right side is the side of the spiritual, the psyche, the soul, as opposed to instinctual life. The right side is closer to consciousness. In Gnostic speculation, movement of the life force to the left is referred to as "descent down to the creation of the physical world"; movement to the right is regarded as belonging to the "upper region" of immortality.[14] The left belongs to the night and darkness, to the mother; the right to the day and light, the father principle.[15] Left is thus the side farther from consciousness, that is, it is the side of the unconscious.[16]

356 According to this symbolism, the eldest son comes up to a mountain, the middle son gets caught by female tricks and lands in a cellar. Both sons reach the anima, each meets up with one of her aspects: to the eldest she reveals

---

[12] See also another Russian tale "The Soldier" where the path to the right leads to heaven and the path to the left leads to hell.
[13] See H. Silberer, *Problems of Mysticism*, New York 1917 pp. 186, 227, 269.
[14] See H. Leisegang, *Die Gnosis*, Leipzig 1924 pp. 175, 320, 363, G. R. S. Mead, *Fragments*, London 1931 pp. 264, 374ff. On the two paths leading into the ancient underworld, see A. Dieterich, *Eine Mithrasliturgie*, Leipzig and Berlin 1923 p. 192, for more on the symbol of crossroads in ancient thought, see H. Usener, *Dreiheit*, Bonn 1903 pp. 338–342.
[15] See here J. J. Bachofen, *Mutterrecht*, Stuttgart 1861 p. 130.
[16] See C.G. Jung, CW 12, *Psychology and Alchemy* ¶166, ¶225.

herself as a copper serpent, to the middle son, who chooses the path of instinctual drives, she appears as a deceitful whore. Copper is a metal associated with Venus,[17] and, referring to the three stages of copper, silver, and gold that is common in Russian fairytales, the copper is the lowest precursor to gold.[18] The snake can be a double symbol, signifying both the spirit (psyche) and instinctual bodily drives. In antiquity the snake was interpreted both as *logos* (see especially the brass serpent that Moses raised up in the desert (Numbers 21: 9), which is later identified with Christ as the *Logos* (John 3: 14). The snake also has a demonic character. The connection of copper to the snake in this tale is a representation of the hidden spirit in Eros; however, it reveals here not the world-changing power, but a rigid attitude. Choosing the road to the right indicates that the eldest son carries a predefined and in itself contradictory image of the anima, partly set by the rational intellect and partly brought up from the unconscious. The tsar responds to this abstract attitude towards life and aliveness as dangerous and says, "What sort of monster did you bring me? It will certainly destroy our kingdom!" The prince, who chooses the path of a one-sided, exclusively intellectual attitude, must fail when meeting up with the unconscious, he can perceive only the instinctual aspects and conceive of things only in thought-out formulas. To the tsar it is clear that this cannot be a treasure from the realm of the soul, it is not the "flowers" that he once plucked, and accordingly he gets infuriated. He tried to gain a better understanding of the unconscious with his auxiliary mental function that is closest to his ego-consciousness, but he is then superior enough to feel the unfruitfulness of this experiment and the inadequacy of the result. Thus, he initiates another venture and sends out his second son in a renewed attempt to reach the source of lost life.

357   The second son – psychologically the second auxiliary function – takes the path to the left, where he must starve for the sake of his steed. This path is diametrically opposite that of the elder son, it is the way of Eros, of feeling. Interestingly, this way (to the left) is not the most opposed to the hitherto conscious mind, thus we must assume that succumbing to unconscious drives

---

[17] See H. Silberer, *Problems of Mysticism*, New York 1917 p. 118, C.G. Jung, CW 13, *Alchemical Studies* ¶228. Some fairytale collectors (for instance, Crawford (1888) note that the copper mentioned in Finnish fairytales was probably "hardened cooper," that is, bronze with which the prehistoric peoples of Europe were well acquainted.

[18] See, for example, the Russian tale "The Duck Maiden" where an eagle carried the hero to the magical realm and they came upon a pillar of copper. "Twenty-five *versts* from this pillar you will find the Copper City." On the orders of the eagle, the hero asked the eagle's sister, who lived there, for "the copper box with the little copper key." Since she refused him, they flew on to a silver column and then fifty *versts* further to the Silver City. The second sister of the eagle, who resided there, also refused to give "the silver box with the tiny silver key." So they flew on to the Golden City and the favorite sister of the eagle, who gave the hero "the golden box with the little golden key." When the hero opened the box, an even larger golden city rose up.
See also "Little Bag, Fill Yourself," "The Knapsack, the Hat, and the Horn," "The Master Maiden," "Kari Woodencoat," "The Tsar's Daughter in the Underground Kingdom" and "The Stolen Daughters" among others.

appears to be relatively close to consciousness, insofar as these represent an extreme, and the conscious mind can only grasp a one-sided attitude. Accordingly, this function apprehends the unconscious by "either–or," and it is impossible, therefore, for the conscious mind to experience the irrational unknown.[19] The second son is held captive in the basement by the treacherous anima figure who turns the bed over on him. He indulges in the pleasures of the senses and then succumbs to the falsehood and deception of such pleasures. The double aspect reveals itself and he falls, as it were, "head over heels" into the depths. The experiences of the two brothers illustrate the opposites that comprise the magical: mountain and cellar, both of which inhibit further development. While the middle brother is held firmly in the abyss, the elder is thrown into prison by his father.

358   Now the function, which is the most undeveloped as seen by worldly consciousness, appears on the scene in the figure of the youngest son. As so often happens in fairytales, the hero is initially depicted as poor,[20] backwards, and/or generally despised. This is here expressed in characterizing Ivan Tsarevich as being naive, coarse, and primitive. In "The Virgin Tsar" the clearest example of this is where the hero, owing to just these very features, can successfully deal with the double aspect of the figures from the magical realm. Ivan Tsarevich declares that with or without the blessings of his father, he will embark on his search. This is because he embodies that part of the personality that can completely escape the control of the worldly consciousness and its will. He deliberately takes over the role of the fool in that he rides away, facing backwards, on the poorest of all the tsar's horses. The worst horse corresponds, through its inferiority in the profane world, to the inferiority of the rider and, like him, who becomes a hero, it transforms into the wonderful steed of the hero after it passes through death and dismemberment. As long as Ivan Tsarevich is in the profane world, he rides backwards and this means that he, seen as a human, is going through a regression,[21] but that his animal nature, the instincts, go forward. This disunity between horse and rider is abandoned once they leave the secular sphere.

359   The journey of the hero is divided into several (actually seven) stations.[22] At the beginning, still at the border of the magical, Ivan Tsarevich sacrifices

---

[19] [See here Jung, "The discriminating intellect naturally keeps on trying to establish their [i.e., the archetypes] singleness of meaning and thus misses the essential point. . . " C.G. Jung, CW 9i, *The Archetypes and the Collective Unconscious* ¶80.]

[20] Poverty is often a prerequisite for the career as hero, the hero must be empty of all secular values. See, for example, the hero in "Dat Könirik von Mornstêrn" who first squanders his father's farm before he begins his journey.

[21] On walking backwards as a regression into the "mother" see G. Róheim, *Spiegelzauber*, Leipzig and Wien 1919 p. 68, fn. 3.

[22] See C.G. Jung, CW 9i, *The Archetypes and the Collective Unconscious* ¶82, The symbolic process is an experience *in images and of images* Its beginning is almost invariably characterized by one's getting stuck in a blind alley or in some impossible situation; and its goal is, broadly speaking, illumination or higher consciousness, by means of which the initial situation is overcome on a higher level.

his horse. This is an important archetypal action. The horse symbolizes instinctual nature, the animal, the partially tamed and subdued unconscious, that is, human instinctual nature. In its destructive form, it is related to the devil. At the same time, as a "mare" it signifies the maternal.[23] By abandoning the bad horse to the crows, he sacrifices, as it were, the regressive, nonvital, "dragging along," sluggish tendencies of the unconscious longing for [re-] immersion into the primordial maternal ground. This sacrifice is the precondition for the creative act.[24] According to the teaching of the *Upanishads*, the world arises through the sacrifice of the horse.[25] Ivan Tsarevich kills his horse, however, to give up the "world" and to enter into the magical. Since the horse is a symbol of one's vitality, so the hero sacrificed only a weak and lame drive that carried him in the secular world. Ivan Tsarevich's real world is the magical realm, the world of the archetypes. For Ivan, the Hindu idea applies that the secular world is illusion, or Māyā, a creation of the all-enveloping deceptive mother. He sacrifices the bond to this world and by this sacrifice gains the whole creative working power of the unconscious.[26]

360   Through the sacrifice of the animal power, the hero himself attains the power of an animal. Even the words, "he roared like an animal in the forest and whistled like a dragon," suggest that he himself has become an animal. Now a new horse comes running up to him, a symbol of his increased strength.[27] Before the sacrifice, the hero is not in union with his horse; this is

---

[23] See C.G. Jung, CW 5, *Symbols of Transformation* ¶370ff, ¶421, ¶450 fn. 56, C.G. Jung, CW 16, *Practice of Psychotherapy* p. 347f.

[24] On the horse as the devouring mother, see C.G. Jung, CW 5, *Symbols of Transformation* ¶395, ¶658, E. Rousselle, *Dragon and Mare*, Princeton 1970 pp. 113–119, and E. Rousselle, "Lau Dsi," *Eranos*, Zürich 1936 p. 192.

[25] See P. Deussen, *Sixty Upanishads*, Leipzig 1921 pp. 382–384 (*Brihadaranyaka Upanishad*, 1 and 2). Compare also the psychological commentary by C.G. Jung, CW 5, *Symbols of Transformation* ¶657–660. For more on the horse sacrifice, see W. Ruben, *Die Philosophen*, Bern 1947 pp. 51–52.

[26] The Norwegian fairytale, "Anent, the Giant Who Did Not Have His Heart About Him" (see also its Russian parallel, "Koshchey the Deathless"), presents an exact parallel to this process. In that tale, the hero sacrifices his shabby nag to a wolf. Having eaten the horse, the wolf becomes so strong that he carries the hero and advises him on his further journey. In the Turkish fairytale, "The Three Sons of the Padishah," the hero chooses the most wretched horse that later becomes a magical helper. In "Youth Without Age and Life Without Death" the hero also selects a miserable sick horse, which later acquires wings. In this tale there is no "sacrifice," the plot focuses on the knowledge that the horse that is disabled in the profane world is transformed in the magical. The choice itself contains the renunciation of the secular world. On the sacrifice of horses to chthonic deities, see Bächtold-Stäubli under *Pferdeopfer* [horse sacrifice].

[27] The whole process of the sacrifice and appearance of the (new or renewed!) horse is depicted in such terse images that it acquires the ambiguity of a dream image. This is a peculiarity of Russian fairytale language, of which Loepfe writes in his afterword:

> The sentences are for the most part unconnected . . . and instead of clausal linkages, an active verb stands at the beginning of the sentence. For example, in the fairytale, "The Little Room," it is said, *pribezala mysz; widit – krinka* ("come mouse; see jug"), for which, to achieve the same impression [in German] I had to use three times as many words, and yet these impressionistic brief phrasings completely capture the whole experience. The rhyme and assonance are lost in translation, and perhaps overly forced because our German verb . . . does not have the same rhyming capability as the Russian. Another phenomenon is the untranslatable asyndetic double word: "He wanted to eat-drink; he sank into grief-sorrow," etc. (A. Loepfe, *Russische*, Olten 1941 p. 192).

expressed, among other descriptions, in that they face opposite directions. At this moment in his development, his being and vitality appear inferior (the fourth function being archaic and infertile in relation to the secular world). After the sacrifice, the hero and his new steed face in the same direction and form a unit. This finds its clearest expression where the fateful separation at the crossroads is no longer even questioned; without hesitation the hero decides to follow the path to death. He is now carried as a whole by the unconscious and served by its animal forces. He himself transforms into a kind of powerful half-animal.[28] In a Russian fairytale, "Siwko-Burko,"[29] the hero gets a fiery hero horse named Siwko-Burko from his dead father, which helps him to acquire the beautiful Yelena, daughter of the tsar. When the simpleton crawls with his Siwko-Burko from left to right through the princess's ear, he is transformed into a handsome prince (and vice versa). In this respect, the horse also has a maternal meaning; one can interpret this movement as a rebirth out of the mother, that is, the unconscious. Thus, the horse is the source of renewal of the instinctual power of the unconscious psyche.

361   The now ever-increasing momentum carries Ivan Tsarevich down the path of death ever deeper into the unconscious, a widespread aspect of the horse symbol.[30] The fire nature of the horse indicates not only the connection to death but also to the devil (the devil is often portrayed with a cloven hoof).

362   The second station leads Ivan Tsarevich to his grandfather's basement, to his ancestors,[31] the realm of the dead. He knows that he needs the magical help of his ancestors if he wants to follow his father's footsteps. (The hero in the Inuit tale, "Siwko-Burko," acts in much the same way and obtains his fiery wonder horse from the ghost of his grandfather who rises from his grave in

---

[28] The new horse now functions as a creative force, which it symbolizes in mythology. Pegasus stamps his hooves and creates a spring. For Germanic traditions, see M. Ninck, *Wodan*, Jena 1935 p. 134, M. Führer, *Nordgermanische*, München 1938 pp. 49–50. See also Wilhelm/Baynes, *I Ching*, Princeton, 1967 p. 273: "The creative works in the horse, the receptive in the cow."

[29] In German, A. Loepfe, *Russische*, Olten 1941 pp. 79–83. See also the parallel from the Caucasus region, "The Fire Horse."

[30] See Jung:
The horse too is a "tree of death," for instance, in the Middle Ages the bier was called "St. Michael's Horse" and the modern Persian word for coffin means "wooden horse." The horse also plays the role of psychopomp who leads the way to the other world – the souls of the dead are fetched by horsewomen, the Valkyries. Modern Greek songs speak of Charon riding on a horse. (C.G. Jung, CW 5, *Symbols of Transformation* ¶427.)

[31] See Bächtold-Stäubli under *Grossvater* [grandfather]:
The position of the grandfather in the family and its relationship to the grandchild is not only characterized by the fact that the grandson is the reincarnated soul of his grandfather, which leads to many magical customs in primitive peoples . . . but also by concepts about the grandparents that often adhere to mythical imprints as much as the "father" and "mother" on par with other symbolic figures found in religious history. . . According to findings from very primitive stages of civilization, the human totem ancestor is the source of a person's soul. When these ancestors retired from the earth, they left behind reincarnating spirit children. . . The grandfather appears as the representative of these ancient ancestors, the carriers of culture, the whole ancestry in general. . ."

the night. The function of Ivan Tsarevich's grandfather parallels the role of the uncle and ancestors in the Inuit tale, "The Strange Boy," who gave the hero fortifying victuals and talismans for his journey north.[32] These carry remnants of primitive rites of renewal, in which the ancestral spirits played a significant role. As Jung writes:

363   The atavistic identification with the human and animal ancestors can be interpreted psychologically as an integration of the unconscious, a veritable bath of renewal in the life-source where one is again a fish, unconscious as in sleep, intoxication, and death. . . The symbolism of the rites of renewal, if taken seriously, points far beyond the merely archaic and infantile to man's innate psychic disposition, which is the result and deposit of all ancestral life right down to the animal level – hence the ancestor and animal symbolism. The rites are attempts to abolish the separation between the conscious mind and the unconscious, the real source of life, and to bring about a reunion of the individual with the native soil[33] of his inherited, instinctive make-up.[34]

364   Often the trip to the ancestor who possesses the water, or the herbs, of life comprises the main goal of the journey. Gilgamesh goes to Utnapishtim to get the herb of life. Here, the primordial ancestor becomes the eternal timeless image of the human being, a model person; as such also a symbol of the Self.[35] The journey to the ancestors as a renewal rite was encountered as the main theme in the Euahlayi tale, "A Legend of Flowers" and the Aztec tale "How Motecuzhoma Sought the Seven Caves."

365   The Navaho origin myth,[36] with its monumental images, contains similar symbolism. Although a detailed discussion of this awesome vision of the Beyond lies outside the scope of this work, we summarize here a short part, "The Brothers Visit Their Father."[37]

366   Estsánatlehi, the Woman Who Changes (or rejuvenates herself), and Yolkaí Estsán, the White Shell Woman, each gave birth to a boy, the

---

[32] In another Russian tale, "The Three Kingdoms, Copper, Silver, and Golden," the hero goes in search of his kidnapped mother and first meets his aged uncle who helps him further, he goes to the copper kingdom, also populated with snakes and continues onwards until he find the anima figure (Elena the Fair) and then frees his mother.

[33] [Literally *Mutterboden* [mother soil].]

[34] C.G. Jung, CW 12, *Psychology and Alchemy* ¶171–174.

[35] See the Finnish epic "Kalevala" where the hero goes into the belly of a monster that is his ancestor to obtain three magic words. The devouring monster is always a symbol of the unconscious in general. See H. Silberer, *Problems of Mysticism*, New York 1917 p. 314.

[36] [This and the paragraphs narrating the tale were originally in a long footnote.]

[37] [The original text can be found in W. Matthews, *Navajo Legends*, New York 1897. The parts below are summarized, except where put in quotes from ¶293 (p. 105) to ¶322, p. 114).]

two hero-brothers. The "brothers" soon embarked in search of their unknown father, the [carrier of the] sun. After shooting at sacred birds, they followed four tracks on a "sacred path." From there, the boys came upon a hole in the ground with a ladder protruding and smoke rising; it was the skylight of the underground chambers of a very old woman, the Spider Woman. She told them of the four places of danger they would encounter on the way: ". . . rocks that crush the travelers who pass between them, reeds that cut people to pieces, cane cactuses that tear humans to pieces, and boiling sands that will cover whatever moves." She gave them talismans to subdue their enemies, a feather of the alien gods, and a life-feather to preserve their lives. She also gave them a magic song about pollen to sooth the anger of their enemies.

367   The brothers went out and indeed met all four dangers. These dangers turned out to be people, but when the brothers sang their pollen song, they were allowed to pass unharmed.

368   At last they came to the house of the Sun. There stood ominous sentinels: two bears, two serpents, two winds, and two lightnings. Again, singing the pollen songs, they were able to pass unharmed. "The house of the Sun God was built of turquoise; it was square like a Pueblo house, and stood on the shore of a great water." The Sun God found and unwrapped the bundle in which the brothers had been hidden, and threw them first upon great, sharp spikes of white shell that stood in the east; but the boys bounded back, unhurt, from these spikes; for they held their life-feathers tightly all the while. He then threw them in turn on spikes of turquoise in the south, on spikes of abalone shell (yellow- iridescent) in the west, and spikes of black rock in the north. The Sun father did not believe they were really his sons and subjected them to a test in an extremely hot sweat lodge heated with first a white, then a blue, and then a yellow, and finally a black boulder. With the help of the Winds the boys survived and the Sun recognized them as his real sons, but not fully convinced, he tested them once again with deadly tobacco smoke, but having been again forewarned by the Wind, the smoke was sweet to them and did them no harm.

369   At last thoroughly satisfied that they were indeed his sons, he asked the boys what they wanted from him. "Oh, father!" they replied, "the land where we dwell is filled with the *anáye*,[38] great demons who

---

[38] [According to Version A, the monsters or *anáye* were all conceived in the fifth world and born of one woman (a granddaughter of First Woman), who traveled much and rarely stayed at home. According to Version B, the monsters were sent by First Woman, who became wary of mankind. See *ibid.*]

devour the people. . . They have eaten nearly all of our kind; there are few left; already they have sought our lives, and we have run away to escape them. Give us, we beg, the weapons with which we may slay our enemies. Help us to destroy them." Their father, Tsóhanoai, carrier of the Sun, led the boys "to the edge of the world, where the sky and the earth came close together, and beyond which there was no world. Here sixteen wands or poles leaned from the earth to the sky; four of these were of white shell, four of turquoise, four of abalone shell, and four of red stone. A deep stream flowed between them and the poles." The brothers crossed this river upon a rainbow bridge blown by the breath of the Wind. The heroes climbed the red pole, which meant the path of war against the demons, with their father [in some versions, the carrier of the sun rode a horse] who "put on his robe of cloud, and, taking one son under each arm, he rose into the heavens."[39] "They journeyed on until they came to Yágahoka, the sky-hole, which is in the center of the sky. The hole is edged with four smooth, shining cliffs that slope steeply downwards, cliffs of the same materials as the wands by which they had climbed from the earth to the sky. They sat down on the smooth declivities, Tsóhanoai on the west side of the hole, the brothers on the east side. The latter would have slipped down had not the Wind blown up and helped them to hold on." . . . Then according to his promise, their father spread a streak of lightning, made his children stand on it, one on each end, and he shot them down to the top of Tsotsil."[40]

370   The hero's journey into the magical realm leads down a big bend from the earth into a subterranean kingdom, and from there to the edge of the world, to where the sky touches the earth and back down again. The square shape of the turquoise house is an orientation in the four directions, and indeed the number four is accented in this tale (and elsewhere in North American tales). (For example, the four footsteps, four sentry animals, or sentinels, four tests, four spikes, four colors, sixteen pillars, the square hole to the earth). This is related to the fact that this is a solar myth and the sun wheel, the symbol of the sun god, is often shown divided into four quarters. Even the ancient god

---

[39] ["Many versions relate that the bearer of the sun rode a horse, or other pet animal. The Navaho word here employed is *lin*, which means any domesticated or pet animal, but now, especially, a horse. Version A says the animal he rode was made of turquoise and larger than a horse. Such versions have great difficulty in getting the horse up into the sky. Version A makes the sky dip down and touch the earth to let the horse ascend. Of course, the horse is a modern addition to the tale. The Navaho People did not see horses until the sixteenth century. Previous to that time it is not known that any animal was ridden on the western continent." (Note no. 118, *ibid* p. 233.)

[40] Mt. San Mateo, Mt. Taylor. *ibid* pp. 322, 114. ["Version A gives, in addition to Tsotsil, the names of three other hills over which Yéitso appeared. These were: in the east, Sa'akéa'; in the south, Dsilsitsí (Red Mountain); in the west, Tselpainali (Brown Rock Hanging Down). – *ibid*, p. 234.]

Helios is related to the four winds, the four cardinal points, the four seasons, and so forth.[41]

371   [The text now returns to the discussion of Ivan Tsarevich's journey.] Only by being strengthened in the grandfather's basement is Ivan Tsarevich capable of taking on the real hero's journey, because the grandfather is the "great father" and, as such, the archetype of the wise old man, the model for the hero, the ageless Self. For this reason, the old wise one often occurs together with the anima figure, or he is one of the figures that the hero meets on the way to the anima.[42] These two figures symbolize the past and the future, because, as Carus pointed out:

372   [O]nly the conscious mind is aware of the *present*, that is, the determination of a point of reference between past and future. When the present has been attained in the development of the conscious mind, past and future become obscure; in contrast, the present does not exist in the unconscious, but the relationship between past and future is all the deeper and more certain.[43]

373   Carus, again:

All growth, formation, destruction, and further development – *this unconscious development* – reveal a most definite and exact relation between what goes before and what follows, and vice versa, even

---

[41] See H. Leisegang, "Schlange," Zürich 1940 p. 190f. On their journey to their father, the hero brothers gain knowledge of their own origin, their own life roots, and in general an expanded awareness. (W. Matthews *Navajo Legends*, 1897 pp. 215–216 notes that the Navahos have two principal systems associating colors with the cardinal points. East always comes first and is white (or black), then south – blue, west – yellow, and north – black (or white) Of the sixteen posts to which the heroes arrive with their sun father, four are turquoise (= blue = south), four are from abalone shell (= light = yellow = west) (see here the note in W. Krickeberg, *Nordamerika*, Jena 1924 p. 394, relating to the Kwakiutl tale, "Raven and the Salmon"), four from white shell and four from red stone. It is likely that the white pillar denotes in this case the East, and that red – according to W. Krickeberg, *Nordamerika*, Jena 1924 p. 342, indicates war – are here assigned to the north instead of the black. Matthews notes, The Navahos explain the annual progress of the sun by saying that at the winter solstice he climbs on the pole farthest south in rising; that as the season advances he climbs on poles farther and farther north, until at the summer solstice he climbs the pole farthest north; that then he retraces his way, climbing different poles until he reaches the south again. He is supposed to spend about an equal number of days at each pole. (*Ibid* p. 233.)
In this story of the hero brothers with the sun god at the red post (which we associated with the north here), we conclude that the story is a myth of the summer solstice. In psychological terms (transferred from the macrocosm to the microcosm), an event at midlife. This conclusion is confirmed by the content of the story: the father recognizes his unknown (with the earth-begotten) hero sons. See L. Frobenius, *Zeitalter*, Berlin 1904 p. 7, who suggests that the ancient Aztec legend of wandering describes the path of the sun god across the four cardinal points of the world. In "The Virgin Tsar," the quaternary structure of space is divided among four people. One of the oldest sun signs in Babylon was also a sign of the soul and of gold, and of everything that is a maximum of perfection, is a quartered circle, or a circle with a clearly designated center. See D. Bernoulli, *Spiritual,* Princeton 1960 p. 316.
[42] See C.G. Jung, CW 7, *Two Essays in Analytical Psychology* ¶374-381, see also C.G. Jung, CW 13, *Alchemical Studies* ¶218.
[43] (C.G. Carus, *Psyche* (English), New York 1970 p. 27.

though it only proves itself as being in a state of constant flux between past and future without a present. This [unconscious] foresight and remembrance, therefore, must indeed be stronger and more certain than in the conscious sphere.

374   Ivan Tsarevich aligns himself with this unconscious continuity when he drinks wine in his grandfather's basement. He communicates with the spirit of his ancestors, and thus he receives the support of the magical realm.

375   After this fortification, Ivan Tsarevich comes to the pillar at the crossroads, that had led his brothers to their ruin. The decisions of the three brothers mirror three attempts to solve the problem of the opposites. At the end of the tale we know that only the choice that embraces the conflict fully, that is, the [conscious] choice to seek death *between* the opposites, will progress along the chosen path.[44] The tension of the opposites that is represented by the cross is the necessary consequence of becoming conscious, through which the human came to stand between animal and God. For this reason, the Gnostics saw the cross as a symbol representing the suffering of the spirit, or spiritual individual, because of the attachment to the material world. Continuing on this middle path between the opposites requires self-sacrifice and passage through death. Success is only possible if the person gives up the ego and entrusts himself to superordinate powers.[45] Although this sacrifice concerns primarily the secular, worldly consciousness, the hero must nonetheless pass through this stage since he represents the human-personal side of the Self. His sacrifice means that the conscious personality surrenders itself for the sake of its higher development. It is the creative forces that press people to undertake this painful restructuring. As the carrier of this conflict situation, Ivan Tsarevich choses the way that lies behind the life of the Tsar, the path straight ahead. Since this direction leads diametrically away from the secular realm and there is no option to take the paths to the left or right, from the point of view of the person coming from the secular life, it appears to be the road to death. At the same time, however, this path has the significance of being a *middle* path between opposites, and as such, it is a road of life because life runs its course between the opposites.[46] That Ivan Tsarevich makes just

---

[44] The motif of the crossroads is present in many fairytales, but the directions do not always have the same meaning. The main point appears to be that the hero decides to choose the path of death. See "Prince Hassan Pasha," "Djulek Batür," "The Three Hunters," "The Story of the Blind King Who Lived in the Western Lands," "Kitschüw," "The Deeds of the Tsar's Son and His Two Companions" and "The Nightingale Gisar."

[45] See C.G. Jung, CW 11, *Psychology and Religion* ¶849 Going through a death ritual with all its anxieties and terrors was also the beginning of the ancient mystery initiations, which were likely intended to lead to a rebirth of personality. [For a review of recent research on the mystery cults, see H. Bowden *Mystery Cults*, London 2010 p. 40ff.]

[46] See C.G. Jung, CW 6, *Psychological Types* ¶192 and R. Wilhelm, *Secret of the Golden Flower*, London 1962 pp. 11–12 on the Tao.

this decision corresponds to his own sense of existence, for he himself is the appointed mediator. Chinese philosophy knows the unity of the mediator and the way by understanding it as a living being, the Tao.[47] With the choice of the way of death Ivan Tsarevich proves his right to follow in the footsteps of his father. He goes, ready for self-sacrifice, whereas his brothers indulged in their opportunistic fantasies – to their own detriment. Ivan Tsarevich sinks selflessly, however, into the unconscious.

376   Thus he enters the realm of the anima; but she appears to him first in the form of the witch-like mother, because for the childlike state of consciousness, the anima still has this appearance. For this reason, the anima figure in "The Knight With the Sinister Laugh" makes it a condition for marriage that the hero fights with the mother-imago. Similarly, Seághan in "The Great Fool from Cuasan" must overcome the mother in her many shapes before he wins the princess. Baba Yaga's house stands on spindle legs and, when called by one approaching from the profane, she turns to face the intruder. She thus connects the two realms. In the tales "The Frog Princess" and "Born of a Fish" her cottage rotates continuously on its own axis (in the latter tale there are actually three huts, one each of brass, silver, and gold inhabited by three sisters – anima figures!). The constant circling of the primordial mother's hut on chicken or spindle legs (indicating the activity of the Great Mother as a spinner, like Maya, creating the veil of this illusory world) symbolizes the cycles of nature, the spiral of growth and decay.[48] By announcing that he does not want to remain forever in the hut, but only one night, Ivan Tsarevich

---

[47] See here Jung:

> The undiscovered vein within us is a living part of the psyche; classical Chinese philosophy names this interior way the 'Tao' and likens it to a flow of water that moves irresistibly toward its goal. To rest in Tao means fulfillment, wholeness, one's mission done; the beginning, end, and perfect realization of the meaning of existence innate in all things. Personality is Tao. (C.G. Jung, CW 17, *The Development of Personality* ¶323.)

See also:

> The savior is always endowed with magical power who makes the impossible possible. The symbol is the middle way along which the opposites flow together in a new movement, like a watercourse bringing fertility after a long drought. (C.G. Jung, CW 6, *Psychological Types* ¶443).

And:

> The psychological point of departure . . . is an increasing split in the deployment of psychic energy, or libido. One half of the libido is deployed in a Promethean direction, the other half in a the Epimethean. As a result, the vital optimum withdraws more and more from the opposing extremes and seeks a middle way. Since the middle position, as a function of mediation between the opposites, possesses an irrational character and is still unconscious, it appears projected in the form of a mediating God, a Messiah. (*Ibid*).

> Thus, "The cross has also the meaning of a boundary stone between heaven and hell, since it is set up in the center of the cosmos and extends to all sides." (C.G. Jung, CW 11, *Psychology and Religion* ¶136 fn. 26).

[48] See Plato's "Spindle of Necessity," which in *The Republic* (10.614-10.621) lies in the lap of Ananke, the goddess of fate and necessity, and is the cause of all turning. See also the dance of the old fairies in "The Piper and the Púca."

expresses the intention as a true hero to go into the jaws of the monster, the mother's body, not to be swallowed up forever, but to be reborn, of which – by his heroic determination – he is certain. By his intrusion he breaks the course of nature and carries conscious awareness and differentiation into the unconscious.

377   The Baba Yaga guards geese, animals of Nemesis, the goddess of inevitable fate, and she stokes the stove with her nose. Like the hut the oven is an image of the womb and in the coarse language with which Ivan Tsarevich greets her, he equates the Baba Yaga herself with the oven. The long nose, with which she stirs the coals, is a phallic attribute like the "cold cruel tooth" of the witch in "The Knight With the Sinister Laugh" (see Volume 1, page 223). The androgynous Baba Yaga embodies the interplay of opposites in the unconscious, male and female, good and evil, dangerous and helpful at the same time.[49]

378   Ivan Tsarevich, as the conscious personality, is apparently well aware of the immense danger of succumbing forever to the spell of archetypal images, threatening to carry him away and dissolve him in their eternal pointless game of opposites. This wisdom confers upon him superiority and further reveals his vocation as a hero. He confronts the witch with her own naturalistic, even obscene coarseness, and takes the wind out of her sails – deflating her initiative – in that he proves himself as a master of the magical realm.[50] Ivan Tsarevich

---

[49] On the death aspect of Baba Yaga see Volume 1, pp. 263-264. The ox (aurochs)-legs of the other two witch-mothers whom the hero meets later, probably also have a phallic meaning. On the male-female character of the great mother goddess, see Przyluski: "We observe that the Great Goddess has in general a tendency to identify herself with time and death. A specific aspect of the Gorgon is that people who look at her are turned to stone, her gaze brings death. She is often depicted as a woman with a beard. This connection of a female body with the features of masculinity shows beyond doubt that the Gorgon, as the androgynous deities of the East, emerged as a fusion of two figures, male and female." (J. Przyluski, "Mutter-Göttin," *Eranos*, Zürich 1939 p. 45ff).

In fairytales the witch sometimes has horns like the devil. See on this W. Laiblin, "Urbild," *Märchenforschung und Tiefenpsychologie*, Darmstadt 1936 p. 138f. See also the Native North American figure of Snēnē'îq who appears as a gum-chewing old woman, in another tale of the same name as a man, and in still another version, as a demon-woman who drinks the fat of dead people ("The Snēnē'îq," F. Boas, *Bella Coola*, New York 1898 p. 83ff). Therefore, the path leads to a symbol of the Self in the center of the magical kingdom through a meeting with the primordial parents or a figure that complements the central character. In "A Foray into the Underworld" two brothers search for their father. The way leads to the underworld and a blind sorceress Kui whom they kill. After further adventures the hero brothers find the bones of their father tended by another old woman. In "The Three Kingdoms, Copper, Silver, and Golden" the search for the mother who was kidnapped by the wind demon leads first to a helpful old uncle, and then to the anima figure. Also, in "The Strange Boy" the hero meets with helpful ancestors on his journey to the anima.

[50] In the case of Ivan Tsarevich, the hero undertakes his journey on behalf of his father and knows keenly how to serve the maternal principle. As a consequence, he gains the help needed to obtain the treasures of the magical realm. In contrast, a legend from the Fiji Archipelago, "The Story of the Sun-Child," tells how the son of the sun, was called to the task of searching for his father. He succumbs to his own headstrong nature, however, and asks for the wrong gift from the moon (the maternal aspect of the unconscious – as mentioned above – is a typical danger for primitives), and so does not get the precious gift that his father had destined for him, but rather something so fascinates him that he perishes as a result of its magical attraction:

> A chief once hid his exceedingly beautiful daughter because he could find a suitor worthy enough to give her in marriage. But then seeing her bathing and resting on the beach, sun falls in love with her. "He loved her and in the course of time a child was born to her, whose

owes his superiority to the sacrifice of his horse by which he attained his animal power. The witch asks whether he came "of his own accord" (a favorite question by Baba Yaga to visiting heroes) to find out if he is a hero for whom the sacrifice was a success. This is because only the one who goes at least partly voluntarily to meet his fate has a prospect of overcoming the unconscious. The very fact that the hero, as the inferior function in the secular world, carries archaic primitive traits, means that he can stand up to the *auseinandersetzung* with the unconscious.[51] Ivan Tsarevich answers by saying that he rode three times against, and once with, his own will, indicating his whole personality, according to which the tsar and his two brothers went against their will, but he took on the quest as his own decision. He owes the witch's submission to his self-assuredness; in the morning she gives him counsel and even lends him her own faithful horse. Thus, he gains the power of the unconscious that carries him further.[52] With progressive success his inhibition decreases, the stone rolls faster and faster. When he meets the second witch, he answers that he only rides twice against his will, and with the third witch he reports in

name she called Sun-child." The boy grew strong and proud "and given to strike other children, like the son of a great chief." One day he was teased by the village children saying that he was a bastard since he did not know who his father was. In a rage, he asked his mother who his father really was. She told him the truth and then he set out in search of his father. In a boat, he sailed to the east where he was closest to his father in the morning. The sun was already rising and said that he could not stop now. But the boy suggested he hide behind a cloud and find a few moments to talk with him. This his father did and told him of the Moon, the Sun's sister, and the boy's aunt. The sun advised that the boy wait for the moon in the night and ask her for one of two things that she kept in her custody. He should ask for the "Melaia" and not for the "Monuia," or he would get into big trouble. In the evening he sailed up to the moon and asked her in stubborn disobedience for the "Monuia." His aunt, the moon, hesitated and doubted that he really wanted this and not "Melaia." She tried to dissuade him from his obstinate wish. He insisted, however, and she reluctantly gave him the Monuia since she felt she must follow the wishes of her brother. But she warned him not to open the package when he was still sailing, but should wait until he landed again on his home shore. On his way he again disobeyed, overcome by curiosity and opened the package. It was a pearl shell, exceedingly beautiful; not white like the shells in our land, but of a shining red, such as he had never been seen before, yea the like of which no man has since beheld; and his heart was glad as he thought how the boys of his town would envy him when they saw it hanging round his neck. But while he was thus gazing upon it he heard a great rushing and splashing over the waters, and, looking up, he saw a multitude of fishes swimming hastily towards him – great whales, and sharks, and porpoises, and dolphins, and turtle, and every other kind of fish – a vast multitude. And they leaped upon him in their eagerness to get at "Monuia" so that in one moment his canoe sank beneath the waves, and the sharks tore him to pieces, and that was the end of Sun-child.

(Told by Ratu Taliaitupou, Lord of Nayau, Fiji archipelago, Fison, *Tales from Old Fiji*, London 1904 pp. 33–39.)

[51] On the common archaic-primitive and even demonic features of heroic figures, see the Norwegian fairytale, "Aspenclog," in which:

The hero, whose mother was an aspen, killed anyone who dared to cut her down. He hired himself out to the king for the sole reward that if the king had no more work for him, then he could give the king three thumps on the king's back. He tamed two bears, overcame the devil, defeated enemies of the king with a mighty oak, and when the king no longer had any more work for him, he give the king his first thump on the back and this shattered the king into a thousand pieces.

See also the title hero in "Djulek Batür."

[52] See the Great Mother figures who at first are hostile, and then become friendly in "Tsetlwalakame" where the hero, Gyī i, returns eyesight to four blind women (ducks), and they become helpful.

detail, with no mention of an aversion at all. The world with its otherness and its resistance lies ever more distant and its influence has become ineffective. The process now plays out deep in the magical realm and there, in the Beyond, the scorned Ivan Tsarevich gradually transforms into a divine hero.

379   The second and third witches surpass the first in age and size. The encounter with the Great Mother, who is actually a single figure, proceeds here in three rhythms, a trinity, the sacred number. But it finds its fulfillment in the number four with the appearance of the anima. This quaternio is like a mirror image of the Tsar and his three sons but in the unconscious.

380   In the Irish tale "The Great Fool from Cuasan" the hero, Cuasan, also had to defeat two giants and then their mother before he fights for a fourth time to finally win the anima. A similar sequence of stages can be found in the Uzbek tale "The Beautiful Dunye" in which the hero wrestles in succession a red, a white, and finally a black *div* (desert demon) before, in a fourth step, he enters the service of the mother of the *div*, a huge witch. After having performed lowly tasks for a long time (like Hercules for Omphale), she shows him the way to conquer the beautiful Dunya. Fairytales often proceed in a triplet rhythm, after which in the fourth spatio-temporal moment the goal is achieved, represented by a symbol of the Self, or there is a peripety and the cycle begins anew as a new approach to win the elusive "fourth."[53]

381   In this fairytale, the fourth position is explicitly shown as the sought-after center. Ivan Tsarevich experiences everything just as the last of the three old Babas Yaga had predicted. He reaches the "Kingdom Under the Sun," a fortressed town that lies just beneath the zenith, the position of the sun at noon. This expresses the idea not only of a spatial but also a temporal midpoint. The relationship of the magical kingdom to the sun is already hinted at by the designation *golden* in the fairytales "The King of the Golden Mountain" and "The Devil with the Three Golden Hairs." In the latter tale, the devil is equated to the sun-bird phoenix. In general, the sun signifies "enlightenment" consciousness, and also the principle of creativity, the source of life, and the ultimate wholeness of the human being.[54] Already for the Stoic philosophers, the sun was a symbol of the "*mens*" (Latin, mind, reason), the conscious mind. The Greek god Mithras-Helios (sun) was, like Christ, the world creating *logos*.[55]

---

[53] Jung writes, ". . . two heterogeneous systems intersect in the self, standing to one another in a functional relationship that is governed by law and regulated by 'three rhythms.' The self is by definition the center and the circumference of the conscious and the unconscious systems." (C.G. Jung, CW 12, *Psychology and Alchemy* ¶312f). See also *ibid*, ¶312f about the dimensions of space-time.

[54] See C.G. Jung, CW 12, *Psychology and Alchemy* p. 112. On the sun as a source of consciousness, see C.G. Carus, *Psyche*, Pforzheim 1846 pp. 209–210.

[55] H. Leisegang, *Die Gnosis*, Leipzig 1924 p. 250. [See also, C.G. Jung, CW 12, *Psychology and Alchemy* p. 112, "We know also that the early Christians had some difficulty in distinguishing ηλιος ανατ ολης (helios anatolis) the rising sun, from Christ." Also Christmas is celebrated three days after the winter solstice, when the sun definitely begins to return, a new birth of the light-bringer, Christ.]

382   The hero meets the sun at its noon position in the center of the magical kingdom. It corresponds, therefore, rather to a midnight sun, that shines in the land of the dead when it is night on Earth. The image of the midnight sun can be found in the ideas of the ancient mysteries. Thus Apuleius professes, "At midnight I saw the sun shining with a radiant light."[56] Insofar as the Baba Yaga belongs to the kingdom under the sun (the Virgin Tsar is her niece!), it is significant that Gorgon, a terrifying mother figure in Greece, was also a symbol of the night sun.[57] In the English fairytale "Childe Rowland" the experience of the magical sun center in contrast to the daily sun is reported as follows:[58]

383   The boy-child Rowland was once playing ball with his two elder brothers and their sister. Rowland kicked the ball so hard it went over the church. His sister, Burd Ellen, went to fetch it, but never returned. The eldest brother then went to the "Warlock Merlin" to ask where his sister was. Warlock Merlin answered that she "must have been carried off by the fairies, because she went round the church widershins.[59] She is now in the Dark Tower of the King of Elfland; it would take the boldest knight in Christendom to bring her back." The eldest brother begged to go search for his sister and after good advice from Warlock Merlin he left, but never returned. Then the second eldest brother tried, and he too never returned. So then Childe Rowland begged to try. His mother, the good queen, was wont to let him go, but he insisted and she gave him a brand and put a good luck spell on it. Warlock Merlin advised him also, instructing him on one thing to do and one thing not to do. The first, he should cut off the head of everyone he meets until he gets to Burd Ellen with his brand. And that he should not eat a bite, nor drink a drop, no matter how hungry or thirsty as long as he was in Elfland. So Childe Rowland said these things over and over again until he knew them by heart, thanked Warlock Merlin, and went on his way. He went along, and along, and still further along, until he came to the land of the fairies. There he asked a rider, then a cow-herd, and then an old woman in a grey cloak for directions. Each time, after they told him, he cut off their heads with his brand. He went on until he came to a round hill with terrace

---

[56] Apuleius, *Golden Ass*, London 1822 p. 207. See also *Psyche* p. II,210 fn. 1. See also the tale "Kaboi" where the people living in the underworld are illuminated by the sun at night. Cf. for the ancient Aztecs, the land of the dead warriors is called the "House of the Sun" (see "The Three Realms of the Dead" (from Sahagun), and M. Graulich, *Myths*, Norman 1997 p. 122). Cf. the figure of the Hyperborean Apollo in H. Leisegang, *Serpent*, London 1955 pp. 255–256.

[57] See *ibid* p. 246f.

[58] [Here summarized. This was in a footnote in the original.]

[59] A German word. The collector, Jacobs, added here "the opposite way to the sun" as an explanation. The storyteller most likely assumed the listener knew what it meant.]

rings and went around it three times "widershins," against the sun, and said the words that the old woman told him, "Open, door! Open, door! And let me come in!" And the third time the door of the Dark Tower did open, and he went in, and it closed with a click, and Childe Rowland was left in the dark.

384   It was not exactly dark, but a kind of twilight or gloaming. There were neither windows nor candles, and he could not make out where the twilight came from, if not through the walls and roof. These were rough arches made of a transparent rock, incrusted with sheep silver and rock spar, and other bright stones. But though it was rock, the air was quite warm, as it always was in Elfland.

385   So he went through this passage till at last he came to two wide and high folding-doors which stood ajar. And when he opened them, there he saw a most wonderful and glorious sight. A large and spacious hall, so large that it seemed to be as long and as broad as the green hill itself. The roof was supported by fine pillars, so large and lofty, that the pillars of a cathedral were as nothing to them. They were all of gold and silver, with fretted work, and between them and around them, wreaths of flowers, composed of what do you think? Why, of diamonds and emeralds, and all manner of precious stones.

386   And the very keystones of the arches had for ornaments clusters of diamonds and rubies, and pearls, and other precious stones! And all these arches met in the middle of the roof, and just there, hung by a gold chain, an immense lamp made out of one big pearl hollowed out and quite transparent. And in the middle of this was a big, huge carbuncle, which kept spinning round and round, and this was what gave light by its rays to the whole hall, which seemed as if the setting sun was shining on it.

387   In the middle was his sister, Burd Ellen. They were so happy to see each other again! But his sister was under the spell of the King of the Elves and could not warn him when he said he was hungry. Rowland almost took a bite to eat, but at the last moment remembered what Warlock Merlin had told him and dashed the bowl. The Elven King entered, announced that he smelled Christian blood, and challenged Rowland to fight him. With his trusty brand, Rowland defeated the giant and made him bring back his brothers to life and to disenchant his sister. Then the four children left the Dark Tower never to return there again.[60]

---

[60] J. Jacobs, *English Fairy Tales*, London 1898 pp. 117–124 [Jacobs added the name "Dark Tower" according to the allusion to this fairytale in Shakespeare.]

388   The symbol of the midnight sun is a mystical enlightenment emerging from the unconscious, often appearing to the conscious mind as strange and foreign.[61] These symbolic connections are only hinted at in "The Virgin Tsar" by the expression, "Kingdom under the Sun" but these links are of major importance since in many fairytales in the center of the magical kingdom such solar allusions arise and are strongly related to the figure of the anima. We see this particularly in parallels to "Ferdinand the Faithful and Ferdinand the Unfaithful" where the sought-after beautiful princess has golden hair, which places her in relation to the sun. This is also the case with the red-haired goddess in "The Wonderful Hair." The radiance that emanates from her is a symbol of the "enlightenment," which she mediates. Köhler dedicated an investigation to the motif of the "golden-haired maiden."[62] The princess that the hero seeks to win is called the "pretty chicken with the golden hair," the "best thing under the sun," the "sun-like princess" or the "daughter of the sun." [63] The quest is a "Journey to the Sun" and so forth. The golden hair of the virgin tsar are thus like sun rays. The "Sun Princess" is apparently an archetypal concept in which two separate principles are, in fact, combined: the *solificatio* as a symbol of the active half of the Self, and the anima, the symbol of the unconscious.[64]

389   The image of the anima in "The Virgin Tsar" is underscored by a rare wealth of symbolic descriptions that emphasize her supra-individual cosmic significance. Her kingdom is surrounded by a wall, like a castle, to mark its inaccessibility.[65] This protective wall around the central mandala, which

---

[61] In India, Yama, the god of death, is the son of the sun god. "The sun is the abode or gateway of deathless life." (H. Zimmer, *Death and Rebirth*, New York 1964 p. 329. Jung writes:

The *solificatio* is consummated on the person of the anima. The process would seem to correspond to the *illuminatio*, or enlightenment. This "mystical" idea contrasts strongly with the rational attitude of the conscious mind, which recognizes only intellectual enlightenment as the higher form of understanding and insight. Naturally this attitude never reckons with the fact that scientific knowledge only satisfies the little tip of personality that is contemporaneous with ourselves, not the collective psyche that reaches back into the grey mists of antiquity and always requires a special rite if it is to be united with present-day consciousness. . . The *solificatio* is infinitely far removed from the conscious mind and seems to it almost chimerical. (C.G. Jung, CW 12, *Psychology and Alchemy* p. 68).

[62] See R. Köhler, "Kleinere Schriften," Vol. 3, Berlin 1900 p. 328. See also a J. Bolte and G. Polívka, *Anmerkungen,* Vol. 2, Leipzig 1915 p. 18.

[63] See *ibid* pp. 19, 20, 22, 26. See also the Latvian song:

The sun's daughter wades in the sea,
One saw only the little crown;
Row the boat, you sons of God,
Save the life of the sun.

(H. Güntert, *Weltkönig*, Halle a. S. 1923 p. 274).

[64] See also the merger of solar symbolism with the image of the anima in the Gnostic figure of the "Virgin of the Light" (Pistis Sophia) (G. R. S. Mead, *Fragments*, London 1931 pp. 476–477 and G. R. S. Mead, *Pistis Sophia*, London 1921 p. 245f.). In the Christian faith, St. Jerome (Eusebius Sophronius Heironymus) compared the Virgin Mary to the sun as the mother of the light. See C.G. Jung, CW 6, *Psychological Types* ¶395 [source of the statement about Saint Jerome is unknown.]

[65] Cf. the wall of an anima figure in Goethe's youth fairytale, "Die neue Paris" [The New Paris], who lives enclosed in a mandala. See also the inaccessibility of the heroine, "The Beautiful One of the Earth," which is symbolized not by a wall, but in a negative dismissive attitude of the anima herself.

envelopes "the inner man," is a widespread symbol, especially among the Gnostics. Thus, according to the concepts of the Ophites, the inner man, as a piece of the primordial man of light, is surrounded by a wall in the fortress of Zion.[66] The Coptic-Gnostic Anthropos [Primal Man] or Monogenes [Only-Begotten] lives within the monad, in the "Mother-City" surrounded by veils in the manner of a protective wall.[67] The wall as an obstacle is seen psychologically as an inhibition and protection.[68] In the center of many Eastern ritual mandalas there is an image of a deity. Also there, the walled castle signifies the unshakeableness and invulnerability of the inner Self.[69] The castle or city as a vessel of the godhead is a maternal symbol. Cities were represented in ancient times as women, and in the Apocalypse, the heavenly Jerusalem is compared to a decorated woman.[70]

390   The center of the mandala corresponds to the calyx of the Indian lotus: seat and birthplace of the gods. This is called the *padma* and has a feminine significance. In alchemy the *vas* is often underscored as the uterus where the "child" is gestated.[71]

391   The central image of the mandala surrounding the sleeping anima figure was already prefigured in the symbol of the crossroads. In Gnosticism, for instance, the cross symbolizes the crucifixion of the world soul in space.[72] The rotating cottage of Baba Yaga also has a mandala character. Hence the mandala motif does not appear here for the first time, but is always present in the unconscious and only, from the point of view of the conscious mind, experienced in different meanings and in various differentiations and

---

[66] See H. Leisegang, *Die Gnosis*, Leipzig 1924 p. 125.
[67] See C.G. Jung, CW 11, *Psychology and Religion* ¶97 and C.G. Jung, CW 12, *Psychology and Alchemy* ¶138. The Coptic text cited is from Baynes pp. 22, 89, 94.
[68] See H. Silberer, *Problems of Mysticism*, New York 1917 p. 60, and also Jung:
> The round or square enclosures built around the center therefore have the purpose of protective walls or of a *vas hermeticum*, to prevent an outburst or a disintegration. Thus, the mandala denotes and assists exclusive concentration on the center, it is a much needed self control for the purpose of avoiding inflation and dissociation.
> ... One might almost say that man himself, or his innermost soul, is the prisoner of the protected resident of the mandala. (C.G. Jung, CW 11, *Psychology and Religion* ¶156–57.)
[69] See here Jung's comprehensive survey in C.G. Jung, CW 12, *Psychology and Alchemy* ¶169, C.G. Jung, CW 13, *Alchemical Studies* ¶31ff, C.G. Jung, CW 9i, *The Archetypes and the Collective Unconscious* p. Plate 36, ¶691. Also R. Wilhelm, *Secret of the Golden Flower*, London 1962 p. 24. On the castle housing the Holy Grail and the old Germanic city-like castle of the gods see M. Führer, *Nordgermanische*, München 1938 p. 22.
[70] On this see this C.G. Jung, CW 5, *Symbols of Transformation* ¶302ff ¶318 fn. 15.
> As "metropolis" the Monad is *feminine*, like the *padma* or lotus, the basic form of the Lamaic mandala (the Golden Flower in China and the Rose or Golden Flower in the West). The Son of God, God made manifest, dwells in the flower. In the Book of Revelation we find the Lamb in the center of the Heavenly Jerusalem. (C.G. Jung, CW 12, *Psychology and Alchemy* ¶139.)
> See also C.G. Jung, CW 9i, *The Archetypes and the Collective Unconscious* ¶156, and Revelation 21, 10-12.
[71] C.G. Jung, CW 12, *Psychology and Alchemy* ¶246, fn. 125.
[72] See "The Acts of Andrew" in G. R. S. Mead, *Fragments*, London 1931 p. 445. [Mead has here "crucifixion of the soul *in matter*," while von Franz and von Beit have "*an Raum*" (in space), therefore their usage is retained.]

significance – when it refrains from drowning out its own activity.[73] As a result of the Tsar's entrusting the continuation of his life adventure to his sons, part of the psychic energy flowed from the conscious sphere – personified by the hero – into the unconscious, whereby the mandala as an image is immediately enlivened, and later actually happens symbolically when Ivan Tsarevich "awakens" the sleeping virgin, the soul-image.

392   The form of the anima is transparent, and this characterizes her as a spiritual being. A similar anima figure appears in other Russian fairytales. In "Koshchey the Deathless" the hero's nurses and governesses sing lullabies to him, "Prince Ivan, when you grow up, you will find your bride. Beyond thrice nine lands, in the thrice tenth kingdom, sits Vasilisa, Kirbit's daughter, in her tower, and you can see her marrow flowing from bone to bone."[74]

393   When the Virgin Tsar breathes, the doors open and close. The breath is the same as hers, she is like the "breeze" of a ghost, spirit breath, or *pneuma*. Almost everywhere, the names for "soul" are connected to the concept of moving air, like a ghostly whisper.[75] The notion of "spirit" (ghost, mind)[76] derives from a similar conceptual space. Leisegang explains it thus:

394   *Pneuma* is . . . initially not spirit (mind), but 'wind,' moving warm 'air.' The view, however, that a pneuma, not a spirit or ghost, but the movement of air, created human life we met in Greek traditional writing and poetry, as well as in the heights of philosophical science.[77]

395   Leisegang also points out that Prometheus sculpted human shapes out of clay and Athena then breathed life into them, and considers the role of *pneuma* in Aeschylus, Euripides, in Orphic beliefs, in Stoicism, and in Aristotle. He continues, noting the connection of the Old Testament *pneuma* of God, which floated over the waters, and the "breath" with which God breathed life into Adam,[78] to the term holy *Pneuma* that reoccurs in the New Testament, signifying the Holy Spirit. Thus, there is a clear link to the idea that this

---

[73] See C.G. Jung, CW 12, *Psychology and Alchemy* ¶329, ¶249.
[74] N. Guterman, (trans.), *Russian Fairy Tales*, New York 2006 p. 485. This motif is also frequent in Yakut folklore. In a tale from the Tundra Yukaghir, "Reindeer Born," a man who is persecuted by a reindeer demon takes refuge in an iron house. "In the house there was a very pretty girl, so pretty that all the food that she swallowed was visible through her transparent body." He marries her and with her help overcomes the demon. W. Bogoras, *Tales of the Yukaghir*, New York 1918 pp. 24–25.
[75] On breath as symbol of vitality and life activity, see Jung:
      "These connections (i.e., between psyche and breath) show how clearly in Latin, Greek, and Arabic, the names given to the soul are related to the notion of moving air, the 'cold breath of the spirits.' And this is probably the reason why the primitive view also endows the soul with an invisible breath-body." (C.G. Jung, CW 8, *The Structure and Dynamics of the Psyche* ¶664.)
[76] [In German, *Geist* can mean ghost, spirit, or mind.]
[77] H. Leisegang, *Die Gnosis*, Leipzig 1924 pp. 193–195.
[78] Genesis 2:7; quoted by Carus, [see below].

pneuma is "life generating, the stuff that creates the world and people." As such, the *pneuma* is the divine in general.[79]

396 In this sense the Virgin Tsar embodies the divine breath of life and is the image of a true *anima mundi*. (In the Uzbek tale, "The Beautiful Dunye," the anima figure is called Dunya (universe, cosmos), and in an Albanian fairytale, "The Beautiful One of the Earth," the princess is called "the beauty of the world."[80] Likewise the anima figure in the Georgian (Caucasus) fairytale, "The Earth Wants to Have Hers," says to the youth seeking immortality whom she finds in a glass house by the sea, "You delude yourself, I was created on the first day of creation, and I am still now just as I was then. They call me: The Beautiful, and I shall forever remain as I am now. You could stay with me

---

[79] Cf. Carus:

> It has often been pointed out that the words for this secret principle of all life are often the same as those for breath: *anima, spiritus,* and *pneuma,* etc. The same sources believed that the figurative [metaphorical] designation was taken from "breath," as one of the most lasting and uninterrupted manifestations of life. But I would nevertheless like to entertain the assumption that the choice of this name has a different meaning, and that it here refers symbolically to the *breath of the Divine,* which creates the body and speech. Already the very remarkable expression in Genesis [King James Version], 2:7: "And the Lord God formed man of the dust of the ground and breathed into his nostrils the breath of life, and man became a living soul," apparently has this meaning. Similarly, "inspiring" also means "to be inspired." Thus the following thought then comes directly to my mind: only those living [creatures] from whom the divine breath is perceived as a divinity, in word and deed, that is, who make it resound (*personare* as intoned by the voices of the ancient actors through their mask), give us the concept of an individual, of a self-governing person who guides his life accordingly to a superior knowledge, that is, a *person*. [Translated from C.G. Carus, *Psyche*, Leipzig 1931 p. 7, consulting C.G. Carus, *Psyche* (English), New York 1970 p. 29.] See also H. Zimmer, *Death and Rebirth*, New York 1964 p. 339 "*Asu,* the principle of life, is etymologically related to *animus, anima,* Greek, *anemos,* 'the wind'; it is an older designation for what was later called *prāna,* 'life breath, vital force'. "H. Zimmer, *Death and Rebirth*, New York 1964 p. 339. Cf. also see L. Lévy-Bruhl, *The "Soul" of the Primitive,* New York 1928 p. 134f, "Sometimes this 'soul' appears in the form of a spirit, a breath. . ."

[80] See *Märchen aus Turkestan und Tibet* p. 63; J. Bolte and G. Polívka, *Anmerkungen,* Vol. 1, Leipzig 1913 p. 50. Kretschmer, in his introductory comments on modern Greece writes:

> Of the female fantasy figures of the modern Greek tale, the figure of the *Beautiful of the World* requires some explanation. . . She appears as the Beautiful One of the World, or the World Beauty, with the Turks and Kurds, as Beauty of the Earth with Albanians and Aromanians (Vlachs), [and] as *La Bella del Mondo* in Italy. . . At first it appears that this figure, like the ancient Greek Helena, personifies the most beautiful woman in the world. But she usually has a more fantastical, fairy-like character, and carries, in the fairytale retold by B. Schmidt, *Griechische,* Leipzig 1877 pp. 79–82, the title: "The Mistress over the Earth and Sea." This figure reminds one of Aphrodite Urania as mistress of the whole world. . . as mentioned in ancient magical papyri. Similar figures are found in Russian fairytales, such as Anastasia the Beautiful, Beautiful Helena with the Gold Trusses, Marda, Daughter of the Sea, (T. Zieliński, *Märchenkomödie,* St. Petersburg 1885 p. 52) where they are attributed to ancient Greek goddesses. The 'Beauty of the World' originates, however, from the Orient. . . " (P. Kretschmer, *Neugriechische,* Jena 1917 pp. x–xi) See also *ibid*: The Beauty of the World is related to the *beautiful one with the seven veils* of the Italian fairytale whose 'beauty shines through the Seven Veils' (Gonzenbach, *Sizilien Märchen,* vol. 1, p. 80f, Comparetti, *Nov. pop. Italian,* vol. I, 55f *La signorina delle sette vele più bella giovane del mondo*) whose name bears an oriental flavor, after *Feraidal - fevai* (J. F. von Hammer-Purgstall, *Rosenöl,* Cotta, Stuttgart and Tübingen 1813 p. 327), in Mohamed's paradise, the beautiful [women] are so lightly clothed that even through the seventy veils with which they are veiled, one still sees the marrow in their legs." (P. Kretschmer, *Neugriechische,* Jena 1917 pp. ix–x, fn. 7.)

forever, but you are not worthy of immortality; eternal life would become loathsome to you!"

397   The rhythmic doors of the chamber of the Virgin Tsar that open and close by themselves represent the two fundamental rhythms of outflowing and inflowing, which underlie everything psychic-living.[81] This is also expressed in the two types, "to realize oneself ever anew," and "to be sunk inside oneself," as Carus[82] called that which later Jung termed extraversion and introversion.[83] In his *Buch des Sängers*, Goethe writes:

398

> In taking a deep breath are two graces:
> To draw air in and let air out. . .[84]

399 Also, in Indian philosophy the rhythm of the breath has mystical significance.

400

> His continuous singing proclaimed his secret being, in and out, sounds the breath '*ham–sa*'. This is also the sound of the Indian word for swan '*hamsa*'; out and in, he says, '*sa-'ham*'. But *sa* means "he" and *ham* (or *aham*) means "I" – thus, "I am he." In this way, the [inhalation and exhalation of the] breath says, "I" – the sensorily tangible innermost power of life that fills the world of the body – am "he," the person that embodies the tangible ego. The other one who fills the world body and lets it arise, and who stands beyond tangible feeling, is just the person who stands beyond in their darkness [waiting to fill themselves with his light].[85]

401   The archetypal motif of breath as the World Soul also combines with the image of the sun as the source of all creative energy. So, in the *Mithras Liturgy*, the generating breath of the spirit comes from the sun, presumably from the "sun-tube."[86] The light, pneumatic, and mandala symbol is also found in the *Upanishads*, for instance, in the *Ātmabodha Upanishad*:

402

> And the city, which is here the Brahman city, the lotus flower as house, the Atman who dwells in it, in the middle of this golden flower, from him springs what is of the nature of cause, the nature of consciousness,

---

[81] [German *Seelisch-Lebendig*.]
[82] See C.G. Carus, *Psyche*, Leipzig 1931 p. 491.
[83] See Jung CW 6, *Psychological Types* and for Goethe's notion of systole and diastole, mentioned by Jung in *ibid* ¶428.
[84] J. W. von Goethe, *Zahme*, Berlin 1960 p. 12, *Buch des Sängers*, "Im Atemholen sind zweierlei Gnaden." [There are two types of grace in breathing.]
[85] H. Zimmer, *Maya*, Stuttgart and Berlin 1936 p. 61. [Translated from the German, for English, see similar discussion in Zimmer pp. 47–50.]
[86] See A. Dieterich, *Eine Mithrasliturgie*, Leipzig and Berlin 1923 p. 7 and C.G. Jung, CW 5, *Symbols of Transformation* ¶487 fn. 19.

consisting wholly of knowledge; that is why it is just like a flash of lightning, its light is like a lamp.[87]

403   In the ancient Iranian religion the concepts of the deity (in the sense of Vedantic *Self* and of the Greek *Nous*) flow into those of the soul.[88] And in ancient Rome the sun[89] was considered to be the "creatrix of all intelligence on earth."[90] It is perhaps not too bold to conclude from the similarity of all the images we have presented that the spiritualized form of anima in "The Virgin Tsar" is to be regarded as one who brings forth life out of herself, who is founded in herself, and who is a life source and inner divine center that mediates the highest enlightenment. Ivan Tsarevich, following in the footsteps of his father, arrives at the sun-like *pneuma* of the world, which is revealed as the source from which all consciousness originates.

404   Among fairytales from the Caucasus region there is one, "The Virgin Queen," which is a very close parallel to "The Virgin Tsar." In this tale (here summarized, with our comments):

405   Three sons of a sick and blinded king searched for the fruit that could heal him in the garden of the Virgin Queen. The two elder sons failed because they mocked an old man who sewed together the cracks in the sun-dried roads (he symbolizes the figure of the helpful old wise one, who works by unifying, tying together.). The youngest son passed over the river of milk, the river of oil, the river of honey, and then to a crystal, and finally to a silver and golden tower. (Note the three rhythms, after which appears the fourth as a new image!) Helped by advice given to him by the old wise man, he opened an iron door with an iron nail, passed through the warning grass by wrapping his feet in grass, and went by the cautioning trees from which he plucked the healing fruits using a wooden pole.

406   Thus, the youngest son collected the healing fruit, but then he wanted to see the Virgin Queen before he left, "even if it should cost him his life." He went up into the tower. On a golden bed she lay, on her forehead she had a star, and a moon shone under her armpit. One could enclose her body with two fingers and when one let go again, she filled the whole earth. At her feet and head stood gold and silver candlelights, in the middle there was a table

---

[87] Deussen, *Sixty Upanishads* p. 807. See also *Brihadaranyaka-Upanishad*, 3, 4th *Brahmanam*, 1: Then Usasta, the descendant of Cakra, asked Yājñavalkya, "The Brahman that is immanent, which is not transcendent, which is inside all beings as a soul, could you explain that Brahman to me?" Yājñavalkya replied, "It is your soul that is inside all beings." "Which, O Yājñavalkya, is inside all?" "That which breathes in with the in-breath, that is your soul, which is inside all. That which breathes out with the out-breath, that is your soul which is inside all; that who breathes in between with the intermediate breath (*vyāna*), that is your soul which is inside all, that which breathes up with the up-breath (*udāna*), that is your soul which is inside all; this is your soul that is inside all." (Deussen, *Sixty Upanishads* p. 454.)

[88] See R. Reitzenstein, *Hellenistic*, Pittsburgh 1978 p. 410, 178 fn. 1.

[89] [The sun is feminine in German, as also in ancient Egypt.]

[90] See Cumont p. 188, see also G. R. S. Mead, *Fragments*, London 1931 p. 56.

set with filled cups and all kinds of delicious food, only "wid-wid milk" was missing.[91] To let the residents of the tower know that he had been there, the youngest son tasted the food, drank from the cups, kissed the sleeping queen three times, and bit her on the cheek. But she did not wake up. The son packed up the fruit and returned to his father.

407　　When the Virgin Queen discovered, with the help of her mirror, what had happened, she gathered her armies from the seven kingdoms and besieged the king, demanding the one who "plucked the fruit from her garden." She tested the two elder brothers, who naturally failed, and discovered the real trespasser. She kissed him six times and bit him on both cheeks, saying, "According to customs and traditions, the one who was stolen from has the right to demand double in return." She healed the sick king and married the hero. They had many children; the boys looked just like their father, and the girls like their mother.[92]

408　　Here the essence of the Virgin Queen is especially well described by the statement that one could encircle her with two fingers and at the same time she could fill the whole world. It is the same image that Hindu philosophy uses when it states that the Atman,[93] is "smaller than small, bigger than big." The anima is here not only associated to the sun, like the Virgin Tsar, but adorned with a star and a moon. Thus, she can also be characterized as "Queen of the Night." The moon is an attribute of Isis as *regina coeli* [Queen of Heaven] and later of the Virgin Mary or the Ecclesia. The moon embodies the female – the earthly, ever-changing, life principle – in contrast to the male, creative, radiant symbol of the sun. The "seven kingdoms" of the Virgin Queen is probably originally a reference to the seven planetary spheres, which she, as queen of heaven, ruled.

409　　The Virgin Tsar, like the Virgin Queen, lies in a bed that rests upon nine pillars. Her cosmic dimension is emphasized by this column-supported bed. According to Gnostic views, the world stands firmly on the four pillars of the elements.[94] The number nine, on the other hand, belongs to the Iranian conceptual sphere,[95] and indeed ancient Iranian beliefs that migrated to Russia probably helped to form the figure of the Virgin Tsar.[96] In the parallel

---

[91] The footnote by the collector, Dirr states "What this 'wid-wid milk' actually is, nobody knows." A. Dirr, *Kaukasische Märchen*, Jena 1922 p. 84.

[92] [Summarized, quoted parts of the tale translated from the German of A. Dirr, *Kaukasische Märchen*, Jena 1922 pp. 84–85.]

[93] [The soul, the Self, see Deussen, *Sixty Upanishads* p. 1.]

[94] See C.G. Jung, CW 11, *Psychology and Religion* ¶97f.

[95] See G. Hüsing, *Iranische*, Leipzig 1909 pp. 22–34, esp. 30.

[96] See R. Reitzenstein, *Hellenistic*, Pittsburgh 1978 *passim* and R. Reitzenstein, *Iranische*, Bonn a. Rh. 1921 *passim* about Iranian concepts of the soul and the divine.

description of the anima in "Koshchey the Deathless," threeness is emphasized in nine, the bride-to-be of the hero lies "beyond thrice nine lands, in the thrice tenth kingdom." Ivan Tsarevich meets a Baba Yaga three times and his journey takes nine days and nine nights. This accentuation of the three springs probably from a primordial sense of the relationship of three in time and space, as rhythm and image, as active-psychic wholeness.[97] Here, in our fairytales, the three in the form of the nine is associated with the feminine, as in the case of the three-headed Hecate, the three Fates (Moirai) or Norns.[98] According to the natural philosophers of the 16th century, the chthonic or female element is the fourth component complementing the Trinity. She symbolizes the body through the Virgin Mary. This was, like the Earth, regarded as the Mother of God.[99] From the name "Marya" of the anima figure in "The Virgin Tsar" it could be concluded that she is related to the Christian Mother of God. The Virgin Mary was represented as a tree life with nine limbs.[100] In contrast to the perfect decade,[101] nine has something incomplete and is related to ten, as seven is to eight and three to four. As mentioned above, the number ten as indicating a completion is hinted at in "Koshchey the Deathless" by the phrase, "in the thrice tenth kingdom."

410   All these remarkable attributes of Marya hinting at cosmic relationships, and her significant name, mark her as a divine figure, the same figure who appears in the various Gnostic systems as a form of the virgin of light. Bousset, in his book, *Die Hauptprobleme der Gnosis* [The Main Problems of Gnosticism], describes the various manifestations of this goddess. According to Leisegang she is the "Virgin Pneuma" that animates the world and lives in a circle of light in the middle kingdom, which bears the word "life."[102] She is identical to the aforementioned Eden, who has a virgin's body above and a snake's below. In other [Gnostic] systems, as Sophia, she is the personified female Wisdom of God, who has fallen into matter and there awaits

---

[97] On this see H. Usener, *Dreiheit*, Bonn 1903 *passim*. For the link with the Christian concept of the Trinity, see C.G. Jung, CW 11, *Psychology and Religion* ¶194-242. See also the nine choirs of angels, "That is why nine circles of angels are found together [group, lit. "camping out" together] like the three times three triads of spirit beings of the Neoplatonists, as well as the three heavenly hierarchies of [Pseudo-]Dionysius the Areopagite, which are themselves divided into triads: the angels, archangels, and princes; the authority, power, and dominion; the Thrones, Cherubim, and Seraphim. . . " H. Leisegang, *Die Gnosis*, Leipzig 1924 p. 17.

[98] For the female triad compare J. J. Bachofen, *Mutterrecht*, Stuttgart 1861 p. 134. See K. Kerényi, *Kore*, Princeton, 1969 p. 56f, on the nine dancers in the Greek *Kore*-cult and the dominance of the number nine there. See also the nine heavens and nine rivers of the Aztec underworld in "The Nine Heavens" [eight heavens are named, the next is unnamed.] W. Krickeberg, *Azteken und Inka*, Jena 1928 pp. 26–27, and "The Three Kingdoms of the Dead" and notes on p. 327.

[99] See C.G. Jung, CW 11, *Psychology and Religion* ¶107.

[100] See W. Laiblin, "Urbild," Darmstadt 1936 p. 94.

[101] "Now the ten is a perfect number." G. R. S. Mead, *Fragments*, London 1931 p. 337. On the important role of the decade in the Kabbalah, see D. Bernoulli, *Spiritual*, Princeton 1960 p. 326f; with the Gnostics, see G. R. S. Mead, *Fragments*, London 1931 pp. 326f, 375f.

[102] See H. Leisegang, *Die Gnosis*, Leipzig 1924 p. 169.

salvation.[103] She carries a variety of epithets, such as "Mother of Life," "Luminous Mother," "higher power," "Holy Spirit," "the man-woman," "*Prouneikos* or the pleasurable," "paradise," "Virgin," "Mother of Grace," "Companion of a Man," "Revealer of the Completed Mysteries," "hidden mother," "Holy Dove" and "Helena." The suffering of Sophia lost in matter, as Leisegang emphasizes, is the central theme of Gnosis.[104] As a cosmic event, her fate reflects the suffering and salvation of the individual human soul.

411   Motifs from ancient mythology live on in several Caucasian fairytales, transformed but still recognizable. The Gnostic myth of the "fallen Sophia" appears to be reflected in the beginning of a legend from the Svaneti, "The Prometheus Legend":[105]

412   Every night at the onset of dusk from the heights of Mount Elbrus,[106] there once resounded down desperate cries of a creature that gave the blacksmith Daredjiani, who lived at the foot of this mountain, no peace. He could not understand where this shouting came from. His curiosity increased until he could bear it no longer; he forged a crowbar and ice pick, and ascended Mount Elbrus. It was very hard and steep going, but with the help of his chisel and pick, he finally reached the top. He looked around and saw at the bottom of a deep chasm, a beautiful woman, crying and shouting. Around her were piles of gold and silver. Without reflecting long, the smith went down and asked the woman why she was crying so. She told him that she was the wife of God, who had thrown her down into that abyss for a crime that she had committed. From then on, Daredjiani frequently visited her, and she conceived a child by him.

413   Due to the frequent absences of her husband, the wife of the blacksmith became suspicious. One day she secretly followed her husband and witnessed his relationship with the woman in the abyss. Out of jealousy she decided to put an end to her rival. Somehow, she found out that the woman acquired her magical power from her hair which covered her body in a dense lichen-like matting. The smith's wife stole up to the abyss and when the woman was asleep, she cut off her hair. When the woman in the abyss awoke, she called the smith to her. She told him without her hair she must die, he should cut the child out of her womb. The smith refused. Then his lover cut open her own belly, brought the child out, and handed it over to the blacksmith.

---

[103] G. R. S. Mead, *Fragments*, London 1931 pp. 334–335.
[104] See H. Leisegang, *Die Gnosis*, Leipzig 1924 p. 383, G. R. S. Mead, *Fragments*, London 1931 p. 470f.
[105] The Svaneti are a people from the mountainous regions of northwestern Georgia.
[106] [The highest mountain in Europe, a dormant stratovolcano on the Russian (Caucasus)-Georgian border.]

Dying, with her last words, she said he should put the child at the crossroads, where it would grow by itself.

414   [This the smith did. Soon thereafter, Jesus Christ, Saint George, and an angel came by and discovered the boy. They baptized him Amiran and said if he thrice broke his word, he would fall into the hands of the devil. The boy grew day by day – even hour by hour! – and very quickly became exceedingly strong. He broke his word three times and landed in the hands of the devil. He conquered all but three of the devil's warriors, but then had no more strength. They bound him up and carried him to the abyss of Elbrus and tied him to an iron post. They also bound a nine-headed div to the same post and put his sword out of reach of both. Amiran and the div tried to let their fingernails grow long enough to reach the sword, but swans came and cut the nails of the div and the devil came and cut the nails of Amiran.] "But the time will come when Amiran will be able to reach his sword, slay the div and free himself. Then for the Svaneti and all Christian countries, the golden age will dawn."[107]

415   The smith has here the same role as Ivan Tsarevich: he becomes the husband of the *anima mundi*, who appears in this story, as in most Gnostic systems, as a female deity, the actual wife of God. The smith is himself an archetype of the demiurgic God. He is also a manifestation of the chthonic god, as can be inferred from the characteristics of the demonic father as discussed in Volume 1. The hero, born from the wife of God, is a Prometheus figure carrying traits of a Messiah. The beginning of this tale is closely related to the above-mentioned Gnostic myth of Justin of Elohim and Edem. The Svaneti tale is such a precise reflection of that myth that one is tempted to think of an historical transmission by way of a southern Russian Gnostic sect. Even the fairytale of the Virgin Tsar – as is clear from the previous description – belongs in the same circle of ideas.

416   The water of life and the water of death that Ivan Tsarevich finds in the garden of the Virgin Tsar are metaphors for a side of the anima's nature: the well, spring, source, and fountain; all have maternal-feminine significance and personify the constantly renewing vital power arising from the unconscious.[108] For example, water is even called "Mother of Life" in a tale from Java. A fountain is often found in the center of a ritual mandala, as the ablution fountains for washing in entryways and courtyards of mosques, and fountains

---

[107] Translated from the German of A. Dirr, *Kaukasische Märchen*, Jena 1922 pp. 238–241.
[108] See C.G. Jung, CW 12, *Psychology and Alchemy* ¶94, ¶157.

in the centers of cloister courtyards.[109] Alchemical philosophy equated the world soul, the *anima mundi*, with the "root of moisture." This was the:

417

> . . . miraculous water, the *aqua divina* or *permanens*, which was extracted from the lapis, or prima materia. . . The water was the *humidum radical* [radical moisture], which stood for the *anima media natura* or *anima mundi* imprisoned in matter, the soul of the stone or metal, also called *anima aquina*. . . [T]he divine water possessed the power of transformation. It transformed the *nigredo* into the *albedo* through the miraculous 'washing' it animated inert matter and made the dead to rise again.[110]

418

It was the spirit hidden in matter that, as *Quinta Essentia*, could be extracted from it as the divine water or tincture. This divine water allegedly came from the super-heavenly waters, those above the firmament (designated as Heaven), which separated these from the waters under the firmament.[111] These upper waters contained the Spirit of God, and were a kind of baptismal water of supernatural and transformative properties.[112] As the alchemical Mercurius this water is both deadly poisonous as well as healing and reviving. In contrast, many fairytales and legends including "The Virgin Tsar," present this double aspect of the one and the same water as a juxtaposition of the source of life and death. Ivan Tsarevich finds on the right (the side of consciousness), the water of life; on the left (the side of the unconscious), the water of death. An example of the same idea is found in of the tale, "The Journey into the Underworld to the Whirlpool Cave Fafá" (summarized):

419

> The hero sought his sister in the realm of the dead. A helpful old woman pulled her out as she floated by in the river of death and dipped her four times in the river of the water of life, "which flowed close by." After each immersion, the old woman guided the girl to look in one of the four directions, and after this orientation in the mandala she became alive again.[113]

420

Here, too, in the other world, the water of life and death lie quite close together. Similarly, in the Norwegian fairytale "The Golden Castle that Hung in the Air," the hero finds in the center of the magical realm a golden palace in which at noon between wild animals one can draw the water of life and of death.[114]

---

[109] See *ibid* ¶155.
[110] C.G. Jung, CW 13, *Alchemical Studies* ¶89.
[111] Genesis 1: 6.
[112] See C.G. Jung, CW 11, *Psychology and Religion* ¶161.
[113] P. Hambruch, *Südsee*, Jena 1921 pp. 246–254.
[114] See "The Story of Jat and Jol," an epic tale from Samoa in Micronesia. There it is told of two water

421   In essence, these two waters, or springs, are two aspects of the same water.[115] In a similar way, the anima herself has two sides, she is a deadly demon and also the inner source of life.

422   As in "Connla and the Fairy Maiden" the anima in "The Virgin Tsar" has the symbol of the Self, here specifically in the form of the rejuvenating apples. The apples of life are often in many myths and legends the goal of the hero's western sea journey. Hercules fetches the rejuvenating apples from the Hesperides in the western garden, and in the Grimm's fairytale "The King's Son, Who Feared Nothing" the hero must also retrieve an apple from the tree of life. These fruits are the hard-to-reach treasure that the hero rescues from the unconscious. Ivan Tsarevich steals them from the anima, like a love pledge in her sleep, because he knows of the dangerous side of the unconscious, which wants to ensnare its fruits again. Next, he leaps with his horse over the inhibitory wall, which represents the inviolability of the center. "Mounting" the wall also has an erotic meaning.[116]

423   Ivan Tsarevich comes to the garden and goes to the two waters (wells) and, following the advice of Baba Yaga, tests their powers on a young raven. He does not expose himself directly to the effects of the waters, he suffers them only through intuition, symbolized by the bird. The raven is his own soul bird, his alter ego,[117] and as a result of his choice to take the path of death – that leads to life – is born by this part of himself, and thus the raven suffers as his soul-bird. In a Finnish story, "The Ox's Son," the hero takes this task on and goes through the transformations himself. The episode with the raven represents how Ivan Tsarevich, at his destination, intuitively experiences dismemberment and rebirth. He thus gains knowledge concerning the effect of the unconscious powers that enable him to approach the anima with certainty.[118]

---

holes, bathing in one of them conferred beauty, strength and valor, but bathing in the other would bring disease and plague. (P. Hambruch, *Südsee*, Jena 1921 p. 193). See also A. Wünsche, *Lebensbaum*, Leipzig 1905 pp. 71–104, and E. Rohde, *Psyche* London 1925 p. III, 390 fn. 1.

[115] See C.G. Jung, CW 5, *Symbols of Transformation* ¶319. On the practice of overturning water vessels to the east and west (i.e., in the direction of birth and death) in the Eleusinian mysteries, see K. Kerényi, *Kore*, Princeton, 1969 p. 74. See also C.G. Jung, CW 6, *Psychological Types* ¶44f on the simultaneously dangerous aspect of the redeeming symbol.

[116] See Goethe's identification in the soldier's song, "Castles with lofty ramparts and towers, maidens proud with scoffing thoughts, I want to win them both!" (J. W. von Goethe, *Faust*, Stuttgart 1949 p. Part 1, Scene 2.) See also Silberer:

> The wall, however, signifies the inaccessibility or virginity of the woman. The wall surrounds the garden. The garden is, however (apart from the paradise symbolism derived from it), one of the oldest and most indubitable symbols for the female body. (H. Silberer, *Problems of Mysticism*, New York 1917 p. 88.)

On the tower as a symbol of virginity, see C.G. Jung, CW 6, *Psychological Types* ¶392f.

[117] Ivan Tsarevich is the anthropos, the divine man, the lover of Sophia. It is probably no coincidence that in Siberian and Pacific North American Inuit mythology, the raven is the embodiment of the God-man. The raven is also the companion and part of Odin, a symbol of the dead in us, and at the same time the messenger of victory and death.

[118] Particularly remarkable is that it is not the water of death that rends the raven apart and not the water of life that revives the bird, but it is Ivan Tsarevich himself who rips the raven limb from limb

424   When he finds the sleeping virgin, he lies with her without waking her up. The phrase "I will let my horse drink by this virgin," confirms the allegorical interpretation of the horse as the hero's instinctive nature and the identity of the anima with the well of life.[119]

425   The anima figure is here, as in "Ferdinand the Faithful and Ferdinand the Unfaithful" or as in "Sleeping Beauty (Little Briar Rose)" or as Brynhildr in the legend of Sigurd, depicted as being asleep; the state of sleep as a fetter corresponds to the unredeemedness from animal form. In the Uzbek tale "The Beautiful Dunye" the heroine sleeps for forty days and forty nights, and no one can awaken her except the wonder-horse, Juz-At (Hundred-Horse).[120] The bed is an encircling mandala, here the inside of the castle.[121] Being asleep, the anima is not "active," but passively hidden in matter, a symbol of the latent creative state of the soul.[122] Through the act of the hero she awakens and is free to enter into the world of consciousness to engage in more fruitful activities. The mandala (the castle), in whose center the anima resides, is the place of transformation, similar to the hermetic vessel. In it, Ivan Tsarevich, the core of consciousness, who lived a shadowy existence in the profane sphere, becomes the Self as the bridegroom of the anima, the divine hero connected to the *anima mundi*. His vocation, his coming under the aegis of a higher authority empowers the true hero to act according to his own law for the sake of immortality.[123] This in turn allows him to devote himself to the deepest unconscious, an activity that is prohibited to non-heroes, and which

---

and the water of death that makes it whole again. This particular logic occurs, however, often in fairytale imagination. This function of the water of death expresses that the state of complete dissolution is already overcome and a step towards rebirth has been made. Thus there are again three stages of transformation and healing: fragmentation, wholeness (by the water of death), and overcoming the paralysis (by the water of life).

[119] [That Ivan Tsarevich rapes the Virgin Tsar and from this she becomes pregnant with twins is taken as an expression of the mystical union (hieros gamos). In her 1953 lectures, von Franz interprets this in terms of masculine psychology and writes: "This reflects the current state of Russian culture, where an over-enlightened attitude admits nothing irrational; everything is seen through the lens of nineteenth-century mechanistic materialism. . . That is raping Mar[y]a." (von Franz, *Animus*, New York 2001 p. 120.]

[120] See G. Jungbauer, *Turkestan*, Jena 1923 p. 65, fn. 1.

[121] In "Ferdinand the Faithful and Ferdinand the Unfaithful" the princess is brought to the ship in her bed.

[122] ["Soul" here in the sense of the world soul, *anima mundi*.] See C.G. Jung, CW 11, *Psychology and Religion* ¶92f on the "dormant demiurge" represented in alchemical philosophy as the image of the deity or the world soul hidden in matter. It was the alchemist's task to revive and extract this spirit, or "Adam," the spiritual man.

[123] Cf. Jung, ". . . The 'son of the mother,' as a mere mortal, dies young, but as a god he can do that which is forbidden and superhuman: he commits the magic incest and thus obtains immortality." C.G. Jung, CW 5, *Symbols of Transformation* ¶394. [This is the CW text, the original text has, "The divine hero and world redeemer performs the forbidden and superhuman and thus obtains immortality."] This is already indicated in that he reached the kingdom under the sun, for the sun is the center of immortality. See Zimmer, "[T]he sun is in the olden days the place of immortality, possession of which is a pledge to a divine ecstatic rapture in death, to her [the sun] rise the blessed." (H. Zimmer, "König der dunklen," Leipzig 1929 p. 209). Cf. also C.G. Jung, CW 5, *Symbols of Transformation* ¶638–639.

then becomes a heroic deed in itself. Ivan Tsarevich's connection to the virgin sun is an entry into the illusion of Maya, of which Zimmer writes:

426   She is the magical sleep-drunkenness of the Lord of the World. . . Everything that lives is infatuated with her and thus spun into existence. The sublime goddess draws with violence even the spirit of the knower into herself and reveals to him the delusion. The Great Maya unfolds all the living world, it is she who graciously grants wishes and helps people to salvation. She is the highest wisdom, the eternal cause of infatuation and the reason for attachment to *samsara* – she alone, the Mistress of the Master of the Universe.[124]

427   In that the Virgin Tsar enfolds Ivan Tsarevich, a complete mandala in the Eastern sense arises, which encloses the god and the goddess in their union.[125] By bowing down to the divine soul asleep in matter and uniting with her, he delivers her from her bondage and awakens her to life.[126] The anima is awakened by the sound of the left hoof of the fleeing hero's horse scraping against the copper parapet of her city walls. Alarm bells often occur in fairytales as "guardians" or warning signs. Bolte and Mackensen in their *Handwörterbuch*, provide a summary in this regard under *Glöckchen* [little bells]: the castle of the virgin is often surrounded by bells that indicate the approach of any human being. Sometimes her bed or her dress are hung with bells that function to a similar end. "In some case, the whole castle is built like a bell such that any contact with the walls causes the whole building to reverberate like a bell. The golden castle in the Hungarian tale resounds if only a hair of a horse's tail touches the open window." In other cases, the bell itself represents the sought-after treasure. This compilation shows that the bell psychologically symbolizes a psychic sensitivity, an auditory clairvoyance in regard to inner stirrings. The bells surround the treasure or the *tremendum* because people take it to be something subtle, which hinders approaching it or becoming aware of its nature. When the virgin's castle is itself a bell, this indicates that the anima, or the space of the anima, represents precisely this psychic receptivity.[127] The sound that shakes the atmosphere around the castle

---

[124] [Alternative translation of the last phrase: "It is she alone who holds sovereignty over Vishnu, the Master of the Universe."] Translated from H. Zimmer, *Maya*, Stuttgart and Berlin 1936 p. 478, 322. For a detailed exposition in English, see Zimmer, *The King and the Corpse*, Princeton, 1972 p. 266ff.

[125] See C.G. Jung, CW 11, *Psychology and Religion* ¶113, ¶136.

[126] On this see C.G. Jung, CW 12, *Psychology and Alchemy* ¶420.

[127] In the Middle Ages there was a widespread legend of the so-called "bell of justice" that every ruler had hung in public so that anyone who felt they had been done an injustice could ring. (See J. Bolte and L. Mackensen, *Handwörterbuch* Berlin 1930, under *Glocke der Gerechtigkeit* [bell of justice]. In India, Buddhist mandalas show *Mâhasukha*, in the upper two of his twelve hands a thunderbolt (*vajra*) as a symbol of the pure doctrine and a bell (*ghanta*) sounding on all sides as a symbol of mercy (H. Zimmer, *Kunstform*, Berlin 1926 p. 79). The bell of justice, like this bell of compassion, confirm the interpretation given above, in that bells represent the fine emotional reactions of the ruler, or of God, to

of the virgin Tsar is an adequate expression for the inner spiritual event. But this feeling-toned signal makes Ivan Tsarevich aware that he has awakened the unknown and strange female, a non-ego. To the masculine conscious mind this is frightening, and Ivan Tsarevich flees.

428   That the anima is awakened at exactly the moment when the Tsar reaches mid-life is, psychologically, according to the rule. For as long as a valid principle governs the conscious mind, the sleeping anima is banned to remain in the unconscious. But if those principles can no longer appropriately function positively as regulating factors, then she comes to life again in her unbridled native nature.[128] Whereas she was previously only latently breathing the rhythm of life [that is, the doors opening and closing], she now breaks forcefully into the conscious sphere in her pursuit of Ivan Tsarevich. Her threat to the Tsar's kingdom mirrors the revenge of the deserted Eden on Elohim, in the aforementioned Gnostic Baruch myth of Justin. The Gnostic narrative also illuminates a point that was insufficiently explained in our tale – Ivan Tsarevich's flight. It is not only due to a fear of the unconscious, but it corresponds to a natural movement of the male spirit "upwards," towards the sphere of consciousness, and a reluctance to remain in the unconscious. Ivan Tsarevich had indeed previously given the Baba Yaga witches notice that he would be staying only one night.

429   But the virgin Tsar follows him on the wings of the wind and is thus further characterized as being pneumatic.

430   During his escape, the three witches give Ivan Tsarevich fresh horses, the same ones that he left behind at each station. Moreover, they aid him further by stopping the pursuing virgin Tsar and engaging her in familial conversation. These scenes reveal the secret identity of the anima image with the mother-imago. The former appears to be a derivative of the mother-imago in as much as the mother is the first carrier of the anima image.[129] The image of the mother lies between the anima and the sphere of consciousness – at the same time interposing itself – and thus often preventing the anima figure from breaking into the realm of the conscious mind. Ivan Tsarevich's conscious attitude towards the world is at first unchanged, since he now returns home and carries on just as before, a figure of ridicule and scorn and the soul still carries the aspect of the shadow and dark mother. The core process of the union of Ivan with the virgin Tsar is still in the deepest unconscious and Ivan Tsarevich's rise to be the immortal partner of the anima, the Self, remains at first unrecognized and without consequences for the secular attitude.

---

all human suffering. This explains the widespread function of the bell as demon exorcist that secured its place in all cultic buildings. (See Bächtold- Stäubli under *Glocke* [bell].)

[128] See C.G. Jung, CW 9i, *The Archetypes and the Collective Unconscious* ¶72.

[129] See C.G. Jung, CW 5, *Symbols of Transformation* ¶406. See also the tale from the Balkan region "The Devil's Deception and God's Power" in which the persecutor is the witch-like mother of the anima.

431   On his way home, Ivan returns once again to the crossroads to free his brother. He has grown and now knows the secrets of the anima and her perishable side, thus he can free his brother together with many fellow sufferers. In doing this he proves himself to be a typical savior-hero who, through his defeat of the monster, the symbol of the devouring unconscious, raises many people out of darkness. Then the envious brother steals the water of life from Ivan Tsarevich as he sleeps, exhausted from his journey. This falling asleep indicates Ivan's difficulty in returning to secular life. The real essential content of the unconscious, that he himself has become by his connection to the anima, cannot penetrate the existing conscious mind, and just at the point where he reaches the threshold, he falls back into the unconscious. This is because consciousness was not ready to receive the new developments, but still held a dismissive and devaluing attitude towards the fourth function.

432   These difficulties are reflected in the so-called return path of fairytale heroes.[130] The former conscious attitude and its affiliated auxiliary functions boast that they now, by theft, claim the power of the unconscious acquired by the function closest to the unconscious. They preserve their irreverent attitude towards the unconscious and the newly established consciousness.[131] But this indicates a presumption of the rational conscious mind, which actually plays into the hands of the unconscious.[132] The conscious mind in its immature worldly attitude does not want to submit to being part of the whole, but tries to retain its previous supremacy. The process of individuation is therefore threatened not only by the unconscious, but is devalued by an envious conscious world.[133] At first Ivan Tsarevich conforms to this situation by letting his horse run wild and sinking into sleep; he also lets himself get robbed without opposition, and once back home, he carries on in pubs and taverns. This states, psychologically, that the hard-won, newly formed personality within the profane sphere again assumes the aspect of the shadow, for the mystical insight of the magical realities that was gained is now perceived by the secular world as foolishness.

433   But the "awakened" soul image begins to act strangely. Not by flight but by ship, the Virgin Tsar surfaces in the secular realm. Here the symbolic indeterminacy of the unconscious appears anew in the light of daily consciousness: the kingdom under the sun can be reached by horse and yet it lies over the sea.[134] Ivan's quest was in fact the night sea journey to the realm

---

[130] ["The technical term for this in mythology is 'difficulty on the return', " (von Franz, *Animus*, New York 2001 p. 118.)]
[131] See Cathal's envious rival in "The Knight With the Sinister Laugh" who boasted that he had killed the snake and brought back the head of the old witch demon, and similar such figures elsewhere.
[132] See C.G. Jung, CW 7, *Two Essays in Analytical Psychology* ¶376f.
[133] See C.G. Jung, CW 9i, *The Archetypes and the Collective Unconscious* ¶256.
[134] See the ship at the end of "Tritill, Litill, and the Birds."

of the underworld sun! That the anima no longer flies, and is no longer vaporous, but travels by ship to the profane world, proves that she has become, as it were, psychologically more real. She appears in the fourth quarter of the year, at midnight and demands the father of her twin boys, to whom she has given birth. In that Ivan Tsarevich carried a piece of male consciousness into the unconscious, the soul has become pregnant.[135] Through this birth, a child of symbolic significance arises. On this Jung writes:

434   Psychologically, it proclaims a new expression of life at its most intense is being created. . . Yet, from that moment, the highest intensity of life is to be found only in this new direction. Every other direction gradually drops aways, dissolved into oblivion.[136]

435   That this new symbol, occurring at the threshold of conscious, appears as a duality (twins) shows that it is in opposition with itself and anticipates the unsatisfactory end of this tale where the old tsar separates from his son Ivan Tsarevich.

436   The Virgin Tsar has become hostile and now threatens to destroy the secular realm by persistent bombardment "with cannons and muskets," that is, due to the wrong attitude of the conscious mind, the unconscious takes on overpowering and dangerous forms. Still, the old Tsar intuits that perhaps all these strange events could indeed be related to Ivan the oven-sitter. Although this one approaches the anima's ship in "ragged uniform" and takes a path "through dirt and rubbish," he is greeted like royalty as a husband and father of the children, because "there one does not inquire," which means that in the realm of the anima, which signifies life, the darkness is not rejected because it is a part of life.

437   At the conclusion of the tale, Ivan Tsarevich recalls his magical abilities in plain words. As in the fairytale "The Poor Miller's Boy and the Cat" the father is strengthened by the undertaking, but the young couple depart and clearly renounce the secular realm. This separation is based on the inability of secular consciousness to grasp the inner process, because it is not able fully to integrate the unconscious events into life. The unconscious pulls the images

---

[135] On the concept of such inner conception in the writings of the Gnostics, Leisegang reports: "Not only creation of the world and birth of the Savior arise from the process of pro-creation, but also the ascent of humans on the path of gnosis is initiated by an act of fertilization. The virgin soul receives the divine seeds of light, becomes pregnant and gives birth to the new, the spiritual human being . . . in himself. Philo the Jew [Philo of Alexandria] says, "Step down onto me all ye right *logoi* of wisdom, copulate with me, let your seed flow into me. And if you see a deep, fertile, and virgin soul, do not pass over her, call her to your work and handling, complete her, and make her pregnant." ([Translated from H. Leisegang, *Die Gnosis*, Leipzig 1924 pp. 31–32. For the original quote of Philo, see *De Somnii*, I, 200.])

[136] See C.G. Jung, CW 6, *Psychological Types* ¶319. See also *ibid* ¶808f.

that its creative play offered back into itself.[137] The correct formula for the relation between consciousness and the unconscious is not found because the conscious mind views the circumstances of the psyche only as a possibility, but not as a covenant and binding task, and refuses to subjugate itself to a supra-personal meaning of life. Consciousness experiences a new life impulse but the actual processes remain obscure to it. It again loses, therefore, the connection to the deeper layers of the psyche in which the divine couple reigns in timeless eternity – as the fundament and, at the same time, the aim of life.

---

[137] On the autonomy of the psyche see C.G. Jung, CW 12, *Psychology and Alchemy* ¶186ff.

◇

Chapter 8
The Blind Padishah

438   A fairytale that has many parallel features to "The Virgin Tsar" is the Turkish tale "The Three Sons of the Padishah":

439   Once upon a time there was an old padishah[1] who had three sons. It came to pass that he fell ill and became blind. He was told in a dream that he could be cured only if someone would take a handful of dirt from some place on earth that had never been trodden by his horse's feet. First, his eldest son went in search of the handful of earth that had never been trodden by his father's horse. He went off and after three months decided he had gone far enough and picked up a handful of earth and brought it back. His father smiled and said, "Son, I used to light a cigarette and reach the spot where you got this dirt before I had smoked it halfway down. My horse has walked on this soil many times!"

440   Next, the second son went, and after six months climbed to the top of a mountain and scraped up a handful of dirt. But alas, this too his father's horse had already passed over. Then the youngest went off to find the dirt that his father's horse had never trodden. He came to an old woman who told him, "When your father left your city in the morning, he ate lunch here in our castle at midday. So, you see, this way you will never find the place that his horse did not tread nor which your father has not already seen with his own eyes." She advised him to go to a certain cave where he would find many horses and choose the reddish brown one with crooked legs and cancer in his shoulder, and to trust wherever this horse would take him. The hero did this and on the way rescued a nest of birds from a dragon, whereupon the mother bird promised to help him in time of need. She also revealed that the reddish-brown horse was that of his father. On the orders of the horse, the hero let himself be transported, with eyes closed, into the realm of an unknown padishah and entered into

---

[1] [Turkish sultan, emperor.]

his service as his thirtieth vizier. The other viziers promptly defamed him, and he received orders to fetch a golden bird. The mother bird that he had saved helped him by driving three golden birds towards him. "Do not be careless like your father was and let the golden birds escape again," said the mother bird to the youth. Following this warning, the young man stood vigilantly at the entrance to a cave, waited, and with great effort was able to catch one of the three golden birds. Then he took leave of the mother bird and with the captured golden bird, mounted the red-brown horse, and rode directly to the palace of the padishah.

441   As a second task, the hero had to climb a tall poplar tree and see what was at the top. The young man, this time following the advice of the red-brown horse, had a smith make a collection of special nails. Then he took a hammer and struck one of these nails into the poplar. He climbed up on this nail and, reaching upwards, hammered another nail in. Thus, he climbed, nail by nail, up the tree. Once at the top he found the plait of a girl's golden hair that a bird had carried there. He climbed back down, returned to the foreign padishah and presented the golden plait. But then the foreign padishah demanded that he fetch the maiden to whom the plait of golden hair belonged.

442   Once again, on the orders of the red-brown horse, he closed his eyes and was transported to an island in the middle of the sea where the golden-haired girl slept, seated on a throne. This girl belonged to a brother of the red-brown horse. The horse advised him to take the whole throne, with the girl in it, bring her back, and then close his eyes. "We will see what God does," said the horse. The young man took the golden-haired maiden in his arms, carried her to the horse, mounted, and shut his eyes. From the other side he heard a voice, "Brother, one time you neglected me in this world; now, the second time, have pity on me." This voice came from the brother of the red-brown perihorse[2] Many years earlier, the father of the young man had come this way to take the maiden. The horse's brother[3] had then let the maiden go. Nevertheless, this time too, the horse's brother had pity, stayed behind in his world, and let the hero take the golden-haired maiden back to the padishah. Now the girl herself imposed three tasks on the foreign padishah. If he accomplished them, then he could call for the wedding and she would marry him. The first task was to fetch a boat (a *kayk*) from a sea island. The padishah promptly

---

[2] "The peris are usually evil spirits in Turkish fairytales." – footnote, F. Giese, *Türkische Märchen*, Jena 1925 p. 303.
[3] [Who evidently had possession of the maiden.]

ordered the young man to carry out this task. The hero went to the red-brown horse and was told to close his eyes and climb on the horse's back. The hero did so and found himself again on an island in the middle of the ocean. The horse then said, "The boat that the padishah commanded you to bring back is here, but do not forget that your reason for taking on all these quests was to retrieve a handful of earth. This place your father has never seen nor did his horse leave a trace. Go, take a handful of earth and put it in your pocket. Then take the boat in your arms and shut your eyes." Again the young man heard a voice. It was the youngest brother of the red-brown horse to which the horse said, "My brother, you are still young, have pity on me. I wish to take this boat and give it to the padishah." The youngest horse-brother had pity and let them take the boat. The young man then took the boat, mounted the red-brown horse and closed his eyes, and found himself across the sea again. He brought the boat to the padishah.

443 The second task given by the golden-haired maiden to the foreign padishah was to bring an iron-headed horse from the sea. Again, the padishah ordered the young man to bring him the iron-headed horse. The hero went to his red-brown horse which told him to put a "batman" (a weight) under each hoof, throw three hides of three oxen upon his back, and glue them down with pitch. "And then we will see if this gets us what we want." The youth did all as he was told. They rode to a beach and he let the red-brown horse go into the sea. After three hours his trusty steed appeared again with the iron-headed horse held tightly in tow by its neck. The youth fitted a bridle around the head of the iron horse, mounted it, and rode to the palace. As they neared the palace, the maiden called out, "Would that you never had come! Where are you going?" The youth turned and saw behind him forty mares following up out of the sea. When they heard the voice of the maiden, the horses stopped where they were.

444 For the third task, the maiden wanted the mares milked and the boat filled with the milk. The padishah again ordered the young man to milk the mares. This the hero did easily and filled the boat with the milk. The golden-haired girl then said to the padishah, "You probably have not yet made the proper ablution for our marriage ceremony, go wash yourself in the milk." He immediately took off his clothes and stepped in the milk bath. But the milk of the mares was poisonous and the padishah immediately died in the bath. Then it was the young man's turn. "Forward, my young one!" said the maiden, "The padishah did not understand the trick of how to properly bathe, but I am sure

you know the trick. Bathe yourself and I will marry you." The youth too, was hopelessly in love with the girl. Just as he was about to step into the milk bath, the red-brown horse held him gently back with his teeth and pulled him to the side. Then he poured something into the bath that detoxified the milk so that the young hero could bathe. He washed himself and stepped out again, completely healthy. He took the maiden in his arms and showered her with kisses. In the end the maiden married the blind padishah's son and they rode back, bringing with them the handful of earth from the island. They carefully laid the earth on the blind padishah's eyes and lo! he could see again. The padishah then placed his son and his new daughter-in-law on his throne and everyone got all that they wished for. And here the story ends.[4]

445   The initial situation of the story is the same as the previous tale "The Virgin Tsar" and portrays the psychic situation of turning inward. The blindness of the old father is an apt metaphor, because the entanglement in the outer world is seen from the inside as blindness.[5] In this fairytale, the blind king orders his sons to bring earth from a place where he has never been. He sends them in strange and mysterious ways out to follow his footsteps, just as the old tsar of the previous tale did, and then further beyond. It turns out that the padishah had made the great hero's quest himself but somehow the golden bird and the golden-haired girl had slipped away from him. This confirms our hypothesis in the discussion of "The Virgin Tsar" that the ego in the first half of life had made a big journey, only with the opposite orientation. At that time, however, the anima remained only a hunch that flashed up in fateful encounters that slipped away again. Only in the second half of life does her true eternal nature reveal itself.

---

[4] [Beginning summarized, translated from F. Giese, *Türkische Märchen,* Jena 1925 pp. 142–149.]
[5] Cf. G. R. S. Mead quotes Philo of Alexandria:
    "Those who are content to worship externals are blind; let them then remain deprived of sight." And he [Philo] adds significantly, that he is not speaking of the sight of the body, but of that of the soul, by which alone truth and falsehood are distinguished from one another. (G. R. S. Mead, *Fragments,* London 1931 p. 67.)
See also Puech pp. 259–260, 264. In the *Mandukya-Upanishad* I, 2:16 it is said:
    In beginningless universal delusion
    Sleeps the soul; when it wakes up
    Then wakes in it the secondless (the non-dual)
    Sleepless, dreamless Eternal.
(Deussen, *Sixty Upanishads* p. 613). And from the *Kaivalya-Upanishad,* Nr. 12:
    When his self is blinded by the Mâyâ,
    He dwells in the body and strives after works,
    In women, food, drink and enjoyments
    He finds satisfaction in the wakeful state.
(*Ibid* p. 793). See also *Cvetâcvatara-Upanishad,* 4: 9, 10.

446   The place on earth, which the padishah never saw, means literally the *terra incognita* of the unconscious, and only from the unconscious can healing of rational consciousness arise.

447   The old woman who supplies the hero with the reddish-brown "perihorse" corresponds to the Baba Yaga, she is the mother-imago in her helpful aspect. The bowlegged horse with cancer resembles Ivan Tsarevich's miserable nag; the helpful instinctual power also appeared in "The Virgin Tsar" in a secular, inferior form. The wretched horse is actually the steed of the father, that is, a crooked and stunted sick life force from which wonders are supposed to emerge. The rescue of the bird's nest from the dragon is a parallel to the well-known motif of the rescue of the virgin anima from the dragon.[6] The padishah's son succeeds in wresting the spiritual from the purely instinctual levels of the unconscious. Later, the mother bird drives three golden birds towards the hero, making four birds in all, a representation of the four functions, whereas here the least developed is not golden, but a helper. (As mother bird this fourth female is simultaneously the feminine-maternal, a fleeting premonition of the anima).

448   First, the hero hires himself out to an unknown padishah as vizier. This padishah behaves in what follows much as the hero's blinded father, that is, as a master, handing out tasks. But this time to wrongfully obtain the magical gifts. He is thus a parallel figure to the paternal padishah, almost a shadow or a double. Since the blind father occurs within a tetrad, he is probably to be regarded primarily as the dominant function, and the employer padishah represents the secular-minded ego: coveting, willful, and self-assertive. Thus here the personality is split into more than one person in order to show more of its aspects: the suffering, the sterile, the conscious mind in need of salvation, the high-handed, overbearing, hostile opponent to inner self-development; and on the other side, the one selflessly seeking the meaning of life, which is embodied by the hero. In the end one padishah is overcome and the other healed. That part of the conscious mind that had to suffer due to its inadequacy is enriched, but the egotistical side must literally be sacrificed. This double aspect belongs to all archetypal figures.[7] The observation and examination of the doubled padishah figure in this fairytale allows us to derive a general law: the doubling of mythological figures means that the double aspect, which belongs to each archetype, appears in independent partial figures.

449   A doubling of the figure embodying the secular attitude was also found in "Ferdinand the Faithful and Ferdinand the Unfaithful" (Volume 1, p. 340). Just as in the present tale, where the father of the hero, on the one hand, who,

---

[6] See "The Great Fool from Cuasan."
[7] [See on this C.G. Jung, CW 9i, *The Archetypes and the Collective Unconscious* ¶413.]

however, in the course of the action completely disappears, and in the employer-king, on the other hand, where the hero was slandered by the shadow figure, as here through the shadowy viziers. In "The Devil with the Three Golden Hairs," in contrast, the attitude of the secular conscious mind was played by the evil master-king, but alone, without a counter-father. Here his redemption-seeking aspect is revealed, however, at the end of the tale in the form of his destiny as the ferryman.

450   The three tasks given by the employer-padishah are easy to interpret considering the previous fairytale: the golden bird is a symbol of the ephemeral-psychic, that hints at the highest values. The golden braids on the tree are a crystallization of the flighty anima image onto the maternal tree symbol, and the golden hair is the halo of the still-invisible sun-virgin.[8] With the third task she herself radiantly appears. She slept (like the Virgin Tsar) in a golden throne on a sea island, that is, in the middle of the great water (just as the Virgin Tsar at the end arrived by ship to the secular realm). In a Nordic fairytale "The Blue Belt" the anima figure is hidden in a little house that floats on the sea, a symbolic expression of her being hidden in the depths of the unconscious.

451   The anima as golden sun-virgin belongs to an invisible brother of the red-brown horse, and later we learn that the boat belongs to another invisible brother of this horse. These three horses correspond to the three sons of the padishah. They are aspects of his animal instincts (components of a lower trinity that stand in opposition to the three auxiliary functions of the conscious personality and at the same time are associated with them). As a whole they form the part of the animal shadow in the personality and correspond to the white horse in "Ferdinand the Faithful and Ferdinand the Unfaithful" in its divine-devilish aspect as a helper and nature demon. In contrast to the shadow in human form (which is closer to the ego), the animal side of the shadow reaches down to the deepest layers of the psyche and mixes in a sliding transition with the figure of the chthonic father deity.[9] Here the horse-brother appears as owner of the anima, who dwells in other fairytales with her demonic father.[10]

---

[8] See the title character in "The Beautiful Dunye" who has forty braids by which she swears, and who desires her must seize hold of them. Therein lies her magical power. See also the German legend referred to by de Gubernatis:

> In the sixth of the *Contes Merveilleux* of Porchat, the young *curioso* sees a nest upon an elm-tree and wishes to climb up. The ascent never comes to an end; the tree takes him up near to heaven. On the summit of the elm-tree there is a nest, from which comes forth a beautiful fair-haired maiden (the moon). (de Gubernatis, *Zoological*, London 1872 p. 244, fn. 2.)

See also C.G. Jung, CW 5, *Symbols of Transformation* ¶368 and ¶396. on the birth of Ra and Mithras from the (sun) tree.
[9] Consider the identity of the little grey-white horse in "Ferdinand the Faithful and Ferdinand the Unfaithful" with the unknown godfather, who is "the good Lord" or "the devil."
[10] See, for example, "The Visit to Heaven" and "The Daughter of the King Vultures."

452   The dark horse-brother, [who guards or watches over the anima on the island], asks the hero not to disregard it "in this world" and that he leaves the anima with him. The theft of the anima and dispatching her into the secular sphere of consciousness signifies, therefore, contempt for the dark nature deity, which is probably why the father's attempt failed. Even now the horse resists this, because he knows the anima is (at least) initially destined for the employer-padishah, the ego oriented to the mundane [world]. But because the hero, who represents the real core of the conscious personality, presents his request together with his friend, the red-brown horse, he obtains the girl. This is because he is also the Self, and thus partakes of both worlds.

453   As in "Ferdinand the Faithful and Ferdinand the Unfaithful," the golden-haired maiden prefers the hero over the padishah and seeks to eliminate the latter. Here she does this by assigning three further tasks that the padishah must perform: obtaining the boat, the iron-headed horse followed by forty mares, and then bathing in their poisonous milk. These three symbols are female (the boat, as a shell, is a vessel, the horse is a maternal symbol and the bathing in poisonous milk is a negative baptism and rebirthing rite). In effect, this means that the person who wants to have the anima must [first] get to know her feminine-enigmatic [profound, hidden, cryptical] and dangerous sides – for him as yet unknown – and then be able to master these. The iron head of the horse suggests that it is not a natural phenomenon, but a monstrous entity of the unconscious, a symbol of a complex fact. Iron is the metal associated with Mars,[11] the iron head therefore displays the hard, destructive, unyielding aspect of instinctual nature. Iron or iron ore is also the precursor of the alchemical gold, thus the horse appears in a sense as the original matter (*prima materia*) of the golden-haired girl. Milk baths in fairytales often play – as will be seen later – the role of redemptive and transformative ritual. But they are apparently only for those who are called, the secular-oriented ego is destroyed in the bath. This is because the unconscious acts destructively towards a presumptuous, high-handed, ego attitude that tries to appropriate the achievements [powers, capacities] of the Self (see "Ferdinand the Faithful and Ferdinand the Unfaithful" and "The Devil with the Three Golden Hairs," among others). The toxic milk corresponds to the enchanted waters of the magical realm that grant life and death, like the *aqua mercurialis* [mercurial water] of alchemy. The hero, as the more comprehensive consciousness in human beings, masters the danger with the help of the red-brown horse, who magically detoxifies the milk. Insofar as the hero represents the inner essence, he participates in the non-human,

---

[11] See H. Silberer, *Problems of Mysticism*, New York 1917 p. 118, 199.

animal friendship with the red-brown horse and thus with the help of natural instincts can overcome the destructive side of the unconscious.[12]

454   On the island, where the hero retrieves the boat, he finds the earth that his father had never touched. In the first half of his life the old, now blind padishah, had ridden this way with his eyes fixed solely on external reality and thus he never reached the home of the mystical anima where the healing *terra incognita* could now be found.[13] In this respect the present fairytale is even clearer than "The Virgin Tsar." The mission to follow the tracks of the father apparently means in this case to go even further beyond where the father traveled and to retrieve new life from the unknown. Ivan Tsarevich did this also, in that he brought back the water of life and the rejuvenating apples, but there it was not so overtly stated whether his father had asked for these or even wanted and needed them. Nor did we learn if his father had ever reached the garden where these treasures lay. In this respect, the Turkish variant offers an explanation and enrichment of the motif. Unlike the end of "The Virgin Tsar," the couple in "The Three Sons of the Padishah" move to the court of the old father and inherit his kingdom (as in "The Three Feathers"). This expresses, as already mentioned, the replacement of the secular attitude by a higher and in general more conscious center. The young newlyweds, symbolizing this inner center, do not disappear again (as in, "The Virgin Tsar") into some hard-to-imagine distant place in the unconscious, but become the life-determining inner core of the personality.

---

[12] See the same motif in "Threeson," a fairytale built on the type of "Ferdinand the Faithful and Ferdinand the Unfaithful." See also the helpful animals in "The Two Travelers."

[13] In "The Adventures of Mrile" (Volume 1, p. 232) a similar motif of following in the father's footsteps is expressed when Mrile sits in his father's chair in the garden and says, "Chair, raise yourself up high like my father's rope when he hung the honey barrel in the virgin forest and in the steppe." This has the same meaning but, in Mrile's case, a negative connotation. There it was a regressive escape to the realm of the mother, whereas here in "The Three Sons of the Padishah" this same regression leads to the encounter with the anima and a rebirth of the personality.

♦

Chapter 9
The Boy and the Snake

455   We find similar images as in "The Three Sons of the Padishah" in a fairytale from the Danube region, "The Boy and the Snake." Later we will compare several parallel versions to enhance the meaning of the theme, but first here is the main version:

456   There was once a poor woman who lived alone with her son. With her spinning she tried to earn what they needed to survive; what she wove at home, the boy took to the market to sell. Once he sold enough to make a whole groschen and happily made his way back home. On the way he encountered some evil boys who were torturing a young snake. He took pity on the snake and said, "Give me the animal for a groschen." The other boys were glad to have the money and made the trade. The boy took the snake and carried it home. When he arrived he called out, "See, mother, what I bought with the money we made!" The mother took one look and shook her head, "O you foolish child, how could you give a groschen for a poisonous snake?" "Let it be, mother, I am sure it will thank me one day!" He took good care of the snake and gave her something of whatever he ate or drank. Gradually the animal grew into a mighty serpent. One[1] day the snake told the boy that she was the daughter of the serpent king and that she would like to take him to meet her father. He would surely repay the boy for the good he had done. They went to the forest and the serpent king agreed to give the boy whatever he wanted. But when the boy asked for his eight-legged white sun horse and the gemstone from the serpent king's crown, this was too much and the snake king refused. When his daughter complained, he promptly swallowed up the boy. His daughter renewed her pleas and seeing that he could not console his daughter the serpent king spat out the boy. But lo! the boy had been transformed into a handsome prince!

---
[1] [Summarized from here.]

457 The serpent king gave the youth the white sun horse and the gemstone and said, "Ride out in the world, and if you have to do something difficult, just tell your horse and it will always help you through. If it is nighttime, however, you only have to place the gemstone on the horse's brow, and you will always have daytime in front of you!"

458 So the boy rode off, and soon they had left the serpent kingdom, for the horse ran faster than the morning breeze and jumped from one mountain peak to another. It was constantly daytime because when the night came, the boy-prince took out the gemstone, which shone all around like the sun. He finally came to the court of a proud king and entered into his service as a huntsman, where he soon became the king's favorite. This rankled the other servants who determined to ruin him.

459 At the edge of a desert in the high reeds lived a wild boar with golden bristles and twelve wild boar piglets. Many hunters had fallen in pursuit of this beast. The envious servants now told the king that the new servant had bragged that he could catch the boar and her young. Promptly the king ordered the young man to capture the animals. With the help of his horse the young man caught the wild sow in a sack painted on the inside with pitch into which the boar stormed in a blind rage followed by her piglets.

460 Back in the courtyard, he opened the sack and the boar with the golden bristles and piglets ran all over but could not jump over the gates. The king heard the cries and grunts and looked outside. How happy he was to see the shining rays reflecting off the golden bristles!

461 As a reward, he invited the young prince to join him at his table. This, however, only annoyed the other servants all the more and they devised a new plan to destroy him. This time they convinced the king that he should fetch the beautiful princess with the golden braids. On the advice of the white sun horse he had a ship built laden with treasures and an exquisite bed.

462 With the treasure the princess was lured to the ship. While she was admiring the splendors on the ship the young man set sail, kidnapping her and delivering her to the king's court. The king was enraptured by her beauty and wanted to make her his queen but she demanded that before she marries him he brings her her royal mares and favorite colt. The horses roamed on an underwater plain and the stallion that watched over them breathed fire and was so strong that nothing could overpower him.

463   The youth was commanded to obtain the horses. On the advice of his horse, he covered his horse with seven buffalo skins and dug a pit in which they hid themselves near the water edge.

464   The white sun horse dared the colt to come up from the ocean depths with his neighing. At the third call the young stallion came rushing, flames spewing, and stormed upon the sun horse. They fought and bit until blood flowed and sand flew, but neither relented the fight. The sea stallion was indeed very defiant and gradually bit through all seven buffalo hides. But he was tiring from the savage struggle. The sun horse still had his own powers and finally overcame the sea stallion. The young man was now able to lead the ocean horses back to the king's palace."

465   But then the princess commanded that the mares be milked and the king bathe in their boiling milk so that he would turn as white as she was. The king ordered the young man to carry out the task. By blowing cold air out of his left nostril the sun horse cooled the scalding milk and the hero bathed and emerged cleansed with his skin white as milk. Upon seeing this, the king jumped into the bath but then the sun-horse blew hot air out of his right nostril of such heat that it brought the milk bath to an immediate boil. The king disappeared in the seething milk and there was soon nothing left of him but white bones.

466   Now the young man stood before the princess with the golden braids and told her about all his exploits. Her heart melted and she agreed to become his wife. Thus, the young man and the princess with the golden braids were married and rose to the throne of the king. What happened to the white sun horse, the colt and the ocean mares, no one knows. But the young king and beautiful queen lived happily together and are still alive today, if they have not yet died."[2]

467   The opening motif of rescue and caring for a despised animal is akin to the motif of "the helpful animal" where a hero meets and spares an animal along his journey that later returns his gratitude by coming to his aid.[3] The snake is, as explained above, a symbol of the chthonic world. Psychologically, this refers to the sphere of psycho-physical reactions. Thus, the daughter of the serpent king is a prefiguration of the anima still deeply immersed in the unconscious

---

[2] Translated from P. Zaunert, *Deutsche Märchen aus dem Donaulande*, Jena 1926 pp. 315–323.

[3] See, for instance, "The Two Travelers," "Ferdinand the Faithful and Ferdinand the Unfaithful," "The Golden Bird" and to a lesser extent "Cinderella" (Greece), and the large set of parallel motifs listed by Aarne in A. Aarne, *Vergleichende Märchenforschungen, Akademische Abhandlung*, Helsingfors 1908 pp. 3–38.

before she appears in human form.[4] The sphere of the unconscious that connects to the material realm is ambivalent and thus often perceived as being evil itself.[5] Fairytales often stress the wisdom of nature and, therefore, portray the snake as a guardian of the treasure or giver of the redeeming mystery. In the present fairytale this ambivalence of the snake symbol is reflected in the friendly attitude of the snake daughter, on the one hand, and the initially hostile nature of the snake king, on the other. He devours the boy and then only later, after he realizes he cannot dismiss the pleadings of his daughter, does he spew him out again, reborn as a dashing hero. Here the night sea journey motif manifests in its simplest classical form. When it appears at the beginning of a larger-scaled fairytale, this motif is a programmatic anticipation of things to come. This is to show the experiencing conscious mind, in symbolic form, that the adventure of the great quest is actually about being reborn out of the dark womb of the unconscious with simultaneous transformation into a new, greater, and more comprehensive personality.

468 After his rebirth out of the snake king, the hero is transformed and even receives what he requested, the white eight-legged sun horse and the gemstone from the crown of the snake king, which brings daylight wherever it shines. The white horse, like the precious stone, belongs in Hindu and Buddhist belief to the seven treasures of the world ruler.[6] They both represent symbols of the Self. The eight feet are not only an expression of his superior and supernatural speed, but the number eight, the Ogdoad, which like the four, is the number of completion, of self-sufficient wholeness. The gemstone that can make daylight shine, is equivalent to the sun itself and is the highest, all-enlightening consciousness that a human can attain when he or she approaches wholeness. This consciousness comes from the assets of the serpent king and embodies the unconscious spirit as a manifestation of the demonic father. It corresponds figuratively to the "midnight sun."[7] The encounter with the unconscious acts

---

[4] See the snake-anima in "The King of the Golden Mountain."

[5] See, for example, the snake in "Golden Feet."

[6] See E. Rousselle, *Dragon and Mare*, Princeton 1970 p. 116 fn. 29. In "The Magic Horse" [a rich and detailed parallel, with motifs similar to the story of Séaghan in "The Great Fool from Cuasan" (see Volume 1, p. 243).] the eight-footed steed who "can speak and possesses great wisdom" was given in gratitude to the hero by its former owner, an old man who had been blind and whom the hero healed. Also, Ferdinand, in "Ferdinand the Faithful and Ferdinand the Unfaithful," receives a white horse from his demonic godfather.

[7] See the underground triad of snake, old man, and stone (with the anima figure a quaternity) in "The Cave Under the Oak":

> Once upon a time there was a man, who would have given anything to make his sick wife healthy again. One day he went in to the forest to fetch wood. He went deeper into the forest and suddenly came upon a huge, very thick, and tall oak tree. He walked all around the tree and noticed a large cave at its base. Twice he tried to go down into the cave, but could not succeed. The third time he managed to enter and found himself at the top of a flight of golden stairs. He stepped down eight golden stairs and groped around in the dark and touched a door handle. He turned it downwards and the door opened. He stepped into a large chamber and, when his eyes got more used to the dark, noticed an old, snow white man. He sat on a stool and at a nearby table sat two maidens who were sewing. Their feet rested on a diamond

like a great illumination and gives the hero the spiritual strength and the knowledge to meet the challenges of the dangerous adventures to follow, which had been anticipated in the image of being swallowed by the serpent king.

469   The next part of the tale is a parallel to "Ferdinand the Faithful and Ferdinand the Unfaithful" and we can, therefore, treat it here briefly. The slanderers represent secular, that is, collective-oriented shadow figures, their wishes and demands can cause corruption but they can also spur higher development. The wild boar with her glistening golden luster is an impressive image of the still undomesticated, half-harmful, half-enlightening power of the unconscious.[8] As a sow, a mother pig, this animal is a symbol of the Great Mother and represents the unconscious in its materiality and also its image-forming function. The number twelve (twelve piglets), like the twelve dark men in "The King of the Golden Mountain" relates to fate in the sense of "realization in time." Thus, the hero reaches a psychic level in which the distinction between inner and outer, psychic and material reality, is suspended and he experiences the natural creative power of the soul.

470   When the hero captures the mother sow, this means that he can include this power of the unconscious in his sphere of consciousness, which brings enlightenment (the court is filled with the golden light). The bag full of pitch is a symbol for the womb, where the pitch is the negative equivalent to gold.[9]

---

footstool. The intruder hid behind the oven and waited to see what would happen next. Suddenly he saw that one snake after another came slithering out of a corner, went to the diamond footstool, kissed it, and wove their way back to their hiding place. Then the old man stood up, also kissed the stool, turned and spoke to the intruder, " O human! How did you enter here?" The man answered, "Chance had it so." The old man spoke further, "You also had good luck that you did not kiss the stool. For had you done that, then I would have smote you to sun dust." Thereupon he gave the man a whole sack full of gemstones. The man was exceedingly happy and made his way back up the golden steps and home through the woods to his wife. He told of his adventure and went off to the pharmacy to purchase medicines to heal her sickness. The apothecary noticed a special smell about the man and asked him where he had been. He promised to give the man all his wealth if he would tell where he had been and what had happened to him. The man then told him openly and truthfully all that he had experienced. Thereupon the apothecary with his son went into the woods with the man. They carried scythes stuck into their belts. When they got to the oak tree, the man climbed up and waited to see what would happen to the other two. Down in the cave, a snake slithered up to the apothecary and cut itself on the scythe. Then came another snake, and a third, and a fourth, fifth, sixth, seventh, and an eighth. All cut themselves, only the eight did not. It hit the oak tree with its tail, the oak tree bent over like a stalk, the man fell to the ground, and was crushed to sun dust. [Translated from F. S. Krauss, *Sagen der Südslaven*, Vol. 1, Leipzig 1883 pp. 237-38.]

Here the chthonic world is represented in four forms. The highest value, the Self, is the diamond stool, which serves the anima figure (in double form). The snakes represent the earthly aspect in the world, the old man represents wisdom. Both worship the stone, the power that supports the world soul. It is an event in the other world. The humans who presage this process can contact the highest value only if they are called. The further course of the tale reveals that this particular man who "had the chance" to witness the intuitive show of a mysterious event, was in the end not an appointed one.

[8] [*Gullinbursti* (meaning "Gold Mane or Golden Bristles") is a boar in Norse mythology.]

[9] On the juxtaposition of gold and pitch, see the two half-sisters in, "Mother Holle." [In the Grimm's

Here again a zoomorphic Great Mother figure is trapped in her own darkness, not with a fight but with a certain knowledgeable, "letting do as she pleases" (that is, permissiveness).

471   The abduction of the princess is also similar to the plot in "Ferdinand the Faithful and Ferdinand the Unfaithful" and means that the unconscious gradually takes shape in the form of the anima and thereby becomes accessible to the conscious mind. The beautiful bed, an image of the receiving container, by which the hero abducts the anima, corresponds to the big sack used by the hero to outwit the wild boar sow. It symbolizes the humble-receptive attitude of consciousness through which the process of catching the wild sow can be repeated at a higher level. With conscious effort, the figures of the magical gradually lose their animal-like, wild aspect and take on a form comprehensible to humans. The dangerous side of the unconscious is, however, not yet overcome, and now enters separately from the anima as an independent force in the figure of the sea colt with his herd of broodmares. This is another form of the impulsive and unbridled animal passion rising up out of the unconscious. The hero does not expose himself to direct combat; it is not the task of consciousness, although it is superior in its ability to handle and control events, to master this given situation. Rather, this particular constellation calls for a stirring, active witnessing, and enduring the suffering, involving the whole personality with its animal nature. Ultimately, it is the sun-horse that defeats the sea stallion in the service of the hero. This battle of the horses vividly symbolizes the clash of opposites, the contrasting nature of the unconscious, out of which basically all deeper life conflicts emerge.

472   The role of consciousness (of the hero) is here interesting: on the one hand, it provokes the outbreak of a latent conflict in the unconscious (through the quest of the hero) by its effort to make conscious some significant unconscious inner contents. On the other hand, it alone cannot bring about any solution, but it can support the positive forces of the unconscious and thus indispensably contribute to the success of the endeavor. In the fairytale, this is figuratively expressed in the fact that the hero assists in the ruse of the sun horse (digging the pit, laying on the buffalo hides). In lending him help that extends beyond what is possible for an animal, they together prove superior to the purely animal (the sea stallion). Thus, the domesticated animal nature won out over the inner wildness that had been aroused by activating the problem of the anima. The conscious mind is able to maintain its leading role, but a further test is in store that symbolically represents a repetition – as if doubly to assure that the point is driven home, or that consciousness has really become aware of the situation and the (potential) development that has

version, they are called *Goldmarie* (Gold Mary) and *Pechmarie* (Pitch Mary). In the English version, the girls are not given proper names, but called the pretty daughter and the lazy daughter.]

taken place. Immersion in the hot bath of mare's milk is an image of enduring in the hellfire of one's own passions. In the previous fairytale, "The Three Sons of the Padishah," the milk was poisoned, however, which indicates a more dispassionate damaging of the conscious mind by the unconscious. This could point to lies, paranoid fantasies, and illusions. This time it gets "under the skin" of the hero himself, that is, the conflict now reaches the threshold of consciousness. From what had been perceived as a hollow torment, emerges a saving instinct that leads the way and should now become an unavoidable conscious suffering. The king-sultan-padishah, the secular conscious attitude of goal-oriented thinking, succumbs to this hot bath of [conscious] suffering. To the hero comes, however, unexpected help; the sun horse who had helped destroy the king, now stands by the hero and cools the hot bath by snorting with his left nostril. The horse proves to be the master of heat and coolness; on the animal level it embodies the balancing and controlling psychic center, the Self. After the union with the princess the horse disappears: the Self as such does not reach the threshold of consciousness, but remains an unknown, an undetected inner power. This figure is like a helpful instinctual force of the unconscious, which becomes activated in dangerous life crises.[10] The anima is included by the conscious mind, however, as an autonomous psychic power in the cycle of life.

---

[10] See the parallel ending (battle of the horses, bathing in the mare's milk, disappearance of the magical horse) in "The Magic Horse".

Chapter 10
The Rose Maiden

473   Another tale from Transylvania, "The Rose Maiden," also has the horses take on decisive actions and can be useful to amplify the earlier tales.

474   Once there was a woman who lived in the forest. One day she came upon a poor orphan boy who had lost his way. She took pity on him and invited him into her home and cared for him like a true mother. When he had grown up he said one day, "Mother, I must go look for the Rose Maiden!"

475   "Oh, but she is far away, my son, and if you should go that way you will meet with great difficulties because she is guarded by a fierce dragon." But the boy had made up his mind and could not be held back. His forest mother gave him a bell and said, "If you ever want something, then ring this bell!" Then he went off and traveled a long, long way. One day he unexpectedly came upon a large swarm of bees. He asked the queen bee if she knew where the Rose Maiden lived. She did not know and she sent out her bees to collect information. Upon their return they reported that they had found no news but when the queen bee counted her bees one was missing. Finally, the missing bee returned. She had been lamed on the way but she brought the desired message that she had been in the neighborhood of the Rose Maiden.

476   She offered to show the boy the way. He readily accepted, and she led him across a huge, wide meadow until they came to a forest. At the other side of the forest, the Rose Maiden lived in a big castle. The boy went there and asked for employment and promptly got a job as geese herder. The boy pastured his flock in the vicinity of the garden. Here he saw the Rose Maiden every day as she walked among the flowers. She was exceedingly beautiful.

477   One day he overheard some courtiers saying that the Rose Maiden went every night to a ball in the city. That evening, he took his bell and rang it. Suddenly there stood before him a copper horse, and beside it lay a copper jacket. He donned the cloak, jumped on the

horse, and rode to the ball where he danced with the Rose Maiden, who she seemed to like the handsome boy. Before the ball was over, however, he stole away, mounted his horse and rode home. The Rose Maiden told her mother about the handsome boy in the copper jacket. The boy had, however, gone back to herding the geese and only furtively glanced into the flower garden. The next night the Rose Maiden again went to the ball. The geese herder again rang his bell, and immediately a silver horse stood ready, and a silver jacket lay next to it. He threw on the jacket and rode into the city to the ball where he again entertained the Rose Maiden, who enjoyed his company. Before the ball was over, however, he hurried away, mounted his horse, and rode off.

478 The following morning the Rose Maiden told her mother about the handsome boy she had spoken with who was dressed in a silver coat. The boy was looking after his geese and only cast sidelong looks to the flower garden. The girl's mother wanted to get behind the secret of the handsome boy, and advised her daughter to take some pitch with her to the ball and when she danced with the handsome boy, to rub it into his hair.

479 The next evening she again went to the ball and this time took the little piece of pitch with her. This time when the geese herder rang his bell a golden horse appeared along with a golden cloak. At the ball, he went right up to the Rose Maiden and danced with her. As her mother had advised, the girl rubbed the pitch into his hair as they danced. The boy did not notice and as usual left the ball before it was over and rode back to his sleeping hut.

480 In the morning, the girl rose again and told her mother of the handsome boy who had come to the dance in a golden cloak, and how she had put some pitch in his hair. On the day, the geese herder went right up to the wall and peaked into the garden. The girl was on the lookout, however, and when she saw him, she noticed the pitch in his hair disheveled. "You are our savior," she cried out joyfully. And when the boy answered, "That I would happily be!"

481 Then the girl's mother spoke and said, "Let us escape while the dragon is asleep! If he awakens, we will be lost." The boy went out and rang his bell three times. At once the copper, silver and golden horses were ready. He sat the Rose Maiden on the golden steed and wrapped her in his golden coat, the mother he mounted on the silver horse and gave her the silver coat. He himself jumped up on the copper horse and put on the copper jacket. Then they all sprang off in haste.

482 In the castle there was a mighty barrel with three iron hoops. The dragon had been hibernating in that cask but was just then waking up. Suddenly one of the hoops sprang apart, then the second, and then the third. Each time a crack resounded as powerful as a thunderbolt. Now the dragon rubbed his eyes and looked around. "Where is my Rose Maiden?" But nobody answered. Then he jumped up and looked in every room and all over the garden, but there was nobody there. He hurried to the stable, jumped on his stallion, saying: "Take me to the thieves as fast as you can!" It was not long before he reached the fugitives.

483 As soon as the dragon approached, they became transfixed on the spot and could not move. Then the dragon thundered, "I could smash you, you little earth worm, but that would bring me no fame." Then he took from the boy, his bell, the copper, silver, and golden horses with the Rose Maiden and her mother, and turned back to the castle. He looked back and taunted the boy, "You could have saved the Rose Maiden if you had a horse, from my mother, like I have. But that will never happen."

484 The dragon went to the castle and climbed back into his barrel to take another long rest. The iron rings themselves closed upon the barrel. The Rose Maiden and his mother were alone again, the girl cared for her flowers by day and no longer went to the ball at night. She always thought of her rescuer. But the boy had set off to find the dragon's mother.

485 On the way he saw a raven that had become entangled in a net. The raven asked the boy, if he would help him out, he would repay in kind one day. The boy freed the bird who flew away. Further along he came upon a fox stuck in a trap who could not get away. "Help me," said the fox, "I will reward you later." The boy set the fox free, and it ran into the woods. Then, when the boy was walking along the shore of a sea, he came upon a large fish that was floundering on the sand. "Put me back into the water! I will reward you later," spoke the fish. The boy did this and soon after he saw a hut in the woods. Here lived the dragon's mother. He knocked at the door and asked if she would take him into her service. "Oh, yes, you shall guard my mare! And what shall I give you as your yearly wage?" asked the old woman. "A foal born in the clouds," said the boy. "So it shall be," replied the old woman, "but if you ever do not bring my mare back home, your life is up."

486 This witch had taken many young men into her service and had killed them all. Next morning, the boy brought the mare out to pasture. She

soon, however, vanished completely from sight. Although he looked long and everywhere he could not find her. Evening was fast approaching. Then he called the raven and said, "Help me if you can!" The bird said the mare was in the clouds and has brought a foal into the world. "Come and sit on my neck, and I will take you there!" The bird flew the boy to the mare and he was able to bring the mare and the foal home. The old woman was surprised. The following morning, he drove out the mare and her foal. Again the mare disappeared with the foal and although he searched every nook and cranny, he could find no trace of them. The fox came by and the boy reported of his distress. The fox spoke right up and said, "They are in a mountain cave and she has brought another foal into the world. Come and sit on my tail and I will take you there." That the boy did, he entered the cave through a fox hole and drove the mare and two foals home. The witch again made big eyes when she saw her mare and the two foals. On the third day, he drove out the mare, this time with the two foals. Again they all immediately vanished from his sight. He sought after them the whole day but could find no trace. When evening came, he came to the seaside and looked sadly into the waters. Suddenly the big fish whose life he had saved swam up and asked him why he was so sad. The boy told all about his plight. The fish said, "She is at the bottom of the ocean and has since given birth to a third foal. If you want, I will take your there!" The big fish took the boy in its mouth and swam to where the mare and her three fillies were. Then the boy drove them all to the shore and back to the old woman's hut. The old woman did not know how this all had happened. She had nowhere else to hide the mare and her foals, and so the boy grazed them on the field until a year was up. Then she said, "Now you can choose a filly," and he chose the eldest. It had grown into a beautiful mare.

487 Then the boy rode on his horse to rescue the Rose Maiden. As soon as he was close, his mare began to neigh. The dragon's young stallion in the barn heard the whinny and started to neigh and stomp the ground so hard that everything began to shake. The dragon awoke in his barrel, as his year's sleep was just ending. The three iron hoops broke with a great bang one after the other. He heard the neighs, jumped up, and ran to the barn. But the stallion had already broken loose and was feverish to run to the mare. The dragon grabbed him by the mane and swung himself up on his back and tried to subdue him. This only excited the young stallion more and he bucked until the dragon fell off. The wild stallion trampled the dragon under his hooves, until he was dead. Then he ran out of the barn, jumped over

the castle wall, and headed out after the mare. When the boy had arrived at the palace, he jumped down from his mare, climbed over the garden hedge, greeted and embraced the Rose Maiden. His mare had turned around and was on her way back to the old woman and the other fillies with the stallion right on her tail. Now the boy was king of the castle and retrieved his bell and his three magical horses again. Then he took the Rose Maiden in marriage and they lived gloriously and joyfully ever after.[1]

488   At the outset of the tale we are told that the hero is an orphan. This characteristic is a typical motif reflecting the hero's outer poverty. Here there is, however, a special nuance that is connected to the idea that a person has two parents, the biological parents and the "spirit" parents, the godfather and godmother. These are often acquired symbolically, for instance, through a baptismal rite. These represent psychologically the parental images in their psychic reality, and so baptism signifies a mysterious rebirth. The mythological motif of the two mothers belongs to the same circle of ideas of self-rejuvenation.[2] The youth of this tale has no biological parents, but only his "spirit" mother in the figure of the forest woman. Thereby he is relatively close to the psychic events following their fateful course. He receives from his forest mother a tintinnabulum [a small chime or handbell] that when rung, fulfills his wishes. Such a role for a bell is rare as a symbol of psychic sensitivity and as such refers here to the hero's connection to the mother. That this bell grants wishes means that the hero's psychic ability is at the same time an aptitude for fantasy, which helps him to achieve his inner goals.

489   The bees that show the way for the hero are, as discussed in the interpretation of the tale "Rakian" (see Volume 1, p. 485), images of the soul. As insects, bees represent the anima at a pre-human stage of development. Bees have an orientation system that may seem unusual to humans. They are therefore good representatives for the unconscious, which in a similar way extends its perceptions out to areas that are foreign to consciousness. Connected to these special sensibilities and standing close to his unconscious perception and orientation skills, the hero lets himself be led by the clairvoyance of love to find the path to the anima. The Rose Maiden is herself like a bee, attending to her garden flowers. The hero's beggarly role as goose herder at the court and his secret rides to the ball are reminiscent of the well-known story, "Cinderella." Taking on this lowly role is an expression of the psychological fact that the inner journey almost always passes through a phase of hardship, adversity, and servitude. The conscious mind must relinquish its

---

[1] Translated from J. Haltrich, *Siebenbürgen*, Vienna 1882 p. 23-24.
[2] See C.G. Jung, CW 5, *Symbols of Transformation* ¶494f.

pride and submit to the demands of the unconscious that appear (from the conscious standpoint) to be absurd and humiliating. But as a result of just this subordination it gains breadth and power, which in our tale is expressed by the hero being recognized as a "golden Prince." The sequence of steps through copper, silver, and gold represents increased refinement or ennobling of metal, a concept from oriental alchemy that flows into many fairytales from eastern Europe, expressing the soul's purification and development process.

490   When the anima is described, as in this tale, as being completely perfect, then usually her darker aspect is present somewhere but as a completely separate figure that carries traits of the archetype of the father or of the shadow. Here, this dark force is embodied by the dragon, who takes his annual sleep in a barrel. This reflects the fact that the demons of the unconscious come only periodically into the light of day. This motif expresses man's perception of the anima as sometimes that which alone can make him happy, and, at other times, as the epitome of a purely demonic being. Thus, the dragon, who seems to be a dark lover of the Rose Maiden,[3] awakens from his yearly hibernation in his barrel and threatens the lovers. The bursting hoops symbolize the self-contained cycle of deepest nature, which appears to be interrupted from time to time. The breaking of these bonds indicates the loosening of psychic inhibitions, which otherwise constrain the dark instinctual powers of the unconscious.[4] The emergence of the dragon is a sudden outbreak of wild dark psychic forces that threaten to destroy the process of becoming conscious of the anima that has been initiated.

491   The interpretation of the dragon as a chthonic deity and as a lover of the Rose Maiden is confirmed by a variant of our tale in the collection of *German Fairy Tales Since Grimm*, "The Princess in the Tree," where the castle of the princess is at the top of a tree and instead of a dragon there is an evil magician. On the wall of a chamber that he was forbidden to enter, the hero finds this sorcerer in the form of a crucified and desiccated raven.[5] The hero gives three drops from a special pitcher to the thirsty raven, with each drop a nail falls out and with the third the raven flies off and kidnaps the princess. The raven represents an evil spirit,[6] which rules over the anima and keeps her too high

---

[3] For another image of this figure see the tale "The Comrade."

[4] See here also "The Frog King, or Iron Henry."

[5] P. Zaunert, *Deutsche Märchen seit Grimm*, Jena 1922 pp. 5-19. This tale is retold in its entirety in English by Jung in C.G. Jung, CW 9i, *The Archetypes and the Collective Unconscious* ¶422–424. See also the crucified ravens in "The Bird with the Nine Heads" where the son of a friendly sea dragon has the shape of a fish and is stapled with four nails to the wall of the cave of an evil nine-headed bird. The hero frees the fish by touching him and they agree to be "brothers." The dragon-father then appears and begins the rescue of the hero. Here the figure of the chthonic deity is split into a benevolent and an evil force: the suffering part is the son, the shadow of the hero (they become "brothers"). This grouping is reminiscent of the devil and the ferryman in "The Devil with the Three Golden Hairs."

[6] See the figure of the raven as a deity among the tribes from eastern Siberia (Chuckchee, Koryak) and the North American Inuit (Tlingit, Haidu, Tshimshian, Kwakiutl), for instance, in the tale "The Raven Legends." According to M. Grünbaum, *Aufsätze,* Berlin 1901 p. 183ff, several legends refer to the "thirst"

above the ground, above reality. He is a spirit preventing the anima from descending into this world and being "realized." The princess also calls him a devil, clearly illuminating his quality as Lord of the Underworld.[7] The sorcerer, or raven is, in contrast to the dragon of the present tale, freed by the hero himself in ignorant pity. This describes the psychological process when the intervention of the conscious mind can unleash the demons of the unconscious. When this happens, the latent antagonistic nature of the unconscious (symbolically represented as the state of being crucified, that is, suspended and strung out between the opposites of the unconscious[8]) becomes an overpowering conflict in which the unconscious threatens to devour consciousness. A fairytale from the Balkans, "The Golden Apples and the Nine Peahens," describes a similar episode:

492   There was once a tsar who took great delight in his garden. Every morning you could see him bending over his flowers or picking the fruit of his favorite tree. This was an apple tree that had the magic property of bearing buds, blossoms, and golden fruit every day. It was known as the golden apple tree. In the morning the first thing the tsar did when he woke up was to look out his bedroom window and to see that all was well with his beloved tree. One morning he was grieved to see that the tree had been stripped of all the golden fruit which had ripened during the night.

493   "Who has stolen my golden apples?" he cried. The palace guards looked everywhere for some trace of the thief but found nothing. The next morning the same thing had happened and every morning thereafter the tree had been stripped of its golden fruit. He called his three sons to him and said, "Is it seemly that a Tsar who has three able-bodied sons should be robbed night after night of his golden apples? Are you willing that this should happen and you do nothing about it?"

---

of the raven (see also F. F. A. Kuhn, *Mythologische Studien*, Vol. 1, Gütersloh 1886 Vol. 1, p. 94 fn. 1, probably because the raven signals rain. In this tale it is of no import, however, since the raven shares thirst with other divine figures of the magical realm in fairytale literature.

[7] In a Russian variant, "Maria Morevna," the evil figure is "Koshchey the Deathless" (also called "The Immortal Koschtschey") the male arch-demon of Russian fairytales. According to C.G. Jung, CW 9i, *The Archetypes and the Collective Unconscious* ¶435, *Morevna* means "daughter of the sea" and Koschtchei Bessmértnoi, "Immortal Old Bones," comes from *koscht* = skeleton, bones, stingy, miser and *pakosth, kaposth* = disgusting, dirty. R. Jakobson, in his afterword to the English edition states, however, that *Koshchey* "signified in Old Russian, as well as in its Turkish prototype, *koschi*, meaning simply "prisoner." The intercourse and struggle of ancient Russia with the nomadic Turkish world bequeathed, in general, many names and attributes to the Russian tales." N. Guterman, (trans.), *Russian Fairy Tales*, New York 2006 pp. 649–650. Both interpretations are consistent with the meaning of the figure in this fairytale.

[8] Gebser etymologically derived the nature of the cross as a "divider of the circle and thus disrupter of destiny," J. Gebser, *Ursprung*, Stuttgart 1949 p. 449 English: Gebser p. 554.) This meaning does not refer, however, to the equal-sided cross in which the raven in the above tale is nailed inside the magical world.

494   The eldest son[9] stood guard but fell asleep and woke up to find the tree robbed. The same happened with the second brother. Then the youngest son offered to stay awake. On the stroke of midnight nine beautiful peafowl flew down from the sky. Eight settled on the branches of the apple tree and began eating the golden fruit. The ninth alighted beside the young prince and changed into a lovely maiden. The young prince fell in love and showered her with kisses. At the first streak of dawn she jumped up, saying she must leave but would return the next night The prince then remembered about the apples and asked the peahens to leave one apple. This he took to his father, who was pleased and did not ask about the particulars of the night.

495   The elder two brothers became jealous that their younger brother had succeeded where they had failed and sent an old woman to spy on him. That night as the prince and the maiden were kissing the witch snipped a lock of hair off the maiden's head, who fled with the peahens. The youngest son then set out in the world and after many adventures found the maiden and married her. One day she had to leave her castle and gave her husband twelve keys to the castle's cellar rooms. He was forbidden to enter the twelfth cellar room but he could not resist. There he found a barrel enclosed in iron rings. From a faucet hole a voice called out, "In God's name, I beg you brother! I am dying of thirst, bring a cup of water!" The tsar's youngest son brought water, poured it through the hole, and one of the iron hoops burst. Again, he heard the voice begging for water, and again he poured water in, and the second iron hoop sprang apart. A third time the voice begged and when the third iron ring broke, the barrel fell apart and a dragon came out, went up through his castle, grabbed the tsarina who had just returned, and flew off.

496   The hero again set off to search for her. He traveled over the world and after many adventures came to the dragon's palace and found the tsarina. They escaped while the dragon was away. But the dragon quickly caught up with the fugitive pair and reclaimed the tsarina.

497   The young man then stole back to the dragon's castle but he realized that if he wanted to rescue his beloved, they needed a swifter horse than the dragon. He asked the tsarina to find out from the dragon where he could find such a steed. The dragon revealed the secret: if a man could successfully pasture the mare and foal of an old witch, then he could choose from her twelve magnificent stallions a horse. He should pick the eleventh, the most mangy one, in the corner of the stall.

---

[9] [The rest of the story is summarized from here.]

498 The hero went in search of the old hag. On the way he successively rescued a fish, a fox and then a wolf. The hero enlisted himself in the service of the old woman and tended her mare and foal. But each time he fell asleep and the mare and foal disappeared. The helpful animals aided him to return the mare and foal, which they transformed into fish, foxes, and wolves. Each time the witch asked what had happened and the mare answered, "I was with the fish (fox, wolf) and a friend of mine came and betrayed me." The hero, having successfully performed his task received his horse of choice, which turned into a beautiful golden steed as soon as he led it into the forest. He then rode back to the dragon's castle, where he rescued his beloved and they rode off together to her kingdom where they lived happily ever after.[10]

499 Here it is clearly shown how the lively participation of the conscious mind unleashes a demon of the unconscious. The unconscious "thirsts" for this sympathy, which is symbolized by the water, and to participate in consciousness.[11]

500 After the dragon's victory the hero of "The Rose Maiden," makes a second attempt to rescue his beloved. This time he frees various animals and thereby enlists their promises of help in the future. He does not go directly to challenge the dragon, but first to its mother. This is significant insofar as the dragon spends a year sleeping in a barrel. The drum, cask, vat, and barrel are all vessels and as such symbols of the womb or of the unconscious as a protective, caring enclosure.[12]

501 Being enclosed in a barrel (negatively) means being locked in the unconscious, far from life, which is why being caged or locked up in a barrel is a common kind of punishment in fairytales.[13] The dragon in the barrel thus indicates that the dark destructive power of the unconscious is connected with the mother image,[14] and thus the hero can defeat the dragon only after he has received the psychic energy, the vital force (that is, the horse) from the mother of the dragon. The pregnant mare in "The Rose Maiden" or the mare and her

[10] From the English of P. Fillmore, *The Laughing Prince*, New York 1921 pp. 107–138 (There called "The Enchanted Peafowl") and the translation from A. Leskien, *Balkanmärchen*, Jena 1919 pp. 96–107. [The latter collector reports that the phrase "In God's name, I beg you brother!" is an ancient call for help of two men standing in deep brotherhood.]

[11] See the "thirst" of the anima figures in "The Three Lemons" and the Spanish variant, "Three Oranges With One Leap" (see Volume 1 p. 442). There also the course of the story concerns the participation of the conscious mind in the fate of the unconscious. See also the collection of reference material in J. Bolte and L. Mackensen, *Handwörterbuch* Berlin 1930, under *Geist aus der Gefangenschaft befreit* [freeing the spirit from captivity].

[12] C.G. Jung, CW 5, *Symbols of Transformation* ¶306 ¶405.

[13] See, for example, "The Strong Son of the Smith," "Brother, Sister, and the Golden-Haired Prince," "Martti" and "The Secret of Bath Bâdgerd." In all these tales the dragon is confined to a barrel as a penalty and to be exterminated.

[14] See the combination of devil and grandmother. Ultimately, they comprise the primordial mythological parents.

foal in "The Golden Apples and the Nine Peahens" is a symbol of the mother herself in animal form[15] and as such is not absolutely evil, but she can be overcome and made subservient. What is devilish here, as so often, is the combination of human conscious or human scheming, which instigates the untamed instinctual drives of the unconscious to become destructive. This is the reason why this aspect of the mother image must be conquered. Then the unconscious in its divine-animal innocence is revealed as a pure force of nature that can be steered. The mare escapes the hero and goes into all three areas of nature: air, earth, and water; and in each of them gives birth to a colt. This means that it is extremely difficult for the conscious mind to capture the unconscious in its creative moment, and yet the mystery of the unconscious is only lifted by experiencing its creations.

502   Air, water, and earth symbolically signify the spiritual, psychic, and physical realms, which represent different aspects of psychic reality. Only those who have apprehended the unconscious in all these aspects gains the superiority of consciousness that makes it possible to overcome the dark machinations of the primordial mother. A raven, a fox, and a fish (in the variants there are other animals, but in principle always a bird, a water, and a land animal). The meaning here is, as always, that the hero mobilizes the support of his own inner animals or animal souls, his animal components, because he has found a harmonious attitude toward them. This is especially clearly stated in the variant "The Golden Apples and the Nine Peahens." When the mare strays under the waters and returns (with the help of the fish, the fox, and the wolf), it tells the witch that the animals were "my friends and they betrayed me."

503   The hero in "The Rose Maiden" acquires the oldest foal, namely the one born in the clouds.[16] This air or cloudhorse is like the sun horse in "The Boy and the Snake" which had been wrested from the deepest layers of the unconscious. It embodies a psychic energy of predominantly spiritual aspects (sun = consciousness, air = *pneuma* = spirit [mind]). In a Romani fairytale, "The Emperor's Three Daughters and the Devil," the horse somersaults when it is handed over to the hero and becomes a horse of gold with twenty-four wings. Gold is like the sun, by whose astrological sign it is so well expressed, a symbol of immutable incorruptible consciousness. The wings indicate the spiritual quality of the power embodied in the horse.

504   The wonderful mare of the dragon mother in "The Rose Maiden" attracts the stallion of the dragon and arouses him to such excitement that he kills the dragon. The attraction that exists between the horses is also symbolically the

---

[15] The mare has already been treated in the chapter on the Great Mother, see "Strong Hans" in Volume I, p. 231.
[16] See Bächtold-Stäubli under *Föhlen* [foal]. "The foal was considered more noble and pure than the horse."

bond of love between the mother dragon and her son, found in other mythological representations as Cybele and Attis or Isis and Osiris, where the son is also the mother's lover. The plausibility of this interpretation is confirmed by a motif from a fairytale from Georgia "The Thrush and the Nightingale" in which the anima figure promises to marry the hero only if her three-legged mare does not fight with his young stallion. Partially summarized, the story runs as follows:

505   Once upon a time there was a king who had three sons. When he was old, he called them all to him because he wanted to know to whom he should hand over his kingdom. He first turned to the eldest, and asked him, "Son, can you build me a church where no one could find a mistake?" The son thought over the matter and said: "No, father, I cannot do that." The middle son's turn came, he was asked the same question and gave the same answer. Then the youngest son was asked, who agreed.

506   The youngest son built a church, and all the people and army found nothing wrong with it. But an old man passing by found the foundation to be a tiny, tiny bit crooked. The son built the church anew. Again, all the people and army came and could find nothing wrong with it. But then the old man passed by and remarked that it was missing a thrush and a nightingale. Despondent, the youngest son decided to leave his country. His father gave him a three-legged horse and the boy donned his armor and went off, moving very slowly since his horse had only three legs. On his way, he met an old man who told him the horse was a very good steed, it only had to be told that it was needed then it would take the prince across the sea to a maiden with golden hair who had a thrush and nightingale. They soon came to the region of the girl with the golden hair. He stole up to her and, just as the old man had told him, when she untied her hair, he wound a strand around his hand and held it tight. "I'm dying," she cried, but he grabbed more strands and held them even tighter. "What do you want from me?" she asked. "I want to marry you!" "Good, I agree." "No, that is not enough," replied the prince, "you must swear to it." She swore. "No," he said again, "you must swear by your thrush and nightingale!" But that she did not want to do. Tighter and tighter he wound her hair around his fingers. "I'm dying," cried the girl again. Tighter he pulled. By the whole world, the heavens, and the sun she vowed to marry him, but not by the thrush and nightingale. He pulled her hair tighter. Finally, she swore by the thrush and nightingale. Then he let go of her hair.

507 "I have sworn to marry you," said the girl, "but I will not unless I have led my three-legged horse together with thine. If the two fight, I will not be your wife. If they do not fight with each other, I am yours." The prince agreed, and they let the two horses meet each other. The animals ran neighing to each other, paused, and rubbed their necks together. For they were mother and son, why should they fight?[17]

508 In the tale "The Rose Maiden" the allusion is to incest, and there the image for this is the dragon in the barrel (that is, the son in the womb). The psychic energy that was previously bound up in the unconscious, in the ring of the game of opposites, is now free thanks to the hero breaking open the ring so that he himself subjugated the mare. The intervention of consciousness has partially yoked the forces of the unconscious; the other parts that cannot be assimilated by the conscious mind, however, destroy themselves. What was previously operating in rhythmic succession (the sleeping dragon in the maternal barrel, and his breaking free by bursting the shackles), now becomes the single decisive event, and the image of the *coniunctio* is lifted onto the human level by the hero winning the Rose Maiden, the anima.

509 At the end of the fairytale "The Boy and the Snake" the two magical horses from the dragon's realm, the sea stallion and the sun horse, run together back to the old witch. In other words, they disappear back into the maternal womb of the unconscious. These horses symbolize the supernatural powers of the unconscious, that manifest only in special situations when the most crucial decisions and life-threatening dangers reach the borders of consciousness. In contrast, the hero gets the copper, silver, and golden magical horses back. These horses embody psychic forces, which belong to the context of the individual personality; they are, as mentioned above, an image for the step-by-step cathartic development of the hero's own psychic being.

510 In the aforementioned fairytale, "The Princess in the Tree" the evil wizard that holds the anima figure captive has a three-legged white mare, who tells him everything he wants to know. In "The Golden Apples and the Nine Peahens" the hero acquires a four-legged colt as a reward for his service to the witch. The white horse of the magician has only three legs because when he first acquired the horse from the witch, her wolves bit off one of its legs. Since the magician represents a "dark" earthy spirit, he does not have the powers to completely wrest himself from the womb of the unconscious. The hero, on the other hand, who embodies the clear and prudent freedom of consciousness, succeeds in making a clean separation of his instinctual driving forces from the destructive powers of the unconscious. This is precisely why he is superior

---

[17] Translated from A. Dirr, *Kaukasische Märchen*, Jena 1922 pp. 35–42. [The tale continues, not trans-lated here.]

to the chaos of the unconscious spirit, which remains threatened by the dark greed of the forces of nature, the wolves.

511   In "The Princess in the Tree" the horses also mediate the union of prince and princess and together they trample the evil sorcerer. Here they do not disappear again into the unconscious, however, but like the white horse in "Ferdinand the Faithful and Ferdinand the Unfaithful" are transformed into a handsome prince and beautiful princess who "repair to their own kingdom."[18] It thus appears that the horses in this tale represent the shadow of the main couple, their otherworldly mirror image.[19]

---

[18] [The original text mentions that they had been changed into horses long ago by the same old hunter or evil wizard who charmed the princess up into the tree.]

[19] For more on this tale and the three- and four-legged horses, see C.G. Jung, CW 9i, *The Archetypes and the Collective Unconscious.* ¶425-55. In addition, see Bächtold-Stäubli under*dreibeinig* [three-legged], H. Usener, *Dreiheit*, Bonn 1903 p. 186ff, and also the compilation of stories with three-legged animals, especially horses, the afterword *Nachträge* to the Sphinx motif by Lessmann in G. Hüsing, *Iranische*, Leipzig 1909 pp. 73–88. See the interpretation of being crippled in the section on the "divine twins."

Chapter 11
The Golden Bird

512   The transformation of the animal helpers into human form is the result of the redeeming acts of the hero. They claim a major place in the well-known fairytale "The Golden Bird" whose beginning is very similar to "The Golden Apples and the Nine Peahens." We will discuss this first, and then an Uzbek fairytale, "Prince Hassan Pasha," which develops along a parallel course. This latter tale we will summarize, mentioning only the differences.[1] Here is the Grimm's version of the tale "The Golden Bird":

513   In olden times there was a king, who had behind his palace a beautiful pleasure garden in which there was a tree that bore golden apples. When the apples were just about ripe to be picked, they were counted, but on the very next morning one was missing. This was told to the king, and he ordered that a watch should be kept every night beneath the tree.

514   The king had three sons, the eldest of whom he sent into the garden; but when midnight came the boy could not keep himself from sleeping and the next morning, again, an apple was gone. The following night the second son had to keep watch; but he fared no better than his elder brother.

515   Now came the turn of the third son to keep watch. The king had not much trust in him, however, and thought that he would be of less use than his brothers. The youth lay down beneath the tree, but kept awake and did not let sleep master him. At midnight he saw a bird with golden feathers alight on the tree, which plucked off an apple. The youth shot an arrow at it and while the bird flew off, the arrow had struck its plumage, and a golden feather fell to the ground. The youth brought the feather to the king, who called his councilors together, and everyone agreed that a feather like this was worth more

---

[1] Most likely the Grimm's version is itself of oriental origin. See also the beautiful Iranian parallel, "The Bird Flower-Triller" and, further, J. Bolte and G. Polívka, *Anmerkungen,* Vol. 1, Leipzig 1913 p. 513f, and G. Weicker, *Seelenvogel,* Leipzig 1902 p. 81f.

than the whole kingdom. Upon this, the king declared that he wanted the whole bird.

516   The eldest son set out to find the bird. He trusted his cleverness. When he had gone some distance, he saw a fox sitting at the edge of a wood, so he cocked his gun and took aim. But the fox cried, "Do not shoot me! In return I will give you some good counsel. You are on the way to the Golden Bird; and this evening you will come to a village in which stand two inns opposite one another. One of them is lit up brightly, and all goes on merrily within, but do not go into it; go rather into the other, even though it seems to be a bad one." "How can such a silly beast give wise advice?" thought the king's son, and he pulled the trigger. But he missed.

517   By evening he came to the village where the two inns were. In one they were singing and dancing; the other had a poor, miserable look. "I should be a fool, indeed," he thought, "if I were to go into the shabby tavern and pass by the good one." So, he went into the cheerful one, lived there in riot and revel, and forgot about the bird and his father.

518   When some time had passed, and the eldest son did not return, the second son set out, also wishing to find the Golden Bird. But he fared no better than his brother.

519   Then the king's youngest son wanted to try his luck. At first his father would not let him go. "It is of no use," said he, "he will find the Golden Bird still less than his brothers, and if a mishap were to befall him, he knows not how to help himself; he is a little wanting at the best." But at last, as he had no peace, he let him go.

520   The prince also encountered the fox which begged for its life in exchange for advice. The youth was good-natured, and said, "Be easy, little fox, I will do you no harm." "You shall not regret it," answered the fox; "and that you may get on more quickly, get up behind on my tail." And scarcely had he seated himself when the fox began to run, and away he went over stock and stone till his hair whistled in the wind. When they came to the village, the youth followed the fox's advice, and, without looking around, turned into the little inn, where he spent the night quietly.

521   The next morning, as soon as he got into the open country, there sat the fox all ready, and said, "Go on quite straight, and at last you will come to a castle, in front of which a whole regiment of soldiers is lying. Do not trouble yourself about them, for they will all be asleep and snoring. Go through the midst of them straight into the castle and go through all the rooms until you come to a

chamber where a Golden Bird is hanging in a wooden cage. Close by, there stands an empty golden cage for show, but beware of taking the bird out of the common cage and putting it into the fine one, or it may go badly with you." With these words the fox again stretched out his tail, and the king's son seated himself upon it.

522 When he came to the castle he found everything as the fox had said. The king's son went into the chamber where the Golden Bird was shut up in a wooden cage, whilst a golden one stood by. Also the three golden apples lay about the room. "But," thought he, "it would be absurd if I were to leave the beautiful bird in the common cage," so he opened the door, laid hold of it, and put it into the golden cage. But at the same moment the bird uttered a shrill cry. The soldiers awoke, rushed in and took him off to prison. The next morning he was taken before a court of justice and sentenced to death.

523 The king, however, said that he would grant him his life on condition that he brought him the Golden Horse that ran faster than the wind. If he were to return with the horse he would receive as a reward the Golden Bird.

524 The king's son set off, but he was sorrowful, for how was he to find the Golden Horse? But then he saw his old friend the fox sitting on the road. "Look," said the fox, "this has happened because you did not give heed to me. However, be of good courage. I will give you my help and tell you how to get to the Golden Horse. You must go straight on and you will come to a castle, where in the stable stands the horse. The grooms will be lying in front of the stable; but they will be asleep and you can quietly lead out the Golden Horse. But of one thing you must take heed: put on him the common saddle of wood and leather, and not the golden one, which hangs close by, else it will go ill with you." Then the fox stretched out his tail, the king's son seated himself upon it, and away he went over stock and stone until his hair whistled in the wind.

525 The prince found everything as the fox had said. He came to the stable in which the Golden Horse was standing, but just as he was going to put the common saddle upon him, he thought, "It will be a shame to such a beautiful beast if I do not give him the good saddle which belongs to him by right." But scarcely had the golden saddle touched the horse than he began to neigh loudly. The grooms awoke, seized the youth, and he was thrown into prison. The next morning he was sentenced to death by the court but when the king heard his tale he

promised to grant him his life, and give him the Golden Horse, if he could bring back the beautiful princess from the Golden Castle.

526 With a heavy heart the youth set out, yet soon found the trusty fox. "I ought only to leave you to your ill-luck," said the fox, "but I pity you, and will help you once more out of your trouble. This road takes you straight to the Golden Castle, you will reach it by eventide. At night when everything is quiet, the beautiful princess goes to the bathing-house to bathe. When she enters it, run up to her and give her a kiss, then she will follow you, and you can take her away with you, only do not allow her to take leave of her parents first, or it will go ill with you."

527 Then the fox stretched out his tail, the king's son seated himself upon it, and away the fox went, over stock and stone, till his hair whistled in the wind.

528 When he reached the Golden Castle, all was just as the fox had said. He waited until midnight when everything lay in deep sleep, and the beautiful princess was going to the bathing-house. Then he sprang out and gave her a kiss. She said that she would like to go with him, but she asked him pitifully to allow her first to take leave of her parents. At first he withstood her prayer, but when she wept more and more, and fell at his feet, he at last gave in. But no sooner had the maiden reached the bedside of her father, than he and all the rest in the castle awoke, and the youth was laid hold of and put into prison.

529 The next morning the king said to him, "Your life is forfeited, and you can only find mercy if you take away the hill which stands in front of my windows and prevents my seeing beyond it; and you must finish it all within eight days. If you do that, you shall have my daughter as your reward."

530 The king's son began, and dug and shoveled without leaving off, but when after seven days he saw how little he had done, and how all his work was as good as nothing, he fell into great sorrow and gave up all hope. But on the evening of the seventh day the fox appeared and said, "You do not deserve that I should take any trouble about you; but just go away and lie down to sleep, and I will do the work for you."

531 The next morning when he awoke and looked out of the window the hill had gone. The youth ran to the king, and told him that the task was fulfilled, and whether he liked it or not, the king had to hold to his word and give him his daughter.

532 So, the two set forth together, and it was not long before the trusty fox joined them. "You have certainly got what is best," said he, "but the

Golden Horse also belongs to the maiden of the Golden Castle. Take the beautiful maiden to the king who sent you to the Golden Castle. There will be unheard-of rejoicing; they will gladly give you the Golden Horse. Mount it and offer your hand to all in farewell, last of all to the beautiful maiden. And as soon as you have taken her hand, swing her up on to the horse, and gallop away, and no one will be able to bring you back, for the horse runs faster than the wind."

533 All was brought to pass successfully, and the king's son carried off the beautiful princess on the Golden Horse. The fox did not remain behind, and when he came up to the youth, he said, "Now I will help you to get the Golden Bird. When you come near to the castle where the Golden Bird is to be found, let the maiden get down, and I will take her into my care. Then ride with the Golden Horse into the castle-yard; there will be great rejoicing at the sight, and they will bring out the Golden Bird for you. As soon as you have the cage in your hand gallop back to us and take the maiden away again.

534 When the plan had succeeded, and the king's son was about to ride home with his treasures, the fox said, "Now you shall reward me for my help. When you get into the wood yonder, shoot me dead, and chop off my head and feet."

535 "That would be fine gratitude," said the king's son. "I cannot possibly do that for you." The fox said, "If you will not do it I must leave you, but before I go away I will give you a piece of good advice. Be careful about two things. Buy no gallows'-flesh, and do not sit on the edge of any well." And then he ran into the wood.

536 The youth rode on with the beautiful maiden, and his road took him again through the village in which his two brothers had remained. There was a great stir and noise, and, when he asked what was going on, he was told that two men were going to be hanged. As he came nearer to the place he saw that they were his brothers who had been playing all kinds of wicked pranks, and had squandered all their wealth. He bought off his brothers, and when they were set free they all went on their way together.

537 They came to the wood where the fox had first met them, and, as it was cool and pleasant within it, whilst the sun shone hotly, the two brothers said, "Let us rest a little by the well, and eat and drink." He agreed, and whilst they were talking he forgot himself, and sat down upon the edge of the well without foreboding any evil. But the two brothers threw him backwards into the well, took the maiden, the horse, and the bird, and went home to their father. There was great

joy, but the horse would not eat, the bird would not sing, and the maiden sat and wept.

538 The youngest brother was not dead. By good fortune the well was dry and he fell upon soft moss without being hurt, but he could not get out again. Even in this strait the faithful fox did not leave him. It upbraided him for having forgotten its advice but nevertheless bade him grasp his tail and keep tight hold of it and then he pulled him up.

539 "You are not out of all danger yet," said the Fox. "Your brothers were not sure of your death, and have surrounded the wood with watchers who will kill you if you let yourself be seen." The youth came upon a poor man sitting upon the road and he exchanged clothes with him. In this way he got to the king's palace unknown.

540 No one knew that he was there, but suddenly the bird began to sing, the horse began to eat, and the beautiful maiden left off weeping. The king, astonished, commanded that all people who were in his castle should be brought before him. Amongst them came the youth in his ragged clothes, but the maiden knew him at once and fell upon his neck. When the king heard the youth's tale, the wicked brothers were seized and put to death, but the prince was married to the beautiful maiden and declared heir to the king.

541 But how did it fare with the trusty fox? Long afterwards the king's son was once again walking in the wood when the fox met him and said, "You have everything now that you can wish for, but there is never an end to my misery, and yet it is in your power to free me." Again he asked to be shot dead and his head and feet chopped off. So the prince did, and scarcely was it done when the fox was changed into a man, and was no other than the brother of the beautiful princess, who at last was freed from the magic spell which had been laid upon him. And now nothing more was wanting to their happiness as long as they lived.[2]

542 As in most of the fairytales we have discussed so far, the totality of the conscious personality is symbolized at the outset. This wholeness is represented in the king as the dominant function of the conscious mind,[3] accompanied by his three sons, the three auxiliary functions. The psychic totality is not only in these four figures, but, among others, comprises also the king's garden and the tree with the golden fruit.

---

[2] J. and W. Grimm, *Complete Grimm's*, London 1975 p. 272-79. Original English translation by Hunt, Grimm (1884, 1910b). This tale is already interpreted in W. Laiblin, *Der goldene Vogel*, Stuttgart 1961 (1961). Our interpretation deviates only in a few points from his.

[3] [In the German original the adjective is *seelische*, here usually translated as "psychic." According to Jung, "psychic" includes both ego and the unconscious (see the next sentence). Since the present usage refers to conscious function, it is translated following Hull's translation of Jung's Collected Works.]

543   This garden with the tree is at the same time that which "nourishes" the ego, the unconscious, the "matrix" of consciousness, which accompanies and nurtures the development of consciousness since conception without the ego being aware of it. Man's secular attitude, symbolized by the king, is that the fruits of this easily accessible garden belong to him. It is only in midlife that he discovers that an invisible being reaps the fruits and benefits from the tree that embodies his inner destiny. The fruits are stolen just at the moment when they are ripe, that is, at the peak of life, at midlife, at a time when the ego least expects it. The bird that enters from an unknown side into the seemingly cloistered area causes the loss of soul that confronts the king with unforeseen problems.[4]

544   Another expression of this state of soul loss at the beginning of the fairytale is found in "The Nightingale Gisar," a variant of the present tale[5] summarized here:

545   A king, who preferred to spend his time in prayer, once built a beautiful mosque, but when he prayed in it a dervish came to him and said, "The mosque is indeed very beautiful, but your prayer is to no avail." In anger, the king had the mosque torn down and a new one built. This was repeated two more times, until the king had no more money. The king's sons heard of his plight and told their father to go into the new mosque and pray, they would wait outside and apprehend the dervish. They did this and asked the dervish why he spoke those words to their father. The dervish answered, "This mosque is beautiful like other fine mosques in the world, but it is missing the nightingale Gisar. If this nightingale would sing inside then it would be like no other mosque in the whole world." The sons asked, "Where is the nightingale Gisar? We want to go and get it!" The dervish replied, "I have heard about it, but where it is, I do not know." The sons let the dervish go, entered the mosque and told their father what they had learned. Then, determined to go and find the nightingale Gisar, they set off, one after the other, on the quest.[6]

546   The plight of the king, formulated by the dervish as "your prayer is ineffective," means that he is far from God. What is missing in his religious life is not pomp and external form (the mosque), but the feeling of being alive, because the

---

[4] See, "My Old Woman Must Be Paid" where the theft of the button by the elf Kidhus causes a catastrophic disturbance to psychic wholeness because it is resisted in the wrong way.
[5] See the same motif in the tale summarized in the previous section, "The Thrush and the Nightingale" (page 239).
[6] [Summarized from A. Leskien, *Balkanmärchen*, Jena 1919 pp. 228–236. English version in Fillmore pp. 177–200.]

nightingale with its song symbolizes the natural expression of emotion.[7] The dervish, who in his annoying way spoils the king's work again and again, is a personification of his shadow. Mendicant ascetics, or wandering dervishes maintain a mystical-ecstatic form of religion, which in its spontaneous expression comes in many ways closer to genuine feeling than the official dogma of the *Qu'ran*. This is why the dervish recognizes the absence of the nightingale even though he does not know where it is. He is too tied to specific forms, however, to be able to procure the sought-after inner value, which is to be found in a realm entirely beyond the human.[8] The path to the nightingale leads to witches, tigers, lions, eagles, and past these to the goal deep in the layers of the animal unconscious psyche.

547   The beginning episode of the Iranian tale "The Bird Flower-Triller" likewise touches upon religious problems. We summarize this tale here:

548   A king once had three sons. The king loved the youngest most and this caused jealousy amongst the brothers. One day the king fell ill. All the doctors of the kingdom were called but none of them could heal the king. Then a doctor came who said there was only one cure, a green fish that carried a golden ring threaded through its nostrils. If this fish were to be caught, his stomach cut out, and a piece put on the heart of the sultan, he would surely recover.

549   Fishermen were ordered to capture such a fish, and when they finally found it, they brought it to the sultan. The youngest son marveled at its beauty. Suddenly he saw that something was written on his forehead, and as he peered closer, he read the words: "There is no God but Allah, Muhammed is the prophet of God, and Ali is his caretaker." At the sight of these words the youngest son, Mälik Ibrâhîm, was deeply moved and said to himself, "Although my father might regain his health by this fish, I cannot kill it," and he threw the fish back into the sea. This act was just what his elder brothers were waiting for, now they could condemn their youngest brother. They reported what Mälik Ibrâhîm had done, and his father the king said, "If Mälik Ibrâhîm is just waiting for me to die so that he can inherit my kingdom, from this hour on I will no longer recognize him as my son and heir." Later Mälik Ibrâhîm learnt from his brothers that there was a bird that every time it trilled (that is, sang), a flower fell from its beak. If they could find this bird and bring it to their father, it would cure the king's heart, like the fish.[9]

---

[7] On the nightingale as a messenger of love, see Bächtold-Stäubli under *Nachtigall* [nightingale]. Her song is considered seductive, passionate and exciting.

[8] [German: *aussermenschlich*.]

[9] [Summarized from the German of Christensen pp. 30–45 (original in A. Christensen, *Iran*, Jena 1939

550   The holy phrase that is written on the forehead of the fish is the *shahada* of Shia Islam, the profession of faith, and therefore belongs to the more mystically-oriented denomination of Islam. This confirms our interpretation above of the nightingale as the emotional expression of religion, where, in this variant, the fish is a parallel to the bird.[10] When the prince, struck by the beauty of the fish and its religious value, decides not to kill the fish, it signals a reverential shrinking back by the conscious mind when confronted with the magical background of life. This is a retreat, at first preventing him from becoming aware of the unknown, unconscious conditions and not leading to the goal, but, on the other hand, it expresses an attitude that will later be very useful to the hero.

551   Another representation of soul loss, which is not as deep, but very apt and witty, is at the beginning of the Uzbek parallel, "Prince Hassan Pasha" (summarized):[11]

552   A sultan had three sons. Without knowing the reason why, he was afflicted with great sorrow. "I do not know what has happened with me," said the sultan, "but I am in an unspeakably sad mood and, at the same time, I am irritated with the whole world." To distract him from his woes, he finally let himself be commanded to ride through his forty gardens, which were the most beautiful gardens in the world. In the fortieth garden, in a small clearing, there stood a huge tree with neither branches nor leaves. He asked his gardener what kind of tree it was. His gardener answered, "Every evening around six o'clock a bud develops and opens at the top of the tree, at seven clock, leaves appear, at nine o'clock, flowers blossom and at midnight, the fruit ripens. Then at this hour, a strange bird flies to the tree and by three o'clock early in the morning, it has eaten all the fruit and then it flies away to return the next night." The sultan, all his sadness gone, ordered his sons to go at night and pick the fruit when it was ripe. None of his three sons succeeded because they all fell asleep. The youngest, prince Hassan Pasha, asked for a second chance and this time managed to stay awake. He took a shot at the bird, which escaped, but one feather fell to the ground. On the feather Hassan Pasha found holy words. The sultan now demanded that Hassan Pasha find and retrieve the bird.[12]

(1939)) and the English version given in Von Franz, *Individuation in Fairy Tales*, New York 2001 pp. 155–160 (with interpretation).]

[10] As mentioned in the notes to this fairytale, Christensen *op. cit.* p. 313.

[11] See a fairytale from the Caucasus region, "The Red Fish," where the initial episode runs parallel to the above tale. The spared fish turns out in the end to be identical to the mysterious helper-friend, the role played by the fox in "The Golden Bird."

[12] This story illustrates, in an interesting way, how a fairytale can make use of various images and link

553 Here fourness is again connected with a garden, the sultan finds the magical tree in the fortieth garden. The number forty, so popular in Turkestani fairytales, is a multiple of four. In itself, the garden is a closed area, a *temenos*, and as such, a mandala. It is of feminine nature, and to the extent that the unconscious mind of a man is feminine, and takes on the figure of the anima, it corresponds to a more nature-like prototype of this figure.[13]

554 In this garden there is a tree full of golden fruit. The image is reminiscent of the western garden with the tree of the Hesperides, and the world-ash Yggdrasil, which bears golden apples guarded by the goddess Idunn. Unlike figures of animals, which would indicate the world of instinctual drives, the tree symbolizes gradual, organic, inner growth. The tree draws its strength from the earth and nourishment from the air, just as human life itself develops, extending between the poles of the material and spiritual.[14] The tree has also feminine-maternal meaning, which is important in "The Golden Bird" in as much as the anima is reached through the stages of bird and horse. The garden with the tree is, as a whole, a precursor of the anima, but in the general form of an unconscious life from which the individual is nourished. The tree is also a symbol of the totality of all cosmic forces.[15] This corresponds to the Hindu idea that the cosmic forces are represented by a tree with branches reaching upwards and roots reaching below. According to Hippolytus' account of the Gnostic Simon Magus, "Of all things that are concealed and manifested, the Fire which is above the heavens is the treasure-house, as it were a great Tree from which all flesh is nourished."[16] The incombustible fruit of this tree is the human soul that is saved in the "storehouse."[17]

555 This corresponds to the Hindu (Vedic) concept that represents the cosmic powers in the form of a tree whose roots are above and branches are below,[18]

---

them together differently without changing the meaning of the plot. Motifs can be easily exchanged as long as they have the same symbolic meaning. Thus, the sought-after treasures can vary in their forms, which, at first thought, leads to seemingly unexpected "relationships" or "affinities," between tales. But only when the dynamic process and the meaning, and especially the final goal, are the same, can one speak of a real relationship between tales. The similitude of some motifs, such as the finding of a treasure in general, or the occurrence of magical birds, or answering feathers, does not in itself permit us to assume that the tales are parallels. On the other hand, clear descriptive differences can be insignificant for the meaning, since these variations are often consequences of cultural influences of the narrator or listening public.

[13] It is characteristic of most Turkestan fairytales that they are long and indulge in large numbers and huge quantities. The reason could be, among others, that these tales are still told today and the exaggerations and voluminousness help to captivate the sensation-oriented imagination of the audience. [The tales were collected in the late 1800s and early 1900s.]

[14] See H. Silberer, *Problems of Mysticism*, New York 1917 p. 88, and also the garden of the anima in "The Virgin Tsar."

[15] See C.G. Jung, CW 9i, *The Archetypes and the Collective Unconscious* ¶198 and on the tree in general, C.G. Jung, CW 13, *Alchemical Studies* ¶304-482. The tree has the significance of rootedness, keeping still, growth, expansion into the air and light realms, and as a connection between heaven and earth.

[16] ["The lower twelve are the World Trees of the Garden of Eden. The Trees are divided into four groups, of three each, representing the four Rivers of Eden. The Trees are evidently of the same nature as the cosmic forces which are represented by the Hindus as having their roots or sources above and their branches or streams below." G. R. S. Mead, *Fragments*, London 1931 p. 194f.]

[17] *Ibid* pp. 171–172.

[18] See H. Leisegang, *Die Gnosis*, Leipzig 1924 pp. 68–69. See also Mead, The manifested side of the Fire is the trunk, branches, leaves, and the outside bark. All these parts of the great Tree are set on fire from

which as *purusha* is a symbol of the world-Self. Since the tree is a symbol of inner knowledge, the enlightenment of Buddha came to him under a tree. In paradise next to the tree of life stands the tree of knowledge. As the world-filling power and *anima mundi*, the tree is a symbol of the Self.[19]

556 The golden fruits of the magical tree also represent the Self, which appears to be still in a multiplicity and not yet unified. They also point to the sun because it is born from a tree, for example, in the beliefs of Mithras religion.[20] As an image of the sun, the apples also mean both life energy and consciousness and often have rejuvenating effects.[21]

557 While in the "The Golden Bird" there is a multitude of fruit (the number of which, however, the king knows) in "Prince Hassan Pasha" only one fruit ripens every night from a single bud on the bare tree, the existence of which the sultan knew nothing. The difference is not large; in one case the king intuits that there is some being that deprives him of his power. In the other case, the sultan simply sinks into melancholy, without being clear about what the cause may be, until he discovers the strange tree in his fortieth garden. The tree is as bare as the sultan is sad, and reflects the lifeless state of his soul. It blooms only at night, when his conscious mind sleeps. In the midnight hour, the fruit ripens, a stage that the sultan has not yet reached. This image shows cohesively and clearly that the solution to his problem lies in a process of psychic development that is contained in the story of the stolen fruit. From the tree grow nocturnal buds, flowers, and fruit. This unfolding anticipates the process of self-development, but so far from the sultan's consciousness that the fruit, stolen as it were from his dream soul, escapes him. His depressed mood is, therefore, a way that he can get into his own depths. He must intervene in the game his unconscious has been playing by itself, breaking the ring in order to realize his inner destiny. The bare, leafless tree is reminiscent of an oriental legend in which it was granted to Adam's son, Seth, that he take a peep into Paradise. There he saw that the tree was withered and in its branches lay a small child.[22]

---

the all-devouring flame of the Fire and destroyed. But the fruit of the Tree, if its imaging has been perfected and it takes shape of itself, is placed in the storehouse (or treasure), and not cast into the Fire. For the fruit is produced to be placed in the storehouse, but the husk to be committed to the Fire; that is to say, the trunk, which is generated not for its own sake but for that of the fruit. (G. R. S. Mead, *op. cit.* p. 172, [order of sentences and quotes exchanged for comprehensibility.]

[19] See the *Mahanarayana Upanishad*, Tenth *Anuvāka*, 20 (Deussen *op. cit.*):
 Higher than he nothing exists,
 always neither smaller nor greater,
 That one stands like a tree rooted in heaven
 Purusha, who fills the whole world.

[20] On this see C.G. Jung, CW 13, *Alchemical Studies* ¶173 and in general, *ibid* ¶304-482. More on the tree of life see also W. Mannhardt, *Wald- und Feldkulte*, Vol. 1, Berlin 1875 p. 45ff, 55f, 242f.

[21] See C.G. Jung, CW 5, *Symbols of Transformation* ¶396, ¶662,¶327f and further fn. 32 to ¶330 and the material cited there.

[22] See, "The King's Son, Who Feared Nothing," J. Bolte and G. Polívka, *Anmerkungen*, Vol. 1, Leipzig 1913 p. 513f. See also [fruit in] alchemy, C.G. Jung, CW 12, *Psychology and Alchemy* ¶449f; H. Silberer, *Problems of Mysticism*, New York 1917 p. 258. See also the fruit of immortality in "Sky O'Dawn," and

558   Even with the Aztecs, Quetzalcoatl's fall from paradise, the original home Tamoanchan, is symbolized by a broken yucca tree.[23] This represents a rupture of harmonious but unconscious development, a splitting off from nature through the dawning of individual consciousness. From the reconnection of the two spheres the higher and fuller personality should then emerge. Flower and fruit symbolize the Self at an unconscious, precursory stage and require a reorientation of consciousness in order to evolve into human form. In the previously mentioned Oriental legend, among many other examples, this is represented in the form of a child.[24]

559   The "Fire Flower" and the "fruit of the fire tree" are also Gnostic symbols of the Self. Mead comments on Hippolytus' account of the beliefs of the Simonians:[25] "The fruit of the Fire-tree and the 'Flower of Fire' are symbols (among other things) of immortal man, the garnered spiritual consciousness of the man-plant."[26] In Mandaeism, the fruit-laden tree is an image of the perfect, complete man, and Paradise, into which God transplanted him, is called "the fruits," as in the hymn, "Life answered me out of the fruits and out of the radiance from afar."[27] This completion is contained *in potentia* in the fruit, and its development from the germ is the task given to the sultan: the unfolding, as it were, of the images embodied in the fruit, as they are then experienced in the following course of the tale. Blossoms or flowering fruit correspond to "germinal vesicle" in Eastern meditation, in which being and life still formed a unity. "This is the reason that all the sages began their work at the geminal vesicle in which outflowing had ceased."[28] There the Self is

---

note to this on page 94. About the Tree of Life, the fruits, and the birds see the mythical material in A. Wünsche, *Lebensbaum*, Leipzig 1905 (1905a). The "holy fruit" is in Chinese meditation a name for the Self. See R. Wilhelm, *Secret of the Golden Flower*, London 1962 pp. 63–64 and C.G. Jung, CW 13, *op. cit.* ¶68, ¶76. Also the ancient Phrygians regarded the father of the universe as a "pre-existing almond which contains within itself the perfect fruit, that moves in the depths, that tears open her [i.e., the depths'] womb and gives birth to her invisible, unamenable and unspeakable child of whom we decree, the Logos-Anthropos." (H. Leisegang, *Die Gnosis*, Leipzig 1924 p. 130).

[23] See A. Wünsche, *Lebensbaum*, Leipzig 1905 pp. 31–36, 242.

[24] Perhaps a mountain palm, or yucca, see, M. Graulich, *Myths*, Norman 1997 p. 195, 213. [A native Aztec image of this broken tree is depicted in the *Codex Boturini*, plate 2. For the German reference, see "Quetzalcoatl's Fall and the Demise of Tollan" and note in W. Krickeberg, *Azteken und Inka*, Jena 1928 p. 342.

[25] On the round fruit as a symbol of the Self, see "Arawanili, the First Medicine Man" and the episode in "A Legend of Confucius:"

    One time in Yangtze a thing washed up on land. It was green and round and as big as a melon. The king of Tschu dispatched a message to Confucius asking what this thing could be. Confucius answered, "The green duckweed in the Yangtze bears fruit once every thousand years. Those who obtain this fruit rule over the entire world." ([translated from the German of R. Wilhelm, *The Chinese Fairy Book*, New York 1921 p. 58, this section not included in the English version.]).

[26] [Followers of Simon Magus.]

[27] G. R. S. Mead, *Fragments*, London 1931 p. 172. On Christ as the fruit of the tree (the cross) in *The Acts of Andrew* see *ibid* page 446. In alchemical philosophy the fruits and seeds of the tree of wisdom (*Book of Enoch*) were called the sun and moon. See C.G. Jung, CW 13, *op. cit.* ¶403, ¶404f.

[28] R. Reitzenstein, *Iranische*, Bonn a. Rh. 1921 p. 136.

represented as a golden flower, also meaning the light, that is, enlightenment.[29] The corresponding symbol in India is the lotus,[30] also in Western psychology the flower appears as a symbol of the Self [31] and Maria is also compared to a blossom.[32] As flowers are specific expressions of feelings, their presence in this fairytale indicates that the central issue concerns the anima problem. Strikingly, in a variant from Styria,[33] "The Birds Phoenus and Floribunda," the anima figure's name (Floribunda) means "the flowering one," and the bird in the Iranian variation "The Bird Flower-Triller" is called the "flower -triller."

560   While the sultan undertakes an inner journey (as far as the fortieth garden), he finds a scene that depicts his inner situation, as viewed from the unconscious, as the consequence of his one-sided development of consciousness: the tree of life is desiccated and it wants the tree to grow a ripe fruit that a predatory bird steals every night. The bird –which is also a soul-image, as mentioned above – is, as a species, exactly the opposite of a tree. Not holding still, and not growing up from the ground, are characteristics of birds; their nature is to be fleety, to move freely in the airy realm. The bird symbolizes, therefore, the spiritual aspect of the Self. In a parallel tale cited in Bolte and Polívka[34], the king had become ill (according to other versions, blind), and nothing in the world could heal him until he first heard (or dreamed) that only through the whistles or singing of the far away phoenix could he be healed.[35] The fact that the bird in the present tale is an anticipatory and preliminary stage of the Self is also indicated by an Armenian fairytale in which the bird wears a luminous stone on its head,[36] which, as stated above, being round, is a symbol of the Self. Furthermore, as the subsequent course of the tale shows, the bird is a preform of the anima. Psychologically, the anima can become for the man, usually unconsciously, the cause of his emotional states, his moodiness, and malaise.[37]

---

[29] R. Wilhelm, *Secret of the Golden Flower*, London 1962 p. 71.

[30] C.G. Jung, CW 13, *op. cit.* ¶13, ¶33-34 and commentaries to mandala images (Figs 6, 9, 26, 37) in C.G. Jung, CW 9i, *The Archetypes and the Collective Unconscious* ¶654, ¶659, ¶680 ¶692. On the holy fruit, see R. Wilhelm, *op. cit.*, London 1962 pp. 63–64.

[31] See the *Chāndogya Upanishad*, VIII, First Khanda,1, Deussen, *Sixty Upanishads* p. 191. Also, the text from the *Ātmabodha Upanishad*, quoted ·above on page 188.

[32] See C.G. Jung, CW 11, *Psychology and Religion* ¶90, ¶315, and C.G. Jung, CW 9i, *op. cit* ¶270.

[33] See C.G. Jung, CW 11 *op. cit.* ¶123, C.G. Jung, CW 6, *Psychological Types* ¶392.

[34] J. Bolte and G. Polívka, *Anmerkungen*, Vol. 1, Leipzig 1913 p. 503

[35] See also, "The Story of the Blind King Who Lived in the Western Lands." J. Bolte and G. Polívka, *op. cit.* p. 506 cite a Maltese parallel, "The Bird Through Whose Song the Old are Made a Year Younger." In a Basque parallel the bird is called, in an English rendition, "The White Blackbird," in the French version, "Le Merle blanc (The White Blackbird)" and the version from Carinthia "Die weisse Amsel" (The White Blackbird). This image corresponds to the German term *weisser Rabe* [white raven] and characterized both the uniqueness of this magical bird and the double aspect of the symbol.

[36] See *ibid* p. 30. Cf. on this motif see also the tale, "The Young Hunter and the Beauty of the World."

[37] See Jung:

The anima is a factor of the utmost importance in the psychology of a man wherever emotions and affects are at work. She intensifies, exaggerates, falsifies, and mythologizes all emotional relations with his work and with other people of both sexes. The resultant fantasies and entanglements are all of her doing. When the anima is strongly constellated, she softens the man's character and makes him touchy,

561   Equipped with this insight, we can recognize the sultan's irritation with all those around him as being an anima mood. Indeed, the story reveals that the reason behind his depression is the bird that is stealing his power. (This is similar to the situation we discussed above in reference to the fairytale, "The *Peaged Arsai* Bird" (see Volume 1, p. 378), in which a bird's thievery also instigated the pursuit of the anima.[38] If the bird represents a figure of the Self that robs the fruit, that is itself a symbol of the Self, then this signifies a game of opposites proceeding within itself in the unconscious namely, the two aspects of the Self: the rooted and the transient. These two aspects are anticipations of the human personifications that appear later in the sibling pair of the anima and her brother, the redeemed fox. But to achieve this human level requires participation of the conscious personality in the form of a reflection.[39] Reflection is, as Jung writes:

562   . . . a privilege born of human freedom in contradistinction to the compulsion of natural law. As the word itself testifies ("reflection" means literally "bending back"), reflection is a spiritual act that runs counter to the natural process; an act whereby we stop, call something to mind, form a picture, and then take up a relation to, and come to terms with, what we have seen. It should, therefore, be understood as an act of *becoming conscious*.[40]

563   Reflection is necessary because the bird's thievery brings an inner slump. The robbery of the fruits resulted in a "loss of soul," as the primitives call this loss of energy.[41] Most often in such cases, the psychic energy migrated inward, attracted by an object in the unconscious.[42]

564   In the Grimm's version ("The Golden Bird"), the conscious personality must exercise great vigilance and exert all its power to discover the cause of soul loss, which is an image in the unconscious that exerts a fascination. It

---

irritable, moody, jealous, vain, and unadjusted. He is then in a state of "discontent" and spreads discontent all around him. (C.G. Jung, CW 9i, *op. cit.*¶144.)

[38] See also "The Artful Eagle" [a tale of winning the anima that begins with the arrival at the king's barn of a flock of possibly predatory birds] in which the eagle turns out to be the son of a wicked witch.

[39] Jung, "So long as consciousness refrains from acting, the opposites will remain dormant in the unconscious." C.G. Jung, CW 12, *Psychology and Alchemy* ¶440.

[40] C.G. Jung, CW 11, *Psychology and Religion* ¶235 fn. 9.

[41] See C.G. Jung, CW 9i, *op. cit.* ¶244, on the loss of the soul, or the loss of the instinctive psyche, due to the ones-sidedness of the conscious attitude. See also *ibid* ¶213f, on "slackening of the tensity consciousness. . . which is felt as listless, moroseness, and depression. One no longer has any wish or courage to face the tasks of the day." See further C.G. Jung, CW 10, *Civilization in Transition* ¶287, C.G. Jung, CW 6, *Psychological Types* ¶383f, C.G. Jung, CW 11, *Psychology and Religion* ¶29. Cf. also the motif of the sick king in alchemy according to which the king and his country become barren, and therefore must be born again C.G. Jung, CW 12, *Psychology and Alchemy* ¶491. See also the ailing Amfortas in the Perceval saga. On a situation of loss as the beginning of the quest, see the heroine's spindle in "Mother Holle," and the golden ball in "Iron Hans."

[42] See C.G. Jung, CW 5, *Symbols of Transformation* ¶253.

follows that the two more developed, dominant functions are overwhelmed by the unconscious, while the one that is closest to this realm gets the job to hold watch at night – according to the law of the "reversed (inverted) world" – that is, able to see, recognize, and comprehend what is taking place. Staying awake is a task often given to heroes in fairytales.[43] This refers to an inner wakefulness, a focused awareness, that does not let itself be overcome by the unconscious. In the religious language of Late Antiquity and Christianity, therefore, "sleep" has become a metaphor for being unconscious, being caught in the [material] world; "being awake" and "awakening," however, became metaphors for religious awareness. Awakening means, therefore, self-reflection, contemplation, and return to the Godhead.[44] When, as in our tale, the prevailing conscious attitude is asleep, "caught in the world," as it were, another soul part awakens, which plays a mediating role between the conscious mind and the unconscious. That is, the hero comes into [conscious] life by making the conscious mind aware of inner processes. "Even sleepers are workers and collaborators in what goes on in the universe."[45]

565 When his youngest son keeps watch, the sultan is able to find out the cause of his unfounded sadness, the theft of his psychic powers by a spirit being. The golden bird is in many parallels, the phoenix.[46] This is a sun symbol, the [new] sun rising up out of the sea. Written on the feather (in "Prince Hassan Pasha") were holy words and on the wings of the phoenix bird is the word φοτ οειδὲς (luminous).[47]

---

[43] See several examples in this work as well as J. Bolte and G. Polívka, *Anmerkungen*, Vol. 1, Leipzig 1913 p. 514. Also Cf. Gilgamesh's slumber that led to the serpent stealing the herb of immortality. Also compare the sleep of the disciples at Gethsemane.

[44] See Mark 13: 35-38. Cf. the sleep of the Savior in the *Hymn of the Soul* [also called *Hymn of the Pearl*] in the apocryphal *Acts of Thomas* [now considered by scholars to refer to Thomas]. The boy is sent to Egypt to retrieve a pearl from a serpent. He falls asleep and forgets his duty to seek the pearl. He is then "awakened" by a letter from the "king of kings." See (in German) H. Leisegang, *Die Gnosis*, Leipzig 1924 pp. 365–368 R. Reitzenstein, *Hellenistic*, Pittsburgh 1978 pp. 58–59 and G. R. S. Mead, *Fragments*, London 1931 pp. 406–414 (Mead translates this as *The Hymn of the Robe of Glory*). On the "awakening" (redemption) in Manichaeism, cf. H. C. Puech, "The Concept of Redemption in Manichaenism," in *Eranos Yearbook* 1936 p. 279, and in Mandaeism and the Iranian traditions, R. Reitzenstein, *op. cit.* pp. 349 and 400. Reitzenstein writes:

> Out of this combination of the concepts of matter and death, spirit and life, it becomes clear that even with the Mandaeans life lies sleeping or sluggish, sunk in the world of matter. It must be *awakened*, life means to be awake. Those concepts, which have been shown to have already been present in the oldest parts of the Avesta. . . and also recur in all Manichean descriptions of redemption, run through the whole Mandaean Book of the Dead. Only the divine caller, the voice, that comes from outside the [material] world can awaken. Its intervention is the crucial factor. (Translated from R. Reitzenstein, *Iranische*, Bonn a. Rh. 1921 p. 51f.)

See also the name of Buddha as "the awakened one."

[45] Heraclitus, Fragment 124, Heraclitus (1994). See also Fragment 15 and comment, "The waking have one world in common, each sleeper turns away to a private world of his own."

[46] See J. Bolte and G. Polívka, *Anmerkungen*, Vol. 1, Leipzig 1913 p. 504. See the fairytales "The Birds Phoenus and Floribunda," "The Bird Wehmus" and "The Bird *Fenus*" (Phoenix).

[47] Bachofen:

> Out of the waters it arises and accompanies, purple and golden are its plumage, on its wings is written φοτ οειδε`ς, because of its nature as light, its watery origin disappears completely. The material substance is entirely transformed to the immaterial. Through the fire all the

566   These are probably the characters that the sultan reads on the feather. The phoenix periodically consumes itself in fire in order to be reborn[48] He therefore knows the secret of ever-renewing life. As stated above, the bird is a symbol of intuitive ideas,[49] fantasies, and the spirit in general. Its relationship with the miracle tree from which it robs, is significant. According to the Egyptian Ra and Roman Mithras cults, as mentioned, the sun was thought to have been born out of the tree. It grows from the World Tree. Thus, when the bird eats the golden fruit, it is a sort of consuming of oneself: precisely that play of opposites of the unconscious that must be broken by a conscious intervention. Because the king has so far ignored his unconscious side, it has become, in the figure of the bird, an autonomous shadow creature that steals from him. It comes from remote regions so that the king, in order to (re)possess it, must expand his inner being. A Turkish tale, "The Story of the Emerald Anka-Bird,"[50] begins with the padishah's apple tree being robbed every night. Only here, the thief is a seven-headed Dev[51] in dragon form that appears at midnight with a roar and howl accompanied by a black fog. He embodies the more bestial-demonic unconscious.

567   In a certain sense, the anima is also contained in the vaguely bird-like quality of our tales, since she appears often first as a bird (motif of the swan maiden).[52] A simpler parallel "The White Dove" relates explicitly how the bird is the anima.

---

dross of mortality is obliterated. From the ashes the son has arisen. The sun imparts its power to myrrh and frankincense from which the consuming fire most beautifully enflames. In this nature the sun bird corresponds completely to the image of Zeus Heliopolis, as the golden griffin corresponded to the Apollonian solar power . . . So we see in the phoenix, the idea of 'the great light power developed to its purest incorporeality and identified with fatherhood.' (J. J. Bachofen, *Mutterrecht*, Stuttgart 1861 p. 24.)

See further Erman:

And still something else should have been on that hill of mud, something that was also into this barren mud world, the egg of a waterfowl. From it a goose broke out, and all was light because it was the sun. With loud gabbles and cackles it flew over the waters. That was the first light and the first sound in the silence and darkness that had until then dominated the world. (A. Erman, *Religion der Ägypter*, Berlin and Leipzig 1934 pp. 61–62.) Cf. H. Leisegang, *Die Gnosis*, Leipzig 1924 p. 267.

[48] In India during the second Vedic period [ca. 800-300 BC] the fire altar was in the shape of a bird. See J. Przyluski, *Erlösung*, Zürich 1938 p. 99.

[49] Homer used the term "winged words" and words were viewed as birds, A. Dieterich, *Eine Mithrasliturgie*, Leipzig and Berlin 1923 p. 113. Cf. the translation of *Logos* as "word."

[50] [The notes to the German collection, F. Giese, *Türkische Märchen*, Jena 1925 p. 303, say that the Anka is a mythological bird like the phoenix.]

[51] [A demon (dêw, daeva), an ancient Iranian word for a supernatural entity with evil character, also ghost, giant, monster, ogre. Div is also used by Tajiks for a huge ape (yeti) with long dirty hair which is believed to live between Afghanistan, China, Kyrgyzstan and Uzbekistan.]

[52] See "Ititaujang," "The Visit to Heaven," "The Daughter of the King Vultures" and "The *Peaged Arsai* Bird." In the Norwegian fairytale, "The Blue Belt" a giant bird in a large egg is the precursor of the anima. See the Russian fairytale, "The Duck Maiden," in which the anima as a duck must be lifted out of the water. In "Queen Crane" the hero, a poor shepherd, refrains from shooting a crane, which promises to help him whenever he calls out, "God aid me, and Queen Crane stay by me, and I will succeed!" See also the wings of the anima figure in "The Virgin Tsar" and "The Three Sons of the Padishah" in which the hero first has to catch a golden bird and later a bird brings him the golden braids of a virgin, whom he then seeks on his quest. See also, "The Disowned Princess," where a bird flies up in a field, making the hero stop and thus discover the grieving dragon princess.

568   Once upon a time, just in front of the king's palace, there stood a great
pear tree. Every year it bore the most beautiful fruit, but as soon as
the pears became ripe, they disappeared, all in one night! Nobody
knew how this happened. Now the king had three sons, the youngest
was considered to be simple-minded and people called him
"Simpleton." The king ordered his eldest son to stand guard under the
pear tree every night for one whole year in order to catch the thief.
This the eldest son did, the tree thrived, and became full of blossoms.
When the fruit began to ripen, he observed it all the more carefully.
Finally, the pears were ready to be harvested the next day. But on this
last night, tiredness overcame the eldest son, and he fell into a deep
sleep. When he awoke, all the fruit were gone.

569   The king commanded his second son to watch every night for a year.
This one did not fare any better than the first. Finally, the king
commanded the youngest son to stand watch every night for a year.
This the Simpleton diligently did. On the last night, he stayed awake
and observed how a white dove came and picked all the pears, one by
one, and flew away with them. When it had taken the last, the
Simpleton followed the bird. The dove flew to a high mountain and
disappeared into a crack in the rocks. The Simpleton looked around
and spied a little grey man. The youngest son spoke to the little man
saying, "God bless you!" The little man answered, "At the moment you
spoke, God blessed me through your words. You have redeemed me!
Go now into that crack in the rocks and you will find your happiness."
The Simpleton climbed through the crack and saw steps leading
downwards. Many, many steps there were as he went down. The steps
came to an end and he made out the figure of a white dove ensnared
in a spider's web. When the dove saw the young man, she began to
break all the binding threads. When she had ripped the last thread
away, there stood a beautiful princess before him. He had also
redeemed her! She happily agreed to become his wife, and he became
a rich king and ruled his country long and wisely.[53]

570   This version shows the anima as a bird caught in the web of unconscious
images, that is, she is pictured here as a fleeting idea that is liberated when it
is recognized to be the actual anima.[54]

---

[53] Translated from J. Bolte and G. Polívka, *Anmerkungen,* Vol. 1, Leipzig 1913 pp. 503–504. [Tale told
by Gretchen Wild in Germany, 1808.]
[54] For further parallels, see in particular the fairytale in which the anima appears as the "bird with the
lovely song" (in "The King's Son and the Bird with the Sweet Song"). See also the "winged woman" of
the Indonesian parallel to the present fairytale, "The Story of the Blind King Who Lived in the Western
Lands." In a Danish parallel to the Grimm's "Ferdinand the Faithful and Ferdinand the Unfaithful" it
is told that the sought-after golden bird transforms into a maiden ("The Golden Feather" (Den gyldne

571   In the above parallels, the youngest son hits the robber bird with his arrow so that a feather falls to the ground. Arrows mean intuitions or ideas, which is why one speaks of "thought arrows." On the other hand, arrows are attributes of Cupid, the god of love, and were interpreted, therefore, as *telum passionis* [the dart of passion].[55] The youngest son, who represents the more naive side of the king, reaches the bird image that was carrying in itself both the unconscious problem and the redemption of the anima by his natural enthusiasm to act. Just this spontaneity leads to the conscious recognition of the problem and, in the end, to establishing the hitherto missing connection to the unconscious. Arrows are also identical with the rays of the sun, so that the sun bird is hit with a piece of its own nature.[56] The function that is least suited to rational life, the fourth function, which stands closest to the unconscious and is in general broadly connected with it, is that function through which the contents of the unconscious can be reached in their figurative, symbolic form. It mediates the connection to what previously appeared only as a passing hint of the Self.[57]

572   At first, the hero salvages only a feather of the bird, a part of the whole. But all his counselors are of the same opinion in recognizing its significance, whereupon the king all the more fervently yearns for the whole bird, for he – the hitherto prevailing conscious mind – would like to acquire the full unconscious power that he now senses. The feathers of the magical bird is a commonly used image in many fairytales. For instance in "Ferdinand the Faithful and Ferdinand the Unfaithful" (see Volume 1 of this work, page 340) the hero, on the orders of his horse, stops to pick up a quill which later, after he joins the service of the king, leads him to fetch the sleeping princess with her writings. In a Danish parallel[58] the image of the princess is depicted on a golden feather. In the Grimm's tale, "The Griffin," the hero has to fetch a tail feather from the mythical bird, similar to the boy in "The Devil with the Three Golden Hairs," who has to pluck out the three golden hairs from the devil's head. In several tales from the Indonesian Archipelago, feathers of a magical bird often transform into humans or treasures.[59] We have already mentioned

---

Fjer), mentioned in J. Bolte and G. Polívka, *Anmerkungen,* Vol. 3, Leipzig 1918 p. 20). See also, "Farther South Than South and Farther North Than North and in the Great Hill of Gold," where the destroyer of the father's fields, who appears at the beginning of the tale, is an enchanted maiden in the form of a dove. The motif of the anima as a dove occurs also at the conclusion of a tale from the Danube region, "Saint Anthony and Charles the Murderer."

[55] See C.G. Jung, CW 13, *Alchemical Studies* ¶278.

[56] On arrows as sun rays see C.G. Jung, CW 5, *Symbols of Transformation* ¶439.

[57] See the fairytale motif in which the hero shoots an arrow with thongs at a castle floating in the air and then climbs up on the straps, (J. Bolte and G. Polívka, *Anmerkungen,* Vol. 2, Leipzig 1915 p. 306.) See also "The Chain of Arrows" from the southern Amazon region, in which the hero-brothers climb on a chain of interlocking arrows that they shot up to heaven and they become the sun and moon, a motif appearing also in adventures of the twins in "The Brothers Visit Their Father."

[58] "The Golden Feather (Den gyldne Fjer)," mentioned in a previous paragraph, see J. Bolte and G. Polívka, *Anmerkungen,* Vol. 3, Leipzig 1918 p. 20. See also *ibid* 22, 25.

[59] For example, in "The Garuda Bird" and "Suri ikuen and the Two Raptors."

the symbol of feathers (as a metaphor for birds) signifying ideas or thoughts; the same meaning is associated with plumage used in headdresses among many indigenous cultures, which are believed to bestow mystical power.

573   Thus the king in our present tale, "The Golden Bird," cannot grasp the bird, that is, he cannot grasp the unconscious psyche, which is in its fullness hidden from him. A thought "occurs" to him (comes into his awareness), however, with the help of his – relative to the secular world – least-developed mental function. And then something does grip him that seems so valuable that he decides to tread the adventurous path indicated by this function. In the parallel tale "Prince Hassan Pasha" there are "holy words" written on the feather. These words are not further clarified in the tale, but most probably hint at "light-sparks," or "light-treasure"[60] meaning that a sign is given to consciousness, indicating that this adventure is to bring him light, that is, *gnosis*. The worldly-oriented, more differentiated, and developed function, as always, does not itself make the journey, since it is not up to the task. By sacrificing its claim to exclusive validity, the total personality reaches the decision to take on, with the help of the fourth function, the night sea journey. In the present fairytale this is expressed by the fact that the king issues a mandate to look for the bird.

574   This delegation of a task is an archetypal situation. This is how Hercules[61] completed his twelve labors in the service of Eurystheus. Thorkill goes to the underworld for king Horm.[62] In the fairytales discussed in this section, the heroes are almost always sent out by the king, signifying that the psychic process of development requires the participation of the ruling conscious attitude.

575   At the edge of the forest (that is, the border to the unconscious) the oldest son meets a fox but scorns its request for mercy and offer of good advice. He shoots at it with his musket and misses his target. The middle son behaves in the same way. The fox represents the animal instincts. Its red color indicates that it belongs to the underworld demons. As pointed out in the title of a Czech variant "The Firebird and the Firefox,"[63] the fox is particularly well-known for his cunning and thievishness[64] and personifies the more

---

[60] [*Light-treasure*, among other terms, is used in Gnosticism, see for example, G. R. S. Mead, *Fragments*, London 1931 p. 528f.]

[61] See C.G. Jung, CW 9i, *Op. cit.* p. 221. See also about such tasks, J. Bolte and L. Mackensen, *Handwörterbuch* Berlin 1930,, under *Aufgabe, schwierige* [tasks, difficult].

[62] This is ascribed by M. Führer, *Nordgermanische*, München 1938 p. 73, to the *Edda* and a legend cited by Saxo Grammaticus.

[63] See J. Bolte and G. Polívka, *Anmerkungen*, Vol. 1, Leipzig 1913 p. 507.

[64] See the fox as an impostor in "The Grateful Fox" and also in the Chané origin myth "The Creation of the World." "Two of the *Tunpas* [giant dead people with superhuman powers], have animal names, *Aguaratunpa* [fox god] and *Tatutunpa* [armadillo god]. There is an intimate relationship between humans and animals" (T. Koch-Grünberg, *Südamerika*, Jena 1921 p. 335). See also "Coniraya." In the latter the fox is also the animal that caused the moon to have spots. See note W. Krickeberg, *Azteken und Inka*, Jena 1928 p. 383. See also the comprehensive compilation in J. Bolte and L. Mackensen, *Handwörterbuch* Berlin 1930, and Bächtold-Stäubli under *Fuchs* [fox].

cunning-wise, agile-versatile aspect of the instincts that pursues its goal in a non-violent way. In the Styrian (*Stiermark*) variant "The Birds Phoenus and Floribunda" the fox says to the hero, "If you are as cunning as the fox, you will win not only the princess, but also keep the horse." When the fox in "The Golden Bird" evades being shot by the elder brothers, this means that its nature cannot be comprehended with rational consciousness. Particularly in China, but not only there, the fox symbolizes the dead soul.[65] In Germanic countries, the fox is also a Fylgia, a witch animal, a companion of devilish creatures and an underworld demon.[66] In China, the fox can also generate the elixir of life from its breath and this allows it to take on human form.[67]

576   In his breath, the fox retains not only the invigorating power of the world, but together with the wolf, is a guardian of secret treasures. The nine-tailed fox is regarded as a divine servant who beguiles people with magic in the form of a beautiful woman.[68] The fox speaks with the voice of the demon who possesses people and uses the female and impure elements to fend off the attacks of the Thunder and the Sky Dragon.[69] The fox is behind harmful spooks and ghosts, and when the fox is the carrier of the elixir of life, then it is revered as the divine old wise one.[70] In South America, as in China, the dead often appeared as foxes.[71]

---

[65] On this motif, see Wilhelm:
> [When one dies] one finds oneself at best in heaven, in the worst case, among the spirits. Such a fox spirit, it is true, may be able to roam in the famous mountains, enjoying the wind and the moon, the flowers and fruits, and taking pleasure in coral trees and jeweled grass. But after having done this for three to five hundred years, or perhaps even a couple of thousand years, his reward is over and he is born again into the world of turmoil. (R. Wilhelm, *Secret of the Golden Flower*, London 1962 pp. 46–47.

See also the tales "The Story of the Blind King Who Lived in the Western Lands" and "The Comrade," in which a ghost takes over the role of the fox in "The Golden Bird."

[66] See Bächtold-Stäubli under *Fuchs*. The fox is a demon also in China. See note to "The Fox-Hole":
> The fox as a demon who can take possession of human beings is a common motif in Chinese folk beliefs. A lot of hysterical phenomena are attributed to the fox and the weasel. Often these hysterical states pass quickly.

(R. Wilhelm, *The Chinese Fairy Book*, New York 1921 p. 385.) [See also the discussion in Von Franz p. 197.]

[67] See note in R. Wilhelm, *The Chinese Fairy Book*, New York 1921 p. 162,
> The thought underlying the story is the belief that the fox prepares the elixir of life out of his own breath, which he allows to rise to the moon. If a thief can rob him of the elixir he gains supernatural powers.

See again Wilhelm:
> According to Chinese folklore, foxes can also cultivate the Elixir of Life; they thus attain the capacity of transforming themselves into human beings. They correspond to the nature demons in Western mythology. (R. Wilhelm *Op. cit.* p. 46 fn. 1.)

[68] See, "The Cave of the Beasts," "Nü Wa," "Ying Ning or the Laughing Beauty."

[69] See "The Fox-Hole," "The Fox and the Thunder," and "Giauna the Beautiful." See also "The Prophet Noah and the Flood." There the blood of the fox, along with that of the tiger and the pig, works like a contaminant.

[70] See "The Friendly and the Bad Fox," "The Talking Silver Foxes," "The Girl Who Was Faster Than Horses." See also the Japanese tale "Kikimimi-Zôshi" about the fox as the lord of the "wisdom of nature" in which two foxes, as a token of their gratitude, give a man a book by which, when he puts it close to his ear, he can understand the language of all animals.

[71] See the Chané tale "The Woman who Followed her Husband to Aguarerente" and the comment by the editor, Koch-Grünberg, where he states:

577   In many fairytales the fox helps the hero and is often clearly a ghost or a haunted being.[72] In two versions of this tale ("The Birds Phoenus and Floribunda" and "Die weisse Amsel" [The White Blackbird]), the fox is the soul of a man that the hero redeemed and buried. Psychologically, this means that the fox is the carrier of a human projection, a piece of the human unconscious.

578   In "The Golden Bird" it becomes clear that the fox initially personifies instinctive cunning and foreknowledge of the future, beyond which is hidden the Self, the higher personality.[73] In the Uzbek parallel "Prince Hassan Pasha" the helpful animal is a wolf. We now continue to tell this tale from where we left off above,

579   An enormous whirlwind of dust approached the hero. Suddenly, a wolf sprang out of the column. He asked the prince for something to eat. Hassan Pasha held out a piece of bread that the wolf grabbed and then disappeared. When the brothers caught up to Hassan, they came upon a crossroads. Nearby they found a stone on which was written: "Whoever takes the road to the left will return happily. Whoever goes straight ahead might return safely, but then again, perhaps not. Whoever follows the way to the right will never return." The elder brothers chose the two more favorable ways and Hassan was left with the path that remained, the way without hope. The wolf appeared again at his side and offered his help as thanks for befriending him earlier. At first Hassan haughtily rejected the offer, but eventually he accepted it.[74]

580   Since the wolf is the hero's helpful animal in many European variants,[75] it may be that the fox is a later arrival and takes the place formerly carried by the

---

    Aguararenta (fox-village) is a village where the dead *anya* live. It lies to the East. In the nighttime the dead who live there take on human form; during the daytime they go around as foxes, rats and other animals or sit in a tree trunk. Every night there is a big drinking orgy in Aguararenta. Alle Chané go there [when they die]. It is their realm of the dead, their afterlife. Some living persons have visited Aguararenta and returned to tell what they saw there. This belief is based on dream experiences that are taken as real-life events. (T. Koch-Grünberg, *Südamerika*, Jena 1921 p. 336, source of the fairytale, E. Nordenskiöld, *Indianer*, Leipzig 1912 pp. 255–257.)

[72] See J. Bolte and L. Mackensen, *Handwörterbuch* Berlin 1930, under *Fuchs*.

[73] On the encounter with the higher personality, see in particular, "The Comrade," which will be discussed in more detail in a subsequent volume of the present work. On animals as symbols of the superior personality, see C.G. Jung, CW 7, *Two Essays in Analytical Psychology* ¶159, and in general, J. Bolte and L. Mackensen, *Handwörterbuch* Berlin 1930, under *Tier* [animal] and especially *Tiergestalt* [animal forms].

[74] On the wolf as a magical helpful animal, see the Norwegian tale, "Anent, the Giant Who Did Not Have His Heart About Him," where the hero sacrificed his horse to a hungry wolf, and it was later carried and advised by the grateful wolf.

[75] See J. Bolte and G. Polívka, *Anmerkungen*, Vol. 1, Leipzig 1913 p. 506, who report of an Alsatian version in which a white wolf appears as a helper. See also *ibid* p. 508f.

wolf. The character of the "The Golden Bird" (Grimm's version) points rather to an oriental origin.

581   The wolf in Greek is λυκος, (lykos),[76] and is related to the word light. The wolf is the animal of the god of light, Apollo, but it also may be a symbol for the fundamental basis of hell, the devil. In ancient Iran the wolf is the animal of Ahriman.[77] In the *Edda* it is said that during the apocalypse, the wolf Fenris would devour the sun and moon:

582   The *Edda* designates that period of time that we are wont to call Judgement Day by the phrase, "the wolf is about" or, "the wolf is on the run" and this signifies the demon of doom, which in some stanzas is called the Fenris Wolf. . . A later North Germanic poem, which tells of the outcome of this battle, reports that Odin is devoured by the wolf. According to other poems it is not Odin but Thor, the fighter of giants, who leads this decisive battle with the wolf that will determine the fate of the world. A third legend says that Tyr, the god of war, must combat a sibling or a variant of Fenris – the wolf Garm – and survive this battle of the Last Days. . . The legend, in its more general and valid form, states that at Judgement Day the great god must enter into the decisive battle against the destructive demon of the wolf. In this struggle, the god succumbs, with the consequence that Heaven and Earth shall perish without hope.[78]

583   The wolf is, as Ninck writes, "a cruel slayer, a pale gray messenger of death and a thief who rips and tears."[79] In alchemy the wolf signifies iron and is the animal of Mars.[80] The wolf embodies affects in their more aggressive and dangerous form than the fox.[81] After all, there is a certain relationship between the two, since Latin *vulpes* [fox], is etymologically related to the German word *Wolf.*

---

[76] See J. J. Bachofen, *Lykische*, Freiburg i. Br. 1862 p. 61ff.
[77] See Cumont p. 140f [The wolf is mentioned in the original German edition, not in the English translation.]. See also, E. Tegethoff, *Französische Volksmärchen*, Vol. 2, Jena 1923 p. vii.
[78] W.-E. Peuckert, *Volksglaube*, Stuttgart 1942 pp. 16–17.
[79] See M. Ninck, *Wodan*, Jena 1935 p. 51. See also, Pausanias' description of Greece mentioning the wolf-ghost Temesa and Pausanius, "Horribly black in color, and exceedingly dreadful in all his appearance, he had a wolf's skin thrown round him as a garment. The letters on the picture give his name as Lycas," (Pausanias, Book 6, 6.11). See also Rohde's mention of the connection to the Athenian hero Lycos who donned a wolf's skin to look like a terrible death-bringing spirit, probably referring to an older legendary figure (E. Rohde, *Psyche* London 1925 p. 153 fn. 114). On the wolf as a demon in general see Bächtold-Stäubli under *Wolf*.
[80] See C.G. Jung, CW 13, *Alchemical Studies* ¶176 fn. 39. Along with the panther and the lion, the wolf belongs to this trinity of evil beasts that Dante meets at the beginning of his descent into Hell.
[81] The fox is also mercurial, that is, cunning, intelligent, agile, and adaptable. The wolf is more Mars- or Saturn-like, that is, more aggressive, dark, and passionate. See A. Fankhauser, *Horoskopie*, Zürich and Leipzig 1939 p. 69,81.

584   The brothers of the hero each personify an animal component (instinct) that gives the hero a superiority [when he is] in nature. Next to the North American hero and culture bringer, Mänäbush, stands his twin brother, who at the request of the good spirits accompanies him as a wolf.[82]

585   The animal companion as shadow is not only the alter ego, but, as it were, the body-soul. To the extent that the human is physical, he or she is like an animal, and comes from the animal world, which is the basis of all conscious development.[83] The mythical ancestors of primitive peoples, therefore, often have a feral form. In contrast to humans, animals live completely independently, beyond good and evil, and follow their own laws. Therein lies their superiority.

586   When, as in this case, the hero, as the fourth function, symbolizes the future conscious personality, his helpful animals represent the not yet human side of his personality that is still bound to the unconscious.[84]

587   A fairytale in which the helpful animals carry practically all the action in the plot, thus clearly showing that they indeed represent an unconscious part of the hero's nature, is "Beg and Fox":

588   There was once a bey (beg)[85] who had nothing but a horse, a hunting hound, and a rifle. He did nothing other than hunt and this was how he provided for himself. One day he went into the mountains with his horse, his rifle on his shoulder and his dog running at his side. When he had come to a flat place, he tethered his horse to a beech tree and continued with his dog into the forest. When he had gone, a fox came to his horse and lay down beside it.

589   The bey was a long time away in the forest. He bagged only a deer. When he returned to his horse, he was surprised to see the fox lying there. He raised his rifle and took aimed at it, but the animal sprang up and begged the bey not to shoot. He only wanted to faithfully

---

[82] See the Navaho myth "The Brothers Visit Their Father" and its continuation in "The Brothers Slay Yéitso." In North America, the coyote ("prairie wolf"), an animal doctor, a divine trickster. See also the tale, "Kagsagsuk," (see page 70) in which a wolf demon strengthens the hero by thrashing him with its tail. See also the note in W. Krickeberg, *Nordamerika*, Jena 1924 p. 369. Also Enkidu, the half-animal companion of Gilgamesh, who is first an enemy but then becomes a trusted companion. See also, H. Zimmer, *Maya*, Stuttgart and Berlin 1936 p. 304 and, on the hero's need for animal assistance when fighting against monsters, when the human is torn [separated from] his self, when he or she is cruelly and unexpectedly robbed of half of his Self, his female soul, when the dearest dream of our soul, when our inner reality is taken from us, and when a reunion with this inner light of our lives seems more uncertain than ever..." (H. Zimmer, *Maya*, Stuttgart and Berlin 1936 p. 285.)

[83] See C.G. Jung, *Children's Dreams*, Princeton 2008 p. 51, C.G. Jung, CW 12, *Psychology and Alchemy* ¶174.

[84] See C.G. Jung, CW 9i, *The Archetypes and the Collective Unconscious* ¶279f and "The animal lump or life-mass stands for the mass of the inherited unconscious [that] is to be united with consciousness." (C.G. Jung, CW 12, *Psychology and Alchemy* ¶184).

[85] [Turkish *beg*, or *bey*, means "lord, nobleman," a title for someone lower in rank than a *pasha* but higher than an *effendi*.]

watch over and protect his horse from harm. The bey was moved by this plea and had mercy on the fox and let him live. He mounted his horse and with the fox, made his way to his home. He prepared the venison and gave the fox the intestines so that he also had something for an evening meal.

590   The next morning, the bey again rode out to hunt and invited the fox along for company. They arrived at a place close to where they were the day before. Again, the bey tethered his horse to the beech tree and asked the fox to watch over the horse and he went again into the mountains to hunt. When the hunter was away, the fox remained by the horse alone. Soon a bear came to them and wanted to slay and eat the horse. Then the fox begged him to refrain and await the return of the hunter. In this way, the hunter might take them home and give both of them a big meal. The bear agreed to this and they both waited for the return of the man.

591   When the bey returned he was astonished to see a bear lying next to the fox and the horse. He again raised his rifle and aimed it at the bear. Again, the fox pleaded with him not to shoot the bear, he also wanted to look after the horse and to be of service to the man. The hunter lowered his rifle and, accompanied by the fox and the bear, made his way to his house. Both animals received meat that evening.

592   The next day the same thing happened. This time a wolf joined the company. Then again, the next day the same. This time a mouse and a mole joined the growing animal crew. Then another wolf joined the group and the bird, Kumrikusha,[86] that was so large that it could carry off a horse and a man. In the evening at his home, the bey gave victuals to all these animals. In the end, a hare also joined the company.

593   At the instigation of the fox the animals decided that their bey should be married. As a wife they chose none other than the daughter of the Tsar. The bird Kumrikusha went to steal the daugher and carried her away. But the Tsar procurred the help of a gypsy who brought the daughter back on a magic carpet, and the Tsar promptly locked his daughter away in a room. Then the fox devised a new plan. Kumriskha carried the fox under its wing back to the Tsar's palace, where the fox transformed himself into a beautiful cat and played under a window and was noticed by the Tsar's daughter. The cat did not let it be caught by anyone and when the Tsar's daugther came to pick it up, Kumriksha again abducted her. Then the Tsar gathered a great army together and

---

[86] A Turkish word, from *kumir* = turtle dove and kuš = bird, A. Leskien, *Balkanmärchen*, Jena 1919 p. 325.

went to war against the animals. Hearing of what was upon them, the fox took up position on his tree-stump from which he instructed the animals: "You bears, wolves, and hares, you go out first. When the Tsar's army has set up its first camp and have started to dine, go and kill all their horses. You hares, go piss in their cannons so that they cannot fire. When the army camps for the second night, you mice, go and chew through the saddles, for the army will have gone and replaced all the horses afresh. At the third night camp, you moles go and dig out beneath the camp a great hole, fifteen cubits wide and twenty cubits deep. Then you kumrikshas go in the morning when the men get up and bombard them from above with stones."

594　And this is how it happened. When the Tsar saw that his whole army was being destroyed, he called out, "Let us return to the palace, this is God's punishment that we have taken up battle against the animals. Let them keep my daughter that they have kidnapped!" At this the army turned around, but found that they were still sinking into the earth. The Tsar called out again, "When God punishes us by collapsing the earth beneath our feet, why then are also stones falling on us from heaven?"

595　One after another, all the Tsar's men died, as did the Tsar himself. Shortly later, the fox exchanged his tree-stump throne for the throne of the Tsar and transferred the palace to Istanbul where he ruled further. The bey gave up hunting and went to live with the fox in Istanbul. He took the Tsar's daughter with him, she remained his wife, and no one ever stole her away again.[87]

596　In this tale, the hero is completely passive and the fox with his crew do everything for him. As a consequence, they take over the throne in Istanbul. This story portrays a very primitive stage of conscious development, where everything happens instinctively. The multiplicity of the animals indicates the deeply unconscious nature of the action.[88]

597　The wolf in "Prince Hassan Pasha" appears in a column of dust, a whirlwind, which emphasizes his (the wolf's) psychic-mental-spiritual side. He is not the animal body, but the nature spirit that dwells in the animal. Spooks, ghosts, or apparitions are often said to be preceded by a cold gust of wind. The Sanskrit word *asu* (= breath, *prana*, life principle) is etymologically related to Latin *animus* (spirit), *anima* (soul), and Greek ανεμος (anemos =

---

[87] A. Leskien, *Balkanmärchen*, Jena 1919 pp. 166–171, from the German.
[88] ["Multiplicity, as such, is characteristic of any inherently unconscious life process," (C.G. Jung, *Children's Dreams*, Princeton 2008 p. 370.)

wind).[89] This helping spirit appears in some fairytales not only as the wolf here does, but in the wind itself.[90] Three old women, representing the three winds, appear as helpers to the hero in a Romansh[91] fairytale.[92] In the Uzbek tale "The Beautiful Dunye" the hero first glimpses the anima as an image in a strong whirlwind, she is the daughter of a red div. According to Anaxagoras and, following him, Ophite cosmogony, the universe arose from a whirlwind in the chaotic primeval waters.[93] This vortex was also the Sun Serpent,[94] because in ancient conceptions the sun was the generator of the wind. In the magical papyri, *Helios-Aeon-Iao-Sabaoth*, was invoked: "Draw close to me, thou who comest from the four winds, thou almighty god who hast breathed the breath of life into man... "[95] In India, too, sun and wind are seen as connected,[96] because the sun, like the wind, is an impregnator (pollinator) and creator, the

---

[89] The Sanskrit root is the same as that for "to be." Nearly all archaic languages have the same word for both breath and wind or air and spirit. Mannhardt lists ancient German and Nordic demons that appear in whirlwinds, W. Mannhardt, *Wald- und Feldkulte*, Vol. 2, Berlin 1877 pp. 82–85, 95-100, 110, 147f. See also H. Zimmer, *Death and Rebirth*, New York 1964 p. 339. See also the meaning of the Greek word *pneuma* for both wind and the divine spirit, H. Leisegang, *Die Gnosis*, Leipzig 1924 p. 193, A. Dieterich, *Eine Mithrasliturgie*, Leipzig and Berlin 1923 p. 116. In the Old Testament, the Spirit of God is called a mighty wind (Isaiah 40: 7), and appears just before Ezekiel has his vision:

> And I looked, and, behold, a whirlwind came out of the north, a great cloud, and a fire infolding itself, and a brightness was about it, and out of the midst thereof as the color of amber, out of the midst of the fire. (Ezekiel 1: 4, King James translation)

And in the second vision, Ezekiel is borne aloft by wind, most often translated as "the Spirit" (Ezekiel 8: 3). See also the references cited in H. Güntert, *Weltkönig*, Halle a. S. 1923 p. 197.

[90] In the Old Testament, the winds are the angels = messengers of God. See Psalm 104: 4 ("He makes the winds His messengers, flaming fire His ministers," (New American Standard Bible translation). See also the Apocryphal *Daniel*, Chapter 14, *On Bel and the Dragon in Babel* verses 35-36 "Then the angel of the Lord took him by the crown, and bore him like a strong wind to the dens of Babel." (Translated from Luther's 16th Century Middle High German: *Da fasset jn her Engel oben bey dem Schopff und füret jn wie ein starcker windgen Babel an den Graben.*).

[91] A Romance language spoken in southeastern Switzerland.

[92] See "The Three Winds" in C. Decurtins, *Drei Winde*, Chur 2002 p. 294. See also the Navaho creator-brother myths, "The Brothers Visit Their Father" and "The Brothers Slay Yéitso" where Niltsi, the wind, whispers warnings and advice to the brothers.

[93] [All this in the mother's womb,] see H. Leisegang, *Die Gnosis*, Leipzig 1924 p. 153. In the Sethian system, "The generative power is called not only 'wind,' but also 'beast,' and 'serpent,' the latter because of the hissing sound it produces, just like the whirling wind." G. R. S. Mead, *Fragments*, London 1931 p. 215. See also the rotating hut of Baba Yaga in "The Frog Princess," among many Russian fairytales. Also the Finnish tale "Born of a Fish."

[94] "[T]he serpent of the universe was the Great Power, the Mighty Whirlwind, the Vast Vortex. . . " G. R. S. Mead, *Fragments*, London 1931 p. 185.

[95] H. Leisegang, *Serpent*, London 1955 p. 223, also *ibid* p. 220 and 224, "Helios and the Aeon, represented as the serpent, are also distinctly associated with the winds in the monuments of the cult of Mithras." See also, A. Dieterich, *Eine Mithrasliturgie*, Leipzig and Berlin 1923 p. 62, where the wind is said to come out of a tube from the sun. See C.G. Jung, CW 5, *Symbols of Transformation* ¶150, C.G. Jung, CW 8, *The Structure and Dynamics of the Psyche* ¶317f.

[96] The *Chandogya Upanishad*, Fourth Chapter, Third part, 1 and 2:

> The wind is, indeed, the gatherer-in-itself. Because when the fire blows away, it enters into the wind; and when the sun sets, it enters into the wind; and when the moon sets, it enters into the wind; and when the waters dry up, they enter into the wind. Because the wind gathers them all in itself. – Thus in regard to the divinity.
> Now in regard to the self. – The breath, indeed, is the gatherer-in-itself. – Because when one sleeps, the speech enters into the breath, the eyes (sight) into the breath, the ears (hearing) into the breath, the *manas* (mind) into the breath. Then the Breath gathers them all in itself. (Deussen, *Sixty Upanishads* p. 121 see also Radhakrishnan p. 404.)

source of life energy.[97] This is relevant to our tale because the wolf in the Mediterranean region, as mentioned before, is the animal of the sun god Apollo-Helios. Thus, this wolf is a spirit, a source of becoming conscious, which is still hidden in animal form. He is also a symbol of the Self, which, particularly in Eastern mandalas, is sometimes represented as a vortex, an image that expresses its self-activating function.[98] Meister Eckhart calls the divine wellspring of the spirit (mind) a vortex.[99] According to Chinese concepts, wind pervades all space and creates manifestation [in space and time], "the streaming of the reality-energies into the form of the idea."[100] Thus the hero is the not-yet-realized image of the human Self, he is its conscious-active half that gains reality first through the connection with the animal and the ensuing adventure-quest. The encounter with the wolf spirit is at first uncanny, because the suspicion of the far-reaching implications gives the hero the shivers.[101] Hassan at first resists, therefore, the wolf's offer of help because the enhancement of personality, which the wolf brings, seems threatening.[102]

598 In fact, the helpful animal represents a wisdom that is vastly superior to human reason, that acts as a guide. In antiquity, the psychopomp Hermes carried this role. In the pantheon of Germanic gods, he corresponds to Odin as wind god and soul guide.[103] In alchemical philosophy, Hermes appears as Mercurius, both as soul guide and as transforming substance.[104] Ruland (*Lexicon alchemyiae*, 1612) defines Mercurius as "spirit which has become earth." He is a spirit that penetrates into the depths of the material world and

---

[97] See C.G. Jung, CW 6, *Psychological Types* ¶336f.
[98] [German, *Eigentätigkeit*.] See Wolff:
   The Self is symbolized, for example, as the centre of the circle and square, whereby it expresses a virtual centre of total psychological situation. . . Its self-activity [German, *Eigentätigkeit*] can be represented as a wheel or vortex, and its non-identifiability with the ego in a form unrelated to the human shape, such as flower or star. The indissolubility and indivisible structure of individuality is sometimes symbolized as a crystal or diamond. (A. Wolff, *Grundlagen*, Berlin 1935 pp. 119–120.)
   See also the whirlwind in "The Piper and the Púca."
[99] See Meister Eckhart (Pfeiffer), *Predigten* Teil 2, Göttingen 1906 p. 233 *Sermon 74* (Acts 1: 4).
[100] Cf. R. Wilhelm, *Secret of the Golden Flower*, London 1962 p. 17.
[101] See C.G. Jung, *Children's Dreams,* Princeton 2008 p. 54 on the subject of how a new insight that reaches far into the future can generate the feeling of cold shivers [in the present]. The whirlwind can also symbolize a strong emotional state of being stricken with terror. The collective can also experience a powerful spiritual effect as portrayed in *The Mabinogion* when Taliesin sang his song prophesying the death of King Maelgwn of Gwynedd in the Yellow Plague: "While he was thus singing his verses near the door, there arose a mighty storm of wind, so that the king and all his nobles thought that the castle would fall on their heads." C. Guest, *Mabinogion*, London/New York (1906) 1937 p. 278.
[102] The characterization of prince Hassan as the fourth function is less clear here than in the Grimm's version ("The Golden Bird"); Hassan is not so poor in the secular world, he is at first wary of the wolf, and does not blindly trust the [spirit] animal. Thus, the gap is less and the lower level of tension is compensated, in a manner typical of the Orient, by a richer use of images.
[103] "Among the Greeks, Hermes is *logos*. He is the conductor and reconductor (the psychagogue and psychopomp), and the originator of souls." G. R. S. Mead, *Fragments*, London 1931 p. 201, E. Mogk, *Germanische*, Berlin and Leipzig 1927 p. 64.
[104] See C.G. Jung, CW 12, *Psychology and Alchemy* ¶404, C.G. Jung, CW 9i, *The Archetypes and the Collective Unconscious* ¶238.

transforms it, a psychopomp, pointing the way to paradise, the goal of the process.[105]

599   As such, he takes the role of the redeemer and represents the Self. If this figure appears in fairytales in animal form, this is because the Self, the core of the personality existing in eternity, takes on an archaic form and, at the same time as being the goal of development, it is the highest imaginable form. This ability to transform is an expression of timelessness or simultaneity of everything unconscious. The unexpected appearance of this figure corresponds to a saving inner voice in a critical moment of a life conflict.

600   In "The Golden Bird" the two elder brothers as the conscious functions scorn that voice that tries to lead them to the goal along dark paths. They even shoot at the fox, that is, they try to reject it. Against its advice they go into a brightly lit inn, and they get stuck there. "Bright" means here "closer to consciousness"; such are the two more developed functions of the conscious personality, because in a brightly lit place you can still see with secular eyes. The two functions represent here the tendency of the conscious mind to grasp only the positive sides that are sensually satisfying, and enjoy only those aspects. Significantly, the inn is in the variant "The Birds Phoenus and Floribunda" replaced by a town called "Full of Pleasure." In Manichaeism the hostel is an image of the body and bodily pleasures.[106] It symbolizes the danger resulting from contact with the animal life as a part of the unconscious, and to fall into its darker side.[107] The behavior of the secular brothers resembles in some respects the attitude of the second brother in "The Virgin Tsar," who winds up in the clutches of a seductive woman. The encounter with the fox, which leads the brothers to a tavern, is meaningful in so far as experiences of the shadow personality impart knowledge of aspects of general human nature.[108] But since the way of psychic development requires serious effort, the simple indulgence in friendly fantasies is fruitless. This is why the elder brothers fail in their quest.

---

[105] [That is, the transformation of what is mortal in one into what is immortal.] C.G. Jung, CW 11, *Psychology and Religion* ¶160, ¶356. See also Marcus Aurelius, *Meditations*, Mount Vernon 1957 p. 5:27, Live with the gods. And he does live with the gods who constantly shows to them, his own soul is satisfied with that which is assigned to him, and that it does all that the daemon wishes, which Zeus hath given to every man for his guardian and guide, a portion of himself. And this is every man's understanding and reason.

[106] See R. Reitzenstein, *Iranische*, Bonn a. Rh. 1921 p. 51.

[107] See J. Bolte and G. Polívka, *Anmerkungen*, Vol. 2, Leipzig 1915 p. 255, 505, where the inn, bath, or hospital is the place where those who have been separated can find each other again by telling their life stories. When the listener in such public and generally accessible places hears the life story of another person, he or she not only takes part in this, but also realizes his or her own parts that have been bound to the collective, and thus finds his or her own nature and being. At the same time this creates a relationship to the others. In "Ferdinand the Faithful and Ferdinand the Unfaithful" the hero in an inn becomes aware of his anima in a prefiguration of the princess, and through this his life takes a decisive turn in that the maiden finds for him a job in the service of the king. In this there is a process of becoming aware of himself, of self-knowledge.

[108] See A. Wolff, *Grundlagen*, Berlin 1935 p. 109.

601   The youngest son in "The Golden Bird" who in the eyes of the father would be of less use than even his brothers, and "was not too bright at the best"[109] and as soon as he meets the fox enters into a relationship with him and follows his advice. He even rides on the fox's tail, meaning that he renders leadership to his instincts. The tail of the fox is a common theme in many fairytales. With it, the fox paves the way, carries the hero or heroine, destroys bridges, or waves obstacles away.[110] When the hero fell into the dry well, the fox leapt down to him and bade him grab hold of his tail and pulled him out. The animal tail plays a special role in alchemical philosophy, which can help us illuminate its meaning. There the transforming substance is a dragon that eats its own tail: the head is the mental (psychic) aspect, and the tail is the material aspect. Both are of the same nature.[111] If the fox and prince riding his horse are considered as a unit, two aspects of the fourth function (opposing the prevailing conscious attitude), then the prince would correspond to the head and the fox to the tail of the mysterious, double aspect of this comprehensive symbol.

602   Instead of the two inns in "The Golden Bird" the three brothers in "Prince Hassan Pasha" come to a crossroads, where they part ways. We met and interpreted the motif of the crossroads already in "The Virgin Tsar." Here it is less developed.[112]

603   In contrast, in "Prince Hassan Pasha" the motif of riding-on-the-animal is given even an additional fine touch: the wolf requires Hassan to sit on his tail, turn "with his back to the front," and hold on tight. Thus, the hero rides backwards into the magical. This is like Ivan Tsarevich's reversed ride into the

---

[109] In "Prince Hassan Pasha" the hero was the first of the brothers to declare his readiness to take on the quest. Then, soon after his departure, his elder brothers decide to do the same. Here, the king equips all his sons equally, there is only a small difference between them: the openness of the youngest to engage in an *auseinandersetzung* with the magical. Hassan was the first to proffer his services to stand guard by the tree. In this tale, the youngest son is less of a simpleton, [called *Dümmling* (little dumb one, stupid, idiot) in the Grimm's tales.] and his father is not so distant from him as in "The Golden Bird." This is apparently because consciousness is less differentiated and thus the tension between the conscious functions is significantly lower.

[110] See J. Bolte and L. Mackensen, *Handwörterbuch* Berlin 1930, under *Fuchs*. See also "The Son of the Old Woman" where the tail of an antelope acts as the wick of a lamp, which gives light (that is, enlightenment) when entering into the unconscious.

[111] See C.G. Jung, CW 13, *Alchemical Studies* ¶105,¶111, C.G. Jung, CW 12, *Psychology and Alchemy* ¶404.

[112] The motif of the crossroads is here portrayed differently and less clearly than in "The Virgin Tsar." The middle way is not the one that goes beyond the play of opposites, rather the way of the undecided, the left path is here that of the unconscious, which may be less harmful since it is easy for something unconscious to slide into the unconscious. The way to the right is the path of going consciously into the unconscious, and, therefore, the way of a dangerous confrontation (*auseinandersetzung*). But since the course of events does not follow the prophecies of the crossroads – as was the case in the Russian fairytale – this motif could be a simple addition, inserted into the tale without much contemplation. In a parallel tale, "The Nightingale Gisar," the motif of the crossroads is also relatively unclear:

> When they had traveled twenty days' journey, they came to a place where three ways met. In the middle of each path was a stone upon which words were written. On two of the ways, it said, "Whoever follows this path will return," and on the third path it was written, "Whoever takes this way will never return."

magical in "The Virgin Tsar." The motif of riding backwards accords with the concept of the unconscious as the "reversed world." This way of riding is a total abandonment of any remaining ego claims, or desires to lead, and a complete giving oneself over to the animals, who look and see where the human cannot. Here Hassan (like Ivan Tsarevich) is still facing the secular, since he is generally more dismissive of the animal than the prince in "The Golden Bird." Riding on the animal is letting-yourself-be-carried by the unconscious, whereby only the question of leadership and control is different. In these present tales, the hero waives all pretense at leading or guiding.[113]

604   The fox now brings his charge to the next stage and advises as a kind of test to stop at a plain, simple guest house. The uneventful night's sleep is like the calm before the storm because from here on all other events develop step-by-step until the deepest place is reached. As the king's son in "The Three Feathers" here too, the youth should always go "straight onwards." The fox foretells the coming events and advises the hero to fetch the golden bird in a wooden cage. The hero's animal guide (as the wolf in "Prince Hassan Pasha") has a knowledge of the future because he is a creature of the underworld and, like dwarves, snakes, and ghosts, knows the future.[114] This is based on the fact that the unconscious is timeless and, in this sense, all developmental phases are simultaneously present. The fox takes over the function of the unconscious psyche, which gives useful ideas, hints, and intuitions. These warnings correspond to having an "odd feeling," a discomfort, a strange premonition. These hints can be experienced when one engages in behavior that goes against the instincts. In spite of this, the prince soon goes against the advice of the fox and puts the golden bird into the gold cage, and thus nearly loses his life. Despite all the mishaps and detours caused by his behavior, the king's son still manages to reach the princess, whom he otherwise would never have won on his own. His disobedience indeed leads him into danger, but he thereby achieves higher goals than if he would have blindly obeyed the fox. In most fairytales, however, the magical demands unquestioning obedience,

---

[113] On such letting oneself be carried by the dark man, half-animal, or animal, see "The Fire-Ball," "The Man from Grimsö and the Bear" and "The Piper and the Púca." In the beliefs of the ancient Mediterranean region, the soul after death is carried to heaven by storm winds. See R. Reitzenstein, *Hellenistic*, Pittsburgh 1978 p. 213, 344.

[114] Ninck writes:

> According to folk belief, many people have coaxed a secret out of a dwarf. Eugel, the dwarf, warned Seyfried-Sigfried about the end, and Alberich, [*Alben* = elves, dwarves; from Indogermanic *albh* = shining, white, in the sense of "light beings."] "king of the dwarves," paves the way for king Ortnit [a legendary king in the Middle High German *Wolfdietrich* Romance legend]. The Dís [mythological female ghosts, spirits, or deities associated with vegetation and fate who can be both benevolent and antagonistic towards mortal people.] warn and point to the right thing and herald death. Basically all these beings know more than the gods themselves. That is, they possess the original knowledge and the gods come to it through them. In light of this, the belief that the dead can mediate wisdom makes sense: they are buried in the earth so partake of deeper "earth" knowledge. [Translated from M. Ninck, *Wodan*, Jena 1935 pp. 219-20.]

and the meaning of this command is that one should sacrifice one's own will and submit to the requirements of the Self.[115] But in many other fairytales it is precisely an act of disobedience that leads – in roundabout ways – to good fortune.[116] The meaning of disobedience is summarized by Carus, "The possibility to err is the first step to realizing the truth, we become aware of the world by making mistakes."[117] This is because disobedience against nature, against the unconscious, serves to become conscious. Nature wants the development of ego consciousness. To exist, the ego must differentiate itself from nature, and stand in opposition to it. This distinction, which gives man his sense of freedom, is identical to disobeying nature. Complete dependence on nature is equal to being undifferentiated, and against becoming conscious.[118] Thus, "disobedience" is necessary both for the maintenance and development of consciousness and for overcoming the bond to the maternal world of the unconscious. But nature belies nature by requiring increased effort, which in turn necessitates a humble turning back to nature and an even deeper penetration into its essence.

605   The fox continues to help the hero despite his repeated disobedience. This is because, although it is a "curser and enchanter," as animal spirit and shadow figure it renders a natural resistance to becoming conscious, yet at the same time it is the personification of the drive to self-preservation and un-conditionally desires life. Consequently, the fox remains loyal to the king's son in a superior, yet friendly, manner.

606   If one looks at the whole problem from the perspective of the total personality, the contrast, prince/fox, indicates a split within the fourth function, or within the shadow itself. There is, on the one hand, a human part, unadapted to the world (the simpleton), and, on the other hand, a wise animal part (the magical animal helper). In so far as the human part still belongs to the realm of the conscious personality, it participates in the individuality and autonomy in relation to nature through which the problem becomes more complex. The tension due to the gap between the human and the purely

---

[115] Meister Eckhart, *Sermon on Matthew, 5: 3*, "If we are to have true poverty, then we must be so free of our own created will as we were before we were created." Meister Eckhart (trans. Davies), *Selected Writings*, London 1994 p. 204.

[116] See, for instance, "First Born, First Wed," "The Lame Dog," "The Three Princesses of Whiteland," "The White Bear King Valemon," "East of the Sun and West of the Moon," "Djulek Batür," "The Story of Ali Cengiz" and, in general, J. Bolte and L. Mackensen, *Handwörterbuch* Berlin 1930, under *Gehorsamsproben* [obedience tests].

[117] C.G. Carus, *Psyche*, Leipzig 1931 p. 143.

[118] See here Aurelius:

> . . . for the [psyche] converts and changes every hindrance to its activity into an aid; and so that which is a hindrance is made a furtherance [to its purposes] to act; and that which is an obstacle on the road helps us [go forwards] on this road.

(Marcus Aurelius, *Meditations*, Mount Vernon 1957 pp. IV–20.) [Brackets refer to the authors' (von Franz and von Beit) own translation from Latin.].

animal part of the shadow facilitates a differentiated unfolding of inner images and experiences.

607   The actual disobedience of the prince is that he does not keep the golden bird in its wooden cage but insists on placing it in a golden cage, whereupon the bird lets out a piercing scream, alarms the court, and let the king arrest the intruder. The cage forms a rigid mandala-shaped frame to confine the elusive bird. Gold is the highest value and is therefore associated with the symbols of the Self and the anima. Since it is inert and unreactive to most acids, it has since time immemorial been a symbol of the eternal and immutable.[119] Gold is thus the invulnerable and unshakeable incorruptibility of a consciousness detached from the world, free from emotional entanglements.[120] Gold as a symbolic concept is associated with the light: thus the golden flower, the highest goal of Chinese meditation, means light and Tao.[121] The fact that the hero places the golden bird in a golden cage shows that he ascribes the highest value to the bird. According to a ubiquitous fairytale truism, however, the most valuable is also the most plain and ordinary.[122] By disobeying the fox, the hero, through his secular misunderstanding, repudiates the simple foundation of the paradoxical unconscious conditions and thereby commits a grave error. Since he comes from and belongs to the conscious world, he is caught in a one-sided conscious mind that cannot deal with opposites.[123] At the same time the hero's reverence of the bird is a recognition of its importance in the positive sense; his attempt to grab the bird is an attempt to "grasp" its nature. But the inability to humble himself and to instinctually accept the paradox of the unconscious, (as the fox advised), causes at first an "arrest" by the unconscious. If he had accepted it, the Self would have been assimilated in an undifferentiated way (through the wooden cage) as an inner intuition (the bird). In a certain sense, he takes it too superficially if he thinks he can simply drag this valued entity into the sphere of consciousness without considering the paradoxical nature of the Self. As a

---

[119] See "The spiritual making of gold" (Angelus Silesius): Then lead becomes gold, then chance tumbles in, With God, I am transformed by God into God. (Translated from the German [Johann Scheffler] Angelus Silesius, *Cherubinischer Wandersmann. Nach der Ausgabe letzter Hand von 1675 Vollst. hrsg. und mit einer Studie "Über den Wert der Mystik für unsere Zeit,"* with an introduction by Wilhelm Bölsche, Eugen Diederichs, Jena and Leipzig 1905 p. 15, no. 102.)

[120] See, C.G. Jung, CW 13, *Alchemical Studies* ¶68.

[121] See, R. Wilhelm, *Secret of the Golden Flower*, London 1962 p. 23f, 30f; and also, J. J. Bachofen, *Lykische*, Freiburg i. Br. 1862 p. 69, where gold is the symbol of the light and sun god.

[122] In his manuscript, *Der goldene Vogel* [The golden bird], on this fairytale, Laiblin emphasizes that accepting the wooden cage would have been equivalent to devaluing and thus sacrificing a (spiritual) concept, since life seeks not perfection but rather completeness [wholeness].

[123] In the next volume of this work we explain that of the two parts comprising the core of the personality, the one hidden in matter, or in the unconscious, (here the fox), is the more persistent and conservative; while the part appearing in consciousness, (here the king's youngest son), has more the character of the creative and formative redeemer. Correspondingly, the prohibitions fit the nature of the fox, and the disobedience, the nature of the hero.

result, it rebels and evades him,[124] until through his painful detours he becomes more conscious.

608   As a consequence of his disobedience and losing the golden bird, the image of the Self as a bird and thus as a fleeting intuition transforms into the image of the horse as a vital creative force, and then into the maiden as precious human emotion and the real soul image. With the horse, the hero commits the same mistake when he puts on the golden saddle. A Spanish fairytale, "The Magician Palermo," can perhaps help us clarify this motif. In that tale, the princess (daughter of the wizard or sorcerer = the devil), tells the hero, who has to tame a wild horse, that the horse is her father and the saddle her mother. Placing the saddle on the horse would thus be a combination of masculine and feminine, a *coniunctio*. The same can be said in retrospect about the bird (the male) and the cage (the receiving, enclosing feminine). It turns out, however, that combining gold with gold, as "like with like," is inauspicious. Rather the opposites: male/female, must still be extended by the pairs, valuable/worthless, beautiful/ugly, in order to produce the greatest possible fruitful tension.[125] The hero cannot bear the tension of the opposites that the fox advises him to bring about, and as a consequence of this weakness, he is soon engulfed by the unconscious. Continuing the Uzbek parallel "Prince Hassan Pasha" from where we left off at the point that Hassan Pasha departs from the crossroads on the road from which "he will never return":

609   The wolf carries Prince Hassan Pasha through a forest and arrived at a city. When evening settled, the wolf spoke to the prince, "Now go into the city! Forty gates you must go through and at each gate sleep two *divs*,[126] But fear not! They will not awake. When you have stepped through the last gate, you will see forty chambers, in which the lord of this land keeps his treasures. These rooms are aligned in two rows. Go along them and count from the left side until you come to the twentieth chamber and step inside. There sit three birds and one is that which you seek. These birds are called *Anka-Kush*[127] and are like great eagles. They are birds of Paradise. Take the birds and quickly go! But do not look behind you. If you look behind you, all will go bad for you."

610   The prince followed exactly what the wolf had told. He went through the forty gates, counted the twentieth room on the left, entered, and

---

[124] On this theme, see the motif of the swan maiden, where the man thinks he can win the anima simply by stealing her swan garments.

[125] See the explanation of the alchemical allegory called th\erns an activation of opposites to overcome the "unfruitfulness" of the land.

[126] Demons similar to *djins* but eviler (*Märchen aus Turkestan und Tibet* p. 295.)

[127] Arabic for *Simurg*, *Kush* means bird (*Märchen aus Turkestan und Tibet* p. 46 and the note on Simurg in *ibid* p. 295.)

there saw the three birds. Hassan Pasha took the three birds and went to the door. But he could not resist his curiosity and looked behind him. There he noticed the golden pedestal upon which the birds had sat. It was of such beauty that he thought it would be a shame to leave it behind. He went back but as soon as he touched the pedestal, a terrific noise broke out, which woke up the forty *divs*. They captured Hassan and brought him to the king of the country.

611 The golden bird is characterized here as a symbol of the Self in that it dwells in the city with forty gates and a palace with forty chambers. The birds are in the middle chamber on the left, that is, in the middle of the unconscious side. The split into three is not significant, it only proves the weaker relationship to the contents of the unconscious, that is, a greater degree of unconsciousness. The trinity contains the one with its two contrasting aspects.[128] Here the bird trinity is clearly set in relation to the sun, and the teller of the fairytale adds that the birds are called *Anka-Kush*, a miracle bird similar to the phoenix. The pedestal on which the three birds sit builds, as a basis, a fourth (as in "The Golden Bird" where the cage represents a second, the opposites) and is connected by a web of invisible threads to bells that awaken the *divs*.[129] These are demons created by God from the smoke of the first fire and were, according to the Sanskrit word *deva* (= Latin *deus* = Greek, θηός (theos) = God), originally in the Avestan language, "beings of shining light." Later on, in Persia, they were considered as evil spirits, horned devils with claws and tails.[130] The three birds and the pedestal together form an image of the Self, the three more developed functions and the fourth, which is the most valuable, and at the same time connected "invisibly" to all the dark powers.

612 Hassan's backward look at the pedestal "arrested" him in the darkness, in the unconscious. The prohibition on turning back is the well-known Orpheus motif[131] that represents a regressive succumbing to the magical or getting stuck in the realm of the mothers.[132]

---

[128] On the "companion" (acolytes) of a god or hero, see the next volume in this work.
[129] These warning chimes are similar to the signal that the hero's horse sends out when its hoof touches the walls around the city of the anima figure in "The Virgin Tsar." These also awaken the whole court and result in the big chase.
[130] See note in *Märchen aus Turkestan und Tibet* p. 295.
[131] And of Lot's wife who looked back at Sodom and was turned into a pillar of salt (Genesis 19).
[132] On being bound to objects of the past Jung writes:
   The demands of the unconscious [the retrospective nostalgia] act at first like a paralyzing poison on a man's energy and resourcefulness, so that it may well be compared to the bite of a poisonous snake. Apparently it is a hostile demon who robs him of energy, but in actual fact it is his own unconscious whose alien tendencies are beginning to check the forward striving of the conscious mind. (C.G. Jung, CW 5, *Symbols of Transformation* ¶458, also *ibid* ¶253-54, ¶351, and ¶455f. See also C.G. Jung, CW 12, *Psychology and Alchemy* ¶55; and on facing or walking backwards, G. Róheim, *Spiegelzauber*, Leipzig and Wien 1919 pp. 68–69, fn. 3.)

613   "Back" refers to the unconscious, the shadow, and the realm of ghosts. The hero must often accomplish his task without turning back or looking away.[133] The symbols in "Prince Hassan Pasha" augment and confirm the interpretation of "The Golden Bird" at the point where the hero does not simply accept what is given to him (and easily carries the birds away), but succumbs to the fascination of deeper and, therefore, more dangerous unconscious values. Partly as a result of their defiance, partly their yearning but unknowing behavior, the heroes of both tales must continue their quest and the *auseinandersetzung* on a still deeper level. The Uzbek tale continues:

614   The king wanted to immediately execute Hassan Pasha but when he heard about the purpose of his journey, he agreed to set him free on condition that Hassan brings him the most beautiful of the forty daughters of the king of a faraway country.

615   Hassan Pasha returned to the wolf in the forest where he becried his lot. The wolf was annoyed that the prince had not followed his advice and left him standing there. But the next day, the wolf offered his help again and took Hassan Pasha on his back to the faraway kingdom. When darkness fell, the wolf spoke to Hassan Pasha. "Go into the city! At the entrance gate there will be a great monster with many heads. Do not fear! Just keep going straight through the gate into the city. There you will come to a large castle in which the forty daughters of the king live. They will all be sleeping. Go inside and count from the left side until you come to the ninth daughter. Then pick her up and carry her back here. But on your way out of the castle, do not turn around. If you do, you will come to harm".

616   Hassan Pasha found everything as the wolf told and he counted to the ninth daughter on the left side, picked her up, and carried her away. At the entrance to the castle, however, he involuntarily turned and looked back. He saw a beautiful scarf that belonged to the maiden. This scarf was woven with gold and silver threads and decorated with precious stones. He thought it would be a pity not to take it too. But as soon as he touched it, a terrific noise broke out and servants came from all sides and grabbed him. He was brought to the king. The king wanted to execute the impertinent thief but when he heard his story he said Hassan Pasha could have the daughter and the precious scarf, if he would bring him the yellow horse that belongs to a *div* who lives in the mountains.

---

[133] Perseus must kill the Gorgon with his face averted. For more examples on looking back causing a paralyzing bond to the unconscious, see the tales "Tiri and Karu," "The Lady of Pintorp" and "The Lord of the Hill and John Blossom."

617   Hassan Pasha returned and told the wolf what had occurred. The wolf flew into anger, smote the prince, but eventually let himself be placated and offered his help.

618   The prince again rode on the wolf's back and on the third day they came to the foot of a high mountain. The wolf told Hassan to climb up the mountain until he reached a house, "Go into that house. There the great *div* sleeps in a large chamber. Around his neck there is a chain of keys. Take this without fear and go away with the keys. You will see many rooms. In the first there are many nails, in the second, a long silk cord, and in the third, the yellow horse. Go into the first chamber and take nineteen nails, and then into the second and cut thirty-eight cubits of silk. Then go to the third chamber where you will find the yellow horse. In a corner of this chamber a large pit has been excavated and nearby there will be a post. When you come in, the horse will neigh loudly. Do not look around, but quickly tie the silk cord around the post and let yourself down into the pit. The *div* will wake up from all the horse's neighing. He will come into the room where the yellow horse is, mount it, and ride out looking for what is disturbing his steed. He will find nothing and then return, put his horse where he had taken it, return to his chamber, and go back to sleep. Wait a while and then with the silk cord, pull yourself up, and stick your head out of the pit. The yellow horse will whinny, the *div* will again wake up, come, and ride out on the yellow horse around his house looking for intruders. But he will again discover nothing, return, put away his horse and go to sleep. Again, stick your head out of the pit. The horse will neigh loudly and awaken the *div* who will again ride out to inspect his environs. This time when he brings the horse to the room, he will take away the bowl of kish (raisin) milk, which is the horse's usual feed, and put dry bones in its place. Then the *div* will say, 'Now you can neigh as much as you want, I will not come, because you have deceived me enough tonight.' Then the *div* will go back to sleep. Now you can come out of the pit, take the bones from the horse, and put back its kish-milk. In this way, you will win the favor of the horse and it will no longer whinny. Then go into the chamber where the *div* is sleeping and nail him to the ground with the nails that you gathered in the first chamber. When he tries to free himself, he will break his back. Then you can mount the yellow horse and ride to me!"

619   Hassan Pasha found everything as the wolf had said and when all had been done, he rode the yellow horse to the place where the wolf was waiting for him. This time the wolf was pleased with how the

enterprise turned out. When they arrived at the king's palace, the wolf transformed himself into a yellow horse and ordered Hassan to take him to the king. Thus, Hassan Pasha won the beautiful princess. Then the wolf turned back into himself and joined the pair.

620 They arrived at the kingdom where they were to fetch the golden birds. Here the wolf transformed himself into a beautiful maiden. Again, Hassan Pasha won the paradise birds, along with the golden pedestal, by a ruse.

621 Here the princess must be fetched, in contrast to "The Golden Bird" (the Grimm's version), *before* the yellow horse, indicating that she represents the highest value, which corresponds well to her elevated position in many older cultures.[134] This tale comes from a culture in which the fine horse of the hero is often valued even higher than a woman. Also, the behavior of the wolf contrasts to that of the fox. The wolf is coarser and rougher, thrashes the prince, threatens to leave him, and can be soothed only with great difficulty.

622 The yellow horse in the Uzbek tale "Prince Hassan Pasha" corresponds to the golden horse in "The Golden Bird" (Grimm's version), because yellow is often seen as equivalent to gold and, particularly in Eastern mysticism, is a Self symbol. Goethe said of the color yellow, "it is the color nearest the light" and "In its highest purity, it always carries with it the nature of the hero."[135] The vision of the yellow color corresponds to a show of light and to illumination which can be equated psychologically to intuition. Thus, the horse (and similarly, the golden bird) represent an intuitively sensed idea of the Self, but represented as animal creativity.[136]

623 In essence, both heroes take on tasks that lead directly to an encounter with the deity of the magical, the great *div*. In "Prince Hassan Pasha" the last big test is the *auseinandersetzung* with the lord of the depths, but in a simpler form than in "The Golden Bird," which is developed in a more differentiated way. By trickery,[137] Hassan wins the sympathy of the *div*'s horse. In

---

[134] Primitive cultures.
[135] J. W. von Goethe, *Theory of Colours*, John Murray, London 1840, translated by C. Lock Eastlake pp. 306–07. On the identity of yellow, gold, and light in China see C.G. Jung, CW 13, *Alchemical Studies* ¶161, fn. 40, "Significantly, the oldest of the Chinese alchemists, Wei Po-Yang, who lived ca. A.D. 140, was familiar with this idea. He said, 'He who properly cultivates his innate nature will see the yellow light shine forth as it should'. " (W. Po-Yang and L. Wu/T. Davis, "An Ancient Chinese Treatise on Alchemy," in *Isis*, 1932 p. 262.)
[136] See the chestnut horse whose galloping brought up a spring in the courtyard of the king in "The Two Travelers," and the horse as a magical companion in "Ferdinand the Faithful and Ferdinand the Unfaithful." See also the role of the horse in the tales "The Princess in the Tree," "The Rose Maiden" and "The Golden Apples and the Nine Peahens." Similarly, in "The Tsar's Daughter and the Dragon" the hero finds three horses with the anima, a black horse with a silver harness, a white horse with a gold harness, and a gray-white horse with a jeweled harness.
[137] On trickery as a component of the motif "contests of transformations," see the next volume of this work.

psychological terms, he cuts off the psychic energy from the father-imago and binds it to himself, thus giving him superiority over the *div*. He gains the power that had previously belonged to the demonic father, who so often in fairytales stands behind the image of the anima. He nails the *div* firmly to the ground, so that the latter, when trying to sit up, breaks his back. This means that, with tremendous effort, Hassan realizes the nature of this all-powerful archetype, that is, he literally "nails" it to the ground, to reality. He is aware of it, knows it, and can control it. The *div* thereby perishes; in other words, this negative image of the father dissolves completely, and the values, the psychic powers, which were symbolized in the yellow horse, become a part of the total personality.

624   In another Uzbek tale, "The Beautiful Dunye," the same central scene is nearly identical, but instead of the *div*, the sought-after anima (the daughter of a *div*) owns the horse, *Juz-At* (= hundred horse).[138]

625   Enriched with some other features, one of the central scenes of "The Golden Bird" takes place at night when the hero intercepts the princess on her way to the bathhouse. This is the only time she leaves the custody of her father and enjoys a few minutes of freedom. The fox advised the hero to grab the maiden, give her a kiss, and then take her with him, without letting her say goodbye to her parents. Of course, the hero manages to carry out all the steps but the last. The beautiful princess pleads that he let her one last time see her parents. The king's son acquiesces and thereby loses her. The night and the bathhouse situation indicate that acquiring the anima happens in the unconscious, and therefore the success of bringing her into the conscious world is conditioned on her not turning back. This is because the danger of slipping back into inaccessible unconsciousness is great. Similarly to Hassan, when he gave in to the attraction of the magical and turned back for the golden pedestal and the precious scarf, the king's son in "The Golden Bird" allows the anima – his soul figure – to turn back. He thus gives in to the anima's resistance to becoming conscious. She thereby falls back into the parental-images, and the hero with her, whereby the whole process of development is called into question. The strength of the parent images accrues from the fact that they are endowed with divine attributes,[139] and psychic energy "sticks" to the memories [that is, the inner images] and wants to keep hold of them forever. Tearing psychic energy away from the sphere of the unconscious leads to inner rebirth. This renewal can only be achieved by sacrificing the retrospective longing before the demonic forces usurp one's whole life force.

---

[138] *Märchen aus Turkestan und Tibet* p. 65.
[139] They are often clearly portrayed in fairytales as parents of the anima, the lord of the magical realm and the Great Mother.

626 In the parallel tale from Albania, "The Nightingale Gisar," the encounter with the anima is portrayed similarly as in "The Virgin Tsar" and its variants. The hero enters the bedroom where the "Beautiful of the Earth" was sleeping:

627 There she had lit four candles and another four were on the table not yet lit. The lit candles had almost burnt out. When the young man came to her, he lit the four fresh candles and put out the burning ones. He took the cage with the nightingale Gisar and walked out. Just as he stepped out the door, everybody in the palace awoke. But before they caught him, his girlfriends [three eagles that had transformed themselves into beautiful maidens] picked him up and brought him back to their house. There they remained together for some time. Then one day the lad said, "Now please take me back to my own country." They brought him to the place [the crossroads] where he had previously separated from his brothers.

628 Later, as in "The Virgin Tsar," the virgin comes to fetch him, and bombards the city of the father-king until the hero comes to her on board her ship.[140]

629 The part about extinguishing and reigniting the candles is significant, since they appear in two groups of four, the number of wholeness. In several fairytales, for instance "Godfather Death," burning candles represent the life of a human being. Lighting new candles is equivalent to a rite of life renewal. The hero's meeting with the Beautiful of the Earth in the mystical marriage, which represents the union of consciousness and the unconscious, creates an inner renewal of the whole psychic personality, and in particular the conscious mind.

630 In "The Golden Bird" no renewing union is, at first, possible because the princess harks back to her parents. Inasmuch as the anima's longing for return symbolizes the regressive tendency of the hero himself, he is also held responsible and must now, as the only possible rescue, perform a fourth task. This last test comprises performing a superhuman task that requires untiring effort. This is needed to wrench himself from the fascination of the unconscious which stands behind the anima. The hero must remove a mountain that blocks the view of the old king. This mountain is an obstacle, a piece of heavy matter, in which the figure of the father is caught, unredeemed. In Gnostic concepts, this image corresponds to the divine *Nous* [mind, intelligence] that in the Creation sank into the physical, material world and needed salvation.[141]

---

[140] This is nearly identical to the ending of "The Bird Flower-Triller."
[141] The crucified raven in "The Princess in the Tree" is an example from fairytales.

631   The unredeemed and handicapped state of the old father-king acts like a mirroring of the often blind and sick king of the upper world, which personifies the ego. He too is blind and sick, so to speak, and requires the action of the hero. The father of the anima symbolizes the blind creative urge of the unconscious, who as it were, seeks the human as the one that can make things real.

632   A fairytale that particularly clearly explores this problem of the mutual redemption of the conscious and the unconscious spheres is a parallel to "The Poor Miller's Boy and the Cat" titled by Bolte-Políka "The Poor Miller's Boy and the Kitten." In summary:

633   An aging miller sent his three sons out on a task: whomever should bring back the best horse would inherit his mill. The youngest son, the simpleton, met up with a little gray man and chopped wood for him a whole year through. As a reward for his honesty and faithfulness, the little gray man gave his best horse. The elder brothers joined up with him on the way home. Because the eldest son had brought back a blind horse, and the middle son a lame one, they banded together, grabbed the simpleton, and shoved him into a limekiln, and took his horse with them.

634   The little gray man came by, pulled him out of the kiln, and anointed him with a healing lotion. The boy quickly regained life and health. He also got his horse back. Then he went to his father. The aging miller did not yet give him the mill, however, but presented all three sons with yet another task: whoever brought back the best shirt would get his mill. Again, the simpleton found the best shirt but on his way home his brothers tied him to a tree, shot him dead, and took the shirt.

635   Again, the little gray man came and brought the boy back to life. When he finally returned to his father, he learned that his brothers had told their father that the youngest son was in alliance with the devil, and had most likely died. The father, seeing his youngest son was confounded and decided to send his three sons out on still another task. He who brought back the best bread would get the mill, because "the devil has no power over bread." This time the simpleton met an old *Mütterchen* [little mother] in the forest. He shared his food with her and she gave him a wishing rod in return. The next day, when he was standing in the middle of a bridge, he dipped the rod down into the water. A little turtle climbed up on it. The simpleton put the turtle in his pocket and carried it along. When later he reached into his pocket, he found a whole roll of coins. Now it all went well with

him. He held the little turtle in high respect, rented the best room in an inn, placed the turtle on a fine bed and went out to find the best bread. After a while he returned without having found what he was looking for. When he looked at the little turtle, it had two beautiful white feet. "Oh my! what could this mean?" he wondered. He put a blanket over the feet to keep them warm. One evening, when he was still musing about how he could find the best bread, he saw someone standing in the shadows, and moving as if they were kneading bread. That night he dreamed that from that dough came the best bread. When he woke up there lay the best bread, right in front of him!

636   He took the bread to his father and everybody had to agree that it was indeed the very best bread. Then the simpleton returned to his little turtle and found a beautiful princess lying next to the turtle. She told him that she was enchanted by her mother and now he had redeemed her. Thereupon she promised to marry him and become his wife, but first she must go home to her father. "Go now to your home," she said, "When you hear the first cannon shot, then I am putting my clothes on; when you hear the second shot, then I am stepping into the coach; the third shot, look behind you and, behind six white horses, I will be coming!" It all happened just like that, the princess came after the third shot and they were wed and lived happily a long time together.

637   Then it came to pass that he let the little turtle, which the princess had taken such good care of all the time, fall into the fire. The princess thereupon became so angry that she spat in his face. He felt so sad about his clumsiness that he dug a hole deep in the ground and decided to live the rest of his life there. Above the entrance he had an inscription made that read, "Here down below no one will find me but God." There, in that deep cave, he lived for many years. The old king, the father of the princess, became sick, and went all over visiting the best doctors and seeking the best medicines, but found nothing that would heal him. By chance he came by the underground cave and was suddenly well again. He looked around and read the inscription, and had his men dig until they reached the opening of the cave deep underground. The man did not want to come out, and the king's men reported back that the man underground only wanted to go to God. But the old king convinced the man underground to ascend. He discovered it was his son-in-law, reconciled him with his daughter, and they lived happily again together for a very long time.[142]

---

[142] Translated from J. Bolte and G. Polívka, *Anmerkungen*, Vol. 2, Leipzig 1915 pp. 466–467.

638   The redemption of the anima from the animal state (here a turtle) parallels the search for the bread (= the physical body and also a necessity of life). Since the old miller no longer appears and the hero becomes in need of redemption, in the second half of the tale he alone represents the core of the personality and consciousness. He does not sufficiently respect the former animal existence of the anima, her amphibious primordial nature. He pushes it aside. In the fairytale this is figuratively represented by his letting the turtle be destroyed in the fire. In consequence, the hero loses contact also with the higher female principle and is thus deprived of his own vitality and activity. He is "buried alive" in the unconscious (the earth as the Great Mother), bound and hidden, just like an unredeemed demon.[143] Through the behavior of the hero, the king also finds himself in distress. The hero allows himself to be raised only by "God" and later acquiesces to the king. This, albeit in a veiled form, indicates the divine nature of the sick old king-father, which corresponds to the primeval chthonic spirit.[144] When the ailing king passes by the spot above the underground cave he is healed, and then it is the turn of the hero to be freed from his (self-applied) spell. The suffering of the king is fundamentally based on his ignoring the nature-bound character of the soul through a one-sided orientation, and also by [ego-]consciousness that is not aware of the importance of accepting the given situation. This behavior (directed by the conscious mind) also exposes the unconscious sphere to suffering.

639   Returning to "The Golden Bird" we see the same dire predicament described where the old king of the magical realm is hemmed in by a mountain and wants to force the hero to remove it, and at the same time, the secular father-king demands the golden bird be brought to him so that he may be healed. This tension between the unconscious and consciousness creates, as it were, in the middle of the stress field the redeeming symbol, which is embodied here in the golden fruits, the bird, the horse, and the sibling pair: fox and anima. The hero, as the "fourth," also partakes, inasmuch as he is the intermediary between the spheres.[145] In this perfectly executed tale, the mirroring of above and below is taken so far that the upper king through his (fourth) son and the lower king through his son (the prince who is enchanted

---

[143] The king does not seem to function, at first glance, like the spiritual principle hidden in matter. But he is to be regarded as such, since he is the father of the anima figure, to whom she had to return for a short time. (Similar to the scene in "The Golden Bird," where the calamity occurs just during the time when the anima visits her parents, that is, when she sinks back into the unconscious (see page 247).

[144] In "The Golden Bird" it is the fox, who later proves to be the son of the lord of the underworld, who contributes essentially to transforming the situation of the ailing figures. In this tale of the miller's son, the figures of the magical helper and his father are united into the single form of the sick king or the father of the anima, and thus the role of helpful fox is passed over to him.

[145] According to Jung's definition, the carrier of the psychic power that in fairytales makes possible the meditation between the spheres could be called the "transcendent function" (C.G. Jung, CW 6, *Psychological Types* ¶824–828).

as the fox), are all ultimately redeemed. That is, the collaboration between the fox and king's son frees them. Through this light that reaches down into the darkness of the unconscious the fox, as daimonion, knows, however, how to master the realities of the unconscious and helps to raise the soul-image into the conscious mind. Thus, a free exchange of power emerges, salvaging the light below, and taking root in life above.

640   The hero is given eight days within which he must complete the fourth and final task of removing the mountain. Seven are spent in the young man's vain attempts, on the eighth day the fox intervenes to save him. The eight is – as already mentioned – a doubling of four, the number of the Self and inner totality, the fox's goal from the beginning.

641   After completing this task – with the fox's help – the youth and the princess begin the return journey, soon to be joined by the fox. This signifies that the regressive movement of psychic energy stops when the symbol is finally attained.[146] The return of the hero is the figurative expression of the fact that consciousness has become aware of what has taken place in the unconscious.[147]

642   On his return journey, albeit with a shortened duration of stay, the king's son passes through exactly the same stations as on his outward path in both "The Golden Bird" and "Prince Hassan Pasha."[148] This is not always the case in fairytales. Often, the way back is experienced wholesale and reported only in summary.[149] The latter is like when one suddenly awakes from a dream.[150] The former shows, however, the difficulties in adapting and integrating what was experienced in the unconscious with previously known conscious patterns in the everyday real world so that it does not remain only something seen intuitively. In the fairytales, the resistance that must be overcome is formulated in two ways: either the prized anima figure does not want to come into the

---

[146] On this see Jung, "With the birth of the symbol, the regression of libido into the unconscious ceases. Regression is converted into progression, the blockage starts to flow again, and the nature of the maternal abyss is broken." (C.G. Jung, CW 6, *Psychological Types* ¶445.)

[147] See the phrase from a sermon attributed to Meister Eckart:

> Aptly says Our Lord, a noble person went into a distant land to win himself a kingdom, and he returned. For human beings must be One. And for that unity, one has to go searching for it – in oneself and yet in One; and it seizes one in one: the human must just simply see God. But he [or she] has also to "come back" and become conscious and aware that he [or she] knows God.

(Meister Eckehart, *Schriften und Predigten,* translated from the Middle High German and edited by H. Büttner, Eugen Diederichs, Jena 1921–1923 p. 97).

[148] Just as in two other tales discussed above, "The Virgin Tsar" and "The Devil with the Three Golden Hairs."

[149] Among the tales already discussed, see "Ngeraod's Bundle," "Hansel and Gretel" and "Tritill, Litill, and the Birds."

[150] On the symbols appearing in such transition processes, see H. Silberer, *Problems of Mysticism,* New York 1917 p. 46 and Herbert Silberer, "Symbolik des Erwachens und Schwellensymbolik überhaupt" in: *Jahrbuch für psychoanalytische und psychopathologische Forschungen,* Vol. 3, ed. by E. Bleuler and S. Freud, Franz Deuticke, Leipzig and Wien 1912 *passim.*

profane world, which expresses a resistance on the part of the unconscious,[151] or, the secular world begrudges the hero what he has accomplished, and what he has won, and pushes him back. In the latter case the opposition comes from the conscious attitude that does not want to accept the reassessment of all prevailing values, which accompany the process of psychic development. The secular-thinking consciousness, with its goals and values shaped by collective attitudes, wants to seize the treasures of the psyche for itself, and to use these in its previous world.[152] Once again, the animal helper steps in to help here and signals the conflict-free mediatory path. Instinct knows no differentiating judgements, not the opposites of consciousness, either yes *or* no, but it leads instead further along the crooked path of nature, which always includes a yes *and* a no. This crooked path is, as it were, the way of the living.

643   Thus, the fox gives advice, both contrary to the unconscious powers that want to keep the treasures for themselves, as well as against the greed of the conscious attitude. First, the fox helps the hero steal the horse and the bird from the two old kings. These are powerless because their deeper roots, the [archetypal] chthonic god in the underworld, has been overcome. But then the fox comes with a strange request to the prince. He asks that the king's son cut off his head and paws. As it later turns out, he would have thereby been transformed into a human, but the hero refuses to acquiesce to his demand. This would have been an act of recognition towards the unconscious instinct that had led him so far. The king's son would have been better off to have asked himself: who actually is this mysterious being that guided him to his goal? But he spares the fox, that is, he protects himself, in that he feels such a "dissecting" self-reflection to be a cruel intervention. He views this requirement with his secular eyes and as a violent destruction of the given situation and does not suspect the possibility of transformation. In the Iranian parallel "The Bird Flower-Triller" the same motif appears at the beginning of the tale: the king's youngest son refuses to kill the healing miracle fish for his father, because a holy phrase[153] is written on its forehead. Here the prince's restraint is justified by religious respect. In addition to reverence, however, making something conscious requires critical reflection of the phenomena and the courage to risk sacrificing the present manifestation in favor of a more adequate one.

644   The fox realizes at once the hero's resistance, revealed in his bonds to secular consciousness, and senses the great dangers that threaten from that world. The animal helper warns the hero, "Buy no gallows' meat and do not sit at the edge of any well." (The "gallows' meat" turns out to be his two condemned brothers. ("Buying" would here mean to set them free.) Then the fox disappears into the forest. Because the hero had failed to carry through

---

[151] For example, in "The King of the Golden Mountain."
[152] On this, see C.G. Jung, CW 6, *Psychological Types* ¶825f.
[153] [A *shahada* of Shia Islam.]

the transforming sacrifice of the fox, it cannot accompany the youth into the secular world. This means that the animal-instinctual aspect of the fourth function is rejected by the conscious mind and thus repressed. Due to this loss of contact with the unconscious, further complications arise and the hero's return takes a detour.[154]

645   The hero arrives at the village from where he set out and which is the border between the secular and the magical. There he buys back his condemned brothers. When all that happens in the fairytale is seen as an intrapersonal drama, this represents a weak sentimentality towards parts of one's own personality. The wrong conscious attitude (shown in the two brothers), which actually has been superseded by the foregoing internal events and is therefore no longer valid and should be rightly extinguished, now returns to life. This means, psychologically, that no lessons were learned, no consequences were drawn from the inner transformations: everything remains as it was. The resistance against the inferior function resurfaces. In the forest near the castle, that is, close to the threshold of consciousness, the envy of the brothers breaks out and they seize the precious things that their brother had brought back and push him into a deep well. This means that conscious tendencies running contradictory to the Self push the fourth function back into the unconscious. This is only possible because the fourth function is split off from the instincts (the fox) and the hero [the conscious mind] has, in the secular world, lost the power to break through, which it possessed when united with the instincts through the unconscious experiences.

646   The assimilation of inner values that the fourth function, with its closeness to the unconscious, mediates for the conscious mind, often meets with difficulties, and herein lies the general psychological meaning of the test encounters along the "way back home" in fairytales. The disappearance of the fox in the forest, and the hero's being shoved off the edge of the well (that is, at the edge of the entrance to the unconscious) correspond to Ivan Tsarevich's sudden exhaustion and sleep in "The Virgin Tsar" on his return journey. (And, for example, Gilgamesh's washing in the well, which allowed the snake to steal the herb of life). In "The Golden Bird" this failure is portrayed not only as a weakness of the hero and attraction to the unconscious, but also as a resistance from the side of consciousness. These two aspects are represented as one and the same process.[155] Psychologically, the Self is always:

---

[154] Laiblin correctly points out (W. Laiblin, *Der goldene Vogel*, Stuttgart 1961 pp. 184–186) the similarities to the archetypal situation described in the *I Ching* , hexagram "Before Completion" [also with the image of a fox] (Wilhelm/Baynes, *I Ching*, Princeton, 1967 p. 248f.)

[155] For more on this common psychological process, see C.G. Jung, CW 12, *Psychology and Alchemy* ¶193f.

647 . . . threatened on the one hand by the negative attitude of the conscious mind and on the other by the *horror vacui* [abhorrence of the vacuum] of the unconscious, which is quite ready to swallow up all its progeny, since it produces them only in play, and destruction is an inescapable part of play.[156]

648 The downfall (in the literal sense) of the hero causes his treasures (the bird, horse, and anima) to lose their vitality, that is, the hitherto dominant conscious attitude (the king) loses its newly won life impulses and the freshly acquired joy of life. He falls back to the same inner state of disinclination and languor as before. The soul (anima) is sad, the life energy (horse) is weary, and the intuition (bird) is silenced.[157]The symbol created by the unconscious cannot be lived because the limitations of the conscious attitude cannot properly assimilate it.[158] If the king were to recognize that he has all these treasures thanks to his son, the simpleton, and that the latter has thus acquired a right to them and even to the king's previous empire, then the inhibitions would dissolve. But he is seen as a "fool" being led around by an animal, and is not yet recognized as a guide to his own inner destiny. The conscious mind still resists the transformation: to accept these new elements [as positive factors in his life] would mean to accept the shadow, the dark alter ego, and the proud conscious mind considers these to be its own negation. Thus, in "The Golden Bird" the hero initially fails again. The Uzbek tale portrays a less differentiated process. We step into the tale at the point where the wolf, disguised as the beautiful princess, appears at the king's court.

649 The king organized a great marriage and according to the customs, the bride wore a thick veil. When the guests had enjoyed their meal, the princess made a transformation and turned into a wolf! She sprang at the king, scratching and biting. All those present ran away as fast as they could. Behind them ran the wolf, who bit not a few in their calves on its way out into the fields where it caught up with the prince and the real princess.

650 Hassan Pasha was invited to spend time at the wolf's castle, but after some time he thought about returning home and remembered his brothers, who had embarked with him on the quest for the mysterious bird. The wolf warned Hassan against his brothers, but despite these

---

[156] C.G. Jung, CW 9i, *The Archetypes and the Collective Unconscious* ¶286.
[157] See a parallel in J. Bolte and G. Polívka, *Anmerkungen*, Vol. 1, Leipzig 1913 p. 503, in which the king can only be healed throughout the singing (German: *Stimme*) of the bird. This shows how important the "mood" [German: *Stimmung* = temperament, spirit, disposition] of the unconscious can be and which senses correspond to the bird's singing.
[158] See C.G. Jung, CW 6, *Psychological Types* ¶310.

warnings the youth went looking for them in a foreign town where they had fallen in hardship and poverty. He freed them both and returned with them to the wolf's castle where the three brothers spent many days enjoying themselves and having good times together. Finally, they prepared for the journey back to their father. As they took leave of the wolf, he whispered in the ear of Hassan Pasha, "Be on guard on your way home! Your brothers have evil in mind and intend you harm!" But the goodhearted Hassan listened only with half an ear to the wolf and did not heed his warning.

651   Then the three brothers set off. When they came closer to their homeland, the elder brothers became spiteful because they had nothing to bring to their father. While Hassan not only found the precious bird, but also had a beautiful bride and a horse.

652   One day, when they took a rest from their journey, the two elder brothers consulted together and decided to take possession of the bird, the bride, and the horse, and to tell their father that they had themselves won these precious things for him. They poked out Hassan's eyes grabbed the bird, the princess, and the horse and left Hassan blind and helpless in the empty desert.

653   No help came to Hassan so he began to fervently pray to Allah. For a long, long time he prayed. Then he heard the voice of the Prophet who said to him, "Forty days must you pray to Allah so that he can send you healing. On the fortieth day, crawl to your right and you will come upon a spring. Wash yourself in the waters and you will be able to see again. Then pray again to Allah to be saved. During the forty days, a bird will bring you nourishment."

654   So it happened and on the fortieth day Hassan crept slowly to his right and came upon the spring where he washed himself and immediately his sight was restored. Then he drank from the spring and set out wherever his eyes led him. In the far distance, he saw a huge column of whirling dust that came towards him. And before he could realize what was happening, there before him stood his trusted servant and companion, the wolf! Then the wolf brought Hassan Pasha to his father's castle, disguised as a gypsy. The lies of the brothers were exposed and the brothers executed. Hassan married the beautiful princess and the wolf took part in the wedding and was treated with great honor. His father, sultan Murad, later handed over the reign of the kingdom to his son Hassan. On each feather of the bird, called the *Anka*, or *Anka-Kush*, some sort of wisdom was inscribed in holy script, and because Hassan Pasha continued to read these words, he learned all the human virtues and became a wise ruler.

655   Unlike in "The Golden Bird" Hassan Pasha is not pushed into a well, but blinded, like the blinding of the tailor by the evil cobbler in "The Two Travelers." The negative-secular forces gain the upper hand and rob the cognitive faculty of its power to see. Help comes here, as in "The Golden Bird," by way of a bird, but it is also portrayed as the voice of the prophet Muhammad, which also – in a higher form – signifies helpful intuition and inspiration by the Spirit.

656   In the Iranian variant "The Bird Flower-Triller" the psychopomp is represented in still another way: by a stone tablet that the hero finds at the crossroads. Reading this, he learns that:

657   Those who come to this crossroads should know that the road to the right is safe and easy, the road to the left, however, is so dangerous that there is no hope that the traveler will return. But should anyone still want to follow the path on the left, they should take this tablet with them." The hero took the path to the left and also the tablet. On his way, the tablet warned him every time he was about to fall for the seductive magic powers of witches and gave him instructions on how to vanquish them. In the *auseinandersetzung* with the third witch, he smashed her head with the tablet; her skull split apart and the spell was broken.

658   This tablet also acts as the voice of conscience and seems to know the inner laws of human beings. Only this knowledge is effective in showing the way through conflict situations, set up by the unconscious, where all the secular rules of conduct fail. The tale tells us, therefore, that it is the voice of instinct (the animal) or the law (the tablet) or of God, which alone helps in the *auseinandersetzung* with the unconscious.

659   In "The Golden Bird" it is the fox that appears as a helper. When the hero sinks back into the unconscious, he approaches the sphere of the fox, thereby creating a new contact with this symbol. The well is dry, so the fallen hero does not sink completely, indicating that after all that has happened, a certain basis, a ground for the inner personality, now exists. It [the inner personality] is no longer at the mercy of the unbounded infinite, but still not wholly free. With its tail, the fox pulls the hero out of the well. As a precaution for the next encounter with the secular, he veils his true nature and returns, as Ivan Tsarevich does in "The Virgin Tsar," to his humble form.[159] Even Hassan comes disguised as a gypsy when he finally returns to his father's court.

660   Once again, the instincts (fox, wolf) save the core personality, which can now free itself and rejoin life in the world. At the same time, secretly and

---

[159] See the hero as a shepherd in "The King of the Golden Mountain" and also the return of Odysseus.

unobserved, the former world-oriented collective attitude reinstates itself. But the feminine feeling, the anima, which has meanwhile been liberated and differentiated by the internal processes, recognizes the actual core of the conscious personality with overwhelming certainty. The anima's relationship with the new and true conscious (fourth function) is then represented archetypally in the image of the "mystical marriage" [*hieros gamos*]. This in itself is a symbol of the Self, in which the opposites come to rest. For example, it is said in the *Brihadaranyaka Upanishad* IV, 3, 21:

661   Because, just as one, embraced by a beloved woman, has no consciousness of that which is outside or inside, so also the spirit, embraced by the self of the nature of knowledge (*prājñend āthanā*, that is, the Brahman) has no consciousness of what is outside or inside. That is the essential form of the same (self) in which it is one with all its desires appeased or fulfilled, one desiring its own self, one without desires and separated (free) from desire.[160]

662   Such a representation of the Self as a hermaphrodite or as a divine syzygy, the divine pair, is a well-known archetypal image.[161] Thus the primeval man-woman Gayomart of Iranian mythology is male-female. As son[-daughter] of the God of Light, he-she fell down into matter and must be freed from the darkness in order to save the human race.[162] According to Talmudic tradition and Valentinian Gnosticism, Adam too was male-female.[163] Just as, on the one hand, the image of the original being as hermaphroditic was projected back into the past, on the other hand, it is also a vision of the goal.

663   As civilization develops, the bisexual primordial being turns into a symbol of the unity of personality, a symbol of the Self, where the war of opposites finds peace. In this way, the primordial being becomes the distant goal of man's self-development, having been from the very beginning a projection of his unconscious wholeness.[164]

664   The symbol of the hermaphrodite also plays an important role as *homo Adamicus* in hermetic philosophy and alchemy.[165] He is Mercurius:

---

[160] Deussen, *Sixty Upanishads* pp. 489–490. [The word "self" is here not capitalized to conform to the published English translation.]

[161] On this, see Jung, "Youth [male] and young girl together form a syzygy or *coniunctio*, which symbolizes the essence of wholeness (as does the Platonic hermaphrodite, who later became the symbol of perfected wholeness in alchemical philosophy)." C.G. Jung, CW 9i *The Archetypes and the Collective Unconscious* ¶326. See also *ibid* ¶120

[162] See C.G. Jung, CW 11, *Psychology and Religion* ¶202f and H. Güntert, *Weltkönig*, Halle a. S. 1923 p. 347.

[163] E. Böklen, "Adam and Qain," *Mythologische Bibliothek*, Leipzig 1907/1908 p. 9ff (nach J. Winthuis, *Zweigeschlechter*, Leipzig 1928 p. 43f, fn. 3).

[164] C.G. Jung, CW 9i, *Op. cit.* ¶294.

[165] On this, see C.G. Jung, CW 11, *Psychology and Religion* ¶47f especially fn. 21.

665   . . . [T]he divine winged Hermes, manifest in matter, the god of revelation, lord of thought, and psychopomp par excellence. . . Mercurius stands at the beginning and end of the work: he is the *prima materia*, the *caput corvi* [raven's head], the *nigredo*; as a dragon he devours himself and as a dragon he dies to rise again as the *lapis* . . . He is the hermaphrodite at the beginning that splits into the classical brother-sister duality and is reunited in the *coniunctio*, to appear once again at the end in the radiant form of the *lumen novum*, the stone. He is. . . a symbol unifying all opposites.[166]

666   The sought-after philosopher's stone was the "round one" and corresponds to the round, bisexual primordial human of Plato.[167] He was the *Rebis* "made of two things," "that unites both male and female nature in itself." He was also represented as brother and sister united in incest.[168] Due to the fact that the Self can appear in hermaphroditic form, representations of the goal in the fairytales can vary from male to female, and to asexual images.

667   In "The Golden Bird" a third character steps between the couple: the fox, which mediates between the male and the female figures. The couple inherit the empire, which signifies that the Self, here reflected in this male-female duality, becomes the inner guide of life, to which all outward things are subordinated. The evil brothers, who personify the resistance to consciousness, are eliminated.

668   The ending of the "The Golden Bird" is not content with the simple "return home with the sought-after treasures" but, according to the slightly higher level of differentiation of this version, the ending includes not only an embellishment, but a sequel with important information. Many years later, the hero meets the fox in the forest again. The fox asks anew that the hero dismember him.

669   The hero still has to free himself from the powers of the unconscious that had hitherto carried him and directed his actions. To become truly conscious requires an act of free will.[169]

---

[166] C.G. Jung, CW 12, *Psychology and Alchemy* ¶404 [Last phrase italicized by von Franz and von Beit.] See also C.G. Jung, CW 11, *Op. cit.* ¶356.

[167] See *Timaeus*, 7, and C.G. Jung, CW 11, *Psychology and Religion* ¶92.

[168] See C.G. Jung, CW 11, *Psychology and Religion* ¶107, fn. 53. See also *ibid* ¶152, ¶161, and ¶161 fn. 72, ¶164 [reference to dream imagery of a patient.]; H. Leisegang, *Serpent*, London 1955 p. 176. On the cult sibling marriages in Iran, see Cumont p. 134 (*Bêl* and *Fides*). Also in Egypt there was the divine couple Isis and Osiris. In Chinese philosophy, the human being inwardly comprises the interaction of *hun*, the animus, who lives in the eyes and is light and mobile, and *po*, the anima, which is localized in the lower abdomen and is the dark, earthbound soul. See R. Wilhelm, *Secret of the Golden Flower*, London 1962 p. 14.

[169] See Jung on the necessity that ego-consciousness has freedom and autonomy:
> In reality, both are always present: the supremacy of the Self and the hubris of consciousness. (This ego-consciousness is, when it exclusively follows itself, always on the way to God-likeness and superman [inflation]. The exclusive recognition of autonomy, on the other hand, leads to a fatalistic childishness and a too worldly and foreign to humanity spiritual

670   This time the hero overcomes his emotional concerns and follows the fox's request and cuts off its head and paws. This sacrifice is part of the common archetype of the sacrifice of the hero's animal brother. In animal sacrifices, the animal stands for the deity itself[170] to whom the animal is sacrificed. Thus, the lamb is the same as Christ, the bull identical to Mithras, and so forth. Jung writes about this:

671   In the case of Zagreus, we saw that the bull is identical with the god and that the bull sacrifice is a divine sacrifice. But the animal is, as it were, only a part of the hero; he sacrifices only his animal attribute, and thus symbolically gives up his instinctuality. His inner participation in the sacrificial act is perfectly expressed in the anguished and ecstatic countenance of the bull-slaying Mithras. He slays it willingly and unwillingly.[171]

672   Thus, this sacrifice is an act of making conscious, whereas this building up of consciousness – it is equivalent to a sacrilege – is to some extent unavoidably bound up with a violation of the magical realm.[172]

673   The sword by which the magical fox is sacrificed is not "merely the instrument of separation, it is also the force that changes" and the *logos*.[173]

---

presumption.) This conflict between conscious and the unconscious is at least brought nearer to a solution through our becoming aware of it. Such an act of realization is presupposed in the act of self-sacrifice. The ego must make itself conscious of its claim, and the Self must cause the ego to renounce it.
(C.G. Jung, CW 11, *Op. cit.* ¶391-92.) [The sentences within parentheses do not appear in the English version of CW 11.

[170] Jung writes:
The animal represents the god himself; thus the bull represents Dionysus Zagreus and Mithras, the lamb Christ, etc. The sacrifice of the animal means, therefore, the sacrifice of the nature, the instinctual libido. This is expressed most clearly in the cult legend of Attis.
(C.G. Jung, CW 5, *Symbols of Transformation* ¶659.) See also, "The ancients were fully aware that the bull torn in pieces in the Bacchic [cult] orgies represented the god [i.e., Dionysus] himself. . . " E. Rohde, *Psyche* London 1925 p. 354, note 35 to Chapter 10.

[171] C.G. Jung, CW 5, *Symbols of Transformation* ¶665.

[172] See the Chinese tale, "The Bird with the Nine Heads," where at the same time as the hero's entry into the realm of the ten-headed demonic bird the heavenly dog bites off one of its heads, leaving nine. The penetration of the hero, who belongs partially to the realm of consciousness ,results in a wounding, that is, a destruction of the completeness of the unconscious.

[173] On the significance of the sword, see Jung:
The divisive and separative function of the sword, which is of such importance in alchemy, is prefigured in the flaming sword of the angel that separated our first parents from paradise. Separation by a sword is a theme that can also be found in the Gnosis of the Ophites: the earthly cosmos is surrounded by a ring of fire, which at the same time encloses paradise. But paradise and the ring of fire are separated by the "flaming sword." An important interpretation of this flaming sword is given in Simon Magus: There is an incorruptible essence potentially present in every human being, the divine *pneuma*, "which is stationed above and below in the stream of water." Simon says of this *pneuma*: "I and thou, thou before me. I, who am after thee." It is a force "that generates itself, that causes itself to grow; it is its own mother, sister, bride, daughter; its own son, mother, father, a unity, a root of the whole" . . . The tree of life is guarded by the turning (i.e., transforming) sword . . . [It] is the transformation of the vital spirit in man into the Divine. The natural being becomes the divine *pneuma*, as in the vision of Zosimos. (C.G. Jung, CW 11, *Psychology and Religion* ¶359).

674   Jung writes:

> Killing with the sword is a recurrent theme in alchemical literature.
> The "philosophical egg" is divided with the sword, and with it the
> "King" is transfixed and the dragon or "corpus" dismembered, the
> latter being represented as the body of a man whose head and limbs
> are cut off. The lion's paws are likewise cut off with a sword. For the
> alchemical sword brings about the *solutio* or *separatio* of the elements
> thereby restoring the original condition of chaos, so that a new and
> more perfect body can be produced by a new *impressio formae*, or by
> a "new imagination." The sword is therefore that which "kills and
> vivifies," and the same is said of the permanent water or mercurial
> water. Mercurius is the giver of life as well as the destroyer of the old
> form. Mercurius . . . too is a sword, for he is a "penetrating spirit"
> ("more piercing than a two-edged sword"!).[174]

675   Through the sacrifice the fox becomes a prince, the brother of the king's
daughter, and is finally "released from the magic charm which had been laid
upon him."[175] The dismemberment of the guiding helpful animal is an act of
self-examination through which the intentions of the instinct that lead to the
goals is made conscious.[176] It is a sacrifice of the former way of life, a self-
sacrifice, through which even the Self wins: it steps out from the state of
unconsciousness and manifests in consciousness.

676   We see it entering into manifestation, freeing itself from the unconscious
projection, and as it grips us, entering into our lives and so passing from
unconsciousness into consciousness, from potentiality into actuality. What it
is in the diffuse unconscious state we do not know; we only know that in
becoming ourself it has become human.[177]

---

[174] C.G. Jung, *ibid* ¶357. See also *ibid* ¶357, C.G. Jung, CW 13, *Alchemical Studies* ¶86(IIIv^bis),
¶89,¶106,¶110, and H. Silberer, *Problems of Mysticism*, New York 1917 p. 38,83f,128f. On the alchemical
sacrifices of the "mother," see in C.G. Jung, CW 13, *Op. cit.* ¶139. The hero of our tale wins the anima
by separating from the father and the brother of the anima through separation from the mother (in the
form of animal nature).
[175] J. and W. Grimm, *Complete Grimm's*, London 1975 p. 279.
[176] Jung writes on this:
> [T]he integration or humanization of the Self is initiated from the conscious side by our
> making ourselves aware of our selfish aims; we examine our motives and try to form as
> complete and objective picture as possible of our own nature. Human nature has an invincible
> dread of becoming more conscious of itself. What nevertheless drives us to it is the Self,
> which demands sacrifice by sacrificing itself to us. Conscious realization or the bringing
> together of the scattered parts, is in one sense an act of the ego's will, but in another sense it
> is a spontaneous manifestation of the Self, which was always there.
(C.G. Jung, CW 11, *Op. cit.* ¶400.)
[177] C.G. Jung, *Ibid* ¶398. See also references in G. van der Leeuw, *Religion in Essence*, Vol. 1 p. 328ff,
and H. Güntert, *Weltkönig*, Halle a. S. 1923 p. 405. See also Bächtold- Stäubli under *Enthaupten, köpfen*
(decapitation, beheading), which relates that in popular German folk belief these events are often
immediately understood as processes of transformation and were therefore performed on dolls at

677   This inner process is illustrated in our tale of the transformation of the fox into a human. As seen from the foregoing, to the extent that fox is a part of the hero, sacrificer and sacrificed are one.[178] This is the reason why the hero feels such resistance against the sacrifice, since he must, through an act of self-knowledge, overcome the animal principle that has supported him so far without calculation for its own sake.[179] The fox calls for and intends the transformation, which is to be achieved through the sacrifice,[180] because it embodies the Self, which demands and needs realization in individual life and needs consciousness to be perceived.

678   The redeemed prince at the end of "The Golden Bird" turns out to be the brother of the anima figure. A similar redemption of a male figure, in addition to the winning of the anima, can be found in the aforementioned fairytale, "The Bird with the Nine Heads," in which the hero enters into the cave of a demon who had kidnapped a princess, and finds a fish nailed to the wall with four nails. "When he touched the fish, the latter turned into a handsome youth, who thanked him for delivering him, and they agreed to regard each other as brothers." Later it turns out that this handsome youth is the son of the dragon king, and he gives the hero great treasures by which the latter wins the princess. The fish that is nailed to the cave wall with four nails is clearly a symbol of the Self still caught in animal and, therefore, unconscious form. This corresponds to the redemption of the helpful white horse in "Ferdinand the Faithful and Ferdinand the Unfaithful" and the helper horses in "The Princess in the Tree." Also, in the Nordic fairytale "Helge-Hal in the Blue Hill" the cat, which aided the hero against the troll, asks the hero to behead him. This done, the cat becomes a prince and marries a sister of the anima figure.[181] This evil enchantment of what is actually a superior soul guide and his need for salvation corresponds to some Gnostic ideas about the nature of the *logos*, that for the Ophites, for example, is a [male-female] intermediary between mind (spirit) and matter.[182]

---

springtime ritual games. In folk legends and tales, beheading appears as a sacred magic ritual. See also Bächtold-Stäubli under *töten* (killing) in which redemptive killing (in fairytales and legends) is a magical counteraction against being enchanted as an animal.

[178] C.G. Jung, CW 11, *Psychology and Religion* ¶342, ¶353, ¶397; C.G. Jung, CW 13, *Alchemical Studies* ¶91. See also J. Layard, *Mythos der Totenfahrt*, Zürich 1938 p. 252 according to which some Aboriginal Australians assume the name of the animal that they sacrifice. See G. van der Leeuw, *Religion in Essence*, Vol. 1 p. Chap. 50, esp. 354ff.

[179] On the psychological meaning and ethical task of such sacrifice, see Jung: "[T]he giver must at least make himself sufficiently conscious of his identity with the gift to recognize how far he is *giving himself up* . . . " C.G. Jung, CW 11, *Psychology and Religion* ¶390, emphasis in original.

[180] See also Ivan Tsarevich's sacrifice of his horse (in "The Virgin Tsar"), whereby this is carried out, however, only at the animal level.

[181] See also "Dat Könirik von Mornstêrn." In this tale, which is a variant of "The King of the Golden Mountain" the torment of the hero during three nights redeems not only the black princess (who becomes white) but also the poodle and her brother, who had joined the hero in his travels and had lead him to the poodle's castle. See also the conclusion of the German tale "The Little Tailor and the Three Dogs."

[182] See H. Leisegang, *Die Gnosis*, Leipzig 1924 p. 132.

679   On the one hand, the *logos* is pure mind, and on the other hand, it can enter into all things. To the extent that the *logos* tarries in matter, it is called "corpse" in Gnosis, in order to emphasize its state of suffering and bondage. At the same time, the *logos* was a god in the upper world. Humans have the task of realizing this "as pure *pneuma*," and as "the inner human" in themselves, which redeems them from involvement with the world.[183] In Manichaeism the mutual redemptive activity is carried out in a special way: the *logos* of light in matter redeems all those called to it, so that they, finding their true self [that is, their "luminous" nature], help to gather together the "scattered" elements of the primordial light-filled human being.[184]

680   The redeemed fox in "The Golden Bird" is a prince and, thus, on the one hand, a mirror figure of the hero, but on the other hand, he is in close relationship to the anima. A secret identity of the fox with the princess is hinted at in that the Old High German word "fox" was feminine, and that in ancient times the fox was probably the female counterpart to the male wolf.[185] But the fox is also a thievish animal that initiates the quest and is thus related to the predatory bird at the beginning of the tale. Moreover, the fox secretly corresponds to the tree as is apparent from the alchemical philosophy, according to which the soul guide Mercurius is, among many things, a tree. The alchemical name for this transformative substance that occurs in many symbolic forms is "root moisture," "spirit of water," "vapor of the Earth," "Adam's paradise tree with four kinds of blossoms that grows out of the sea," "the hermaphroditic monster," "the one and the root of itself" and "the All."[186]

681   The fox is simultaneously an all-generating spirit of nature hidden in the anima.[187]

---

[183] See *ibid* pp. 133–134,145f.

[184] See Puech pp. 256, 284-5. On mutual salvation ("man as both the one to be redeemed and the redeemer") in alchemy, see C.G. Jung, CW 12, *Psychology and Alchemy* ¶414f. See also the encounter with the heavenly double after death in R. Reitzenstein, *Hellenistic*, Pittsburgh 1978 pp. 206f. and especially 518. "Obviously there is here an underlying sense of duality and separation and yet again of the belonging-together or even the union of two things . . . " See also pp. 354f. (German), 445, and especially 70 on individual self and world self. For more on mutual redemption in fairytales, see the next volume of this work.

[185] See Bächtold-Stäubli under *Fuchs* (fox).

[186] See C.G. Jung, CW 13, *Alchemical Studies* ¶173. See also C.G. Jung, CW 11, *Psychology and Religion* ¶358f and also other names of *lapis philosophorum* such as, "Elixir vitae . . . quintessence, light, east, morning . . . living fountain, fruit tree . . . Adam, human, *Homo altus* . . . brother, son, father, *Father mirabilis*, king, hermaphrodite, *Deus Terrenus* (Lord of the Earth), Salvator, Servator, *filius macrocosmi* and so on." (C.G. Jung, CW 13, *Alchemical Studies* ¶203.)

[187] A poetic portrayal of such a figure (to explain more is beyond the scope of this work) is the dwarf Oberon in the legend "Huon of Bordeaux":

  Huon, a knight at the court of Charlemagne, is forced to take a trip to Babylon. On the way other knights joined him and they traveled together. One day Huon and the other knights found themselves in the enchanted forest of elf-king Oberon (Auberon) lying between Jerusalem and the Red Sea. As the weary Huon rested under an oak, he saw a little hunch-backed man coming towards him, who was "as beautiful as the sun on a summer's day." A silk coat covered him, all adorned with golden ribbons. A bow was in his hand, with which he always bagged game, a horn made of pure ivory by fairies on an island in the sea hung around his neck. One fairy had given him the gift that whoever heard the horn sound would

682   The anima and her accompanying spirit sometimes appear at the beginning of a fairytale as a pair, the male figure carries primarily the aspect of the shadow, and to a lesser extent, the spiritual soul guide. This original unity is usually split apart in the course of the fairytale.[188]

683   That the fox is actually identical to the anima and the secret precious treasure follows from the parallel Uzbek tale "Prince Hassan Pasha."[189] At the end, the wolf is only honored at the court of Prince Hassan, not redeemed by an act of sacrifice and transformed into human form. Thus, the whole process of development remains stuck at a lower level. Although the essence of the animal helper is not seen through and recognized, his identity with the sought-after treasure is wonderfully revealed in this version. In order for Hassan to keep his precious winnings and not have to give them to the contracting kings, the wolf transforms himself temporarily into the prized horse and, later, into the beautiful maiden. Each time it suddenly transforms

---

be made healthy on the spot, even if that person was close to death. A second fairy added another power: whoever hears the horn, their hunger and thirst would be immediately quenched. A third fairy declared that whoever heard the horn should start to sing, no matter how heavy their cares were. Finally, a fourth fairy gave the horn one more power: wherever the horn sounded, be that in a far land, Oberon would hear those tones in his own city of Monmur. Oberon called out to the knights in a loud voice: "You men who have crossed my woods, be greeted by Oberon, Lord of the World! I adjure you by God's majesty, in oil and chrism, in holy baptism salts, in all that God has created, I beseech you: answer my greeting!"

It was said that when one engaged in a conversation with Oberon, one could never leave the forest again. Thus the Knights tried forthwith to ride away without greeting Oberon, but he inhibited their escape by touching his horn, thus creating a great storm. As they continued on their way, they found themselves on a narrow bridge and right in front there stood Oberon! Again he summoned them in the name of God to speak with him. But the knights rode right past him without speaking. Then he appeared again in front of the riders. This time he promised to help the knights if they were to talk to him. Huon greets him, and asks why he is following them, Oberon responds, "I love you more than any other human . . . because of your integrity." He, Oberon was the son of Julius Caesar and the fairy Morgana. He had been bewitched by a fairy (who had been left out at his birth) into a small and hunchbacked dwarf. A second fairy tried to right this curse and gave him the ability to see what is in people's hearts and to know their secret thoughts. A third fairy gave Oberon the power to fulfill every wish and to quickly move from place to place, to make all animals obedient to him through a special sign, to know all the secrets of paradise, and to hear the choirs of angels. "Never in my life will I age, even if I wish to die. My place at God's side is reserved." (Huon receives from Oberon the horn and a miracle goblet that provides wine without limit to whomever is without sin. With Oberon's help, the horn, and the goblet, which in the further course of the tale acts as the conscience of people, Huon continues on his quest with many adventures. In the end he returns to the forest and with Oberon's blessing takes his place as king of the forest.)

[188] See "The Disowned Princess," "Makonaura and Anuanaitu," "Ititaujang," "Tapairu, the Beauty from the Land of the Fairies" and "The Jack-of-all-Trades of the Plains." Jung writes:

The shadow corresponds to a negative ego-personality and includes all those qualities we find painful, embarrassing, or regrettable. Shadow and anima, being unconscious, are then contaminated with each other, a state that is represented in dreams by "marriage" or the like. But if the existence of the anima (or the shadow) is accepted and understood, a separation of these figures ensues . . . The shadow is thus recognized as belonging, and the anima as not belonging, to the ego.

(C.G. Jung, CW 12, *Psychology and Alchemy* ¶242, fn. 118.)

[189] And also, for example, from the Czech variant "The Firebird and the Firefox." See J. Bolte and G. Polívka, *Anmerkungen*, Vol. 1, Leipzig 1913 p. 507.

back, becoming again the bad wolf, biting and scratching everybody that stands in the way of its escape. Also in another Danube variant, "The Bird Wehmus," the fox transforms itself into a jewelry store laden with treasures, in which he kidnaps the princesses. After being redeemed, he marries one of the maidens and gives the hero the other to have as his wife.[190] The magical companion is thus of the same substance as the precious treasure, like the "philosopher's stone" in alchemy, which sometimes appears as "friend" and soul guide.[191] Similarly, the helping voice of Allah in "Prince Hassan Pasha" can be considered as a different aspect of the same wolf because he is characterized as *pneuma* by the cloud of dust and an inspiring spirit. Only here, according to the later stage of religious development, the "animal doctor" is split into a helpful divine voice and an animal. The wolf possesses a castle in which Hassan repeatedly recovers from his travails before returning home. This castle gives Hassan power (as Anthaeus acquired by contact with the earth). The wolf is thus the lord of the inner mandala from which all power flows out. It is passionate nature and instinct, in which the divine mind, or divine spirit, is simultaneously hidden and acts as a guide.[192]

Thus, the Self is expressed in "The Golden Bird" through a whole series of symbols: the initial quaternity [tetrad], the garden, the tree, the golden fruit, the nocturnally blossoming flowers, the birds, the horse, and the virgin with her animal-brother-prince. It manifests in these different images as the tale unfolds, but it is at the same time ever-present. The manifold variety of images in which the Self appears is because, as a transpersonal piece of the psyche-soul, it is practically without boundaries.[193] The main symbol of the Self in "The Golden Bird" is the fox prince who bridges the opposing tendencies of the conscious mind and the unconscious and furthers the psychological process of transformation with the goal of uniting the opposites. The Self symbol as a psychic phenomenon encompasses both the corporeal and the

684

---

[190] The Lithuanian tale "The Fool and the Wolf who was his Friend" gives more examples of the transformative ability of the wolf.

[191] See examples in C.G. Jung, CW 9i, *The Archetypes and the Collective Unconscious* ¶238f,¶246 and also see Jung:

> I conjecture that the treasure is also the 'companion,' the one who goes through life at our side – in all probability a close analogy to the lonely ego who finds a mate in the self, for at first the self is the strange non-ego. This is the theme of the magical traveling companion of whom I will give three famous examples: the disciples on the road to Emmaus; the warrior Arjuna and his guide and charioteer Krishna driving to the Battle of Kurukshetra (*Bahagavad Gita*); and Moses and the mystical guide al-Khidr (Khidr) in the 18th sura of the Qur'an . . . the *lapis* is nothing less than a good friend and helper who helps those that help him, and this points to a compensatory relationship.

(C.G. Jung, CW 12, *Psychology and Alchemy* ¶155.) [The 18th sura (*The Cave*) presents a narrative where Khidr accompanies Moses and tests him about his oath to not ask any questions.]

[192] See C.G. Jung, *Children's Dreams*, Princeton 2008 p. 229, and, C.G. Jung, CW 8, *Spirit and Life* ¶642-43, about the appearance of the spirit as an autonomous phenomenon: "Psychologically, the spirit manifests itself as a personal being, sometimes with visionary clarity. . . " Thus, this spirit is a kind of higher consciousness, superior to ego-consciousness.

[193] See C.G. Jung, CW 11, *Psychology and Religion* ¶390f.

mental side of the unconscious, always a symbol of a principle that unifies the opposites.

After human ego-consciousness has had the psychological experience of a divinity expressed in the transformation of the Self-symbol,[194] and has passed through this development, it can then take a place behind a superior
685 consciousness. This is reflected in the final situation of "The Golden Bird" where, just as at the beginning, there is a quaternity of people present: the old king, the son, his bride, and the fox prince. In contrast to the initial quaternity, however, the female element is now included,[195] which creates a three-dimensional earthy reality.

The first tetrad is therefore only an unconscious anticipation of the Self in the spiritual realm, which in the course of the processes that follows becomes a [psychic] reality.
686 In contrast to the Grimm's version, the fourth figure in the quaternity in the Uzbek tale "Prince Hassan Pasha" remains an animal. According to the narrator's cultural setting, this state is not perceived as a painful enchantment.
687 As a result of the redemption of the animal brother as the shadow aspect of the Self, which finally crowns a richly decorated and, consequently, realized sequence of archetypal motifs, we consider "The Golden Bird" to be more highly differentiated than many other fairytales.[196] It tells not only of a connection to the female-maternal world of the unconscious and through that wins a renewal of life, but also by the drama of the self-sacrifice of the male archetype (*anthropos*) hidden in the animal, the figure of a superior spiritual being is made conscious and its instinctive aspect stripped, so that in consciousness *both* aspects, the female *and* the male, the hermaphroditic Self, pictorially appear and its comprehensive wholeness is shown in its entirety. The king's son – as the fourth function of the conscious personality – links with one of those parts (the anima), and he thus becomes a bridge that leads to the Self. He stands so close to the fox prince, indeed they act together almost as a unity, that he may *also* be considered as the "inner primordial human," which is why many people see the mystical marriage of the fourth with the princess to be the ultimate and complete goal. The fox prince is like a doubling of the king's son, which serves to illustrate some non-human aspects of the

---

[194] See Jung:
> But precisely because the new symbol is born of man's highest spiritual aspiration and must at the same time spring from the deepest roots of his being, it cannot be a one-sided product of the most highly differentiated mental functions but must derive equally from the lowest and most primitive levels of the psyche. . . From the activity of the unconscious there now emerges a new content, constellated by thesis and antitheses in equal measure and standing in compensatory relation to both. It thus forms a middle ground on which the opposites can be united.

(C.G. Jung, CW 6, *Psychological Types* ¶824-25.) *Ibid* ¶441f.
[195] See the entrance of the female mandala at the end of "The Three Feathers."
[196] In comparison, note the castle of the unredeemed wolf in "Prince Hassan Pasha," the mandala symbol, remains in the unconscious, that is, more bound to the material.

Self. In other words, the hero (whether he be the "youngest" or a single character) and his demonic shadow helper (whether a spirit, a ghost or an animal) are jointly operating, cooperative aspects – the conscious and the unconscious, the non-human – of the one unified core of the personality, the Self.[197] (In the tales of primitive peoples the hero is, however, often a human and an animal at the same time.)

---

[197] Compare, for instance, "Puss in Boots" and "Ferdinand the Faithful and Ferdinand the Unfaithful."

Chapter 12
The Golden Castle that Hung in the Air

688   The Norwegian tale, "The Golden Castle that Hung in the Air," ends with the sacrifice and redemption of the helpful animal and also combines rich imagery with many individual motifs of the tales we have just discussed.

689   Once upon on a time there was a poor man who had three sons. When he died, the two eldest went out into the world to try their luck; but as for the youngest, they would not have him come along at any price. "You are fit for nothing but to sit and hold fir tapers, grub around in the ashes, and blow up the embers; that is what you are fit for." "Well," said the Ashlad – for that was what his brothers called him – "then I must go by myself."

690   [The two elder brothers rested in a large forest; there an old hag came out from a hillock and asked for something to eat, but they laughed at her and give her nothing. They went on and arrived at a royal court and were taken into service there.]

691   After his elder brothers had started out from their home, the Ashlad gathered together what crumbs his brothers had thrown aside, and put them into his little knapsack. He also took with him the old gun which had no lock, for he thought it might come to some good along the way. Thus equipped he set off. When he had wandered some days, he too came to the big woods that his brothers had passed through, and as he was tired and hungry, he sat down under a tree that he might rest and eat. But he had his eyes open and looked about. As he opened his knapsack, out of the corner of his eye, he caught sight of a picture hanging in a tree, and on it was painted the likeness of a young maiden. The girl looked so lovely that he could not keep his eyes off of the picture. So he forgot both food and knapsack, and took down the painting and lay there and just stared at it. Just then up came the old hag out of the hillock. She hobbled along with her stick, her nose and mouth met, and her head shook. She begged for a little food, for she had not a morsel of bread in her mouth for a hundred years. At least, that was what she said. "If that is true, granny, then it is high

time you had a little to live on," said the lad, and with that he gave her some of his crumbs. The old hag said no one had ever called her granny all these hundred years, and she would in turn be as a mother to him. Then she gave him a grey ball of wool. He only had to roll it before him and he would come to whatever place he wished. But as for the painting, she said he should not bother himself about that, he would only fall into ill luck if he did.

692 The Ashlad nevertheless took the painting with him and behind the ball of wool reached the royal court where his brothers served. There he was assigned to the stable master and found recognition for his diligent work and love of horses. He hung the picture on the hayloft where he slept and spent every free moment in front of it. The brothers, who often were punished for their laziness, became jealous and told the stable master that the Ashlad was an idolater and did not believe in God. It came to the ears of the king, who was constantly sad because his three daughters had been carried off by a troll. When he went to investigate and saw the picture, he recognized it as a portrait of his youngest daughter. The brothers forthwith claimed that the Ashlad had told everyone that he could get the king his daughter back, whereupon the king ordered the Ashlad to carry out what he had boasted about. So, following the ball of wool, the Ashlad returned to the old hag in the forest and asked for her advice.

693 She said he must take with him his gun, and three hundred chests of spikes and horseshoe nails, three hundred barrels of barley, and three hundred barrels of groats, and three hundred butchered pigs, and the carcasses of three hundred oxen. Then he was to roll the ball of wool before him until he met a raven and a baby troll, and then he would be all right, for they were both of her kin.

694 The lad did as the old hag bade him. He went to the king's manor and took his old gun with him, and he asked the king for the spikes and the nails, the groats, and the pig and ox meat. He also requested the horses, the men, and the wagons to carry them in. The king thought it was asking a great deal, but if it meant he would get his daughter back, he would give him whatever he needed, even if it were half of his kingdom. When the lad had fit himself out, he rolled the ball of wool before him again, and with his laden carts and horses and men, he had not gone for many days when he came upon a high hill, and there sat a raven high up in a fir tree. The Ashlad went up close under the tree and then he pretended to aim and pointed his musket at the raven.

695   "No, no," cried the raven, "do not shoot me, do not shoot me, I will help you." "Well," said the Ashlad, "I never heard of anyone who boasted that he had eaten roasted raven, and since you are so eager to save your life, I may as well just spare it." He threw down his gun, and the raven came flying down and said, "There, up on that mountain there is a troll child who is walking up and down, for he has lost his way. I will help you go up there, and then you can lead the child home. When you get to the troll's house, the parents will surely offer you all the grandest things they have, but you should not heed them a pin. Mind that you take nothing else but the little grey donkey that stands behind the stable door."

696   The boy followed the raven's advice, brought the troll child back to its home, was reluctantly given the grey donkey, and together they traveled onwards. After many days they came to a blue mountain. The donkey knew they had somehow to go through. A unicorn ran up threateningly but, on the donkey's advice, was placated with twenty oxen and twenty pig carcasses. After gobbling them up the unicorn drilled a hole in the mountain so quickly that they could hardly follow it. Then they rewarded the unicorn with twenty more swine. After some time the donkey asked the Ashlad if he saw anything up ahead. When the lad answered, "Only sky and mountains," they moved on. Later the donkey asked again and this time the Ashlad responded that he saw a little star glittering in the distance. They traveled further. The grey donkey asked again and the Ashlad said that he saw something ahead that shone like the moon.

697   "It is not the moon," said the donkey, "but the silver castle we are bound for. Now, when we get there, you will see three dragons lying in watch at the gate. But they have not been awakened for hundreds of years and so moss has grown over their eyes." "I almost think I shall be afraid of them," said the Ashlad. "Oh, do not say that," said the donkey; "you have only to wake up the youngest, and toss a couple of score of ox carcasses and butchered pigs down its gullet. Then I dare say it will talk to the other two, and you will be allowed to enter the castle."

698   [After a long time they reached the castle, which was cast entirely of silver. The Ashlad followed the donkey's advice, the dragons were appeased and let him walk into the castle. It was very beautiful but all the rooms were empty except the last, where the princess sat spinning. She was happy and surprised that a "Christian" had come, but warned him against an evil troll with three heads. When the boy was not afraid and wanted to stay anyway, she told him to take a sip from a

bottle from which the troll always drank. Doing that, the Ashlad was able to swing the big rusty sword behind the door. When the troll arrived, he began to complain that something smelled like "Christian meat," but before he could finish his sentence, the boy cut off all three of his heads. Despite her joy the princess soon became heavy-hearted, for she pined for her sister, who had been stolen by a troll with six heads and lived in a golden castle "three hundred miles on the other side of the world's end." The Ashlad was not put out one bit, he would go and fetch both the princess and the castle. So he took the sword and the flask and got on the donkey, and bade the dragons follow him and carry the meat, grain and nails. Soon he sawsomething shining like a little star, then like the moon, and finally like the sun.]

699 "That," said the donkey, "is the golden castle we are bound for, but outside it lives a huge serpent that bars the way and keeps watch and ward over the castle."

700 "I think I shall be afraid of it," said the Ashlad. "Oh, do not say so," said the donkey, "we must spread over it heaps of twigs and branches, and lay between them layers of spikes and horseshoe nails, and set fire to them all. And then we shall be rid of it."

701 After a long time they came to where the castle hung in the air, but the serpent lay wound underneath it and barred the way. So the lad gave the dragons a good meal of ox flesh and salted swine so that they would help him, then they spread heaps of boughs and wood over the serpent, and laid between them layers of spikes and nails. When it was done, they set fire to the pile and burned the serpent alive in a fire at white heat.

702 When that was done, one of the dragons flew under the castle and lifted it up, and the two other dragons went up high into the sky and loosed the chains and hooks that it hung by, and then they lowered the castle down to the ground. When that was done the Ashlad went inside and found everything far grander than in the silver castle, but he could find no one until he came to the innermost chamber, and there lay a princess lying on a bed of gold. She slept so soundly as though she were dead. But she was not, even though he was not able to wake her. She was as red and white as milk and blood. And just as the Ashlad stood there gazing at her, the troll came rushing in, shouting, "Huff! I smell the smell of Christian flesh in here." "That might be," said the Ashlad, "but you need not sniff around and snort about that; you shall not have to suffer long." And with that he hacked off all of its heads as though they stood on cabbage stalks. Then the dragons took the golden castle on their backs and flew home with it. They

were not long on the way and soon set it down side-by-side with the silver castle, so that it shone both far and wide.

703   When the princess of the silver castle came to her window in the morning and caught sight of the golden castle, she went there at once, but when she saw her sister lying there and sleeping as though she were dead, she became very sad. Then she said to the Ashlad that they would never get life into her sister unless they found the Water of Life and Death. The Water of Life and Death was to be found in two wells that hung on either side of a golden castle that hung in the air, nine hundred miles beyond the world's end. There the third and youngest sister dwelt.

704   The Ashlad thought there was no other way, he must go and fetch it, and before long he was on his way. This time he and the donkey travelled far and farther than far through many realms, across field and forest, over mountain and moor, over land and sea until the Ashlad said, "Now I see something that shines like the sun." "That is where we are bound," said the donkey, "that is the golden castle that hangs in the air, there is the Water of Life and Death and there lives a princess who has been stolen by a troll with nine heads. But all the wild beasts in the world lie there and keep watch and block the way."

705   "I almost think I am afraid of them," said the Ashlad. "Do not worry," said the donkey, there was no danger if he would only make up his mind not to linger there, but to set off on his way back as soon as he had filled his flasks with the water. For the castle grounds could only be entered for one hour in the day, and that hour began at high noon. If he did not make ready in time and get away within that hour, then beasts would tear him into a thousand pieces.

706   [It was at the stroke of twelve when they reached the castle, where lay all the wild and savage beasts but they all slumbered like logs and stones, and the Ashlad came to each of the wells and filled his flasks with the Waters of Life and Death.]

707   After he filled his flasks, he looked up at the castle, which was made of the purest gold. It was the grandest he had ever seen, and he thought it would surely be even grander still inside. "Pooh! I have plenty of time!" thought the Ashlad, "I can always look about for half an hour." He opened the great door and went in. Inside it was finer than the finest, and as he went from one magnificent room to another, he marveled at how they were all closely hung with gold and pearls, and everything that was costliest in the world. But no one was to be seen. At last he came into a chamber where there lay a princess on a

bed of gold, just as though she were dead. And this princess was as grand as the grandest queen, she was red and white as blood and snow, and more beautiful than anything he had ever seen, except for a picture; for indeed, it was she who was painted in the picture he had found in the forest! Then the Ashlad forgot both the Water he had come to fetch, the wild beasts, and the castle. He could only gaze at the princess. He thought he could never have his fill of looking at her; but all the while she slept as though she were dead, and he was not able to wake her.

708 [Towards evening the troll came, smelled Christian flesh but again the Ashlad curtly cut off his nine heads.] But after this was done, the Ashlad was so weary that he could not keep his eyes open. So, he laid down on the bed by the side of the princess. Even though she slept both night and day as though she would never wake again, at the stroke of midnight she would wake up for the twinkling of an eye. On this night when she awoke, she found the Ashlad next to her and she told him that he had set her free. However, she must bide there for three more years. If she did not come to him then, he would have to fetch her.

709 When it was one o'clock in the afternoon the Ashlad woke up again, and the first thing he heard was the donkey braying and making a stir, so he thought he would get up and set off. Before he went, he cut a breadth out of the princess's skirt, and took it away with him. But he had loitered so long that the beasts began to wake and stir, and by the time he had mounted his donkey, they stood in a ring round him. Then the donkey said he must sprinkle on them a few drops of the water of death. As he did so, in a trice they all fell down headlong on the spot, and never stirred a limb any more.

710 On their way home, the donkey said to the Ashlad, "Mark my words, when you come into honor and glory, you will forget me and all that I have done for you, so I will be down on my knees with hunger." "No, no, that shall never be," said the lad.

711 When he reached the castle of the eldest princess and gave her the Water of Life, she sprinkled a few drops on her sister and woke her up, and then there was great joy. They travelled back to the king, and he too was glad because two of his daughters had returned. But soon he went about pining and longing for his youngest daughter. As for the Ashlad who had brought the princesses back, the king made him a mighty man and deemed that he was to be the first in the land after the king himself. But there were many who were jealous that the Ashlad should have grown to be such a man of mark, and one of them

was the Red Knight, who coveted the eldest princess. He got her to sprinkle a few drops of the water of death over the Ashlad so that he fell into a deep sleep and lay as dead.

712 [When the three years were over, in the fourth a foreign warship arrived and on it was the youngest sister with her three-year-old son. She announced that she would not set foot on land unless they send her the one who had come to her in the golden castle. They sent a noble courtier to the ship, but when the princess asked the child who was playing with a golden apple, "Can that be your father, my son?" he answered, "No, my father does not crawl about like a cheese maggot!" Then they sent the Red Knight but he fared no better than the first, and the princess sent word back to the king that if they did not make haste and send the right man, then it would go ill with them. They were forced to find the Ashlad and, seeing him dead asleep, they sprinkled Water of Life on him. He awoke and went down to the ship of the princess. The Ashlad did not make deep bows, he only nodded his head and took out from his pocket the piece of cloth that he had cut out of the skirt of the princess in her golden castle.] "That's my father! That's my father!" cried out the boy, and gave him the golden apple he was playing with. Then there was great joy and happiness all over the realm. Soon word got around what the Red Knight and the eldest princess had done to the Ashlad. The king became outraged and decreed that they both should be rolled down a hill, each in a cask full of spikes and nails. But the Ashlad and the youngest princess pleaded that their lives be spared and so they were reprieved with harsh reprimands.

713 Now it happened that one day, as they were about to begin the bridal festivities, the Ashlad and his princess stood looking out of their castle window. Spring was beginning and it was just when the stable servants were turning out the horses and cows after long winter. The last that came out of the stable was the donkey, but it was so starved that it hobbled out of the stable door on its knees. Then the Ashlad was pierced to his heart because he had forgotten about the donkey. He rushed down to the stable and begged forgiveness from the donkey. He did not know how to make it up to the poor beast. But the donkey said the best thing he could do was to cut off his head. The Ashlad was loath to do this, but the donkey begged so hard and pleaded so genuinely that he had to yield, and at last, he sliced the donkey's head off. As soon as the donkey's head fell to the ground, the donkey was transformed. He had been enchanted into the form of a donkey by witchcraft, and now there stood a handsome prince! He asked for and

received the hand of the second princess, and now all fell into an even more joyful wedding feast. There was so much rejoicing that it was heard and talked about for years over all the seven kingdoms.

714   Then they built themselves houses,
And stitched garments to make one swoon,
And had so many children
That they reached up to the moon.[1]

715   In our discussion of "The Three Feathers" we drew attention to the need to realize the Self through the connection with the earth and the female principle. The present tale illustrates this, in that the highest value, as the title states, initially hovers in a castle between heaven and earth and only through the help of the donkey does it gain earthly reality. In the very beginning we learn that the father of three sons has died, that is, the conscious attitude hitherto adapted to collective life is no longer adequate to serve the goals of the second half of life; new sources must flow in from elsewhere. This searching attitude in secular life is subsequently borne by the king who appears later.

716   The hero-to-be is called the Ashlad, again clearly indicating that he is the less-developed psychological function. Ash represents the dirt that adheres to the boy acquired during his lowly chores in the house; he is a male Cinderella.[2] Bolte and Mackensen relate this name to the Transylvanian *Iesch-poder* [ash powder] that is sprinkled on participants in the Ash Wednesday sacrament.[3] Thus ash takes on the meaning of the ancient religious gesture of mourning – a reminder of earthly transcience. According to Genesis, ash or dust is the substance of the human body.[4] Ash also plays a role in alchemy, it is matter purified by fire in its "chemically most accessible form."[5] Thus ash is an apt metaphor for the despised son as a symbol of the psychic function, connected with the chthonic world and its treasures.

717   At the first encounter with the old hag, who appears out of "hillock" (in some versions, "a clump of grass"), the three brothers are confronted for the first time with the mother imago, behind which lies a world with which an *auseinandersetzung* is inevitable. With her need for bread and nourishment,

---

[1] [The translation, shortened and edited from various online English versions. This variant is from the Kristiansund area, as told by a seaman on board the corvette *The Eagle* and collected by Asbjørnsen in 1850.]

[2] On the name, see J. Bolte and G. Polívka, *Anmerkungen,* Vol. 1, Leipzig 1913 pp. 182– 185.

[3] See J. Bolte and L. Mackensen, *Handwörterbuch,* Berlin and Leipzig 1930–1934 under *Aschenputtel* [Cinderella], note 12.

[4] Also, with the Aztecs, see W. Krickeberg, *Azteken und Inka*, Jena 1928 p. 6, "World Time Age" according to which Quetzalcoatl created humans on day seven from wind and ash. See also M. Graulich, *Myths*, Norman 1997 p. 109 citing the *Histoyre du Méchique* where the first human couple was born from Quetzalcoatl's ashes and bones.]

[5] See H. Silberer, *Problems of Mysticism*, New York 1917 p. 123, and, "Despise not the ash, for it is the diadem of thy heart, and the ash of things that endure." *Rosarium philosophorum*, folio $L_3 V$ cited in C.G. Jung, CW 13, *Alchemical Studies* ¶183.

the old one indicates her desire to be part of human life.[6] Psychologically, this represents a hint from the unconscious of the necessity to transform threatening mental patterns into positive forces by connecting them to real life. Only the youngest sees the picture of the beautiful maiden hanging in the tree (also a mother figure), with which he falls in love. This is the first flash, an intuition of the anima, but it is still an abstract image, floating above the ground. The mother image still carries within it the anima and the connection to reality. The picture hanging on the tree is like an anticipation of the golden castle hanging in the air; the anima is still an ideal dream image far from reality. The old hag's warning about the image represents a small resistance by the mother image to the relationship with the anima. This resembles the initial resistance of the Baba Yaga figures to Ivan Tsarevich's pressing advances to the princess in "The Virgin Tsar."

718   The appearance of the anima first as an image is similar to the hero's vision in "The Beautiful Dunye" in which he sees the beautiful *div* daughter in the enchanted garden.[7] The Beautiful Dunya later has her picture hung above the city gate and thus she finds her husband again. This motif corresponds to the psychological fact that the anima figure is an inner mental image, a reflection that the man carries in the psyche.[8]

719   That the anima's image is hanging visible on the tree of life means it can be perceived by the conscious mind as the image of a deity, about which Zimmer writes:

720   [A] figure of the divine is a fixed point, like a concave mirror, which catches and focuses the rays that want to break out from the intangible inner life of the believer. As a concave mirror it polarizes this and radiates it [back out] as a burst of light into the eye of consciousness in a way that it would not otherwise be seen. The mirror gives [his or her inner life] a charitable, transformed, and speaking form.[9]

---

[6] See our interpretation of bread in the discussion of "The Two Travelers" and the request for food by the magical helper in "Tritill, Litill, and the Birds" and "Prince Hassan Pasha."

[7] See also "Prince Shaadot," where in pursuit of a deer, the prince is lured into the garden of an old man in whose house he gazes at a painting of a maiden of such beauty that he pleads with his host to tell him the name of the beautiful one and where she lives. He finally finds her after an adventurous quest. See also "The White Bride and the Black Bride," "Faithful John," "The Story of the Halva Merchant" and "The Story of Cefa and Sefa." See more examples in J. Bolte and L. Mackensen, *Handwörterbuch* Berlin 1930, under *Bild* [image].

[8] On the anima image, see Jung:

This image is fundamentally unconscious, an hereditary factor of primordial origin engraved in the living organic system of the man, an imprint or "archetype" of all the ancestral experiences of the female – in short, an inherited system of psychic adaption.

(C.G. Jung, CW 17, *The Development of Personality* ¶338.) See also C.G. Jung, CW 6, *Psychological Types* ¶810, and, "Every psychic process is an image and an 'imagining', otherwise no consciousness could exist and the occurrence would lack phenomenality," C.G. Jung, CW 11, *Psychology and Religion* ¶889.

[9] H. Zimmer, *Weisheit Indiens*, Darmstadt 1938 p. 43.

721 This image is just a first light of awareness in the conscious mind of that mysterious essence of the soul personified by the anima.

722 The royal court at which the Ashlad arrives and where he finds a job in the stables, means the sphere of the profane attitude. After some time, he is vilified by his brothers who indict him as a worshiper of idols. This accusation is not without some ground, because, as we have seen in the section above on the magical daughter, the anima comes from the archaic and non-Christian layers of the human psyche.[10] The slander of the brothers corresponds in its malicious character to the cobbler in "The Two Travelers." This represents a shadow characteristic. The two brothers, who embody the two auxiliary functions of the conscious mind, are thus also a manifestation of the shadow that is split into a duality. The shadow is here negative mainly because – standing between consciousness and the unconscious – it represents an internal conflict. This shadow comprises both the instinctual drives of the unconscious-animal without its innocence, and the single-mindedness of the conscious mind without its clarity and freedom. The auxiliary functions are here similarly unclear in their tendencies and correspond to human shadow emotions and impulses. The king recognizes his youngest and long-lost daughter in the picture that the Ashlad had hung in his space in the attic. Here, as in "Tritill, Litill, and the Birds," the anima at the profane court is portrayed as the daughter of the dominant conscious collective attitude. This is because in the course of human life she belongs to both worlds and stands between them, thus nourishing the life of secular consciousness and forming – unconsciously in the first half of life – the background to all experience. The initial situation of the anima at the secular court is similar to that in which the king in "The Golden Bird" and the sultan in "Prince Hassan Pasha" possess the golden fruit or midnight blossoming flower in the garden before they were stolen. The theft of the anima by a troll in "The Golden Castle that Hung in the Air" corresponds to the loss of the soul through the robber bird appearing at midnight in "The Golden Bird" and means that the Self symbol must be won anew from the unconscious. The trolls are nature demons of the forest and mountains and embody the archaic impulses of the unconscious farthest from the conscious mind, where the human merges with the animal, and finally with all of nature. Since only like can overcome like, the hero, on the advice of the old forest woman, takes with him all the help from the animals that will assure his success against the trolls. Led by the gray ball of wool, a gift from the old woman that had already led him to the royal manor, the hero comes to the raven that further helps him. The gray ball is in many Nordic tales a tool of trolls and can even be one of their manifestations. With a knot,

---

[10] See, for example, "Trunt, Trunt, and the Trolls in the Mountains" where a mother-anima giantess enchants the man who slowly looses his faith in God and in the end believes only in "Trunt, Trunt and the trolls in the mountains."

bundle, or ball of twine trolls lure humans[11] or show them the way. (A ball or an apple can serve the same purpose).[12] With the ancient Germans it was used to aid ecstatic rapture.[13] As the round inner center, this ball of yarn is a symbol of the Self.[14] The yarn itself symbolizes the thread of fate, insofar as the Self only manifests in time; in the course of human life, through the fateful occurrences in the life of an individual.[15]

723   Woven into the concept of thread, here a kind of Ariadne's thread,[16] is the idea of passing unchanged through everything and giving orientation in life's labyrinth, whereby is meant the providential guidance of the Self that emerges out of the unconscious. The ball of yarn still has a ghostly appearance and only in the image of the raven and donkey does it take on the more conscious form of the animal soul guide; of being instinctively driven.

724   The raven that is spared like the fox in "The Golden Bird" advises the hero to choose the donkey behind the stable door as the gift for returning the lost troll-child. In following this advice, both by returning the child and choosing the donkey, the hero shows his adherence to nature and his friendly attitude towards the unconscious, from which he obtains its support.

725   The raven, as the bird of the gallows and the battlefield, belongs to the beasts of the devil and witches and is here a relative of the old forest woman. It embodies intuitions arising from the dark layers of the unconscious. That the hero indeed has landed in the realm of the ambivalent spirits, that is, figures of the collective unconscious, follows from the appearance of the wild unicorn that bores tunnels in mountains, devours oxen, and gobbles up pigs, and also by the other animals that the hero meets. With the help of his little donkey, however, he comes through all these adventures unscathed.

---

[11] See "The Troll Wedding" where the editor notes, "Curious, also, is the belief that trolls like to turn into skeins of yarn when disturbed, and then roll swiftly away." C. Stroebe, *Norwegian Fairy Book*, New York 1922 p. 53. See also "The Comrade" and "The Forest Woman."

[12] See "The Princess with the Twelve Pairs of Golden Shoes," "First Born, First Wed," "The Farmer and the Golden Sun," "The Mill That Mills Everything," "Ingebjörg and the Good Stepmother," "Horse Goldmane and Sword Battlefeather" among other tales.

[13] See M. Ninck, *Wodan*, Jena 1935 p. 285f. See also "Witch Pastor" where a witch who is to be burned pulls out a gray ball of yarn, throws one end up into the sky and and climbs up on it like a cat into the heights and is never seen again.

[14] See "My Old Woman Must Be Paid," "Connla's Sea-Journey" and "Connla and the Fairy Maiden."

[15] See Bachofen:

The fabric of the telluric creation becomes the thread of fate, the yarn, the human lot, Eileithyia, the midwife, the good weaver to Moira, who surpasses even Kronos in age. Thread appears in its redemptive, rescuing function in connection with the Dionysian Ariadne-Aphrodite; and destructive to those who split the shrine of the Erinyes, and those who had entrusted themselves to its protection in the Cylonian affair [Athens, 632 BC] (Translated from the German, J. J. Bachofen, *Gräbersymbolik*, Basel 1859 p. 312.) [Bachofen may be referring to the rope that Cylon's followers tied to a column in the temple of Athena, which broke, leading to their massacre. The leaders of the angry Athenians were later stained with a curse for breaking their promise not to kill Cylon's people.]

[16] [Ariadne, goddess of the labyrinth in Crete, having fallen in love with the sacrificial victim Theseus, gives him a ball of thread with which he can find his way out of the labyrinth.]

726   The donkey (ass) is an animal with a double meaning. For example, the evil Egyptian god, Seth, has – mainly in later dynasties – the head of a donkey.[17] In the ancient world, the donkey was considered the mount of Dionysus and was a symbol of lust.[18] The donkey bone or leg (*Eselsbein* [donkey bone]) and the jenny [female donkey] also belonged to the goddesses Lamia, Hecate, and Empusa. They had a donkey's leg or a bone of manure, both of which symbolized the fruitful power of the earth.[19] Thus, the donkey in a broader sense means the male power of creation.[20] According to the *Bundahishn*,[21] "there is a monstrous three-legged ass that stands in the heavenly rain-lake, Vourukasha; his urine purifies its waters, and at his cry all useful animals become pregnant and all harmful animals drop their young."[22]

727   The unicorn stands in a remarkable relationship to the donkey and was even often seen as a one-horned donkey. Jung has given a detailed presentation of the symbol of the unicorn in *Psychology and Alchemy*.[23] In Christian allegory, the Church Fathers borrowed the image of the unicorn from Psalms 29:6 and 92:10, and used it as a symbol of the strength of Christ, that is, the *Logos* or God, specifically the "wrathful" Old Testament [Yahweh]. In addition, the unicorn also symbolizes the power of evil, as it is said to be a maverick, wild, and cruel beast. In this manner it became an image of the devil. In alchemical symbolism, however, the unicorn represents the *spiritus vitae* that aids resurrection. This accords with the belief from antiquity that the powder of the horn of the unicorn is an alexipharmic or a potency drug. From this it follows that the unicorn is a symbol of the daemonic forces of nature, the power of God that is also revealed in "the wild impulsiveness of instinctual nature within man."[24] Alchemical philosophy noted particularly the penetrating effect of the unicorn. It is a "spirit that penetrates everything

---

[17] See J. J. Bachofen, *Mutterrecht*, Stuttgart 1861 p. 148, and J. J. Bachofen, *Gräbersymbolik*, Basel 1859 p. 385f. See also, the chained ass of Typhon (another name for Seth), according to Plutarch (P. Cassel, *Der Neue*, Leipzig 1936–1938 p. 304f.), and Bächtold-Stäubli under *Esel* [donkey]. In German tradition and belief, the donkey is a demonic animal. "The wild ass is a sign of the devil." (E. G. Graff, *Diutisca*, Stuttgart/Tübingen 1829 p. 27. Lucifer as a three-legged donkey haunts the region of the Rhön (on the mountain *Eselborn* [born of a donkey], ghosts appear in donkey shape, a donkey guards the treasure of the devil. See C.G. Jung, CW 12, *Psychology and Alchemy* ¶539. A donkey appears in the Uzbek fairytale, "The Prophet Noah and the Flood," (G. Jungbauer, *Turkestan*, Jena 1923 p. 191. Even the *djinns* (genies) and the evil *paris* sometimes take the form of a donkey. See *ibid* Note p. 293 and *ibid* "The Treasures of the Devil," p. 34.
[18] See Apuleius, *Golden Ass*, London 1822, J. J. Bachofen, *Mutterrecht*, Stuttgart 1861 p. 20.
[19] See J. J. Bachofen, *Gräbersymbolik*, Basel 1859 pp. 388–389.
[20] See C.G. Jung, CW 16, *Practice of Psychotherapy* ¶340, and on the priapic nature of the ass, see de Gubernatis, *Zoological*, London 1872 p. 283f, 288f, J. J. Bachofen, *Gräbersymbolik*, Basel 1859 p. 385ff. The donkey was a symbol of stupidity in Egypt and Greece.
[21] [Bundahishn means "Primal Creation" and is the name traditionally given to the encyclopedic collection of Zoroastrian cosmogony and cosmology (trans.)].
[22] C.G. Jung, CW 5, *Symbols of Transformation* ¶428, C.G. Jung, CW 12, *Psychology and Alchemy* ¶535f, de Gubernatis *op. cit.* p. 294.
[23] See C.G. Jung, CW 12, *Op. cit.* ¶518ff, See also generally Bächtold-Stäubli and J. Bolte and L. Mackensen, *Handwörterbuch* Berlin 1930, also under under *Einhorn* [unicorn].
[24] [See, for instance, Job 39: 9–10.]

solid."[25] This explains the role of the unicorn in our fairytale in which with its immense strength it tunnels through the mountain that blocks the way.

728   The hero plays off the opposites embodied in the unicorn and donkey [that is, his own opposing natures] against each other; he defeats the wildness of the unicorn with the wildness of the donkey that has been made to serve him. More precisely, he himself is carried by a piece of unrestrained daemonic natural power, through which he subordinates all other natural powers and defeats like with like [*similia similibus*].[26] In fact, this is a moral conflict situation by which any concession to nature (such as riding the troll's donkey) unleashes nature's animal ferocity, which then becomes threatening. (At each appearance of wild animals the hero says he is afraid, and is thereupon reassured by the donkey.) But it is just those very forces of nature that enmesh people in these passionate affairs that can also carry people over all obstacles and gradually bring about the superiority of humans over the animal instinctive.

729   Feeding the unicorn with oxen and pigs is a sacrifice to propitiate the wild powers necessary to manage such a dangerous conflict. The sacrificed animals originated with the king. Thus, they represent an offering by the secular conscious attitude. The hero does not make a sacrifice, because he himself is a half- daemonic being, a part of the Self. To achieve a relationship with the anima, the conscious mind has to abandon a piece of its goal-oriented thinking.[27] Pig sacrifices were offered to the subterranean powers in general. Thus, the hero, as that part of consciousness that serves the Self, takes vital power from the secular attitude to use it for the realization of the inner personality.

730   The unicorn bores through the blue mountain, behind which lies the magical realm of the anima. This mountain means an inhibition, an obstacle. It symbolizes the dense impenetrability of the unconscious, which opens only to a passionate mental effort (that is, the unicorn). According to the legends of the ancient Germanic gods, Odin, like the unicorn, penetrated the thickness of matter as he forced the giant Baugi to pierce the rock of the *Hnitbjorg* (=*Schlagberge* ["Strike" or "Hit Mountains"]) with the wonder-drill Rati (rodent), whereupon he slipped into the shape of a serpent. Once inside the mountain, he spent three nights with the giantess Gunnlöð who let him drink the rich mead of poetry, which he later gave to humans.[28] The mountain also

---

[25] C.G. Jung, CW 12, *Op. cit.* ¶524

[26] See Numbers 22: 21–33, where Balaam's ass sees the angels of God blocking the way, prompting it to turn aside. This incites Balaam's anger because he misjudged the ass's turning aside as an act of disobedience.

[27] On the anima as a mediator of the perception of things that would otherwise remain in the dark, whereby a certain "dimming of consciousness" is needed, see E. Jung, *Animus and Anima*, Putnam 1985 p. 49f. [Exact quote not yet found in the English edition, the German reference is E. Jung, "Beitrag zum Problem des Animus" in *Wirklichkeit der Seele*, Zürich 1934 p. 331f.]

[28] See M. Ninck, *Wodan*, Jena 1935 p. 320 on the original meaning of spirit [German: *Geist*] as an angry

stands for an obstacle that, once overcome, makes one happy. In the Grimm's fairytale "Donkey Cabbages" a cloud carried the hero away as he was sitting on the summit of a mountain and later set him down in a garden of magic cabbages. This expresses falling into ecstatic rapture into the unconscious, the boundless realm of fantasy, after having made the effort of climbing. The mountain symbolizes in these cases an inner rigidity, above which one can rise with the momentum of spiritual experience. The blue color of the mountain signals its ghostly nature and indicates that it is an inhibition arising from the unconscious.

731   Once the mountain obstacle is surmounted with the help of the unicorn, the hero arrives in succession to the silver, moon-like castle, the golden sun castle that hangs in the air, and the third, also golden castle with the Waters of Life and of Death. Although the image of the anima is here split into three figures and reached in three stages, all these motives are to be understood as an expression for *one* psychological fact. Even the ambivalent title evidently that refers not to the last castle but instead to the second, shows that there is in fact only *one* central motif. It is expressed as three stages for the sake of embellishment,[29] the third – and most important – castle brings no increase in the valuable substance (that is, gold). The golden castle of anima and the wells of life and death are symbols that often appear together in fairytales (see, for example, "The Virgin Tsar"). The alchemist Zosimos describes the central mystery of the alchemical work as a temple of white stone that sparkles like the sun and is guarded by a dragon. Inside is a well [fountain, spring] at which a brazen man [". . . you will soon have him as a golden man."] sits beside the sought-after treasure.[30] Just as when a dream presents a similar image several times, as if it is circling around a central idea that it wants to bring closer to consciousness, so also here the castle with the anima appears in different variations that all indicate different aspects of the same underlying motif.

732   The three dragons of the first castle submit to serving and helping to oust the dragon of the second castle. Here again we encounter the expression of making natural forces subservient through the medium of "like conquers like." To begin with, the hero wakes up the dragons, the youngest first. The passions slumbering in the unconscious, and also the destructive nature of the unconscious, should not be ignored or circumvented in the process of becoming conscious when the conscious mind penetrates into the un-conscious. This is because they could easily burst forth with unsurmountable

---

outburst and linguistically related to the Old Norwegian root verb *geisa* = rage (of fire and passion) and Gothic Old English *us-gaisjan* (to go wild, to be beside or outside of oneself), with the basic meaning "to get excited."

[29] In the anthroposophical teachings of Steiner the three manifestations of the anima correspond to the sensation psyche, the reason [intellect], and the conscious mind. See R. Meyer, *Weisheit Schweizer*, Schaffhausen 1944 p. 88.

[30] See C.G. Jung, CW 13, *Alchemical Studies* ¶87 (III, i, 5).

ferocity. They must be first recognized in their nature and tamed accordingly. At the third castle with wild animals, all hell is let loose. But the hero survives by subduing the animals with the Water of Death. With his knowledge of the two faces of life and a sense of the danger of death that he has obtained from the unconscious, coupled with his disengagement from entanglements in profane life, he is able to overcome the fierce passions. Through his advancing to the wells with the Waters of Death and Life, and then on to the anima, the hero gains knowledge of the nature of the forces of destruction and construction, and is therefore superior to the blind impulsiveness of inner nature.

733   The hero also defeats the many-headed trolls, which embody the character of the chthonic deity as "Lords of the Animals" with the magical sword of discernment that the anima plays into his hand. This sword symbolizes the instrument of conscious differentiation. It is rusty because it has lain so long unused, that is, it was deep in the unconscious. Rust is a symbol of destruction, and here expresses the fact that [the tool of] knowledge is unclear and sick as a force when it remains in the darkness of the unconscious and in the possession of nature demons. Only when the sword is used in the hands of a human does it become a real weapon.

734   The second castle is attached to chains descending from the heights and in this way it floats in the air. The dragons carefully unhook it and place it on the ground. Here something psychologically meaningful occurs as dragons represent chthonic being and essence, the deeply unconscious reactions of human nature. Usually the dragon symbolizes the obstacle to be overcome that separates the hero from the golden treasure or the virgin. In this case the dragon symbolizes the terrible mother, the regressive tendency of the unconscious that blocks the way of inner development.[31]

735   This natural basis that remains in eternal standstill must be overcome in order to reach higher consciousness, which always entails a detachment from nature. The dragon (lindworm, wyvern or serpent) is also a part of the anima herself; often she has a dragon tail, or she must be redeemed from a total dragon form, or (as in *Cupid and Psyche*[32]) she lives with a dragon-shaped being.[33] In this case, the anima represents all parts of the unconscious, from its deep, dark aspect to its higher, human side. Our present tale contains both forms: on the one hand, the dark animal in the form of the lindworm and the wild animals that must be overcome. On the other hand, the image of the anima comprises simultaneously the guarding dragon and the princess

---

[31] On this C.G. Jung, CW 7, *Two Essays in Analytical Psychology* ¶261, H. Silberer, *Problems of Mysticism*, New York 1917 p. 128f, and M. Ninck, *Wodan*, Jena 1935 p. 245.
[32] A story in Apuleius, *Golden Ass*, London 1822.
[33] See R. Reitzenstein, *Hellenistic*, Pittsburgh 1978 p. 270f.

floating in the air.[34] These two parts form a conceptual unit. The actual form of the anima is on the one hand, too high and far from reality, a fantasy image of ideal femininity; and on the other hand, she takes the form of the chthonic serpent.

736   The lowering of the castle brings about a balance of these opposites. With the aid of the instinctual aspect of the unconscious, the ideal image of the anima is brought into the realm of real experience, whereby only then is she actually "realized" and can work effectively.[35] In "The Three Sons of the Padishah" the anima is initially in an ideal, "too high" position. Before he can get to the anima "beyond the sea," the hero must first bring down a golden plait of hair from a tree. The braid is, as part for the whole, the anima herself, but in the form of hair, she is a mere thought, an idea, or a fantasy being without physical reality. In the aforementioned German fairytale, "The Princess in the Tree," the hero found the anima by climbing up a high tree for days. On the second day he came to a large village built into the tree where the inhabitants wanted to stop him. But he said, ". . . I have to climb up to the braid. . . " Here "braid" (pigtail, plait) means the top, and by this expression, the tree is considered to be identical to the anima. Once at the treetop where "the sun was high in the sky," the hero reached an ancient palace where he found a maiden who had been condemned by an evil wizard to this inaccessible place. When she told him her story, the boy said, "He could have condemned you to a lower place!" The tale continues, "But that did not help him much, now she sat up high and had to stay there. And because the princess was a nice and pretty girl, he decided not to return but to remain there and keep house together with her in the castle."[36] Here this floating and hovering on high with the anima is portrayed as a maladjustment, an unredeemed state,[37] because it is as much about living an unconscious existence, just as if she were in the depths of the sea. In the same sense a tale from the Balkans, "The Tsar's Daughter and the Dragon," tells how a princess was kidnapped by a dragon to live in a tower that "was neither in heaven nor on earth." The hero cut a thong from butchered horse, with an arrow shot the thong high up in the tree, and then used the thong to climb up to the princess. In this case, being in an unconscious state has a spiritual aspect. This contrasts

---

[34] This corresponds roughly to the belief of the Daena in the ancient Iranian religion, who as a second ego resides in the heavenly place, but nevertheless depends on the earthly deeds of humans and through this relationship either becomes more beautiful or is disfigured into a whore. See H. Zimmer, *Maya*, Stuttgart and Berlin 1936 p. 192f.
[35] For more on this, see the alchemical idea of the "sowing of gold in the earth" or its dissolution in alchemy, through which the "true gold" or the elixir [or tincture] of life comes into being. A saying of the alchemical "Hermes" is in the same vein: "It is necessary that at the end of the world heaven and earth be united: which is the philosophical Word," quoted in C.G. Jung, CW 12, *Psychology and Alchemy* ¶462.
[36] [Translated from P. Zaunert, *Deutsche Märchen seit Grimm*, Jena 1922 pp. 5–7.]
[37] See also, "The Wooden Eagle" and "The Winged Prince."

to an unconscious state that emphasizes a driven, instinctive, and impulsive character. In "The Golden Castle that Hung in the Air" the dragons manage to balance the tension between the chthonic dragon and the ethereal, divine aspect of the anima image. By placing themselves subservient to the hero, they are not only a part of the anima, but are to be understood as part of the hero, whose nature has much in common with that of the dragon.[38] The dragon is the carrier of the action and is the bridge between the hero and the anima.[39]

737　　　As in "The Virgin Tsar" the hero arrives at the castle of the princess at noon and only at this time can the magical waters be drawn. The symbolism is the same in both tales: only in the maturity of midlife is the conscious encounter with the mysterious psychic forces possible and necessary in order to enlighten the kingdom through the light of that realm and to unfold the light radiating from that realm into this life. And just as in the Russian tale, the hero sleeps with the princess and then leaves her. She wakes up just before he goes, however, and promises to follow him or to have him brought to her in three years' time. The evil and persecutory side of her nature is depicted in this tale as being split into the wild animals, which swarm around the young man as he hastens away and that he must eliminate with the Water of Death.

738　　　The hero cuts a piece of the princess's garment and takes this with him back to the donkey as a piece of evidence by which to identify her. His animal guide now reminds him not to forget his service when he comes into good fortune. The donkey knows that the secular attitude can gain an upper hand and even resist what has been won, as in "The Golden Bird." The Red Knight as a slanderer corresponds to the elder secular brothers in that tale. Here again the shadow coincides with the figures of the auxiliary functions. The red color also indicates the personification of unbridled passion. But, as already mentioned, it only becomes dangerous and acts in an evil manner when it is combined with profane functional thinking and develops from animal savagery into human devilry.

739　　　The arrival of the third princess, the actual anima figure, by ship in the fourth year and the scene of her recognition of the real hero, mirrors the action in "The Virgin Tsar." Again, psychic experience affects the design of real life at a relatively late stage. The golden apple and the little son who hands it over are symbols of the Self, which represent, in different images, the union of opposites and the inner renewal of life.

740　　　In "Ferdinand the Faithful and Ferdinand the Unfaithful" the king, as the embodiment of the dominant secular attitude, tried to claim the anima for himself and was, therefore, beheaded by her. In "The Golden Castle that Hung in the Air" this problem is not raised because here the anima is the daughter

---

[38] For more on this, refer to C.G. Jung, CW 5, *Symbols of Transformation* ¶575f.
[39] Moreover, the dragon or ouroboros as the alchemical Mercurius is identical with the Waters of Life and Death, see C.G. Jung, CW 13, *Alchemical Studies* ¶105.

of the old king. So, the marriage between the hero and the princess is consummated as the longed-for union of opposites in which the secular intellect takes only a limited part because the union of soul and spirit is an eternal and timeless event.

741   This is followed by the final episode with the donkey's sacrifice and his redemption, which corresponds to the sacrifice of the fox in "The Golden Bird." That the hero left the donkey to starve is equivalent to forgetting the fox and pushing him into the forest (the unconscious). To starve something means to pay no attention to it; to lend no mental energy to something and to give it no place in one's life. The donkey is hungry for human life and begs, like the fox, to be killed. (The fox even said that there was no end to his misery in his life in the forest.)[40] Through the dismemberment, the helpful animal is transformed into a prince, the symbol of the Self in human form and a double of the hero. Then follows a triple wedding, whereby the three female figures, like the three men, are actually split-off parts of a single psychic image; on the one hand, the anima, and on the other, the animal-shadow-hero. The fox prince and the enchanted donkey are closely related to the master of the magical world. The fox-prince is his son and the donkey-prince, because of his relationship to the unicorn, is not just a part of the hero, but also a part of the troll and his animals. Afterall, the hero found the donkey in the troll's stable.

742   The identity of the hostile trolls with the dangerous helpful animals and a wise soul guide as a third figure, occurs in another Nordic fairytale, "The Three Dogs." The course of the tale is similar to the one just discussed, but in simplified form:

743   Once upon a time there was a king who went forth into the world and fetched back a beautiful queen. After each of their three daughters were born, a strange-looking old woman appeared and prophesied that the mountain troll would come and fetch them if they were ever to play in the open before their fifteenth year. Thereupon the king gave strict orders to keep his daughters beneath the roof of the castle. The princesses grew up to become the most beautiful maidens, then war broke out and the king had to leave. One day the princess looked out the window at the garden and felt a great desire to play with the lovely flowers. They begged and begged their guards to let them go until they got their way. No sooner were the maidens beneath the open sky, than a cloud came down and bore them off. All attempts to find them were fruitless. The grieving king sent out a commandment that whoever

---

[40] On the motif of the prince enchanted into a donkey, see the Grimm's tale, "Donkey Cabbages," and J. Bolte and G. Polívka, *Anmerkungen*, Vol. 3, Leipzig 1918 p. 3f.

liberated his daughters should have one of them as a wife and half the kingdom in addition. Among many others, two boastful princes set out to search for the princesses.

744 Far, far out in the wild wood, there lived a poor widow with only one son who drove his mother's pigs to pasture every day. As he crossed the fields, he whittled himself a flute, and amused himself playing it. And he played so sweetly that he warmed the cockles of the hearts of all those who heard him. One day, an old man came along, with a beard so long and so broad that it hung far below his girdle accompanied by a large, powerful dog. He noticed that the fellow would like to have the dog and said: "That's why I came, I want to exchange my dog for one of your pigs." The lad agreed to the deal, and as the old man said goodbye he added that the dog was not like other dogs. "His name is 'Take Hold!' and whatever you tell him to take hold of, he will seize, even though it were the grimmest of trolls." Thereupon they parted, and the youth thought that fortune had indeed favored him.

745 When the boy went home and introduced his new dog to his mother, she became exceedingly angry. The youth told her to calm herself; but all in vain, the longer he persisted, the more furious she became. Then since he did not know what else to do, he called out to his dog: "Take hold!" At once the dog ran up, seized the old mother and held her so tightly that she could not move. But otherwise he did her no harm. And now she had to promise her son to make the best of the matter, and then they were friends once again.

746 The next day, when the lad played the flute again in the forest, the dog danced so well that it was like a miracle. Again, the old man with the grey beard came, this time with another dog, and again the boy traded him for a pig. "You have reason to be well satisfied with your purchase, for this dog is not like the other dogs. His name is, 'Tear!' and if you give him something to tear, he will tear it to pieces, even though it were the grimmest of trolls." At home, his old mother was no less angry than she had been before. But this time she did not venture to beat her son, because she was afraid of the great dogs. Yet, as is usual, when women have scolded long enough, they stop of their own accord and that is what happened in this case. The youth and his mother made peace with each other; although the mother thought to herself that the damage done could not well be repaired.

747 On the third day in the woods, both dogs danced wonderfully and again the grey-bearded man came with an even bigger dog. The boy traded his last pig, and the old man explained that the dog's name is

"Hark!" and his hearing was so keen that he heard everything that happened, though it be happening many miles away. "He even could hear the grass and the trees grow." The lad was delighted. Back home, his mother acquiesced to his desire to see the world and the next day he took leave with his three dogs. He came to the heart of a sombre forest. There he met the grey-bearded man again and greeted him as "Grandfather." The old man advised him to "Keep right on going till you come to the royal castle, and there your fortune will take a turn." And with that they parted. The youth followed the old man's advice and for a time wandered on straight ahead. When he came to a tavern, he played his flute and let his dogs dance, and was never at a lack for bed and board and whatever else he might want. Finally, he reached the town where the king had issued his proclamation. The lad went to the castle and had his dogs dance in front of the king, who became happy for the first time in seven years since the disappearance of the princesses. When the boy said what he wanted most was to search for the king's daughters, the king grew gloomy, saying it was no use, but if the boy was successful at delivering one of his daughters, he would not break his word.

748 So, the lad took leave and passed through many broad kingdoms. One day Hark! reported that the king's daughter was spinning in a high mountain and that the troll was not at home. When they got close to the mountain, Hark! said, "There is no time to lose. The troll is only ten miles away, and I can already hear the golden horseshoes of his steed ringing on the stones." The youth now ordered his dogs to break down the door into the mountain, and they did. As he stepped into the mountain, he saw a lovely maiden, sitting in the mountain hall, winding a golden thread on a golden spindle. The youth went up and greeted the lovely girl. Then the king's daughter was much surprised and said: "Who are you that dare to venture into the giant's hall? During all the seven long years I have been sitting here in the mountain I have never yet seen a human being." And she added, "For heaven's sake hasten away before the troll returns home, or else your life will be forfeit!" But the youth was unafraid and said that he would await the giant's return without fear. When the giant arrived in a terrible fury the boy had his dogs tear him to pieces.

749 In the same way he also freed the second king's daughter; then he sought out the third. He found her sitting in the mountain hall, weaving a web of gold. This maiden was lovely beyond all measure, with a loveliness exceeding all the youth had ever thought to find on earth. He went up and greeted the lovely maiden. The king's daughter was much surprised and said, "Who are you that dare to venture into

the giant's hall? During all the seven long years I have been sitting here in the mountain I have never yet seen a human being." And she added, "For heaven's sake, hasten away before the troll comes, or else your life will be forfeit!" But the youth was full of confidence and said he would gladly venture his life for the king's lovely daughter.

750 The third troll had, however, already heard of the fate of his brothers and thought it advisable to fall back upon cunning and treachery, for he dared not venture into an open battle. For that reason he made many fine speeches and was very friendly and smooth with the youth. Then he told the king's daughter to prepare a meal in order to show the guest his hospitality. Since the troll knew so well how to talk, the youth allowed himself to be beguiled by his smooth words and forgot to be on his guard. He sat down to the table with the giant, but the king's daughter wept secretly and the dogs were very restless though no one paid them any attention.

751 When the boy became thirsty, the giant replied, "On the mountain-top is a spring in which bubbles the clearest wine but I have no one to fetch it." The youth answered, "If that be all that is lacking, one of my dogs can go up." Then the giant laughed in his false heart, for nothing suited him better than to have the youth send away his dogs. The youth ordered Take Hold! to go to the spring, and the giant handed him a great tankard. The dog went, yet it was easy to see that he did not go willingly; and the time passed and passed and he did not return.

752 After a while the giant said, "I wonder why your dog stays away so long? Perhaps you would let another of your dogs go and help him, for the way is long and the tankard is heavy." The youth did not suspect any trickery and agreed. He told Tear! to go and see why Take Hold! had not yet come. The dog wagged his tail and did not want to leave his master. But the youth did not notice and drove him off himself. Then the giant laughed heartily, and the king's daughter wept, yet the youth paid no attention; he was merry and at his ease, played with his sword, and dreamt of no danger.

753 Again, his dog did not return and he told his third dog to hurry to the spring. But Hark! did not want to go and instead crept whining to his master's feet. Then the youth grew angry and drove him off by force. And when the dog reached the top of the mountain it shared the fate of the others: a high wall rose round about him, and all three dogs were imprisoned by the giant's magic power.

754   Now that all three dogs were gone, the giant stood up and suddenly looked altogether different. He took down a long sword from the wall, and said, "Now I will do what my brothers did not do, and you must die at once, for you are in my power!" Then the youth was frightened, and he regretted that he had allowed his dogs to leave him. He said, "I do not ask for my life, since in any event the time will come when I must die. But I would like to repeat the Lord's prayer, and play a psalm on my flute, for such is the custom in my country." The giant granted his prayer but said that he would not wait long. So the youth kneeled and began to play his flute until it sounded over hill and dale. And that very moment the magic wall was broken and the dogs were freed. They came rushing on like the stormwind. The youth at once rose and said, "Take Hold!, seize him! Tear! and Hark! tear him into a thousand pieces!" And the dogs flung themselves on the giant and tore him into pieces. Then the youth took all the treasures, including the princess, hitched the giant's horses to a gilded wagon, and drove off as fast as he could.

755   When the king's daughters met again there was great joy, and all thanked the youth for delivering them from the power of the mountain trolls. The youth fell in love with the youngest princess, and they promised to be true to each other. So the king's daughters passed on their way with music and merriment of every kind, and the youth served them with all the honor and courtesy due maidens of gentle birth. And while they were underway the princesses toyed with the youth's hair, and they tied their golden rings in his locks for remembrance.

756   On the way, they met the two wanderers; the youth stopped his wagon and asked them who they were and whence they came. The strangers answered that they were two princes, and had gone forth to search for the three maidens in the mountain. But fortune had not favored them and now they had to return home. When the youth heard this, he felt sorry for the two wanderers and asked whether they would like to ride with him in his handsome wagon. The princes thanked him for his offer and they drove on together. But out of envy the two princes attacked the youth and strangled him. The princes threatened the princesses with death if they did not keep quiet. When they arrived at the king's castle, he welcomed them with joy and great festivities.

757   In the meantime, the poor youth lay as if dead in a gorge in the forest. Yet he was not dead, and his faithful dogs lay about him, kept him warm, and licked his wounds, not stopping until their master came back to life again. When he was once more well and strong, he set out

and after many difficulties came to the royal castle in which the princesses dwelt.

758   When he came to the great hall, the whole court was full of joy and merriment, and there was the sound of dancing and string music. That surprised him greatly, and he asked what it all meant. A serving man answered, "You must have come from far away, since you do not know that the king has regained his daughters who were in the power of the mountain trolls. Today is the oldest princess's wedding day. But the youngest daughter does not want a husband and weeps the livelong day, although no one knows why." Then the youth felt happy once more for he knew that she loved him and had kept faith with him.

759   The youth went to the keeper of the door, and bade him tell the king that a guest had arrived who would add to the merriment of the wedding festivities by showing his dogs. This was to the king's liking, and he ordered that the stranger receive the best possible treatment. When the youth stepped into the marriage hall, the whole wedding company were astounded by his skill and his manly bearing, and all agreed that so handsome a youth was rarely seen. When the king's three daughters recognized him, they jumped up from their table and flung themselves on his neck. The princes then thought it best to make themselves scarce and left. The king's daughters told all how the youth had freed them, and about the rest of their adventures. To show all that their story was true they found their rings among his locks.

760   Now when the king heard of the trickery and treachery of the two strange princes, he grew very angry and had them driven ignominiously forth from the castle. But he received the brave youth with great honor, as he had deserved, and he was married to the king's youngest daughter that same day. After the king's death, the youth was made king of all the land, and a gallant king he was. And there he lives with his beautiful queen, and is reigning happily to this very day. And that is all I have to do with it.[41]

761   The interpretation of this tale and its motifs follows the main lines discussed so far. The resistance of the mother against the hero and his way, his humble origins, the need to free the anima figure from the bonds of the unconscious and the realm of the shadow, are familiar problems. Even the intervention against the hero at the end of the fairytale by the shadow figures corresponds

---

[41] K. Stroebe, *The Swedish Fairy Book*, New York 1921 pp. 167-86, some parts summarized. See the similar tales "The Little Tailor and the Three Dogs," "The Three Dogs," and the two helpful dogs, called "North" and "South" in "The Tale of the Two Dogs."

to that of the brothers in "The Golden Bird" and the Red Knight in "The Golden Castle that Hung in the Air."

Only the figure of the magical helper shows new features; it is split into the dogs on the one hand, and the old wise one, "the grandfather," on the other hand. This is like the wolf in "Prince Hassan Pasha" that acted like Allah's second voice. The hero exchanges pigs for the dogs, they replace the animals that belonged to the mother. The pigs represent an inferior manifestation of the unconscious. By trading them for dogs, which are not to the mother's liking (because they lead to the detachment of her son), the hero (ego consciousness) reaches a higher level. Dogs are the most domesticated of all animals, and represent a driving instinctual force of the unconscious that obeys the [conscious] will. While pigs represent chthonic gods and are associated especially with the mother goddess, they also stand for being caught in blind impulsiveness and hedonism.[42] The dog has the advantage of its great sense of smell and a devoted faithfulness to humans. It therefore embodies a drive that is confident, composed, and controlled. In many religions the dog is a guardian of the underworld and a soul guide,[43] since it is the guiding instinct in the unconscious.[44] As the embodiment of instinctual life, a dog is also often understood to be a personification of the devil. For instance, in Goethe's *Faust*, Mephisto appears as a poodle.[45] Unlike the pig, which symbolizes a lower aspect of the instinctual drives, the dog in the present tale obeys the hero and can even dance to his flute, that is, submit to his feelings.[46]

---

[42] On the pig as the animal of Demeter see J. J. Bachofen, *Der Bär*, Basel 1863 p. 8. See also Kerényi:
The pig is Demeter's sacrificial animal. In one connection where it is dedicated to the Eleusinian mysteries, it is called δε΄λφαξ (*delphax*), the "uterine animal" of the earth, just as the dolphin was the "uterine animal" of the sea. It was customary for Demeter to receive a pregnant sow as a sacrificial offering. The mother animal is a fit offering to the Mother Goddess, the pig[lets] in the pit a fit offering to her vanished daughter. As symbols of the goddess, *pig* and *grain* are perfect parallels. Even the decomposed bodies of the pigs were drawn into the cult: the noisome remains were fetched up again, put on the alter, and used to make the sowing more fruitful.
(K. Kerényi, *Kore*, Princeton, 1969 p. 119.) See also Wilhelm/Baynes, *I Ching*, Princeton, 1967 p. 273.
[43] On the significance of the dog for the ancient Germanic peoples, see M. Führer, *Nordgermanische*, München 1938 p. 83; for the Aztecs, "The Three Kingdoms of the Dead"; for the Inca, "The Other-world"; for Iran, C.G. Jung, CW 5, *Symbols of Transformation* ¶354; for the Greeks, *Ibid* ¶577. In general, see Bächtold-Stäubli under *Hund* [dog]:
In spite of the fact that the dog is the oldest domesticated pet, and more than any other animal that animal on which people depend, it is regarded with great superstitious shyness. Because of its superior nose and all-around sensitivity, the dog is considered able to sense future happenings. . . In general the dog is considered able to see ghosts and spirits. If a dog nudges close to its master along a nightly walk, it means that ghosts are close by. . . also particular to dogs are their pitiful barking, whining, and howling that presage evil and death.
(H. Bächtold-Stäubli Vol. H, p. 419.)
[44] In the Spanish parallel "The Three Dogs" the dogs have the names "Sun," "Moon" and "Morning Star," and are actually angels, that is, messengers of the unconscious.
[45] See J. J. Bachofen, *Mutterrecht*, Stuttgart 1861 p. 11; K. Kerényi, *Kore*, Princeton, 1969 p. 130.
[46] See also another Spanish tale, "The Flute that Brought Everyone to Dance":
Two elder brothers make fun of their younger brother who is forced to be a shepherd since he is incapable of doing anything better. An old woman gives him a flute, which, when played, causes all his sheep and goats to dance until exhaustion. In spite of this they remain healthy

763   That flute music is related to feeling, and thus to the anima, is shown in an Irish fairytale "Diarmuid Donn and the Magic Flute" in which the hero goes to the Orient to get, among other objects, a magic flute that is actually a sorceress (the anima). Anyone who hears her coming with her flute music falls sound asleep. She also possesses the Water of Life and is conquered by the hero. According to other fairytales, playing the flute gives the hero power over dwarves and leprechauns who help him to gain the anima figure,[47] or she becomes pregnant with his music, so that she must marry him. This indicates the phallic significance of the flute. To the extent that the hero can differentiate his feelings so that he can express them, he gains a certain mastery over the uncontrollable and instinctive impulses of the unconscious. The hero who, through his magical music is master of nature and animals, is an archetype, which is revealed in figures such as Orpheus, Pan, and other pastoral gods. (Even the Pied Piper of Hamelin conjures with the flute, although his signs augur doom. He does not embody the allowance of being positively guided, but instead the enticing aspect of the bottomless unconscious.)[48]

764   Like Orpheus, the hero of our tale succeeds through the strength of his flute playing to subdue the forces of the evil nature powers and break the magic of the trolls, and also to gain the service and aid, first of the old man, and later his three dogs. The dogs even bring him back from death, so they represent distinct invincible natural powers. In some fairytales the dog companion of the hero or heroine reveals himself to be an enchanted prince, as the fox in "The Golden Bird."[49] He thus resembles a dark brother of the anima concealed in animal dress. Just as the fox prince represents a son of the ruler of the underworld, the dogs in our tale are, as it were, children of that old grey-bearded wise one who knew how to bring about "the turn in the fate of the hero." He wrapped his dark, wise plans in the seemingly inconsequential gift of the wonderful dogs, through which he released the hero from his mother and her pigs, and led him out on his great adventure. The old man and the dogs are actually a single being, together they represent a kind of light

---

and fat. When the master and later the mistress of the sheep and goats call for a demonstration of the flute-playing, they also dance along with shepherd and animals. But then they dismiss the shepherd, and soon thereafter the sheep and goats die from grief. Back home, the boy acquires pieces of gold from selling grapes that stick in his baskets and bags until he dances them out with his flute music. The same thing happens again with eggs that bring in so much revenue that he and his father become rich and he no longer needs the flute. Out of jealousy his elder brothers rob him but gain no luck with their thievery.
Here the flute is the creative power of the unconscious. Sometimes through playing his flute, the hero can make demons so tired that they serve him. See "The Twelve Pieces." This means that all the destructive forces of the unconscious are subject to the rhythm of positive feeling.
[47] See the tales "The Gnome," "The Living Kantele" and "The Wonderful Flute."
[48] See the deadly effect of the song in the tale from the Yahuna people of Columbia, "The First Pashiuba Palm."
[49] See for instance, "The White Dog from the Mountains," "The Lame Dog" and "The Three Little Birds."

of nature, the *lumen naturae*, a superhuman and subhuman divine and animal-like spirit from the unconscious, which leads to the realization of destiny in the service of the Self.

◊

Chapter 13
The Red Swan

765   The unconscious identity of the archetype of the dark father and the brother of the anima appears very clearly in a fairytale from the Ojibwe People of North America, "The Red Swan":

766   Odjibwa[1] was the youngest of three brothers.[2] Their father had been a hermit and had died when the boys were very young, they had to learn to fend for themselves alone as best they could, for they knew of no other human beings. One day while hunting, Odjibwa was blinded by a red glow in the sky and heard a human voice. He followed the sound and, coming to a lake, he saw a beautiful swan whose plumage shone red in the sun. The young hunter shot all his arrows without hitting the bird. He then hurried to his home and fetched three magic arrows from his dead father. Even with the magic arrows he missed the swan. With great effort, he shot the last magical arrow and it hit the swan in the neck. The swan remained still and then slowly took wing and flew off toward the setting sun, taking the third arrow with it. Odjibwa was swift of foot and chased after the swan. He ran all day. He ran and ran until just before nightfall he came to a village. The chief of the village invited Odjibwa into his lodge and soon offered the handsome young man his daughter as a wife. The daughter was not pleased with this idea, and neither was Odjibwa, who resolved to leave at dawn. But he asked the daughter about the swan, and she told him she had seen it fly past and pointed out the direction.

767   All the next day, Odjibwa ran in that direction and at nightfall came to another village where the chief also offered him his daughter. She received him kindly, but once again Odjibwa decided to follow the

---

[1] Odjibwa here (spelled with a "d") is a personal name, the tale itself comes from the Ojibwe or Chippewa, a large Algonquin tribe that historically lived around the Great Lakes region.

[2] That there are three brothers is unusual for tales from North America. Most often there are *two* or *four* brothers, or *one* hero differs from a multitude or group. The trinity, as well as the arrows, is from European and Near Eastern influence and is only rarely found in tales from other continents. In spite of this, the story contains so many otherwise authentic traits that we can ignore this abnormal threesome.

swan instead, and the daughter pointed the way. The next night, Odjibwa came across an old man living alone. This was a magician who made a kettle appear with food in it that was continually replenished. The old man fed Odjibwa and explained that the red swan had passed this way many times, and those who had followed had never returned. But, he said, Ojibwa would succeed if he was strong of mind. The next night Odjibwa encountered a second old man who fed him, and on the fifth evening a third old man hosted him and explained that the red swan was the daughter of a wealthy magician who valued his daughter almost as much as he valued his wampum treasures.

768 This wealthy magician had once worn a scalp of wampum, but some other Indians had asked to take it so that their chief's daughter might be cured of a mysterious sickness. Finally, he had agreed and had given them the scalp, leaving his own head raw and bloody. But those other Indians had never brought it back to him. His daughter, the red swan, had been enticing young men ever since then to get her father's scalp back. Whoever succeeds, this second old man explained, will get the red swan for his wife. The next day, Odjibwa set forth and soon enough came across a lodge from which the sounds of a man groaning could be heard. There he found the magician with the raw and bloody head. Behind a partition in the lodge came a rustling sound and Odjibwa wondered if it might be the red swan. But before he could find out, the old magician asked to hear Odjibwa's dreams. Only after he had told many dreams did the magician shout, "Yes, that is it! Now I know you will get back my scalp for me."

769 So again Odjibwa set forth, and soon came to another village where many people were shouting and performing a war dance around a high post. On the post the scalp was waving in the wind. Odjibwa changed himself into a hummingbird and flew near the scalp. Fearing he might be detected, he changed again into a tuft of down and floated onto the scalp. He untied it from the post and floated off, then he transformed himself into a hawk, and carried the scalp back to the magician's house. Once there, he slammed it firmly onto the old man's head, almost killing him with pain. But it fit perfectly and the old man was suddenly transformed into a handsome young man, his former self. He invited Odjibwa to stay and showered him with treasures. Out of courtesy, Odjibwa never mentioned the red swan, and neither did the magician. On the day Odjibwa was to leave, the magician brought her forth, now she was a beautiful young woman, so beautiful she was

nearly unearthly. The magician told Odjibwa to take her with him as his wife. Odjibwa took his new wife, who had been the red swan, with him back on his journey home to his brothers. Along the way he passed through the two villages he had visited, and the chiefs sent their daughters along with him. When Ojibwa and his bride came home, he presented the women to his brothers as their wives and everyone lived peacefully for a long time.

770 But then Odjibwa's elder brothers began to upbraid him for having taken their deceased father's magic arrows, and they urged him to procure others. Their object was to get him away, so that one of them might get his wife. Then Odjibwa set forth to go and look for the arrows. After traveling a long way he came to an opening in the earth and descending, went down into the abode of the departed spirits. The country was beautiful, the extent of it was very great, the boundaries were lost in the distance. Odjibwa saw animals of various kinds in abundance. The first animals he came close to were buffalo that addressed him as human beings. They asked him what he came for, how he had descended there, and why he was so bold as to visit the abode of the dead. He told them he was in search of his father's magic arrows to appease his brothers. "Very well," said the leader of the buffaloes, whose whole form was nothing but bone. "You have come to a place where a living man has never before been. You will return immediately to your tribe, for your brothers are trying to dishonor your wife, and you will live to a very old age and die happily. You can go no further in these abodes of ours."

771 With the aid of his guardian spirits, Odjibwa returned the way he had come. After wandering a long time in quest of information to make his people happy, he one evening drew near to his village; after passing all the other lodges he finally came to his own. There outside, he heard his brothers at high words with each other; they were quarreling for the possession of his wife. She had, however, remained constant and true. Odjibwa wordlessly placed the magic arrows to his bow, drew them to their length and laid the brothers dead at his feet. Thus, ended the contest between the hermit's sons, and a firm and happy reunion was consummated between Odjibwa and the red swan.[3]

---

[3] [Summarized from David Leeming, Jake Page, *The Mythology of Native North America*, University of Oklahoma Press, Norman 1998 pp. 177–179, originally printed in H. R. Schoolcraft, *Myth of Hiawatha*, Philadelphia 1856 pp. 161–179. Schoolcraft revised the original text to be in a more "acceptable, literary" form, but it is still the most extensive version available.]

772   In this tale, the hero is not the fourth in a group because there is no father present,[4] only three brothers, as in "The Golden Castle that Hung in the Air." The two elder brothers embody a secular group, the collective thinking attitude, while the hero is a typical solar hero figure.[5] As such, his fate is the image of the course of inner human life[6] because the sun is a symbol of the autonomously moving center within the human being[7] and thus an image of the source of consciousness.[8] In ancient times it was, therefore, interpreted as the spirit of the universal god of the cosmos.[9] Similarly, in India, the sun is a symbol of the Atman in the world, and this divine spirit appears in the image of the wild swan, Hamsa.[10]

773   The two brothers of the hero might well represent the two companion figures typical for the sun god. Thus, for example, the sun in Greek mythology is accompanied by the Dioscuri, who, alternately inhabiting the upper and lower worlds, symbolize the two hemispheres through which the sun traverses. The one is mortal, the other immortal. In Syria, the acolytes are interpreted as the morning star and the evening star.[11] On several Mithras monuments,

---

[4] [Although the father does not play any active role, his having been a hermit colors the whole story. Thus, this tale could be considered to fit into the category of a foursome: the father and three sons.]

[5] See the sun as the hero in Psalm 19: 5-6:

> Their sound has gone forth through all the earth, and their words to the end of the world. In them hath He set a tabernacle for the sun, which is as a bridegroom coming out of his chamber, and rejoiceth as a strong man to run a race. His going forth is from the end of the heaven, and his circuit unto the ends of it; and there is nothing hid from the heat thereof. (21st Century King James Version.)

[6] On this, see C.G. Jung, CW 5, *Symbols of Transformation* ¶553 and also:

> Just as the sun, by its own motion and in accordance with its own inner law, climbs from morn till noon, crosses the meridian and goes its downward way towards evening, leaving its radiance behind it, and finally plunges into all-enveloping night, so man sets his course by immutable laws and, his journey over, sinks into darkness, to rise again in his children and begin the cycle anew. The symbolic transition from sun to human is easily made. . . " (C.G. Jung, CW 5, *Symbols of Transformation* ¶251.)

See also:

> The sun, rising triumphant, tears himself from the enveloping womb of the sea, and leaving behind him the noonday zenith and all its glorious works, sinks down again into the maternal depths, into all-enfolding and all regenerating night. This image is undoubtedly a primordial one, and there was profound justification for its becoming a symbolical expression of human fate: in the morning of life the son tears himself loose from the mother, from the domestic hearth, to rise through battle to his destined heights. Always he imagines his worst enemy in front of him, yet he carries the enemy within himself – a deadly longing for the abyss, a longing to drown in his own source, to be sucked down to the realm of the Mothers." (*Ibid* ¶553.)

[7] On this see Jung: "In the microcosm the balsam dwells in the heart, like the sun in the macrocosm . . . Like the sun in the heavens, the balsam in the heart is a fiery, radiant center." C.G. Jung, CW 13, *Alchemical Studies* ¶188. Cf. the representation of the sun as a sunflower (a mandala) in H. Leisegang, *Serpent*, London 1955 p. 196, and fn. 8.

[8] On this, see C.G. Jung, CW 5, *Op. cit.* ¶141, C.G. Jung, CW 13, *Op. cit.* ¶37f.

[9] See H. Leisegang, *Serpent*, London 1955 p. 200, H. Leisegang, *Die Gnosis*, Leipzig 1924 p. 72.

[10] See the image of the sun swan in Deussen, *Sixty Upanishads* p. 325, Śvetāśvatara Upanishad, 6:15 "The one swan in the midst of this universe, he entered as fire in the billows of water." and Cūlikā Upanishad, 1 "The bird, radiating, eight-footed, three-strained, eternal jewel, having flames of fire, wandering twofold, everyone sees him [as the sun-bird] and sees him not." *Ibid* p. 67.

[11] See J. Przyluski, "Ursprünge," in *Eranos*, Zürich 1939 pp. 31–32, J. Przyluski, "Mutter-Göttin," in *Eranos*, Zürich 1939 p. 44; C.G. Jung, CW 5, *Symbols of Transformation* ¶596 fn. 182. On the companions

the figures of Cautes and Cautopates, stand to his left and right; one with raised, the other with lowered torch. One is often associated with the bull and the other with scorpion, that is, with the equinoctial points, so that one represents the rising, the other the setting sun.[12] Similarly, Odjibwa's two brothers are related to him, they portray parts of his soul split into opposites. Towards the end of the tale, therefore, they could take the upper hand and threaten to dissolve his irrational unity. They behave similarly to the two secular brothers within the four-function group, in that being connected to the secular conscious attitude, they resist the hero's drive to develop further. In this tale a differentiation of the four functions, and, therefore, a distinctly rational worldly relatedness – a "dominant ego consciousness" – does not appear to exist. From this it can be concluded that the whole process is still largely occurring in the unconscious itself. The tale seems to reflect a process wherein the conflict between the tendency to wholeness against the tendency to fall into the opposites takes place within the unconscious. The lapse-into-the-opposites constitutes a profane group, that is, from it arises secular consciousness, and it represents typical collective responses that disrupt the original unity and impede the hero's attempts to unify the personality. At the same time, this group of two hostile brothers personifies the shadow, as in "The Virgin Tsar," "The Golden Bird" and "The Golden Castle that Hung in the Air."[13]

774   In comparison with the last two tales, there are fewer important and actively supporting figures in the present tale. There is neither king nor father, so that the personification of the conscious mind flows together with the actively creative conscious core in the figure of the hero. Together with the brothers, this "solar hero" embodies the archetype of consciousness. The manifestation of an archetype in primitive myths is generally characterized by the combination of several aspects of the same archetype into one form or symbol. For the sake of clarity on a higher level, these aspects are often split into different figures or symbols. This could well be explained as an unintended consequence of a developing consciousness with an increased ability to differentiate. Closely associated with this problem is the question of the division, in fairytales, of the male characters into one, two, three, or four persons. In some cases, the male carrier of the plot – the hero – can be a single figure without a split-off shadow, and even without a human helper or opponent who completes the quest. In other cases, the development is

or acolytes of the deity or divine hero, see the detailed discussion in the section on the divine twins in the next volume of the present work.

[12] See C.G. Jung, CW 5, *Symbols of Transformation* ¶294ff. Cf. also *ibid* on the two thieves flanking Christ and other examples.

[13] This results in the subtle problem that the shadow represents a figure of the unconscious and also of the secular attitude.

determined by two figures: by the hero and a shadowy divine helper or opponent, or also by a foursome, for instance, a father and three sons. In the tale "The Red Swan" we meet an intermediate stage: the triad of the hero and his two brothers. Considering the above discussion of the quaternity we can say that here there is no tension of opposites within the group representing consciousness, that is, between a superior function and the figure of the youngest brother that we identify with the undeveloped function. In this case, the core of the personality (hero) is sensed as the whole ego, and includes the differentiated and primitive, emotionally-conditioned reactions to the external and internal world. The focus here is not on the problem of the renewal of the old attitude that has become sterile and a new ego personality arising out of the previously despised inferior function, rather the hero is a solar hero, who, as the sun, arises ever anew. The problem of the constantly necessary renewal of consciousness is solved without a conflict in the conscious mind by nature itself.

775   That does not resolve the conflict, however, between goal-oriented collective thinking and the requirements of individual development. It is true that the prevailing and most developed function usually aligns with collective goal-oriented thinking (in many fairytales the father-king goes along with the hostility of the evil brothers against the youngest son, or the king himself comes up with the hostility on his own account). However, it is not identical with it as such. Following from our interpretation of the quaternity above, it must be assumed that the two auxiliary functions tend to serve collective thinking, or the "secular" attitude, to a high degree. This can be explained as follows: the undeveloped function is by nature unadapted to the collective; the differentiated function likewise. It is those functions that are to a certain extent less in the focus of the personality and therefore go unnoticed by the individual that adapt to collective views and secular attitudes. The paralyzing poison of a collective attitude that inhibits all steps towards individuation creeps into the relatively neglected areas of life, and thus constitutes a kind of shadow personality that operates on the threshold of consciousness.[14] This "secular shadow" differs from the animal-demonic shadow opponent of the hero: it is another aspect of this archetype. Now we can formulate the psychological significance of the triad of the hero and two brothers: this trinity symbolizes, as hinted above, the conscious personality and the shadow. Here it is beginning to separate into a secular and a magical aspect, according to the general principle that any doubled appearance of an archetype (also as

---

[14] Carus writes, "Through consciousness a large part of the functions belonging to the unconscious sphere are given a certain order and regularity, which is, however, very easily violated if the generally ruling, internally directed, irrefutable laws of the unconscious do not prevail, but rather a consciousness that is not yet enlightened by the light of reason. . . " (C.G. Carus, *Psyche*, Leipzig 1931 pp. 170–171.

duality, twinship, or twoness) represents its gradually manifesting opposite aspect. The conflict is within the group of three that seems to precede that between the differentiated function and the undeveloped function. Only when this *auseinandersetzung* has taken place does the complete quaternio of the components of consciousness become apparent.

776   In "The Red Swan" there is a conflict between the conscious mind and the unconscious (the hero against the anima and her father) and a conflict between individual experience and secular attitudes (the hero against his brothers). This is not a conflict between a trained, fine-tuned instrument of conscious awareness and an undifferentiated (even if conscious) reaction (such as between king and youngest son). Even when the father is mentioned, he is already dead, that is, certain abilities that the conscious mind can differentiate, which once stood in the service of life, are indeed there but do not form an independent complex within the conscious personality. This personality is unbroken and only the hostility of the shadow opposes it, which in its duality indicates that a new differentiation is in the making.

777   Odjibwa is called by a swan whose plumage glittere" red in the sun and that spoke with a human voice. It flies away in the direction of the setting sun and lures him away from his brothers. The enticement of the hero into the magical by a hunted animal, which often represents the anima or an animal precursor of the anima, is a common motif in fairytales.[15] For instance, the Uzbek tale "The Beautiful Dunye" (summarized):

778   An old king on his deathbed warned his three sons not to hunt on the eastern side of the empire. When they transgress the prohibition, they are lured by a saiga[16] into a garden where they are poisoned by a witch. Only the youngest son tricks the witch into drinking her own poison, whereupon she dies. In the garden he is approached by a strong whirlwind and in the distance sees a beautiful maiden, the daughter of a *div*. After many adventures, he finally wins the maiden, the Beautiful Dunye.

779 Here too the anima first manifests as a saiga, in animal form. As we mentioned in the previous section, the anima is merged with nature, especially with instinctual nature. The allurement is actually a fascination that emanates from the spiritual background and moves in unknown spheres.[17]

780   In the same way the hero Odjibwa is fascinated by the wonderful red swan. The swan is a common image in Hindu mythology, and symbolizes the breath

---

[15] See the literature cited in J. Bolte and G. Polívka, *Anmerkungen*, Vol. 2, Leipzig 1915 p. 345f.
[16] [A kind of antelope.]
[17] See here again C.G. Jung, CW 12, *Psychology and Alchemy* ¶439.

of the Atman [the Self; the universal God] whose mantra, "*so ham hamsah*" is interpreted as "I am he." The word *hamsa* also means swan.[18] The homeless wild swan is the symbol of the metaphysical-transcendent aspect of the soul.[19] Even Brahman can appear with a team of swans or by himself as a swan.[20] He is, as Zimmer says:

781

A symbol of the divine that pervades the world and does not enter into it . . . A symbol of the intangible unbound, which carries the small world of the human body to its innermost being, and of the all-pervading finest power in the worldly body."[21]

782 The swan is therefore a symbol of the *anima mundi*. Even in Germanic mythology the swan maiden is a symbol of the anima.[22] At the same time it is a symbol of the sun and thus the world-fertilizing creative force.[23] The sun is often presented as a bird or as being winged,[24] it is the phoenix, which renews itself again and again.[25] In this sense, the red swan corresponds to the golden bird in "The Golden Bird"[26] and also the winged *anima mundi* in "The Virgin Tsar." The red swan lures the hero to the west and leads him to a night sea journey. Even in ancient belief the swan is a guide at the ascension,[27] and in

---

[18] See H. Zimmer, *Maya*, Stuttgart and Berlin 1936 p. 61.

[19] See H. Zimmer, "Yoga und Maya," in Corona, München and Berlin 1934 p. 387ff.

[20] See H. Zimmer, *Maya*, Stuttgart and Berlin 1936 pp. 52, 142, 300, 415.

[21] *Ibid* p. 61, see also the *Śvetāśvatara Upanishad*, 3: 18:
> In the city with nine gates,
> he was living as a swan, roaming the universe outside,
> he is the ruler of the whole world,
> of whatever that is immobile and mobile.

Deussen, *Sixty Upanishads* p. 314, slightly changed based on *Śvetāśvatara Upanishad* fn. 2, and the original German text of Deussen and *ibid* 6:18:
> The one swan in the midst of the universe,
> he entered as fire in the billows of water.
> Only he who knows him, escapes the realm of Death;
> here is no other way to go [attain deliverance].

Ibid p. 314. [The English translators, Bedekar and Paisule, note that the first two lines may refer to the setting of the sun in (behind) the sea.]

[22] See M. Ninck, *Wodan*, Jena 1935 pp. 167, 280, 283, (Brynhild replies to Sigurd "like a swan on the waves," p. 294f). On the swan as a soul bird see E. Tegethoff, "Amor und Psyche," in *Philologie und Volkskunde*, Bonn and Leipzig 1922 p. 91.

[23] See Jung, "The sun symbol of the bird rising from the water is preserved etymologically in the idea of the singing swan. *Swan* derives from the root *sven*, like 'sun' and 'sound'," C.G. Jung, CW 5, *Symbols of Transformation* ¶538, 235 fn. 40. See also *ibid*, ¶136ff and on the bird-sun relationship in alchemy, see C.G. Jung, CW 13, *Alchemical Studies* ¶188.

[24] On the sun-bird Garuda in India, see H. Zimmer, *Maya*, Stuttgart and Berlin 1936 p. 395; also H. Leisegang, *Serpent*, London 1955 p. 209ff; A. Erman, *Religion der Ägypter*, Berlin and Leipzig 1934 p. 61f.

[25] See J. J. Bachofen, *Mutterrecht*, Stuttgart 1861 p. 24.

[26] On this, see *Atharva-Veda*, XX, 8,18:
> His wings span a thousand days,
> He flies as a golden bird in the sky,
> In his bosom, he holds all the gods;
> Thus he wanders about, overlooking the nature of beings (after P. Deussen, *Allgemeine*, Leipzig 1894 p. 321).

[27] See J. J. Bachofen, *Orphische Theologie*, Basel 1867 p. 20.

Germanic mythology it is a symbol of the ecstatic retreat.[28] To a certain extent it embodies the desire for life renewal.[29]

783   Insofar as Odjibwa is a typical solar hero and the story is about the self-renewal of the solar principle through the night sea journey, he is also psychologically identical with the swan as the sun bird. The solar hero represents human consciousness as a radiation or emanation of the unconscious. If now the anima also has the quality of the sun, this means that a piece capable of consciousness is in the unconscious, not connected to the ego, which is why it appears in a non-human form. The bird symbolizes potential consciousness in the form of a hunch, a notion, or a desire, a troubled inner quest for unknown goals. This form of the anima is the symbol of the changeable and the restless, and of being called. It represents connection to a third unexpected new aspect of the sun symbol, the darkened "old" sun in the land of the dead.

784   Odjibwa can only strike the swan with his father's magic arrows, because the relationship to the ancestors must be taken up to reach the unconscious.[30] The arrows represent ideas and thoughts that can "hit" the essence of the swan, that is, in a moment of intuition Odjibwa "catches hold" of the idea that the swan is his new goal in life that he has now to follow. Arrows are also characteristic attributes of the sun god or hero.[31] The three arrows correspond to the three brothers, two remain in the secular world, the third is drawn by the swan into the magical realm. Insofar as the two brothers represent the opposites in Odjibwa's nature, he cannot hit his target with their arrows, that is, an intuition or idea caught in the opposites; only out of his own unity can he strike the swan. Arrows are also weapons of the god of love [Cupid], and Odjibwa hits the swan, as it were, with the arrow of his desire, his love, which gives him the true intuition. The red color of the swan indicates not only its affiliation with the magical, but also the fact that this experience is carried with feeling and passion.[32]

785   At each of five stations along the trail the hero meets with chiefs and old men. These ancestral spirits act – as do all the figures at stations – partly in an inhibitory way, tempting the hero to linger there, and partly – in accordance with their double aspect – as magical helpers. They are like premonitions of a fantasy already involved in deeper layers with the imminent experience. These

---

[28] See M. Ninck, *Wodan*, Jena 1935 p. 256f.
[29] On the swan in general, see Bächtold-Stäubli under *Schwan* [swan].
[30] See the fortification Ivanko retrieves in his grandfather's basement in "The Virgin Tsar" and the magical objects that the hero in "The Beautiful One of the Earth" finds in his father's cellar.
[31] See C.G. Jung, CW 5, *Symbols of Transformation* ¶439ff. and the fairytale "Tiri and Karu" where arrows from the sun fall to the earth in T. Koch-Grünberg, *Südamerika*, Jena 1921 p. 281.
[32] Odjibwa's killing of the bear (before seeing the swan) is like the killing of the cayman brother of the anima in "Makonaura and Anuanaitu." Odjibwa is shaken by this murder – possibly of a totem animal – and slides into the unconscious and consequently receives the first hint of the anima.

are reflections, aspects of that distant sorcerer, the father of the anima. Along with this, at the first two stations, the hero meets with anticipations – in the figures of the chiefs' daughters – of various aspects of the human form of the anima.

786   The way goes backwards, over the ancestors, to the father figure in the unconscious. It turns out that the father deliberately lured the hero with his daughter, the red swan, because he needed someone to carry out the work of his redemption. This temptation of the anima into the other world has been the undoing of many young men, because the anima and her accompanying father-brother-demon belong to the realm of the dead. Thus, in the Egyptian myth, the sun god reaches Sokaris, the god of death from Memphis in the west, a waterless sand desert full of snakes, and even his solar barque must first turn into a snake. As a beetle he becomes the morning sun and leaves his old body back in the underworld.[33] In the Orphic mysteries the sun also has two aspects: that of the day star and that of the night star, the latter which lights up the realm of the dead.[34] A further image of the night sun is the Gorgon to whom the myste must descend to experience the transformation,[35] and who turns those who behold her into stone.

787   The old sorcerer that Odjibwa encounters, confronts him first as father and then, after his rejuvenation, as the brother of the red swan. He is a manifestation of the old wise one and lord of the magical kingdom. The red swan is a form of the same archetype, and as such both are symbols of the Self. The connection between these representations is the phoenix that can arise anew from the ashes and, as a bird, is a symbol of the spirit. The anima also possesses wisdom of the past, and is changeable, and immortal. The anima's wisdom is embodied in the old wise one. This form of the father, to which the anima seems to be bound, is a symbol of the spirit that pervades her and shines behind her. When the hero approaches this male figure he then comes to the fore, so that the female aspect of the unconscious transforms into the male, into an image of the Self.

788   The old wizard is in a state of suffering because his enemies had robbed him of his wampum scalp, and he expects that the hero will get it back. Wampum are white and purple shell beads fashioned from the shell of the North Atlantic channeled whelk or quahog, or the Western North Atlantic hard-shelled clam. Woven belts of wampum commemorated treaties or historical events; they were used as memory aids for oral traditions, and also

---

[33] See A. Erman, *Religion der Ägypter*, Berlin and Leipzig 1934 pp. 17, 233 and 234. According to Zimmer, "Yama, the god of death, is the son of Vivasvant, the sun god, 'he who shines in all directions'." H. Zimmer, *Death and Rebirth*, New York 1964 p. 329.
[34] See H. Leisegang, *Serpent*, London 1955 pp. 255–256.
[35] *Ibid* p. 246f.

for social transactions and marriages. This scalp is also a colorful ray cap, which signifies the very essence of the Old God.[36] On the symbol of headgear, Jung writes:

789   The hat, as a covering for the head, has the general sense of something that epitomizes the head. Just as in summing up we bring ideas "under one hat" (*unter einen Hut*), so the hat, as a sort of leading idea, covers the whole personality and imparts its own significance to it. Coronation endows the ruler with the divine nature of the sun, the doctor's hood bestows the dignity of a scholar. . . Encircling the head, the hat is round like the sun-disc of a crown and, therefore, contains the first allusion to the mandala.[37]

790   The possibility of transformation, which lies hidden in the hat symbol, is particularly evident in the Germanic idea of a magic hood which causes ecstatic rapture,[38] a state of going berserk, and generally causes change of shape.[39] The wampum scalp in our fairytale has a similar significance, since it confers continual rejuvenation to the wearer.[40] Jung also writes:

791   In general, flaying signifies transformation from a worse state to a better [state], and hence renewal and rebirth. The best examples are to be found in the religion of ancient Mexico. . . The prototype of this renewal is the snake casting its skin every year. . . In [Zosimos's] vision the skinning was restricted to the head [that is, scalping] and this can probably be explained by the underlying idea of spiritual transformation. Since olden times shaving the head has been associated with consecration, that is, with spiritual transformation or initiation. The priests of Isis had their heads shaved quite bald, and the tonsure, as we know, is still in use at the present day. This "symptom" of transformation goes back to the old idea that the transformed one becomes like a newborn babe (neophyte, *quasimodogenitus*) with a hairless head. In the myth of the night sea

---

[36] Cf. the sun symbol that the Hopi created from colorful feathers and corn husks in "The Coming of the Hopi from the Underworld."

[37] C.G. Jung, CW 12, *Psychology and Alchemy* ¶53. In this same paragraph, Jung refers to the hero in Meyrink's *The Golem* who puts on the hat of somebody else and becomes entangled in foreign experiences. According to W. Mannhardt, *Wald- und Feldkulte*, Vol. 2, Berlin 1877 p. 85, there is a German popular saying that there is witchcraft in a whirlwind but if you can throw a hat into it, the wind will stop. Thus, the hat establishes supremacy over the demonic.

[38] [German: *entrücken*.]

[39] See M. Ninck, *Wodan*, Jena 1935 p. 88,150, M. Führer, *Nordgermanische*, München 1938p. 31f.

[40] Another amplification is the story of Siegfried in the *Edda*. This hero kills the dragon Fafner and eats his heart, and this gives him the power "to win the magic cap through whose power Alberich had changed himself into a serpent – an allusion to the motif of rejuvenation by casting the skin." C.G. Jung, CW 5, *Symbols of Transformation* ¶569.

journey, the hero loses his hair during his incubation in the belly of the monster, because of the terrific heat.[41]

792   The luminous wampum shells of the scalp indicate the sun nature of this headwear.[42] This wampum scalp was stolen from the sorcerer, and from thence on he was at the mercy of the suffering of human creatures, with age and pain.

793   The magician's suffering is a parallel to the father's state of seeking salvation in "The Golden Bird." There, the aging father's eyesight was bad and in other versions he was ill. (See also the wound of the Fisher King, Amfortas). Our interpretation of that motif is that the suffering of the god of the depths is related to a one-sided development of consciousness of human beings. "The Red Swan" portrays a similar theme: humans have stolen the radiant thing, the solar power, from the daemonic father. This process is equivalent, for example, to the theft of fire by Prometheus for the sake of human consciousness. Prometheus is a son of the maternal-chthonic world, and his theft becomes a guilt because there is a primordial hostility between the world of the gods of light and the dark maternal earth-principle. Usurping the sparks of wisdom from the chthonic world calls forth the revenge of the spirit realm. This is why Adam and Eve, persuaded by the serpent as chthonic daemon to steal from the tree of knowledge, must also leave Paradise and learn to suffer. The tragedy of the ancient sun god, who is subject to the negative-magical feminine principle, is particularly well-illustrated in the myth of the ancient Egyptian solar deity, Ra.[43] According to the well-preserved hieroglyphs from the temple of Edfu, Isis molded a snake from the drool of the aging Ra and some earth, and set it out where Ra would pass on his daily journey. The snake bit him and its poison caused him terrible pain. Isis offered to heal him if he told her his secret name. At first he refused, but the pain became so great that he finally agreed, and so Isis gained his powers.[44] Like the father of the red swan, Ra too, is threatened by earthly rebels whom his son, Horus, appearing as a winged solar disc, subdued. One text states, "Then Horus-Behedti returned in his divine form as a colorful falcon and as the great winged sun in the boat of Re-Horakhty."[45]

---

[41] C.G. Jung, CW 11, *Psychology and Religion* ¶348. See the legend "The Fig Tree," according to which people die because one of the twin brothers, as his soul was rising to heaven, misheard his dead father calling out to him, "Change your skin! Change your skin!" He thought his father was saying "Stop [living]!" Only the snakes, lizards and the Mulatta tree still hear the call.

[42] On the meaning of the scalp, see C.G. Jung, CW 5, *Op. cit.* ¶268, and the phallic meaning of the hat, *ibid* ¶183. See also the Freudian view of scalping as a substitute for castration in Otto Rank, "Das Inzest-Motiv in Dichtung und Sage," in *Grundzüge einer Psychologie des dichterischen Schaffens*, Franz Deuticke, Leipzig and Wien 1912 p. 296 fn. 1. This idea emphasizes only the sacrifice, the loss, and does not take into account the possibility of rebirth.

[43] [Also called Re, Re-Horakhty, and later merged with Horus, and Amun-Ra.]

[44] See G. Roeder, *Urkunden*, Jena 1923 p. XXI.

[45] See *ibid* p. 121f. On page 135, *ibid*, Roeder mentions that two snakes or acolytes accompanied Horus.

794   It is likely that in "The Red Swan" there is a similar situation; the multiplicity of enemies of the ancient sun god means a dissolution into the darkness of the night world, the sphere of the unconscious that is associated with death and suffering; just as the animal garment of the anima reflects being entangled in the magical world.

795   The anima is aware of the suffering of the god, and, therefore, relentlessly attracts the hero into his realm to attain his salvation. The swan maiden, who embodies the love of the human soul for the spirit lying hidden in creation, is a female spirit mediating between the old one in need of redemption and the sun hero.[46]

796   Odjibwa is instructed to retrieve the wampum scalp, thereby giving life back to the magician.[47] The post with the cap is like a martyr's stake upon which a part of the ancient sun god is hung and tortured [lit. martyred].[48] This corresponds to a state of being suspended in conflict with matter and held captive in the material as the maternal world. The repeated motif of the timeless and continual suffering of the sun god reflects psychologically a condition to which the hero himself is exposed during his night sea journey. Odjibwa beholds, as it were, the antithesis of his own heroism; his efforts are consequently the work of self-redemption and self-transformation. To obtain the scalp, he assumes the shape of a bird. His ability to transform into an animal parallels, in other tales, the duality of the hero and his animal brother. At a primitive level, these two characters are a unity, in that it is easy for indigenous people to imagine the transformation of a human into an animal. In these fairytales, the hero can be a human and an animal at the same time. Odjibwa becomes a hummingbird, whose colorful head feathers correspond to the colorful wampum scalp. Here again, like is pitted against like. As a bird he adapts to the nature of the anima, that is, he is dematerialized and becomes a colorful hovering winged creature. As the feather into which he transforms next, this process of becoming spirit goes even further. He is now unassailable for material evil. According to the Native Americans, feathers have not only the meaning of thoughts or ideas, but also of sun rays, that is, of creative and psychic power.[49] In this form the hero succeeds in letting himself be carried by the wind (that is, spirit breath!) and to reach the desired treasure, which he, now as a *Kakak* [goshawk], carries away over the heads of the enraged

---

[46] See the Irish tale "The Knight With the Sinister Laugh" in which the anima wants a relationship with the hero only if he saves the knight with the sinister laughter from the power of the witch.

[47] First, he is asked to tell his dreams. This is a test of the relationship to the magical, which is probably a projection of real Ojibwe cultural traits. To become a shaman, you must have dreams calling you to that profession and, in turn, only shamans are considered to have "big" dreams. The magician's testing of Odjibwa in this way illustrates a transfer of secular methods into the magical world.

[48] The desecrated sun god is himself on the stake as *pars pro toto*, in the primitive form of thought as *participation mystique*. He suffers in the mockery of his light being split off from him.

[49] See L. Lévy-Bruhl, *How Natives Think*, New York 1966 pp. 100, 124–125.

people. His appearance as a bird of prey corresponds to the personification of the Egyptian god Horus as a falcon.[50]

797   Although the violent slamming of the rescued wampum scalp onto the head of the old magician causes the latter at first to faint from the pain, he then appears renewed as the brother of the red swan. His long-endured suffering is ended by a suggested killing and, in this way, he is reborn with the help of a human. Completely parallel to our fairytale, alchemical philosophy expresses the rejuvenation of the father through the process of transformation. Silberer notes the identity of father and son in the alchemical work and understands "that the father is a state, or a psychic potentiality, of the 'son,' whom the latter has, in himself, to conquer."[51] He cites the alchemist Ruandus who quotes the *Turba Philosophorum*, "O what a wonderful nature, for here is the father become the son and born again."[52] This refers to a Gnostic tradition preserved by the Syrian writer Philoxenus of Mabug (about 500 A.D.): " 'The Ancient of Eternity is a boy,' that is to say, he is forever young."[53] Also in the legends of Mithras there appears such a "two as one" unity of father and son. There Mithras is the father, Helios is his son and his *Logos* through which the world was created.[54] Another parallel is the relationship between Osiris and Horus or Harpocrates: Osiris is the descending sun, Horus is the rising sun; and both are soon husband, soon son of Hathor-Isis.[55]

798   After the old magician's rejuvenation, he is no longer the father, but the brother of the red swan, a beautiful youth, and is thus an image of the hero himself. This idea of two hero figures of the same nature had a ritual function in many cultures, for example, in the Sanctuary of the Great Gods, in Samothrace, which were later philosophically reinterpreted by the Gnostics. Hippolytus in the Refutations V, 3, writes:

799   In the mysteries that were celebrated among them, the Samothracians expressed that Adam was the primordial man. In the holy of holies of the Samothracians there are also the statues of two naked men, having both hands stretched aloft towards heaven and their erect penises directed upwards, like the statue of Hermes on Mount Cyllene. These statues are images of the primordial man and the reincarnated pneumatic (spiritual) man, who is very much like him [that is, co-essential].[56]

---

[50] See G. Roeder, *Urkunden*, Jena 1923 pp. 122, 205; also, "Further to these different conceptions of the sun is yet still another, the sun as a hawk or a falcon-headed god, Horus," (A. Erman, *Religion der Ägypter*, Berlin and Leipzig 1934 p. 18, see also *ibid* 51.)

[51] H. Silberer, *Problems of Mysticism*, New York 1917 pp. 257–258.

[52] *Ibid* p. 258; C.G. Jung, CW 12, *Psychology and Alchemy* ¶446.

[53] See G. R. S. Mead, *Fragments*, London 1931 p. 397, see also the manifestation of Merlin as a boy in Heinrich Zimmer, "Merlin," in *Corona*, 9. Jahr, no. 2, München and Berlin 1939 p. 144.

[54] See H. Leisegang, *Die Gnosis*, Leipzig 1924 p. 250; A. Dieterich, *Eine Mithrasliturgie*, Leipzig and Berlin 1923 p. 120.

[55] See C.G. Jung, CW 5, *Symbols of Transformation* ¶356f.

[56] Translated from H. Leisegang, *Die Gnosis*, Leipzig 1924 p. 126.

800   This is the theme of the double (similar to the hero and fox in "The Golden Bird"), which is discussed in the section on the divine twins in a later volume of the present work.

801   Jung explains the situation where the Self appears as a wise old man and consubstantially as his son, psychologically as individuation. It appears, on the one hand, as the synthesis of a new unity (in "The Red Swan" the regeneration of the old magician), "which previously consisted of scattered particles," (that is, the theft of the wampum scalp and the old one's ensuing debilitation), and:

802   . . . on the other hand, as the revelation of something which existed before the ego and is in fact its father or creator and also its totality. Up to a point we create the Self by making ourselves conscious of our unconscious contents, and to that extent it is our son. . . But we are forced to make this effort by the unconscious presence of the Self, which is all the time urging us to overcome our unconsciousness. From that point of view the Self is the father.[57]

803   The primordial human being, according to Gnostic views, is man/woman, male/female, since he/she is created out of the marriage of spirit (*nous*) and matter (*physis*).[58] Thus, in "The Red Swan" the old magician shares a divided room with his daughter-sister, the red swan, and the sound of her wings can always be heard. The old wise one, as the sage of the way and soul guide from the depths of the unconscious, is an image of the archetype of inspiration that contains the secret of the Self. Whereas he embodies a static principle, the anima is involved in the world.[59] She is a part of the Earth and at the same time rooted in heaven and in the earth. When an image of the anima appears spiritualized as Sophia [the Wisdom of God], the old wise one merges completely with her into one being. In the course of "The Red Swan" a trinity of figures appears: the double that emerges from the old one, the anima, and the hero. The anima plays a mediating role through which the two aspects of the Self are brought closer together. Through his active involvement in the conflict situation, the hero has the task of clearing up the darkness surrounding the old man, but also of breaking the bond between him and his daughter-sister. This corresponds to dissolving the initial marriages of the anima figure with the shadow, as they appeared in fairytales we have discussed above.[60] But the old man in "The Red Swan" is more than just the shadow. This

---

[57] C.G. Jung, CW 11, *Psychology and Religion* ¶400.
[58] See H. Leisegang, *Die Gnosis*, Leipzig 1924 p. 132.
[59] On this see C.G. Jung, CW 6, *Psychological Types* ¶368f.
[60] For instance, in "Tapairu, the Beauty from the Land of the Fairies" see also "Ititaujang," where the connection to the shadow emerges at the end. See also "The Shoes were Danced to Pieces."

is revealed in that the course of action follows his ultimate intentions. Through this he is raised from the ordinary shadow to a psychopomp (like the fox in "The Golden Bird") and reveals himself as a hidden aspect of the Self.[61]

804   The redeemed magician gives the hero many treasures, and finally, after a brief hesitation, the anima, that is, the life force. She is now freed, as it were, from a dead latent state (bound to the god of the underworld), into activity (connected to the new solar hero).[62] The reluctance is comparable to the resistance of the invisible brother of the red-brown perihorse in "The Three Sons of the Padishah," in releasing the anima, when it says: "Brother, once you neglected me in this world; this time, have pity on me." This corresponds generally to the tendency of the father, or shadow-brother of the anima, to keep her in the unconscious (or the retrospective longing of the anima when leaving her father, for example, in "The Golden Bird"). As was shown in the section on the magical daughter, this bond is the reason why the hero's quest is often coupled with a journey to the fathers and brothers of the anima.[63] Apparently, behind the anima stands the problem of the redemption of the animal brother, through which the problem of psychological development is raised onto a more differentiated level.

805   The renewal of this side of the Self is completed by the central processes of Odjibwa's act of redemption, but this leaves the brother of the swan still back in the unconscious. (In the German version given in H. Kunike, *Prärie-Indianer*, Berlin 1923, the youthful now-redeemed magician [the brother of the red swan] notices gloomily that his "duty" held him there and forbade him to accompany Odjibwa, indicating a bond to the unconscious.) Psychologically, therefore, a gradual blurring sets in on the return stations where the hero picks up the chiefs' daughters for his brothers. Later the brothers turn hostile, forcing the hero to go on a second quest. This secular resistance corresponds to the psychological stage in "The Golden Bird" in which the hero refused to dismember the fox so that it disappeared into the unconscious and eventually his brothers threw the hero into the well. In "The Red Swan" the brother of the anima is redeemed, but his being left back in the magical obviously indicates a lack of knowledge of the Self on this side, which does not enter into permanent connection with the conscious sphere. Perhaps it is because of this imperfect realization of the Self in secular life that Odjibwa must embark on a second quest.

---

[61] [As an aid to understanding this secret identity of the old wise one with the anima, a quote by Jung might be helpful, "The wise old man, the superior master and teacher, the archetype of the spirit, . . . symbolizes the pre-existent meaning hidden in the chaos of life. He is the father of the soul, and yet the soul, in some miraculous manner, is also his virgin mother." (C.G. Jung, CW 9i, *The Archetypes and the Collective Unconscious* ¶74).]

[62] The hero carries creative (solar) energy into the unconscious and thereby rejuvenates (through the scalp) the magician and in return wins the swan, who also embodies solar energy.

[63] See, for example, "Makonaura and Anuanaitu," "The Visit to Heaven," "The Daughter of the King Vultures," "Ititaujang" and "Rakian."

806   At the urging of his brothers, Odjibwa must now fetch the three magic arrows of their father that they accuse him of having used for his own benefit. That the brothers prevail is in accordance with their meaning as we have so far interpreted: they represent the aspect of irreconcilable opposites in the sun hero himself. He is threatened by a disintegration in the unconscious. Thus, he sets out for a second time and passes through a hole in the ground into the realm of the dead. The buffalo spirit is most likely a totem god. The identity of the dead with animals is a general perception among indigenous cultures. That the buffalo god appears to Odjibwa as a skeleton and warns the hero, means that a disintegration into the opposites is deadly, since all life involves a collaboration between the irreconcilable. Degeneration into the opposites would end in stagnation and death for the figure of the hero, equivalent to succumbing to the shadow. Disintegration into the opposites is also shown by the buffalo god's hint about the home of "the good" and "the evil." By heeding this warning, Odjibwa succeeds in overcoming the brothers and uniting with the red swan, who mediates anew the earthly realization of the Self.

807   This fairytale relates the continually recurring inner events of the figure of the sun hero as the human Self: self-renewal through immersion in the suffering of the world, self-assertion against disintegration into the opposites caused by the shadow, and unification with the female-earth principle.

◆

Chapter 14
The Story of Djihanishah

808   As shown in "The Red Swan" and "The Golden Bird," the connection of the archetype of the old wise one to that of the anima reveals a peculiar mirror-image relation between the father figure in the magical and the father figure in the secular world. These two represent the unconscious, on the one hand, and on the other, the collective conscious attitude. This sometimes odd and paradoxical relation is clearly illustrated in the following fairytale, "The Story of Djihanshah." The course of this tale completely overlooks, however, the problem of the animal shadow and the demonic father, and thus from that side, an unexpected disaster results and the hero's quest ends negatively.

809   There was once a padishah called the Djihanishah, who said, "I want to find the other end of this world," and took soldiers and provisions with him on a boat across the sea. Underway he met with a big storm, and lost all his food and soldiers. He alone survived. After three or four months the Djihanishah finally reached land. He came to a village and remained there as a guest. One day when he arose, he heard a crier calling out, "Is there anybody here who would like to earn a new suit, a lot of money, and a pretty girl for an hour's work?" Since the Djihanishah was in need, he said, "I want to do this!" and the man gave him a suit, money, and the girl. Then the man said, "Come, I will take you to the place." He gave the Djihanishah a horse, mounted one himself, and took along ten other horses and two people. Thus, they went into the mountains, came to a rocky place, and dismounted from their horses. The man killed one of the horses, slit open its belly, took out the entrails, and said to the Djihanishah, "Take your clothes off." The Djihanishah asked, "Then what should I do?" "You will climb into the belly of the horse, sleep for an hour, and tell me what you have seen in your dreams." The Djihanishah undressed and climbed naked into the belly of the horse. Then the man sowed up the belly and went to hide in an ambush.

810   From the top of a nearby mountain great birds flew down, picked up the dead horse with the Djihanishah inside and flew with their bounty to the top of a mountain. The birds shredded the horse and ripped open its belly. But when the Djihanishah stepped out, they scattered in all directions. The Djihanishah looked around and saw that he was not at the same place where he climbed into the dead horse's belly. He went to the edge of a cliff and looked around. Down below he saw the people with the horses. The man called up to him, "Throw down a few stones from up there and I will tell you how you can climb down." The Djihanishah threw some stones down, which the people collected but then they went back to their village. The Djihanishah eventually found a way to descend. He took two bones in his hands as supports for the steep descent. On the path down, the way ended abruptly. He found himself standing at the height of two minarets above the ground. He had no choice but to throw himself down. Allah saved him from sure death and the Djihanishah fell unconscious on the ground. When he came to himself, he saw that he had climbed down at sunrise and at sunset regained consciousness. It was impossible to reach this place from land or from sea. In the distance he spied a castle. All around he searched for a way, soon he found one and made his way to the castle. Once there, he opened the door and entered. There he found a man with a white beard. When this man saw the Djihanishah he rose up and asked him, "But my dear son of man, how did you find your way here?" The Djihanishah told him what had happened and the man with the white beard who lived there in the castle said, "My son, take this key, open any door but that one there. In three days I will return. But do not open that door." Then the old one with the white beard left.

811   As soon as the Djihanishah was alone, he opened one door after another and looked inside. When he came to the door that he should not open he thought to himself, "Oh well, I have experienced so much misfortune, I will open that door also, come what may." He opened the door and stepped inside. In the middle there stood a water fountain surrounded by a rose garden. he heard nightingales singing. Behind all the other doors he had opened there was nothing so beautiful and in those places no nightingale sang. The Djihanishah went for a walk around the fountain and then sat down under a rose tree. A dove flew down and sat on the stone wall at the pool of water. The Djihanishah watched as the bird transformed into a maiden, then another dove flew down, and then another. All three doves turned into maidens. The oldest one said to the others: "Look around and see if there is a human around." The youngest said, "Since the time of

Sultan Soliman, no human being has come here. Let us take our clothes off." When the youngest one undressed, the Djihanishah saw her beauty, lost his senses, and fainted. These doves came once a year to this fountain, bathed themselves, and then flew away. This time too, after they had bathed, they left again.

812 When the old man with the white beard returned, he noticed that the Djihanishah was nowhere in the castle. He looked all over and could not find him. Then he thought, "Maybe he has opened the door I said not to open and has gone in there. Then surely misfortune has befallen him." The old one went into that room and looked around the garden around. He found the Djihanishah laying on the ground under a rose tree and shook him until he returned to his senses. "What happened to you?" "Oh, Father, I will do anything you want, just tell me how I can find the youngest of the maidens. I will serve you all my life, just procure that girl for me." The old man answered, "Those were *peri*.[1] They come here once a year and bathe in the pool and then go away. But if I am here, they do not come. They only come when I go to govern the birds, then they come, in the form of doves. If you wait a year, they will come again, just as they did before. When the youngest has taken off her clothes, remove them and keep good hold of her no matter how hard she pleads, until she has given birth to a child for you."

813 The Djihanishah waited a year. When one year had passed, the lord of the castle again gave him the key. The Djihanishah went into the garden and hid under a tree again. The doves came and took off their clothes, the Djihanishah stole the garments of the youngest dove and went back and sat under the rose tree. After they had bathed, the older maidens found their clothes, dressed, and flew away. The youngest was flustered. When she saw the Djihanishah with her clothes and pleaded with him that if he were to return her robes, she would belong to him. But the Djihanishah waited until the lord of the castle returned. The youngest maiden said to the old man, "Marry me to this Djihanishah." But the Djihanishah said, "Only when my father is present will I join in marriage with you." The owner of the castle warned him under no circumstances to give back her clothes. The maiden took him on her back and flew with the Djihanishah into the air. She pointed down to the city below and asked, "What city is that?" the Djihanishah replied, "That is the city of my father." The girl descended with him to the ground. The Djihanishah's father and

---

[1] F. Giese, *Türkische Märchen*, Jena 1925 p. 303, note 9. In Turkish the *peris* are almost always evil spirits.

mother had not seen their son for three years and now he appeared with a beautiful girl.

814   The Djihanishah now ordered, "Split a marble stone." In the crack he put the clothes of the girl. "Now a castle shall be built," he commanded. The marble stone he made into the cornerstone of his new castle. He let the castle be built and the wedding be prepared. When the castle was finished and all the arrangements for the wedding ready, he bade the maiden to enter. When she came inside, she smelled the odor of her clothes, found the marble stone at the base of the castle, pulled them out, and flew up on a windowsill and remained there. When the *Hodjas*[2] led the Djihanishah into the castle in prayer, he could not find the maiden in her room. He thought, "Am I in the wrong room, or am I confused?" When he turned around, the maiden said, "You are not confused, I am here on the windowsill." He said, "Come down!" She answered, "When the padishah of the birds as a Hodja led us to our marriage ceremony, you said, 'My mother and father may now see that their wish is fulfilled!' Now your mother and father have seen their wish fulfilled, but not mine! If you love me and want to have me, then you must come and visit me in the Periland of my father!" And with these words, she flew away.

815   The Djihanishah wept and all the relatives and parents came and said, "We would like to give you the daughter of this-and-this vizier." But nothing helped. The maiden went to her parents and related the story of all that had happened. Her father said, "Oh my daughter, that was the son of a king. You were meant for him, you should not have flown away." The girl answered, "I hope that he searches and finds me, or dies for my sake. And besides, he must be found in the castle of the padishah of birds in the garden with the fountain and rose trees." According to these words her father sent two peris out to find the old padishah with the white beard and the Djihanishah.

816   The Djihanishah once again boarded a boat, just as three years earlier, and sailed again to that land. There the barker cried out, "A suit, a thousand piasters, and a pretty girl for one hour of work!" The Djihanishah took on the job, the suit, the money and the girl, mounted a horse, and rode up into the mountains. Just as before, he took off his clothes, and let himself be sewn into the belly of the dead horse. The big birds came and carried him up to the top of the mountain. They pecked open the horse, he stepped out and the birds all scattered. When the Djihanishah looked around and saw the

---

[2] *Ibid,* p. 303, note 1: the title of a spiritual person.

people below, they cried out, "Throw a stone down and we will tell you how to climb down." The Djihanishah did not throw a stone down because the last time the people had deceived him. The stone weighed as much as an Osman *oka* and was worth its weight in gold. Like the first time, he took two bones as supports and slowly climbed down. When he came again to the height of two minarets from the ground, saw no path and no crevices in the cliff, he threw himself down and collapsed, unconscious.

817 When he again came to himself and looked around, he saw the castle, and went there. Inside, he found the old man with the white beard, and kissed his hands and feet. The old man knew that the girl had escaped. Her father had sent two peri messengers to find the youth. He asked the bird [that is, the old man, the padishah of the birds], "do you know of the land of the peris?" The bird answered, "I do not know of it, but there is a great bird, called the Emerald Bird whom we can ask. He called the Emerald Bird[3] and asked. The Emerald Bird answered, "When I was still a young bird in the nest, my mother took me and flew to the border of Periland. I know this border, but I will not go beyond." To fly from here, the castle of the padishah of birds, all the way to the border of Periland would take three months; from that border to the city where the father of the maiden lives would take another six months." The lord of the castle filled a water bag with twenty *okas* of water and packed another bag of meat, strapped them to the back of the Djihanishah, and helped him mount the Emerald Bird. He also wrote a letter to give to his elder brother who lived a month's travel away. He was also a padishah of birds. The old man with the white beard then told the Djihanishah, "When the bird, upon which you sit, cries out 'Tshkak!' then give him a piece of meat. When he calls out 'Tshunk!' then give him some water." To the Emerald Bird he said, "Fly the Djihanishah to my elder brother. Then fly back."

818 The Emerald Bird flew the Djihanishah to the elder bird padishah, gave him the letter, and returned. The elder brother read the letter: "Put this Djihanishah on a strong bird and write a letter to our eldest brother that he should find another bird to take the young man to the land of the Peris." This brother then called together all his birds, picked the strongest, set the Djihanishah upon it, and gave him the message. This bird then flew to the eldest brother. There the Djihanishah mounted another bird who flew him on and set him down at the border of Periland. There the Djihanishah met the two peris whom

---

[3] While the Emerald Bird in "The Story of the Emerald Anka-Bird" is a kind of a phoenix, it could well be understood as such in this tale (cf. *Ibid*, p. 303, note 13).

the father of the girl had sent out to find him. They said to one another, "This is the one whom our peri padishah is looking for." They took hold of him, without causing any pain, and brought him to the peri maiden's father. This one said, "I am satisfied," and ordered the wedding ceremony be prepared and consummated. When all was finished, he brought the Djihanishah to the nuptial chamber and there he attained his wish.

819   After some time had passed, the Djihanishah longed to visit his father. He put his wife on peris and sent precious gifts along with them. When they flew through the air, they looked down and saw a place with meadows and fields in the barren land below. The wife asked to stay there for the night. They stepped down from the air and tarried in this place. As they leisured, the wife went to the water to wash her back. There on the shore she removed her clothes. As she stepped into the water, a wolf came out of the forest and killed the woman. When the husband learned that a wolf had eaten up his beloved wife he began to weep and never stopped. He would go neither to his father, nor to the parents of the girl, but remained at a that place, crying until he died.[4]

820   The tragic end of this fairytale is actually already anticipated at the beginning when the hero succumbs to the deceptive shadowy figures of the crier and his cohorts who entice him with money and a beautiful girl, and then shamefully take advantage of him for their own enrichment. They represent the dominance of the shadow, an inner evil greedy side of the personality, that drives him into the belly of an animal. As a result, he falls into the power of birds of prey, that is, avaricious plans through which he lets himself be completely carried away.[5] This journey is an immersion into the unconscious under a negative sign (although entering naked into the body of an animal is a pre-stage to rebirth). Even the storm at the beginning of the voyage indicates an overly powerful dominance of the chaotic unconscious. In spite of this, the tale continues positively onwards, the hero's fate is still undecided, and it is an open question whether or not this intrusion of the unconscious [by means of the storm] has, in the end, a renewing and redeeming effect. The hero lets himself fall from the mountain, in an intentionally passive way, down into the unconscious. This courageous attitude, a kind of *amor fati*, at first transforms the negative aspect of the unconscious, and the hero reaches the castle of the helpful old man with the white beard.

[4] See the close parallel "The Prince and the Swan Maiden" and the weaker variant "How the King's Son Wins Back his Runaway Wife."
[5] On this we noted that a group of men also appears as shadow figures in "The Beauty of the World."

821   In the centre of the castle lies a rose garden with a pool of water. The whole scene represents a mandala, which according to Jung can be regarded as:

822   . . . the actual – that is., effective – reflection of a conscious attitude that can state neither its aim nor its purpose and, because of this failure, projects its activity entirely upon the virtual center of the mandala. The compelling force necessary for this projection always lies in some situation where the individual no longer knows how to help himself in any other way.[6]

823   The symbol of the rose garden occurs often in medieval alchemy. It is the place of transformation,[7] and from the fountain gushes forth the Water of Life.

824   The roses that bloom in the garden of our tale are symbols of feeling;[8] the rose is, therefore, often an attribute of the beloved, an aphroditic symbol,[9] and as a mandala the birthplace of the gods. Also, the flower is an earthly reflection of the sun and in the flower God descends living and fruitful into matter.[10]

825   Like the rose, the garden is a feminine symbol; it is the place of healing and resurrection, and as a mandala, the vessel of rebirth into a divine being. The symbols of the fountain and the spring are related to that of the garden.[11] As a symbol of the flow of life, the fountain is essentially related to the image

---

[6] C.G. Jung, CW 12, *Psychology and Alchemy* ¶249. See also the images in, C.G. Jung, CW 11, *Psychology and Religion* ¶90, ¶109.

[7] C.G. Jung, CW 12, *Op. cit.* ¶235 and figure 84; further:
     For the garden is another *temenos*, and the fountain is the source of 'living water'
. . . The plan of the *temenos* with the fountain developed under the influence of early Christian architecture into the court of the mosque with the ritual wash-house in the center. . . We see much the same thing in our Western cloisters with the fountain in the garden. . . The center and the circle, here represented by fountain and garden, are analogues of the *lapis*, which is among other things, a living being. (*Ibid* ¶155.)

[8] See the tale, "The Story of the Crystal Palace and the Diamond Ship," where the princess, as a child, walked in a rose garden, and later demands of her passionate admirer, the prince, that he build a golden bridge and decorate it with real roses and at one end wait for her. Only then will she come to him.

[9] See "The City of Roses" in which the city of roses is the goal of the hero's quest. See C.G. Jung, CW 5, *Symbols of Transformation* ¶628f, H. Silberer, *Problems of Mysticism*, New York 1917 p. 88, M. Ninck, *Wodan*, Jena 1935 p. 262f, 341f.See

[10] See C.G. Jung, CW 12, *Psychology and Alchemy* ¶139; "The lotus is the eternal birthplace of the gods. It corresponds to the Western Rose, in which the King of Glory sits, often supported by the four evangelists, who correspond to the four points of the compass."C.G. Jung, CW 11, *Psychology and Religion* ¶123. See C.G. Jung, CW 6, *Psychological Types* ¶392 on the Rose as an attribute of the Virgin Mary and the Song of Songs 2: 1: "I am the rose of Sharon, and the lily of the valleys." See also the rose as symbol of the Self in the children's legend, "The Rose": Once a child went to fetch wood in the forest and there met another child who helped her industriously pick wood and carry it home. The little girl told her mother who did not believe her until one day she brought back home a rose and said that the beautiful child had given it to her and had told her that when it was in full bloom he would return. The mother put the rose in water. One morning her child could not get out of bed. The mother went to the bed and found her dead, but she lay there looking very happy. On the same morning the mother found the rose in full bloom. (J. and W. Grimm, *Complete Grimm's*, London 1975 pp. 819–820.)

[11] See C.G. Jung, CW 12, *Op. cit.* ¶155f and figure 56. See also A. Wünsche, *Lebensbaum*, Leipzig 1905 p. 85f on the invigorating power granted by the fountain of the Norse goddess Huldra or German goddess Holda [Frau Holle, Bertha, Pertha] that holds the souls of the dead and is in a "beautiful blue garden."

of the anima[12] and appears in conjunction with her in "The Virgin Tsar" and "The Golden Castle that Hung in the Air." Consequently, the fountain also has maternal meaning and carries secret wisdom and timeless events.[13]

826   Insofar as the garden, the spring, and the old wise one can all be symbols of the living, mysterious, preserving and guiding spirit,[14] we can interpret them as one being. The helping psychopomp in this fairytale is sometimes described as a man, sometimes as a bird, and also the lord of the birds. (In the tale "The Red Swan" the old one is the father or the brother of bird). This shapeshifting, this changeableness, emphasizes the spiritual essence of the old wise one, who, as the epitome of inspiration, holds the keys that lead to the secret mandala center. For he is the general principle behind which all other images are concealed and can thus hide them and at the same time prevent them from spontaneously breaking into the realm of consciousness. This figure that represents – from the human perspective – natural, inherited wisdom, disappears once a year and goes into the realm of the birds to reign there. Thus, the old man loses his human form, that is, the spiritual, guiding principle vanishes from the field of human experience and returns to being a part of the general spirit of nature.[15]

827   A similar movement is attributed to Dionysus: Several legends circulate about the disappearance of the god into another world and his return to the world of people. Every second year his reappearance is celebrated. This very arrival, his "epiphany," is the reason and occasion for the feast.[16]

---

[12] C.G. Jung, CW 12, *Op. cit.* ¶94,¶157 on the mystery of the fountain symbolizing passion and, as a spring with its connection to the underground, the instinctual world.
[13] On the fountain of Mimir [a gigantic being of great wisdom in Norse mythology.] see C.G. Jung, CW 5, *Symbols of Transformation* ¶319f, ¶566 fn. 107, C.G. Jung, CW 9i, *The Archetypes and the Collective Unconscious* ¶319f,¶156, and J. Przyluski, "Ursprünge," Zürich 1939 pp. 13–16. On Mimir's fountain see also M. Ninck, *Wodan*, Jena 1935 p. 180,227, esp. 296:

> What goes on in the depths enters into all that happens, what comes out of the deep, knows of the interrelationship between all that goes on. Trees and springs are full of pearls of wisdom, as are the spirits of the deep, giants, monkeys, the dís [plural, Norse goddesses, protectresses, and guides of the dead.] and the dead. (M. Ninck, *Wodan*, Jena 1935 p. 296.)

See also the Inca tale "Pachacuti Inca Yupanqui and the Sun God" in which Yupanqui, a historical Inca king, met his father, the sun god, as he rose up from a spring and revealed Yupanqui's future to him. See also, "The Shepherd and the Princess of the Sun":

> Once the sun princess fell in love with a shepherd. When she appeared to him, he thought she was the embodiment of one of the four crystal clear springs that had a great reputation in his region. When she returned to her castle, the princess was so much in love with the shepherd that she did not know what to do. "A songbird, by the name of Checollo [a small bird like a nightingale] came to her and told her to sit between four fountains. There she was to sing what she had most in her heart. If the fountains repeated her words, then she might safely do what she wanted." (Markham p. 411.)

On the significance of the mercurial water in alchemical philosophy, see H. Silberer, *Problems of Mysticism*, New York 1917 p. 161, C.G. Jung, CW 13, *Alchemical Studies* ¶86 (III, i, 3), ¶89, ¶97. It is the water of transformation into a spiritual being.
[14] For the alchemic view on this, see C.G. Jung, CW 12, *Psychology and Alchemy* ¶409.
[15] Thus, according to oriental concepts, the souls of the dead become birds when they pass into the afterlife.
[16] E. Rhode, *Psyche*, London 1925, Volume 2, pp. 12-13.

828   ... [T]here is no reason to see in this disappearance and reappearance of the godhead. . . any allegorical symbolization of the destruction and renewal of vegetation. The godhead is in the real and literal sense temporarily distanced from humanity, tarrying in the realm of the spirits. So Apollo, according to Delphic legend, retreated at times from the world of humans, he was then in the land of the Hyperboreans, inaccessible to humans by foot or ship. . . Sometimes Dionysus also went into the underworld, the realm of spirits and the souls. . . Why Dionysus sojourned in the realms of the soul in the underworld is clear enough, it is after all *his* kingdom. And so one understands why Dionysus is also the Lord of Souls. . . and why he can be accorded such clear epithets of Hades. His true religion, exported from Thrace, but in Greece greatly altered, retained this figure of Lord. . . of souls and spirits, and was partly retained in some Greek local cults and in the Orphic Dionysus cult.[17]

829   In our present tale, "The Story of Djihanshah," the old man does not manifest, like the Greek gods, in this world among people, but between a faraway magical region in which he does occasionally retreat, and a psychic world on this side that lies in the unconscious but is reachable by consciousness, like a certain region of the magical close to secular life. The old one's affiliation to the unconscious, his sovereignty there, is more strongly stressed than with Dionysus. A quote from Carus may contribute to better understanding the concept of a periodic immersion of a divine figure into distant realms of the unconscious:

830   [E]verything belonging to the conscious life of the soul does not always remain in consciousness, but returns periodically into the unconscious. . . *As long as it is unconscious*, the previously conscious content must come into closer rapport with the general than it was before and *suffer a certain degree of change*. . . A return into the unconscious furthers and strengthens individual concepts, thoughts and sequences of thoughts. The ancient myth of Anteus, the son of the earth, who gained new strength in every contact with his mother, is repeated in the relationship between every person and his or her unconscious. This is especially borne out by the undeniable *regeneration (of the conscious soul) in sleep*. Sleep is a regular return into the unconscious, mainly for this reason. "Sleeping on something" if even only for a short period, often can clarify an obscure thought or reveal a missing connotation. Even memories, long since faded,

---

[17] *Ibid*, p. 12 footnote 2 for further examples.

often awaken clearly and poignantly within the soul after consciousness sinks for a short period into the unconscious. This happens because there is in the unconscious a greater *generalization of life*, and, therefore, everything that is immersed in the unconscious somehow shares in this generalization.[18]

831 The temporary disappearance [of the divine figure] into the kingdom of the birds thus means a resolution of the old ways for the purpose of self-renewal.[19] Both his situation in a secularly accessible layer of the magical realm, and his need to immerse himself in a rhythmic journeying to distant lands and back, lend this figure the character of being unredeemed. In his bird phase, the old man leaves the human realm, so that, as it were, the spiritual principle completely disappears and thus creates a gap, an openness to the side of the unconscious. During this state of internal transition, an inner transformation, the three *peri* maidens appear as doves in an enclosed garden.[20] These fairies or nature spirits, personifications of the anima, are like female manifestations of the spirit principle that was previously personified by the wise old man. In an Uzbek tale "Prince Shaadot" the old man himself is in the garden where the unhappy and unsuccessful lover lands in his search for the anima figure who lives far away. The similar situations, one with the anima figures, and the other with the wise old man in the garden, illustrate the secret kinship of these two archetypes already discussed above in relation to "The Red Swan." In Manichaeism the otherworldly soul part of humans is also represented, on the one hand, as a maiden of light and, on the other hand, as the wise guide or god of light.[21] When in "The Story of Djihanshah" the spirit [that is, the old

---

[18] Translation based on C.G. Carus, *Psyche* (English), New York 1970 pp. 64–65 with emphasis in the original expanded by von Franz and von Beit.

[19] This contrasts with parallel figures of the same archetype, which are banished to the underworld and only periodically appear [in the upper world of the conscious mind], such as the dragon in "The Rose Maiden" and also those whose special aspects seek the connection to the upper world, like the ferryman in "The Devil with the Three Golden Hairs." The myths surrounding the Greek god Dionysus sometimes emphasize his disappearance, and other times his reappearance. For instance, E. Rohde, *Psyche* London 1925 pp. 536–536, points to his affiliation with the underworld. He thus stands between those characters who rarely disappear, like the old man in "The Story of Djihanshah" and those who only rarely appear. It is only a short step from these figures to those as in "The Prince and the Swan Maiden" in which the hero comes to an old man shackled to a wall with heavy iron chains, who begs to be freed from his bonds, or as in "The Golden Apples and the Nine Peahens" in which the dragon is bound in a barrel or, as in "The Princess in the Tree" in which the raven is nailed to a wall. It always is a question: to what extent does human consciousness know of the spirit hidden in nature and how much and in what way does it let this spirit participate in her or his life, and can and will she or he surrender to its guidance? The fairytale depicts the different levels of consciousness in the situation and the effects of the chthonic deity and the degree to which it is unredeemed.

[20] See the discussion above on the rhythmic appearance of the anima in the shape of geese.

[21] See R. Reitzenstein, *Iranische*, Bonn a. Rh. 1921 pp. 5 and 28:
"When death," teaches Mani, "approaches a complete (or truthful) person, the primordial god sends a light God in the form of a guiding wise one and with him three gods and a water vessel, the clothing, the head covering, the crown, and the wreath of light. With them comes the virgin, like the soul of this complete (true) one. The devil of greed and lust also appears with other devils. As soon as the honest one sees these, he invokes the goddess *who takes the form of the wise one*, and the other three gods to help him, and they now approach him." See

man, padishah of the birds] sinks into the depths of the unconscious, the female-earthly aspect of the unconscious, with her charming and alluring mysterious fairies, takes the place of the old wise one. This vision moves now in front of the image of the spirit divinity, since the anima is the mediator between the conscious mind and that seemingly unattainably distant guiding spirit of nature.

832   The *peri*-nixies appear at the center of the mandala in the water fountain, again pointing to a renewal out of the unconscious, since this contact with the source of life takes place just at the time when the old man is seeking new strength [power] in the underworld. The anima appears first as a trinity of doves. Bächtold-Stäubli under *Taube* [dove] write:

833   The dove comes from Mesopotamia, where it is the sacred animal of Ishtar, goddess of the feminine principle, animal fertility, and birth, equivalent to the Greek goddess Aphrodite. Therefore, the dove also appears as a symbol of the latter.[22]

834   In Christian belief the dove represents, however, the Holy Spirit, the Sophia, and the World Soul.[23] In "The Golden Bird" the dove was a manifestation of

---

also *ibid*, p. 30f.: Enigmatic is the figure of the maiden, who is similar to the soul of the deceased (the true, the complete person). Apparently she is identical to the goddess that has taken on the form of the wise one, that is the Redeemer God. For the first statement [allegation] Yast 22, 5-11, from the *Zend-Avesta* provides an explanation. Evidently this female figure corresponds to a much older Iranian belief. There, Zarathrusta asked Ahura Mazda where does the soul abide on the third night after death. Ahura Mazda answered: "It takes its seat near the head, singing the Ustavaiti Gâtha and proclaiming happiness: 'Happy is he, happy the man, whoever he be, to whom Ahura Mazda gives the full accomplishment of his wishes!' . . . At the end of the third night, when the dawn appears, it seems to the soul of the faithful one as if it were brought amidst plants and scents: it seems as if a wind were blowing from the region of the south, a sweet-scented wind, sweeter-scented than any other wind in the world. And it seems to him as if his own ego were advancing to him in that wind, in the shape of a maiden fair, bright, white-armed, strong, tall-formed, high-standing, well-breasted, beautiful of body, noble, of a glorious seed, a maid in her fifteenth year, as fair as the fairest things in the world. And the soul of the faithful one addressed her, asking: 'What maid art thou, who art the fairest maid I have ever seen?' And she, being his own ego, answers him: 'I am you, your ego, O youth, (I am) your good thoughts, your good words, and your good deeds. . . " (Darmesteter pp. 315–316.) [Reitzenstein (*op. cit.* pp. 30–31) comments that he translates *daena* not as religion or the thinking personality or "conscience," as Darmesteter does, but rather as "Self."] After further questions and answers with a reference to the service of the deceased for his soul, The soul of the righteous one – we must assume now united with his ego [i.e., the maiden] – ascends in four steps through the stations of good thoughts, good words, and good deeds, up to the infinite light (*Ibid* p. 31.)
See also p. 54: Thus, in a short song, *Genza*, I, 113, 12, the souls says of itself:
    I go towards my image,
    and my image comes to me;
    It kisses and hugs me,
    as if I was returning from captivity.
It is the Manichean idea of the guiding wise one, the maiden, "who is like to the soul of the elected one."
[22] On the dove as a soul-image see also Bächtold-Stäubli and O. Tobler, *Epiphanie*, Kiel 1911 p. 28ff and G. Weicker, *Seelenvogel*, Leipzig 1902 p. 26f.
[23] See this G. R. S. Mead, *Fragments*, London 1931 pp. 423–424; C.G. Jung, CW 11, *Psychology and Religion* ¶126, *Ibid* ¶336.

the anima.[24] The dove is, therefore, an apt symbol of the anima in her sensual, seductive, and spiritually stirring nature. A meeting with this figure becomes a dangerous mystical experience. Therefore, the old wise one forbids the hero from entering the central room that leads into the garden; apparently because he suspects that the hero is not mature enough for the experience on account of his overly strong bond to the secular world.

835   The old man with the white beard holds the key to the special room. This is a means to tap into the unknown, and thus this image indicates here the right way to enter into the secret meaning of the unconscious. In the Gnostic text, *Pistis Sophia*, this term is used for the mysteries of the kingdom of heaven, which brought Jesus to save people, and which he calls a key.[25] In Luke 11: 52 the image of the key is also used: "for ye have taken away the key of knowledge: ye entered not in yourselves, and them that were entering in ye hindered." [King James Version]. In the realm of symbols[26] the key is generally an attribute of the anima and the old wise one as psychopomp figures, who mediate the "mysteries" of the unconscious.[27] Therefore, the key was an attribute of the sun god Aion (eternal life)[28] and later of Saint Peter, who guarded the gates to the kingdom of heaven.[29] In alchemical philosophy even the Philosopher's Stone is itself sometimes called the key because "the round thing was in possession of the magical key which unlocked the doors of matter."[30] This is the key of knowledge that opens the Paradise of Joy.[31]

836   In most fairytales a catastrophe follows immediately after entering the "forbidden room" (more on this motif in the next volume), but here the negative consequences develop only gradually. Next, the old wise one goes

---

[24] See J. Bolte and G. Polívka, *Anmerkungen,* Vol. 1, Leipzig 1913 p. 503f. In alchemical thought the dove was a symbol of the soul of the substance, an anima of matter. See C.G. Jung, CW 11, *Psychology and Religion* ¶150, and *Ibid*¶443.

[25] H. Leisegang, *Die Gnosis,* Leipzig 1924 p. 386, "For this cause, therefore, have I brought the keys of the mysteries of the kingdom of heaven." [also in G. R. S. Mead, *Pistis Sophia,* London 1921 p. 289.]

[26] [In the original German *psychischer Bilder* (psychic images).]

[27] See C.G. Jung, CW 9i, *The Archetypes and the Collective Unconscious* ¶73f.

[28] See A. Dieterich, *Eine Mithrasliturgie,* Leipzig and Berlin 1923 p. 66.

[29] Hecate as a gatekeeper of Hades also possessed the key as an attribute. See C.G. Jung, CW 5, *Symbols of Transformation* ¶577fn. 135 See further the fairytale "The Youth Who Wanted to Win the Daughter of the Mother in the Corner" in which the rat princess had a keychain on her tail. Also, in the Grimm's tale "Ferdinand the Faithful and Ferdinand the Unfaithful" the hero's mysterious godfather gave him a key to the castle, which held the white horse . See also *Faust* Part 2, Act 1 where Mephisto gives Faust a key to find the Mothers.

[30] C.G. Jung, CW 11, *Psychology and Religion* ¶92.

[31] H. Silberer, *Problems of Mysticism,* New York 1917 pp. 212, 381, 383 [where he quotes extensively from the Christian mystic Jane Lead (1624-1704)]. Here is the original quote:

    This is Wisdom's Key, which will make our Hands drop with sweet smelling Myrrh upon the handle of her Lock. Which while I was opening her Privy-Door, with this Key, my Soul failed within me, and I retained no strength; my Sun of Reason, and the Moon of my outward Sense were folded up, and withdrew. I knew nothing by my self, as to those working Properties from Nature, and Creature, and the Wheel of the Motion standing still, another moved from a Central Fire; so that I felt my self Transmuted into one pure Flame. Then came that Word to me, "This is no other than the Gate of my Eternal Deep." (*Jane Lead's Spiritual Encounters – Journal Entries: 1670-1675,* "In the Month of August.")

along with the inevitable and lends the hero his support, like the fox in "The Golden Bird" that continues helping the hero despite his repeated disobedience.

837   The padishah of the birds advises the hero to steal the animal guise from the dove maiden he desires. This is a significant extension of the swan maiden motif discussed above. There, the theft of the animal garb emerged as a violent invasion of consciousness into the realm of the unconscious, and this intrusion sometimes has unfortunate consequences. At other times, however, it initiates a quest that leads to higher awareness. In "The Story of Djihanshah" this violation of the laws of nature by the conscious mind corresponds to an inner spiritual tendency, which in turn itself arises from nature. Thus, this verifies the alchemical saying, ". . . Nature triumphs over nature. . ."[32] Even the seemingly arbitrary human attitude that "sets itself against nature" corresponds to a transpersonal meaning, that is, the creative will of the spirit of nature to become conscious.[33]

838   The hero meets three anima figures in the rose garden, of whom he chooses the youngest. This splitting of the anima into several figures means that she is still contaminated with the unconscious. The multitude of characters indicates a predominance of the unconscious-female relative to the hero. This superiority causes the counter-reaction of the hero who does not, as the maiden suggests, agree to marry in the castle-mandala and have a child with her. The child as a Self symbol would have guaranteed the *unio oppositorum* and would have prevented the subsequent disintegration, which results from the indecision of both lovers. Because the hero proposes to first go to his parents in the secular world, he breaks the protective circle of the [garden] mandala, which would have been the proper place for the union. As the mandala symbolizes by nature closure and wholeness, it has, as mentioned above, the purpose of preventing an inner process from disintegrating. It supports an "exclusive concentrating on the center; the Self." It "expresses completeness and union."[34]

839   The hero asks to return to his parents and lets himself be carried there by his bride-to-be. There he orders that a castle be built and hides the maiden's clothes in a foundation stone. His actions here represent an attempt to transpose the soul image, as the highest value, and the union with it, into the secular sphere of consciousness, thereby the unconscious part, the anima, quickly flies away again. As in "Rakian," "The Daughter of the King Vultures," "The Visit to Heaven" and "The Witchdoctor Makanaholo," the hero attempts to follow the anima and sets out again on a quest. This, again, is achieved with

---

[32] *Ibid* p. 202 [cited as a quote from Pseudo Democritus that Berthelot translated.]
[33] On this, see the parallel representation of this motif in "The Swan Woman" and "The Young Count and the Witch's Daughter."
[34] C.G. Jung, CW 11, *Psychology and Religion* ¶156, ¶136.

the help of the old man or bird padishah, his brothers, and the Emerald Birds, and this time, all the way to the primordial [archetypal] image of the Lord of Periland, the god of the magical realm.[35] This father figure also desires to unite his daughter and the hero, and even makes allegations to her concerning her outlandish conduct. But the maiden demands to be sought, and insists that the hero follows her even if he must die on her behalf. The anima wants the hero to find her in the same place as before. She insists on the mandala center between the two kingdoms and that the hero exerts himself on her behalf! (In general, the anima problem shifts to the forefront whereas the male father figure becomes split, undifferentiated, and less important.)[36] Hardly has the hero finally obtained the anima than a counter movement again sets in. Now he wants her to visit *his* parents afresh. The result is an indecisive, swinging back and forth between consciousness and the unconscious, in which the whole adventure becomes barren and meaningless. During the return journey, the previously helpful aspect of the unconscious transforms back into destructiveness, which had earlier been embodied by the crier and his robber cohorts. At a stop in fields and meadows on the way, a wolf tears up the peri wife when she goes to wash her back. This is a repeat of the motif of bathing anima in the fountain in the rose garden, and has here the meaning of a temporary entering into the unconscious. But this time no revival of life follows, because the bathing does not take place in a closed *temenos*, but in public waters, where the powers can flow through.

840   The peri-maiden is torn to pieces by a wolf bursting forth from a nearby forest. This rapacious robber is a symbol of passion, and his demonic possession in this tale points, on the one hand, to the dark side of the anima (by being devoured, she becomes the wolf), and on the other hand, the dark counterpart to the white-bearded, helpful old man. The wolf in "Prince Hassan Pasha" helps and acts along the same lines as the voice of Allah. These are two forms of magical wolf helpers on two different levels. In "The Story of Djihanshah" there is, however, a complete split into opposites: the otherworldly power has transformed into an inner corruptor; and the hero, by remaining undecided and weeping endlessly at the place between the two kingdoms, perishes miserably. The attempt at a spiritual development of the personality has failed, and the hero, as the core of consciousness, dissolves.[37]

---

[35] On this progression, refer to the steplike journey through the three Baba Yaga figures to the anima in "The Virgin Tsar."

[36] This might also be related to the psychological particularities of the narrator's culture.

[37] In the tale "The Freeloader" the hero is torn apart by a wolf as a result of his laziness and hubris. Not the hero, but the secular ego experiences a similar end when it wants to arrogate to itself the values of the unconscious without making any efforts on its own. Thus ,the king at the end of "The Devil with the Three Golden Hairs," who originally delegated the task to the hero, oscillates endlessly back and forth. Likewise in "Murmur Goose-Egg," when the king refused to give the hero his just reward for accomplishing all the deeds that the king commissioned, the hero threw the king into the air with a backpack of provisions "and if he has not come down yet, then he, together with the knapsack, is floating

841   This is the result of a certain weakness and indecision, already foreshadowed at the beginning where the hero lets himself be duped by the robbers, in his powerlessness against the anima figure. It also manifested in his attachment to his parents that prevented him from following the counsel of the old wise one and to unite with the dove girl in the mandala center and to father a child with her. Had he followed this advice, despite the unfavorable conditions, the hero would still have had the possibility to turn the events in his favor (as, for example, in the modern Greek parallel "The Prince and the Swan Maiden." There the hero defeats the enemy of the swan maiden's father and as reward wins the hand of his daughter. He returns with his new wife to his home).

842   Thus, the hero's basic psychic structure, expressed at the outset, decisively sets the course of his fate. While the many twists and turns of real human life make such a development seem in general less succinct and like a passive rolling along, fairytales prefer to refrain from the details of the developmental process in time and space and the consequent inhibitions and new attitudes. They tend to focus on the portrayal of the archetypal – that is, the timeless – basic patterns. Thus, many fairytales are like a stripped-down statement of the inner psychological development. But there are also fairytales that present real life problems in ever new forms, similarly to dreams that circle the same fundamental problem through a repeating theme in different forms. This gives the impression of spiral, where the same basic theme is dealt with in ever deeper layers, illuminating the problem in different ways. Such repetitions can enrich the fairytale, and this is perhaps partly why fairytales – especially from the East – are often spun out into a seemingly endless string of single episodes.

---

between heaven and earth to this very day." (C. Stroebe, *Norwegian Fairy Book*, New York 1922 p. 196
The Grimm's tale "The Young Giant" ends in a similar fashion.

Chapter 15
Djulek Batür

843 An example of a meandering tale is the great quest-journey of the hero Djulek Batür. The course of the adventure in itself shows little development, although the theme here is also the search for the most precious value. This great value is represented by many different symbols, thus giving the impression of endless repetition and seemingly epic delays that manifest in a variety of images always expressing the same meaning. Formally, these seem like different fairytales just strung together, but at closer inspection the episodes are woven together in a completely meaningful way.[1]

844 Just as the dream always captures a central problem in an astonishingly well-formulated way, so the course of this tale from Tashkent (Uzbekistan) is so rich in images, the performances required by the magical so varied, the tests of obedience, behavior, courage, the suffering and struggle so luxuriantly ornamented, that the tale grows to epic proportions, abounding in colorful adventures.[2]

845 There once was an old couple who had three sons. The youngest was called Djulek Batür. The father had a mare that gave birth every year to a foal but would then inexplicably disappear on the very same night. The eldest son offered to stay up all night the next time the mare gives birth and see what happens. But he fell asleep. The next year, the second son tried and also failed. Then Djulek Batür wanted to try, but his brothers made fun of him. His father reluctantly let him try. So Djulek Batür went and watched the mare. Nothing happened and after midnight he grew sleepy. He took a knife out of his pocket, made a cut in his little finger, and scattered some salt into the wound. The burning pain did not allow him to sleep. When the mare gave birth

---

[1] The inner essence of a dream is similar to that of a fairytale. On the correspondence of a dream series to a fairytale series, see Jung:

> In dream series, the [individual] dreams are connected to one another in a meaningful way, as if they were trying to give expression to a central content from ever-varying angles. To touch this central core is to find the key to the explanation of individual dreams. It is not always easy, however, to delimit a dream series. It is a kind of monologue taking place under the cover of consciousness. (C.G. Jung, *Children's Dreams*, Princeton 2008 p. 3.)

[2] [To do it justice, the tale is translated here with only minor shortening.]

to a foal, Djulek Batür noticed that something came in from the side door and picked up the foal. The boy drew his arrow, aimed, and shot. The tail and little finger of a *div* fell to the ground.[3] Morning broke, the muezzin sang out from the minaret. Cheerfully, Djulek Batür ran to the house of his family. "Now, my son, what news do you bring?" asked the father. "Father, the mare gave birth and something entered from the side door and took the colt away. I shot an arrow and a finger of the *div* and the foal's tail fell to the ground. Go and see for yourself!" The father went to the stall and found something lying on the ground that looked like the corpse of a camel. "When this is just the little finger, how monstrous the *div* must have been! You are a good and courageous young man, my son!" and with that he slapped the boy's shoulder. Then Djulek Batür spoke up, "Father, if you allow, I would like to go and search for the foal!" "Are you crazy, my son? You are my wisdom, the whites under my pupils, the light of my face, the power of my soul, my only son. There is no relying on your brothers." But when Djulek Batür insisted his father agreed, resigned and sad. Djulek Batür baked himself some oatmeal, packed it in his knapsack, let himself be blessed by his father and mother, and took his leave. Just on his way, to his great astonishment, he saw his brothers running after him. "Whither are you going, younger brother?" They asked. "I go to fetch our horse and I will find it and bring it home." The elder brothers now thought, "When our younger brother goes off, why should we, his elder brothers, stay here?" And they decided to join him. They rode together as a threesome for a long time all over the land. Forty days and forty nights passed, and they came to a crossroads where three roads branched off. In the middle of the parting of ways stood a stone upon which it was written: "Whoever goes to the right will come back, whoever goes straight may either return or maybe not, and whoever goes to the left will surely never return." The eldest brother took the road to the right, the middle brother chose the way straight ahead, and Djulek Batür went on the third path, along which those who traveled would never return. Let

---

[3] On *divs* see Jungbauer:
Like the *jinns* [also spelled *djinns*], *divs* are a species of demons, only eviler. God created them from smoke that rose from the first fire. The *djinns* came from the flames, and the angels from the light of this fire. [The *Qu'ran* (15:27) mentions that the *jinns* are made of a smokeless and "scorching fire."] This belief of the Sartens on the origin of the *divs* betrays their origin from general Indo-European concepts of the divinity of fire and light. The Indo-European root *dev* means the light of the divinity and in Sanskrit *dewa*, is linked to *deus* [God] in Latin, and with Greek *theos*, etc... *Divs* look like a hairy devil with horns on their heads, with large bared tusks, claws on their hands and feet, and a long tail. *Divs* possess an unusual power, are often of enormous size, and are considered to be invincible. (*Märchen aus Turkestan und Tibet* p. 295.)

us now leave the elder brothers to go on their way and listen to what happened to Djulek Batür!

846   Djulek Batür went on without adjourning, without stopping, and without resting. After forty days and forty nights, he came to a hill. He looked around and saw a garden fence at three day's distance. He went off in this direction. When he reached the garden, he entered forthwith. The garden was. . . Oh, wonder of wonders!

847   There in the sunlight lay a sky-blue lake,
White roses and blood-red clover floated on its waters.
From golden trees hung fruits sweet and heavy,
Parrots perched and flew, chattering loudly all around.
And nightingales sang, so wonderfully and ever so fine,
Silken carpets invited one to enjoy gentle slumber.
And colorful embroidered pillows, soft and swollen with down lured one to recline.
It was so beautiful, so delightful – a wondrous fairytale realm.

848   Djulek Batür was exceedingly tired, he completed his washing ritual, spoke the prayers of gratitude, and lay himself down to sleep. Scarcely had his head touched the pillow than a serving maiden passed him by.

849   She had just gathered water in a golden vessel that she carried in her hand. When she saw the young man lying by the shore of the lake, she was astonished and ran to her mistress and reported,

850   Hear what I proclaim, highest fairy!
By the sky-blue lake sleeps a young man fair of face.
From whence he came, I do not know.

851   Then the *pari*[4] put on her golden shoes, drew her gossamer dress together, sharpened her rosy red lips, and made off to see the stranger herself. When she found him lying by the shore of the lake, she spoke the words:

---

[4] On the *pari*, see Jungbauer:
Usually appearing in the company of *divs, paris*. . . are friendly, helpful, but sometimes treacherous and greedy. Already in the *Zend Avesta* they come under the name *pairika* as female fiends or ogres. According to Parsi belief, with its richly-endowed demonology that offers a fruitful ground for the formation of fairytales, the *paris* are fairy-like beings who have turned away from the realm of darkness and strive towards the light. The name Fergana – the fertile valley in southeastern Turkestan [today's Uzbekistan and Tajikistan.] – was also known as *Peri*-chana (Fairyland). (G. Jungbauer, *Märchen aus Turkestan und Tibet* Jena 1923 p. 295-96.)

852

In what garden do you blossom, flower?
Over what fields do you sing, nightingale?
What lets you have no peace in your little nest?
What brings you here to this enchanted valley?
When little flies come flying here,
They immediately scorch their little wings,
Their legs burn away as they fly by,
Now a little man comes into this magical land.
How dare you? Tell me freely,
Without fear and without shame!

853

Djulek Batür replied curtly and coarsely, "First, do not talk to a person when he is hungry; second, not with one who is naked; and third, not with a tired one. I am hungry, naked, and tired. Leave this talk aside and tell me where I can get something to eat!" The *pari* spoke, "There in front of you lies a bowl with seven handles full of cooked pilaf. Just above us there is a house where you can go and eat fried mutton from seven rams. Afterwards you may go into a chamber where there are seven ovens with freshly baked bread. Eat your fill and then come outside and let us speak together!"

854

Djulek Batür immediately sat up and gobbled the pilaf from the bowl with seven handles in seven gulps. He went to the house and quaffed down the mutton from seven rams in seven chews, and then swallowed the bread from the seven ovens in seven swallows. He then scraped all the crumbs together and finished off these too. He went back out to the *pari* and said, "Oh *Pari*! Have you not somewhere hidden a piece of bread? A corner of my stomach is empty." "Oh fool," she scolded. "Have you eaten everything?" "Ach... I am still hungry! Can you not go and look?" She went up into the house and saw that there was no pilaf, no meat, and no bread anywhere. When she returned, Djulek Batür asked, "To whom does this place belong?" She answered, "The Black Div." "From whence will he come?" She spoke,

855

From there, from the steppe, in a flash,
From the island he comes, like a whirlwind.

856

Djulek Batür went to meet the *div* and hid under a bridge. Suddenly in the distance, the Black Div appeared. Chased by mighty dust clouds, he stormed forth. But when his horse came to the bridge, he stopped, stood stock still, and refused to cross. The Black Div spoke to his black steed, "Do you sense the Djulek, is that why you do not want to go over?" Then up sprang Djulek Batür, incensed because the *div* had pronounced his name so dismissively, without the second part: Batür. He cried out, "Is this Djulek you speak of, the slave of your father? What is your pleasure: shooting or wrestling?" "Your father would shoot, with you I will wrestle," answered the Black Div. He immediately jumped off his horse and fought with the young upstart. Djulek Batür lifted the *div* up in the air, dashed him to the ground with great force, and struck off his head. He cut a bushel of hair from the horse's forehead and said, "Go now, horse of my eldest brother!" Then he moved on; forty days and forty nights he wandered without resting or stopping. With God's help, he came to the foot of a white hill, tucked his shirttail under his belt, wiped the dust from his loins, and came to the edge of a spring. After completing the ablution and speaking his prayers, he went to the top of the hill and looked around. Again, he saw a garden fence. He proceeded in that direction and came to a garden. . .

857   Oh wonder of wonders!
        There in the sunlight lay a sky-blue lake,
        White roses and blood-red clove floated on its waters.

858   [This garden is described in the same verses as before. A servant maid came to fetch water. As she knelt at the lake, she spied the young man and, leaving the water vessel standing there, rushed to her *pari* mistress and reported what she had seen. A beautiful *pari* woman came again with her golden shoes and asked what he was doing there. He answered curtly and coarsely that he was hungry, naked, and tired. She again directed him to food. This time the bowl had fourteen handles, there were fourteen pieces of mutton, and fourteen loaves of bread from fourteen ovens. When he asked to whom the place belonged, she answered, "To the White Div."] "And from whence does he come?" asked Djulek Batür.

859   From there, from out of the steppe, from the island,
        In the roaring storm, he comes.
        "And one further question, *how* will he come?" asked Djulek Batür.
        In snow and ice, as cold as the winter night,
        Storming and raving, he blasts across the bridge.

860   Again, Djulek Batür hid under the bridge. Suddenly an icy cold wind arose, snow began to fall, and a great snowstorm raged. When the *div* came up to the bridge, his dogs refused to cross over and stood still. "Heh!" complained the White Div, "Why do you not want to go over the bridge, do you smell something here, like the Djulek?" Djulek Batür sprang out from his hiding place and called, complaining and challenging, "How dare you address me like that, what will you have: shooting or wrestling?" The *div* answered, "Shooting is for your father,

I shall wrestle with you." They fought furiously for three days and three nights. Finally, Djulek Batür raised the *div* in the air and threw him to the ground and cut his head off. Then he went to the *div*'s horse, kissed it on both cheeks, and said, "Go now! You will belong to my second brother!"

861 Again, Djulek Batür wandered for forty days and forty nights, and came again to the foot of a hill from which he beheld a garden fence all made of gold. He went forth and came to a splendid golden gate. He went in and lo! Oh wonder of wonders!

862 There in the sunlight lay a sky-blue lake,
White roses and blood-red clover floated on its waters.

863 The garden place is again described with the same verses as before. Djulek Batür saw a golden bower, inside a throne, and on the throne a maiden of unearthly beauty. Yet he was tired and wanted to sleep. Again a servant maid came to fetch water. As she knelt at the lake, she spied the young man and, leaving the water vessel standing there, rushed to her *pari* mistress and reported what she had seen. Again, the beautiful *pari* put on her golden shoes, primed her rosy red lips, and went to see the intruder for herself. She spoke the same verses, Djulek Batür answered in his gruff way, and she offered him forty bowls of pilaf, the meat of forty mutton, and forty loaves of bread. The young man hungrily ate all the pilaf, the meat, and the bread, and then he demanded more. She went into the house and saw that there was nothing more to eat. She went out again and spoke to the young man. Djulek Batür asked, "To whom does this place belong?" "To the Red Div." "And from whence comes the Red Div?"

864 From there, out of the steppe,
From the island he comes, in the roaring storm.
Over the bridge of copper, he crosses the sea,
The Red Div comes, bringing untold woe.

865 Djulek Batür asked one further question, "In what *form* will he come?"

866 As hot as the sun, a flaming hero, he will scorch the Earth.
And everything that moves thereupon will perish in his blazing fire.

867 Djulek Batür went and hid under the bridge. Suddenly the air became hot, the earth began to glow red, and then it burst into flame. All living things were burnt to death. The Red Div came galloping through the flames, but suddenly his steed stopped dead at the bridge. "Heh!" chided the Red Div, "Do you smell the scent of something, maybe like the Djulek, and is that why you balk at crossing the bridge?" And he

struck the horse with his whip. Djulek Batür jumped out from his hiding-place and cried out, "Is somebody like Djulek maybe the slave of your father that you speak his name so rudely? Will it be shooting or wrestling?" The Red Div sprang down from his horse and they grabbed hold on one another. The fight went on for seven days and seven nights. They wrestled like lions, they chained themselves together like tigers, they plowed up the earth like farmland. No one could throw the other. Finally, both wanted to take a drink and they let go of each other. Djulek Batür ran first to the lake and drank it dry. When the Red Div arrived, there was only one gulp left and he could not quench his thirst. Djulek Batür, fully strengthened by the water, returned strong as a lion, opened wide his arms, and grabbed the Red Div. He lifted him up and threw him onto the ground. Then he jumped upon the *div*'s chest and, with one stroke, hewed off his head.

868 "God be praised and thanked. I have reached my goal!" cried out Djulek Batür, rejoicing. He kissed the horse twice on the forehead, leaped up on its back, and rode back to the garden. There Djulek Batür remained many days with the fair *pari* maiden. Then he became homesick and began to sigh. The *pari* maiden spoke, "Oh you, how I wish I could take on your illness,[5] do you have better friends than I?" "No, but we were three brothers who set off on this journey together. One went the way of sure return, the other took the path that might bring return but might not, and I took the way from which one never returns. I have a dear mother and a dear father. I was thinking: how are they doing now? And that is why I sighed so." "Would you like to go visit them?" asked the fair *pari* maiden. "Yes," he said. He took the maiden, gathered the necessary belongings and money, and set out. On the way back to his home, he picked up the *pari* of the White Div and the *pari* of the Black Div with all their treasures, and took them along, too.

869 When Djulek Batür arrived at the crossroads where the three ways parted, he pitched three tents, waited a week for news of his brothers, then left the three *pari* maidens and rode on his pitch-black horse to look for his brothers. He first followed the path on which one would surely return and, after he had found the eldest brother, they went on the path from which one may or may not return. They came to a city and in the bazaar found his second brother selling bits of bread.

---

[5] A common figure of speech expressing the greatest love, as when one is prepared to take on the illness of their loved one to make him or her well again. (G. Jungbauer, *Märchen aus Turkestan und Tibet*, Jena 1923 p. 95.)

Djulek Batür took him in, bought him beautiful clothes and the three returned to the crossroads to the tents, horses and treasures.

870   The two elder brothers had recognized each other back at the bazar. Now they saw the magnificent tents, the uncountable treasures, and the horses numbering as many as sheep dung. Tied to six posts were six heroic *bide*[6] that restlessly circled the posts and trampled the ground. Evening fell and the three *pari* maidens brought three bowls of pilaf and placed them in front of the brothers. During the meal, Djulek Batür asked the men, "Tell me, from whence do you come?" The eldest brother answered, "I come from such and such city, and the second brother said, "I come from such and such city." Djulek Batür then asked, "And why did you come to this land?" They said, "When we first came here, we were three brothers. Right at this crossroads we parted ways. One of us went along the way from which one would surely return, the other upon the way which one may or may not return, and our youngest brother went on the path from which there is no return. Now two of us are back here where the ways parted. We do not know if our youngest brother lives or not."

871   Then Djulek Batür revealed himself to the amazed brothers by showing them the wart on his forehead and on his back the mark of Saint Ali's fingers. While Djulek Batür slept in the tent with the *pari* maidens, the elder brothers discussed how they could harm him and they could return to their father wealthy and as the performers of heroic deeds. They tied the sword to the tent, sharp edge inwards, mounted two horse and rode past the tent crying "Djulek Batür, wake up! Thieves have taken all your things and are riding away with them!"

872   Djulek Batür awoke abruptly from a sweet sleep, ran out the tent entrance and both his legs were cut off by the sharp sword. Lying moaning on the ground and with doleful cry, he called out, "Ach, my brothers, you have done your work and I lie here helpless! Slaughter two horses, put the meat in the skin of one and from the other skin make a *turzuk* (water hose) and fill it with water." The brothers did as he requested, slaughtered the two horses they had ridden, put the meat of one in the skin of the other and from the skin of the second they made a *turzuk* and filled it with water. They laid this on the ground next to Djulek Batür, took the three *pari* maidens and all the tents and treasures, and moved on.

---

[6] [Mares that had never given birth and were, therefore, light and fast of foot, counted among the best of horses. *Ibid* p. 98.]

873   He laid and laid and laid there. At one time he thought he saw a blind man pursuing a *saiga*.[7] Sometimes the *saiga* ran in front of the blind man, sometimes the blind man ran in front of the *saiga*. Djulek Batür called out, "You blind one, if you want to eat some meat, then come to me!" The blind one came, ate some meat, and remained with Djulek Batür. Some time went by. Then Djulek Batür saw a man without arms who could see. He was running, chasing a *saiga*, but without any luck. Djulek Batür called out to him, "Oh you armless seeing one, if you would like to eat some meat, then come here!" This one came too. Djulek Batür shot the *saiga* with an arrow. Together, they prepared the catch and ate.

874   One day, Djulek Batür said, "The way we live here really makes no sense." They took counsel on what they should do. The blind one and the armless one spoke to Djulek Batür, "You are the eldest, do what you think is best." Djulek Batür told them to go into the city, find a girl, a kettle, and household items. The two went into the city and brought back a girl, a kettle, and the other things. There they lived together as a foursome and called the girl, who took care of the household chores, "Sister." One day they brought the sister a cat and told her that even if she had one last breadcrumb left, she must share it with the cat. She promised to do this. The three men went off to hunt and the girl remained at their home.

875   The maiden searched all over the living room and found a raisin. She called the cat, but the animal did not come. She called again, but still no cat. So, then she ate the raisin herself. But suddenly the cat came meowing and asked, "What is it that are you eating?" The girl answered, "I am eating nothing." "When you have nothing to eat, then why did you call me? Look, you are still chewing something!" said the cat. The girl replied, "I found a raisin and called you, but you did not come. I called again and you still did not come, so I ate the raisin myself." The cat became very angry, and to make sure that the brothers beat the girl when they came back, it ran to the stove, dug up the ashes, urinated on the burning coals, so the fire was quenched. Then it ran out of the hut with its tail raised.

876   When the time came for the men to return, the sister prepared the kettle to cook pilaf for her brothers. But when she went to blow on the coals, she saw that they were cold. She then went up on the roof of the house and looked all around. In the distance, she spotted smoke

---

[7] [A kind of antelope once common across the steppes of Uzbekistan and Mongolia, now almost extinct.]

rising and made off in that direction. The smoke came from the entrance to a large cave. The maiden went to the cave. There she saw a large courtyard and, in the middle, a monstrous, ghastly old woman, who was roasting lice in a kettle with forty handles and then gobbling them up. "*As-salam alaikum*, dear Mother," greeted the maiden. "*Wa salam alaikum as salam!*"[8] responded the old one. "You are lucky that you greeted me thus. Were it not proper, I would have bent you into two pieces and swallowed you in one bite!" The maiden then asked, "Could you spare me a glowing coal?" The old one said, "First, louse my hair twice, my head is itching terribly!" The old woman laid her head on the knees of the girl, but then suddenly grabbed her, bit into her leg and began greedily to suck her blood. Afterwards she said, "Oh, that was delicious, my Daughter," and gave her a handful of roasted lice and also a piece of glowing coal. As the young girl went home, the lice fell out of her breast pocket so that all were dispersed by the time she got home. But at the places where the lice fell, bushes grew up, and thus marked the way. The girl took the coal, kindled the fire, and cooked the pilaf so that it was ready for the three men when they returned in the evening.

877   The next morning, the brothers again went forth to hunt, but around noontime the old woman came and asked the girl, "Now, my Daughter, what are you doing?" "Nothing," said the girl. "Then louse my head two times!" said the old hag. The maiden went through the old woman's hair but that one threw the dress of the girl up and began greedily to suck her blood again. Then she went away. So it went for many days. Each time the brothers went away, the old hag would come and suck the girl's blood. One evening, Djulek Batür noticed that the girl's face was pallid and white. He asked her, "Sister, what happened to you? You are deathly pale!" "Nothing has happened," the girl said. "When nothing has happened, then you should be red and fat from the meat of the saiga we have brought." "No, really, nothing has happened," repeated the girl. But Djulek Batür then spoke more strongly, "I will kill you if you do not tell me. Did one of the brothers or somebody else abuse you?" The girl told him everything that happened, exactly and truthfully. Djulek Batür instructed the seeing armless one to stay in the hut and catch the old woman when she returned and then to call him. The old woman came, threw herself at the armless man and sucked out his blood. He complained to Djulek Batür about what happened. Then Djulek Batür appointed the blind

---

[8] [The appropriate Arabic greeting and the proper response, equivalent to "May peace be upon you," "And unto you be peace."]

man to stand guard. But the old woman came and sucked the blood from the blind man putting her head on his knee.

878 Then Djulek Batür spoke, "We will have to do it another way. You two go to a certain place, there is a pit there. Hide in that pit. When the old hag comes, I will grab her and call out. Then come immediately!" And to the sister he said, "Heat up some water in the kettle and begin to wash my shirt. When the old one comes in, then say to her, 'Dear Mother, when I go to fetch water, there is no one who puts wood on the fire, and when I put wood on the fire, there is no one to fetch water. Bring me water and lay wood on the fire!' But first, dig a hole just behind the door!" The girl dug a pit behind the door and Djulek Batür climbed in and told the girl to cover him with twigs. It was noontime when the old hag came. The girl stood up and said, "*As salam alaikum*, dear Mother! My eyes have been looking all the time for somebody to come. When I go to fetch water, there is nobody here to put wood on the fire and when I watch the fire, then there is nobody to go fetch water. Give me two pitchers of water and put some wood on the fire!" The old one went to the stove. Then Djulek Batür crept out of his hiding place. The old one cried out "*Ainaljai*,[9] Long have I searched for you and could never find you." But he grabbed her and held her tight. He took his sword in one hand and dragged her by the hair out of the house and tied her by her hair to forty posts. Then he called for the blind one who had hands and the armless one who could see, and the sister, who had run away.

879 Then Djulek Batür ordered the old hag first to swallow the girl. This she did. Then he ordered her to let the sister out again. She let her out. The sister was transformed into a beautiful *pari*, her countenance was a mirror image of the sun. Then Djulek Batür ordered the old woman to swallow the blind one who had hands and then to let him out again. This she did. The blind one came out and could see. Then Djulek Batür commanded her to swallow the armless one and then to let him out again. This she also did and the armless one came out with two healthy arms. Then Djulek Batür spoke, "Now, brothers and sister, all three of you take a sword in your hand! When she swallows me and refuses to let me out again, then immediately cut off her head and slice her whole body into pieces. If you hesitate even a tiny bit, she will digest me!" They all promised. Then Djulek Batür ordered the old woman to swallow him. This she did. But then she did not want to let him out again. "Let him out!" all three cried out. But the old woman remained

---

[9] "I love you." (G. Jungbauer, *Märchen aus Turkestan und Tibet*, Jena 1923 p. 104, footnote 1.)

sitting stiffly with gaping eyes. And then the three all together lifted their swords up and struck off her head. Then they cut her body up into pieces. But nowhere was Djulek Batür to be seen! They looked all over. Then they heard a little voice calling out, "Little finger, little finger!" Immediately they cut open the little finger and out stepped a completely healthy Djulek Batür with two perfectly good legs. But the head of the old hag rolled away and cried out, threatening incessantly, "I will get you yet, I will get you yet!" Djulek Batür ran after the head but it disappeared into a deep well. The three held counsel on what to do. Then Djulek Batür told the one-who-had-been-blind to take a sword and tie himself to a rope and they would let him slowly down into the well. "I will do this," he said. They tied a rope around his middle and let him down. But he had not reached halfway when he was overcome with heart palpitations from fear of the darkness. With all his life power he called out, "Oh I am dying! Oh pain, I am burning up!" And they pulled him up again. Then Djulek Batür said to the one-who-now-had-arms, "You are no longer without hands, you can certainly let yourself be lowered without panicking." "That I will do." He tied the rope around his belt, took the sword and let himself be lowered down. He was not yet at the middle and began to scream pathetically, "Help the helpless, help!" And so they pulled him back out. Djulek Batür became irate and decided to take the job on himself. He said, "If I also start to cry out, 'I am dying,' or 'I am burning up,' then do not pull me out! And when I finally get to the bottom and give the top a shake, then pull up everything that I have tied to it!" He shut his eyes tightly and let himself be lowered into the well.

880   Djulek Batür reached the bottom and opened his eyes. When his eyes grew accustomed to the darkness, he spied a hollow cavity with a dome. When he looked closer, he discovered a small door. He opened it and entered into a golden hall in the middle of which sat a *pari* next to a cradle. In the cradle lay the head of the old hag and the *pari* was rocking the head. Djulek Batür called out, "Ai, beautiful *pari*, what are you doing there?" "Nothing," she said. "Is that so? Is that which is in the cradle really nothing?" he asked. The *pari* said, "Somebody killed the old woman. If I rock the cradle for forty days, then the old one will become alive and complete again. Then she will destroy the murderer and his whole family up to the fortieth member." "Aha! In that case I will help you," said Djulek Batür. He could hear how the head babbled, "I will get you, I will get you yet!" Djulek Batür grabbed the head by the hair, twisted it around his hand and bashed it with all his power to the ground. Then he took his sword and cut it up into tiny pieces until no trace of the head remained. Djulek Batür looked

at the *pari* and asked her, "What do you say now?" She answered, "May your illnesses be mine! What more can I say? You are mine and I am yours. God has forced me to wait for uncountable years in this well. But now He has given me my beloved!"

881 With these words she led Djulek Batür into her inner chambers. But he did not want to lose any time and spoke, "You must know that three people, my two brothers and my sister, are waiting for me. I cannot spend any time with you here." The *pari* said, "Good! Let them pull us up and I will follow you." But Djulek Batür was mistrustful and worried that she would not come after him. Then she spoke, "Ai, Djulek Batür, may your disbelief dry up! Be careful! If I come up first and your brothers see me, then they will not pay any more attention to you. If they no longer lower the rope back down to you, then go in this door, into a chamber in which two horses are standing. If you mount the white horse, you will ride into the upper world, if you sit upon the raven black horse, you will fall through seven layers of the earth into the underworld." Djulek Batür tied the rope around a box in which the *pari* sat and shook the rope. The bothers pulled the box up. When they saw the box, they were very curious and immediately opened it. They beheld the *pari*! Her forehead shone like the full moon, her eyes were as two shining suns, her beauty was so radiant that it could illuminate the darkest of all rooms. In their wonderment the brothers forgot all about Djulek Batür. Each one of them wanted to possess the *pari* and they engaged in a bitter dispute. Then the *pari* maiden took a clump of earth, blew on it, spoke the highest names of God, and threw the clump far away. Immediately it transformed into a high earthen wall. She then picked up a stone and said, "Whoever can throw this stone over the wall, to him I will belong."

882 Let us take leave of them at that place, with their trouble throwing the stones, and look at what happened to Djulek Batür.

883 Djulek Batür waited at the bottom of the well and saw that the rope did not come down for him. He waited some more, but the rope still did not come down. "Look at that! It has happened just like the *pari* said," he spoke to himself. He turned and went to the horses. With a strong jerk, he opened the door wide, two dragon-like horses menacingly stretched their muzzles out towards him. Djulek Batür was not afraid and jumped onto the white horse. But the horse collapsed beneath him. Then he mounted the pitch-black horse. This one leapt head over heels and galloped off through seven layers of the Earth and descended into the Underworld.

884 There, Djulek Batür came upon an old man in a field plowing with oxen. "*As salam alaikum*, dear Father," greeted Djulek Batür. "*Wa alaikum as salam*," answered the old one, and added, "Oh, misfortune, oh dire need!" "What are you missing, dear Father?" asked Djulek Batür. "Shhh, shhh, my Son, speak very quietly!" warned the old man. "What is going on here, Father?" Djulek Batür again asked. Then the old one whispered back, "Look, my Son, there are two tigers here and when they hear our voices, they will come and eat our cattle." Djulek Batür responded, "Dear Father, do you accept me as your guest?" The old grey one answered, "Oh yes, my dear Son! That I would like very much to do. A guest is a gift from God." Whereupon Djulek Batür replied, "Good, Father! I have been wandering many days without eating, I am very hungry. Bring me from your house a bowl of groats and two cakes of bread! In the meantime, when you are fetching the food, I will slowly plow the fields with your oxen." "Good, my Son," answered the old man, "drive them slowly onwards and meanwhile I will go to the house and fetch you something to eat."

885 Djulek Batür took the ploughman's rod and drove the oxen. After some thirty steps, he began to yell loudly at the oxen, "Heeya, heeya! Move it, move on, my Cattle!" After he had plowed the field once in the even, and once in the odd direction, two young tigers appeared and threatened to eat and drink everything up. But Djulek Batür let the oxen off the reigns and took the two tigers by their ears and harnessed them to the plow. Then he drove them on, scolding and beating them with the rod. "Are you the ones," he cried out with another bash of his rod, "who do not let the people have the time to blink and come and eat their cattle?"

886 Before the old man had brought the bowl of groats, Djulek Batür had plowed the whole field three times, and even the fields of neighboring people. When the old man returned and saw the strange plow team, he stood still, amazed, and did not trust to come closer. Djulek Batür called out, "Come, dear Father, you need not be afraid!" The old man saw the oxen grazing peacefully and the sweat-drenched tigers standing obediently in front of the plow. "By the will of God, my Son, what have you done here?" he called out, amazed. Djulek Batür replied, "Oh Father, may God grant you health!" Then the old one said, "My Son, you are a courageous youth!" Djulek Batür left the plow and went to eat. Before doing this, Djulek Batür had charged the tigers to leave the old one, his descendants, and all his neighbors in peace. He let them go with the words, "If you do not let the people here live in peace and work their fields in peace and quiet, then no matter how

far away I am, I will know it and come and crush your skulls and destroy all your progeny and your whole species." After he had eaten, the old man spoke, "Request of me whatever you want!" "Oh Grandfather, what should I ask of Thee? Just tell me where may I find the way to the light upper world?" Then the old man answered, "That, my dear Son, I unfortunately do not know myself. Go to the king of this land, maybe he can tell you."

887 Then Djulek Batür went to the king of that land. On the way he saw a how a man tied up a maiden and a sheep, put them inside a black tent, and how the man then ran away. Djulek Batür went to the tent. But there the maiden spoke out, "Youth, my life is at its end! I am destined to die! That is why they have brought me here. But you should not perish for my sake. Return to the place from whence you came." Djulek Batür asked, "Why did that man tie you up and put you in this tent?" She answered, "A terrible dragon ravages and devastates this land of my father. Every day we must sacrifice a virgin to this dragon. Now there are no longer any virgins left in our country but I. So now I must be sacrificed." Then spoke Djulek Batür, "I want to see him with my own eyes. But I have not slept in a long time. Let me lie on your knees and rest a bit. When the dragon comes, then wake me up!"

888 Djulek Batür laid down on the knees of the girl and slept deeply. Soon the dragon approached. He had eyes like torches, and with his scorching breath, annihilated everything in his path.[10] No matter how hard she tried, the maiden could not awaken Djulek Batür. She became terrified and shed bitter tears. These fell on Djulek Batür's eyelids and because of their bitterness he awoke. Springing up, he called out, "What is it?" The girl pointed to the dragon, "There! There!" "When he comes," thought Djulek Batür, "then we are ready," and he went out of the tent and dressed his sword. There stood the dragon and with one snort he sucked Djulek Batür into his mouth. Djulek Batür went down the dragon's throat and came right out his other end. But during his passage through the dragon, Djulek Batür had held out his sword and had sliced the dragon into two halves. He took a strip of the dragon's skin and gave it to the virgin as a bag and then he lay down on her knees for another deep sleep.

889 In the meantime, the girl's father, the king, wanted to send someone out to find out what happened to his sacrificed daughter, but no one dared to go there. Then the king commanded his ministers to find a

---

[10] Jungbauer notes, "For the people of Iran and neighboring lands. . . the dragon by its breath can draw in animals from afar, and they fall by themselves into his throat. Then the dragon winds itself around a large tree stump or stone and thus crushes the bones of the swallowed animals." (*Ibid* pp. 296-97.)

man who lived in the royal city, known as a coward, and to tie him with a rope forty ellen long to a horse and send him out to reconnoiter. The coward who was tightly tied to the horse wept loudly and held up a sword in his trembling hand. He came shaking in fear upon the dead dragon and poked around with his sword. Once convinced that the dragon was indeed dead, he cut off a piece of flesh and rushed back to the king and requested a *sujintsi* for bringing the joyful news. But the king then demanded that he bring his daughter. The coward then went and fetched the girl. The king erected a tent for the marriage of the coward and his rescued daughter. The girl asked, "Father, what are you doing here?" He answered, "I want to marry you to the one who killed the dragon!" "But Father," she cried out, "The one who really killed the dragon is lying motionless asleep by the black tent." Then the king sent for Djulek Batür and offered him his daughter in marriage. But our hero spoke, "What should your daughter bring me?" The king responded, "I will give you my kingdom and all that I possess." "What should I do with all your possessions and your kingdom?" "Then ask me for whatever you want!" Djulek Batür hastened to respond, "Now know what I ask: send me back into the upper light world!" Then the king answered, "Neither I nor any of my people can do this. Only Simurgh can do this.[11] This bird has its nest in a plane tree up there under that mountain near a spring."

890   Djulek Batür rode to the indicated plane tree, dismounted from his horse, and rested beneath the tree. There he fell asleep from the exhaustion of the past days. Suddenly he was awakened by the fearful cries of the Simurgh's nestlings. "Tchirr-prr, tchrr-prr!" He raised his head and saw a dragon which was creeping up the tree with snakelike movements. Djulek Batür jumped up, drew his sword, and struck the beast, cutting it into pieces. He threw the meat to the Simurgh's nestlings. The little birds ate everything up but the head, which they put aside for their mother. Then the Simurgh bird came flying towards its nest and saw something lying under the plane tree. She believed it was the dragon that comes to devour her chicks each year but the fledglings presented her with the dragon's head. Simurgh ate the head, flew down from the plane tree and held her wings over the head of Djulek Batür so that he could sleep peacefully in the shade. He slept for seven days and seven nights. When he awoke, he saw something like a black roof over his head. That was Simurgh who immediately spoke up, "My son, fear not! Rather ask of me whatever you want!"

---

[11] The simurgh is the Iranian phoenix, known also to the Turkic people of Central Asia; a female, benevolent, mythical bird, like the German griffin, or the Barunda bird of the Hindus. (*Ibid* p. 296.)

Djulek Batür responded without pleasantry, "If that is the case, then I wish that you fly me to the upper, light world."

891 Then Simurgh cried out, "Oh my child, you have chosen my weakest side! You have given me a difficult task. But since you have done me a good deed, I will fulfill your wish. Go and slaughter forty fat horses, bring the flesh from all forty in the skins of twenty and stitch from the other twenty horses skin sacks and fill them with water." After Djulek Batür had prepared everything, Simurgh spoke, "Now put everything on my back! When I ask for water, you must give me water, and when I ask for meat, you must give me a piece of meat."

892 When everything was ready, they took off. Simurgh rose high up and flew, and flew, and flew. Then she asked for water and Djulek Batür gave her meat. When she asked for meat, Djulek Batür gave her water. And so it went, back and forth. Then the meat was all eaten up but the entrance to the light world was still a spear's throw distant. Simurgh asked again for meat. Djulek Batür spoke, "I wish not that we fall," and cut a piece of meat from his own loin and gave it to the bird. Simurgh ate the meat and flew into the upper world and set Djulek Batür down and asked, "When I requested meat, you gave me water; when I asked for water, you gave me meat. And what kind of meat did you give me just before the last stretch? Tell me the truth, or I will throw you down into a place more sinister than where you were before!" Then Djulek Batür spoke, "Yes, you asked for meat and I gave water, you requested water and I gave you meat. When we were close to the end and the meat was all gone, I cut a piece of my own flesh and gave it to you." Uncover yourself, I want to see for myself," commanded Simurgh. Djulek Batür showed her his loin. Simurgh put a piece of meat, which she had kept under her tongue at the place where Djulek Batür had cut from himself. She licked it and his wound grew together. Then said the bird, "Go now and may God guide you well."

893 Djulek Batür now went to the well into which his brothers and sister had let him down and looked around. The sister was in the meantime returned to her homeland. He saw the two men trying to throw a stone over a wall, but they could not do it. The third person was sitting there and watching them. Djulek Batür went closer and asked, "My good youths, what are you doing here?" They answered, "The *pari* promised herself to him who throws a stone over the wall, but we have not managed to do that yet." "Wait," said Djulek Batür, "Let us see if I can." He picked up a stone and threw. It flew three ellen [cubits] higher than the wall and fell down behind. "And now what, my good youths?"

894   They responded, "For us, promised is promised; the *pari* belongs to you." Upon which Djulek Batür asked, "Then why did you come here?" They answered, "We had a brother named Djulek Batür, through whose help we regained our eyesight and arms. He let himself down into the well on a rope and there he found the *pari* and sent her up. We were blinded by her beauty and could do nothing but try to win her for ourselves and forgot our brother." "Would you now recognize him if you saw him?" asked Djulek Batür. He drew his sword and called out, "Shall I now strike the both of you down on the spot? What evil have I done unto you, that you never let the rope back down in the well? But since we so long lived together and shared bread and salt with one another, I will let you free. Go from whence you came!"

895   Djulek Batür took the *pari* and went with her to his home. They wandered long and far. After many days and many nights, they came into his homeland, and went to the house of his father. There they saw preparations for a great feast. Forty kettles were standing at forty places. He asked a man there for what occasion the feast was planned. He received the answer, "The brothers of Djulek Batür brought back three *pari*s from the way from which one will never return. They wished to make the *pari*s their wives, but the *pari*s asked for a period of grace. Today is the end of this grace period and tonight they will celebrate their marriage." "Wait, I will first heat up the kettles a bit more," said Djulek Batür. He took some tongs. But instead of sandalwood beneath the kettles, he put the man in the fire. Before one could say *ana man*[12] he had thrown forty people into the forty fires. The other people spoke broke into uproar, and all fled.

896   The old father, who was sitting in a corner, was blind. Djulek Batür drew saliva from his mouth and moistened his father's eyes, and his father could see the light again. His mother was also blind. Again, Djulek Batür drew saliva and wetted her eyes and she could see again, too. After they had greeted one another weeping in joy, Djulek Batür asked, "What has happened here?" The father answered, "Your brothers told us they went on the way from which one would not return, destroyed the *div*, and thus gained great wealth and riches. But Djulek Batür, who had gone down the way from which one returns, found nothing."

897   Djulek Batür called for his two brothers and spoke, "Be well, my dear brothers! Truly, that must have been a surprise for you, to have indeed

---

[12] ["That's it." *Ibid* p. 115.]

come back on the path from which one does not return, you invincibly strong guys! Did I sell bread cakes at the bazar?" he asked, turning to face his middle brother. "Did I sit at the oven of the *Kaljanaz* and tend the fire, day after day, for a few crumbs of groat, and drink dishwater to survive?" He asked his eldest brother, "Do you not fear God, and shame yourself before the people? You sliced off the legs of a man like me, who had done you so much good, and left him for a merciless death out on the steppe." He spoke further, "Father, whomever shoots from this bow into the centre of the target, is the one telling the truth and is in the right. Whomever is lying and in the wrong, they will kill themselves. Thus, we will decide the case and in this way no one can raise a complaint against me." The father agreed to Djulek Batür's suggestion and spoke, "Good, my sons, shoot!" The eldest brother took the bow and arrow and shot. The arrow missed the center, turned around, and hit him in the forehead. He fell down dead on the spot. "Shoot!" said Djulek Batür to his middle brother. This one took the bow and arrow and shot. But this arrow missed the target, also turned and came back, and killed him too.

898   Djulek Batür now celebrated his own marriage to the *pari* and gave a feast that lasted forty days and forty nights at which all the people of the land regaled and delighted. Thus, he had reached his goal and found luck in life.

899   May the good reach its goal but the evil find its dishonor. May we all also reach our goals! Amen, King of the worlds![13]

900   At the outset of this epic fairytale, we have again the quaternity of a father and his three sons. (The figure of the mother is scarcely mentioned and can be overlooked in this context.) The father, who embodies the prevailing dominant conscious attitude, is blind, the youngest son enters the scene and becomes the redeemer of the entire personality. Djulek Batür's generally blunt, gruff, and coarse behavior reveals that he represents the least-developed function.

901   The *div's* theft of the foal from the stable of his father corresponds to the robbery of the apples in "The Golden Bird" and, as in that tale, symbolizes an invasion of the unconscious into the sphere of the conscious personality, a loss of the soul; but it is also a calling, an evocation, to embark upon a quest.

902   Again, it is only the youngest son who does not let himself be overcome by sleepiness or the unconscious. That is, the fourth function is most likely to

---

[13] For a similar long saga, see the Latvian tale "Kurbads" about a folk hero who was born magically from a white mare and performed many great deeds. This narrative contains variations on many of the motifs occurring in "Djulek Batür." L. Frobenius, *Zeitalter*, Berlin 1904 p. 33, writes on the subject of mythical and fairytale heroes not always representing historical events and personalities.

succeed in perceiving hints and subtle indications in the dim light of the unconscious and in forwarding them to consciousness. Djulek Batür cut his own finger in order to stay awake, demonstrating his willingness to make sacrifices. The robber turns out to be a *div*, whose little finger the hero shoots off with an arrow. Fingers embody creative formative power. This is why the Greek Dactyls, [literally "fingers," δα´κτμλοι] who were archaic dwarves and forger deities, were the first teachers of Orpheus and inventors of the Ephesian magical formulae and musical rhythms.[14] According to widespread superstition, the little finger is the seat of secret knowledge. Thus, Djulek Batür had received on his back a mark of the five fingers of the holy saint Ali like a prophecy of his quest into the unconscious.

903   The meaning of the crossroads where the brothers separate corresponds to the one in "The Virgin Tsar" and "Prince Hassan Pasha." As in those tales, Djulek Batür also chooses the path of death. The arrangement of the paths is, however, somewhat different than in other tales. The way to death is on the left, that is, it leads deepest into the unconscious, while in "The Virgin Tsar" it is the middle one that leads straight into the conflict.[15] After a certain complete time (expressed here by the number forty), the hero arrives at a hill that divides the border area from the innermost-magical, and from there he reaches a garden surrounded by a fence, a sign of another differentiation. Forty is a common number in fairytales from central Asia and consists of 10 x 4, where ten, like four, signifies wholeness or completion.[16] Ten indicates the quaternity (here in a diversity) and wholeness. The enclosed garden is a mandala, and thus a symbol of the Self. It is regarded by Muslims as an image of the place of heavenly joys. The 88th surah of the *Qu'ran* describes the garden of the blessed and may have served as a model for the verses of the story:

904   In it there is a flowing spring,
       In it are couches raised high,
       Goblets set in place,
       Cushions, in rows closely intertwined,
       And colorful carpets, all spread out.[17]

---

[14] See C.G. Jung, CW 5, *Symbols of Transformation* ¶183 and ¶136. On the importance of the little finger in particular, see J. J. Bachofen, *Mutterrecht*, Stuttgart 1861 p. 130f. Cf. also the tale from the Bakairi people of South America "Keri and Kame" in which the mother becomes pregnant with the hero brothers by swallowing finger bones. See also tales in which the heroes learn the language of birds or gain other wisdom from putting a finger in their mouths, for example Sigurd (Siegfried) and Gwion Bach in the *Taliesin* legend, C. Guest, *Mabinogion*, London/New York (1906) 1937 p. 263. See in general, J. Bolte and L. Mackensen, *Handwörterbuch* Berlin 1930, under *Finger*.

[15] That the path to the right is the path to death in "Prince Hassan Pasha" may be due to a corrupt tradition, unless the motif in this form is not founded in local beliefs.

[16] For more on ten in Iranian traditions, see G. Hüsing, *Iranische*, Leipzig 1909 pp. 23–33.

[17] *Qu'ran* verses 12–16. There is a rhymed German translation given in G. Jungbauer, *Turkestan*, Jena 1923 p. 307.

905 A piece of Arabic love poetry has found its way into this unusually poetic description of the garden, with its hidden, mystical-religious content.[18] The *pari*'s warning about naive mystical devotion to the vision of paradise and self-abandonment to love-death is at the same time a warning of the danger lurking behind the magical aspect of the anima. The love garden of the *paris*, where the limbs of all humans and animals are burned, is the same as the witch's garden in "The Beautiful Dunye" but here viewed in the negative sense. For this reason, Djulek Batür meets the *pari* with his self-confident coarseness and stresses his earthly needs to counter a dissolution into ecstasy. Thus, like the way in which Ivan Tsarevich in "The Virgin Tsar" acts towards the Baba Yaga figures, Djulek Batür shows himself in this tale as master over the powers of the unconscious.

906 Djulek Batür's great appetite is a markedly demonic trait,[19] which characterizes him as a hero, which according to his essence is a human personification of the Self. Eating means "to-take-into-one's-self," to ingest, assimilate, incorporate, and integrate unconscious powers or forces projected onto the outer world. An Egyptian pyramid text tells how this large increase in power occurs; the arrival of the dead prince in heaven is described as follows:

907 The sky weeps, the stars quiver, the warders of the gods tremble and their servants flee when they see the king arise as a spirit, as a god who lives on his fathers and takes possession of his mothers. His servants have caught the gods with a lasso, have found them good and dragged them forward, bound them, cut their throats, and taken out their entrails, have cut them in pieces and boiled them in hot cauldrons. The king devours their magic power and eats their souls. The great gods are his breakfast, the medium gods his midday meal, the lesser gods his supper, and the old gods and goddesses he uses as fuel. The king devours everything that comes in his way. He swallows all greedily, and his magic power becomes greater than all magic. He is an inheritor of might more than all other inheritors; he becomes the lord of heaven, for he ate all the crowns and all the armbands, he ate the wisdom of every god.[20]

---

[18] On the image of the fly which burns itself in the light, see Goethe's poem, inspired by the Persian poet Hafiz, *West-Eastern Divan* (or "Book of the Singer"), "Tell it, the wise alone … " [that is, "the wise alone speak of it"], Goethe, *West-Eastern*, London & Toronto 1904 p. 19.

[19] See Jungbauer's note to "Djulek Batür": "Great appetite [overeating] is otherwise a characteristic of witches, giants, and demonic beings." *Op. cit.* p. 307. See also the many tales in which the hero has a great appetite, for instance in "Knos," "Murmur Goose-Egg," and "Fionn and Lorcán."

[20] A. Wiedemann, *The Realms of the Egyptian Dead*, London 1902 pp. 31–32. See also, A. Dieterich, *Eine Mithrasliturgie*, Leipzig and Berlin 1923 p. 105. See the same text in another wording in G. Roeder, *Urkunden*, Jena 1923 p. 191ff; also, L. Lévy-Bruhl, *How Natives Think*, New York 1966 p. 264. On the eating and drinking traits of the god Thor, see E. Mogk, *Germanische*, Berlin and Leipzig 1927 p. 87.

908   Eating as a test of heroism is evident in the tale "The Two Brothers" where,

909

> There were once two brothers, the younger was a cunning and courageous hero, the elder one also, but he was slighter and had a good heart. The younger went out into the world "looking for fear" and came to a shepherd who told him that if he were a hero then he should be able to eat an oven full of bread and drink a kettle full of milk. The younger brother tried but could not manage and later was devoured by the dragon mother. The elder brother then set out to find his younger brother, successfully passed the eating and drinking test of the shepherd, and moreover ate all the apples and pears in the garden of the mother dragon. She invited him into her kitchen and asked him to help blow the fire to heat the kettle. In contrast to his younger brother, who followed the dragon mother and was eaten by her, this brother retorted, "Since when is the custom to ask a guest to blow in the fire, aren't you ashamed to use me as a bellows?" The mother dragon replied, "Don't you see we have no servants, blow into the fire just a little bit!" But the hero took his battle club and smashed her into two pieces and freed his brother.[21]

910   Psychologically this shows – especially in the pyramid text quoted above – that the kernel of the new conscious personality gains more and more power and attracts the scattered forces of the unconscious to itself and develops into a superhuman being.

911   The elemental or unbridled nature of the hero is a motif in many fairytales.[22] This is evident in Ivan Tsarevich's rudeness towards the Baba Yaga figures in "The Virgin Tsar," in Seaghan's rough awkwardness in "The Great Fool from Cuasan," and in the hero's behavior in the Latvian tale "Strong Hans." A particularly dramatic example is found in the Norwegian tale, "Aspenclog," in which the hero, the son of an aspen tree, enters into the service of a king but with his unbridled strength he performs the tasks assigned to him with such ferocity that it spells the end of the king himself. He even intimidates the devil and ultimately smashes the king to pieces. This tale shows to some extent the negative aspect of heroism as raw, primitive violence. The same unconscious forces that drive humans to higher consciousness can erupt as undomesticated emotions and destroy the personality from within.

---

[21] Translated as summarized from W. Aichele, *Zigeunermärchen*, Jena 1926 pp. 174–176.

[22] For instance, the Grimm's "The Young Giant" and the variations thereof in J. Bolte and G. Polívka, *Anmerkungen*, Vol. 2, Leipzig 1915 p. 285ff, also "Hans One and a Half" (the name refers to the hero's excessive strength), "God's Son-In-Law and the Judge," "Rustam," "The Prometheus Legend" (Akhanazi-Georgia), "The Prometheus Legend" (Georgia), "The Prometheus Legend" (Svanetian), "The Mare's Baby," "The Ox's Son," "Ivanko the Bear's Son" and "Baldak Borisievich."

However, tamed and subjected to conscious reason, they can also successfully counter the demonic sides of the unconscious, as with Djulek Batür.

912   In "Djulek Batür" there now follows the battles with the *div*s where the hero defeats one after another, a black, a white, and a red *div*.[23] The first *div* is like a dark wind of the steppe that comes from an island, the second is a personification of winter, and the third is the scorching summer heat of the sun. Thus, all these *div*s are characterized as nature demons. The island *div* is reminiscent of the figure of Balor in "Balor and the Birth of Lugh." The order of colors: black, white, and red, and also these colors individually, have a far-reaching symbolic significance. Black has since ancient times been the color of mourning and renunciation.[24] It is often assigned to the chthonic gods of the dead and nocturnal demons. [25]Thus, the "Black One" is a name of the devil.[26] In ancient Egyptian religion, Seth, as a black pig, injures the eye of Horus.[27] The black *div* thus embodies the unconscious as something still dark, undefinable. As wind he indicates in particular the mental and emotional aspect. The *div* is like a storm of dark passions, which were aroused by the image of the *pari*. This is the reason why Djulek Batür so rudely and coarsely rejects the sensual advances of the lovely maiden.

913   The white *div* is, corresponding to its color, the opposite pole of the black *div* and is, therefore, secretly identical to it. The contrast black-white, which attends so many forms of the unconscious as a double aspect,[28] in general signifies the light and dark sides of the same figure, the opposites such as life and death, becoming and withering, good and evil, etc.[29] The English word "black," is related to German *blank* = pure, and French *blanc* = white, in which the paradoxical similarity of extreme opposites is manifested.[30] Black is obscure and opaque and consequently symbolizes the fearsome aspect of the unconscious, whereas white, which like black is "not a color," indicates indeterminacy in the sense of untouched, unspoiled by the profane world. It symbolizes, therefore, innocence, the ideal, apotheosis, and, in contrast to the dark power of the unconscious expressed symbolically in blackness, it is more the penetrating, clear (ice cold!) of spiritual power. As a result of this concordance of both black and white with respect to the indeterminacy of the

---

[23] See the same motif in the reverse color order in "The Beautiful Dunye."
[24] See Bächtold-Stäubli under *schwarz* [black].
[25] See M. Führer, *Nordgermanische*, München 1938 p. 9ff, H. Zimmer, *Maya*, Stuttgart and Berlin 1936 p. 417. Cf. also the black poodle in Goethe's *Faust* as a manifestation of Mephisto [that is, the devil].
[26] See the "black villain" in "The Piper and the Púca."
[27] See G. Roeder, *Urkunden*, Jena 1923 p. 271.
[28] See the black and white ravens on Odin's shoulder. M. Führer, *Nordgermanische*, München 1938 p. 82 describes the ancient Germanic goddess Hel as half black, half white. See also the Orphic Urei half black, half white or red in J. J. Bachofen, *Gräbersymbolik*, Basel 1859 p. 13f.
[29] See *ibid* p. 38.
[30] See M. Ninck, *Wodan*, Jena 1935 p. 174.

unconscious, white is also the color of the underworld.[31] The deep waters of the Germanic [Norse] primordial Well of Urdr[32] colors everything snow-white.[33]

914   After Djulek Batür confronts the magical world in the aspect of contrasting colors that both tend to emphasize its vagueness, imprecision, and indeterminacy, he meets the red color as the clearest and most pronounced manifestation of that sphere, and which is the hardest to overcome and control. Just as the white *div* represents a contrast to the black, the red *div* who follows is an antithesis to the white figure, which is emphasized by the progression from cold to hot. A ghastly foreboding of the unconscious triggers cold shivers. Jung once said, "When we are mentally taken by somebody into a region where we no longer feel at home, we speak of ice-cold heights of the intellect."[34]

915   The unconscious is at the same time also a place of infernal heat, which is why in many depictions of the underworld people are tortured simultaneously by frost and heat.[35] Whereas cold is a freezing up from fear, indicating an inward-looking emotion, heat symbolizes the outbreak of passion, the fire of desire and instinctual drives, and thus is close in meaning to the color red, in which demons often appear. Colors are associated with particular emotions, and, as Jung says:

916   Emotion is the moment when steel meets flint and a spark is struck forth, for emotion is the chief sources of consciousness. There is no change from darkness to light or inertia into movement without emotion.[36]

917   For Djulek Batür the problem of the dangers lurking behind the lure of the unconscious are, for the time being, resolved after the defeat of the red *div*.

918   The combination of the colors black, white, and red is a common and typical attribute for figures of the unconscious.[37] Particularly in the symbolic

---

[31] See C.G. Jung, *Children's Dreams*, Princeton 2008 pp. 214–215. See also the fairytale "The Mountain of the Fair Women," "How Motecuzhoma Sought the Seven Caves," (where Aztlan, the Land of the Dead, means "The White") and "Rakian."
[32] [In the *Prose Edda*, the Urðarbrunnr is cited as one of three wells existing beneath three roots of Yggdrasil that reach into three distant, different lands.]
[33] See M. Ninck, *Wodan*, Jena 1935 p. 180.
[34] See C.G. Jung, *Children's Dreams*, Princeton 2008 p. 54. On the concept of cold in the unconscious and the association of clarity with whiteness, see "The Wide Halls of Crystal Coldness," (Volume 1 of this work, p. 32) in the Chinese fairytale "The Lady of the Moon."
[35] See, for example, "How a Scholar Chastised the Princes of Hell" and Dante's *Inferno*.
[36] C.G. Jung, CW 9i, *The Archetypes and the Collective Unconscious* ¶179.
[37] See this color sequence in the compilation of fairytales, legends, and ballads in R. Köhler, "Kleinere Schriften," in *Volkskunde, Vol. 3*, Berlin 1900 p. 581ff, especially no. 65, "The White, the Red, and the Black Cock." On these three colors as characterizing the Land of the Dead , see A. Thimme, *Märchen*, Leipzig 1909 pp. 36–37.

representations of medieval alchemy, in which the process usually goes through three stages, these colors appear together. These three stages are: the *nigredo*, the blackness, a symbol of utter destruction and dissolution in the unconscious; the *albedo*, the white, a state of cleansing, purification, and transfiguration, and new innocence and receptivity; and the *rubedo*, redness, a symbol of active and lively re-emergence. This is then a combination, *coniunctio*, of the white female and red male elements.[38] The color combination of black, white, red is – exactly as each of these colors individually – characteristic of the Beyond and of demons. Thus, for example, the Aztec underworld is "The Land of the Red and Black."[39] In many tales from North America, red and white animals guard the entrance to the underworld.[40] Also the angels of the Apocalypse unleashed by the Book of Seals (Revelations 6: 2-5) ride on a white, a red, a black, and a pale horse. According to the Indian philosophy of the Jains, the color of the soul is determined by its predominating constituents (*gunas*) and can be white, red, or black.[41] It is conceivable that similar ideas are reflected in Central Asian mythology. In "Djulek Batür" all three colors are assigned to the demonic enemies of the hero and have, therefore, negative connotations. That means that there is no relationship between the conscious core of the personality (represented by the hero) and the forces of the unconscious indicated by the three colors. Only when they are completely distant and separated from consciousness do they take on such inhuman shape and are characterized by such exaggerated and destructive power.

919   Djulek Batür waits for the *divs* under a bridge. As explained before, the bridge signals a weak point in the continuity of consciousness, a place where transition and transformation takes place and, therefore, where invasions of the unconscious threaten.[42] It is significant that the *divs* believe that shooting is a matter of Djulek Batür's father, and wrestling is the battle choice with Djulek Batür himself. Here, shooting means a meeting with arrows, that is, with intuitions or thoughts from afar, as befits the rational conscious mind. But because the hero represents the fourth function, which is the farthest from the rational intellect, he is well-placed to deal with the unconscious on a more physical, bodily level. Djulek Batür defeats the first *div* by lifting him up off

---

[38] See H. Silberer, *Problems of Mysticism*, New York 1917 p. 54, 103, 125f, 368; Rousselle pp. 68–69; C.G. Jung, CW 13 *Alchemical Studies*¶124, C.G. Jung, CW 11, *Psychology and Religion*¶164.

[39] See W. Krickeberg, *Azteken und Inka*, Jena 1928 p. 332 [for an English source, see M. Graulich, *Myths*, Norman 1997 p. 202 . See also, the Aztec Anales de Cuauhtitlan, which state that Quetzelcoatl left Tollan to go to *Tlillan Tlapallan* ("The Land of the Red and Black") where he would cremate himself and pass on to the other world]

[40] For instance, "The Strange Boy" or "Flight to the Moon."

[41] See E. Abegg, *Indische Psychologie*, Zürich 1945 p. 105.

[42] See the Púca's attack on the piper at the bridge in the Irish tale, "The Piper and the Púca," and the battle between the powerful hero with the dragon on the bridge in the Russian tale "Ivan the Cow's Son."

the earth. This is reminiscent of the Antaeus motif insofar as the hero separates his opponent, in this case a demonic shadow figure, by detaching him from the connection to the whole unconscious and thus from the overwhelming power of that background. Thus, he is able to conquer the negative aspect of the shadow and can appropriate its vital force: the horse. Since preponderance of the shadow psychologically severely limits freedom of will, overcoming this imbalance is a prerequisite for winning the anima, the highest virtue.

920   This struggle with the shadow and the attainment of the anima occurs in a magnificent swelling rhythm of threes. The trinity of the *divs* and the anima figures correspond to the now-familiar triad of unconscious figures, for instance the three Baba Yagas of the Russian fairytale, "The Virgin Tsar."[43] The number three is male and indicates the active-creative principle.[44] Bachofen writes of the three: [I]n it lies power itself, the expression of which contains the double movement, the alternation of becoming and decaying (that is, the duality of the opposites).[45] Psychologically, three indicates movement related to emotion and drive. (Note the unruliness of the *divs*.) Insofar as three also indicates the movement of time – past, present, and future – it expresses fate. The triad of Hindu gods, Brahma, Rudra and Vishnu, corresponds to the three powers of creation: will, knowledge, and action; or sun, moon, and fire.[46] The physiology and psychology of China knows this trinity in the image of the three rivers in the human being: the germ, the breath, the genius.[47] In the West, these views correspond to Gnostic speculation about a primordial being comprised of the principles of spirit, soul, and body.[48] Between the father = spirit (mind) and the mother = matter stands the world soul, which, upon entering into the world, is subjected to suffering. On the microcosmic scale, this corresponds to the threefold human soul.[49] In some Christian-Gnostic systems the world in need of redemption is even defined as the "Tripartite."[50] The three *div* and three anima figures are symbols for these unconscious formative impulses that, with their powerful

---

[43] See the triple rhythm in the tales "Trunt, Trunt, and the Trolls in the Mountains," "The Great Fool from Cuasan," "The Three Feathers," "The Golden Bird," "The Golden Castle that Hung in the Air" and "The Three Lemons," among many others.

[44] On the problem of the three and the four in general, see, C.G. Jung, CW 12, *Psychology and Alchemy* ¶310-322, C.G. Jung, CW 11, *Psychology and Religion* ¶116-124.

[45] J. J. Bachofen, *Mutterrecht*, Stuttgart 1861 p. 134.

[46] See V. C. C. Collum, "Schöpferische Mutter-Göttin," in *Eranos*, Zürich 1939 p. 316f. These signify the three basic properties (*gunas*) of *Prakrti* (nature): *sattva* (creation), *rajas* (preservation), and *tamas* (destruction). According to the *Baghavad Gita*, *sattva* encompasses the qualities of goodness, passion, and darkness, (or goodness, light, and harmony). See also C.G. Jung, CW 9i, *The Archetypes and the Collective Unconscious* ¶158; D. Bernoulli, *Spiritual*, Princeton 1960 pp. 315–316.

[47] See E. Rousselle, "Spiritual Guidance" in *Spiritual Disciplines*, Princeton 1960 p. 71.

[48] See D. Bernoulli, *Op. cit.* p. 315

[49] See H. Leisegang, *Die Gnosis*, Leipzig 1924 p. 118,320. See also the reference above to Carus on the threefold division of psychic energy into cognition, feeling, and volition.

[50] See *ibid* pp. 143–144 on the belief of some Gnostics that the cosmos is a unity consisting of three principles.

driving forces, threaten to overwhelm the ego-personality. Djulek Batür defeats the last fiery *div*, which embodies the strongest and most dangerous outburst of passions, by managing to drink the lake dry before the *div*, and thus to withstand his heat. His knowledge of the polarity of all unconscious manifestations stands him here in good stead. Even in the storm of the most ardent passion he can deploy the opposite, coolness, thus assuring him the upper hand. While the black *div* personifies confusion, disorientation, and dark forebodings, the white *div* represents freezing up; shuddering in fear of the unknown. The red *div* symbolizes burning desire, from which Djulek Batür rescues himself by balancing this out with the nature of the unconscious, symbolized here by water. The union with the anima can then take place, which is always coupled with the problem of the return, and which is spun out in particularly rich detail in this tale. The return journey is initiated by various attempts to connect the newly gained insights to the old secular attitude. This – in the form of the brothers – arrogates to itself the increase in growth of spiritual values gained in the unconscious, so that an inflation of the rational conscious mind arises.

921   A new motif in our presentation so far is the dismemberment of the hero by the secular elder brothers. They maliciously place a sword so that Djulek Batür cuts off his own legs when he runs out of his tent, thus treacherously simulating a self-mutilation. As in previous tales, Djulek Batür is partly responsible himself through his guileless, naive trust and his wish to help his secular brothers. In "The Golden Bird" this characteristic was even more strongly accentuated in that the hero refused to dismember the fox, which may indicate his lingering ensnarement in secular notions. In "Djulek Batür" the suffering of the hero is particularly enhanced, however, and it is even implied that he inflicted this suffering on himself.

922   In many fairytales, the confrontations on the return journey, like here, are not a clash between the hero and the differentiated or dominant collective function, but rather the two elder brothers or a figure like the red knight in "The Golden Castle that Hung in the Air" place themselves in the way of the hero. This means that in such cases, where neither the whole conscious attitude to life nor the inferior function – insofar as it is only nature and occurs in the "naive" hero – acts in a negative or evil way, but rather that the evil actually arises out of a half-conscious psychic (mental) state, in which nature is falsified by the conscious mind and consciousness is clouded by nature. This constellation in the present tale corresponds to that in "The Red Swan," in that the tension here, as there, is between the hero and the two brothers. There the brothers represent the opposites, that is, parts of the hero's shadow that have fallen into a more secular and a more magical attitude. In contrast, the conflict with the differentiated function is missing. The outcome of this conflict is, however, not necessarily dependent on the collective views, but is rather a

consequence of the differentiated function's lack of understanding of the realities of the unconscious. This function is, therefore, unable to become the conscious core of the personality. In some fairytales the father succumbs, however, to the whisperings of the secular brothers, thus showing that the differentiated function, the previous way of life, is also dependent on collective beliefs. This is explained by the generally immense power of the collective [community], which van der Leeuw contrasts with loneliness. This is the "feeling of insecurity," the fear that overcomes people when they approach the edges of their lives.[51]

923   Primitive man . . . thinks and acts collectively. Without his fellows the individual is nothing. His family, his tribe acts in him. Man cannot live "alone." There is only the great dread. To be alone is to die. . . [Today we still become "primitive" as soon as we feel ourselves among the mass of living humanity. . .] Thus, whoever is severed from the community cannot live, homesickness gnaws at his soul . . . It is not the "I" that has been damaged, but the "we" that has been shattered . . . Life is essentially a single whole and the communality of society is precisely the power of life.[52]

924 To override these natural laws is so difficult that only those called to the task can succeed. Such a hero, as a symbol of the personality striving for maturity, must find a middle position, both between the differentiated adaptation to the legitimate claims of the rational outer world and the demands of nature in the inner psychic regions of the soul, and between the collective powers in their secular aspect as well as in their magical setting. The duality of the brothers indicates that they personify two opposing powers; the secular often functions both as collective-rational and as negative-magical, thus requiring a special effort in order to bring about further development. But because the Self is the root of *all* these forces and also nourishes the intermediate forms, it is ultimately "its own enemy."[53] To this extent, Djulek Batür's suffering is actually a self-dismemberment in that the Self compels the ego into self-sacrifice.[54] This happens here, however, with a negative sign; the sacrifice is not an ethical act of self-reflection, but an unwanted event, arranged by the shadow.

---

[51] G. van der Leeuw, *Religion in Essence*, Vol. 1 p. 242. [The direct citation is: "Loneliness is the culmination of the insecurity and care wherein we live. Hence its terror arises whenever we approach the boundaries of life and experience most intensely its powerlessness and uncertainty. . ." An alternative translation of van der Leeuw's German could be: "Loneliness is the enormity of insecurity and danger; the cause of the anxiety that overcomes a man when he approaches the boundary of his life."]

[52] [Translation based on the German of von Franz and von Beit and the English translation of G. van der Leeuw, *op. cit.* pp. 243–244.]

[53] See the *Srimad Bhagavad Gita* VI, 5: "For this self is the friend of oneself, and this self is the enemy of oneself.

[54] See C.G. Jung, CW 11, *Psychology and Religion* ¶397 and 398.

925   In itself, dismemberment of the primordial human, or of the hero's image of the Self that is still vested with demonic features, is an archetype commonly reflected in myths and fairytales. In this manner, Osiris and Dionysus were dismembered.[55] In alchemy, the division (*separatio*) of the mercurial dragon or lion plays a central role as a prerequisite to further development. Many creation myths tell of the world arising from the dismemberment of a primordial being.[56] Moreover, the dismemberment of the magical helper – as in "The Golden Bird" and "The Golden Castle that Hung in the Air" – is formally the same motif. As mentioned, in "Djulek Batür" this has to be evaluated negatively, however, since the action happens out of the realm of semi-consciousness and does not appear to be clearly intended either by the unconscious or by the conscious mind.

926   Precisely at the crossroads is where Djulek Batür loses his legs through dismemberment, and it is limbs that connect one to the earth, that is, to reality. According to Bachofen,[57] the leg or foot often symbolizes the fertilizing power of the earth. Djulek Batür is lamed and deprived of his life spirit,[58] and thus the Self is again cut off from the sphere of secular life to which it is striving to return. This creates a state of indecision, which in some ways recalls the tragic demise of the hero in "The Story of Djihanshah." Actually, the newly emerging consciousness is again swallowed by the unconscious, which is why it soon reappears in the form of the evil mother (the witch). Dismemberment is a characteristic representation of the prevalence of the unconscious, since it corresponds to disintegration into the particles of creation.

927   A blind and then an armless man join Djulek Batür, then a girl whom they call sister is added, creating a companionship of four people.[59] They are each dependent on the others; individually they are only parts without means. This new tetrad constitutes the inner Self, which is designated as a quaternity. In this respect Djulek Batür's efforts to attract these comrades to himself is an attempt to build up a new inner wholeness. On the other hand, the fact that the Self appears neither in *one* character nor in a fourfold *complete* person, indicates that the Self has fallen apart and fragmented into pieces as a result of repression by the rational conscious mind. Since each part is dependent on the other for that which they are lacking, the lamed figures reflect not only the situation of the Self, but also that of the ego. The new quaternity that now

---

[55] On Osiris see C.G. Jung, CW 12, *Psychology and Alchemy* ¶416fn. 36, H. Silberer, *Problems of Mysticism*, New York 1917 p. 77f, 200f; and on Dionysus, see C.G. Jung, CW 13 *Alchemical Studies* 91. Cf. also C.G. Jung, CW 11, *op. cit.* ¶400.

[56] See the sacrifice of Purusha in the *Bark'he Soukt*, Deussen, *Sixty Upanishads* p. 893ff, and that of Ymir in H. Güntert, *Weltkönig*, Halle a. S. 1923 p. 326ff.

[57] See J. J. Bachofen, *Gräbersymbolik*, Basel 1859 p. 389.

[58] To be crippled corresponds to a certain degree to castration. On this, see C.G. Jung, CW 5, *Symbols of Transformation* ¶356 and Dr. Aigremont, *Fuss- and Schuh-Symbolik*, Leipzig 1909 in general.

[59] On the following sections of this tale with the cripples and the blood-sucking witch, see the Russian/Ukrainian parallels given in J. Bolte and G. Polívka, *Anmerkungen*, Vol. 1, Leipzig 1913 p. 311.

emerges is an unconscious wholeness, for it can neither walk, nor grasp, nor see. That is, it cannot take action in any way or discern, and it lacks any connection to the sphere of secular consciousness and real life. In as much as the quaternity, when it arises as a symbol of the Self, expresses its character as constituent of the conscious mind, it cannot be complete if it does not set real life as its goal. The company of cripples acts as a mirror image of the secular brothers and behaves accordingly even after the parts are healed. (The "sister" is a somewhat pallid anima figure.) The secular brothers seem to have been replaced by two new characters, because here the situation no longer concerns the functions of consciousness, but the disintegration of the Self into opposites in the unconscious. The emergence of the archetypal quaternity and the avoidance of a fragmentation into infinitely many parts indicate that a new consciousness is trying to emerge.

928   Hunting the saiga by the cripples is like a motif out of a droll or bawdy comedy.[60] It shows the paradoxical and still ineffective nature of the new attempt at individuation. In Chinese oracle language, however, the lame who can walk, and the one-eyed man who can see, represent adaptation and persistence in an irregular situation.[61] In the situation of the present fairytale something similar is presented: the healing of the cripples comes about after they have gone through the innermost realms of darkest nature.

929   The three cripples order their "sister" to keep a cat and to share all her food with it. She cannot uphold this requirement and her breach of this commandment leads to the involvement with the vampire-like witch, who initially threatens the quaternity but then heals the lamed men through a rebirth event. The incident with the cat thus leads to an *auseinandersetzung* with the Great Mother in her threatening aspect. The cat is a manifestation of this archetype, and probably because of this demonic background the three men demand that the cat be appeased at all costs. The girl's indifference indicates an imperfection of the anima, which forms a parallel to the defective nature of the cripples. The anima has lost her capacity to mediate between the conscious mind and aspects of the unconscious, a skill which, for example, she had as the *pari*. The weakness of the Self represented by this particular foursome provokes, therefore, the exaggerated power of the unconscious in the form of the witch. The cat symbolizes not only the positive anima (as in "The Poor Miller's Boy and the Cat") but is also identical to the witch. This relationship appears in mythological parallels where the cat is considered to be the animal of witches. For instance, the cat is the companion animal of Frau Holle, Freya, and the Greek mother goddesses.[62]

---

[60] See more on this in *ibid*, Vol. 3, Leipzig 1918 p. 116.

[61] See Wilhelm/Baynes, *I Ching*, Princeton, 1967 p. 208ff, Hexagram 54, Kuei Mei, The Marrying Maiden.

[62] Also, the cat is the companion animal of the Baba Yaga. See the Russian tale "The Miracle Sleigh." For more on the cat as the witch and soul animal, see O. Tobler, *Epiphanie*, Kiel 1911 p. 46f.

930   When the cat out of spite extinguishes the hearth fire, this only worsens the girl's offense, so that she gets even more entangled in the power of the dark demonic animal powers. The hearth fire has since ancient times been taboo, and sacred to the chthonic mother goddess. In ancient Greece, it was associated with the cult of Hestia, and in Rome with that of Vesta.[63] The cat exacerbates the disintegration into the unconscious by interrupting the cultic connections to the Mother Goddess. Its evil, spiteful deeds are almost symbolic of this decay. Since the witch is the guardian of the fire, the girl has to go to her to fetch the embers, that is, the psychic energy, and conjures up the whole demonic possession of the magical world.[64] The battle that ensues corresponds to Djulek Batür's first fight with the *divs*, only the *auseinandersetzung* with the Great Mother proves to be more engulfing, complex, and consequential than the overcoming of the dubious shadow spirits in the unconscious. The witch approaches and takes advantage of the girl (and later the men too), first with the request that her head be deloused, but then like a vampire, she also sucks the maiden's blood. That demons demand delousing as a humiliating service, is a frequent motif. In "Mother Holle," a parallel tale of Grimm's, the old woman, as "a little red mother," requests that the heroine delouse her. Dragon or animal princes sometimes require to be deloused.[65] Through the act of delousing, a state of *participation mystique* with the witch arises since it is common among natural people to eat the lice they pick. Thus, the one performing the

---

[63] See Bächtold-Stäubli under *Herdfeuer* [hearth]. Van der Leeuw writes:

> We find the forms of worship of the power of fire most beautifully and systematically developed in ancient Rome; they originated in the primeval domestic cult, wherein the hearth was entrusted to the care of the women (the later vestals), while the father of the family appeared as the priest of the flame and his sons (*flamines*) as the kindlers. Fire is the object of the oldest family worship, wherein the power of the communal essence is concentrated; and on the first of March, at the commencement of the old Roman year, the fire was extinguished and immediately rekindled. Thereby prosperity was ensured for another year. In this state the hearth fire (*vesta*) became the deepest mystery, on which the community's security depended. . . In modern Calabria too, in case of death, the fire on the hearth is allowed to expire, while according to old German custom the flame was revived on special festive days, or when "sinking fortune made it evident that a renewal was necessary." (V. Grönbech, *Vor Folkaet*, 11, 1912, p. 57) An Indian tribe had to pay, by its gradual decline, for a girl's carelessness in permitting the fire to go out (K. Knortz, *Märchen und Sagen der nordamerikanischen Indianer*, 1871, No. 60). These examples afford ample proof that the idea of the potency of fire extended very far, and was by no means limited to Indo-European peoples. Fire's living power protects against evil influences. . . (G. van der Leeuw, *Religion in Essence*, Vol. 1 pp. 62–63.)

On the significance of the hearth, see van der Leeuw *ibid* p. 397.

[64] See the parallels from India and Tripoli in J. Bolte and G. Polívka, *Anmerkungen*, Vol. 1, Leipzig 1913 p. 460f. See further details and parallels in A. Wesselski, *Versuch*, Reichenberg i. B. 1931 p. 80ff and the relatively bland fairytale, "The Seven Brothers."

[65] See J. Bolte and G. Polívka, *Anmerkungen*, Vol. 1, Leipzig 1913 p. 207 J; *ibid*, Vol. 2, Leipzig 1915 p. 298; and *ibid*, Vol. 3, Leipzig 1918 p. 41.

delousing ingests the blood of the one being deloused.[66] The lice make up, therefore, a connecting bridge between the witch and the four cripples like the shrubs that later grow up along the way. Lice are bloodsuckers like the witch, they are even her representation, and in this manner a mutual attachment is formed. In fairytales witches are often described with vampiric traits. Bloodsucking is a depiction of an actual property of the unconscious, whereby a person is deprived of psychic energy (as can be observed in cases of neurosis). Prolonged exposure to the mercy of the unconscious can bring about a total dissolution of the personality. In "Djulek Batür" there is the danger that the Self gradually gets completely swallowed up by the unconscious, a peril that the hero conquers because he decides to meet it voluntarily. The motif of letting-oneself-be-devoured-by-the-mother corresponds to the hero's night sea journey in the belly of the dragon or whale.[67] Before he goes into her, he ties her hair to forty poles. Her crying out "I love you, my son!" is significant, emphasizing the devouring and overbearing maternal love.[68] (The same idea is behind the Manichean doctrine that the darkness burned itself in love of the light and therefore sought to devour it.)

931   Tying up the witch's hair symbolizes banning or exorcising her powers.[69] Her psychic power really vests in her hair, and later in her head. Djulek Batür nails down, so to speak, her evil intentions and thoughts, so they cannot slip away or transform. He can then look them in the eye, question them, and thus deflate their power. This is followed by a fourfold repetition of the motif of being devoured and reborn in the dragon-whale. Only Djulek Batür is no longer spewed out by the witch but must be cut free from her little finger by his companions. Since the little finger, as a phallic symbol, has the meaning of creativity, the image of the hero hidden in the little finger of the witch corresponds to the idea of the Self hidden in the unconscious, and at the same time, that of the motif of the male companion of the Great Mother figure. Since Djulek Batür comes, however, from the sphere of the conscious mind and represents the reflection of the Self in consciousness, being stuck in an identification with otherworldly powers is highly dangerous. Because he cannot overcome the witch independently from inside her, he is dependent

---

[66] See L. Lévy-Bruhl, *The "Soul" of the Primitive*, New York 1928 p. 120f. See also the Warao tale "The Sun, the Frog, and the Firesticks."
[67] For more on this motif in general see C.G. Jung, CW 5, *Symbols of Transformation*. See also the close Russian parallel, "The Blind and Legless Hero," in which two crippled brothers forced the Baba Yaga to give them the waters of healing and the waters of life through which they became healthy again.
[68] On this see the devouring love in the Warao tale "The Story of Haburi."
[69] See Jungbauer: "In a tale recorded by Ostroumov. . . the unusual strength of the heroine lies in her hair with a thousand tresses." (*Märchen aus Turkestan und Tibet* p. 303). This is reminiscent of Samson's hair, which is also the source of his strength.

on external support, and still the head of the old hag escapes and rolls away and the quest must continue until the demon is definitely defeated without the help of others.[70] The head, as something "round," is a symbol of the Self and represents, therefore, the essential nature of the human being and also its regenerative power.[71] In our tale, the head of the witch contains, as it were, the quintessence, the real meaning of the unconscious that is hidden in the mother archetype, and which, as yet unrecognized by Djulek Batür, slips into the unconscious (the well).[72]

932   And so, the third circuitous journey begins. Here Djulek Batür's now healed comrades take on the role of the secular brothers. It turns out that they cannot go down into the well, but claim that they are burning up. Only Djulek Batür, who has already overcome the *divs*, makes the trip with eyes closed and perceives neither fire nor other horrors. The comrade-brothers succumb to the Maya; the illusion of the unconscious. One representative parallel to this is an episode in the Irish tale, "The King's Son and the Bird with the Sweet Song," in which three brothers let themselves descend into a well, one after the other. The elder two saw giant people coming after them with blood-red lances and quickly asked to be pulled up again. When the hero went down the well, he met a small man with a skewer whom he immediately grabbed and held down until the man said, "Let go, Son of the King! I'm not your enemy, but propitious to every brave man. Before you, two men were here, but they lacked courage." The little man then became the hero's magical helper.

933   Just how the unconscious changes its aspect when approached properly is shown by an episode from a Balkan tale, "The Twelve Pieces." The hero has to defeat a dragon with his flute, that sets everyone dancing when he plays on it.

934   As soon as the dragon saw the tsar's son coming, he called out, "You are the one that I have long been searching for!" The dragon launched fiery arrows, but the horse of the tsar's son knelt and the arrows flew harmlessly overhead. The tsar's son then threw his lance at the dragon, but it broke in two and did the dragon no harm. He tried with one weapon after another, all to no avail. In the end he stood there, empty-handed. The dragon laughed and stormed up to him. Then the tsar's son took out his flute and began to play. All living things everywhere around them began to dance, the dragon hissed and began to tremble, and gradually became smaller and smaller until it

---

[70] The rolling head of the witch is reminiscent of the rolling skull in the Native American tale "Skull Acts as Food-Getter."

[71] See C.G. Jung, CW 11, *Psychology and Religion* ¶366f.

[72] See also, "The Bald Goose-Herder," where a witch devours one of the hero brothers. The other brother, who later defeats the witch, splits her head open and finds his brother who is alive, along with his horse and loyal panthers.

was just like a little bubble that jumped up and down. The tsar's son was quick to run up to it, stomped on the bubble with his left foot, and the bubble burst. The devil's power was ended.[73]

935 Neither weapons of consciousness nor the rational intellect were able to tame the monster, but the inner life of feeling and the fearlessness that swelled from within abruptly disarms the devouring unconscious rendering it easy to overcome. Once again, we see here that the unconscious reflects the attitude with which the conscious mind perceives it.

936 We find another parallel to this motif in the Grimm's tale, "The Gnome,"[74] which tells of a king who was a great lover of all kinds of fine trees:

937 He had a particular liking for one special apple tree. He was so fond of this tree that he wished whomever took apples from it to land one hundred fathoms deep underground. One day, the king's three daughters were walking in his garden and came upon this apple tree completely laden with ripe fruit. The youngest had such a desire to taste these apples that she could not resist. She knew of her father's feelings for the tree but thought that he loved her so much, he would never wish her harm. So, she plucked a big red apple and it was so delicious she enticed her elder sisters to do the same. As soon as all three had tasted the apples, they sank deep into the ground, "where they could hear no cock crow." Three young huntsmen set out to search for the princesses, one at a time. The first came upon a little man who begged for a piece of bread. The huntsman gave a piece of his bread to the little fellow, who let it fall to the ground. The little man then asked the huntsman to pick it up for him. As soon as the young huntsman bent down to fetch the piece of bread, the little man seized him by the hair and gave him a good beating. The second fared no better. Neither told the others any details of what had happened. Then came the turn of the youngest huntsman. When the little man asked him to pick up the bread he had let fall, the young huntsman said, "What! Can you not pick up that piece yourself? If you will not take as much trouble as that for your daily bread, you do not deserve to have it!" When the little fellow complained, the young huntsman grabbed him and gave him a thorough beating until he agreed to reveal where the king's daughters were hidden.[75]

---

[73] From the German of A. Leskien, *Balkanmärchen*, Jena 1919 p. 176.

[74] See also "The Three Brothers and the Dwarf," "The Stolen Daughters," and the middle section of, "The Bear Hans."

[75] For more examples of such rebellious behavior, see the tale "The Golden Bird." See also the Danish parallel, "Strong Jack," "The Fairies on the Gump," and the test of courage in "Canonbie Dick and Thomas von Ercildoune."

938 He revealed that the princesses lived in the kingdom of a thousand gnomes in a well without water. The little man also warned him that his two companions would not deal honorably with him and he should retrieve the maidens alone. The little man then gave exact instructions and disappeared. When the youngest hunter returned to his comrades, they asked him what had happened and he reported honestly but did not mention the final instructions. The other two grew green and yellow with jealousy and insisted they try to get the princesses all together. But just as the little man predicted, as soon as they were let down in the well, they rang a bell and asked to be hauled up again. Only the youngest went down to the bottom, found a nine-, a seven-, and a four-headed dragon each of which one of the maidens was delousing. He cut off their heads and freed the maidens. They were overjoyed and embraced him. Then he had his comrades draw up one after another of the maidens. When it came to his turn to get in the basket, he remembered the gnome's words, put a heavy stone in the basket, and then rang to have it raised up. Sure enough, his comrades raised the basket only halfway up, then they cut the rope and let it fall down again. They heard it crash and were sure that he was dead, and went to the king with the princesses, making them promise to say it was they who had rescued them. Meanwhile, the youngest hunter wandered about the underground chambers and came upon a flute. But he was so sad he left it hanging. Only after wandering around so long that the ground became smooth and flat from his steps did "other thoughts come to his mind, and he took the flute from the wall." When he played a few notes, ten elves suddenly appeared. A few more notes and ten more appeared. They asked what he desired and he said to go up to the surface of the earth again. So, they all grabbed him by the hair and flew with him up to the surface of the well. He went to the palace and arrived just as the wedding of the princesses to his comrades was about to be celebrated. When the princesses saw him, they all fainted, whereupon their father, the king, suspecting the newcomer had done something evil to them, ordered him to be imprisoned. But when the maidens returned to their senses, they pleaded with their father to free the young huntsmen. When their father asked why, they said they could not tell. "Then tell it to the stove," he said. This they did, but the king listened on the other side of the closed door and heard everything. Then he ordered the two older huntsmen to be hung and gave his youngest daughter to the youngest huntsman to be his wife.[76]

---

[76] [Summarized from J. and W. Grimm, *Complete Grimm's*, London 1975 pp. 420–424.

939 In both these fairytales, it is only the hero who reaches the depths of the well, meaning that only the fourth function can "get to the bottom," the real essence of the unconscious. There Djulek Batür finds the anima, who in the depths of the unconscious (in contrast to the "sister") attains her mysterious and divine *pari* aspect. She is rocking the witch's head like a child in a cradle. We have already mentioned the intimate connection between the mother imago and the anima. The deepest meaning or essence (head) of the maternal image leads the hero to the anima, since the anima experience is for a man the fascinating core in the unconscious. There lie the roots of his creative powers and the meaning that he is searching for. But whereas the anima is often accompanied by a circular or round thing, a symbol of the Self in its positive aspect,[77] here the head expresses its negative aspect. It is the mysterious treasure in the negative-magical form, similar to the previously mentioned "rolling skull" motif. The ambiguous, iridescent nature of the anima proves that she fosters this negative side (she cradles the witch's skull) and even tries to further its growth! This is a parallel to the association of the anima with devilish spirits. The hero must destroy this dangerous aspect of the anima. He grabs the old hag's head again by the hair, but this time thoroughly finishes his job by cutting it up into pieces with his sword, after which the *pari* recognizes him as her "redeemer." In the *pari*'s attempt to bring about a union with Djulek Batür lies the tendency, characteristic of the anima, to bind the hero firmly in the unconscious. Djulek Batür's goal is, however, to bring what he has experienced in the depths back into the world of consciousness, for only through this can he complete his path of individuation. But in doing this he also puts up barriers separating himself from the anima and loses the connection to her. Thus, he is forced to embark on long detours and new adventures. At first, he tries too quickly to reach the light, conscious side and thus succumbs to the one-sidedness of his pursuit. As a consequence, the white horse collapses beneath him and he must take the black steed to even greater depths. He must first experience the double aspect of the unconscious in a more lasting, permanent way so that he can stand on his own feet; as master of the situation, with respect to the *pari* as a demonic being, on the one hand, and on the other hand, towards the secular world.

940 According to Jungbauer, the collector of these Uzbek tales, the section of "Djulek Batür" that transpires in the underworld is based on ancient traditions and should be considered, therefore, as an original, independent episode that was added on.[78] In fact, a parallel from Bulgaria, "Saint Georg, Lamia, and the Snake," begins with a variant on the episode of the white and black mounts, which appear here as two rams. They are in a well, and the white one steers

---

[77] See, for instance, "Connla and the Fairy Maiden."
[78] See "Notes" *Märchen aus Turkestan und Tibet* p. 308.

up towards the light, the black one leads down into the dark underworld. On the other hand, four other parallels, the modern Greek tale, "The Goldapple Tree and the Descent into Hell," the Udi variant of the Rustam legend called "The Thrush and the Nightingale"[79] and the Turkish fairytale, "The Story of the Emerald Anka Bird,"[80] where the adventure begins with a black and white animal and is the continuation of a previous journey. Most of the longer fairytales were probably a concatenation of several shorter stories, sometimes the "seams" connecting the episodes are apparent. Although in Djulek Batür the subsequent annexations might have been added by the storyteller for literary reasons, the psychological sense is certainly present. This psychological consistency ensured that this particular combination of fairytales remained popular in many different regions.

941   The idea of the light and dark riding animals (in the version from the Caucasus mentioned above, they are a white ram and a black he-goat, in the Turkish and modern Greek versions, a white and a black sheep) expresses in archetypal simplicity the two basic currents of psychic energy in the unconscious, which can be described as extraversion and introversion. But all conceivable pairs of opposites are associated with them, such as good and evil, heavenly and earthly, and so forth. Plato used this pair in the image of the chariot of the soul drawn by two horses, the good white one that strives upwards to the light, and the wild black one pulling downward. A similar idea is the struggle between the black demonic horse Apaosha and the star Sirius as the white horse Tishtriya in the Persian *Zend-Avesta*.[81] In ancient Germanic beliefs the light elves opposed the dark elves, the male deity Dag [day], with his team of white horses, opposed Nott [night], the giant's daughter, with her black team.[82] In India, Krishna and Balarâma were born of a white and black hair from the head of Vishnu.[83] Also Chinese philosophy concerns itself with the dynamic balance between the light-dark, male-female primordial principles of yin and yang.

---

[79] Here there are three horses, a black one, that tries to kill its rider, a white one that leads up to the light, and a red one that takes its rider downwards.

[80] See also "The Wise and Valiant Prince" where the hero, in the depths of the well, must make the choice himself with the phrase, "The white ram conquers the black" or vice-versa, as he sees fit. See also "The Young Hero and the Dragon Mother" and J. Bolte and G. Polívka, *Anmerkungen*, Vol. 2, Leipzig 1915 pp. 307, 314, where an Arabic parallel from *One Thousand and One Nights* is mentioned in which the hero meets a black bull and red bull. [Bolte and Polívka surmise this may be the basis for many other versions.]

[81] The *Hymn of Tishtriya* mentioned in C.G. Jung, CW 5 *Symbols of Transformation* ¶395. ["Tishtriya is the star Sirius, which brings drought and is the leader of the stars against the planets. Stars and planets belong, respectively, to the worlds of Ahura Mazda and Angra Mainyu. The *Hymn of Tishtriya* is a description of the production of the rain through the agency of Sirius (the star, Tishtriya). It has to struggle against the Daeva of Drought, Apaosha. At first, Tishtriya is overcome but then ultimately wins." (Darmesteter, *The Sacred Book of the East*, Oxford 1883 pp. 92–109).]

[82] See M. Führer, *Nordgermanische*, München 1938 p. 10.

[83] See E. Abegg, "Krishnas Geburt," in *Mitteilung*, Zürich 1937/1938 p. 35.

942   The fateful tendency "downwards," that opposes the conscious will of the hero, is even more clearly emphasized by the motif of the somersaulting horse. This is reminiscent of the capsizing little boat in "The King of the Golden Mountain," which seemingly surrenders the hero over to the power of the devil, and also the overturning bed in "The Virgin Tsar" by which the seductive female figure imprisoned Ivan Tsarevich's brother in her basement. With the overturned horse Djulek Batür is also confronted anew with the problem of his instinctual drives.

943   He is taken seven fathoms deep and meets there an old man plowing, who is threatened by two young tigers, and afterwards a king whose daughter is just about to be eaten by a dragon. Thus, he is presented twice with escalating expressions of the same problem: that the unconscious forces supporting human cultural work are threatened by the chaotic forces of nature. It is these forces (that is, the black horse) that continue to drive Djulek Batür back into the depths, the very forces that he must overcome to make the return journey. His renunciation of the king's daughter proves that for him it is no longer about winning the anima, but overcoming his untamed natural impulses. That the father figures of the underworld are suffering or are in need of redemption corresponds to the situation in "The Golden Bird." The old man ploughing, who must constantly fear the tigers, is a striking image of the threat to every human cultural event by the "unharnessed" forces of the unconscious, the passions.[84] The duality of the tigers points to an unconscious dynamic system of nature powers that are not only evil but ambivalent, and can therefore be made to serve positively by Djulek Batür's heroic act.[85]

944   The freeing of the virgin about to be sacrificed to a dragon is a widespread motif and is discussed above in association with the Irish tale, "The Great Fool from Cuasan." A novelty in the present tale is that Djulek Batür overcomes the dragon from within; he lets himself be sucked inside and during his passage slices the beast in half with his drawn sword. This form of overcoming the monster has been discussed extensively by Jung[86] (Another close parallel is the story of how Krishna defeats a demonic stallion by stretching his arm into its mouth and ripping it in half.)[87] Conquering the demon from the inside is an image of the right way to tackle tasks set by the unconscious: the hero, as the core of human consciousness, lets himself literally be sucked in by the demonic power that erupts from the psychic

---

[84] See the Hindu concept of yoga as a yoking or harnessing of unconscious impulses.

[85] See the legend of Jason plowing the field with the *Khalkotauroi*, bronze-hoofed, fire-breathing wild bulls. And also the Polish and Ukrainian parallels to the Grimm's fairytale, "The Young Giant," cited in J. Bolte and G. Polívka, *Anmerkungen*, Vol. 2, Leipzig 1915 p. 291.

[86] See C.G. Jung, CW 5, *Symbols of Transformation* ¶307-310 and ¶374, ¶572. Further examples are found in the fairytales "Why the Boa Constrictor Does Not Eat People," "Faithful and Unfaithful," "Big Raven and the Wolf," "The Prometheus Legend (Georgia)," "Assipattle and the Stoor Worm" and "The Lambton Worm."

[87] See H. Zimmer, *Maya*, Stuttgart and Berlin 1936 p. 357f.

sphere. This total and unconditional commitment makes it possible for him to realize (by means of the sword as a cutting or analytical cognitive faculty) the ambiguity or paradox of threatening psychic powers (the two halves of the dragon), so that the hero, standing outside of the opposites, emerges as the freely choosing, sovereign master of the battle situation. Overcoming the dragon from within is a counterpart to subjugating the tigers from the outside. The latter represent the necessary willpower to withstand the unconscious, the former, the equally necessary volitional task. And with this enormous deed, Djulek Batür frees the treasure, represented by the virgin, which was threatened by the instinctual unconscious, and which as life itself, has the highest value. Only the rescue of this anima figure who symbolizes the blossoming in the depths of the unconscious, entitles the hero to return to the upper world. This journey through the night sea monster, as the crowning deed of all his acts, signals the turning point in Djulek Batür's quest even if the way back brings still more *auseinandersetzungen* [confrontations]. Djulek Batür defeats the dragon, which signifies the definitive overcoming of the regression,[88] thanks to his full recognition of its paradoxical meaning. This feat is framed, and thus accentuated, by his deep sleep before and after the undertaking. The sleep of the hero is known from many myths and indicates that the struggle with the unconscious requires a tremendous effort by the conscious mind. At the same time, the regenerative force that empowers the strength and cunning of the hero, also comes from the unconscious. He is awakened only by the bitter tears of the virgin. Tears express emotional pain and indicate extreme danger, here they are the driving force behind the hero's great deed. If the initial sleep had functioned to invigorate as well as to put the work at risk, the second sleep is also dangerous, for when the hero recovers from his battle, he loses the treasure he had won. This corresponds to the course of action in "The Virgin Tsar," "The Golden Bird" and other tales in which false heroes intervene to wrongly claim the treasure for themselves. It symbolizes the unavoidable danger of sliding back into the machinations of the shadow, against which only a constant wakefulness can help.

945   That Djulek Batür rejects the princess that he rescued and refuses to take her with him to the upper world may have to do with the loose stringing

---

[88] Jung writes on this:

The principle of progression and regression is portrayed in the myth of the whale-dragon worked out by L. Frobenius, *Zeitalter*, Berlin 1904 (1904), (*Das Zeitalter des Sonnengottes*)... Entry into the dragon is the regressive direction, and... its attendant event symbolize the effort to adapt to the conditions of the psychic inner world. The complete swallowing up and disappearance of the hero in the belly of the dragon represents the complete withdrawal of interest from the outer world. The overcoming of the monster from within is the achievement of adaption to the conditions of the inner world, and the emergence ("slipping out") of the hero from the monster's belly... symbolizes the recommencement of progression. (C.G. Jung, CW 8, *The Structure and Dynamics of the Psyche* ¶68).

together of several individual stories.[89] Formally, Djulek Batür must find his way back to the three *paris*. Psychologically, there is also the meaning that Djulek Batür's path of development involves only his return to the upper world and does not deepen and expand the anima experience, which could chain him down. Also, in this fairytale a single anima figure is not essential considering their multiple occurrences. The anima is in principle largely assimilated in the form of the *paris*, and a repetition of the theme of making the anima conscious is unnecessary and apparently does not correspond to this narrative level. (A higher level of anima awareness would be an exposition focusing on the *auseinandersetzung* with a *single* anima figure.)

946   In the next episode, Djulek Batür must gain the favor of the Simurgh bird by overcoming a dragon that threatens her children. For the third time a battle takes place in which the psychic nature of the unconscious must overcome the forces of regressive instinctual drives. The first battle was against subjugation, the second for knowledge, and the third to disentangle from the dark powers. The Simurgh is a well-known figure in Near Eastern mythology. Jungbauer, the collector of the German edition of the Turkestani tales, notes:

947   The legendary bird Simurgh, the German griffin, the Bharunda bird of the Hindus, was known among the Persians, from which the designation [Simurgh] was transferred to various Turkish peoples, Kyrgyz, Bashkirs, Tatars, and others with minor changes in vowel constituents. Thus, we meet names like Samrak, Samruk, Samrau, and Samurak. To the Arabs, the bird is known by the name Anka, which means a bird with a long neck. The Persian word Simurgh can be explained as "the silver bird"; the bird with shiny, silver feathers. According to popular belief, this bird is so large that if it spreads its wings out fully, it blocks out the sun. Its wings contain all the colors of every bird in the world, and on its neck is a white stripe like a collar. It lays gigantic eggs and lives for two thousand years. It has such power that it can carry away a camel or an elephant.[90] According to some traditions, it has a human face. All Muslims ascribe to it the ability to speak."[91]

---

[89] See the differently configured version of similar motifs in a Kyrgyz legend reported in B. Schweitzer, *Herakles*, Tübingen 1922 p. 213, according to which the hero, to rescue his abducted wife, fought and killed a seven-headed monster at the bottom of the well. For the return flight he is dependent on the bird since the other two heroes are too weak to pull up him and his wife, along with their entourage. See also L. Frobenius, *Zeitalter*, Berlin 1904 pp. 139–144 and the tale from *One Thousand and One Nights* cited by J. Bolte and G. Polívka, *Anmerkungen,* Vol. 2, Leipzig 1915 p. 314 where the hero also protects the children of the roc from a snake. In gratitude the roc flies him to the upper world.
[90] See also the second voyage of "Sinbad the Sailor," where the hero lets himself be carried by a great roc – note by Jungbauer.
[91] *Märchen aus Turkestan und Tibet* p. 296. See more material in de Gubernatis, *Zoological*, London 1872 p. 188f.

948   For the Sufi mystics, similarly to the Hindu wild swan Hamsa, Simurgh acquired the meaning of the inner Self or God.[92]

949   When the bird Simurgh carries Djulek Batür out from the underworld, it shows that Djulek Batür gained intellectual freedom, wisdom, and superiority through his struggles and adventures. The bird lives in a plane tree near a spring, and is, or rather her children are, threatened by a dragon. The spring in the unconscious can be interpreted as the source of life, and associated with it is the archetypal image of the enmity between bird and snake. This is a symbol of the opposition between spirit [mind] and nature, an image often combined with the tree as a symbol of inner becoming [individuation]. Another representation of this conflict is that of the Germanic world ash, Yggdrasil: in its crown lives an eagle and a dragon devours its roots, and these two are constantly feuding.

950   When Djulek Batür breaks this vicious cycle by killing his instinctually-driven side, he wins freedom. But having trusted a superhuman demonic spirit, and letting himself be carried by it, he is to a certain extent identified with it. On the final flight to the upper world he is again close to the danger of crashing down during this passionate, uplifting spiritual swing to the heights, or at least of failing to reach his goal. (We have already met this motif of the danger of not reaching the goal due to the exhausted stock of nourishment in "The Thrush and the Nightingale" and "The Three Brothers, Three Sisters, and the Half-Iron Man"; and it is evidently presumed in the variants mentioned above.) In all these cases the hero must sacrifice "his own flesh" to survive the journey.

951   Unlike most other parallels, in the present Uzbek version Djulek Batür gives the Simurgh meat when she asks for water and water when she asks for meat. Only at the end, just when they approach the sphere of consciousness, does he give meat (from his own body) when asked for meat. Like the "disobedience" in "The Golden Bird," such arbitrary actions on the part of the hero express the independence of the conscious mind. That the bird's powers threaten to fail towards the end of the flight indicates the enormous effort it takes to reach the threshold of consciousness. At first the conscious mind humbly waives its claim to independence and supremacy, the sacrifice of meat [his own flesh]. The meaning of this is analogous to the commitment at the beginning to fight the dragon in order to liberate the king's daughter. And also in this case the problem posed by the unconscious is resolved: the connection between the core of consciousness and the sustaining spirit of the unconscious

---

[92] Van der Leeuw writes:
   Similarly, the "thirty birds," whose pilgrimage is described by the sufi Fariduddin Attar, at the goal find only themselves: *Simurgh* (a term meaning "thirty birds"). God is a mirror in which everyone views himself. "So they vanish in Him forever, as the shadow disappears in the sun." (Van der Leeuw p. 504, italics in original, internal quote is from Field, *Mystics and Saints of Islam*, p. 131ff.)

is so profound that the secular world can be reached in health and the problems there can be put in order.[93]

952   Once again in the upper world, Djulek Batür finally wins the *pari* who had been waiting for him by heaving the stone far over the wall, an accomplishment which his struggling companions apparently could not manage. The *pari* had created this wall from a lump of clay by breathing on it and speaking the name of God. This episode clearly expresses the creative power of the anima. To the extent that the stone is generally a symbol of the Self, this scene describes a test of how the hero can fare with his own self, or put even more simply, how he can deal with himself.[94] The wall may well represent the border to the unconscious, to the realm of the anima. Only one who has achieved the right relationship to the Self can get over this wall and thus gain the anima. Casting the stone is the equivalent of a pronouncement of fate,[95] and Djulek Batür proves that he can overcome the obstacles that stand in the way of his connection with the *pari*, that he can reach "the other side," and this is because he now knows this other side.

953   Djulek Batür's homecoming brings some well-known motifs: thanks to his completed inner journey, he has become a healer and cures the blindness of his elderly parents.[96] (Compare here bringing the carpet back to the old king in "The Three Feathers," the horse to the old miller in "The Poor Miller's Boy and the Cat," and the water of life and the apples to the tsar in "The Virgin Tsar," among others.) The secular brothers are again punished by a kind of divine judgement (similar to eliminating the healed cripples by throwing the stone), their arrows fly back to them, that is, they perish by their own evil intentions.[97] It is as if by bringing the Self to light the collective-secular tendencies are extinguished without a fight, freeing the total personality and dissolving the negative bond with the brothers.

954   Only the hero can master the ever-changing game in such a quest with its string of new challenges and demands to adapt to the unconscious. With its magnificent portrayal in mythic images, this fairytale answers the question:

955   "How can I best live in the dance of life with this wisdom of the unconscious and still preserve myself?" This task demands to be

---

[93] For more on the symbolism of the return journey and thresholds in general, see H. Silberer, "Symbolik des Erwachens," Leipzig and Wien 1912 *passim*.
[94] Cf. Nietzsche, "O Zarathustra, thou stone of wisdom, thou sling-stone, thou star-destroyer! Thyself threwest thou so high, but every thrown stone *must* fall! Condemned by thyself, and to thine own stoning: O Zarathustra, far indeed threwest thyself, thy stone – but upon thyself will it fall back!" [F. Nietzsche, *Thus Spake Zarathustra*, Wordsworth, 1999.]
[95] See the epic Russian tale, "Ivan the Cow's Son," where three brothers throw a ball into the air to see which one will be the eldest. Cf. on the relationship of betting games, winning lots, and pronouncements of an oracle, see, J. Huizinga, *Homo ludens*, Amsterdam 1939 p. 80f.
[96] The significance of saliva as an "appurtenance" and soul-substance see, L. Lévy-Bruhl, *The "Soul" of the Primitive*, New York 1928 pp. 115–127, and Bächtold-Stäubli under *Speichel* [saliva].
[97] On the same motif in Hindu myth see, H. Zimmer, *Maya*, Stuttgart and Berlin 1936 p. 177.

solved anew each day, to satisfy the ever-changing equations between the will of the I, which should secure and preserve itself, and the rhythm of the circle dance that requires faithful devotion to its constantly changing form. The unconscious in us, always ready with a wink to guide us into danger and then to rescue us, laughing silently over every formula it gives us, over every enlightenment from its darkness, and when we hold the answer tight and think, 'now I have it, now no trouble will come over me again' . . . Because it is a wisdom just like any other, it holds for a time, but is pure delusion for all other times; what it whispers for the next step in the dance, it whispers only for this moment and no other.[98]

---

[98] *Ibid* p. 167f.

Chapter 16
The Magician Palermo

956 A fairytale that reflects this repeated *auseinandersetzung* with the unconscious, but each time with a new and different constellation and with an astonishing variety of images, is the Spanish tale "The Magician Palermo":

957 Long ago there lived a prince who was greatly given to gaming. He gambled away all his possessions, and when he had lost everything he left the palace in despair. He had heard of a magician who was so powerful that he could do anything he wished. The name of the magician was Palermo. "How I wish that I had the power of the magician Palermo!" moaned the prince. "Then it would be easy to regain all that I have lost."

958 Suddenly the prince heard a voice at his elbow. "What is it that you want?" said the voice. The prince fell upon his face on the ground. "I am a foolish, stupid prince who has gambled away all his possessions. If I only knew how to regain my losses I'd be the happiest prince in the world," said he. "I'd also be wise enough to take better care of my property in the future."

959 "I am the magician Palermo," said the voice. "I will give you a bag containing a thousand pieces of silver. You must pay it back to me within the year. Every time you play with these silver pieces of mine you will win. You will soon be a rich prince again, so it will be easy for you to restore the silver. The difficult part of the affair is that you must pay it back to me where I live. That is far, far away beyond the sea. At the end of your journey I promise you one of my own daughters for your wife."

960 "Agreed!" cried the prince. "My heartiest thanks for all that you are doing for me!" When the prince returned to the palace his luck had changed. Every time he played with the pieces of silver which the magician Palermo had given him, he won. He played until he had not only regained all that he had lost but also until he had won a great fortune in addition. Then he set out to find the house of the magician

Palermo to pay back the thousand pieces of silver, according to the agreement.

961   The prince traveled about, asking everyone he met where the palace of the magician Palermo was to be found. No one knew how to direct him there. Finally he came to the palace of the little birds. They had not even heard of the magician Palermo, and did not know the way but directed the prince to the palace of the big birds.

962   At the palace of the big birds, the birds had heard of the magician Palermo, but also did not know the way. However, at last the eagle came flying home. He had been to the palace of the magician Palermo and agreed to take the prince there but warned that the journey would be difficult. "One flies for days and days, seeing nothing except the salt water." They needed to take the meat of a horse and a sheep, and the prince had to feed the eagle a quarter of horsemeat or mutton when he asked for it. Even though they made these provisions, the journey took so long that they ran out of meat and prince allowed the eagle to pick some meat off his thigh. At last they reached the palace of the magician Palermo.

963   The eagle bid him to call "Help me, o eagle!" whenever he was in difficulty and flew off.

964   The prince entered the magician palace and repaid his debt. The magician also remembered his own promise to give the prince his daughter, but first he wanted to put the prince to the test. The magician ordered him to plow up a mountain, sow it with wheat, and harvest it, and then make a little cake out of the wheat for the magician to enjoy for breakfast.

965   In his need, the prince called to the eagle, upon which a beautiful maiden appeared to him. She was the youngest daughter of the magician Palermo and called Luisa. She explained that the magician set the impossible task because he did not want to let her go, but that she would complete the task on his behalf. The next morning the mountain had been plowed and planted and harvested and the magician's daughter gave a little cake made out of the wheat to the prince. It was wrapped in a napkin and placed on a tray ready for him to serve to the magician Palermo for breakfast.

966   When the magician saw the little cake on the platter he ran to the window. There he saw the mountain converted into a freshly harvested field. He was surprised but then he set a second task. This time the prince had to break in the wild black horse. Again the prince went out into the field and asked help of the eagle. The magician's

daughter immediately came in answer to his call. When she heard the new task given to the prince she said, "In the morning place a saddle, bridle, and stirrups upon the black horse and lead him out into the field. Cut a big sharp stick. The black horse is my father, the saddle my mother, the two stirrups my two sisters and I am the bridle. Take your stout stick and beat the horse, the saddle, and the stirrups, but be sure that you do not beat the bridle. That would be beating me."

967   The next morning the prince led the black horse out into the field. He gave a terrible beating to the horse, the saddle, and the stirrups, but he never touched the bridle. After the beating, the black horse was entirely tamed. It was easy for the prince to mount him and ride him. When the prince put the horse in the stable and entered the palace he found the magician Palermo, his wife, and his two eldest daughters sick in bed with their bruises. Luisa was as well as ever, and because of this her father was suspicious that she had helped the prince.

968   The magician therefore set a third task. This time, the prince had to find a ring that had belonged to the magician's grandmother and had fallen into the sea and return it to the magician. Again the prince called on the help of the eagle and again Luisa appeared at his side. When she heard that the magician Palermo had asked for the ring she knew that her father was suspicious of her having given aid to the prince.

969   "You will have to kill me and cut my body into pieces in order to get this ring out of the depths of the sea," she said. "Only be sure that when you cut me into pieces you tie the pieces up in a cloth and do not lose any of them. Despite his great resistance, the prince did as Luisa commanded him. When he tied up the pieces of body in the cloth, however, he let a tiny piece fall to the ground unnoticed. Soon the sea rose in great waves. Out of the waves came Luisa with the ring upon her finger, however, her little finger was missing. When the prince delivered the ring to the magician Palermo the magician was greatly surprised. Now, the magician Palermo led the prince to his three daughters to choose his bride, but he blindfolded the prince's eyes. However, the prince was able to choose Luisa because he recognized her by her missing little finger. The magician was then compelled to give the prince Luisa as his bride,[1] but he swore that the pair would pay a heavy price.

---

[1] [The version by Eells ends here with a happy homecoming on the backs of four great eagles. The German translation used by Von Franz continues and is also used here.]

970   That evening, they made their escape. Luisa ordered the prince to go to the stable where he would find two horses. The fat one runs thirty miles in an hour, the thin one forty. He had to saddle the latter.

971   In the meantime Luisa spat in a vessel. Her father was calling to her and she answered him each time. When they escape, he would know that she was not there when she would stop answering him. Her spittle, however, would answer for her until it dried up, thereby giving the pair a headstart. When the prince returned with the horses, Luisa noticed he had saddled the wrong horse. However, there was not enough time to change horses.

972   They mounted the slower horse and made their escape. In the meantime, the magician Palermo called out again, "Luisa, Luisa!" and her spittle answered, "Your wish, father?" And this continued for a while. But then the spittle began to dry up and from call to call the echo became weaker, until it finally ceased altogether.

973   Upon discovering the pair's escape the magician went in pursuit on the forty-miler horse and soon caught up with them. But Luisa changed their horse into a garden, the prince into a gardener, and herself into a head of lettuce. She ordered the prince to play dumb if the magician asked him anything.

974   And just what she said really happened. The magician came, saw the gardener and asked, "My dear fellow, have you seen a man and a woman riding by here on a fat horse?" "I have only this salad, but it is good," said the prince. "I am not talking about that, I want to know if you saw two people traveling on horseback!" "This year the crops are not so good, maybe next year they will be better," answered the prince again, looking at the fields.

975   "To the devil with you!" said the magician and returned to his castle, and told his wife what had happened. "You are really an idiot!" his wife said to him. "The garden was the horse, the head of lettuce was our daughter, and the prince was the gardener!"

976   The magician then mounted his horse again, and galloped off in pursuit. Soon he had almost caught up again. This time Luisa turned the horse into a hermitage, the prince into a hermit and herself into the picture of a saint. Soon the magician Palermo arrived at that place and asked, "Dear hermit, have you seen two young people riding past on a fat horse?"

977   "Oil for the lamp, oil for the lamp!" "I am not talking about that, but if you have seen two people riding by on horseback!" "Soon it will all be burned down, soon all burned down!" The magician sent all the

doves to the devil, and turned back home swearing heavily to himself. As the mother heard the story, she said, "The hermit was your son-in-law and your daughter was the picture of the saint. Go, ride again after them and this time, bring back what you have found."

978 The magician angrily took on the chase again and swore they would not evade him this time. Soon he had caught up with them again. Luisa took out an egg and threw it onto the ground. It transformed into an ocean that separated themselves from the father. When the magician arrived at the shore, he looked across the expanse and saw that he could not overtake them, so he called out to the youth, "When you touch a dog, or when an old woman embraces you, you will forget Luisa." He then turned back to his castle.

979 The young pair continued on their way and came into the prince's country. But before they arrived at the palace, the prince said to Luisa, "Wait for me here, I am going to get the carriage and everything that is necessary for you to enter the city, as is proper for us." She warned him not to go without her but the prince promised to be careful.

980 The prince was cautious not to embrace anyone when he returned home. He ordered the carriage and gathered an entourage to greet his wife. Then he rested a while for he was very tired and while he lay asleep his old grandmother entered and embraced him and when the prince awoke he had forgotten about his wife.

981 In the meantime, Luisa had waited in vain for him and when she noticed that he would not return, she went into the city and hired herself out as a cleaning woman in the service of a rich couple. This couple had a beautiful daughter. As time passed, the prince fell in love with this daughter and asked for her hand in marriage.

982 As the day of the wedding approached, Luisa suggested to her mistress that she set up a puppet show with the puppets that she owned. The mistress thought this a good idea and ordered Luisa to prepare the puppets. Luisa set to work and made clothes for the puppets. For one woman puppet she made clothes like those she had worn when the prince left her at the edge of the city. For the man puppet she made clothes like those the prince had worn on that day he went to make preparations for her entry into the city.

983 The wedding day came and when the whole company had gathered, they entered the room where the puppet theater was ready. Luisa hid herself behind the stage. One of the puppets carried a cane and said to the other, "Christoph, do you remember that you went looking for

the castle of the magician Palermo and that an eagle had flown you there on its wings?"

984 "No," answered the puppet that was clothed as the prince. He promptly received a blow from the cane. The real prince, sitting in the audience following the puppet show, suddenly cringed. He felt the blow just as if he himself had received it. The puppet with the cane continued, "Christoph, do you remember how the magician ordered that you plow up a mountain, sow it with wheat, and harvest it. Then you made a little cake out of the wheat to give the magician with his breakfast chocolate?"

985 "No," And again the puppet and the real prince received a blow from the cane. "Do you remember the black horse you had to tame?" "No." "Do you remember you had to fetch a ring that had fallen into the sea?" "No."

986 Even when the real prince felt the blows, he spoke no word. Luisa, speaking as the puppetmistress then said, "Do you remember that my father, pronounced a spell and said that you would forget me when an old woman embraced you?" As the male puppet got another blow, it broke into a thousand pieces. The real prince felt such great pain that he jumped up and pressed his hand to his forehead, and what had happened returned to his mind. Thus, the prince found back his Luisa. The other woman suddenly lost her groom, and was left standing alone by the puppet show. Now this tale is over and we are going home.[2]

987 The beginning of this tale is reminiscent of the Swedish tale "Lasse, My Servant" in which the hero also squanders all that he owns and thus falls into great distress; this being the precondition for his adventure-quest. For this is when the human being turns to the irrational powers of his soul, as in this tale where the prince seeks out the magician. This is similar to the Spanish fairytale "The Beauty of the World" in which the hero also gambles away his kingdom. Palermo the magician is, as it turns out in the course of the tale, the father of the anima figure and thus a manifestation of the spirit hidden in nature or in the unconscious. But the story also contains hints that he is the shadow of the hero. This is evident when we compare this tale with the aforementioned "The Beauty of the World" in which the hero appeals to the "gentleman" for help, the same man to whom he has lost everything. This gentleman cheats him in exactly the same way as the merchants trick the hero

---

[2] [Eells pp. 159-173 (English, first part) and H. Meier and F. Karlinger, *Spanische*, München 1991 pp. 50-62 (German, second part). Tale shortened.]

in the tale "The Story of Djihanshah." The Lord of the Magic Castle turns out later to be an evil black man. Whereas in "The Beauty of the World," the personal shadow and the deity of the magical world are portrayed as separate figures, in "The Magician Palermo" they are united into one person.

988   In a parallel French version, Richard the farmer's son accepts the help of the devil to aid his impoverished father. The devil's condition is that he must return the empty sack that held the money to the "Black Mountain" otherwise Richard would forever belong to the evil ones. Riding on a raven, Richard arrives but only by sacrificing a piece of his own flesh to the bird when the meat supply is consumed. After the raven leaves him at the foot of the black mountain he comes upon a fountain in which three daughters of the devil are bathing. He steals the clothes of the most beautiful one and manages to win her love. (The tale continues in parallel to the course of "The Magician Palermo" where the devil sets impossible tasks and the couple must flee.)[3]

989   In a Roma tale "The Green Man" (summarized):

> A young miller named Hans was an expert at gambling with cards. One day he won against a stranger who had bet a castle. When Hans lost the next game, the stranger said, "You must now seek my castle. My name is the green man who lives in no-man's-land. And if you do not find my castle within one year and one day, I will strike off your head." From an old woman Hans received a ball of yarn that guided him and a horse, and set off in search of the green man's castle. He reached a lake where he observed three white birds as they removed their plumage and went bathing. The hero took the feather clothing of the last bird and refused to give it back unless the bird carried him across the lake to the castle of the green man. She carried him across and there changed into the daughter of the green man. When the green man discovered them, he confronted them with a series of impossible tasks (similar to those of the magician Palermo) that the maiden helped the young miller to accomplish. Through this he won the young man and after the death of the green man they lived together in his castle.

990   These two parallels mix the motifs of "The Story of Djihanshah" and "The Magician Palermo." In both tales the heroes' secular shadow and their magical father are personified by one and the same person. (The green man is a nature spirit, his castle is a mandala. Whoever loses against this shadow figure in the game of life must laboriously seek its treasures.) Already in "The Devil with the Three Golden Hairs" we noted how the figure of the ferryman unified a

---

[3] G. Huet, *Les contes*, Paris 1923 p. 18ff. The second of these tasks will be recounted below.

figure of the demonic underworld with the shadow. Just as the images of the Great Mother and the anima represent two different archetypes but sometimes are identical, so also the figures of the demonic father and the shadow are two different beings (such as in "The Golden Bird") but they often merge into one and the same guise. Psychologically put, the experience of the shadow can signal the encounter with the most powerful forces of unconscious demonic possession.

991   At the beginning of "The Magician Palermo" the hero receives from his demonic opponent the bag with the winning silver pieces. This shows that by making contact with the unconscious, he gains an immense superiority in the world. But he must pay for this superiority, because the way into the inner reaches of the psyche is no cheap method to reign over the world (although this gift was one of his goals), but rather it leads into the distant world of unknown horrors on the "other side." Therefore, the prince must undertake the great quest or, put differently, the conscious mind is forced to render due justice to the hidden background of its own personality. Here also, the Spanish tale "The Beauty of the World" describes an appealing scene: the hero, left alone on an island and desperate with thirst, begins to dig for water with his bare hands. After a long and painstaking endeavor, he arrives at a magnificent *and* dangerous magic castle. He who never wants to accomplish anything in the world is forced by fate to gain access to the unconscious with his last efforts. The quest takes the hero in "The Magician Palermo" first to the castle of the small, and then of the big birds where he finds the guiding eagle. The multiplicity of birds suggests that the hero is initially overwhelmed by a mixture of intuitive ideas, hunches, and thoughts emerging from the unconscious, and this situation only improves when the multitude gradually consolidates into the symbol of the eagle as a unified spiritual directive.

992   In most myths the eagle is a solar bird, for example, as the theriomorphic personification of the Hyperborean Apollo.[4] In this sense, it is a symbol of the winter and night sun, that is, a kind of consciousness, or a spirit of the unconscious. For this reason, the eagle is often represented in fairytales as a demon of the depths.[5] Even more often the eagle is the carrier and guide for the hero in his journey into or out of the unconscious.[6] As such he is a psychopomp figure in animal form like the fox in "The Golden Bird," except that the eagle embodies more the psychic-spiritual, and less the instinctual-animal, directives in the unconscious. In its mythological relationship with

---

[4] See J. J. Bachofen, *Orphische Theologie*, Basel 1867 p. 20; A. Dieterich, *Eine Mithrasliturgie*, Leipzig and Berlin 1923 p. 54 and *ibid* p. 184 *Seelenvogel* [soul bird]. See also H. Leisegang, *Serpent*, London 1955 pp. 243–44.

[5] See, for example, in "The Strange Boy" and "The Three Fairies."

[6] For example, in "The Duck Maiden," "The Artful Eagle," "Balai and Boti," "The Beauty of the World" and "The Mountain of the Golden Queen."

the phoenix, it is also a symbol of self-renewal.[7] This nuance is mainly due to the oft-depicted mythological dichotomy of eagle and snake (as mind and body). More rarely, but therefore also more remarkable, is the motif of the secret identity of eagle and the anima that appears in the present tale.[8] This is the typical connection of the anima with animal helpers or with the demonic father god, which to a certain extent embodies the masculine-psychic [spiritual] element in the anima. (Seen psychologically, this is an intellectual factor in both men and women that represents their shared unconscious psychic connection.)

993   The same episode with the birds that show the way, and the eagle that carries the hero, is also found in the fairytale "The Beauty of the World." There, an extensive interim episode is inserted, however, that replaces the difficulties and problems that come later in "The Magician Palermo," summarized here:

994   The hero was imprisoned by an evil but friendly black man who spared his life if he agreed to work for him. Having nothing to lose, the hero accepted the offer and the man showed him around the castle. The black man warned the hero not to enter one chamber where the Beauty of the World lay in an enchanted sleep. To get to her, one had to pass horrible man-eating lions, whirling hammers, a giant grinding millstone, and a huge snake.[9] Naturally the hero became bored with his tasks and entered the forbidden chamber. There he vanquished the fierce guarding lions by throwing them his hat, the whirling hammers with his jacket, and the furiously spinning millstone with his waistcoat, and to the dreadful snake guard he sacrificed his hard leather shoes. The snake choked on the hard leather and this gave the hero the chance to pull out his knife and cut off its head. Then he found the sleeping Beauty of the World and awakened her from enchanted sleep with a kiss.

995   The figure of the black man brings new perspective to the figure of the wise old one in "The Story of Djihanishah," who despite his "light aspect" appears as the demonic father deity. Only from his temporary disappearance in the bird kingdom is it inferred that he was not redeemed. Through the parallel figure of the black man that appears here, the unredeemed dark demonic side

---

[7] See J. Bolte and L. Mackensen, *Handwörterbuch* Berlin 1930, under *Adler* [eagle].
[8] Also in "Muhammad, the Shepherd, and the Pari Princess." See further examples in J. Bolte and L. Mackensen *op. cit.*, under *Adler*.
[9] This figure of the black man illuminates anew the character of the old man with the white beard in "The Story of Djihanshah," who was also the padishah of the birds. In spite of his "light" aspect, we interpreted this figure initially as a demonic father deity and only from his temporary disappearance into the bird kingdom did we acknowledge his unredeemed aspect. The appearance here of a parallel character in the figure of the black man further indicates and clarifies the unredeemed character of the dark demonic side.)

is now made clear. The sacrifice of pieces of his clothing signifies the abandonment of attitudes that do not really belong to one's real nature. These are pieces of the persona, the outer mask that one tends to show when dealing with the outer world and thereby concealing one's inner essence. Only when these outer garments are sacrificed, can the hero penetrate to the anima. The dangers that lie here in ambush are embodiments of the hazards carried by these attitudes since they can also appear as devouring beasts. The hammer and the millstone are similar to the widespread motif of the clashing cliffs and symbolize the risk of being crushed between the opposites, to succumb to despair when faced with the paradox.

996   The anima figure then flies forth as a dove and the hero must go in search of her afresh. He finds her in the "Garden of the Three Oranges." He tries to capture her by staying awake but he cannot manage this, and she escapes him again. Now he has to go and seek her in the "Castle of Three Golden Almonds." Here we see again the clear parallels between the black man and the old man in "The Story of Djihanishah"; they both tend gardens in which the anima comes to bathe as a bird. The inability-to-stay-awake motif, which is in other tales a shortcoming of the secular brothers, here as in the other tales, indicates a weakness of consciousness, whereby the hero loses his capacity to concentrate on the unconscious and thus cannot grasp its contents, particularly the anima. Here, this weakness is motivated by the effect of the shadow or the chthonic god. This figure embodies the unfathomable darkness of the unconscious, which confuses the conscious mind and makes it impossible to grasp and comprehend the psychic content. Now follows a bird episode that appears earlier in "The Magician Palermo." In that version, after the hero reaches the enchanted castle and the anima, new difficulties are encountered and struggles with the Lord of the Underworld ensue, while in "The Beauty of the World" the hero wins the anima relatively easily.[10]

997   We now return to the discussion of, "The Magician Palermo." With respect to their content, the impossible tasks that are delegated to the hero are reminiscent of Djulek Batür's taming of the tigers and plowing the fields in the underworld. Here, it is done through the cultivation of the natural, undomesticated powers of the unconscious through labor (plowing, sowing, harvesting, and so forth) on the one hand, and, on the other hand, by exerting outer energy (breaking in the wild black horse). It is instructive to understand the essence of the motif that the black horse is the magician, the saddle his wife, the two stirrups are two daughters, and the bridle is Luisa. The family embodies in its entirety the untamed wildness of instinctual life, which, decomposed, comprises the anima, the mother imago, and the demonic father god as the divine spirit in nature. The totality of these archetypal figures

---

[10] Extracts translated from H. Meier and F. & Karlinger, *Spanische*, München 1991 pp. 63–74.

initially constitutes the unconscious vitality of a human being. In that the hero protects the positive side (anima) and overcomes the negative side, he proves to be a superior man of knowledge; at the same time this knowledge has been mediated and channeled from the unconscious by the anima. It must be added that the hero has more or less unconsciously meandered through the situation without recognizing the power that has led him to take the correct action. He is given the task, therefore, of dismembering her to get the ring, that is, to consciously "analyze" who and what he is dealing with. The lost ring of Palermo's grandmother is a symbol of the Self in its quality of being the unifying element between the opposites. This power that binds all together,[11] that was initially in the deepest layer (that of the instincts) of the unconscious (Great Mother) is now completely lost in the unknowable (the sea). This is an image indicating that the right connection to the unconscious in its feminine-maternal aspect is missing. To the extent that the hero consciously dissects the figure of the anima and, on the other hand, is committed to the primordial maternal ground – a paradoxical act that combines exact conscious intellectual dissection with devoted immersion – he gains a new a relationship to his soul. This time it is with the ring, a unifying symbol, so that a permanent connection is possible, which is why the magician can no longer stand in the way of the marriage. The loss of the anima's little finger, the sign by which he regains her in the test of recognition, indicates that, in spite of all efforts, a piece of the anima remains in the unconscious,[12] and cannot be consciously comprehended by the hero. The little finger is a symbol of natural, intuitive knowledge,[13] and the fact that he let a tiny piece fall to the ground unnoticed thus shows that the hero cannot grasp something of the natural and superior wisdom of the woman, and that he does not quite possess it. This also follows from the subsequent peripeteias.

998   In the variant mentioned by Huet, the devil sets the hero to tests, it is the task for the second day that is of most interest to us:

999   The hero, Richard, must climb to the top of a high marble tower that is as smooth as glass, and bring down a nest. When Richard cannot climb it, the girl has him dismember her and boil her pieces in a large kettle. According to her previous instructions, he makes a ladder out of her bones. After he has climbed the tower and retrieved the nest, he puts the bones on the earth back into right place. He performs the task as required and the maiden comes back to life. Only he forget the

---

[11] [See the saying in Tolkien's *Lord of the Rings* "The one ring to bind them all."]
[12] See "The Six Swans."
[13] See the [German] saying, "the little finger told me so." In this respect, as already indicated, the little finger is a phallic, and consequently, creative symbol that represents here a psychic (intelligence) in the female soul-figure (as also personified by the eagle).

bone of the little toe, over which the girl just laughs. When the next night comes and he must choose which one of the three daughters he would like to marry, he chooses the one who only has four toes on one foot. (Then follows the escape to his parents who live "in a Christian place.")[14]

1000   The differences compared to the same episode in "The Magician Palermo" are minor but still interesting. The nest, which probably contains eggs, is a mandala, a symbol of the Self. For human beings, that is the conscious mind, [full awareness of the Self] is unattainable. The boiling of the dismembered anima in the kettle corresponds to the immersion in the sea in the Spanish version, because the kettle, especially when filled with water, is a symbol of the unconscious in the maternal sense, just as is the sea. The bone ladder graphically represents how a man – here with the help of the anima –makes the effort step by step to meet the challenges of the unconscious. Just like Antaeus life is regained from contact with the earth. The little toe takes the place of the little finger. That the girl laughs at her missing finger may be because she foresees the advantage this will give the hero in differentiating her from her sisters. It could also be because she savors the quiet triumph that a part of her being will never be grasped by the conscious mind.[15]

---

[14] See G. Huet, *Les contes*, Paris 1923 p. 18ff.

[15] There is also a Samoan version "Siati" (originally sung in verses):

There was a youth called Siati noted for his singing. A serenading god came along, threw down a challenge, and promised him his fair daughter if he was the better singer. They sung, Siati beat him, and off he went to the land of the god, riding on a shark belonging to his aunt. They reached the place. The shark went in to the shore, set him down, and told him to go to the bathing-place, where he would find the daughters of the god, the one was called Puapae (White Fish),and the other Puauli (Dark Fish). Siati went and sat down at the bathing-place. The girls had been there, but had gone away. Puapae had forgotten her comb, returned to get it, and there she found Siati. "Siati," said she, "why have you come here?" "I have come to seek the song-god and get his daughter to be my wife." "My father," said she, "is more of a god than a man; eat nothing he hands you, never sit on a high seat lest death should follow, and now let us unite." Siati and Puapae were united in marriage, but they went off to live elsewhere. The god sent his daughter Puauli to Puapae to tell her husband to build him a house, and that it must be finished that very day, under a penalty of death and the oven. Siati cried, but his wife Puapae comforted him, said she could do it, and off she went and built the house, and by the evening was weeding all around it. In came another order, and that was for Siati to fight with the dog. The fight took place and Siati conquered. Next the god had lost his ring, and said Siati must go to the sea and find it. Again, Siati wept, and again his wife cheered him. "I will find the ring," said she, "only do what I tell you. Cut my body in two, throw me into the sea, and stand still on the beach until I come back." He did so, cut her in two, threw her into the sea, she was changed into a fish, and away she went to seek for the ring. Siati stood and stood, sat and lay down, stood again, and then lay down, and went off to sleep. Puapae returned, she was thrown up by the fish and stood on the shore. Siati awoke by the splash of the seawater on his face. She scolded him for not keeping awake, and then said: "There is the ring, let us go with it in the early morning." And in the morning off the two went to her father. That very morning the god called his daughter Puauli and said, "Come, take me on your back, and let us seek Siati that I may eat him." Presently they started back, Siati and Puapae were coming. Puapae and Siati threw down the comb and it became a bush of thorns in the way to intercept the god and Puauli. But they struggled through the thorns. They threw down a bottle of earth, and that became a mountain; and then they threw

1001   In "The Magician Palermo" the hero's lack of mastery surfaces when he chooses, against the advice of the anima, the slower horse for their escape and thereby provokes a new threat by the magician. This means that the spirit of the unconscious is still a threat and the ego (the conscious mind) is still not up to it. Thus ensues the "magical flight," psychologically an attempt to repress a non-assimilable inner content. The magical flight transpires here partly in the form of a series of shape-shiftings by the fugitives in which not only magical barriers arise, but the fleeing pair also change themselves into various guises in order to remain undetected.[16] Psychologically, the escape episode represents an example of how the conscious mind is transformed by contact with the unconscious: the conscious mind absorbs and is transformed by inner contents, just as those inner contents take in and incorporate conscious elements. When the conscious mind changes its attitude, so does the unconscious change the face that it turns towards consciousness. Then, in this new situation, the *auseinandersetzung* begins anew but on another level.

1002   This transformation of the unconscious shows itself here in that the mother imago gradually replaces that of the father as the persecutor. The first hint of this is that the wife of the magician sees through the tricks of the fugitives. Then, second, it is the grandmother of the hero who erases his memory of Luisa with her embrace. Also, the figures that the fugitives take on are not accidental. The garden and the hermitage represent a confined space, a mandala. The protected circle serves to make the conscious mind invulnerable against the disintegrating powers of the unconscious, in our case

---

down their bottle of water, and that became a sea and drowned the god and Puauli. Puapae said to Siati, "My father and sister are dead, and all on account of my love for you; you may go now and visit your family and friends while I remain here, but see that you do not behave unseemly." He went, visited all his friends, and then he forgot his wife Puapae. He tried to marry again, but Puapae came and stood on the left side. The chief called out, "Which is your wife, Siati?" "The one on the right side." Puapae then broke silence and cried out, "Ah, Siati, you have forgotten all I did for you!" and off she went. Siati remembered now all that had happened, darted after her crying, and then fell down and died. (Turner pp. 102-104). Noteworthy here is the splitting of the anima into a positive and a negative form, both assigned to the demonic father god. The anima-daughters are figured as carrying (that is, sustaining, supporting) powers of the god of the depths. They actually take the place of the demonic mother. This version especially clearly illustrates the tendency to represent the anima as being bound to the father deity. The light anima figure, in order to get the ring, is further divided. This recorded version does not clearly state whether only one part or both parts become fish. In any case, the image corresponds to the fragmentation in the previous versions. Because she transforms into fish shape she is more linked to the magical than the anima figures of the other versions and also draws the hero into that world. Her submergence causes Siati to fall asleep, because the weak state of consciousness of the primitive is dependent on the luminosity of the unconscious. He shows that he (the ego, the conscious mind) is barely involved in the solution of the problem. (In some fairytales, the anima advises the hero to sleep, however, while she works her wonders. In these cases, the task is to be solved by the unconscious with the conscious mind asleep. Here, in contrast, the anima figure is very annoyed about Siati falling asleep, according to the psychic situation of the primitive, where one must aspire to more consciousness.) Had he been more wakeful, this might have helped him later to remember her, or she would have broken through to repair his phase of slipping back, and he might have remained alive.

[16] See the magical flight in "The Water-Nixie," "The Wonderful Hair" and the transformation flight in "Wila Remain Wila," "Kitschüw," and "The Sea King and Vasilisa the Wise," among others.

this is represented by the magician who creates panic in the face of incomprehensible fantasies and overwhelming dark emotions. The garden is a protective reserve created by the intellect against wild nature; the hermitage a cultic sanctuary against direct contact with the unfathomable darkness of the passions.

1003   The third protective measure that the anima conjures up against the magician is an egg, from which arises an uncrossable sea. The egg, as "the round thing"; a seed, germ, and embryo, is a symbol of the Self. In alchemical symbolism, the egg signifies the primeval chaos and the *semen mundi* [the seed of the world]; it is thus an image of the World Egg.[17] The egg has the same cosmogonic meaning here as in other areas of mythological lore. Thus, according to Orphic doctrine, the world is created from a primordial egg; from the top half heaven, from the bottom, the earth.[18]

1004   As such the egg is a parable of the world and also matter itself.[19] Likewise, according to the Hindu view, the world emerged from the self-begotten egg of Prajapati, the "Lord of Creation," in which he broods and hatches himself.[20] Similar ideas are found also among the ancient Egyptians and Persians. From all these amplifications it is apparent why in the present tale a sea might arise from the egg, because water is also mythologically the primordial matter of the world.[21]

1005   The above amplifications indicate that the egg represents the totality of the unconscious *in potentia*. For this reason, the egg in fairytales is often portrayed as the secret center of the life force, in which, according to primitive concepts, the soul is preserved outside the body. As a Self symbol and as the all-encompassing totality of the unconscious, the egg appears most evidently in fairytales associated with a sought-after jewel or the castle of the princess.[22] So, also in the present tale, the unconscious is itself overcome by the

---

[17] See also C.G. Jung, CW 9i, *The Archetypes and the Collective Unconscious* ¶290.
[18] On the importance of the philosophical egg in alchemy, see C.G. Jung, CW 13, *Alchemical Studies* ¶109 and ¶188., C.G. Jung, CW 11, *Psychology and Religion* ¶92.
[19] See J. J. Bachofen, *Gräbersymbolik*, Basel 1859 p. 21.
[20] See C.G. Jung, CW 5, *Symbols of Transformation* ¶588f. See also the *Chandogya Upanishad* 3,19,1:
    This world was, in the beginning, non-being; this (non-being) was the being. The same originated. An egg then developed itself. It lay there, as long as a year. Thereupon, it split itself; of both shells of the egg, the one was of silver, the other was of gold. (Deussen, *Sixty Upanishads* p. 117.)
See also the references to the Latvian cosmogony in J. Bolte and L. Mackensen, *Handwörterbuch* Berlin 1930, under *Ei* [egg]:
    The Latvians believed, for example, that from the mouth of the primordial god the word escaped as a breath of wind. From the wind an eagle arose, which died in the conflict with the god. His blood became the sea, his body became the mud. One half of the egg contained in the eagle became heaven, the other the earth, divided into waters and mud.
See also F. Lukas, "Ei," Berlin 1894 pp. 227–243.
[21] "Since [in alchemy] water and egg are synonymous. . . " and "because the egg surrounds everything that is within it, and has in itself all that is necessary." C.G. Jung, CW 13, *Alchemical Studies* ¶109, fn. 71). The alchemists noted that possessing all that one needs is an attribute of the divine.
[22] See "The Stolen Daughters," "The Egg and the Jewel," "Sa'd and Sa'îd," and "Dawn, Evening, and Midnight."

unconscious. But the aspect of the Great Mother is not yet fully incorporated into consciousness, and, therefore, danger still threatens. The unconscious as destructive storm spirit is defeated, but it still stands in the way of individuation as the inertia of matter. For now, the prince forgets his bride, he leaves her stranded at the edge of the city to fetch a carriage for her, "befitting" her entrance into the city. The prince's attitude is still too worldly and secular and, as in "The Golden Bird" and other fairytales, this calls forth a balancing movement, a new relapse into the unconscious. This sinking back is portrayed here by the motif of forgetting. The unconscious – personified by the image of the Great Mother– cuts the conscious mind off from its memory of what was experienced in the unconscious, thereby causing a splitting of the psychic sphere, the loss of the anima. But she remembers well and recalls the past back to the prince using a puppet show. That is, the soul [psyche] portrays the past events to the conscious mind by reproducing them; by playing them out in front of it. Since these images are inside the prince himself and reflect his inner life, he feels the participation with the performing dolls, and "wakes up." Awakening is an image for becoming conscious, and only now does the conscious mind recognize the whole series of past events, and through this, it now wins a permanent and intimate relationship with the soul.

◇

Chapter 17
Endings – the Meaning
of the End of a Fairytale

1006 The fairytales discussed above reveal the great variety of motifs that appear under the theme of the "quest," where sometimes the way into the unconscious is a problem, or sometimes the return; at times gaining the anima is key, or the redemption or the conquest of the shadow, and sometimes the conflict with parental images is the central motif. Occasionally there is even a chain of seemingly separate tales, such as in "Djulek Batür"; a series of images strung together so that they seem like a dream series that express an unconscious developmental process in the psyche.[1] Whereas the dreams of an individual describe a process that even with the best goal-oriented efforts will never reach an end within a human lifetime – and this end is only hinted at in a few single dreams – the sequence of motifs in a fairytale necessarily have to come to a formal conclusion. The specific way in which these endings are depicted, indicate from the psychological point of view the extent to which the tale represents a process of individuation, or only describes basic approaches or possibilities that cannot advantageously be put to use by the conscious mind.

1007 Of the many possible fairytale endings, a key one is the "end in the magical," where the hero disappears with the anima in the realm of the unconscious. In such an instance, it is as if at the beginning an impulse goes out from the magical, the fairytale spreads its treasures in a plethora of images, but then the events seem to collapse again into themselves while the secular sphere sometimes even suffers a loss. Examples of this are found in the Chinese tale "Help in Need," in which the hero finally goes off with the Dragon Princess to the realm of the dead or, "The Disowned Princess," where Liu I adjourns to immortality in Lake Dunting. Withdrawing into the eternal realm of the anima is a particularly common motif and is also found in "The Fire-Ball," "Connla and the Fairy Maiden," "Rakian," "The Poor Miller's Boy and the Cat," "The King of the Golden Mountain," "The Virgin Tsar," and "Stupid Ivanko." Whereas in the above examples there is no negative assessment placed on this ecstatic retreat into the unconscious, at most an expression of a general

---

[1] See C.G. Jung, CW 11, *Psychology and Religion* ¶53f.

tragic mood, there are other fairytales in which the disappearance into the other world is represented as a disaster, be it death or madness.[2] We find examples of this in the tales "Trunt, Trunt, and the Trolls in the Mountains," "Blue-Jay Visits his Sister Io'i in the Land of the Dead," "The Star," "Makonaura and Anuanaitu," and "The Mermaid and the Great Dubhdach." These different assessments of a symbolic situation follow from the fact that all symbols can be experienced both negatively and positively. In worldly life [reality], ecstatic rapture manifests itself, if not as death or mental illness, then as a daze, stupor, or obsession. Even more subtle is the disappearance into a particular social role or an identification with an "inner vision," in which the person is apparently lost to the social circle. Other profound "changes of mind" (such as sudden conversions):

1008   . . . originate in the attractive power of a collective image. . . [and] can cause such a high degree of inflation that the entire personality is disintegrated. This disintegration is a mental disease, of a transitory or a permanent nature, a "splitting of the mind," schizophrenia. . . This pathological inflation naturally depends on some innate weakness of the personality against the autonomy of collective unconscious contents [in other words, the archetypes].[3]

1009   However, fairytales are usually not about the description of pathological psychic processes, rather they only touch upon this area when they reflect painful events that threaten the human soul, suspended between the divine and the secular worlds and required to partake of both. The opposition of these poles creates a mysterious and pregnant tension that requires withstanding extreme power. Of this, Carus says:

1010   In that the conscious spirit of man, when he wants to surrender himself thoroughly and intimately to the relationship to a supreme; to something immeasurable, unconscious, finds himself unconditionally and forever absorbed in a peculiar mystical opposition of consciousness and unconsciousness; he cannot other than, with all longing, behold a great mystery, an eternal mystery; a mystery to which he may be smashed to pieces and be irretrievably lost as one

---

[2] See also a tale from the Pemon (Arecuna) people of South America, "Eteto," a frightening story that depicts the tragic destruction of the conscious personality overwhelmed by the shadow, which well-nigh evokes psychiatric images.

[3] See C.G. Jung, CW 7, *Two Essays in Analytical Psychology* ¶233. See also C.G. Jung, CW 5, *Symbols of Transformation* ¶448f on the underground world of memories, the paradisal state of infancy, and with those memories the hopes sought as a replacement for the abandoned threatening upper world.

tries to raise oneself to the highest degree, and yet in that moment he may be capable of redeeming himself forever.[4]

1011 There are two ways to philosophically appraise identification with, or losing oneself to the unconscious, as a way out of the conflict between this world and the hereafter. Thus we must evaluate the "end in the magical " in different ways, especially since we must consider the culture and ideals of the land where each particular fairytale originates. Just as the individual, so also do fairytales have recourse to other possible solutions. Thus, for example, the hero in the end sometimes enters into the magical realm, but the realm is then "transformed" and freed from all evil spirits. This is described, for instance, in "The Mountain of the Golden Queen," "Lasse, My Servant," and "The Great Fool from Cuasan." Thus, according to our interpretation, the fairytale indicates that entering into the unconscious does not constitute a mindless sinking or succumbing, but rather that a (conscious) psychic struggle and development process preceded this, which puts every later permanent or temporary sojourn in the unconscious into a harmonious relationship with the individual's secular life. A piece from the unconscious is wrested away, made accessible and made "livable"; its treasures realized and brought across into daily life. The unconscious is no longer threatening but reachable, and the opposites are no longer in tension. In the former case, on the other hand, the fairytale appears to represent a recurring cycle in the unconscious, in which the end touches the beginning.

1012 The above type of fairytale closure that ends "in the magical" contrasts with the "end in the secular" type.[5] With the latter type too, there are several nuances. In many primitive tales the hero merely returns to the secular realm, either with nothing, or simply with the relief and joy of having escaped from the devouring unconscious, for example in "The Strange Boy" or "The Mountain of the Fair Women." (Compare also the undecided fate in "The Story of Djihanshah," in which the hero remains between the spheres and even loses everything.) Or the hero brings some gain, bags some game, acquires a

---

[4] Carus continues:

> The former [getting lost] will happen when he or she is led astray by mock images [simulacra] of this supreme and eternal, or if they get lost in the madness of groping to know what is in itself unknowable. One can reach the latter transformation only when one has the courage to gaze at the unconscious as such, and to surrender oneself intimately to the infinite, and at *another time, through the power and depth of love,* able to fill and conquer the abyss and the unfathomable of something quite immeasurable and mysterious, and in this way achieve a perfect and complete, beautiful and pure relationship with that mystery. (C.G. Carus, *Psyche,* Leipzig 1931 p. 401.)

Italics are from the source (Carus). [The translation purposely follows the original text literally, trying to reflect the exceedingly dense but poetic language.]

[5] It would be interesting to study the psychology, ethnology, and cultural history of the peoples from which different fairytales emerge and to compare which people prefer the end in the magical, which in the profane, and why.

magical object, or wins the anima figure herself. To the type of unsuccessful meetings with the unconscious also belong those with a magical marriage that end with a separation, such as in "Ititaujang," "The Sealskin," "The Mermaid and the Great Dubhdach," "Una, the Elfen Girl," "Why Honey is So Scarce Now" or "The Tiger Changed into a Woman" among others. On the other hand, we find examples of winning a permanent prize or asset in the form of hunting success, new cultural goods, or an increase in shamanistic power, for example, in "Flight to the Moon" (reindeer), "The Lady of the Moon" (music, songs), "A Legend of Flowers" (flowers), "How Motecuzhoma Sought the Seven Caves" (gifts), "The Piper and the Púca" (music), "Women's Words Part Flesh and Blood" (gems), "The Visit to Heaven" (corn), or "Kagsagsuk" (heroic-shamanistic powers).

1013   In all these cases the winnings that were brought back symbolize new levels of consciousness wrested from the unconscious. The prize most valued is, however, the anima, who often brings other treasures with her. In this respect, the anima is one of the most important personifications of the unconscious in a man. She signifies a lasting contact with his inner world, and thus a secure and permanent source for life renewal, expansion of consciousness, and individuation. This relationship even contains a hint of immortality. For these reasons, the anima is very often linked to symbols of the Self: she lives in a mandala, she tends the round thing or the gold, she possesses the pills of immortality or the rejuvenating apples, she guards the water of life, or weaves with a golden thread, and so on. She is, therefore, largely identical to the Self. Associated with her manifestation is a metaphorical wealth of psychological differentiation, and thus psychic "benefits" that augment her figure. For example, the redemption of her animal brother, as in "The Golden Bird" and "The Golden Castle that Hung in the Air." In these tales, a higher level of consciousness is gradually reached, whereas in simpler fairytale narratives the masculine helping powers are contained within the hero, as in "The Red Swan" and "Djulek Batür," or they are natural forces and remain as such, for instance in "Tritill, Litill, and the Birds" or "Prince Hassan Pasha."

1014   When a tale ends with a safe return to secular life, new issues arise that are seldom encountered in tales that end in the magical realm. Expressed figuratively, some examples are the punishment of the old father or the secular brothers, or the problem of succession to the throne. For, what is considered from the inside to be the greatest gain may look from the outside like something damaging. Thus, the old king, who represents a former way of life, must leave the hero half or all of his kingdom. Or if the old king stands in opposition to the new attitude, he may even be eliminated (as in "Ferdinand the Faithful and Ferdinand the Unfaithful" or "The Devil with the Three Golden Hairs"). In other cases, the negative, collectively-oriented tendencies within the personality, its "halfheartedness" or secular brothers, are, in many cases, killed, even if the prevailing [conscious] attitude is initially retained. Thus, the Self becomes a destroyer of some aspects that have reigned before. The division of the kingdom, or the rules of succession (in the sense of the division of time rather than space) means, as already mentioned, a shift in emphasis within the personality, through which the supremacy of rational ego-consciousness is reduced in favor of the Self. What is confusing in interpreting the hero as a symbol of the Self is, however, that this figure often nearly coincides with the figure of the shadow, in as much as the hero as the fourth and the inferior function is connected with the unconscious so that he embodies a bridge to the Self.[6] At the same time, however, it is clear that he personifies the human ego-consciousness, especially when, as in "The Golden Bird," he is associated with an animal brother, who in this case takes over the role of the shadow, the alter ego. This paradox is intrinsic to the nature of the Self, of which it can be empirically stated that it is the ego *and* the non-ego, the ego *and* the superordinate or supraordinate inner personality; in short, that which is symbolized by wholeness.[7] The more differentiated fairytales (such as "The Golden Bird") depict an image of the hero that is divided into "two different figures" that are nonetheless related. In those fairytales that emerge from a more primitive psychic level, the paradox is visible in that the individual components of the hero: his animal side, his *Dümmling* side, his limited ego side, are not separated from his divine side into individual figures, but are still embodied in one single figure. In this respect, the Self is, as Jung writes, an entity superordinate to our conscious ego, and, "[h]owever much we may make conscious, there will always exist an indeterminate and indeterminable amount of unconscious material which belongs to the totality of the self."[8] Thus, in interpreting the figure of the hero we must keep in mind that he symbolically represents a psychological element that is not totally comprehensible.

1015   According to Jung, in psychological development, the Self has the character of a source point, or origin, of spiritual life, and also, a result or the goal that is to be attained. The Self:

1016   . . . is the most complete expression of that fateful combination we call individuality, the full flowering not only of the single individual, but of the group, in which each adds his peroration to the whole.[9]

---

[6] See C.G. Jung, CW 12, *Psychology and Alchemy* ¶31.
[7] See also C.G. Jung, CW 7, *Two Essays in Analytical Psychology* ¶399 on the Self and the conscious mind as a part of it, as a center between consciousness and the unconscious.
[8] See C.G. Jung, CW 7, *Two Essays in Analytical Psychology* ¶274.
[9] *Ibid* ¶404.

As something divine, in general and also individually, the "hero" is an adequate symbol to personify the divine and the demonic in human nature. And as such the fairytale hero appears in conjunction with other Self symbols. A beautiful combination of hero and "the roundness" can be found, for example, in an Arabic parallel to "The Gnome"[10] where the hero carries with him the garments and the castles of princesses in the shape of a ball. From this it follows that the Self includes in itself at the same time the symbols of the feminine, belonging to the anima (just as the anima figure has a masculine-spiritual side). In alchemical philosophy the Self is often shown as a hermaphrodite.

1017   For this reason, there is no difference in its nature, but rather only in the image when instead of the hero, a female figure carries the action of the plot, as in the case with the fairytales that will be considered in the next volume.

---

[10] J. Bolte and G. Polívka, *Anmerkungen,* Vol. 2, Leipzig 1915 p. 314.

Bibliography

Aarne, Antti, *Vergleichende Märchenforschungen. Akademische Abhandlung*, Druckerei der Finnischen Literaturgesellschaft, Helsingfors 1908.

Abegg, Emil, "Krishnas Geburt und das indische Weihnachtsfest" in: *Mitteilungen der Geogr.-Ethnogr.-Gesellschaft*, Vol. 38, 1937/1938, pp. 29–57.

– *Indische Psychologie*, Rascher Verlag, Zürich 1945.

Abt, Regina and Bosch, Irmgard/Mackrel, Vivienne, *Traum und Schwangerschaft. Eine Untersuchung von Träumen schwangerer Frauen*, Daimon Verlag, Einsiedeln 1996.

Aichele, Walther (editor), *Zigeunermärchen*, (*MdW*), ed. by Fr. v. d. Leyen and P. Zaunert, Eugen Diederichs, Jena 1926.

Aigremont, Dr., *Fuss- und Schuh-Symbolik und -Erotik: Folkloristische und sexualwissenschaftliche Untersuchungen*. Mit einem Geleitwort von Dr. Friedrich S. Krauß, Deutsche Verlags-Aktien-Gesellschaft, Leipzig 1909.

Altmann, Christine (editor), Kleine Märchenzeitung Schweizerischen Märchen-Gesellschaft SMG, 3. Jahrgang, Mai 1998.

Apuleius, *The Metamorphosis or Golden Ass of Apuleius*, W. J. Cosby, Universal Press, London 1822, trans. by Thomas Taylor.

Ashliman, D. L. (ed.), *The Grimm Brothers' Children's and Household Tales* (*Grimms' Fairy Tales*), Princeton University Press, Princeton NJ 1998-2009.

Aurelius, Marcus; George Long, Translated by (ed.), *The Meditations*, The Peter Pauper Press Inc., Mount Vernon 1957.

Bachofen, Johannn Jakob, *Myth, Religion, & Mother Right, selected writings of J.J. Bachofen*, Bollingen, Princeton Universtiy Press, Princeton, NJ 1973.

– *Versuch über die Gräbersymbolik der Alten*, Bahnmaier's Buchhandlung (C. Detloff), Basel 1859.

– Das Mutterrecht: Eine Untersuchung über die Gynaikokratie der alten Welt nach ihrer religiösen und rechtlichen Natur, Krais & Hoffmann, Stuttgart 1861.

– Das Lykische Volk und seine Bedeutung für die Entwicklung des Altertums, Herder'sche Verlagsbuchhandlung, Freiburg i. Br. 1862.

– Der Baer in den Religionen des Alterthums, Ch. Meyri, Basel 1863.

– Die Unsterblichkeitslehre der orphischen Theologie auf den Grabdenk-mälern des Alterthums. Nach Anleitung einer Vase aus Canosa im Besitz des Herrn Prosper Biardot in Paris, dargestellt von Dr. J. J. Bachofen mit einer Tafel in Farbendruck, Felix Schneider's Buchhandlung, Basel 1867.

Bächtold-Stäubli, Hanns, *Handwörterbuch des deutschen Aberglaubens*, W. de Gruyter & Co. Bd. I–VII, Berlin and Leipzig 1927–1936. Vol. VIII–X, Berlin 1936–1942. editor unter bes. Mitwirkung von E. Hoffmann-Krayer and Mitarbeit zahlreicher Fachgenossen.

Barnstone, Willis, and Meyer, Marvin, *The Gnostic Bible*, Shambhala Publications 2003.

Baumann, Dieter, "Individuation in the Spirit of Love" in: *The Fountain of the Love of Wisdom: an Homage to Marie-Louise von Franz*, ed. by Emmanuel Kennedy-Xypolitas, Chiron Publications, Wilmette, Illinois 2006, pp. 167–176.

Baynes, Charlotte, translator, *A Coptic Gnostic Treatise Contained in the Codex Brucianus* (Bruce Ms. 96. Bod. Lib. Oxford), Cambridge Univ. Press, Cambridge (UK) 1933.

Beit, Hedwig von, *Das Märchen. Sein Ort in der geistigen Entwicklung* [The Fairytale. Its place in Spiritual Development], Francke Verlag, Bern and München 1965.

– *Symbolik des Märchens*, Band I, 8. Auflage, Francke Verlag, Tübingen 1997.

Bernoulli, Rudolf, "Zur Symbolik geometrischer Figuren und Zahlen" in: *Eranos-Jahrbuch 1934: Ostwestliche Symbolik und Seelenführung*, hrsg. von Olga Fröbe-Kapteyn, Rhein-Verlag, Zürich 1935, p. 369–415.

– "Spiritual Development as Reflected in Alchemy and Related Disciplines" in: *Spiritual Disciplines: Papers from the Eranos Yearbooks*, Princeton University Press, Princeton NJ 1960, Bollingen XXX-4, pp. 305–340.

Berthelot, Marcellin, *Collection des ancien alchimistes grecs*. Volume 2, Georges Steinheil Éditeur, Paris 1888.

Boas, Franz, *The Mythology of the Bella Coola Indians*, Memoirs of the American Museum of Natural History, New York 1898.

Böklen, Ernst, "Adam und Qain im Lichte der vergleichenden Mythen-forschung" in: *Mythologische Bibliothek*, Vol. 1, no. 2, ed. by d. Ges. f.

vergleichende Mythenforschung, J. C. Hinrichs'sche Buchhandlung, Leipzig 1907/1908.

Böklen, Ernst, "Die 'Unglückszahl' Dreizehn und ihre mythische Bedeutung" in: *Mythologische Bibliothek*, Vol. 5, no. 2, ed. Ges. f. vergleichende Mythenforschung, J. C. Hinrichs'sche Buchhandlung, Leipzig 1913.

Bogoras, Waldemar, *Tales of the Yukaghir, Lamut, and Russianized Natives of Eastern Siberia*, Anthropological Papers of the American Museum of Natural History, New York 1918.

Bolte, Johannes, and Polívka, Georg, *Anmerkungen zu den Kinder-and Hausmärchen der Brüder Grimm*, Vol. 1, Dieterich'sche Verlagsbuchhandlung, Th. Weicher, Leipzig 1913.

– *Anmerkungen zu den Kinder-and Hausmärchen der Brüder Grimm*, Vol. 2, Dieterich'sche Verlagsbuchhandlung, Th. Weicher, Leipzig 1915.

– *Anmerkungen zu den Kinder-and Hausmärchen der Brüder Grimm*, Vol. 3, Dieterich'sche Verlagsbuchhandlung, Leipzig 1918.

– *Anmerkungen zu den Kinder-and Hausmärchen der Brüder Grimm*, Vol. 4, Dieterich'sche Verlagsbuchhandlung, Leipzig 1930.

Bolte, Johannes and Mackensen, Lutz, *Handwörterbuch des deutschen Märchens*, Volume 1–2, W. de Gruyter & Co., Berlin and Leipzig 1930/1934.

Bousset, Wilhelm, *Hauptprobleme der Gnosis*, Vandenhoeck & Ruprecht, Göttingen 1907.

Bowden, Hugh, *Mystery Cults of the Ancient World*, Thames & Hudson Ltd, London 2010.

Brill's New Pauly (Greek-English Dictionary), Pauly, Leiden and Boston 2003.

Carus, Carl Gustav, *Psyche, zur Entwicklungsgeschichte der Seele*, Flammer und Hoffmann, Pforzheim 1846.

– *Psyche, zur Entwicklungsgeschichte der Seele*, Kröners Taschenausgabe, Nr. 98, mit einem Nachwort, ed. by R. Marx, Alfred Kröner Verlag, Leipzig 1931.

– *Psyche Part One: The Unconscious*, Spring Publications, New York 1970, Trans. by R. Welch.

Christensen, Arthur (ed.), *Märchen aus Iran*, (*MdW*), ed. by Fr. v. d. Leyen, Eugen Diederichs Verlag, Jena 1939.

– Goldapfelsins Tochter: Märchen aus Persien, Diederichs 2009. 253, 951.

Collum, V. C. C., "Die schöpferische Mutter-Göttin der Völker keltischer Sprache, ihr Werkzeug, das mystische 'Wort,' ihr Kult und ihre Kult-Symbole," in: *Eranos-Jahrbuch 1938: Gestalt und Kult der "Grossen Mutter,"* hrsg. von Olga Fröbe-Kapteyn, Rhein-Verlag, Zürich 1939, p. 221–324.

Copenhaver, Brian P., *Hermetica*, Cambridge University Press, Cambridge (UK) 1992.

Crawford, John Martin, *The Kalevala, the Epic Poem of Finland into English*, The Robert Blake Company, Cincinnati 1888.

Cumont, Franz, *The Oriental Religions in Roman Paganism*, Open Court, Chicago 1911.

Danzel, Theodor-Wilhelm, "The Psychology of Ancient Mexican Symbolism", in: *Spiritual Disciplines: Papers form the Eranos Yearbooks*, Princeton University Press, Princeton NJ 1960, Bollingen XXX-4, pp. 102–114.

Darmesteter, James, translator, "The Zend Avesta", Part II (SBE23), in: *The Sacred Books of the East*, Müller, Friedrich Max (Ed.), Volume 23, Clarendon Press, Oxford 1883.

Decurtins, Caspar, Die drei Winde. *Rhätoromanische Märchen aus der Surselva*, Desertina, Chur 2002, ed. by Ursula Brunold-Bigler.

Deussen, Paul, Allgemeine Geschichte der Philosophie, mit besond. Berücksichtigung der Religionen, Volume 1, F. A. Brockhaus, Leipzig 1894.

– *Sechzig Upanishad's des Veda*, F. A. Brockhaus, Leipzig 1921.

– *Sixty Upanishads of the Veda, two volumes*, Motilal Banarsidass, Delhi 1980/1997, translated by V.M. Bedekar and G.B. Palsule.

Dieterich, Albrecht, *Eine Mithrasliturgie*, ed. by Otto Weinreich, B. G. Teubner, Leipzig and Berlin 1923.

Dirr, Adolf (ed.), *Kaukasische Märchen, (MdW)*, ed. by Fr. v. d. Leyen and P. Zaunert, Eugen Diederichs, Jena 1922.

Dixon, Roland, *Maidu Myths* in: Bulletin of the American Museum of Natural History, 17 (2) [1902], pp. 33–118.

Dossetor, Robert Francis, Gawain and the Green Knight, The Myth of an Intuitive, London 1942.

Eckhart, Meister, *Meister Eckhart, Selected Writings*, Penguin Books, London 1994, Trans. by Oliver Davies.

Eells, Elsie Spicer, *Tales of Enchantment from Spain*, Harcourt, Brace and Company, New York 1920.

Eggert, Charles A. (ed.), *Goethes Das Märchen*, D. C. Heath & Co., Boston, New York, Chicago 1904.

Enzyklopädie des Märchens. Handwörterbuch zur historischen und vergleichenden Erzählforschung, Walter de Gruyter, Berlin 1979.

Erman, Adolf, Die Religion der Ägypter. Ihr Werden und Vergehen in vier Jahrtausenden, Walter de Gruyter, Berlin and Leipzig 1934.

Fankhauser, Alfred, *Horoskopie, Orell Füßli*, Zürich and Leipzig 1939. 272

Fillmore, Parker, *The Laughing Prince, A book of Jugoslav Folk and Fairy Tales*, Harcourt, Brace & World, Inc., New York 1921.

Fison, Lorimer, *Tales from Old Fiji*, Alexander Moring Ltd, London 1904. 176

Franz, Marie-Louise von, *Animus and Anima in Fairy Tales*, Shambala, New York 2001.

-*Aurora Consurgens, A Document Attributed to Thomas Aquinas on the Problem of Opposites in Alchemy*. A Companion Work to C. G. Jung's *Mysterium Coniunctionis*. translated by R. F. C. Hull and A. S. B. Glover, Princeton University Press, Princeton NJ 1977, Bollingen Series, LXXVII.

– *Erlösungsmotive in Märchen*, Klösel-Verlag, München 1980

 Individuation in Fairy Tales, Shambala, New York 2001.

Number and Time, Reflections Leading Towards a Unification of Depth Psychology and Physics, translated by Andrea Dykes, Rider & Company, London 1974.

– Psychologische Marcheninterpretation, Verlag Stiftung fur Jung'sche Psychologie, Kusnacht 2012.

– The Interpretation of Fairy Tales (An Introduction to the Psychology of Fairy Tales), Spring Publications Inc, New York 1970.

– The Psychological Meaning of Redemption Motifs in Fairytales, Inner City, Toronto 1980.

– *Symbolik des Märchens*, Verlag Stifting fur Jung'sche Psychologie, Kusnacht 2015.

Franz, Marie-Louise von, "Marie-Louise von Franz im Film von Francoise Selhofer" in: *Jungiana*, Reihe A Band 2, 1989.

Frobenius, Leo, *Das Zeitalter des Sonnengottes*. Erster Band, Georg Reimer, Berlin 1904.

Führer, Maria, Nordgermanische Götterüberlieferung und deutsches Volksmärchen. 80 Märchen der Brüder Grimm vom Mythus her beleuchtet, Neuer Filser-Verlag, München 1938.

Gebser, Jean, *Ursprung und Gegenwart. Erster Band. Die Fundamente der aperspektivischen Welt*, Deutsche Verlags-Anstalt, Stuttgart 1949, Beitrag zu einer Geschichte der Bewußtwerdung.

Gebser, Jean, *The Ever-Present Origin, 2nd edition*. Ohio University Press, Athens 1991, authorized translation by Noel Barstad with Algis Mickunas.

Gerber, Irene, "Yonec. Zu einer Märchendichtung der Marie de France" in: *Jungiana*, Reihe A, Band 9, 2000, pp. 53–96.

Giese, Friedrich (ed.), *Türkische Märchen, (MdW)*, ed. by Fr. v. d. Leyen and P. Zaunert, Eugen Diederichs, Jena 1925.

Goethe, Johann Wolfgang von, *Faust. Der Tragödie erster und zweiter Teil*. Mit dem Urfaust und einer Einl. v. Reinhard Buchwald, Alfred Kröner Verlag, Stuttgart 1949.

   Goethe's Theory of Colors, John Murray, London 1840, translated by Charles Lock Eastlake.

– *West-Eastern Divan*, J. M. Dent & Sons Ltd., London & Toronto 1904, translated by Edward Dowden.

– "Zahme Xenien." *Poetische Werke*. Berliner Ausgabe, Volume 2, Berlin 1960.

Graff, Eberhard Gottlieb, *Denkmäler deutscher Sprache und Literatur, Volume 3*, F. G. Gotta'schen Buchhandlung, Stuttgart/Tübingen 1829.

Graulich, Michael, *Myths of Ancient Mexico*, University of Oklahoma Press, Norman 1997, translated by Bernard R. Ortiz de Montellano and Thelma Ortiz de Montellno.

Grimm, Jakob, Theodor Grimm, *The Complete Grimm's Fairy Tales*, Routledge and Kegan Paul, London 1975.

Grimm, Jacob Ludwig Karl, *Grimm's household tales with the author's notes by Jacob Grimm*, G. Bell & Sons, London 1884, 1910, Translated by Margaret Hunt.

Grünbaum, Max, *Gesammelte Aufsätze zur Sprach- und Sagenkunde*, ed. by Felix Perles, S. Calvari & Co., Berlin 1901.

de Gubernatis, Angelo, Zoological Mythology or the Legends of Animals, Volumes 1 and 2, Trübner & Co., London 1872.

Güntert, Hermann, Der arische Weltkönig und Heiland. Bedeutungs-geschichtliche Untersuchungen zur indo-iranischen Religionsgeschichte und Altertumskunde, Max Niemeyer, Halle a. S. 1923.

Guest, Charlotte, *The Mabinogion*. Translated by Charlotte Guest, Introduction by Rev. R. Williams. M. A. Everyman's Library, Ed. by Ernest Rhys, J.M. Dent & Sons Ltd. / E.P. Dutton & Co. Inc., London / New York (1906) 1937.

Hall, Charles Francis; Nourse, J. E (ed.), *Narrative of the Second Arctic Expedition made by Charles F. Hall*, U.S. Naval Observatory, Government Printing Office, Washington D.C. 1879.

Hall, A. W. (ed.), *Icelandic Fairy Tales*, Frederick Warne & Co., London 1897.

Haltrich, Josef, Deutsche Volksmärchen aus dem Sachsenlande in Siebenbürgen, Verlag von Carl Graeser, Vienna 1882.

Hambruch, Paul (ed.), Südseemärchen aus Australien, Neu-Guinea, Fidji, Karolinen, Samoa, Tonga, Hawaii, Neu-Seeland and a., (MdW), ed. by Fr. v. d. Leyen and P. Zaunert, Eugen Diederichs, Jena 1921.

– *Malaiische Märchen aus Madagaskar und Insulinde, (MdW)*, ed. by Fr. v. d. Leyen and P. Zaunert, Eugen Diederichs, Jena 1922.

Hammer-Purgstall, Joseph Freiherr von, *Rosenöl*, Cotta, Stuttgart and Tübingen 1813.

Hartlaub, Gustav Friedrich, "Mythos und Magie der Schlange" in: *Atlantis*. Länder, Völker, Reisen, no. 10, Oktober 1940, p. 566–574.

Hempel, Hans, *Das Frau Holle-Märchen und sein Typus: eine vergleichende Märchenstudie*, Ph. D thesis, Universität Greifswald, Greifswald 1923. 712

Heraclitus, Heraclitus, The Complete Fragments, Translation and Commentary and The Greek text, Middlebury College, Internet 1994, Trans. by William Harris.

Horton, Alice/Bell, Edward (eds.), *The Lay of the Nibelungs, metrically translated from the Old German text*, George Bell and Sons, London 1901.

Hüsing, Georg, *Die Iranische Überlieferung und das arische System*, ed. by d. Gesellschaft für vergleichende Mythenforschung, mit Nachträgen von H. Lessmann, Volume II, 2, Mythologische Bibliothek, J. C. Hinrichs'sche Buchhandlung, Leipzig 1909.

Huet, Gédéon, *Les contes populaires*, Ernest Flammarion, Paris 1923.

Huizinga, Johan, Homo ludens. *Versuch einer Bestimmung des Spielelementes der Kultur*, Pantheon Akademische Verlagsanstalt, Amsterdam 1939.

Isler, Gotthilf, "Jung, Carl Gustav" in: *Enzyklopädie des Märchens*, Band 7, Lieferung 2/3.

– "Franz, Marie-Louise von" in: *Enzyklopädie des Märchens*, vol. 5, installment 1.

Jacobs, Joseph (ed.), *English Fairy Tales, 3rd edition*. David Nutt, London 1898.

Jegerlehner, Johannes, *Am Herdfeuer der Sennen, Neue Märchen aus dem Wallis*, aus dem Volksmund gesammelt, A. Francke, Bern 1929.

Jung, Carl Gustav, *Children's Dreams, Notes from the Seminar Given in 1936–1940*, Lorenz Jung and Maria Meyer-Grass (editors), translated by Ernst Falzeder and Tony Woolfson, Princeton University Press, Princeton 2008.

– "Address on the Occasion of the Founding of the C. G. Jung Institute, Zurich, 24 April 1948" in: *The Symbolic Life*, CW18, 2nd edition, Princeton University Press, Princeton 1969.

– "Basic Postulates of Analytical Psychology" in: *The Structure and Dynamics of the Psyche*, CW8, 2nd edition, Princeton University Press, Princeton, 1970.

– "Concerning the Archetypes, with Special Reference to the Anima Concept" in: *The Archetypes and the Collective Unconscious*, CW9i, 2nd edition, Routledge and Kegan Paul, London, 1969.

-"Concerning Mandala Symbolism" in: Read, Sir Herbert et al. (eds.): Collected Works, Vol 9i: *The Archetypes and the Collective Unconscious*, CW9i, 2nd edition Princeton University Press, Princeton, p. 355–384.

– "Concerning Rebirth" in: *The Archetypes and the Collective Unconscious*, CW9i, 2nd edition, Princeton University Press, Princeton ,1969.

– "The Development of Personality" in: *The Development of Personality*, CW17, 2nd edition, Princeton University Press, Princeton 1971.

– "Foreword to Suzuki's 'Introduction to Zen Buddhism'" in: *Psychology and Religion: West and East*, CW11, 2nd edition, Princeton University Press, Princeton 1975.

– "The Meaning of Psychology for Modern Man" in: *Civilization in Transition*, CW10, 2nd edition, Princeton University Press, Princeton, 1970.

– "On Psychic Energy" in: *The Structure and Dynamics of the Psyche*, CW8, 2nd edition, Princeton University Press, Princeton, 1970.

– "On the Psychology of the Unconscious" in: *Two Essays on Analytical Psychology*, CW7, 2nd edition, Princeton University Press, Princeton, 1971.

– "Paracelsus as a Spiritual Phenomenon" in: *Alchemical Studies*, CW13, 2nd edition, Routledge & Kegan Paul, London, 1967.

– "The Phenomenology of the Spirit in Fairy Tales" in: *The Archetypes and the Collective Unconscious*, CW9i, 2nd edition, Princeton University Press, Princeton, 1969.

– "The Philosophical Tree" in: *Psychology and Alchemy*, CW13, 2nd edition, Routledge & Kegan Paul, London, 1967.

– "The Practical Use of Dream Analysis" in: *The Practice of Psychotherapy*, CW16, 2nd edition, Princeton University Press, Princeton, 1985.

– "A Psychological Approach to the Dogma of the Trinity" in: *Psychology East and West*, CW11, 2nd edition, Princeton University Press, Princeton, 1975.

– "The Psychological Aspects of the Kore" in: *The Archetypes and the Collective Unconscious*, CW9i, 2nd edition, Princeton University Press, Princeton, 1969.

– "Psychological Aspects of the Mother Archetype" in: *The Archetypes of the Collective Unconscious*, CW9i, 2nd edition, Princeton University Press, Princeton, 1969.

– "Psychological Commentary on 'The Golden Flower'" in: *Alchemical Studies*, CW13, 2nd edition, Routledge & Kegan Paul, London, 1967.

– "Psychological Commentary on 'The Tibetan Book of the Dead'" in: *Psychology East and West*, CW11, 2nd edition, Princeton University Press, Princeton, 1975.

– *Psychological Types*, CW6, 2nd edition, Princeton University Press, Princeton, 1970.

– "The Psychology of the Child Archetype" in: *The Archetypes and the Collective Unconscious*, CW9i, 2nd edition, Princeton University Press, Princeton, 1969.

– "The Psychology of the Transference" in: *The Practice of Psychotherapy*, CW16, 2nd edition, Princeton University Press, Princeton, 1985.

– The Relation between the Ego and the Unconscious in: *Two Essays on Analytical Psychology*, CW7, 2nd edition, Princeton University Press, Princeton, 1971.

– "The Soul and Death" in: *The Structure and Dynamics of the Psyche*, CW8, 2nd edition, Princeton University Press, Princeton, 1970.

– "Spirit and Life" in: *The Structure and Dynamics of the Psyche*, CW8, 2nd Edition, Princeton University Press, Princeton, 1970.

– "The Spirit Mercurius" in: *Alchemical Studies*, CW13, 2nd edition, Routledge & Kegan Paul, London, 1967.

– "The Stages of Life" in: *The Structure and Dynamics of the Psyche*, CW8, 2nd Edition, Princeton University Press, Princeton, 1970.

– "The Structure of the Psyche" in: *The Structure and Dynamics of the Psyche*, CW8, 2nd Edition, Princeton University Press, Princeton, 1970.

- *Symbols of Transformation*, CW5, 2nd edition, Princeton University Press, Princeton, 1967.

- "Transformation Symbolism in the Mass" in: *Psychology and Religion: West and East*, CW11, 2nd edition, Princeton University Press, Princeton, 1975.

- "The Visions of Zosimos" in: *Alchemical Studies*, CW13, 2nd edition, Routledge & Kegan Paul, London, 1967.

Jung, Carl Gustav and Kerenyi, Carl, *Essays on a Science of Mythology: The Myth of the Divine Child and the Mysteries of Eleusis*, Princeton University Press, Princeton, NJ 1969.

Jung, Emma, "Ein Beitrag zum Problem des Animus" in: *Wirklichkeit der Seele: Anwendungen und Fortschritte der neueren Psychologie,* ed. by C. G. Jung, Rascher & Cie. A.G. Verlag, Zurich 1934, p. 296–354.

- *Animus and Anima, two essays*, Spring Publications, Inc., Putnam Connecticut 1985.

Jungbauer, Gustav (ed.), *Märchen aus Turkestan und Tibet, (MdW)*, ed. by Fr. v. d. Leyen and P. Zaunert, Eugen Diederichs, Jena 1923.

Kappes, Alison, "Bibliographie von Marie-Louise von Franz" in: *Jungiana*, Reihe A Band 2, 1989, pp. 33–46.

Kennedy-Xypolitas, Emmanuel (ed.), *The Fountain of the Love of Wisdom: an Homage to Marie-Louise von Franz*, Chiron Publications, Wilmette, Illinois 2006.

Kerényi, Karl, Kore, in: Essays on a Science of Mythology: The Myth of the Divine Child and the Mysteries of Eleusis, Princeton University Press, Princeton 1969, pp. 101–155.

Koch-Grünberg, Theodor (ed.), *Indianermärchen aus Südamerika, (MdW)*, ed. by Fr. v. d. Leyen and P. Zaunert, Eugen Diederichs, Jena 1921.

Köhler, Reinhold, "Kleinere Schriften" in: *Kleinere Schriften zur Neueren Litteraturgeschichte Volkskunde und Wortforschung, Band 3*, ed. by Johannes Bolte, Verlag von Emil Felber, Berlin 1900.

Krauss, Friedrich Salomon, Sagen und Märchen der Südslaven, in ihrem Verhältnis zu den Sagen und Märchen der übrigen indogermanischen Völkergruppen, Volume 1, Verlag von Wilhelm Friedrich, Leipzig 1883.

Kretschmer, Paul, *Neugriechische Märchen, (MdW)*, ed. by Fr. v. d. Leyen and P. Zaunert, Eugen Diederichs, Jena 1917.

Krickeberg, Walter (ed.), *Indianermärchen aus Nordamerika, (MdW)*, ed. by Fr. v. d. Leyen and P. Zaunert, Eugen Diederichs, Jena 1924.

– Märchen der Azteken und Inkaperuaner, Maya und Muisca, (MdW), ed. by Fr. v. d. Leyen, Eugen Diederichs, Jena 1928.

Kuhn, Franz Felix Adalbert, Mythologische Studien. Vol. 1, Die Herabkunft des Feuers und des Göttertranks, Vol. 2, Hinterlassene mythologische Abhandlungen, ed. by Ernst Kuhn, C. Bertelsmann, Gütersloh 1886 (Vol. 1), 1912 (Vol. 2).

Kunike, Hugo (ed.), Prärie-Indianer-Märchen, nach deutschen und amerikanischen Quellen, Axel Juncker, Berlin 1923.

Laiblin, Wilhelm, "Urbild der Mutter" in: Laiblin, Wilhelm (ed.): *Märchenforschung und Tiefenpsychologie*, Wissenschaftliche Buchgesellschaft, Darmstadt 1936, pp. 100–150.

– "Der goldene Vogel. Zur Symbolik der Individuation im Volksmärchen" in: *Jugend zwischen Gestern und Morgen – In psychotherapeutischer Sicht*, Ernst Klett Verlag, Stuttgart 1961, Institut für Psychotherapie und Tiefenpsychologie, p. 137–187.

Laistner, Ludwig, *Das Rätsel der Sphinx. Grundzüge einer Mythengeschichte*, Verlag Wilhelm Hertz, Berlin 1889.

Lang, Andrew (ed.), *Custom and Myth, 2nd edition*. Longmans, Green, and Co., London 1885.

Layard, John, "Der Mythos der Totenfahrt auf Malekula"[The Myth of the Death Journey on Malekula] in: *Eranos-Jahrbuch 1937: Gestaltung der Erlösungsidee in Ost und West (2)*, ed. by Olga Fröbe-Kapteyn, Rhein-Verlag, Zürich 1938, p. 241–291.

Leade, Jane, *A Fountain of Gardens*, J. Bradford, London 1696.

Leeming, David and Page, Jake, *The Mythology of Native North America*, University of Oklahoma Press, Norman 1998.

Leeuw, Gerardus van der, *Religion in Essence and Manifestation: A Study in Phenomenology, Volumes 1 and 2*, Harper & Row Publishers, New York 1963, Trans. by J. T. Turner.

Leisegang, Hans, *Die Gnosis, Kröners Taschenausgabe Vol. 32*, Alfred Kröner Verlag, Leipzig 1924.,

– "Das Mysterium der Schlange. Ein Beitrag zur Erforschung des griechischen Mysterienkultes und seines Fortlebens in der christlichen Welt" in: *Eranos-Jahrbuch 1939: Die Symbolik der Wiedergeburt in der religiösen Vorstellung der Zeiten und Völker*, ed. by Olga Fröbe-Kapteyn, Rhein-Verlag, Zürich 1940, p. 151–250.

- "The Mystery of the Serpent" in: *The Mysteries: Papers from the Eranos Yearbooks 2*, Routledge & Kegan Paul, London 1955, Book ordered from Colibris 23 January 2014, pp. 194–260.

Leskien, August (ed.), *Balkanmärchen aus Albanien / Bulgarien, Serbien und Kroatien, (MdW)*, ed. by Fr. v. d. Leyen and P. Zaunert, Eugen Diederichs, Jena 1919.

Lévy-Bruhl, Lucien, *The "Soul" of the Primitive*, Macmillan, New York 1928.

- *How Natives Think*, authorized translation by Lilian A. Clare (1926), Washington Square Press, Inc., New York 1966.

Lévy-Strauss, *Structural Anthropology*, Basic Books, New York 1963, Trans. by Claire Jacobson and Brooke G. Schoepf.

Liddell and Scott, *A Greek-English Lexicon*, Clarendon Press, Oxford 1843, 1985 printing.

Loepfe, Alfred, *Russische Märchen*, Otto Walter, Olten 1941.

Löwis of Menar, August von (ed.), *Russische Volksmärchen, (MdW)*, ed. by Fr. v. d. Leyen and P. Zaunert, Eugen Diederichs, Jena 1921.

Lüthi, Max, "Psychologie des Märchens. Märchendeutung. Zu einem Buche Hedwig von Beits" in: *Neue Zürcher Zeitung*, Literatur und Kunst, Sonntag, 12. April, Blatt 4, 1953.

- "Besprechung von Band II. Gegensatz und Erneuerung" in: *Neue Zürcher Zeitung*, Nr 2806/7, 1957.

Lüthi, Max (ed.), *The European Folktale: Form and Nature*, Indiana University Press, Bloomington & Indianapolis 1982, trans. John D. Niles.

- "Hedwig von Beit" in: Enzyklopädie des Märchens 2.

Lukas, Franz, "Das Ei als kosmogonische Vorstellung" in: *Zeitschrift des Vereins für Volkskunde*, 4 1894, Nr. 1, pp. 227–243.

Mannhardt, Wilhelm, Wald- und Feldkulte, Vol. 1: Der Baumkultus der Germanen und ihrer Nachbarstämme. Mythologische Untersuchungen, Gebrüder Borntraeger (Ed. Eggers), Berlin 1875.

- Wald- und Feldkulte, Vol. 2: Antike Wald- und Feldkulte aus nordeuropäischer Überlieferung, Gebrüder Borntraeger (Ed. Eggers), Berlin 1877.

Marcinowski, Johannes Jaroslaw, "Gezeichnete Träume" in: *Zentralblatt für Psychoanalyse. Medizinische Monatsschrift für Seelenkunde*, II 1912, Nr. 9, pp. 490–518.

Markham, Sir Clements, *The Incas of Peru*, 2nd edition. E. P. Dutton and Company, New York 1912.

Matthews, Washington, *Navajo Legends*, Houghton, Mifflin and Company, Boston and New York 1897, Memoires of the American Folk-Lore Society.

Mead, George Robert Stow, *Pistis Sophia, A Gnostic Miscellany*, 2nd edition. John M. Watkins, London 1921.

- *Fragments of a Faith Forgotten*, 2nd. Ed. John M. Watkins, London 1931.

Meier, Harri/Karlinger, Felix (eds.), *Spanische Märchen, (MdW)*, ed. by Fr. v. d. Leyen and P. Zaunert, Eugen Diederichs, München 1991.

Meister Eckhart, *Deutsche Mystiker des vierzehnten Jahrhunderts. 2. Vol.*: Meister Eckhart, Teil 2, ed. by Franz Pfeiffer, Vandenhoeck & Ruprecht, Göttingen 1906.

- *Schriften und Predigten, aus dem Mittelhochdeutschen übers.* and ed. by Herman Büttner, Eugen Diederichs, Jena 1921–1923.

Meyer, Rudolf, *Die Weisheit der Schweizer Märchen*, Columban-Verlag, Schaffhausen 1944.

Mogk, Eugen, *Germanische Religionsgeschichte und Mythologie*, 2nd edition. W. de Gruyter & Co., Berlin and Leipzig 1927, Sammlung Göschen.

Nietzsche, Friedrich Wilhelm, *Thus Spake Zarathustra*, Gutenberg.org, Online 1997/2008, translated by Thomas Common, Wordsworth Classics of World Literature. 455

Ninck, Martin, *Wodan und germanischer Schicksalsglaube*, Eugen Diederichs, Jena 1935.

Nordenskiöld, Erland, *Indianerleben*, Verlag von Albert Bonnier, Leipzig 1912.

Novalis, *Fragmente*, Erste vollständige, geordnete Ausgabe, ed. by Ernst Kamnitzer, Wolfgang Jess Verlag, Dresden 1929.

Petsch, Robert, Formelhafte Schlüsse im Volksmärchen, Weidmann 1900.

Peuckert, Will-Erich, *Deutscher Volksglaube des Spätmittelalters*, Sammlung Voelkerglaube, ed. by Claus Schrempf, W. Spemann Verlag, Stuttgart 1942.

Picard, Charles, "Die Grosse Mutter von Kreta bis Eleusis" in: *Eranos- Jahrbuch 1938: Gestalt und Kult der 'Grossen Mutter'*, ed. by Olga Fröbe- Kapteyn, Rhein-Verlag, Zürich 1939, p. 91–119.

Po-Yang, Wei and Wu, Lu-Chiang/Davis, Tenney L., "An Ancient Chinese Treatise on Alchemy Entitled Ts'an T'ung Ch'i" in: *Isis*, 18 1932, Nr. 2, pp. 210–289.

Przyluski, Jean, "Die Erlösung nach dem Tode in den Upanishaden und im ursprünglichen Buddhismus" in: *Eranos-Jahrbuch 1937: Gestaltung der Erlösungsidee in Ost und West* (2), ed. by Olga Fröbe-Kapteyn, Rhein-Verlag, Zürich 1938, p. 93–136.

– "Ursprünge und Entwicklung des Kultes der Mutter-Göttin" in: *Eranos-Jahrbuch 1938: Gestalt und Kult der "Grossen Mutter,"* ed. by Olga Fröbe-Kapteyn, Rhein-Verlag, Zürich 1939, p. 11–34.

– "Die Mutter-Göttin als Verbindung zwischen den Lokal-Göttern und dem Universal-Gott" in: *Eranos-Jahrbuch 1938: Gestalt und Kult der "Grossen Mutter,"* ed. by Olga Fröbe-Kapteyn, Rhein-Verlag, Zürich 1939, p. 35–57.

Puech, Henri-Charles, "The Concept of Redemption in Manichaeism" in: *The Mystic Vision: Papers from the Eranos Yearbook 1936 – The Shaping of the Idea of Redemption in the East and the West*, Joseph Campbell (Ed.), Bollingen Series XXX, Princeton NJ 1970, pp. 247–314.

Radhakrishnan, *The Principle Upanishads*, George Allen and Unwin, Ltd., London 1953/1968.

Rank, Otto, "Das Inzest-Motiv in Dichtung und Sage" in: *Grundzüge einer Psychologie des dichterischen Schaffens*, Franz Deuticke, Leipzig and Wien 1912.

– *The Myth of the Birth of the Hero*, trans. Gregory C. Richter and E. James Lieberman, John Hopkins University Press, Baltimore MD 2004.

Rasmussen, Knud, Across Arctic America, narrative of the Fifth Thule Expedition, Putnam's Sons, New York 1927.

Reitzenstein, Richard, *Das iranische Erlösungsmysterium. Religionsgeschichtliche Untersuchungen*, A. Marcus & E. Weber's Verlag, Bonn a. Rh. 1921.

– *Hellenistic mystery-religions their basic ideas and significance*, Pickwick Press, Pittsburgh 1978, translated by John E. Steely.

Rink, Henry, Tales and Traditions of the Eskimo, with a sketch of their habits, religion, language and other peculiarities, William Blackwood & Sons, Edinburgh & London 1875.

Roeder, Günther, Urkunden zur Religion des alten Ägypten, Religiöse Stimmen der Völker, ed. by Walter Otto, Eugen Diederichs, Jena 1923.

Rohde, Erwin, *Psyche: the cult of souls and the belief in immortality among the Greeks*, Transl. W. B. Hillis, Kegan Paul, Trubenr & Co., Ltd., London 1925 (reprinted 2019 Martino Fine Books).

Róheim, Géza, *Spiegelzauber*, Vol. 6, Internationaler Psychoanalytischer Verlag, Leipzig and Wien 1919, Internat. Psychoanalytische Bibliothek.

Rousselle, Erwin, "Lau Dsi's Gang durch Seele, Geschichte und Welt. Versuch einer Deutung" in: *Eranos-Jahrbuch 1935: Westöstliche Seelenführung*, ed. by Olga Fröbe-Kapteyn, Rhein-Verlag, Zürich 1936, p. 179–205.

– "Dragon and Mare, Figures of Primordial Chinese Mythology" in: *Mystic Vision, Papers from the Eranos Yearbooks, Volume 6*, Princeton University Press, Princeton 1970, pp. 103–119.

– "Drache und Stute, Gestalten der mythischen Welt chinesischer Urzeit" in: *Eranos-Jahrbuch 1934: Ostwestliche Symbolik und Seelenführung*, ed. by Olga Fröbe-Kapteyn, Rhein-Verlag, Zürich 1935, p. 11–33.

– "Spiritual Guidance in Contemporary Taoism" in: *Spiritual Disciplines: Papers from the Eranos Yearbooks*, Princeton University Press, Princeton NJ 1960, Bollingen XXX-4, pp. 59–101.

Ruben, Walter, *Die Philosophen der Upanishaden*, A. Francke AG, Bern 1947.

Schiller, Friedrich, Über die ästhetische Erziehung des Menschen, in einer Reihe von Briefen, J. G. Cotta'sche Buchhandlung, Stuttgart 1879.

Schmidt, Bernhard, *Griechische Märchen, Sagen, Volkslieder*, Teubner, Leipzig 1877.

Schopenhauer, Arthur, Transcendent Speculation on the Apparent Deliberateness in the Fate of the Individual, in: Parerga and Paralipomena: short philosophical essays, Volume 1, Oxford University Press, Oxford 1974, pp. 199–224.

Schweitzer, Bernhard, Herakles: *Aufsätze zur griechischen Religions- und Sagengeschichte*, J. C. B. Mohr (Paul Siebeck), Tübingen 1922.

Sébillot, Paul, "Littérature orale de L'Auvergne" in: *Les Littératures populaires de toutes les nations, Volume 35*, J. Maisonneuve, Paris 1898, pp. 1–393.

Schoolcraft, Henry R., The Myth of Hiawatha, and other oral legends, Mythologic and Allegoric, of the North American Indians, J. B. Lippincott Company, Philadelphia 1856.

Silberer, Herbert, "Symbolik des Erwachens und Schwellensymbolik überhaupt" in: *Jahrbuch für psychoanalytische und psychopathologische Forschungen, Vol. 3*, ed. by Ernst Bleuler and Sigmund Freud, Franz Deuticke, Leipzig and Wien 1912, p. 621–660.

– *Problems of Mysticism and Its Symbolism*, Moffat, Yard and Company, New York 1917, Trans. Smith Ely Jelliffe.

Silesius, Angelus [Johann Scheffler], *The Cherubinic Wanderer*, Paulist Press, New Jersey 1986, trans. by Maria Shrady.

Stroebe, Klara (ed.), *The Swedish Fairy Book*, Frederick A. Stokes Company, New York 1921, Trans. Frederick H. Martens.

Stroebe, Clara (ed.), *The Norwegian Fairy Book*, Frederick A. Stokes Company, New York 1922, Trans. Frederick H. Martens.

Tegethoff, Ernst, "Studien zum Märchentypus von Amor und Psyche" in: *Rhein. Beitr. and Hülfsbücher z. germ. Philologie and Volkskunde, Band 4*, ed. by Th. Frings, R. Meissner, J. Müller, Kurt Schroeder, Bonn and Leipzig 1922.

– *Französische Volksmärchen 2: Aus neueren Sammlungen, (MdW)*, ed. by Fr. v. d. Leyen and P. Zaunert, Eugen Diederichs, Jena 1923.

Thimme, Adolf, *Das Märchen. Handbücher zur Volkskunde*, Verlag von Wilhelm Heims, Leipzig 1909.

Thurnwald, Richard, "Primitive Initiations- und Wiedergeburtsriten" in: *Eranos-Jahrbuch 1939: Die Symbolik der Wiedergeburt in der religiösen Vorstellung der Zeiten und Völker*, ed. by Olga Fröbe-Kapteyn, Rhein-Verlag, Zürich 1940, pp. 321–328.

Tobler, Otto, *Die Epiphanie der Seele in deutscher Volkssage*, Christian-Albrechts-Universität zu Kiel, Kiel 1911, Inaugural-Dissertation.

Trebitsch, Rudolf, *Bei den Eskimos in Westgrönland. Ergebnisse einer Sommerreise im Jahre 1906*. (Nebst einem ethnologischen Anhang v. Dr. M. Haberlandt), Dietrich Reimer, Berlin 1910.

Turner, George, **Samoa, A Hundred Years Ago And Long Before**, University of the South Pacific, London/Samoa 1884/1984 ⟨URL: http://www.gutenberg.org/files/14224/14224-h/14224-h.htm⟩.

Usener, Hermann, *Die Sintfluthsagen, Religionsgeschichtliche Untersuchungen*, dritter Theil, Friedrich Cohen, Bonn 1899.

– *Dreiheit: Ein Versuch mythologischer Zahlenlehre*, Carl Georgi Universitätsdruckerei, Bonn 1903.

– Kleine Schriften. Arbeiten zur Religionsgeschichte, B. G. Teubner, Leipzig and Berlin 1913.

van Baarda, M. J., "Het Loda'sch in vergelijking met het Galela'sch dialect op Halmaheira, Gevolgd door Loda'sche Teksten en Verhalen"[The Loda Language in Comparison with the Galela dialect of Halmaheira followed by Loda Texts in Translation] in: *Bijdragen tot de Taal-Land-en Volkenkunde van Nederlandsche-Indië*, Martinus Nijhoff, Gravenhage 1904, p. 317–496.

Weicker, Georg, Der Seelenvogel. In der alten Literatur und Kunst. Eine mythologisch-archaeologische Untersuchung, B. G. Teubner, Leipzig 1902.

Wesselski, Albert, *Versuch einer Theorie des Märchens, Prager Deutsche Studien, No. 45*, E. Gierach and H. Cysarz eds. Sudetendeutscher Verlag Franz Kraus, Reichenberg i. B. 1931.

Wiedemann, A., *The Realms of the Egyptian Dead, Volume The Ancient East, No. 1*, Translated by J. Hutchison, David Nutt, London 1902.

Wilhelm, Richard (ed.), *The Chinese Fairy Book*, Frederick A. Stokes Company, New York 1921, Trans. Frederick H. Martens.

- *The Secret of the Golden Flower, a Chinese Book of Life*, Routledge & Kegan Paul, London 1962, trans. from German by Cary F. Baynes.

- *The I Ching or Book of Changes*, Princeton University Press, Princeton, NJ 1967, trans. Cary F. Baynes.

Winthuis, Josef, Das Zweigeschlechterwesen bei den Zentralaustraliern und anderen Völkern. Lösungsversuch der ethnologischen Hauptprobleme auf Grund primitiven Denkens, Volume 5, Forschungen zur Völkerpsychologie und Soziologie, Verlag von C. L. Hirschfeld, Leipzig 1928.

Wisser, Wilhelm (ed.), *Plattdeutsche Volksmärchen, (MdW), Vol. 1*, ed. by Fr. v. d. Leyen and P. Zaunert, Eugen Diederichs, Jena 1922.

Wolff, Antonia (Toni), "Einführung in die Grundlagen der komplexen Psychologie" in: *Die kulturelle Bedeutung der komplexen Psychologie. Festschrift zum 60. Geburtstag von C. G. Jung*, ed. by Julius Springer, Psychologischer Club Zürich, Berlin 1935, p. 3–168.

Woodman, Marion and Bly, Robert, *The Maiden King: The Reunion of Masculine and Feminine*, Henry Holt and Company, New York 1998.

Wünsche, August, Die Sagen vom Lebensbaum und Lebenswasser. Altorientalische Mythen, Verlag von Eduard Pfeiffer, Leipzig 1905.

Zaunert, Paul (ed.), *Deutsche Märchen seit Grimm, (MdW), Vol. 1*, ed. by Fr. v. d. Leyen, Eugen Diederichs, Jena 1922.

- Deutsche Märchen seit Grimm, (MdW), Neu Ausgabe, bearbeitet von Elfriede Moser-Rath, Eugen Diederichs, Köln 1964.

- Deutsche Märchen aus dem Donaulande, (MdW), ed. by Fr. v. d. Leyen and P. Zaunert, Eugen Diederichs, Jena 1926.

Zieliński, Tadeusz, Die Märchenkomödie in Athen, Abdruck aus dem Jahresbericht der Deutschen Schule zu St. Annen, Buchdruckerei der Kaiserlichen Akademie der Wissenschaften, St. Petersburg 1885.

Zimmer, Heinrich, Kunstform und Yoga im indischen Kultbild, Frankfurter Verlags-Anstalt A.G., Berlin 1926.

– "Der 'König der dunklen Kammer'". In drei Verwandlungen vom Rgveda bis Tagore, in: Zeitschr. d. Deutschen Morgenländischen Gesellschaft, ed. By G. Steindorff, F. A. Brockhaus, Leipzig 1929.

– "Yoga und Maya", in: Corona, 4. Jahr, 4. no., ed. by Martin Bodmer, Verlag der Corona, Zürich. R. Oldenbourg, München and Berlin 1934.

– "Maya" der indische Mythos, Deutsche Verlags-Anstalt, Stuttgart and Berlin 1936.

– Weisheit Indiens. Märchen und Sinnbilder, L. C. Wittich Verlag, Darmstadt 1938.

– "Merlin", in: Corona, 9. Jahr, no. 2, ed. by Martin Bodmer, Verlag der Corona, Zürich. R. Oldenbourg, München and Berlin 1939, p. 265–279.

– Myths and Symbols in Indian Art and Civilization, ed. Joseph Campbell, Pantheon Books, Bollingen Foundation, New York 1946, Bollingen Series VI.

– Death and Rebirth in the Light of India, in: Campbell, Joseph (ed.): Man and Transformation: Papers from the Eranos Yearbooks, Volume 5, Pantheon Books, Bollingen Foundation, New York 1964, pp. 326–352.

– The King and the Corpse, Tales of the Soul's Conquest of Evil. Princeton University Press, Princeton NJ 1972.

Zingerle, Joseph und Ignatz, Kinder- und Hausmärchen aus Süddeutschland, Regensburg 1854.

Index of Authors

Tegethoff, E., 111, 212, 282, 390
Thimme, A., 332, 390
Tobler, O., 20, 33, 303, 338, 390
Tolkien, J. R. R., 23
Trebitsch, R., 58, 390

Usener, H., 11, 69, 76, 126, 149, 189, 390

Weicker, G., 191, 303, 391
Wesselski, A., 21, 339, 391
Wiedemann, A., 329, 391
Wilhelm, R., 72, 85, 92, 124, 130, 135, 143, 202, 203, 210, 217, 222, 235, 240, 272, 338, 391

Winthuis, J., 239, 391
Wolff, A. (Toni), 10, 45, 217, 218, 391
Wünsche, A., 153, 202, 299, 391
Zaunert, P., 3, 16, 82, 110, 171, 182, 264, 375

Zimmer, H., 13, 53, 71, 145, 146 154, 155, 213, 216, 257, 264, 282, 284, 288, 331, 346, 350, 392
Zingerle, J. and I., 21, 392
Zosimos, 241, 262, 384

Index of Fairytales

Subject Index